Cambridge Guide to Cognitive Behavioural Therapy (CBT)

This book provides a concise and up-to-date guide to Cognitive Behavioural Therapy (CBT), from the history and supporting theory through to the most recent empirical evidence and practical aspects of delivery. Starting with an overview of the structure of CBT, practitioners can utilise this detailed guide to deliver therapy in clinical practice, whilst its coverage of various adaptations of CBT, such as group therapy and working with older adults, allows therapy to be tailored to different settings with different timeframes attached. The book covers all the major CBT protocols necessary to work with a wide range of common mental health conditions, and delivers a comprehensive resource for a wide range of practitioners providing practical approaches, goals and strategies to manage mental health problems using CBT.

The book is part of the Cambridge Guides to the Psychological Therapies series, offering all the latest scientifically rigorous and practical information on a range of key, evidence-based psychological interventions for clinicians.

Jessica Davies is a British Association for Behavioural & Cognitive Psychotherapies (BABCP) accredited practitioner, supervisor and trainer. She qualified as a CBT therapist in 2013 from the Institute of Psychiatry, Psychology and Neuroscience, and has since worked in NHS Talking Therapies (National Health Service Talking Therapies) (NHSTT), student services and private practice. She is currently Portfolio Co-director for the Masters in Clinical Associate in Psychology Degree Apprenticeship and CBT Lead for the Doctorate in Clinical Psychology, both at the University of Exeter. In addition, she works as a research therapist for the Accept Clinic at the Mood Disorders Centre, and is Associate Editor of the BABCP journal *Behavioural and Cognitive Psychotherapy*.

Paul Salkovskis is Professor of Clinical Psychology at the University of Oxford. From April 2018 he has been Director of the Oxford Centre for Psychological Health, the Oxford Institute for Clinical Psychology Training and Research and the Oxford Cognitive Therapy Centre, at the University of Oxford and Oxford Health NHS Foundation Trust. He is President of BABCP and Editor in Chief of the BABCP journal *Behavioural and Cognitive Psychotherapy* and Honorary Fellow of the Association.

Professor Ken Laidlaw, PhD, is a clinical psychologist with world-leading expertise in the psychology of ageing, CBT for older people and attitudes to ageing. He is Emeritus Professor in Psychology at the University of Exeter and part-time Consultant Clinical Psychologist within the Clinical Psychology service in NHS Highland in Scotland. In 2025 he was made an honorary Fellow of the BABCP in recognition of outstanding contribution to the development of CBT in the UK. Ken is widely published in peer-reviewed academic journals and is the author and co-author of a number of influential books on CBT with older people, emotional disorders in late life and clinical geropsychology. He has worked as a clinical psychologist with older people in the NHS both in England and Scotland for more than three decades and in clinical psychology training since the late 1990s, leading two different doctoral training programmes in clinical psychology. He has been responsible for developing manuals for various clinical trials and led the development of a cross-cultural Attitudes to Ageing Questionnaire (AAQ), which was trialled in no fewer than 20 countries across the world.

Cambridge Guides to the Psychological Therapies

Series Editor

Patricia Graham
Consultant Clinical Psychologist, NHS Lanarkshire, UK

The go-to resource for up-to-date, scientifically rigorous, and practical information on key, evidence-based psychological interventions.

This series of clinical handbooks provides clear and concise guides to understanding and delivering therapy, and offers clinicians a handy reference for matching a specific therapy to a particular patient. Each book follows a consistent style, with chapters on theory, technique, indications, and efficacy, so that healthcare professionals can move seamlessly between different volumes to learn about various therapies in a consistent, familiar, and trusted format. The books also provide guidance on relevant adaptations for each therapy, such as for children, adolescents, and older people, as well as different methods of delivery, such as group interventions and digital therapy.

Books available in the series

Cambridge Guide to Schema Therapy
Robert N. Brockman, Susan Simpson, Christopher Hayes, Remco van der Wijngaart, Matthew Smout

Cambridge Guide to Psychodynamic Psychotherapy
Adam Polnay, Rhiannon Pugh, Victoria Barker, David Bell, Allan Beveridge, Adam Burley, Allyson Lumsden, C. Susan Mizen, Lauren Wilson

Cambridge Guide to Mentalization-Based Therapy (MBT)
Anthony Bateman, Peter Fonagy, Chloe Campbell, Patrick Luyten, Martin Debbané

Cambridge Guide to Interpersonal Therapy (IPT)
Laura Dietz, Fiona Duffy, Patricia Graham

Cambridge Guide to Cognitive Behavioral Analysis System of Psychotherapy (CBASP)
Massimo Tarsia, Todd Favorite, James McCullough Jr

Cambridge Guide to Dialectical Behaviour Therapy (DBT)
Jim Lyng, Christine Dunkley, Janet Feigenbaum, Amy Gaglia, Michaela Swales

Cambridge Guide to Acceptance and Commitment Therapy (ACT)
Chris Graham

'This guide is a must-have for any mental health professional who uses cognitive behavioural therapy in their practice. Written by internationally regarded CBT researchers, teachers and clinicians, it not only provides the reader with concisely written instruction on how to deliver CBT for a variety of mental health conditions, but also neatly links such guidance to the powerful theories and evidence that underpin the application of CBT. A wide range of disorders is included, each with multiple CBT models expertly summarised and contrasted. Other chapters consider the application of CBT to different populations and settings. Both those new to CBT and expert practitioners will find this volume an essential text that supports their practice for years to come.'

Richard Meiser-Stedman Department of Clinical Psychology & Psychological Therapies Norwich Medical School University of East Anglia

'A thoroughly enjoyable book, written by notable thinkers and experienced psychotherapists with a long history of working with populations across different age ranges. It clearly and robustly reviews the theoretical, methodological and practical arguments that make CBT an evidence-based practice for adults, including older adults dealing with issues such as depression or anxiety. The book also offers compelling counterarguments to the widespread ageist belief that psychotherapy is ineffective with older adults. It has strong applied value, as it presents the therapeutic process in a highly practical way, with excellent examples illustrating therapy goals, techniques and structure. Across its chapters, the book covers a wide range of disorders as well as case examples of therapy applied in various contexts and populations – including children, older adults and caregivers of family members with dementia, couples, and both group and computer-based interventions. I recommend it both for students or early-career therapists and for professionals interested in strengthening their knowledge and practical resources.'

Professor Andrés Losada Baltar Professor of Clinical Psychology Rey Juan Carlos University Spain

Cambridge Guide to Cognitive Behavioural Therapy (CBT)

Jessica Davies
University of Exeter

Paul Salkovskis
Oxford Health NHS Foundation Trust and University of Oxford

Ken Laidlaw
University of Exeter and NHS Highland

CAMBRIDGE
UNIVERSITY PRESS

CAMBRIDGE
UNIVERSITY PRESS

Shaftesbury Road, Cambridge CB2 8EA, United Kingdom

One Liberty Plaza, 20th Floor, New York, NY 10006, USA

477 Williamstown Road, Port Melbourne, VIC 3207, Australia

314–321, 3rd Floor, Plot 3, Splendor Forum, Jasola District Centre, New Delhi - 110025, India

103 Penang Road, #05–06/07, Visioncrest Commercial, Singapore 238467

Cambridge University Press is part of Cambridge University Press & Assessment, a department of the University of Cambridge.

We share the University's mission to contribute to society through the pursuit of education, learning and research at the highest international levels of excellence.

www.cambridge.org
Information on this title: www.cambridge.org/9781009088350

DOI: 10.1017/9781009090940

When citing this work, please include a reference to the DOI 10.1017/9781009090940

First published 2025

A catalogue record for this publication is available from the British Library

A Cataloging-in-Publication data record for this book is available from the Library of Congress

ISBN 978-1-009-08835-0 Paperback

Contents

Foreword

I was delighted to be asked to write the foreword for this sure-to-be influential textbook on CBT. It has an ambitious scope, as it covers most of all the established evidence-based protocols we have for CBT across conditions and across populations. This is important, as it is now well-established that CBT is the gold standard for the psychological treatment of common mental health conditions, and as such a contemporary textbook is needed to guide the next generation of therapists through the extensive and expanding field, and to assist those therapists with more experience to stay contemporary with clinical practices and skills in CBT. The authors are well-known to me and have invested their professional careers in education, research and clinical work to enhance the outcome of CBT. My own career started in education before psychology, but the synergies between the two as life-enhancing and life-changing are very powerful. Books can play an important part in our educational and professional development, so I applaud the authors' mission to educate and train and to make accessible the best evidence available to the readers through the pages of this book. I welcome this textbook for its thorough scope of coverage and for providing a logical and coherent structure. The different sections of the book make it easier for readers to navigate directly to the information they need. It is a rich resource, with references, tables, tips and hints, and graphics all made practical by case examples throughout. By itself, this book won't make you a better therapist, but it can be a valuable and practical support on your own journey to becoming the type of therapist that is well-versed in the evidence-base and well-grounded in the principles, practice and ethos of the empowering, compassionate, therapy we know of as CBT.

Judith S. Beck

A Note from the Series Editor

I remember when I first met Sarah Marsh, editor at Cambridge University Press – it seems like a lifetime ago now. We met at a café in central Edinburgh in June 2017 to discuss an idea that she had to create a series of books focussed on evidence-based psychological therapies. The idea was simple – the books would be attractive to a trainee and simultaneously to an expert clinician. We wanted to enable readers to conceptualise a psychological difficulty using different theoretical models of understanding, but not become overwhelmed by the volume of information. We saw the need for a series of books that could be easily read and yet would examine complex concepts in a manageable way.

So, when Sarah asked me if I would become the Series Editor, I couldn't say no. What we could never have predicted back then, when making early plans for the series, was that we would soon face a global pandemic. There were days when we didn't even know whether we could leave our house or if our children could go to school – the world effectively stopped. Yet through all the chaos, uncertainty and fear, I saw the determination and successes of those around me shine through. I was in awe of the resilience of my own son, Patrick, who lived his adolescence in 'lockdown'. I watch him now and the young man he has become – he walks tall with a quiet confidence. I am so proud as he and his friends laugh together and now enjoy what most of us had previously taken for granted: their freedom at university. In a similar way, I watched the many authors of these books, most of whom are busy and tired clinicians, continue to dedicate their precious time to this venture – an incredible achievement through a most challenging time. They each welcomed me into their academic, clinical and theoretical worlds, from all over the globe. They have all been an honour to work with. I would personally like to thank every contributor and author of this series for their hard work, determination and humour even in the darkest of days. Despite all the unknowns and the chaos, they kept going and achieved something wonderful.

I would like to thank Sarah, and Kim Ingram at Cambridge, for giving me the opportunity to be Series Editor. I have loved every minute of it; it has been a longer journey than we anticipated but an amazing one and for that I am incredibly grateful. Sarah and Kim are my friends now – we have literally lived through a global pandemic together. It has been my absolute pleasure to work together and in collaboration with Cambridge University Press.

Patricia Graham

Chapter 1

An Historical Overview of Cognitive Behavioural Therapy

Learning objectives after reading this chapter:

- After reading this chapter you will have a historical overview of CBT and begin to appreciate how elements of this therapy developed over time.
- You will be able explain CBT to clients in a more enriched way as you appreciate the fundamental principles of this approach.
- You will be better able to appreciate the uniqueness of CBT as a psychotherapy and differentiate it from other structured evidence-based therapies.
- You will have a better knowledge about how behavioural and cognitive elements of CBT interact to enhance treatment.

Introduction

The Spanish Philosopher, George Santayana [1], reflected, 'Those who ignore history are doomed to repeat it' (p. 45). This should contain particular resonance for therapists as we witness clients recount episodes of past and present events that appear to resonate with other episodes of imagined failings. One may also reflect that an understanding of how CBT developed, and an appreciation of historical antecedents and milestones in establishing the fundamental principles of CBT, provide a greater appreciation of how to make therapy sessions bespoke but within guidelines. A firm understanding of how CBT developed and the important principles that helped set it apart from other therapies available at the time allows one an insight into what are the important theoretical elements and how the concepts of cognitive change allied to behavioural change has been so crucial to the creation of a mainstream standard psychological treatment – forget that and perhaps we forget the heart of what we do. This chapter allows you some insights that may enhance your theoretical and conceptual coherence as a CBT therapist.

Landmark Developments for CBT: Cognitive Therapy

In the form most commonly applied in the UK, CBT arose out of the work of Aaron T. Beck in the late 1950s and early 1960s when he developed Cognitive Therapy (CT), now more commonly known as Cognitive Behavioural Therapy or CBT. The first and arguably most important landmark development in the founding of CT is the explicit commitment to psychotherapy as science [6]. The adherence to an evidence-based approach is fundamentally important and should remain so to any practitioner of CBT. Beck drew heavily on the scientific orientation of behavioural approaches and was also appreciative of the cognitive orientation of peers such as Albert Ellis, but differences in philosophy and adherence to protocol-driven approaches resulted in CBT and rational-emotive behaviour therapy (REBT) sharing some roots but taking different paths [2,3]. Without question Beck was also heavily influenced by his original training as a psychoanalyst. Initially as a young man, Beck was more interested in neurology as a medical intern and as this specialism required a rotation in psychiatry he was, *reluctantly*, introduced to the area that would quickly become his life's passion and work. In 1954, Beck joined the Department of Psychiatry at the University of Pennsylvania (PENN) in Philadelphia and he started to conduct research seeking to prove the efficacy of psychoanalytic psychotherapy. Beck noticed, and was intrigued by, the importance thoughts appeared to play in the maintenance of depression in his clients. As he sought to find more effective methods to help his clients overcome their problems he moved further away from the theory and practice of psychoanalysis (for an excellent first-hand account see [4]).

From the beginning, Beck sketched out the nature of negative cognitive distortions as being spontaneous, requiring little effort to generate, plausible, mood congruent, idiosyncratic and self-perpetuating [5,7]. Cognitions were to be tested and evaluated rather than simply disputed providing a strong collaborative approach to CBT from the outset. As Beck developed his model of psychopathology he explored and described the impact of cognitive distortions identified as self-generating and punitive reflecting negative themes such as failure, inadequacy and so on [see 7,4]. Beck set out to chart a coherent intervention for psychotherapy to systematically challenge distortions by differentiating the theme of cognitions in the content-specificity hypothesis where for example anxiety generating cognitions revolve around themes of threat while depression generates cognitions revolving around themes of failure and rejection [8].

To Beck, it was evident in depression and the anxiety disorders that there were mood-congruent biases in recall and general memory biases for negative events [see 9 for review] that maintained these conditions. The Beck model proposed a stress-diathesis as helpful for understanding idiosyncratic predispositions for the development of common mental health conditions [6]. Simply put the diathesis reflects predisposing, underlying (and usually latent – i.e. not yet activated) vulnerabilities that when activated by a matching, or congruent stressor, leads to activation of a depression or anxiety disorder. Beck noted 'Early adverse events foster negative attitudes and biases about the self, which are integrated into the cognitive organization in the form of schemas; the schemas become activated by later adverse events impinging on the specific cognitive vulnerability and lead to the systematic negative bias at the core of depression' [10, p. 970]. Thus, latent diatheses (vulnerabilities) when activated facilitate the core beliefs, or schemata, through which individuals process their experiences and which determine emotional and behavioural responses to situations and stimuli. To simplify, Beck's approach to CBT has three main elements:

- Cognitive processing errors
- Errors in cognitive content
- Beliefs and idiosyncratic appraisals/pre-existing vulnerabilities (schema activation in a stress-diathesis)

As Beck's approach developed apace his theoretical, conceptual and intervention approach so deviated from psychoanalytic and psychodynamic principles that his approach was rejected by his psychoanalyst peers [11]. By helping his clients recognise the interactions of thoughts, feelings, behaviours and physical sensations a method of treatment was developed that alleviated distress and promoted active and positive behavioural and cognitive change. At this point in the development of CBT, Beck was influenced by the cognitive approach to depression pioneered by Albert Ellis [12,13] and he was also influenced by behavioural theories of depression [14] developing behavioural activation (BA) and Seligman's theories of learned helplessness [15]. Around this time Beck [16,17] created an elegantly simple formulation for the development of depression or anxiety symptoms that was easily grasped and understood by clients especially as the linked strategies to deal with negative affect and cognition were so elegantly and simply connected and easily implemented in daily life as homework strategies. For example when a client says 'I see myself as weak now, I just keep expecting things to go wrong for me and I suppose I give up when I hit a hurdle.' The CBT therapist is able to help a client reflect not just on what is said but on the impact of these if they were to act as if the thoughts were 100% valid. Being able to introduce clients to thought monitoring and challenging while introducing related behaviour change via behavioural experiments (e.g. homework, pleasant event scheduling, etc.) is a very powerful set of interventions. To the extent that this can seem such a simple technique one must bear in mind the warning by Beck [18], 'Cognitive and behavioural techniques often seem deceptively simple' (p. 46). Something so apparently simple but so powerful is unlikely to work without the professional skills, experience and humanity of therapists. Cognitive Behavioural Therapy is not delivered by technicians but by knowledgeable, compassionate and competent therapists.

The simplest four components model of CBT, where thoughts (cognitions) are seen to create negative affect (feelings such as sadness or fear) with behavioural consequences (self-isolation, avoidance), and consequent physical sensations (fatigue/sleep disturbance, butterflies in the stomach) is commonly known as the hot cross bun model. The example here is of a man who has developed health-related anxiety linked to sensations in his legs when he goes out for a walk (Figure 1.1). He becomes concerned that he may become stranded and unable to seek help with catastrophic consequences imagined.

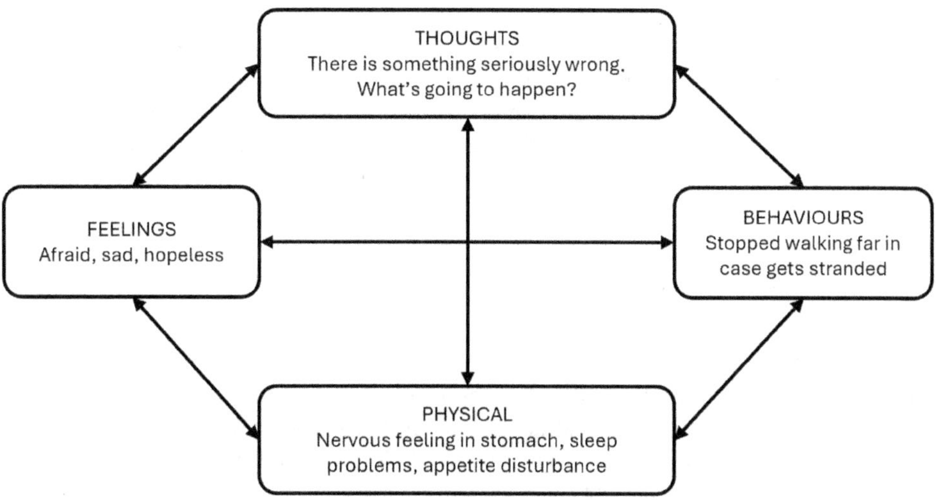

Figure 1.1 The four central components of CBT.

We are aware that when we change one element of this model we change all elements. It may be hard to recognise how revolutionary this approach was to managing common mental health conditions such as depression and anxiety when it was first proposed. What was also revolutionary at the time was the collaborative nature of the therapeutic relationship with the client. The therapist was not seen as the omniscient expert sagely directing the client to make changes in their life but takes the role more of the equivalent to a sports coach empowering the client to take control of their thoughts, feelings and behaviour. In doing so, Beck accepted Carl Rogers' tenets of warmth, genuineness, unconditional acceptance and empathy (congruence) and these bedrock elements of CBT have remained key to good effective CBT ever since [19]. Beck outlined his approach into a systematic format for psychotherapy that he called CT, that emphasised a scientific, evidence-based, open, transparent, collaborative psychotherapy where clients were empowered to help themselves in the here and now. Hammen [20, p. 1067], a significant researcher into CBT, wrote her reflections on the change that CBT brought about as follows:

> The cognitive revolution that had enormous impact throughout psychology during the late 1960s and 1970s, took the form of a virtual tidal wave in clinical psychology. Increasing numbers of investigators – now armed with a major theoretical perspective as well as new research diagnostic criteria with high reliability – applied Beck's model to the measurement and study of cognitive processes as they contributed to depression and to the treatment of depressed individuals.

While recognising similarities in approach between CT and BT [5], Beck [16,17] differentiated CT from Behavioural Therapy for depression and emphasised the importance of cognitive restructuring for symptom relief. These historical antecedents remain fundamental for a good outcome to this day. They also emphasise that CBT therapists ought to have a strong appreciation of the strengths and values of other forms of psychotherapy that demonstrate a methodological approach to scientific evaluation [16,17,18].

In the UK, pioneering work by David Clark and Paul Salkovskis, amongst others at Oxford in the 1980s, took the fundamentals of Beck's model of psychopathology and developed elegant condition-specific models for the anxiety disorders guiding treatment interventions [3]. Empirical research demonstrated the power of CBT to help people overcome a range of anxiety disorders and CBT is now recognised as a frontline treatment for many common anxiety conditions. A number of concepts around emotional regulation, attention deployment and so on, became useful in other clinical presentations besides anxiety disorders, with the result that CBT has become a more complete treatment approach for common mental health conditions and as such is National Institute for Health and Care Excellence (NICE) recommended for a number of these conditions.

Landmark Developments for CBT: Scientific Evaluation of Cognitive Therapy

By the 1970s Beck had published some key scientific treatises on the models for CT but he provided evidence for the efficacy of CBT as a treatment for depression in a landmark paper in 1977 [21] and a bestselling treatment handbook [18] and as CT became extensively evaluated across the world, for a range of psychological conditions, CT became more commonly known as CBT in the process.

Beck continued to refine the approach and philosophical orientation of CBT and set in stone an emphasis on the importance of scientific validation of CBT as a treatment intervention. Beck conducted the first randomised controlled trial (RCT) of CBT for depression in 1977 [21]. This seminal paper was amongst the first to demonstrate that a psychological treatment could be more efficacious than a physical treatment (antidepressant medication) for depression. As Beck and colleagues compared CBT to tricyclic antidepressant medication at the correct dosage this test was a very robust one for any type of psychotherapy and helped establish the empirical nature of CBT as an evidence-based protocol driven therapy.

In 1977, Beck and research colleagues [21] proved for the first time that a psychotherapy (talking cure) such as CBT could perform better than medication in the treatment of depression. This amazing finding was quickly replicated by Ivy-Marie Blackburn and colleagues in Edinburgh in 1981 [22]. By 1982 CBT was shown to help older people manage depression too and by the mid 1980s David Clark and Paul Salkovskis were leading the way in showing that CBT was the first-line treatment for anxiety disorders. Consequently, interest in CBT as an efficacious treatment took off where nowadays CBT is seen as a mainstream treatment for common mental health conditions.

The principles of CBT and the structured nature of this approach specified by Beck ensured it was more amenable than other forms of psychotherapy for evaluation in scientific studies such as RCTs and ensured its wider evaluation across a range of mental health conditions and with a range of clinical populations. The paper by Rush and colleagues [21] also helped launch a new journal, *Cognitive Therapy and Research*. The treatment manual for this study was published in 1979 as the highly influential book by Beck and colleagues called *Cognitive Therapy of Depression* [18]. At this time the early pioneers of CBT were seen as being part of an innovative and radical approach to mental health treatment.

The Importance of the Behavioural Model of Depression and Behavioural Activation for CBT

The behavioural model for depression has a simple but effective approach to understanding and treating depression where a substantial portion of the most salient positive reinforcers in an individual's life are considered to be interpersonal in nature. Lewinsohn was the early pioneer of behavioural treatments for depression and his influence is still very evident in contemporary protocols for BA [24,25].

Lewinsohn's behavioural model of depression [24,25,26] is very simple, suggesting that when depressed individuals engage in less social interaction and less positive social interactions, this results in an increased frequency of negative events and a reduction in positive events that in turns acts as the antecedent condition with depression as the outcome. Behavioural activation constructed collaboratively with clients is the key component of any behavioural intervention, and many CBT interventions, for depression and anxiety.

Reduction in engagement in valued roles and goals in a person's life is a key antecedent to the development of depression.

A landmark paper by Jacobson and colleagues [27] ignited a debate about the key treatment elements of structured psychological therapies. This intriguing study addressed the question as to what are the effective treatment ingredients of CBT for depression. The study compared 152 people who met criteria for major depressive disorder who were randomly allocated to receive either BA alone, or BA with activation and challenging dysfunctional thoughts (Automatic Thoughts (AT) condition) or full CBT that included challenging core beliefs delivered by four experienced CBT therapists. Contrary to expectations, BA performed as well as full CBT at the end of treatment and at six-month follow up. Gortner and colleagues did a longer follow up in 1998 and demonstrated no differences between treatment conditions in terms of relapse prevention. Behavioural activation, AT or CBT were all equally effective as a treatment for depression. What was intriguing about this study was that all three conditions produced equal amounts of change in activity, dysfunctional cognitions and reductions in attribution of negative events due to core beliefs. The main effect of this paper was to provide an impetus to the development of BA as a standalone treatment and provoke further examination of necessary theoretical components of CBT.

Due to the nature of BA strategies this treatment can be learned relatively quickly and can be effectively delivered by people with less psychotherapy training [28] which has led to its wider adoption with a range of clinical populations.

While earlier models largely ignored cognitions more modern BA protocols recognise their importance [24,25]. Lejeuz and colleagues [23] developed the behavioural activation treatment manual for depression which emphasised focus on values, roles and goals and also emphasised the therapeutic alliance by focussing on meaningful treatment rationales linked to an individual's problems. Martell and colleagues [29] incorporated a more formulation-like approach (Trigger, Response, Avoidance Pattern – TRAP), into BA models via functional analysis focussing on understanding context, the role and function of avoidance behaviours and translating negative consequences of behaviour into powerfully reinforcing positive actions. The 'cognitive' type approach adopted in the Martell model of BA sees the interaction of cognition and behaviour as follows, 'The behavioral activation therapist accepts her client's thinking, but encourages clients to look at the context of thinking rather than at the content of thoughts' [29, p. 64]. Meaningful behavioural engagement with a more context-dependent understanding of reinforcement contingencies, and sophisticated cognitive behavioural interdependencies in contemporary accounts of BA, provide for a more sophisticated articulation of the behavioural model for depression.

> Beck [5] noted CT and BT share common elements as they are much more structured, are symptom focussed, with an emphasis on the 'here and now', use direct reports from clients without need for interpretation and distress is a result of maladaptive reaction patterns with a focus on maintaining factors rather than on origins of symptoms.

Behavioural Activation on its own appears to be efficacious [24,28] and as an intervention has a number of effective ingredients (mediators of effect) but this can be more complex to quantify [30, p. 27]. Nevertheless, having a client become more engaged in activities that may provide a tangible sense of achievement and noticeable positive impacts on affect directly challenges an individual's negative appraisals and can act as a motivator to engage in more pleasurable activities. Once 'activated' a person may notice that their self-esteem improves, their relationships improve and a more positive self-sustaining cycle starts. Behavioural Activation and CT are complementary processes and BA is an essential effective ingredient of any treatment plan within CBT.

Lewinsohn's behavioural model for depression [14,26] suggests a vicious cycle develops as a person becomes depressed. As a person's mood becomes lower, reduced engagement in activities and hobbies that previously were experienced as pleasurable and enjoyable results in further reduction in activity overall and the increased opportunities for rumination. As depression becomes more established the potential availability of reinforcers becomes reduced for the person as they can become increasingly aversive for others to interact with them, and as a consequence. the depressed person becomes more isolated and alone. This can result in more time dwelling on negative thoughts and a consequent impact on mood and behaviour.

Concluding Remarks

All formats of CBT therapies share a rich history with a common thread of being scientific, evidence-based and collaborative, problem focussed and structured. Cognitive Behavioural Therapy has never stopped developing since its inception in the 1960s and over that time a more sophisticated understanding of mechanisms of change has seen new variants of CBT emerge. Since the first paper demonstrated efficacy for CBT there has been an explosion in publications demonstrating evidence across settings, across the lifespan, range of clinical conditions and across all common mental health conditions. So much has been done but much more remains to be done and each generation of CBT therapists will add to the strength of this community. As CBT is increasingly more widely applied with more clinical populations than ever before CBT increasingly is recognised as a frontline mainstream treatment approach for common mental health conditions.

Further Reading

The following sources provide more in-depth coverage of topics raised in this chapter.

Beck, A. T., Rush, A. J., Shaw, B. F., & Emery, G. (1979). *Cognitive Therapy of Depression*. New York: Guilford Press. The classic text which sets out the fundamental principles for the application of CBT. A must have.

Beck, J. S., & Fleming, S. (2021). A brief history of Aaron T. Beck, MD, and Cognitive Behavior Therapy. *Clinical Psychology in Europe*, 3(2), Article e6701, https://doi.org/10.32872/cpe.6701. A more personal account of the history of CBT providing insight into our primary trailblazer.

Dimidjian, S., Barrera, Jr. M., Martell, C., Munoz, R. F., & Lewinsohn, P. M. (2011). The origins and current status of behavioral activation treatments for depression. *Annual Review of Clinical Psychology*, 7, 1–38. A comprehensive and collaborative account of BA written by the key originators.

Lewinsohn, P., Munoz, R., Youngren, M. A., & Zeiss, A. M. (1992). *Control Your Depression*. Revised and expanded. New York: Prentice-Hall. Another absolute classic guide to behavioural treatment of depression written for clinicians. A must have.

References

1. Santayana, G. (1905). *The Life of Reason: Reason in Common Sense.* New York: Charles Scribners & Sons.
2. Padesky, C. (2003). Science and philosophy: Comparison of cognitive therapy and rational emotive behavior therapy. *J. Cognitive Psychotherapy*, **17**(3), 211–224.
3. Ruggiero, G. M., Spada, M. M., Caselli, G., & Sassaroli, S. (2018). A historical and theoretical review of cognitive behavioral therapies: From structural knowledge to functional processes. *J. Rat-Emot. Cognitive-Behav Ther.*, **36**, 378–403.
4. Beck. A. T. (2019). A 60-year evolution of cognitive theory and therapy. *Perspect. Psychol. Sci.*, **14**(1), 16–20.
5. Beck, A. T. (1970). Cognitive therapy: Nature and relation to behavior therapy. *Behav. Ther.*, **1**, 184–200.
6. Clark, D. A., & Beck, A. T. (1999). *Scientific Foundations of Cognitive Theory and Therapy of Depression.* New York: Guilford Press.
7. Beck, A. T., & Ward, C. H. (1961). Dreams of depressed patients: Characteristic themes in manifest content. *Arch. Gen. Psychiatry*, **5**, 462–467.
8. Beck, A. T. (1963b). Thinking and depression: I. Idiosyncratic content and cognitive distortions. *Arch. Gen. Psychiatry*, **9**, 324–333.
9. Kircanksi, K., Joormann, J., & Gotlib, I. H. (2012). Cognitive aspects of depression. *Wiley Interdiscip. Rev. Cogn. Sci.*, **3**(3), 301–313.
10. Beck, A. T. (2008). The evolution of the cognitive model of depression and its neurobiological correlates. *Am. J. Psychiatry*, **165**, 969–77.
11. Beck, J. S. & Fleming, S. (2021). A brief history of Aaron T. Beck, MD, and cognitive behavior therapy. *Clin. Psychol. Eur.*, **3**(2), Article e6701.
12. David, D., Cotet, C., Matu, S., Mogoase, C., & Stefan, S. (2018). 50 years of rational-emotive and cognitive-behavioral therapy: A systematic review and meta-analysis. *J. Clin. Psychol.*, **74**(3), 304–318.
13. Ellis, A. (1995). Changing rational-emotive therapy (RET) to rational-emotive behavior therapy (REBT). *J. Rat., Emot., Cog. Behav. Ther.*, **13**(2), 85–89.
14. Lewinsohn, P. M. (1974). A behavioural approach to depression. In R. J. Freedman, & M. Katz (Eds.), *The Psychology of Depression* (pp. 157–174). Oxford: Wiley.
15. Seligman, M. E. P. (1975). *Helplessness: On Depression, Development and Death.* San Francisco: Freeman.
16. Beck, A. T. (1967). *Depression: Clinical, Experimental, and Theoretical Aspects.* Philadelphia: University of Pennsylvania Press.
17. Beck, A. T. (1976). *Cognitive Therapy and the Emotional Disorders.* New York: Meridian.
18. Beck, A. T., Rush, A. J., Shaw, B. F., & Emery, G. (1979). *Cognitive Therapy of Depression.* New York: Guilford Press.
19. Nienhuis, J. B., Owen, J., Valentine, J. C., Winkeljohn Black, S., Halford, T. C., Parazak, S. E., et al. (2018). Therapeutic alliance, empathy, and genuineness in individual adult psychotherapy: A meta-analytic review. *Psychotherapy Res.*, **28** (4), 593–605.
20. Hammen, C. (2006). Stress generation in depression: Reflections on origins, research, and future directions. *J. Clin. Psy.*, **62**(9), 1065–1082.
21. Rush, A. J., Beck, A. T., Kovacs, M., & Hollon, S. (1977). Comparative efficacy of cognitive therapy and pharmacotherapy in the treatment of depressed outpatients. *Cog. There. Res.*, **1**, 17–37.
22. Blackburn, I. M., Bishop, S., Glen, A. I. M., Whalley, L. J., & Christie, J. E. (1981). The efficacy of cognitive therapy in depression: A treatment trial using cognitive therapy and pharmacotherapy, each alone and in combination. *Br. J. Psychiatry*, **139**(3), 181–189.

23. Lejuez, C. W., Hopko, D. R., Acierno, R., Daughters, S. B., & Pagoto, S. L. (2011). Ten year revision of the brief behavioral activation treatment for depression: Revised treatment manual. *Behav. Modif.*, **35**(2), 111–161.

24. Dimidjian, S., Barrera, M., Martell, C., Muniz, R. F., & Lewinsohn, P. M. (2011). The origins and current status of behavioral activation treatments for depression. *Annu. Rev. Clin. Psychol.*, **7**, 1–38.

25. Kanter, J. W., Puspitasari, A. J., Santos, M. M., & Nagy, G. A. (2012). Behavioural activation: History, evidence and promise. *Br. J. Psychiatry*, **200**(5), 361–363.

26. Lewinsohn, P. M., Munoz, R. F., Youngren, M. A., & Zeiss, A. M. (1978). *Control Your Depression*. Englewood Cliffs, NJ: Prentice-Hall.

27. Jacobson, N. S., Dobson, K. S., Truax, P. A., Addis, M. E., Koerner, K., Gollan, J. K., Gortner, E., et al. (1996). A component analysis of cognitive-behavioral treatment for depression. *J. Consult. Clin. Psychol.*, **64**, 295–304.

28. Richards, D. A., Ekers, D., McMillan, D., Taylor, R. S., Byford, S., Warren, F. C., et al. (2016). Cost and outcome of behavioural activation versus cognitive behavioural therapy for depression (COBRA): A randomised, controlled, non-inferiority trial. *Lancet*, **388**(10047), 871–880.

29. Martell, C. R., Dimidjian, S., & Herman-Dunn, R. (2010). *Behavioral Activation for Depression: A Clinician's Guide*. New York: Guilford Press.

30. Janssen, N.P., Hendriks, G-J., Baranelli, C. T., Lucassen, P., Voshaar, R.O. Spijker, J., & Huibers, M.J.H. (2021). How does behavioural activation work? A systematic review of the evidence on potential mediators. *Psychotherapy. Psychosom*, **90**, 85–93.

Chapter 2

The Supporting Theory of Cognitive Behavioural Therapy

Learning objectives after reading this chapter:

- This chapter acts as a clear guide to your theoretical understanding of CBT to enhance your knowledge across protocols, clinical populations and clinical presentations.
- You will gain a working knowledge of the theoretical basis of Beck's model CBT and how theories and models remain important for advancing clinical practice.
- You will be able to more effectively apply CBT across protocols as you will have a better elaborated account of how this therapy has integrated elements across conditions and client presentations.
- You will become knowledgeable about the theoretical mechanism of change in CBT.
- You will become more skilled in using theoretical principles of CBT to stay true to execution of treatment protocols.

Introduction

There is no single model of CBT and in many ways CBT might be more usefully thought of as an umbrella term to describe a range of therapies that share common philosophical orientations, structures and aims [1]. The class of therapies considered as CBT share an orientation towards treatment change [2] describing their commonalities. Nevertheless, the form of CBT most associated with a particular theoretical perspective is the form developed by Aaron T. Beck, with the greatest emphasis on the centrality of theory [3,4] sharing the greatest insights into the mechanism of change in CBT [5].

Kurt Lewin famously wrote, 'There is nothing so practical as a good theory' [6]. The benefit of theories and models for treatment are that they describe and explain current phenomena/experiences and allow us to make sensible predictions for the occurrence of future behaviours or consequences when planning interventions in treatment. Theories can be understood, 'as bodies of knowledge that are broad in scope and aim to explain robust phenomena' [7, p. 336].

While theories describe and explain, models are more specific and can be considered as maps to guide treatment endeavours [8]. Beck's model of psychopathology, also known as the longitudinal model of depression, is commonly used as a formulation/conceptualisation framework. The information contained in the Beck theoretical model of psychopathology can be synthesised into the elements of a formulation with the worksheet (Figure 2.1) providing an example of how theory can be translated into practical therapy work.

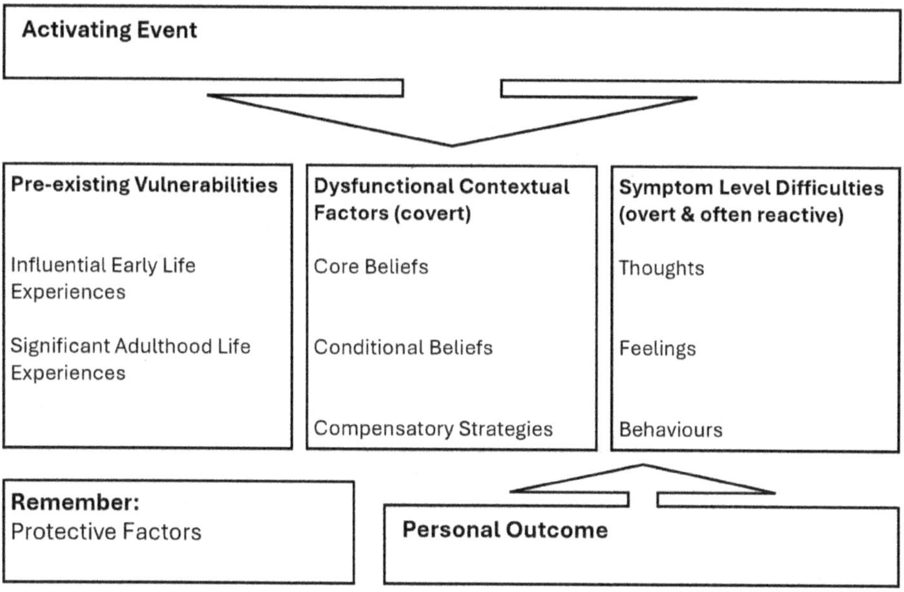

Figure 2.1 Beck model applied as a formulation worksheet (source: Laidlaw, K. (2015) *Cognitive Behaviour Therapy for Older People: An Introduction*. London: SAGE Publications). Reproduced with permission from SAGE Publications.

A good example of a model based on a theory would be the Clark [9] approach to understanding and treating panic disorder. Prior to development of cognitive theories for anxiety disorders efficacious treatments for phobias existed [10] and were largely behaviourally oriented. Clark [9] provided a more cognitive and emotional account of how anxiety disorders impacted on individuals. These theories explained anxiety phenomena and models laid the path for treatment interventions facilitating a whole series of treatment innovations and better treatment outcomes across the range of anxiety disorders.

Applying the Theory of CBT in Practice

In CBT an important starting point for understanding the theory of CBT is that an individual's appraisal of their experience (phenomena), rather than the experience itself (noumena), is what determines its impact. This idea is best encapsulated in the words of the stoic philosopher Epictectus who said, *Men are disturbed not by things, but by the view which they take of them.* What Epictectus seems to be saying is that we all, uniquely and idiosyncratically, make sense of our experiences in our world, and that two people can experience the same phenomena in completely different ways.

The Cognitive Model of Psychopathology: Underlying covert level operators such as core and conditional beliefs (schemas) interact with pre-existing vulnerabilities (the diatheses) when confronted by a matching or congruent activating stressor and the individual becomes at the mercy of negative automatic thoughts with associated emotional, behavioural and physical sequelae. At the start of treatment people may not be aware of schemas or core beliefs and the role they play in the generation of negative cognitions. As such the theory of CBT is communicated via interim formulations shared with our clients.

In many respects how we think and make sense of everyday experiences and the environments we interact with is a consequence of how, and what, we have learned over the course of our lives. How one thinks about a situation influences emotional responses and may determine mood-congruent behavioural responses with associated physiological responses. In the CBT model, physical and psychological experiences of an individual reflect the two sides of the same coin with our physical and psychological state indivisibly connected.

In the CBT model there are structural elements (core beliefs (schemata), conditional beliefs, Negative Cognitive Triad (NCT)) and information processing errors (cognitive specific errors of thinking, preferential negative attentional encoding biases, emotional regulation deficits) as shown in this simple schematic (Figure 2.2).

Understanding the elements of the model helps communicate rationales for treatment interventions with our clients. To that extent we all need a good theory to share with our clients. The theoretical idiosyncratic process of an individual making sense of and responding to stimuli is outlined in Figure 2.3.

Figure 2.3 calls our attention to important elements in the activation of emotional distress and emphasises that the personal meaning attributed to experiences is crucial for therapists to understand. Simply put it is the meaning we attach to events that determines individual impact, with meaning processed via schema which are themselves products of our life experiences. Thus, using Figure 2.3 may teach our clients that rigid belief structures (schema) can bias our thinking and overcoming our vulnerabilities by using cognitive and behavioural strategies could become an effective way to prevent further episodes of psychological distress.

In the Beck model, schemas are meaning and knowledge representation structures and inform how we process information, explaining choices we make and reactions we produce,

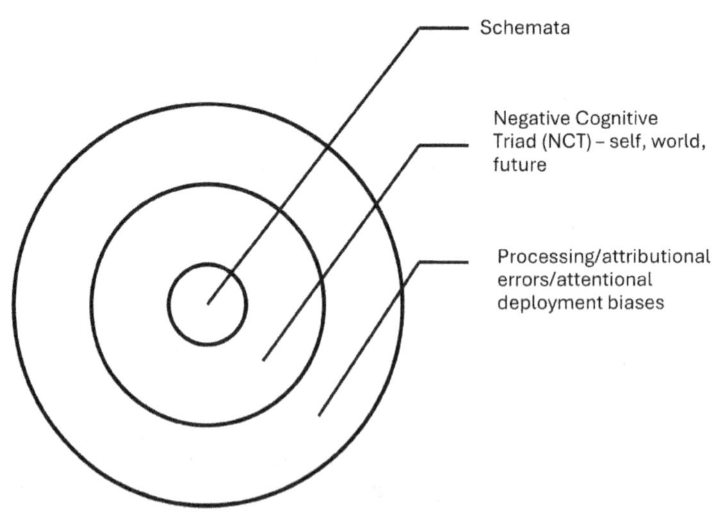

Figure 2.2 Fundamental structure and process of Beck's model of psychopathology.

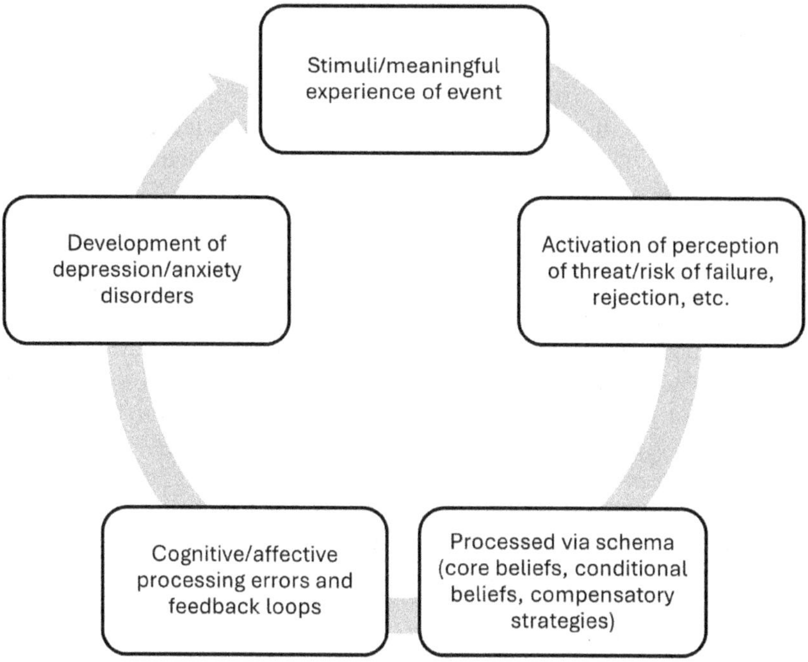

Figure 2.3 Stress-diathesis negative loop.

in the context of an individual's own mental model. Clarke and Beck [11, p. 79] explain schemas as follows, 'As hypothetical structures containing the stored representation of meaning, schemas are pivotal in guiding the selection, encoding, organization, storage and retrieval of information within the cognitive apparatus [of individuals].'

Beck Stress-Diathesis Model of Psychopathology

The Beck (stress-diathesis) model of CBT describes the enduring and pre-existing vulnerabilities (the diatheses) that form part of an individual's psychological make-up [12] formed as a result of the experiences of the individual over the course of a lifetime, placing them at increased risk of arousal of negative emotions. The diatheses (dispositions) are considered latent (and maladaptive) until activated by a stressor. Activation of schemas often results in significant distress to the individual. Once activated an individual is prone to making information processing errors as is evident in the content of negative automatic thoughts. Biased and faulty information processing results in specific cognitive biases evident in the characteristic thinking errors such as selective abstraction, dichotomous thinking and so on [3]. Additionally Power and Dalgleish [13] propose a dual process theory which suggests there are two modes of processing, a fast automatic mode of emotion processing (think of a time when you got a fright at something you noticed from the corner of your eye) and a slower more effortful mode of processing. Thus, after we have recognised a trick of the light we can process that there was no real threat [14]. In this approach emotion and cognition are inextricably linked but the two different processing modes may sometimes be in conflict which may explain how it is that sometimes our clients produce an enhanced risk response to a situation which can be justified by post-hoc emotional reasoning. Consistent with a dual-process model, Clark and Beck [11] recognise different availability and accessibility of schema content. Over recurrent episodes of depression or of anxiety conditions schemas may become so coherent and consolidated that activation may become more easily triggered [3]. Thus, information that is more integrated and connected will have a great accessibility for individuals. As such individuals with previous episodes of distress may have a faster negative response to specific stimuli.

The Beck model provides a framework for understanding how an individual preferentially processes data in a distress-laden way, while explaining and predicting content of cognitions coherent with self-punitive themes outlined in the NCT. Traditionally in CBT, schema content is formed from early life experiences but these can also be developed from formative adulthood experiences. This may be an oversimplification as research suggests there may be a stress-generation process possible for people with depression being likely to interact with stressors in a bidirectional manner [15]. Complimentary to the stress-diathesis in CBT, the stress generation model of depression [16] suggests individuals who are depressed are not passive in the way they interact with stressors in their environments such that it may make it more likely that people living with depression experience a greater frequency of aversive events as they are proactive actors in the construction of their own lives. Thus context as well as content of cognitions and negative schemata are important considerations when applying treatment protocols.

The meaning of events are processed via schemata (schemas) which are similar to the concept of beliefs. As Beck and Haigh [17, p. 6] state, schemas are 'a generic label to represent a variety of schema-related constructs such as assumptions, expectancies, fears, rules, and evaluations influencing memories and associations' [17, p. 6]. Schema are often latent but maladaptive until a matching, or congruent, stressor (activating event) is encountered by an individual. Commonly therapists talk of schemas and beliefs interchangeably. Beliefs can be recognised as conditional and unconditional (core). Core beliefs are primitive, rigid, inflexible ideas or images, that are stated in absolute terms, such as I am bad, toxic, and so on. Core beliefs are powerfully held but under-processed beliefs that become processed as conditional beliefs, so called, because they often take the form of 'if . . . then' type statements. This intermediary class of belief is often the rule by which a person operates in their environment. For instance, a person who has the core belief 'I am bad' may have the intermediary (conditional) belief '*If* I let people get close to me *then*, they will find out about me and reject me.' These beliefs are very often self-referential and negative self-attributions can often maintain distress.

A further class of intermediary belief are the compensatory beliefs [18]. For instance if a person states 'I am bad' the compensatory belief is 'I must protect myself from rejection.' The compensatory strategy may be to sabotage relationships with other people when they appear to be getting too close, or to become excessively self-sacrificing of one's own needs to avoid feared rejection. When developing a formulation with our clients it is important that early experiences are linked to specific core beliefs that are in turn linked to specific conditional beliefs and linked to compensatory strategies so as to provide the client with a coherent theory of the development and maintenance of current problems.

The person may not be aware of having maladaptive schemata (core beliefs) and as such the Beck model takes this into account by noting two different levels. The first level is overt and is at the level of thoughts, feelings and behaviour (overt and observable) usually

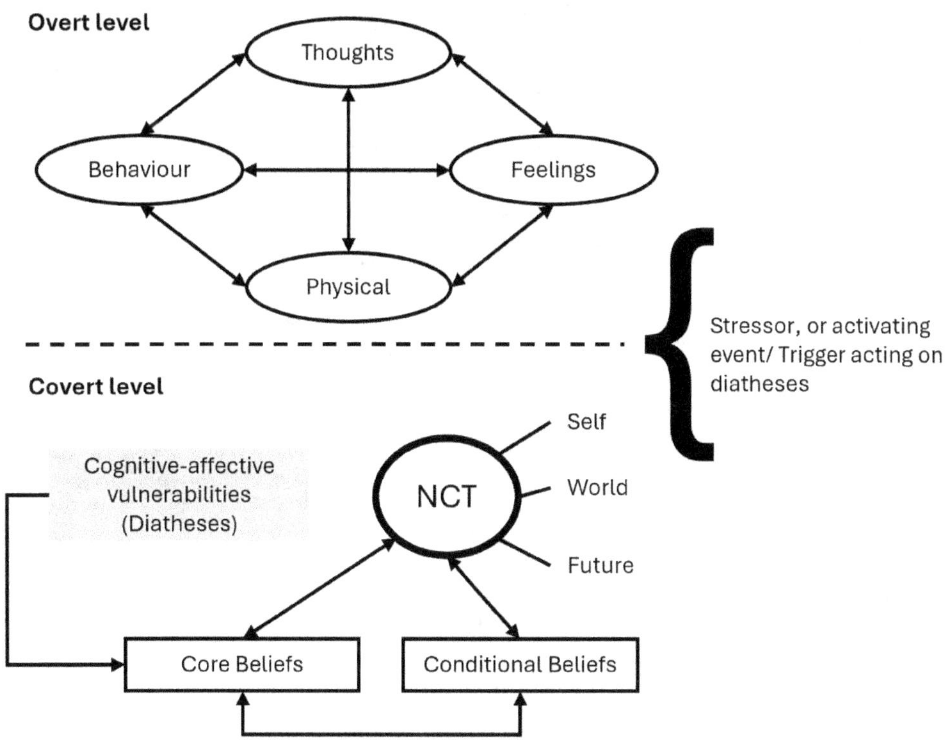

Figure 2.4 Beck's psychopathology model for CBT. Source: Author's own.

articulated by the client when describing the nature of their problems. The second level is covert level and immediately accessible or recognised by the individual. This comprises core beliefs and conditional beliefs. The schematic for Beck's model of psychopathology (see Figure 2.4) visually represents the main elements of the Beck model for CBT.

How the two levels (overt and covert) of the Beck model interact is illustrated in Figure 2.5. This shows that negative thoughts while automatic are not entirely random during depression and anxiety. For example, people with anxiety disorders may be prone to enhanced thoughts of threat, whereas people with depression may be prone to thoughts of loss or failure. Therefore cognitions are considered to be connected to the content of schemata. Figure 2.5 shows that a person with a schema of being worthless will be prone to specific cognitions which are likely with specific sequalae.

Information Processing Errors in the CBT Model

An important element of the cognitive model of psychopathology is the concept of negative automatic thoughts which are central to distress experienced by individuals during an episode of depression or of an anxiety disorder. Interventions designed to target biased thought processing and reasoning to help an individual recognise, measure and challenge erroneous unhelpful cognitions is known as cognitive restructuring [17]. This can be

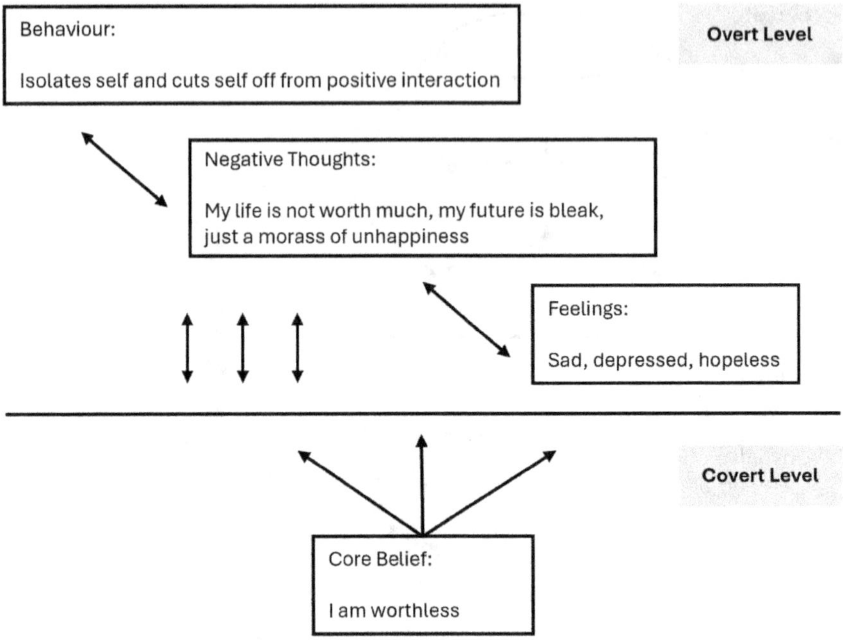

Figure 2.5 Negative thoughts and their underlying covert structure.

achieved via a number of different means within therapy using cognitive (e.g. thought-monitoring) and behavioural (behavioural experiments) strategies.

Within the Beck CBT model, thoughts are considered to be absolute and pervasively negative which is termed the negativity hypothesis [11]. Alongside this, the exclusivity hypothesis suggests the relative absence of any positive thinking around events and experiences. The negativity hypothesis is evident in the negative cognitive triad.

The Negative Cognitive Triad

The negative cognitive triad or NCT [3] constitutes thoughts client hold about themselves, their experiences and their future (in the form such as I am, people are, the future is), reflecting a non-random negative bias. The NCT reflects a negative processing style where anxious and depressed individuals habitually engage in negative and pessimistic appraisals that undermine their efforts to address problems, regulate their affective responses and reinforce negative expectations for current and future personal activity. The NCT can be observed in what this client says to her therapist when describing herself, 'I've not made any progress as a human being [Self]' and 'I think so little of myself. I can't make any changes if I can't help other people [World], there's no point in being around [Future].'

The NCT is restricted to a negative view of self in regard to intrapersonal evaluation [11], and a negative view of the world reflected via the self in relation to others and a negative view of the future in relation to a pessimistic expectation about outcome within an intrapersonal reference (as in the example above). In a somewhat similar approach, the hopelessness theory of depression [19] posited that individuals who experience depression are prone to make attributions that are *global, stable and internal* where a person thinks that their problems have developed because of their incompetence (global attribution, e.g. nothing will ever work out for me) and that these are characteristic of the person and not likely to change (stable attribution; why do I always do this), and are internal attributes that will negatively impact across all areas of life (e.g. I am a mess up).

In the CBT model the content-specificity hypothesis proposes that different mental health conditions (e.g. the anxiety disorders, depression, etc.) can be characterised by specific negative symptomatic cognitive content. For example, depressed individuals are prone to assume failure, while anxious individuals are prone to assume threat to what they do or are expected to do (3, 17). The primacy of negative cognitions does not suggest that presence of negative thoughts causes depression or anxiety, but it suggests that increase in the intensity and frequency of negative thinking will have a consequence in terms of aspects of psychological distress, for example, thoughts have an impact on feelings, behaviour and physiological responses.

When individuals process situations, as schemas may be activated, one should expect there to be characteristic themes evident in the content of thinking (cognitive distortion) and interested readers may wish to look at the early work of Beck [20] for some clear examples of cognitive distortions. These habitual thinking errors have been extensively studied and described. Table 2.1 gives examples of common cognitive distortions.

Consequently when working with cognitions therapists should expect clients to espouse a consistent and coherent apperception of lack of resources to successfully overcome any future situation (in the case of depression) or a lack of resources to deal with threat (in the case of anxiety). In effect the magnification of risk and minimising of personal resources mitigates against client motivations and optimism for overcoming their current problems which also translates into a negative expectation for successful treatment outcome. In anxious or depressed individuals there is a selective attentional bias that encourages the pathological view individuals hold about themselves and their actions [11]. This becomes a negative maintenance cycle that makes it difficult for individuals to believe that change is possible and contributes to the maintenance of a spiral of despair. An example is from Jennifer, aged 68 years old. She experiences low mood and generalised anxiety. During a bank holiday weekend, Jennifer has been on her own for a few days without any family or friends calling in on her. At the end of this period she attended her regularly scheduled appointed with her therapist and said this when asked how she had been since the last session.

> 'I don't matter! I feel more neglected, down, alone, vulnerable' . . . When the therapist asked her what happens when she thinks she doesn't matter [indirectly differentiating feelings from thinking], she replied, 'I phone the Samaritans when I feel desperate' . . . [a good example of self-defeating and self-fulfilling biases evident in a person's thinking which increases their sense of vulnerability]. Jennifer goes on to state, 'I felt terrible, terrible loss. I went to the cinema, drank a bottle of gin when I got home and then I phoned Samaritans about 5.30pm' . . . The more she calls for help the worse she feels about herself as it brings about feelings of shame as she says, 'How am I going to learn now you are wasting your time. If I never learnt now [to cope on my own], typical old woman.'

In this exchange one might look for themes that suggest evidence for schemata, or core beliefs that individuals may use to 'filter' experiences [21,22] in a congruent and habitual manner [3]. Activation of core beliefs may be evident when Jennifer says 'The feeling of deep loneliness and that nobody cares about me; it's been there all my life. It's real to me.' It appears Jennifer has a core schema about being unlovable, and being inadequate. At her

Table 2.1 Common Cognitive Distortions in CBT

Cognitive distortion	Description of distortion	Example of distortion
Arbitrary Inference ***(aka discounting the positive)***	Drawing a specific conclusion in the absence of evidence or evidence to the contrary	Client joins a new book club and thinks everyone must think I am an idiot as everyone else seems to focus on a specific episode in the book that client thought was peripheral to the main plot.
Selective Abstraction ***(aka mental filter)***	Focussing on a detail out of its context while ignoring more salient information	Client gives a presentation at work. Ignores all the positive comments ('they are just being nice') and ruminates on one (constructive) comment from their boss about smiling more when talking. Thinks should start to look for a new job.
Dichotomous Reasoning ***(aka all or nothing thinking)***	Propensity to categorize all experiences in one of two categories	Client's friend cancels a trip to visit for her birthday, and thinks, 'She doesn't care for me, I am all alone in the world.' (Friend's daughter has been taken into hospital unexpectedly.)
Overgeneralisation	Making more of the evidence than is warranted. A single event is used to generate a wider negative conclusion	Acquaintance walking across the street fails to say hello. Client thinks, 'Nobody wants anything to do with me now because they know I am mentally ill (seeing a psychologist).'
Personalisation	Propensity to relate external events to oneself	Client finds out their son is getting divorced and thinks it is his fault, 'I let my son down, I didn't act as a better role model. I didn't show them enough love when I should have.'
Jumping to Conclusions (***aka fortune telling, mind-reading)***	Somewhat like a combination of arbitrary inference and selective abstraction where negative experiences in the here-and-now generate a sense of hopelessness for the future.	Client who is very stressed at work completely 'blanked' on details of a technical specification they were explaining to potential customers and is now worrying they are at the early stages of dementia (they have 'seen' the signs of dementia as their eldest aunt became forgetful and she is now in a nursing home).
Filtering: Magnification and minimisation	Exaggerating (magnification) is taking the significance of an event to extremes whereas	

	down-playing (minimising) the personal significance of an event is usually applied when something positive is turned neutral or negative.	Minimisation: Client completes a behavioural experiment and says 'It's no big deal most people can do this without thinking about it.' Magnification: Client has an argument with their wife and says, 'I ruin everything, she must be sick of me and will be looking for a way out of our marriage.'
Awfulising ***(aka Catastrophising)***	The propensity to think the worst possible outcomes for situations. Often the person ignores contradictory evidence hence often linked with emotional reasoning	Client has bought a new house and notices damp in one room and thinks, 'I have made a foolish buy here, I will lose all my savings in this money-pit!'
Emotional Reasoning	Intensity of emotional response in situations is taken as an indicator of factual measure of danger/risk and assumes this means certain fears are about to be realised.	Client has a panic attack 'out of the blue' and assumes that they are going to die, says, 'You don't feel so afraid unless there is something serious about to happen.'

Other Types of Distortions:

Thought-Action Fusion. Common in OCD where a person thinks that having a thought is as bad as engaging in the action, especially powerful where actions are repulsive to the person (see Shafran, R., Thordarsen, D.S., Rachman, S. (1996). Thought-action fusion in obsessive compulsive disorder. *J. Anxiety Dis.*, 10 (5), 379–391).

Baseline Distortions. Can be more common when people have a physical condition and make unhelpful comparisons with how life was before illness. For example, in stoke person compares how life was before their stroke and finds current circumstances unsatisfactory but this is not a valid comparison as the person should compare current functioning to the day after their stroke and not before it so they can appreciate the progress they have made (see Broomfield, N., Laidlaw, K., Hickabottom, E., Murray, M., Pendrey, R., Whittick, J., & Gillespie, D. (2011) Post-stroke depression: The case for augmented Cognitive Behaviour Therapy. *Clinical Psychology & Psychotherapy: An International Journal of Theory & Practice*, 18 (3), 202–218).

most bleak moments she completely believes 'Nobody cares for me . . . ' despite multiple pieces of evidence to the contrary.

Conclusions

This chapter provides a concise review of the main theoretical elements of Beck's cognitive model. The emphasis has been primarily on depression but this is because the elements of the model are more simply described with a depression frame of reference rather than adding elements of different models for the different anxiety disorders. However the principles are the same and the blueprint for the theory of CBT was first laid down by Beck with reference to depression so we feel we are following a well-trodden path that is hopefully maximally useful as an introduction to the theory of this powerful form of therapy we share with our clients.

Further Reading

The following sources provide more in-depth coverage of topics raised in this chapter.
Relatively recent papers by Beck summarising CBT theory and models:

Beck, & Haigh, E.A.P. (2014). Advances in cognitive theory and therapy: The generic cognitive model. *Annual Review of Clinical Psychology*, **10**, 1–24.

Beck, A. T. & Bredemeier, K. (2016). A unified model of depression: Integrating clinical, cognitive, biological, and evolutionary perspectives. *Clinical Psychological Science*, **4**(4), 596–619.

Beck, A. T. & Dozois, A. J. A. (2011). Cognitive therapy: Current status and future directions. *Annual Review of Medicine*, **62**, 397–409.

Clark, D. A., & Beck, A. T. (1999). *Scientific foundations of cognitive theory and therapy of depression*. New York: Guilford Press.

The authoritative text summarising the theoretical basis for CBT presented definitively in Beck's own words. A must-read book for all CBT therapists.

Joormann, J. & Tanovic, E. (2015). Cognitive vulnerability to depression: examining cognitive control and emotion regulation. *Current Opinion in Psychology*, **4**, 86–92.

References

1. David, D., Cristea, I., & Hofmann, S. G. (2018). Why cognitive behavioral therapy is the current gold standard of psychotherapy. *Frontiers Psychiatry*, **9**, 4.
2. Mennin, D. S., Ellard, K. K., Fresco, D. M., & Gross, J. J. (2013). United we stand: Emphasizing commonalities across cognitive-behavioral therapies. *Behavior Therapy*, **44**(2), 234–48.
3. Beck, A. T., & Bredemeier, K. (2016). A unified model of depression: Integrating clinical, cognitive, biological, and evolutionary perspectives. *Clinical Psychological Science*, **4**(4), 596–619.
4. Beck, A. T., & Dozois, D. J. (2011). Cognitive therapy: Current status and future directions. *Annual Review of Medicine*, **62**, 397–409.
5. Lorenzo-Luaces, L., Keefe, J., & DeRubeis, R. J. (2016). Cognitive-behavioral therapy: Nature and relation to non-cognitive behavioral therapy. *Behavior Therapy*, **47**(6), 785–803.
6. Lewin, K. (1952). *Field theory in social science: Selected theoretical papers by Kurt Lewin*. London, UK: Tavistock.

7. Fried, E. I. (2020). Theories and models: What they are, what they are form, and what they are about. *Psychological Inquiry*, **31**(4), 336–344.
8. Smaldino, P. E. (2020). How to build a strong theoretical foundation. *Psychological Inquiry*, **31**(4), 297–301.
9. Clark, D. M. (1986). A cognitive approach to panic. *Behaviour Research and Therapy*, **24**(4), 461–470.
10. Barlow, D. H., Allen, L. B., & Choate, M. L. (2016). Toward a unified treatment for emotional disorders. *Behaviour Therapy*, **47**, 838–853.
11. Clark, D. A., & Beck, A. T. (1999). *Scientific foundations of cognitive theory and therapy of depression*. New York: Guilford Press.
12. Ingram, R. E., Miranda, J., & Segal, Z. V. (1998). *Cognitive vulnerability to depression*. New York: Guilford Press.
13. Power, M. J., & Dalgleish, T. (2015). *Cognition and emotion: From order to disorder*. 3rd ed. London: Routledge.
14. Power, M. J. (2010). *Emotion-focused cognitive therapy*. London: Wiley-Blackwell.
15. Liu, R.T. & Alloy, L.B. (2010). Stress generation in depression: A systematic review of the empirical literature and recommendations for future study. *Clinical Psychology Review*, **30**(5), 582–593.
16. Hammen, C. (2006). Stress generation in depression: Reflections on origins, research and future directions. *Journal of Clinical Psychology*, **62**(9), 1065–1082.
17. Beck, A. T., & Haigh, E. A. P. (2014). Advances in cognitive theory and therapy: The generic cognitive model. *Annual Review of Clinical Psychology*, **10**, 1–24.
18. Beck, J. S. (2011). *Cognitive behavior therapy: Basics and beyond*. 2nd ed. New York: Guilford Press.
19. Liu, R. T., Kleiman, E. M., Nestor, B. A., & Cheek, S. M. (2015). The hopelessness theory of depression: A quarter century in review. *Clinical Psychology*, **22**(4), 345–365.
20. Beck, A. T. (1970). Cognitive therapy: Nature and relation to behavior therapy. *Behavior Therapy*, **1**, 184–200.
21. Joormann J., & Gotlib I. H. (2010). Emotion regulation in depression: relation to cognitive inhibition. *Cognition and Emotion*, **24**, 281–298.
22. Davis, D. J. A., & Rnic, K. (2015). Core beliefs and self-schematic structure in depression. *Current Opinion in Psychology*, **4**, 98–103.

Chapter 3

Efficacy of CBT: A Brief Outline and Review

This chapter will help you to be able to:

- Describe in brief a comprehensive overview of the evidence-base for CBT across the range of common mental health conditions.
- Critically appraise the evidence-base for CBT for depression and the anxiety disorders.
- Exercise choice for your treatment approach based on the evidence-base for CBT.
- Use the evidence-base for CBT to support the use of CBT where treatment protocols are lacking or are under-developed.
- Be better equipped to function more confidently as an evidence-based clinician by appraising yourself of outcome literature for CBT.

Introduction

Cognitive behavioural therapy is the most systematically evaluated form of psychotherapy with numerous clinical guidelines recommending its use for common mental health conditions [1]. CBT has established itself as the gold standard evidence-based psychotherapy [2] and is recommended in NICE guidelines (UK) and in APA guidelines (see [3]) as an efficacious mainstream treatment for depression and anxiety disorders including PTSD [4]. CBT is efficacious with adults [1,7], children and adolescents [5,6], older people [8,46,47] and across a range of conditions (e.g. Parkinson's disease [48]; eating disorders [10] etc.). This chapter provides a brief overview of the empirical basis for CBT and should equip you with sufficient guidance to understand how the empirical evidence stacks up for CBT across a range of common clinical conditions.

Adding to the overall sense of efficacy for CBT as an evidence-based treatment, Fordham et al. [11] conducted a comprehensive panoramic meta-analysis of systematic reviews and meta-analyses of CBT. The panoramic approach adopted by Fordham et al. [11] is in effect *a systematic review of the most robust systematic reviews of CBT*. Their review included 494 peer-reviewed published reviews comprising 221,128 participants providing clinical evidence for CBT outcome. Fordham et al. [11] concluded the quality of reviews were poor and as such focussed their analyses on high-intensity delivered CBT. Consistent results across studies confirmed CBT is efficacious and improves quality of life with symptomatic improvements maintained for 12 months after the end of treatment. Overall, this broad review provides further evidence for the wide applicability of CBT as an evidence-based psychological intervention.

Evidence-Based Practice

Adhering to the evidence-base is not just important as part of CBT's 'DNA', it is also important because at some point clinicians will be required to consider treatment interventions where there is not necessarily a consensus on treatment approaches, or where, inevitably there are gaps in the scientific evidence for conditions, populations or individual circumstance, or where no treatment protocols exists despite clinical need (e.g. post-stroke anxiety, Knapp et al. [12]). In this scenario clinicians should be guided by the principles of evidence-based practice or clinical guidelines [3,13]. To defer on using evidence is to resort to opinion and as Bertrand Russell once famously said, 'The fact that an opinion has been widely held is no evidence whatever that it is not utterly absurd.' To take one example it used to be a widely held opinion that CBT with older people would be less effective and that older people would not benefit from CBT as they were too set in their ways and lacked the cognitive flexibility to benefit from CBT, however evidence from clinical trials and more naturalistically from Improving Access to Psychological Therapy (IAPT) (NHS talking therapies) services shows this to be manifestly false and moreover evidence from older people who receive CBT via NHS talking therapy services report better outcomes with less attrition (drop-out) than compared to data for working age adults, see Chaplin et al. [14] and Saunders et al. [15]. Thus, CBT therapists need to remain resolutely evidence-based practitioners to ensure they can support change in all the client groups we work with and to avoid potential risk of therapeutic drift [16].

Evidence-based practice (EBP) requires that people use the best available evidence and in so doing must exercise critical appraisal of evidence as it exists, as well as taking account of factors pertaining to services, culture, and individual characteristics and preferences (see [13] for review). As such EBP is a complex action on the part of the therapist as applying this requires the clinician to rely, at least in part, or their clinical experience or treatment-specific expertise. This chapter aims to help CBT therapists augment and enhance their treatment specific expertise to promote individual client choice and satisfaction for treatment but interested readers may wish to consult Singel et al. [17].

While we often talk about the effectiveness of CBT in a range of settings and with different populations, what we are usually referring to is efficacy outcome. in clinical research trials efficacy is quite different from effectiveness. Thus we should more properly talk about efficacy. Effectiveness trials are usually conducted in more naturalistic clinical settings, considered more 'real-world conditions' and have less strict conditions associated with efficacy trials. There may be looser constraints to eligible participants than one may typically find in efficacy trials. Singel et al. [17] provide a simple way of defining the difference between the two types of trials: efficacy answers the question whether the interventions works under ideal circumstances and effectiveness answers the question whether the intervention works in real world clinical practice.

Understanding Meta-Analyses

To be able to independently and autonomously make sense of data from Meta-Analysis a quick primer may be useful (for more in-depth detail see Cuijpers [18], available free at www.pimcuijpers.com/blog/meta-analysis/). Meta-Analyses (MA) take a number of research papers examining a similar issue (e.g. CBT treatment for depression) and by combining them together, results can be magnified so that we can see if a treatment works. It is more powerful to combine studies together as we gain a much larger sample size and we can see more clearly whether treatments are efficacious. This is done by calculating effect sizes of all studies combined. It is an efficient means of considering what treatments work best under which set of circumstances. In MA it is usual to compare one form of treatment with another treatment (comparator) with effect sizes calculated to quantify and compare the effect to other treatments or control conditions. Thus, MA has become very common within CBT research as a tool to demonstrate strength of the evidence base of CBT compared to other psychotherapies, placebos, medication, waiting-lists etc. An effect size (ES) is calculated very simply by subtracting the mean (average) scores for CBT from the mean scores for the control or comparison condition and then dividing this figure by the pooled standard deviation (variability of spread of scores across both treatment groups). Cohen [49] provided a helpful rule of thumb when he suggested that an ES of 0.2 is small, an ES of 0.5 is medium and an ES of 0.8 and above is large. In reality, most ES quoted in research papers are a little more complicated as corrections for sample sizes are often taken account of. Hedges' G is often reported instead of Cohen's d so as to provide a less biased result when small samples sizes are used. As well as taking note of effect sizes in MA, results are often interpreted in terms of heterogeneity (variability of scores) of the studies entered into MAs. Usually I^2 is quoted as an index of this heterogeneity on a relative scale, with scores of 25% considered small, scores of 50% as medium and scores of 75% and above as large and likely to be problematic. Thus ES with large I^2 scores need to interpreted cautiously.

Reading charts and graphs in MAs can also look intimidating to the uninitiated as Forrest Plots are often the primary means of representing summary data outcomes. Despite looking a little on the scary side with lines, numbers, bars, and other items, Forrest plots are relatively simple to make sense of. A Forrest plot has a central vertical dividing line which is usually assigned a value of zero. To the left of this dividing line scores are usually represented as negative (e.g. −2, −.5, etc.) and to the right scores are positive. Usually ES are displayed graphically as a box (or square) for each individual study in the MA with lines protruding from either side. Horizontal lines extruding from the box indicate confidence intervals (CI). Where the box falls in the graph indicates both strength and direction of effect. For example if we are comparing the efficacy of CBT for depression to that of a waiting list control condition, ES in the form of box would appear on the right side of the Forrest plot if CBT is more efficacious in comparison to a control condition. The boxes vary in size as these are weighted average scores representing relative contribution to the overall effect size for the MA. Larger size indicates larger relative contribution to overall ES. Usually shorter CI are linked with larger box sizes in Forrest plots. On the bottom of the Forrest plot there is a diamond which represents the overall (pooled) effect size for the MA. This 'bottom-line' figure is usually what people turn to first as it indicates what the effect size is for the MA comparison. The diamond is usually quantified as a score indicating strength of ES and we can use Cohen's helpful rule of thumb to interpret this.

Not everyone agrees with MA as quality of reports depend very much on the quality of the data being entered into the calculations and the methodological precision of the researchers. Some MAs can be criticised for poor comparisons to the treatment condition a researcher wants to show is efficacious. This can sometimes be portrayed as comparing apples to oranges. Bias is also easy to import into MAs. The Cochrane review research group have produced guidelines for producing robust MA [19], and with QUOROM (Quality of

Reporting of Meta-analyses: [20]) updated in 2009 by Moher et al. [50] to PRISMA (Preferred Reporting Items for Systematic Reviews and Meta-analyses) guidelines for meta-analyses of controlled trials are readily available.

CBT Evidence Base

Evidence for the efficacy of CBT as a psychological treatment for depression has always used randomised controlled trials (RCTs) and latterly systematic reviews and meta-analyses as the foundational evidence upon which to establish CBT as a scientifically robust mainstream treatment intervention. The National Institution for Health and Care Excellence (NICE) recommends CBT for treating depression and the anxiety disorders [21]. Much of the evidence from RCTs are considered to meet the gold standard of evidence in medicine proving that treatments work reliably, consistently and effectively. While RCTs are not perfect as they are often performed in conditions quite different from standard clinical practice they constitute a robust test of any form of psychotherapy outcome and constitute the best evidence that can be generated. Comparisons in RCTs are often carefully chosen and all extraneous variables that may bias outcome for either comparison condition in an RCT are controlled as best can be. Individual RCTs may not be able to tell us much about process issues in CBT but they do provide us with a surety that our procedures, techniques work and justify following protocols as best we can in routine practice.

Randomised controlled trials applied in clinical settings aim to evaluate whether a treatment works. In the case of CBT RCTs usually compare CBT to another treatment such as another psychotherapy, treatment as usual or medication and or/placebo treatment conditions. Some RCTs user weaker comparisons such as a control conditions like waiting list. Allocation of research participants (usually patients who consent to take part in research evaluations) is done entirely at random and is not under the control of the researcher. This is done so that certain client characteristics such as age, gender, duration of time living with a condition, and so on are distributed evenly between the treatment groups. This hopefully avoids a bias favouring any treatment group and means that generally we should be able to say that any treatment differences between groups will have occurred as a result of the psychological treatment under test. It is usual in RCTs that CBT delivery is strictly controlled and monitored to ensure it is delivered optimally according to manuals and protocols. Evaluation usually follows a standardised procedure using appropriate psychometric measures (e.g. PHQ9, BDI-II etc.) and it is common for follow-up to occur after the end of treatment. Randomised controlled trial evidence is considered the strongest evidence for psychological therapy efficacy.

Evidence from individual RCTs have always been a key part of the story of treatment efficacy but systematic reviews and meta-analysis are also important sources of evidence. As these tend to appraise and summarise the evidence from a number of studies rather than basing outcome on a single trial they are excellent means of comprehensively reviewing evidence of CBT for specific conditions and specific populations. For the purposes of this chapter meta-analyses and systematic reviews will be the primary source consulted and reviewed here.

CBT Evidence for Depression

The original RCT evaluating the efficacy of CBT for depression was conducted by Beck and colleagues in the 1970s [22] and became the first treatment trial to demonstrate that a psychotherapy (CBT) alone could be a superior treatment compared to physical treatments for depression (i.e. medication). Forty-one moderately to severely depressed participants were randomly allocated to receive either CBT or medication (impramine), with the majority reporting suicidal ideation and a sizeable minority having been depressed for more than one year prior to entering the trial. Over treatment both groups reported symptomatic improvement, with CBT participants reporting significantly stronger treatment response compared to medication and with fewer numbers of participant drop-out. At the end of treatment 79% of CBT participants reported a marked or complete improvement (BDI scores less than 9), whereas only 23% of the medication group reported similar levels of improvement. Treatment gains and treatment differences were maintained at six-month follow-up. This study was so ground-breaking that results were initially doubted but it has laid down a clear pathway to scientific evaluation of CBT and a clear result for the efficacy of CBT for many others to follow.

Another major evaluation of the efficacy of CBT for depression was the US-based treatment of depression collaborative programme (TDCRP) sponsored by the NIMH in the 1980s [23,24]. This significant national clinical trial often known as the TDCRP study compared four supervised and manualised treatment groups CBT versus IPT (interpersonal therapy) versus medication (imipramine) plus clinical management, versus pill-placebo plus clinical management across three different treatment sites each with specific expertise in the active treatment conditions. The TDRCP did confirm CBT as an efficacious treatment for depression but it did not outperform IPT, and medication performed best of all conditions when considering more severely depressed participants. When comparing treatment outcome for less severely depressed participants medication and IPT did better than CBT and CBT did not outperform placebo plus clinical management. Overall CBT performed relatively poorly in the TDRCP but there are indications there was variability in performance across different sites and with more severe populations CBT performed better and more consistent with expectations. The TDRCP study was controversial at the time and results remain disputed. Elkin et al. [24] subsequently wrote a paper to address some of the key issues following on from the original TDCRP study and re-iterates one of the key findings that medication plus placebo performed particularly well. Steve Hollon and colleagues followed up the trial methodology of the original TDCRP in a number of studies and showed that for severe depression CBT is more efficacious than medication, or IPT or placebo and that people who respond to CBT are less likely to relapse following treatment making it a more cost-effective treatment than antidepressant medication over time (for more detailed outcome see [51,52,53,54]). Reviewing efficacy of CBT for depression Hollon [25] lays out a very well-reasoned review outlining concerns about the adequacy of the TDRCP which raises caution over how much weight the findings of one study should carry. The substantial body of treatment trials conducted by Rob DeRubeis and Steve Hollon at the turn of the millennium (see Hollon [25]) did help restore the status of CBT as an efficacious treatment for common mental health conditions.

Dobson [55] conducted one of the first meta-analyses of CBT for depression and while results strongly favour CBT this paper is less cited nowadays as the analyses failed to consider therapist allegiance and as such outcome may have been biased towards CBT. Other early meta-analyses [56] clearly demonstrate that CBT for depression produced strong results with CBT being as efficacious as behaviour therapy (BT) and marginally more efficacious than medication. Both Gloaguen [56] and Butler [57] demonstrate CBT's superiority to waiting list.

Butler et al. [26] produced a comprehensive analysis of CBT across populations and clinical conditions which provided an overall strong case for the efficacy of CBT at that time. CBT for depression was considered more efficacious than placebo, medication and wait list conditions. Comparisons to other forms of psychotherapy are more nuanced in interpretation as the data did not allow definitive conclusions to be reached and partially this was to do with a low number of comparative studies and the lower amount of efficacy data generated for some other forms of psychotherapy.

Cuijpers et al. [27] conducted a meta-analysis of strictly defined CBT for depression with 112 studies meeting inclusion criteria with 65% of the studies being RCTs comparing CBT with a control condition (wait-list, TAU, placebo, etc.). Overall the quality of studies entered into the MA was 'questionable' for the majority of studies and when the MA was conducted on highest quality studies only the effect size (ES) was lower for the MA as whole. Nevertheless, ES was large at 0.71 overall for this MA and moderate (0.53) when only looking at high quality studies. However, CBT even when less optimally applied is still nevertheless efficacious. CBT compared to medication was reviewed in 20/115 studies with no difference (ES = 0.03) observed for CBT meaning there is no difference in efficacy between treatments. Likewise, when compared to other psychotherapies on the whole CBT is not superior in RCTs. However, comparisons are very small for other psychotherapies so one must exercise a degree of caution when interpreting current results. While these results may seem a little underwhelming it indicates that CBT works as well as the mainstream treatment for depression and that other psychotherapies who adopt an evidence-base approach such that they can meet criteria for evaluation in an RCT provide good treatment alternatives in depression. As such while there is no question of the efficacy of CBT for depression especially as the CBT is the most extensively evaluated form of psychotherapy perhaps a more balanced view of the true efficacy of CBT can be determined by MAs adopting strictest quality criteria.

In a follow up to the review by Cuijpers and colleagues in 2013, since it has been noted that CBT is the most commonly evaluated form of psychotherapy, Cuijpers et al. [1] examined the efficacy of CBT in a further comprehensive MA that compared outcome between CBT and other psychotherapies and medication (and combination) across age groups, clinical populations, and so on. The majority of studies entered into this review focussed on adults with depression in various clinical settings with less than 10% of the sample represented by children and young people. CBT was compared in a range of formats, individual, group, guided and unguided self-help etc. Results overall are encouraging as CBT reported large effect sizes (0.79) when compared to treatment as usual and/or waiting list conditions. At 10–12 month follow-up moderate effect sizes (0.49) were reported for CBT suggesting gains are maintained after the end of treatment. In comparison to other psychotherapies as with the review by Cuijpers et al. [1] differences in outcome are minimal with effect sizes reported at 0.06 but at longer term follow-up small to moderate differences in outcome (ES = 0.34) appear suggesting differential impact of having CBT. As previously found by Cuijpers et al. [28], it appears CBT is more efficacious when delivered in combination with medication. Although the number of studies are small it appears there is evidence that combined CBT and medication is not more efficacious than CBT both at end of treatment and at follow-up. This very comprehensive review provides a lot of interesting evidence for practitioners but despite its comprehensiveness there are still a number of gaps in our knowledge so one must always proceed cautiously but nevertheless CBT looks to have established a strong track record of efficacy as a treatment for depression.

Cuijpers et al. [28] produced a network MA (also known as mega-regressions) comparing a number of forms of psychotherapy and medication for depression. Network meta-analyses (NMA) can incorporate a very large number of studies and allow multiple comparisons in a way standard meta-analyses cannot. In this NMA, CBT was the most commonly applied form of psychotherapy. Results showed combined psychotherapy and medication produces the strongest treatment outcome and there was no difference in treatment outcome for either psychotherapy or medication alone. Similar results were reported when looking at achieving remission and when treating chronic or treatment-resistant depression, thus medication plus psychotherapy appears to be the first rank treatment approach for depression. Cuijpers et al. [28] also examined acceptability of treatment and while again results suggest combined treatment is acceptable, psychotherapy alone is more acceptable to patients than medication alone. 'Findings from this paper clearly show that combined treatment is the best option in moderate depression, and in routine clinical care it would be better to consider psychotherapy as the first choice when only one treatment is offered to a patient' ([28], p. 102).

Summary: Evidence for CBT for Depression

CBT is undoubtedly an evidence-based and mainstream treatment for depression and has been extensively evaluated in more four decades of RCTs of CBT alone and in combination with medication, clinical trials, naturalistic studies of outcome, meta-analyses and systematic reviews. CBT is recognised as efficacious in NICE guidelines and has been made available nationally out free of access in the NHS in England since 2008 via NHS Talking Therapies (previously IAPT) services. Substantial clinical outcome data has been generated by NHS Talking Therapies outside of the narrow confines of research settings showing CBT to be of enormous benefit to the very many thousands of people receiving help with depression. There remains much work to do to ensure that more complex presentations of depression and depression in the presence of other contexts or conditions is optimally effective for reducing distress. Nevertheless the early promise and hopes for CBT expressed by the authors of the first ever RCT of CBT [22] seem very well justified.

CBT for Anxiety Disorders

In their recent panoramic meta-analysis, Fordham et al. [11] reported CBT as overall moderately efficacious for anxiety disorders in their subsample of 34 papers cutting across 12 anxiety conditions. This should come as no surprise to most psychological practitioners as it is evident that CBT provides clients with a way of understanding and overcoming anxiety generating thoughts and affect [58]. The first evidence for psychological therapy as an effective intervention to alleviate distress comes from the anxiety domain. Based on the principles of classical conditioning from learning theory, that is, that what can be learned (via paired stimuli), can be unlearned, Wolf [29] taught people to develop relaxation skills and then help people become desensitized to feared stimuli by repeated systematic graded exposure, via a hierarchy of feared situations, which resulted in symptomatic relief (see [30] for a thoughtful account of Wolf's legacy for CBT). It would be remiss to fail to mention the pioneering work of Professor Mary Cover Jones in the 1920s especially as Wolf considered her the mother of behaviourism and Rachman [31] contextualises the importance of her work in applying behaviourism as therapeutically viable. As an early pioneer of BT she produced a positive demonstration of how conditioning as extinction could be used to treat fears and phobia in 'little Peter'. She successfully treated his fears and established principles of treatment for others to follow [32]. Behavioural approaches while radical in their own right provided interventions to reduce symptoms of anxiety disorders that neglected to incorporate non-observable elements such as cognition. Rachman [31] provides an excellent and interesting account of the historical developments of cognitive and behavioural approaches and outlines the opposition early psychologists faced when proposing treatments for anxiety disorders. Such a personable account written by Rachman as one of the leading protagonists in what we all take for granted, the ability for psychologists to provide psychological treatments, is highly recommended reading. Beck's concepts and therapeutic interventions became part of behavioural approaches to the treatment of anxiety disorders [59] and in the UK the treatment models and protocols developed by David Clark and Paul Salkovskis provided great advances for clinicians to treat anxiety disorders. As treatment protocols became more refined and focussed across different anxiety conditions, more cognitively oriented approaches held sway, and it became clear that relaxation was not a necessary component of anxiety treatment [33]. In the UK, David Clark and his colleagues focussed attention on understanding and treating panic disorder (PD) with agoraphobia and established a specific model for PD that established principles of CBT for anxiety disorders more generally [33,34]. As Rachman [31] notes at page 5, 'Clark's admirably succinct theory is of historical significance because it became a model for the cognitive analysis of various manifestations of anxiety, and the effectiveness of the therapy deduced from the theory, is impressive.'

The large corpus of research conducted to establish CBT as an evidence-based treatment for the anxiety disorders can be efficiently reviewed via the most substantive systematic reviews and meta-analyses (see [11,35,36,60]).

Cuijpers et al. [35] conducted a comprehensive meta-analysis that considered the relative efficacy of CBT for GAD, social anxiety disorder (SAD) and PD in comparison to a control condition. The outcome for each condition was primarily calculated using psychometrically robust and valid measures of anxiety, for example, the Beck Anxiety Inventory (BAI), State-Trait Anxiety Inventory (STAI) and the Hamilton Rating Scale for Anxiety (HAMA) across 2477 participants in 42 RCTs that met inclusion criteria. CBT was compared to other placebo conditions, waiting list, treatment as usual (excepting psychotherapy), and so on. Individually delivered, group delivered and professionally supported guided self-help formats were included in the review. Results perhaps unsurprisingly showed that outcomes for panic disorder reported stronger scores on the BAI compared to that for SAD and GAD. CBT efficacy overall across the three types of anxiety disorders reported large effect sizes but data indicates that PD may report better CBT outcomes than SAD and GAD. This outcome requires careful consideration as outcome was measured using generic measures of anxiety and there were differential levels of methodological quality and in some anxiety conditions there are smaller numbers of clinical trials. In a separate meta-analysis, Cuijpers et al. [37] reported that CBT for anxiety disorders (GAD, SAD, PD) reported large effect sizes when compared to waiting list control, but moderate effect sizes when compared to treatment as usual and placebo control conditions.

Papola et al. [36] conducted an inclusive systematic review and network meta-analysis comparing ten different psychotherapies in terms of outcome for PD. The three best performing psychotherapies for PD were BT, CBT and short-term psychodynamic psychotherapy. After accounting for data biases potentially inflating treatment outcomes (75 out of 136 included RCTs were considered to have some indice of bias) only CBT and BT remained efficacious in comparison to treatment as usual.

Summary: Evidence for CBT for the Anxiety Disorders

CBT reports strong results for the treatment of anxiety disorders and can be justifiably considered a first-rank mainstream treatment to reduce symptoms and distress associated with the range of anxiety conditions. Anxiety treatment can be considered the foundation base for the establishment of evidence-based principles of psychological treatment. CBT has a long tradition in establishing, enhancing and extending the evidence-base for the treatment of the anxiety disorders. While more work can be done on the relative efficacy of CBT for the different anxiety disorders there is much for clinicians to celebrate as they can invest confidence in existing CBT protocols for the anxiety disorders.

CBT with Older People

Evidence for the efficacy of CBT with older people is strong and comes from a range of sources including RCTs [28,37,38,39,46,47,61], naturalistic data from NHS taking therapy services [14,15] and systematic reviews [45]. CBT with older people also shows good potential for depression and anxiety in dementia (see [40] for review). CBT is efficacious with dementia caregivers, with Kwon et al. [62] reporting data from a meta-analysis showing good outcome for depression in dementia caregivers and Hopkinson et al. [41] noting in their meta-analysis that caregivers who received CBT reported significant reductions in levels of depression and stress. Innovative applications of CBT are being pioneered in residential care settings with depressed older people with promising results [42,43].

Contrary to opinion CBT is not less efficacious with older people and indeed data from audits of outcome from NHS talking therapies suggests older people do rather well in comparison to working age adults when it comes to recovery and attrition. Saunders et al. [15] reported outcome data for people receiving therapy across eight IAPT services across London and noted better outcomes for older people in comparison to working age adults. Saunders et al. [15] summarized this data by noting that older people were 30% more likely to recover after a course of treatment compared to outcome reported for working age adults. Moreover, older people required *fewer* sessions than working age adults and attrition from treatment was much *lower*. When Saunders et al. [15] took account of the impact of physical illnesses (long-term conditions (LTCs)) on outcome, these had much more negative impact on treatment outcome with working age adults compared to older people.

Contrary also to meta-analyses by Covin et al. [44] and Gould et al. [46,47], suggesting that CBT may be less efficacious with older people, meta-analyses report no differences in psychotherapy outcome between older people and working age adults Cuijpers et al. [28,45].

Looking at specific age-related outcomes for CBT two meta-analyses adopt specific age comparisons when examining treatment outcome. Kishita and Laidlaw [38] conducted a meta-analysis comparing CBT outcome for GAD between older people and working age adults. This meta-analysis adopted an approach to explicitly focus on outcome in age groups within a single meta-analysis. Thus outcome studies for CBT for GAD comparing across age groups used the same outcome metrics and the same inclusion and methodology criteria. By doing so a more precise deliberation on the question of whether treatment outcome for GAD was different for older people. Kishita and Laidlaw [38] reported no statistically significant treatment differences.

Werson et al. [39] used a similar methodology to that reported by Kishita and Laidlaw [38] and this time compared outcome for CBT for depression between older people and working age adults. This meta-analyses compared 37 RCTs and 3499 participants. Overall for this meta-analysis, CBT reported better outcome in comparison to active and passive control conditions. When comparing outcome for CBT for depression between the age groups there was no significant difference. Werson et al. [39] concluded that CBT practitioners should expect equivalent outcomes for older people and as such there is no justification for older people to be denied access to evidence-based treatments such as CBT.

Final Summary and Conclusions

This chapter cannot hope to cover all instances in which an evidence-base has been generated for CBT so interested readers are advised to also consult specific specialist texts for this purpose with some key reading sources outlined at the end of this chapter. As a result, in order to provide readers with a sufficiently contemporary and reasonably comprehensive review of the efficacy of CBT we have focussed primarily on outcomes for CBT with the common mental health conditions. CBT has a substantial evidence-base and has been more extensively evaluated compared to other forms of psychotherapy. To an extent that is because the structural elements of CBT lend themselves to explication via manuals and treatment protocols. In other respects it is because of the CBT founders' belief in the need to create a scientific therapy. As CBT practitioners we are fortunate to have an extensive evidence-base but it is by no means exhaustive or complete and there remains much research to be conducted to support the work we do and to extend the beneficial reach to a range of clinical populations with as yet unmet need.

Further Reading

The following sources provide more in-depth coverage of topics raised in this chapter.

Some recent comprehensive reviews of the efficacy of CBT across a range of conditions and population can be consulted:

American Psychological Association. (2019). Clinical practice guideline for the treatment of depression across three age cohorts. www.apa.org/depression-guideline.

Bhattacharya S, Goicoechea C, Heshmati S, Carpenter JK, Hofmann S. Efficacy of cognitive behavioral therapy for anxiety-related disorders: A meta-analysis of recent literature. *Current Psychiatry Reports*, 2023;**25**:19–30. https://doi.org/10.1007/s11920-022-01402-8.

Cuijpers P, Miguel C, Harrer M, Plessen CY, Ciharova M, Ebert D, Karyotaki E. Cognitive behavior therapy vs. control conditions, other psychotherapies, pharmacotherapies and combined treatment for depression: A comprehensive meta-analysis including 409 trials with 52,702 patients. *World Psychiatry*, 2023;**22**:105–115.

David D, Cristea I, Hofmann SG. Why cognitive behavioral therapy is the current gold standard of psychotherapy. *Frontiers Psychiatry*, 2018;**9**(4). https://doi.org/10.3389/fpsyt.2018.00004.

Fordham B, Sugavanam T, Edwards K, Stallard P, Howard R, das Nair R et al. The evidence for cognitive behavioural therapy in any condition, population or context: A metareview of systematic reviews and panoramic meta-analysis. *Psychological Medicine*, 2021;**51**:21–29. https://doi.org/10.1017/S0033291720005292.

Fukomori M, Kikuchi T, Zhou Y, Hittori S, Kudo T. Network meta-analysis of the effectiveness of psychotherapies with or without medication for treating adult depression. *Acta Neuropsychiatrica*, 2024;**36**(6):423–437.

Werson A, Meiser-Stedman R, Laidlaw K. A meta-analysis of CBT efficacy for depression comparing adults and older adults. *Journal of Affective Disorders*, 2022;**319**:189–201.

References

1. Cuijpers P, Miguel C, Harrer M, Plessen CY, Ciharova M, Ebert D, Karyotaki E. Cognitive behavior therapy vs. control conditions, other psychotherapies, pharmacotherapies and combined treatment for depression: A comprehensive meta-analysis including 409 trials with 52,702 patients. *World Psychiatry*, 2023;**22**:105–115.
2. David D, Cristea I, Hofmann SG Why Cognitive Behavioral Therapy is the current gold standard of psychotherapy. *Frontiers Psychiatry*, 2018;**9**(4). https://doi.org/10.3389/fpsyt.2018.00004.
3. American Psychological Association. (2019). Clinical Practice Guideline for the Treatment of Depression across Three Age Cohorts. www.apa.org/depression-guideline.
4. Bhattacharya S, Goicoechea C, Heshmati S, Carpenter JK, Hofmann S. Efficacy of cognitive behavioral therapy for anxiety-related disorders: A meta-analysis of recent literature. *Current Psychiatry Reports*, 2023;**25**:19–30. https://doi.org/10.1007/s11920-022-01402-8.
5. Arnberg A, Ost, L-G. CBT for children with depressive symptoms: A meta-analysis. *Cognitive Behaviour Therapy*, 2014;**43**:275–288.
6. Oud M, de Winter L, Vermeulen-Smit E, Bodden, D, Nauta, M, Stone, L, et al. Effectiveness of CBT for children and adolescents with depression: A systematic review and meta-regression analysis. *European Psychiatry*, 2019;**57**:33–45.
7. Cuijpers P, Noma H, Karyotaki E, Cipriani A, Furukawa TA. Effectiveness and Acceptability of Cognitive Behavior Therapy Delivery Formats in Adults With Depression: A Network Meta-analysis. *JAMA Psychiatry*. 2019;**76**(7):700–707.
8. Werson A, Meiser-Stedman R, Laidlaw K. A meta-analysis of CBT efficacy for depression comparing adults and older adults. *Journal of Affective Disorders*, 2022;**319**:189–201.
9. Dobbin RD, Mann SL, Intern A, Gara MA, Menza M. Cognitive behavioral therapy improves diverse profiles of depressive symptoms in Parkinson's disease. *International Journal of Geriatric Psychiatry*, 2019;**34**:722–729.
10. Linardon J, Wade TD, de l Piedad Garcia X, Brenna L. The efficacy of cognitive-behavioural therapy for eating disorders: A systematic review and meta-analysis. *Journal of Consulting and Clinical Psychology*, 2017;**85**:1080–1094.
11. Fordham B, Sugavanam T, Edwards K, Stallard P, Howard R, das Nair R et al. The evidence for cognitive behavioural therapy in any condition, population or context: a metareview of systematic reviews and panoramic meta-analysis. *Psychological Medicine*, 2021;**51**:21–29. https://doi.org/10.1017/S0033291720005292.
12. Knapp P, Campbell Burton CA, Holmes J, Murray J, Gillespie D, Lightbody CE, Watkins CL, Chun HY, Lewis SR. Interventions for treating anxiety after stroke. *Cochrane Database of Systematic Reviews*, 2017;**5**(5):CD008860. https://doi.org/10.1002/14651858.CD008860.pub3.
13. American Psychological Association. (2021). Professional Practice Guidelines for Evidence-Based Psychological Practice in Health Care. www.apa.org/about/policy/evidence-based-psychological-practice-health-care.pdf.
14. Chaplin R, Farquharson L, Clapp M, Crawford M. Comparison of access, outcomes and experiences of older adults and working age adults in psychological therapy. *International Journal of Geriatric Psychiatry*, 2015;**30**:178–184.
15. Saunders R, Buckman JEJ, Stott J, Leibowitz J, Aguirre E, John A, et al. Older adults respond better to psychological therapy than working-age adults: Evidence from a large sample of mental health service attendees. *Journal of Affective Disorders*, 2021;**294**:85–93.
16. Waller G, Turner H. Therapeutic drift redux: Why well-meaning clinicians fail to deliver evidence-based therapy and how to get back on track. *Behaviour Research and Therapy*, 2016;**77**:129–137.
17. Singel AG, Higgins PDR, Waljee AK. A primer on effectiveness and efficacy trials. *Clinical & Transactional Gastroenterology*,

2014;**5**:e45, https://doi.org/10.1038/ctg.2013.3.

18. Cuijpers P. *Meta-Analyses in Mental Health Research: A Practical Guide.* Amsterdam: Vrije Universteit Amsterdam; 2016.
19. Higgins J, Green S. (Eds.) Cochrane Handbook for Systematic Reviews of Interventions: Cochrane Book Series; 2019. https://doi.org/10.1002/9780470712184.
20. Moher D, Liberati A, Tetzlaff J, Altman DG, Preferred reporting items for systematic reviews and meta-analyses: the PRISMA statement, 2009. *BMJ*, **339**, b2535.
21. Clark DM. Implementing NICE guidelines for the psychological treatment of depression and anxiety disorders: The IAPT experience. *International Review of Psychiatry*, 2011;**23**(4):318–327.
22. Rush AJ, Beck AT, Kovacs M, Hollon S. Comparative efficacy of cognitive therapy and pharmacotherapy in the treatment of depressed outpatients. *Cognitive Therapy and Research*, 1977; **1**:17–37.
23. Elkin I, Shea MT, Watkins JT, Imber SD, Sotsky SM, Collins JF, et al. National Institute of Mental Health Treatment of Depression Collaborative Research Program: General effectiveness of treatments. *Archives of General Psychiatry*, 1989;**46**:971–982.
24. Elkin IE, Gibbons RD, Shea MT, Shaw BF. Science is not a trial (but it can sometimes be a tribulation). *Journal of Consulting and Clinical Psychology*, 1996;**64**(1):92–103.
25. Hollon SD. Cognitive and behaviour therapy in the treatment and prevention of depression. *Depression & Anxiety*, 2011;**28**:263–266.
26. Butler AC, Chapman JE, Forman EM, Beck AT. The empirical status of cognitive-behavioral therapy: A review of meta-analyses. *Clinical Psychology Review*, 2006;**26**:17–31.
27. Cuijpers P, Berking M, Andersson G, Quigley L, Kleiboer A, Dobson K. A meta-analysis of cognitive-behavioural therapy for adult depression, along and in comparison with other treatments. *Canadian Journal of Psychiatry*, 2013;**58** (7):376–385.
28. Cuijpers P, Karyotaki E, Eckshtain D, Ng MY, Cortesellinia KA, Noma H, Quero S, Weisz JR. Psychotherapy for depression across different age groups: A systematic review and meta-analysis. *JAMA Psychiatry*, 2020;**77**(7):694–702.
29. Wolf J. The systematic desensitization of neuroses. *Journal of Nervous and Mental Disease*, 1961;**132**:189–203.
30. Carona C, Ramos K, Salvador C. Psychotherapy by Reciprocal Inhibition: Wolpe's unique legacy to the evolution of cognitive-behavioural therapy. *British Journal of Psychiatry Advances*, 2023;**29**:218–222.
31. Rachman J. The evolution of behaviour therapy and cognitive behaviour therapy. *Behaviour Research and Therapy*, 2015;**64**:1–8.
32. Rutherford A. Mary Cover Jones: Behaviorist as personologist. *The Feminist Psychologist*, 2000;**27**(3):22–23.
33. Salkovskis P, Clark D, Hackmann A. Treatment of panic attacks using cognitive therapy without exposure or breathing retraining. *Behaviour Research and Therapy*, 1991;**29**:161e166.
34. Clark DM. A cognitive approach to panic. *Behaviour Research and Therapy*, 1986;**24**:461e470.
35. Cuijpers P, Gentili C, Banos RM, Garcia-Campano J, Botella C, Cristea IA. Relative effects of cognitive and behavioural therapies on generalised anxiety disorder, social anxiety disorder, and panic disorder: A meta-analysis. *Journal of Anxiety Disorders*, 2016;**43**:79–89.
36. Papola D, Ostuzzi G, Tedeschi F, Gastaldon C, Purgato M, Del Giovane C, et al. Comparative efficacy and acceptability of psychotherapies for panic disorder with or without agoraphobia: Systematic review and network meta-analysis of randomised controlled trials. *British Journal of Psychology*, 2022;**221**: 607–619.

37. Cuijpers P, Cristea IA, Karyotaki E, Reijders M, Huibers MJH. How effective are cognitive behaviour therapies for major depression and anxiety disorders? A meta-analytic update of the evidence. *World Psychiatry*, 2014;**15**:245–258.

38. Kishita N, Laidlaw K. Cognitive behavior therapy for generalized anxiety disorder: Is CBT equally effective in adults of working age and older adults? *Clinical Psychology Review*, 2017;**52**:124–136.

39. Werson A, Meiser-Stedman R, Laidlaw K. A meta-analysis of CBT efficacy for depression comparing adults and older adults. *Journal of Affective Disorders*, 2022;**319**:189–201.

40. Orgeta V, Leung P, del-Pino-Casado R, Qazi A, Orrell M, Spector AE, Methley AM. Psychological Treatments for Depression and Anxiety in Dementia and Mild Cognitive Impairment. Cochrane Database of Systematic Reviews 2022, Issue 4. Art. No.: CD009125. http://doi.org/10.1002/14651858.CD009125.pub3.

41. Hopkinson MD, Reavell J, Lane JA, Mallikarjun P. Cognitive behavioral therapy for depression, anxiety, and stress in caregivers of dementia patients: A systematic review and meta-analysis. *The Gerontologist*, 2019;**59**(4):e343–e362, https://doi.org/10.1093/geront/gnx217.

42. Bhar DS, Koder D, Jayaram H, Silver M, Davidson T. Addressing mental health in aged care residents: A review of evidence-based psychological interventions and emerging practices. *Advances in Psychiatry and Behavioral Health*, 2022;**2**(1):183–191.

43. Chan Y, Bhar S, Davison T, Doyle C, Knight B, Koder D et al. Characteristics of cognitive behavioural therapy for older adults living in residential care: A systematic review. *Aging & Mental Health*, 2021;**25**(2):187–205. http://doi.org/10.1080/13607863.2019.1686457.

44. Covin R, Ouimet AJ, Seeds PM, Dozois DJA. A meta-analysis of CBT for pathological worry among clients with GAD. *Journal of Anxiety Disorders*, 2008;**22**(1):108–116.

45. Cuijpers P, van Straten A, Smit F. (2006). Psychological treatment of late-life depression: a meta-analysis of randomized controlled trials. Int J Geriatr Psychiatry, 21(12),1139–49.

46. Gould RL, Coulson MC, Howard RJ. Cognitive behavioral therapy for depression in older people: A meta-analysis and meta-regression of randomized controlled trials. *Journal of American Geriatric Society*, 2012;**60**:1817–1830.

47. Gould RL, Coulson MC, Howard RJ. Cognitive behavioral therapy for anxiety disorders in older people: A meta-analysis and meta-regression of randomized controlled trials. *Journal of American Geriatric Society*, 2012;**60**:218–229.

48. Alnajjar, A.Z., Abouelmagd, M.E., Krayim, A., AbdelMeseh, M., Bushara, N. Nabil, Y. (2024). Efficacy of cognitive behavioral therapy for anxiety and depresson in Parkinson's disease patients: An updated systematic review and meta-analysis. Neurol Sci., 45 (11), 5277–5290

49. Cohen J. A power primer. *Psychological Bulletin*, 1992;**112**(1):155–159.

50. Moher D, Liberati A, Tetzlaff J, Altman DG, The PRISMA Group. Preferred Reporting Items for Systematic Reviews and Meta-Analyses: The PRISMA Statement. *PLoS Med*, 2009;**6**(7):e1000097. doi:10.1371/journal.pmed.1000097.

51. DeRubeis RJ, Hollon SD, Amsterdam JD, et al. Cognitive therapy vs medications in the treatment of moderate to severe depression. *Archives of general psychiatry*, 2005;**62**:409–416.

52. Hollon SD, DeRubeis RJ, Shelton RC, et al. Prevention of relapse following cognitive therapy vs medications in moderate to severe depression. *Archives of General Psychiatry*. 2005;**62**:417–422.

53. Hollon SD, Thase ME, Markowitz JC. Treatment and prevention of depression. *Psychological Science in the Public Interest*. 2002;**3**:39–77.

54. Hollon SD, Stewart MO, Strunk D. Enduring effects for cognitive behavior therapy in the treatment of depression and anxiety. *Annual Review of Psychology*, 2006;**57**:285–315.

55. Dobson KS. A meta-analysis of the efficacy of cognitive therapy of depression. *Journal of Consulting and Clinical Psychology*, 1998;**57**:414–419.

56. Gloaguen V, Cottraux J, Cucherat M, Blackburn I. A meta-analysis of the effects of cognitive therapy in depressed patients. *Journal of Affective Disorders*, 1998;**49**:59–72.

57. Butler AC, Chapman JE, Forman EM, Beck AT. The empirical status of cognitive-behavioural therapy: A review of meta analyses. *Clinical Psychology Review*, 2006;**26**:17–31.

58. Salkovskis PM. Cognitive-behavioural treatment for Panic. *Psychiatry*, 2007;**6**(5):193–197.

59. Beck AT, Emery G with Greenberg RL. *Anxiety Disorders and Phobias: A Cognitive Perspective*. New York: Basic Books; 1985.

60. Bhattacharya S, Goicoechea C, Heshmati S, Carpenter JK, Hofmann S. Efficacy of cognitive behavioral therapy for anxiety-related disorders: A meta-analysis of recent literature. *Current Psychiatry Reports*, 2023; **25**:19–30. https://doi.org/10.1007/s11920-022-01402-8.

61. Holvast F, Massoudi B, Voshaar RCO, Verhaak PF. Non-pharmacological treatment for depressed older patients in primary care: A systematic review and meta-analysis. *PLoS One*, 2017;**12**(9): e0184666.

62. Kwon OY, Ahn HS, Kim HJ, Park KW. Effectiveness of cognitive behavioral therapy for caregivers of people with dementia: A systematic review and meta-analysis. *Journal of Clinical Neurology*, 2017;**13**(4):394–404.

Chapter 4

What Is Cognitive Behavioural Therapy?

In this chapter we will help you to be able to:

- Define CBT.
- Explain the key processes within CBT.
- Describe the key features of good CBT as described in therapy rating scales.
- Consider how to best incorporate the key components of CBT in terms of structure, style and content.

Introduction

CBT stands for Cognitive Behavioural Therapy; that is, it is a self-change process (Therapy) focussed on what we think (Cognitions) and what we choose to do (Behaviours). It is based on the central concept that our emotions are caused by how we think and what we do in response to situations, and so changing what we think and do will change how we feel. CBT is a structured, evidence-based therapy, but it also values the interpersonal relationship between therapist and patient. Good CBT balances a focus on content, structure and style, providing a safe and supportive space for patients to make significant and long-lasting change.

What Is CBT?

CBT is not actually a single therapy, but rather a group of approaches unified by a focus on cognitions and/or behaviours [1]. As discussed in Part I, CBT started as a range of cognitive therapies and behavioural therapies, based respectively on the cognitive and behavioural theories of general human functioning. These have since been combined in many modern approaches to take account of both behaviours and cognitions, as well as how they interact with each other. While there are many versions of CBT still practised, this book will focus predominantly on Beckian CBT – that is, therapy based on the works of Aaron Beck [2,3]. However, other schools of thought will be represented in treatment for specific problems (e.g. behavioural activation approaches for depression in Chapter 20) [4].

The key aims of CBT are to help people to achieve their goals and overcome the problems that they wish to focus on. As such, it is problem-focussed and goal-oriented; see Chapter 5 for more about goals and aims of CBT. This is true both across therapy as a whole and within a session – each session aims to explore an agreed problem or concept, with the aim that the patient will have learnt something by the end of the session which they can apply moving forwards to help overcome that problem [5].

Key Processes in CBT

For most patients seeking CBT, the end goal is to be able to live a functional life where they can successfully confront scenarios which might otherwise cause distress. CBT approaches aim to achieve this by modifying behaviours, modifying thinking and solving problems [2].

Behavioural change processes are based on the concept that individuals react to situations based on their previous experiences, and this leads to short-term and long-term consequences [6]. For those with a psychological difficulty, this will invariably involve reacting in a way that aims to provide short-term relief, but leads to long-term maintenance of the issue (for example, with fear [7], or depression [8]). As such, changing what we do in relation to a given trigger changes how we feel when next confronted with that trigger [9]. So, CBT looks at the different things the patient does in response to situations, such as avoidance, withdrawal or the use of safety behaviours, and explores how the person can modify their behaviours to reach their goals and feel less distressed long-term.

The cognitive model is based on the idea that how we feel in a situation is not just based on the situation itself, but on how we think about this situation – what interpretation we make of it, and what predictions we have [3]. This is true for everyone, and we will have typical and recurring ways of reacting to similar scenarios, which we have learnt over time, and which shape our behaviours as well as our emotions. Cognitive change is focussed on the concept that changing how we think about scenarios will then change how we feel about the scenario, so will feel better both in the moment and when next in a similar scenario. CBT looks at the specific thoughts we have in situations, and helps us to come to new perspectives which lead to more adaptive behaviours and helpful emotions. Over therapy, the focus will often shift from looking at specific thoughts to the more general rules and assumptions they make, and may explore and help to change their most central and fundamental beliefs are – their core beliefs (see Chapter 7 for more detail about the flow of therapy through these different levels of cognition). Within each of these levels, we will also want to explore how changes in behaviour can disconfirm our current thoughts or support our new perspectives.

A common third strand of CBT therapies involves problem solving. All people are confronted with practical problems in their lives to some degree, which cause distress and difficulties, and for which there may be no easy and obvious solution. By exploring these situations, and what options are available, we can feel confident that we are making the best choices available to us. Finding the best possible solutions to problems allows us to shape our lives so as to minimise unhelpful distress and difficulty while still achieving desired goals. For more information on each of the areas above, see Chapter 6.

All of the above processes are true for all individuals. That is, CBT does not see mental health issues as qualitatively different from normal human experience, but as part of a continuum. As such, CBT can be a useful way of viewing almost any behavioural cycle a person is stuck in, which leads to distress or impacts their functioning.

Features of Good CBT

CBT is a fundamentally evidence-based approach and lots of research has been focussed on what drives it to be effective. Each disorder has its own priorities and features (see Part III) but there are fundamentals across all CBT regarding how to do the therapy well. These features are then looked for to appraise therapy quality, both for trainees to prove competence, and in trials to evidence that it was done to a sufficient standard. There are a number of different appraisal tools, but the most commonly used are the Cognitive Therapy Rating

Table 4.1 A comparison of the items in the CTRS and CTSr

Cognitive Therapy Rating Scale (CTRS)	Cognitive Therapy Scale, Revised (CTSr)
Agenda	Agenda Setting and Adherence
Feedback	Feedback
Understanding	
Interpersonal Effectiveness	Interpersonal Effectiveness
Collaboration	Collaboration
Pacing and Efficient Use of Time	Pacing and Efficient Use of Time
Guided Discovery	Guided Discovery
	Eliciting Appropriate Emotional Expression
Focussing on Key Cognitions or Behaviours	Eliciting Key Cognitions
	Eliciting Key Behaviours
	Conceptual Integration
Strategy for Change	Application of Change Methods
Application of Cognitive-Behavioural Techniques	
Homework	Homework Setting

Scale (CTRS) [10,11], and the Cognitive Therapy Scale, Revised (CTSr) [12,13]. Both measures correlate with each other and appear to assess whether therapy is being done well, in so far as they correlate with subsequent patient outcomes [14].

There are several major differences in the items defined in each of the two scales, as shown in Table 4.1. There are also minor differences in the exact definitions of each item, with some concepts broadened in one or the other.

While the scales may appear quite different on first glance, the main variations are about how much weight is given to each concept, and where marks for each concept are given. All 14 items appear to be key to providing high-quality therapy, and so all will be explored below, following the guidance from the two scale manuals [10,13].

Agenda: CBT sessions should focus on what matters to the patient, and at the same time, on what the therapist knows can help (suitable target problems). A good, shared agenda is an agreement that the session will be focussed on such areas, with suitable time available for each topic to be explored productively. Said agenda should be prioritised and then followed, with deviations noted and discussed – either to come back to the agenda, or to amend it if a more important topic has been uncovered. How to do all of this effectively will vary depending on the patient, the problem, and the stage in treatment. For more information on ways to set agendas in therapy sessions at different stages of treatment, see Chapter 7.

Feedback: It is vital in any collaborative, voluntary therapy that the patient has made sense of what is happening and wants to continue to engage in the process. To review these two things, feedback should be elicited to understand what sense the patient has made of the session, and how they feel about the experience of therapy. Any issues or confusion can then be explored and worked upon. Eliciting feedback should be a regular process, but is especially important when major new concepts have been introduced or where the patient appears confused or concerned about what is being explored.

Understanding: For the therapist to help a patient, they need to understand what the patient is saying (both implicitly and explicitly) and empathise with how they are feeling and how difficult their problems may be for them. As such, the therapist should also give feedback to demonstrate their own understanding of the patient and show empathy for the resultant emotional and situational difficulties a patient is experiencing. This is different from sympathising, where the therapist focuses on how they would feel in the situation, or colluding, where the therapist agrees with the patient's unhelpful thoughts and behaviours. Instead, it is about actively listening to the patient, making sense of why they would be feeling the way they do given their thoughts, and then empathising with this.

Interpersonal effectiveness: In order to be willing to discuss personal issues in full and take risks in what they disclose and try to do, a patient needs to feel safe. As such, while CBT does not consider the therapeutic bond as all that is needed for change as in some other approaches (such as in person-centred therapy [15]) it is nonetheless strongly valued as necessary. Good therapy is where the therapist is appropriately warm and genuine, as well as being professional and showing confidence in the approach being taken.

Collaboration: Therapy should be genuinely collaborative. The two main reasons for this are both that the patient will learn and change more if they are an active part of the process, and because the patient is genuinely the expert in their experiences and problems, and so will enhance the therapy if given choices in the right points. On the other hand, therapists should also value their own expertise, and so not give the patient choices where the patient has no reason to know what will work best, and the therapist does. Great therapy is where both the patient and the therapist are working together with a common goal and a genuine trust in each other's expertise. CBT aims for the patient to eventually be able to use the relevant techniques for their problem themselves, so over the course of treatment the therapist should increasingly let the patient determine how to manage problems and apply techniques, to let them become skilled at doing so independently.

Pacing and efficient use of time: Therapy as a whole aims to be time limited, and aims to help patients manage their problems and reach recovery as quickly as possible so they can live their lives. Pacing within a session is about keeping at the patient's learning speed – not labouring the point, but also not going too fast for the patient to keep up, so they get as much as possible from the time. Sessions should be focussed on discussion and activities that will help the change occur, to ensure time is used efficiently. See Chapter 7 for how a typical session should be structured to achieve this.

Guided discovery: This is the primary discussion style used in CBT, where the patient is helped to find their own more helpful perspectives (see Chapter 6 for more information on this). Good CBT will use this style for most of the time, moving to a more didactic approach only when there is information that the patient cannot gain access to by other means. Therapists should rarely – if ever – appear to be debating their patients or persuading them, as this will put the patient on the defensive, and may entrench the very perspectives that are causing the problem.

Eliciting appropriate emotional expression: Generally, one of the fundamental aims of most patients is to 'feel better' – that is, to have fewer or less negative emotions and more positive emotion. Therapy thus needs to focus on the emotions being experienced in response to different thoughts and behaviours to make this link, and help the patient to feel better more often.

Change within sessions is also enhanced by being at the right emotional level – too cold, and the changes won't connect to feeling differently, too hot, and the patient won't be able to think and act in a way to make changes at all.

Eliciting key cognitions: In CBT (as opposed to pure BT) the meanings, predictions and interpretations behind one's behaviours and emotions are central to understanding and changing the problem. Therapy should involve explicitly eliciting these and noting them as thoughts. Good therapy focusses on thoughts that are central to the problem being worked on – the key cognitions that drive the problematic behavioural and emotional cycles that the patient has come to therapy to change.

Eliciting key behaviours: Likewise, good therapy focusses on the main recurring behaviours that reinforce or maintain these key cognitions. By eliciting these and making sense of how they connect to the cognitions and emotions above, the patient can better make sense of their problems, and how to make a change.

Conceptual integration: Therapy should be based on a shared and central understanding (formulation) of the problem the patient wishes to solve. Good therapy ensures that the thoughts and behaviours being worked on, the method for working on them, and the resultant homework being devised, all connect to this shared understanding – that is, the therapy is conceptually integrated. Great therapy maximises the advantages of this, by ensuring the patient makes links to how specific changes can be applied more widely, and how abstract changes can be made concrete. See Chapter 8 for more information about how to formulate.

Strategy for change: Therapy is a change process, and so sessions should be predominantly focussed on creating change, not simply reviewing changes occurring outside of sessions. There are many different strategies for creating such change (see Chapter 6) and each type of problem will have its own list of specific targets and techniques that can maximise change. Good therapy is where the best of these are picked and implemented by the therapist dependent on the material the patient has brought. See Chapter 8 for a general discussion of how strategies are chosen, as well as Part III for the specific strategies recommended for each problem type.

Application of change methods: Just as it is important that the right techniques are picked, so too it is important that the methods are used skilfully. Skilful in-session change allows for the therapist to adjust the process as it's happening and to review it immediately after, so as to ensure maximal learning for the patient in ways that out-of-session change may not achieve. See Chapter 6 for a description of the key features of the main techniques, and tips of how to make them more effective.

Homework: All therapy sessions should include a review of the previous week's homework tasks, and a plan for the week ahead. Great therapy ensures that these tasks are custom tailored to the exact changes the patient wants to make and are devised and reviewed in a way to maximise engagement, learning and change. See Chapter 7 for how homework should be incorporated into sessions.

Concluding Remarks

Modern cognitive behavioural therapy is a range of approaches based on the early cognitive and behavioural theories, which have been combined together to create a robust way of helping patients to change their unhelpful cognitive-behavioural cycles. Good CBT involves understanding these theories and how the patient idiosyncratically fits into this, in order to collaboratively work with them to make the changes they need. CBT should be structured and focussed, while maintaining a warm and genuine bond with the patient, so as to help them feel safe to engage. The key features of good therapy, as explored in the most commonly used rating scales, cover the content, structure and interpersonal style of a therapist, as all three aspects are needed for effective CBT.

Further Reading

Beck, J. S., & Beck, A. T. (2020). *Cognitive Behavior Therapy: Basics and Beyond.* 3rd ed. New York: Guilford Press.

Young, J., & Beck, A. T. (1980). *Cognitive Therapy Scale.* Unpublished Manuscript.

James, I., Blackburn, I., & Reichelt, F. (2001). *Manual of the Revised Cognitive Therapy Scale.* Unpublished Manuscript Newcastle Cognitive Behavioural Therapy Centre Newcastle UK.

References

1. Gaudiano, B. A. (2008). Cognitive-behavioural therapies: achievements and challenges. *Evid Based Ment Health*, **11**(1), 5–7.
2. Beck, A. T. (1964). Thinking and depression: II. Theory and therapy. *Arch Gen Psychiatry*, **10**(6), 561–71.
3. Beck, A. T., Rush, J., Shaw, B. F., & Emery, G. (1979). *Cognitive Therapy of Depression.* New York: Guilford Press.
4. Martell, C. R., Dimidjian, S., Herman-Dunn, R. (2013). *Behavioral Activation for Depression: A Clinician's Guide.* New York: Guilford Press.
5. Beck, J. S., & Beck, A. T. (2020). *Cognitive Behavior Therapy: Basics and Beyond.* 3rd ed. New York: Guilford Press.
6. Skinner, B. F. (1938). *The Behavior of Organisms: An Experimental Analysis.* D. Appleton-Century Company, incorporated.
7. Mowrer, O. H. (1947). On the dual nature of learning: A re-interpretation of 'conditioning' and 'problem-solving'. *Harv Educ Rev*, **17**, 102–148.
8. Lewinsohn, P. M. (1978). *Control Your Depression.* Prentice-Hall.
9. Wolpe, J. (1958). *Psychotherapy by Reciprocal Inhibition.* Stanford University Press.
10. Young, J., & Beck, A. T. (1980). Cognitive therapy scale. https://beckinstitute.org/wp-content/uploads/2021/06/CTRS-Manual-2020.pdf.
11. Vallis, T. M., Shaw, B. F., & Dobson, K. S. (1986). The Cognitive Therapy Scale: Psychometric properties. *J Consult Clin Psychol*, **54**(3), 381–385.
12. Blackburn, I. M., James, I. A., Milne, D. L., et al. (2001). The revised cognitive therapy scale (CTS-R): Psychometric properties. *Behav Cogn Psychother*, **29**(4), 431–446.
13. James, I., Blackburn, I., & Reichelt, F. (2001). *Manual of the Revised Cognitive Therapy Scale.* Unpublished manuscript Newcastle Cognitive Behavioural Therapy Centre, Newcastle, UK.
14. Kazantzis, N., Clayton, X., Cronin, Timothy J., Farchione, D., Limburg, K., & Dobson, Keith S. (2018). The cognitive therapy scale and cognitive therapy scale-revised as measures of therapist competence in cognitive behavior therapy for depression: Relations with short- and long-term outcome. *Cogn Ther Res*, **42**(4), 385–397.
15. Rogers, C. R. (1980). *A Way of Being.* Boston: Houghton Mifflin.

Chapter 5

The Goals of Cognitive Behavioural Therapy

In this chapter we will help you to be able to:

- Explain the overarching purpose of any CBT treatment process.
- Consider the rationale for having therapy goals.
- Define the most important features of a good goal.
- Collaboratively create a set of goals with individual patients.
- Determine the key targets of treatment from a therapist perspective.

Introduction

At its core, the actual aim of every course of cognitive behavioural therapy is to reduce an individual's distress and improve how they are functioning. While this general goal is shared, the precise nature of what needs to change will be unique to each patient, and working out what these specific goals should be is important in ensuring that therapy is targeting the right factors.

Good goals have been defined many ways across the CBT literature, but there are some shared key features. Taking all this into account, this chapter will explore how and why to set effective goals with patients, and then how to use both these and an understanding of CBT to determine the most important therapeutic treatment targets.

The Aims of CBT

The very concept of a psychological disorder, as defined since the Diagnostic and Statistical Manual, 4th Edition, includes within it that the patient experiences 'clinically significant distress or impairment in social, occupational, or other important areas of functioning' [1]. This distress or impairment in functioning is what patients almost always come to therapy to change, and it is the overarching aim of CBT to reduce this distress and improve overall functioning.

As explored in Chapter 4, CBT sees this distress and functional impairment as the result of the dysfunctional cognitive behavioural cycles that the patient is stuck in. As such, the process by which CBT achieves its general aim is by exploring and then collaboratively modifying these cognitive and behavioural patterns as needed. However, it is key to remember that neither enhanced understanding nor modification of a patient's beliefs and behavioural strategies is the end goal itself; the aim is to help them feel better and live the life they want.

The Purpose of Goal Setting

So, why is it important to set specific goals, rather than simply sticking to a vague plan of helping people feel better?

First, goals help to clarify what changes are needed in a patient's situation. While psychological disorders can affect many areas of an individual's life, it isn't a given that all areas need changing. In defining and assessing the problem, therapists can often gather a vast list of possible issues and treatment targets, potentially stumbling upon secondary disorders or underlying traits that the patient may have, as well as the issue they wanted to resolve. By agreeing specific goals that the therapy should work towards, it can become clearer which problems the patient has described are genuinely problematic for them, and so focus the therapy more effectively.

Goals can also be important in focussing the patient onto what they will get from therapy, and so enhance their motivation to engage. In many disorders, one of the most effective short-term methods of reducing distress can be avoidance or withdrawal. In contrast, therapy often requires confrontation and engagement, and in the short term these can increase distress. As such, therapy with the aim of distress reduction alone will be hard to evidence, as while the techniques should eventually reduce distress, over the short-term things may appear to be deteriorating. In contrast, clear goals of what they might be doing or achieving differently due to therapy gives something to work towards and makes it clear why avoidance and withdrawal can't get them there.

Goals can also be helpful as therapy progresses, in allowing for both therapist and patient to reflect on the progress that has been made. It can be easy for both therapist and patient to lose sight of what has changed in therapy, as current functioning quickly becomes the new normal. By looking back at what was considered a difficult goal only a few weeks or months prior, the level of change and the effectiveness of the therapy becomes much clearer. Of course, this can also be achieved through various standardised questionnaires or measures, but goals give a more meaningful version of this for the patient.

Last, setting goals results in people feeling better. A meta-analysis of 15 different studies into the effects of goals setting found that it had a significant positive effect on treatment outcomes [2]. Importantly, these treatment outcomes were largely defined as reduced symptoms and improved functioning; exactly what the patients have typically asked for to start with.

Features of Good Goals

Good goals have been defined in many ways both within therapy and in the world in general. One popular method for goal setting is the SMART acronym, as first proposed in the field of management [3]. Initially standing for Specific, Measurable, Assignable, Realistic and Time-Related, it is now most typically applied in the field of therapy as Specific, Measurable, Achievable, Relevant and Time-Limited.

While these concepts can each have merit, there are also other factors to consider. First, good goals are not simply time-related, but also cover a range of different timescales, from short-term goals that can be the target of a quick win, to long-term visions that inspire significant and permanent change. It is important to note that while having staged goals is useful, it may be counterproductive to try and define an agreed timescale for these goals, as the rate of therapeutic change is hard to predict by either party, and patients may, by the nature of their disorder, have overly negative views of the rate of possible change.

Many would argue that goals should also connect to a patient's personal values. All individuals have values; that is, all people have concepts and constructs that are important to how they live their life in a broad and enduring manner [4]. Helping a patient live a life that better aligns with their values is considered key to many of the third wave versions of CBT [5,6,7]. Conversely, inflicting our own values on our patients is generally accepted to be unhelpful for a range of reasons [8]. As such, considering what the patient values either prior to, or as part of setting goals, can help ensure goals are not just relevant to the patient, but of genuine value to them.

It can also be helpful to elaborate on the meaning of achievable. Patients with certain presentations may not be able to see much hope for change at the start of therapy, and thus asking them what they think will be achievable may rule out a lot of otherwise useful goals. A better concept thus is whether the target in question is concerned with their own actions. For example, getting a job or getting married requires the input of others, and often a measure of luck. In contrast, applying for jobs and attending any offered interviews, or going on a proposed double date, might be something the patient can do, were they to feel differently. Achievability also needs to consider the limitations of therapy. There are many goals a patient might have that are achievable with the right support; however, good therapy goals will be those where the key changes needed are cognitive and behavioural.

One final addition to good goal setting is the concept of the goals being positive. Just as avoidance is the fastest way to reduce distress, it is also the fastest way to reduce most unhelpful behaviours that a patient might want to drop. As such, goals such as 'don't check', 'don't worry' and 'don't clean' may be counterproductive at promoting the kind of change that will enhance functioning, as they are most easily achieved by avoidance and withdrawal, the two things known to maintain almost all problems long-term. Goals should thus be about what the patient will do, not what they will stop.

How to Set Collaborative Goals

All of the above might feel somewhat overwhelming, if not to the therapist, then often to the patient. As one of the purposes of goal setting is to motivate the patient and increase their engagement, it is important to have a patient-friendly way of creating goals. This will generally occur in three stages – defining how the problem is currently impacting the patient's values, creating a list of key goals and then elaborating this list to include various time frames.

To create the list of goals themselves, a patient-friendly process can simply be to ask, and if necessary, repeat, the question:

> 'If [problem] was no longer interfering with the things you value in life, **what would you do differently?**'

Each of the words in bold can be used to focus the patient onto a more useful goal as follows:

What (specifically) – this word aims at ensuring the goal is a clear discrete thing. Sometimes patients will initially reply with a general answer, such as 'everything' – responding by asking for more detail, what specifically they would do differently, can then define this.

Would – this word aims at ensuring it's both a positive activity, and that it's an activity they would choose to do, not just be something that they could do, or feel they should want to do. By noting what they've said they wouldn't do, or they could do, or they should do, the question can then be repeated, stressing, 'what **would** you do?'

You – if their goals are about what how others would behave towards them, this word helps to highlight it's about their actions, not others.

Do – by emphasising do, the question focusses the patient on what would change in their behaviour, rather than on their feelings or thoughts. Behavioural goals are by their nature more measurable than cognitive or emotional ones, and also prevent goals that are avoidance compatible.

Differently – goals need to involve change. However, they don't always need to be whole new activities, but might instead be about what activities will be done in a more functional way.

To see how this applies in practice, consider the following interaction.

THERAPIST: 'If OCD was no longer interfering with the things you value in life, what would you do differently?'

PATIENT: 'Oh, I'd feel so much better, I'd be so relaxed.'

THERAPIST: 'Okay, so you'd *feel* better and more relaxed. And what would you *do* differently?'

PATIENT: 'Well, I wouldn't be washing so much like I do now.'

THERAPIST: 'So you wouldn't be washing how you do now. And in comparison to how you wash now, what would you do *differently*?'

PATIENT: 'I'd just wash my hands like other people do – like for 20 seconds after I've been out.'

THERAPIST: 'So would that be a valuable goal to work towards – to be able to go out, and then wash your hands for no more than 20 seconds?'

PATIENT: 'Yeah, that'd be a big change.'

THERAPIST: 'Okay, so that seems like a useful goal then. What else would you do differently?'

As the list of goals grows, the therapist may want to direct the patient to consider other time frames. For example, if the patient has given mostly short-term goals which require minor changes, the therapist may want to preface the goal question with 'and in the longer term, if the problem was totally resolved'. Alternatively, if the patient has given only goals which require major change, the therapist may want to redirect by asking 'and more immediately, if therapy were to start helping with the issue, what do you think might be the first thing you would do differently?'

Finally, to give a benchmark for therapy, it can be helpful to review the patient's current ability to achieve each of the goals. A simple 0–10 rating scale of how difficult they would find it to carry out each goal can be used. This can be helpful especially when patients have an all-or-nothing image of change, by exploring what difficulty rating they would see as a significant improvement, and by then later reflecting on how the numbers have changed.

Therapist Treatment Targets

Once the therapist knows what the patient is focussed on achieving in therapy, they will then need to consider what the specific behaviours and cognitions are that need exploring. Some of the more basic therapeutic targets include:

- Moving from negative and 'primitive' thinking to more balanced 'mature' thinking [9].
- Reducing avoidance of feared stimuli.
- Responding to negative beliefs in a way that tests their veracity.
- Engaging in activities which reinforce desired beliefs.

Beyond this, the more recent proliferation of disorder-specific protocols has helped to pin down more specific treatment targets for any given presentation. For example, in Dugas' protocol for Generalised Anxiety Disorder (see Chapter 14) the generic aim of 'engaging in activities which reinforce desired beliefs' could be more specifically defined as 'dropping approach and avoidance strategies to increase tolerance of uncertainty'. Throughout Chapters 10–21, these specific aims of each treatment protocol have been summarised.

It is important to note that these specific therapeutic targets can sometimes seem to be at odds with what the patient initially wants from treatment. Part of socialising the patient to the concept of CBT is thus to make sense of why these therapeutic targets are key to their goals – how making these changes will result in them being able to do the things they want to do while feeling the way they want to feel. These concepts are central to Chapters 6 and 8, which respectively explore the techniques used in CBT to achieve change, and how these are linked to a shared understanding of the problem.

Concluding Remarks

Therapy aims to treat distress and improve functioning, both because this is what defines something as a problem in the first place, and because this is what patients want. Defining clear behavioural goals has been shown to help with this. There are many important features to a good therapeutic goal, which go beyond SMART acronyms. By setting goals collaboratively, both patient and therapist can be clear on the focus for therapy. Therapeutic treatment targets can then be determined by therapists based on a combination of the patient's goals and a cognitive-behavioural understanding of drivers of the problem. By determining these treatment targets, and using a shared formulation to help the patient see the purpose of such targets in achieving their behavioural goals, CBT can be both evidence-informed and genuinely tailored to the patient's needs.

Further Reading

Tryon, GS, & Winograd, G. Goal consensus and collaboration. In Norcross, JC (ed.), *Psychotherapy Relationships That Work: Evidence-Based Responsiveness*. 2nd ed. (pp. 153–67). Oxford: Oxford University Press; 2011.

References

1. American Psychiatric Association. *Diagnostic and Statistical Manual of Mental Disorders: DSM-IV*. American Psychiatric Association; 1994.
2. Tryon, GS, Winograd, G. Goal consensus and collaboration. In Norcross, J. C. (ed.), *Psychotherapy Relationships That Work: Evidence-Based Responsiveness*. 2nd ed. (pp. 153–167). Oxford: Oxford University Press; 2011.
3. Doran, GT. There's a SMART way to write management's goals and objectives. *Manage Rev*. 1981;**70**(11):35–36.
4. Schwartz, SH. Are there universal aspects in the structure and contents of human values? *J Soc Issues* 1994;**50**(4):19–45.
5. Martell, CR, Dimidjian S, Herman-Dunn, R. *Behavioral Activation for Depression: A Clinician's Guide*. New York: Guilford Press; 2013.
6. Strosah, KD, Hayes, SC, Wilson, KG, Gifford, EV. An ACT Primer. In: SC Hayes, KD Strosahl (Eds.), *A Practical Guide to Acceptance and Commitment Therapy [Internet]* (pp. 31–58). Boston, MA: Springer US; 2004. https://doi.org/10.1007/978-0-387-23369-7_2.
7. Dunn, BD, Widnall E, Reed N, Owens C, Campbell J, Kuyken W. Bringing light into darkness: A multiple baseline mixed methods case series evaluation of Augmented Depression Therapy (ADepT). *Behav Res Ther*. 2019;**120**:103418.
8. Patterson CH. Values in counseling and psychotherapy. *Couns Values*. 1989;**33**(3):164–176.
9. Beck AT, Rush J, Shaw BF, Emery G. *Cognitive Therapy of Depression*. New York: Guilford Press; 1979.

Chapter 6

The Specific Techniques of Cognitive Behavioural Therapy

In this chapter we will help you to be able to:

- Describe the different techniques available in CBT.
- Consider the purpose of any given technique in relation to the maintenance cycles it interrupts.
- Tailor interventions to individual patients, considering their unique strengths and needs.

Introduction

CBT is a model known most for its techniques – thought challenging, activity planning, problem solving, to name but a few – and they have been used far outside of comprehensive therapy. The use of specific techniques, and the tailoring of these to various disorders, has been a significant part of what has made CBT so testable, and which allows for comparatively rapid dissemination of the approach. These tools have their roots in both the behavioural and cognitive schools which have led to modern CBT, and cover both the stages of socialisation and intervention.

A general description of this range of tools, and how each is typically applied to a problem, will be the focus of this chapter. Along with this will be a consideration on the purpose of the tools, and how they can thus be tailored to apply best to the patient in question, following his or her idiosyncratic formulation.

Socialisation Techniques

The first set of techniques that will typically be used with a patient are those aiming at socialisation; that is, helping a patient to understand and consider an alternative way of viewing their difficulty. Formulation, of course, is the start of this, and the many aims of formulation are detailed in Chapter 8. However, formulation alone largely helps the patient to see what the problem already is, and so further socialisation techniques can be vital in helping the patient to also see what the solution might be, and how therapy can help change things from what they are, to what they could be.

Psychoeducation

Psychoeducation – that is, educating the patient on the parts of psychology that affect their problem – is the simplest form of socialisation, and occurs in some form in almost all CBT treatment. The topics that a therapist may educate their patient on include:

- How the brain itself works (including fight or flight responses, how memories are processed, how tiredness and sleep work).
- The biological and psychological effects of drugs and medication (both those used for mental health issues and those taken recreationally).
- The biological and psychological effects of exercise (such as the thermogenic, endorphin, monoamine, distraction and/or self-efficacy hypotheses [1]).
- The role of behaviour in conditioned responses and habituation.
- The impact of selective attention and processing (such as in GAD [2]).
- The impact of prior experiences on our core beliefs [3].

Each patient seen will need a different combination of these topics to help them engage in change. Even within each topic, the specific information needed will depend on the problem being worked with, and the overarching model being followed. Every patient will also have their own starting set of information, which may need only minor additions to it, or may need a significant exploration and re-evaluation.

As such, it's important not to see psychoeducation as a one-size-fits-all standardised process. For psychoeducation to work well, therapists should start from considering the unique patient in front of them, and their exact understanding of themselves and the world. This can then be compared to how the therapy ahead will view the issue, so that psychoeducation can be targeted to filling in the gaps as required.

For example, imagine two patients were to start therapy for depression on the same day – let's call them Sally and Jane. Sally is a recent psychology graduate, with a good grasp on medication effects and the concepts of classical and operant conditioning. She has felt unlovable ever since her mother left when she was three years old, and so strives to always do her best in everything, to ensure she has some value in the world. Whenever she feels low, she simply to aims to do more to prove her value and help others, convinced that this will give her the neurochemical kick she needs. She also expects other to meet high standards and is quick to give up on anything that doesn't show results.

Jane, meanwhile, is a mother of two grown children, and had always been relatively happy until they left home, and she hurt her back. Her doctor prescribed her some powerful painkillers at the time, which left her feeling jittery afterwards, and so she is highly concerned about what the newly prescribed antidepressants will do to her, given that 'her brain is clearly prone to addiction'. She is generally very inactive, seeing everything she could do as not worth the effort, and so often spends the day in bed, watching TV and comfort eating.

Sally and Jane have been diagnosed with the same disorder, prescribed the same medication, and will be treated using the same overall CBT protocol – Beck's Cognitive Therapy of Depression [3]. However, the psychoeducation that Sally and Jane could benefit from will be very different. While targeted information about addiction, brain chemicals and SSRIs could be useful in helping with Jane's fears of medication, Sally would likely either see this as further evidence that her 'do more' system was a good one, or could lose faith in therapy altogether as it was only telling her what she already knew. Conversely, an exploration of the impact of relaxing and self-compassionate behaviours on self-esteem is likely to be more relevant to Sally than Jane.

Further information on the specific psychoeducation useful in each disorder can be found in the treatment overviews throughout Part III, with examples of how this has been tailored to the patient in the various case studies.

Metaphors

Metaphors are not a concept that is unique to CBT; they are a fundamental part of almost all human communication. The purpose of metaphor is to help us to make sense of something that is unfamiliar, or intangible, or just too complex, by comparing it to something more familiar, more concrete and more easily understood.

In CBT, the actual concepts being explored can be extremely complex, and to attempt a literal understanding of the exact mechanisms can be beyond the grasp of science itself. Even when the science and theory is well understood, therapists often take years of study to fully comprehend it. Clearly, this will not be a helpful process to employ with our patients, and so this is where metaphor comes in. Metaphor bridges this gap, taking something that is known to the patient, and using their understanding of this to make sense of whatever therapeutic concept needs explaining.

As an example of this, consider the concept of neuromodulation on habitual thinking patterns. The exact biochemistry involved in strengthening and weakening neural pathways, and how this interacts with consciously controlling one's thought patterns, is incredibly complex, and is beyond the scope of most therapy training courses, let alone most therapy sessions. In contrast, the following metaphor would be accessible to any forager or lover of the countryside, in only a couple of minutes:

THERAPIST: 'Imagine you are walking in the countryside, and there are two paths ahead. The one to the left is the one you have always taken – it is well trodden, and so the ground is smooth and the brambles that encircle it are far back from the edges. The path doesn't really take you where you want to go, but it's easy to follow, it's comfortable. The path on the right is newer, and you haven't walked down it in years. The ground has lots of weeds and grass on it, and the brambles have closed in from all sides. However, you can see it would take you exactly where you want to be.

How do you think it would be, taking the right-hand path for the first time?'

PATIENT: 'Difficult and uncomfortable. You'd have to force yourself through, and it'd be slower going.'

THERAPIST: 'Yeah, that's what I'd expect too. I'm wondering though, if you kept taking that new path, every time you went there, what would happen over time?'

PATIENT: 'Well, the pathway would start getting easier – the ground would get worn in, and the brambles would end up further back, like the left-hand path.'

THERAPIST: 'And what would happen to the left-hand path?'

PATIENT: 'It would get to be just like the right-hand path used to be, it would become the difficult one.'

THERAPIST: 'And this is just the same as what we find with new pathways in our brain. When we try to go a new way, to think differently, it can be harder, bumpier, uncomfortable even. But if we keep following that new path, that new way of thinking about ourselves, or the world, it can become easier and more comfortable, until it's smoother than our old paths.'

This is just one metaphor, to explain one concept to one subset of patients. In total, there are as many metaphors in the CBT literature as there are ideas to make sense of, and then as many more as there are different things to compare to them. For a fuller exploration of at least some of these metaphors, both in terms of how to use them, and to start building your own therapeutic library, please see *The Oxford Guide to Metaphors in CBT* [4].

Theory A/B

For many problems, the aim in CBT is to help the patient discover news ways of thinking that are more helpful for them. The therapist starts from the position that the patient's current thoughts appear to be unhelpful for them, and that there is likely to be a more helpful set of thoughts that the patient can discover. What this new set of thoughts might be is either unknown or can be found simply by testing the validity and helpfulness of the original set of thoughts (see the sections on Guided Discovery and Cognitive Restructuring).

However, in some problems, the theories and beliefs the patient is following may be hard to fully disprove. Moreover, there can be a specific alternative theory which the therapy would give as the more helpful alternative, but which the patient would struggle to find alone. In these cases, the therapist may need to offer this theory themselves, and then help the patient compare the two theories directly; this is theory A/theory B [5]. It aims to help the patient leave their unfalsifiable theory behind, by offering a more believable and more clearly provable theory for the patient to live by.

This approach can be used for both socialisation to therapy as a whole, and for more specific thoughts that the patient is stuck on. One of the most common examples of its use in some models for OCD, to offer an alternative theory as to why they are experiencing their intrusions and compulsions [6]. Theory A will be unique to each patient, but at its heart will be the idea that the problem is due to being in danger. This has been the theory that they have followed so far in life, and it will be at the heart of their formulation. To help them let go of this theory, they need a credible alternative, and the model would suggest that this Theory B, which again will be unique to each patient in its detail, is centred on the concept that they are oversensitive to danger. While the idea of being oversensitive to danger may be one that the patient has heard before, it is unlikely that they will have fully explored how this alternative could credibly explain all their symptoms, and how it could make sense of the complex problem they are experiencing. By exploring this, they can start to get distance from Theory A, and start to see this as a thought to be examined, not an inescapable fact.

Intervention Techniques

Once a patient has a sense of how their problem might be maintained, and has been socialised to the concepts of how therapy might work with this, it is time to start helping them to make a change. There are a range of ways in which CBT does this – a range of 'change methods' for the therapist and patient to try out. Each method will link to a specific maintaining pathway within the patient's formulation, and will be aiming to break this and form a new, more helpful cycle instead.

Cognitive Restructuring

As described in Beck's seminal work, cognitive therapy is based upon the idea that a person's emotions are caused not by what happens to them, but by what they think [3,7]. This idea is not new, as explored in Chapter 1, but what was unique to cognitive therapy was the concept of exploring and challenging these thoughts specifically to change how one thinks.

This is the basis of cognitive restructuring; the structured exploration and questioning of a person's problematic cognitions regarding a situation, or area of their life, or life overall, in order to help them find a more helpful way of thinking about it. To do this, the therapist and patient will need to work through a number of steps.

First, the problematic cognition needs to be identified, so that there is a clear focus to the restructuring – it isn't generally a good idea to simply explore the whole situation and all their opinions about it as one. This cognition needs to be more than a description of fact, it needs to be believed, it needs to lead automatically to a problematic emotion and it needs to be significant enough to the patient that it is worth spending time on. Getting a rating on how much the thought is believed, and how strong the given emotion was as a result, can be helpful here.

Once the cognition has been identified and rated, it then needs to be examined from both sides. It is generally helpful to start from the same side as the patient; the reasons why they believe this. While it might seem strange to do this, to add fuel to the emotional fire, it is an important part of the process. Cognitive restructuring aims for balanced, helpful thinking, not overly positive thinking, and finding the reasons why the negative thought exists will help.

Next the arguments against the thought can be explored. This is the area where the patient is more likely to struggle, and so the therapist will generally help them to consider various avenues, considering not just empirical evidence against their belief, but also any logical or pragmatic issues with believing it. A list of possible avenues to explore can be found in the Box – this is by no means exhaustive, and each thought will benefit from a different combination of these, ideally adapted and tailored to the specific scenario.

Using the collected evidence, an alternative belief can then be devised. This new, balanced belief should take into account both sides of the evaluation, and can often be devised by summarising one side, then adding the word 'but' or 'however', and then summarising the other. The aim is not to be overly positive, but to create a statement which provides relief from the extreme distress the patient was feeling and can be genuinely believed as true. For example, the initial cognition of 'I'll never get a job' should not simply become 'I'll get a job soon', as the patient can't know this is true, so won't be able to believe it. It could however be transformed into 'It's difficult to get a job right now, however I have lots of valuable skills so will likely find something eventually if I keep applying.' This option accepts the reality the patient is in, and allows for the inherent uncertainty of the future, but is far less distressing than the original.

Questions to evaluate negative thoughts

Empirical:

- What evidence do you have against this thought?
- Have there been any situations where this didn't hold true?
- Is there anything that happened that seems to go against this?

Logical:

- Is it possible to do as you are thinking you should?
- Are there any other ways to make sense of this?
- How would you view this if it was your friend in the situation?
- How would others view this situation?

Pragmatic:

- How helpful is it to view the situation this way?
- What impact did thinking this way have on what you did?
- What impact did thinking this way have on how you felt?
- What impact did thinking this way have on the situation?
- What would be a more helpful way to view the situation?
- If you viewed the situation differently, how would that have impacted you?

Finally, it can be helpful to re-rate the belief in the original belief, as well as in the new belief and the level of distress. This helps the therapist to see how effective the process has been for the patient, and if any further adaptations are needed. It also helps the patient to see the value of the process, to encourage its use in the future, in and out of sessions.

Restructuring a cognition can occur at any level of belief (NATs, assumptions or core beliefs). With more firmly held, deeper levels of cognition, additional tools are likely to be needed, such as using data logs, role plays, and pros and cons lists, to name but a few. For further information on this, see the specific protocol descriptions in Part III. Alternatively, an excellent exploration of these tools in general can be found in the book *Basics and Beyond* [8].

Guided Discovery

As with cognitive restructuring above, guided discovery is a process by which Socratic questions, summaries and reflections are used by the therapist to help guide a patient to discover new information, which they had previously not connected together, and which could help them with the concept that had been maintaining their problem. The therapist does not have to have a predefined alternative belief that they are aiming for the patient to arrive at, and indeed true guided discovery does not have any goal in mind beyond finding something that will help the patient make more adaptive choices.

This wider use of Socratic questioning – to guide discovery rather than simply challenge a belief – was most notably defined by Christine Padesky, in which she provides the following definition of Socratic questions as used for guided discovery [9]:

- They are questions that the patient can answer with their current knowledge;
- The questions cause the patient to pay attention to something they weren't currently considering, but which is relevant to the issue at hand, and;
- The questions generally move the patient from concrete information to more abstract concepts.

Due to this, the questions should eventually allow the patient to either re-evaluate their past thinking, or come to a new solution or plan, based on the application of the previously unconsidered information. Ensuring this occurs is important; while guided discovery doesn't have a specific goal in mind, it is key that the therapist helps summarise the new information as it is found, and guides the patient to apply this to the initial issue.

Guided discovery can occur throughout therapy sessions. While agenda setting, therapists can use guided discovery to help the patient realise that they do in fact have a useful item to add, or that out of the three concerns they were planning to discuss, actually one will be most useful. During homework review, guided discovery can help a patient see that there were reasons why the homework did not go to plan, and so discover a new plan for the week ahead. During homework setting, guided discovery can find the best possible way to apply the session's learning to the patient's life. For each of these to truly be guided discovery, the therapist must be asking the patient questions that fit the concept above, not simply leading the patient to the therapist's own pre-planned outcomes.

Exposure for Habituation

Exposure is a behavioural approach, which is based on the concept of Pavlovian extinction of fear due to repeated exposure to the feared stimulus without experiencing any negative consequences. The basic steps in exposure are to determine the situations or triggers that evoke fear in the patient, and then to encourage the patient to systematically expose themselves to these, without any avoidance or distraction. The patient needs to stay in this situation for a sufficient period of time to experience the lack of negative consequence, as this causes the link between the trigger and fear to weaken. By repeating this over several occasions, the fear response to the trigger or situation can be increasingly extinguished. To measure the effect of the work, subjective units of distress scale (SUDS) ratings are taken before, during and after each exposure exercise.

While basic exposure to real (in vivo) scenarios is effective in simple phobias, adaptations are needed to help it apply in other disorders. The two most commonly used changes are imaginal exposure, and exposure with response prevention (ERP).

Imaginal exposure, as the name suggests, is where the feared stimulus is imagined rather than experienced in vivo. To be effective, the process of imagining needs to again be prolonged, and kept in mind vividly, and as such often incorporates the use of a script to be read, detailing the scenario. However, while this narration is useful, its key is that the patient is using this to aid their imagery of the feared concept, not listening passively. Imaginal exposure can be used for two main reasons. The first is where exposure to the feared stimulus is difficult or impossible, or will inevitably cause a negative consequence (thus reinforcing the fear rather than weakening it). This could include situations such as a fear of dying, or of vomiting, which are both inherently aversive. The second reason for using imaginal exposure is where it is the image itself that is feared. This is highly relevant in disorders such as post-traumatic stress disorder and generalised anxiety disorder, where avoidance of feared mental images is believed to be a maintaining factor of the problem as a whole [10,11].

Exposure with response prevention varies from standard exposure in that the patient is asked to expose themselves to a feared stimulus, and then explicitly prevent themselves from using their usual responses (such as checking, washing or mental acts). This variation to the process is key in disorders where the feared triggers are most managed by such responses, as in OCD, as it ensures that both the fear to the stimulus is reduced, and the urge to use compulsions on future exposure. For more detail on this, see Chapters 15–18.

Behavioural exposure approaches, including these adaptations, have now been successfully tested in almost all disorders where anxiety plays a maintaining role, and as such, are a primary intervention in a number of the disorder-specific protocols (see Part III for a range of examples of this).

The use of hierarchies as a method of grading exposure for habituation has been well established, and is employed in most protocols that use this intervention. However, the empirical value of this is harder to evidence. In a recent study, those receiving graded exposure according to a hierarchy did not show any greater improvement over those where exposure varied randomly across stimuli [12]. Moreover, both this and other trials have shown that more variable exposure appears to lead to a more persistent reduction in fears following therapy [13,14]. Furthermore, and contrary to what might be expected, more patients dropped out of studies where the exposure followed a graded process. All of this calls into question whether hierarchies are actually of therapeutic value in habituation, or are simply a therapist habit.

Behavioural Experiments

Behavioural approaches to anxiety, as described above, can be highly successful, and as noted, there are many protocols which thus use exposure in a behavioural way. However, as these protocols were rolled out, therapists began to find patients where it didn't seem to cause the hoped-for changes; where the patients' cognitions seemed to block Pavlovian extinction [15], and where safety-seeking behaviours used by patients during exposure prevented these cognitions from changing [16].

From this, an alternative, cognitive approach to exposure was developed. While classical cognitive therapy tests out beliefs primarily through discussion and cognitive restructuring, this focussed on testing out or changing a patient's beliefs through experience – a behavioural experiment.

The use of the word experiment is fitting; behavioural experiments, like those in science, should have a clear hypothesis to test where possible, and should try and control any variables that might otherwise prevent a clear conclusion from being drawn. As such, most experiments will be set up with the patient by first discussing what the prediction is to be tested, and what outcomes would show that prediction to be right or wrong. The set up will also include exploring what factors will need to be controlled to truly test it. This might mean running through the situation a set number of times, or for a set duration. It also means dropping any of the patient's safety-seeking behaviours that will otherwise be seen as an alternative reason for the outcome.

Picking the right thing to test out is a key role of the cognitive therapist when using behavioural experiments. Importantly, the belief being tested needs to be part of what is maintaining the patient's problem, or would lead to their recovery. Disorder-specific cognitive protocols which use behavioural experiments help with this, as they define the key cognitive themes for each disorder, and the general ways in which each theme can be experimented with (see Part III). However therapists should also be creative with experiments, going beyond the standard experiments wherever needed to test the exact thing the patient believes [17].

Active behavioural experiments in anxiety disorders can seem similar to their behavioural cousin, exposure for habituation, and indeed both often involve exposing the patient to the same situations, and avoiding use of the same behaviours, resulting in a reduction in fear. However, the detail of each is quite different. In behavioural experiments, the focus is on the risk being taken, and whether that risk seems worth the possible new information to be gathered. In behavioural exposure, the focus is instead on the anxiety being experienced, and whether this is tolerable. This may explain why more cognitive approaches are generally preferable in problems such as panic disorder, where beliefs about the dangerousness of sensations are likely to cause avoidance and reluctance to behavioural exposure, and yet are readily disproved with a cognitive approach.

Behavioural experiments can also be done without direct exposure to feared stimuli. These observational experiments instead involve collection of data through surveys, allowing the testing of beliefs about the experiences or opinions of others. Such observational experiments are key when the cognition is focussed on hidden outcomes, such as other people's secret opinions, or is focussed on situations that cannot easily be accessed (for example, how others behave in job interviews). However, using surveys instead of direct experience should be done with care; indirect data is rarely as compelling as actually experiencing reality, and avoiding experiments where they are feasible can reinforce the sense of danger.

Behavioural Activation

At its heart, behavioural activation is about helping an individual to change what they spend their time doing day on day, to change how they feel. While there are many variations to the process (see Chapter 20 for different ways in which this is applied in depression, as well as Chapter 19 for how a similar process is used in PTSD) there are common features to all. Namely, the process will involve exploring what the patient currently does, and how this impacts their mood and/or cognitions, and then experimenting with new behaviours to see what works better. Generally, it will start with making smaller changes, and then building up to larger and more effortful changes as motivation and mood improves. It will also try to encourage a wider range of activity, including those that spark pleasure as well as those giving a sense of achievement, and those that result in a sense of closeness to others.

Importantly, it is not necessarily about doing more. Many depressed individuals may have a lack of activity in life, but equally many others are actually doing too much, albeit in a very narrow range of behaviours. For the latter group, being told that their mood is caused by not doing enough is likely to rupture the therapeutic relationship, as well as being obviously untrue. Instead, it can be helpful to consider in all cases that it is about doing differently; be that by dropping some housework to make space for a bubble bath, or by dropping some time spent in bed to do the washing up. In either case, the individual is dropping one activity for another, according to what will bring them a greater overall sense of wellbeing.

On the surface, the foundation for behavioural activation can appear self-explanatory – do things that make you happy, and you'll be happier. However, the full rationale for why this approach works is greater than that, and understanding this can make it easier to engage patients, as well as enhance its effectiveness.

First, depression often involves a loss of motivation to engage in previously enjoyed activities and a drive to avoid effort, distress or risk. One theory for this is that due to a reduction in engaging in rewarding activities, there is less associated positive reinforcement, and so the behaviour becomes extinguished [18]. Meanwhile, unhelpful behaviours, which allow the individual to avoid aversive experiences, are carried out frequently, and so become strongly negatively reinforced. By changing this and choosing to engage in a rewarding activity, the patient will re-experience the missing positive reinforcement, and so automatically strengthen the tendency to engage in this activity in the future. At the same time, they will stop having their unhelpful avoidance-based activity reinforced, lessening their tendency to repeat that.

Understanding this rationale can help when starting the work with patients, as it helps to make sense of why they aren't feeling motivated to make these changes naturally. It also helps give hope that this will change if they can take the first step; by making even small changes, the tendency to avoid and withdraw will be lessened, and the motivation to engage will increase.

On a parallel track, depressogenic behaviours also drive depressogenic thoughts, and vice versa. For example, if an individual believes they are unlovable, they may avoid being around others, or replying to contact attempts. Over time, this results in others drawing away, reinforcing the 'I am unlovable' belief. If they reverse this, and attempts to socialise again, there is the opportunity to have this belief contradicted by friends appearing happy to see them. This version of behavioural activation, where the behavioural changes actively open the patient up to opportunities to disconfirm their depressogenic beliefs, is central in Beck's original therapy for depression, the so-called cognitive model.

Yet another reason for the success of behavioural activation is in creating variety of activity. Often a precursor to depression is the restriction in activity range which results in emotional wellbeing being overly driven by the success/enjoyment of those activities [19]. If something then goes wrong with those activities, there is little else to fall back on to maintain a sense of worth or wellbeing, and so the individual can become depressed. Many of us will have experienced this during periods of excessive focus on our own lives, such as when studying for an important qualification. As other aspects of our lives are ignored, our sense of wellbeing becomes increasingly focussed on how we are doing with our studies. This is fine so long as the studying goes well, but can be disproportionately distressing if we struggle, or fail an assignment. This is often why students are encouraged to have a work-life balance, and likewise in behavioural activation, simply broadening the patient's focus and range of experiences can lessen the distress of a single area going wrong.

Finally, behavioural activation can help by focussing on bodily cycles. Humans experience a complicated range of hormonal and chemical changes throughout the day, which tend to be regulated by some of our activities (especially sleeping, eating and exercise), and which can be disrupted by depression. This then in turn dysregulates our drives to engage in those activities, resulting in the classic depressive symptoms of hypersomnia/insomnia, changes in appetite and psychomotor retardation/agitation. As direct control of our hormones would be difficult, behavioural activation starts from the opposite angle – manually control eating and exercise, and limit sleeping opportunity to a preferred sleeping window. This can reverse the unhelpful dysregulation, bringing a wide range of cycles back under control, and so lift mood.

Problem Solving

Problematic situations are an inevitable part of life, and how effectively we solve problems will inevitably impact us, both practically and emotionally. Many people, due to prior experiences or feared consequences can become ineffective problem solvers, and so a useful intervention can be to enhance this skill. This won't mean that patients suddenly find easy and perfect solutions to the difficulties they face in life, but it will mean that they can feel more confident about the choices they make, and make choices that result in the best possible consequences for the circumstance.

First proposed as either a complete treatment or component of wider work, problem solving therapy is based on behavioural and social learning theory, as well as borrowing from early cognitive theory [20]. Its aim is to aid patients in being able devise a variety of possible solutions to a given problematic situation and increase the likelihood that the best solution will be chosen and employed. This can be done by using, and teaching patients to use, five key processes:

- Development of a positive problem orientation
- Defining the problem and goals
- Generating solutions
- Evaluation and choosing a solution
- Reviewing and refining solutions

Development of a positive problem orientation: Effective problem solving starts with adaptive reactions to encountering a problem. If problems are viewed as abnormal or unmanageable, they will inevitably cause more distress than if they can be viewed as a normal part of life that the individual will be generally able to solve. If patients ignore or avoid acknowledging problems, then they will likely become more problematic than if noted earlier. If patients automatically respond to problems by doing nothing, or impulsively using the first solution available, they will likely miss out on the opportunity to implement an effective solution. For example, solving financial issues will be almost impossible while a patient is focussed on how unfair it is to have to deal with money worries (negative problem attitude), or while they are avoiding opening bills (lack of problem awareness) or repeatedly taking out new credit cards (impulsively problem solving).

Thus, developing a positive problem orientation involves focussing on each of these issues in turn, and using psycho-education and/or cognitive restructuring techniques to help the patient believe that problems are a normal, manageable part of life, which they do not need to ignore, avoid or impulsively solve. This may not be easily believed at first, and the therapist may need to negotiate with the patient to simply act as though this is true to start with. Subsequent practice with the remaining steps should help the patient build evidence of their problem-solving ability, which in turn should then make it easier to see problems as normal and manageable, and to resist avoidance or using a less effective solution impulsively when future problems arise.

Defining the problem and goals: This process is about being specific and comprehensive about what a problem is – rather than defining the problem as 'I'm broke' or 'my outgoings exceed my income' defining it as 'my current income is X, and my average outgoings are Y, and there are no expected changes in any of these numbers, and as such I fear that I am going to go broke, lose my house and car, and end up on the street. I also don't feel able to do anything social, as I am always worrying about the cost'. This step may involve data gathering, to get the problem more clearly defined. It also involves defining the key goals – in the case above to have a balanced budget and to be able to socialise regularly.

Generating solutions: Once the problem has been defined, the next step is coming up with possible solutions – that is, ways of changing the situation so that it stops being problematic to the patient. To do this effectively the patient should be instructed to use classic brainstorming rules [29]; namely, to let ideas be as strange as they wish, to postpone any critique of ideas until they have a full list (if the solution would in some way solve the problem, it stays!), to aim for as many ideas as possible and to experiment with combining ideas or editing them to create new options. By brainstorming this way, patients are more likely to find more good solutions, as well as become more open to the idea that there are multiple solutions to any problem. In addition to all the solutions the patient has come up with, it can often be helpful to add their current solution – do nothing. This helps in ensuring that this solution isn't picked de facto due to avoiding making a choice – either it will genuinely be the best solution, or it will clearly be worse than picking something and trying it.

For our patient above, such a list might have 'rob a bank, get a lodger, economise on optional monthly spending, increase earnings by working more hours, re-mortgage the house, invite people to social events that don't have any cost, get a lodger and work more hours, get a lodger and re-mortgage the house, do nothing and hope the situation resolves itself'.

Evaluation and choosing a solution: Evaluating solutions is often done in two stages. The first stage is to quickly review the list, and get rid of any options that have such a high cost that they are certain to be rejected. The remaining solutions are then evaluated in more detail, looking at the positive and negative consequences both short term and long term, and for both the individual and those around them. Therapists should ensure that the emotional, time and effort-based costs of each are also considered. As a rule of thumb, all solutions will have at least one negative consequence – if they didn't the patient would have already taken action.

For our example patient, initial screening cut out robbing a bank and re-mortgaging the house. Further analysis noted consequences such as having to share space, the time involved in each solution, possible social benefits to a lodger, and whether the solution was feasible long term. By going through these, each patient will end up picking the solution that fits best for them – for the patient who deeply values personal space, working more hours might fit best, whereas another patient who is generally feeling isolated may be able to kill two birds with one stone by finding a lodger. In either case, the therapist's role is not to promote one solution or another, but to encourage the patient to make a choice and put it into action.

Reviewing and refining solutions: Once an option has been chosen and implemented, the final stage is to seek out information on whether it has solved the problem, so that the patient can decide whether to continue with the solution, refine or edit the solution, or stop and try out a new solution. Therapist and patient together will need to define this stage as any other; what information does the patient need to access to see if the solution is working, and when is a good point to review this?

In the case above of getting a lodger, as in many cases, reviewing the solution is likely to be in multiple parts. First, could the solution be implemented (could a lodger be successfully found)? Second, did implementing the solution achieve the main goal (did income become higher than outgoings)? Last, how did the consequences of the solution compare to the predictions (did this result in more social opportunities, and how did sharing space feel compared to predictions)?

By going through each of these parts, patients can improve their decision making for the future, and feel comfortable making choices, safe in the knowledge that they can adapt as new information arises. In turn, this will naturally reinforce the positive problem orientation initially proposed, making problem solving as a whole more natural and automatic.

Skills Training

The key tenet of cognitive behavioural therapies is that distress and problematic cycles are maintained not by fundamental deficits in the patient, but by their thoughts and responses to situations. A nuance to this is that with some problems, patients may not have learnt how to action certain responses, due to their prior cognitive-behavioural cycles. In these situations, cognitive behavioural therapy may be enhanced by the addition of specific skills training.

Skills training incorporates a wide range of possible options, depending on what the patient most needs to be able to do to act in accordance with their new beliefs. Common examples of the kinds of skills patients may need across multiple disorders include attention training, relaxation, assertiveness and sleep hygiene, and each of these have been described in detail in numerous other texts.

Whichever skill is being taught, the key focus of the therapist should be on ensuring that the skill is actually needed, and that using it will help the patient to live in accordance with their new beliefs. For example, teaching relaxation techniques to a patient with panic disorder may appear helpful, but using them would go directly against the belief that panic isn't dangerous and can be let pass. Conversely, helping a patient with generalised anxiety disorder, who is trying to increase their belief that they can tolerate and control anxiety, may benefit greatly from relaxation techniques which allow them to do so.

Imagery

Much of the therapeutic work above has considered cognition in terms of verbal thoughts. However, mental processing often involves a second track, which is more sensory and experiential – a track we describe as imagery. Said imagery features strongly in various disorders (e.g. depression in cancer patients [21], phobias [22] and bulimia [23]), it can correlate with the severity of the problem [24] and exposure to imagery can even treat some problems [25].

So, as imagery can be part of both the problem and the solution, it is useful to ask about it. Images are often connected to areas of particularly high emotion, and so such emotion can often be the first clue that it may be helpful to ask about imagery. To start this, simple questions about what the patient is imagining, what images or pictures come to mind at that point, can be helpful. From this, it is then important to add detail and help the patient to connect fully to the image; this can be done by simply requesting more information, asking the patient to describe across any and all senses what it is that they imagine.

Once the image itself has been captured, the meanings of the imagery can then be determined. Said meanings include both the direct meaning of the content and the meta-cognitive meaning of having an image at all. For example, an individual with OCD might have an image of the oven catching fire. The meaning of the content might be 'the house will burn down'. The meaning of having the image at all might be 'this means I didn't turn the oven off; I wouldn't have had such a strong image unless it was true'. Just like with verbal cognitions, images can then evoke emotional and behavioural responses, and it can be helpful to capture these too, so as to fully understand the importance of the image in the patient's difficulties, and to make sense of how the imagery is being reinforced. For more information on this, see the chapters on Social Anxiety Disorder (Chapter 13), OCD (Chapter 16) and PTSD treatment (Chapter 19), all of which tend to have imagery as a central aspect of the difficulty.

Having captured the imagery and all of the associated meanings, behaviours and emotions, the therapist then has a range of options. Many of the tools above – psychoeducation, exposure for habituation, cognitive restructuring, behavioural experiments – can be used to help break the links between imagery and distress. Beyond this, as images are, by their nature, imaginary, therapy can also involve changing the images directly. This might involve changing the image into something more realistic, or widening the image to add in the more tolerable next steps, or even having someone enter the imaginary situation to help. It can also involve creating fully alternative images, such as the more likely alternative outcome, or a hoped-for positive possibility [26].

A word of caution; while images can be a powerful cognitive process for most, they are not a universal experience [27]. Aphantasia, the inability to visualise mental images (and for some, the paired inability to recall sounds, smells or other sensory memories), is thought to occur in around 2–5% of the population [28]. A larger group, while being able to form mental images when needed, will nonetheless think purely in words by nature, which can be surprising for those therapists who are strongly visual thinkers themselves. As such, while asking about imagery is important in therapy, so too is accepting that there won't always be an answer and adapting future questions to match.

Concluding Remarks

There are a wide range of techniques available in within the CBT umbrella of therapies, allowing therapists to help their patients with socialisation, behavioural change, cognitive shift, developing skills, problem solving, and engaging with imagery. Any given patient will need their own unique subset of these, dependent upon the specific difficulties they are experiencing, and their own idiosyncratic maintenance cycles. The following chapters will consider how these tools fit within therapy (Chapter 7) and how tools can be best selected based on the patient's formulation (Chapter 8).

Essential Reading

Beck, JS, Beck, AT. *Cognitive Behavior Therapy: Basics and Beyond*. 3rd ed. New York: Guilford Press; 2020.

Padesky CA. *Socratic questioning: Changing Minds or Guiding Discovery.* A keynote address delivered at the European Congress of Behavioural and Cognitive Therapies, London (1993, September).

Hackmann A, Bennett-Levy J, Holmes, EA (Eds). *Oxford Guide to Imagery in Cognitive Therapy.* Oxford: Oxford University Press; 2015.

Rouf K. *Oxford Guide to Behavioural Experiments in Cognitive Therapy.* Oxford: Oxford University Press 2004.

References

1. Craft LL, Perna FM. The benefits of exercise for the clinically depressed. *Prim Care Companion J Clin Psychiatry*. 2004;**6**(3):104–111.
2. Hirsch CR, Mathews A. A cognitive model of pathological worry. *Behav Res Ther*. 2012 Oct;**50**(10):636–646.
3. Beck AT, Rush J, Shaw BF, Emery G. *Cognitive Therapy of Depression*. New York: Guilford Press; 1979.
4. Stott R, Mansell W, Salkovskis P, Lavender A. *Oxford Guide to Metaphors in CBT: Building Cognitive Bridges*. Oxford: Oxford University Press; 2010.
5. Salkovskis PM, Kirk J. Obsessive-compulsive disorder. In: Christopher G. Fairburn & David M. Clark (eds.), *Science and Practice of Cognitive Behaviour Therapy* (pp. 179–208). New York: Oxford University Press; 1997.
6. Bream V, Challacombe F, Palmer A, Salkovskis P. *Cognitive Behaviour Therapy for Obsessive-Compulsive Disorder*. Illustrated ed. Oxford: Oxford University Press; 2017.
7. Beck AT. Thinking and depression: II. Theory and therapy. *Arch Gen Psychiatry*. 1964;**10**(6):561–571.
8. Beck JS, Beck AT. *Cognitive Behavior Therapy: Basics and Beyond*. 3rd ed. New York: Guilford Press; 2020.
9. Padesky CA. *Socratic Questioning: Changing Minds or Guiding Discovery*. A keynote address delivered at the European Congress of Behavioural and Cognitive Therapies, London (1993, September).
10. Hembree EA, Foa EB. Posttraumatic stress disorder: Psychological factors and psychosocial interventions. *J Clin Psychiatry*. 2000;**61**:33–39.
11. Borkovec T, Inz J. The nature of worry in generalized anxiety disorder: A predominance of thought activity. *Behav Res Ther*. 1990;**28**(2):153–158.
12. Jacoby RJ, Abramowitz JS, Blakey SM, Reuman L. Is the hierarchy necessary?

Gradual versus variable exposure intensity in the treatment of unacceptable obsessional thoughts. *J Behav Ther Exp Psychiatry*. 2019;**64**:54–63.

13. Rowe MK, Craske MG. Effects of varied-stimulus exposure training on fear reduction and return of fear. *Behav Res Ther*. 1998;**36**(7–8):719–734.
14. Lang AJ, Craske MG. Manipulations of exposure-based therapy to reduce return of fear: A replication. *Behav Res Ther*. 2000;**38**(1):1–12.
15. Clark DM. A cognitive approach to panic. *Behav Res Ther*. 1986;**24**(4):461–470.
16. Salkovskis PM. The importance of behaviour in the maintenance of anxiety and panic: A cognitive account. *Behav Cogn Psychother*. 1991;**19**(1):6–19.
17. Rouf K. *Oxford Guide to Behavioural Experiments in Cognitive Therapy*. Oxford: Oxford University Press; 2004.
18. Ferster CB. A functional analysis of depression. *Am Psychol*. 1973;**28**(10):857–870.
19. Rehm LP. *Behavior Therapy for Depression: Present Status and Future Directions*. Academic Press; 1981.
20. D'zurilla TJ, Goldfried MR. Problem solving and behavior modification. *J Abnorm Psychol*. 1971;**78**(1):107–126.
21. Brewin CR, Watson M, McCarthy S, Hyman P, Dayson D. Intrusive memories and depression in cancer patients. *Behav Res Ther*. 1998;**36**(12):1131–1142.
22. Pratt D, Cooper MJ, Hackmann A. Imagery and its characteristics in people who are anxious about spiders. *Behav Cogn Psychother*. 2004;**32**(2):165–176.
23. Somerville K, Cooper M, Hackmann A. Spontaneous imagery in women with bulimia nervosa: An investigation into content, characteristics and links to childhood memories. *J Behav Ther Exp Psychiatry*. 2007;**38**(4):435–446.
24. Speckens AEM, Hackmann A, Ehlers A, Cuthbert B. Imagery special issue: Intrusive images and memories of earlier adverse events in patients with obsessive compulsive disorder. *J Behav Ther Exp Psychiatry*. 2007;**38**(4):411–422.
25. Foa EB, Steketee G, Turner RM, Fischer SC. Effects of imaginal exposure to feared disasters in obsessive-compulsive checkers. *Behav Res Ther*. 1980;**18**(5):449–455.
26. Hackmann A, Bennett-Levy J, Holmes EA, (Eds.) *Oxford Guide to Imagery in Cognitive Therapy*. Oxford: Oxford University Press; 2015.
27. Zeman A, Dewar M, Della Sala S. Lives without imagery: Congenital aphantasia. *Cortex*. 2015;**73**:378–380.
28. Faw B. Conflicting intuitions may be based on differing abilities: Evidence from mental imaging research. *J Conscious Stud*. 2009;**16**:45–68.
29. Osborn, Alex (1953). *Applied Imagination: Principles and Procedures of Creative Problem Solving*. New York, New York: Charles Scribner's Sons.

Chapter 7 The Structure of Cognitive Behavioural Therapy

In this chapter we will help you to be able to:

- Explain the structure of CBT as a whole, including the purpose of each stage of therapy.
- Effectively structure a treatment session of CBT, so as to ensure the best possible experience for patients.
- Develop a strong therapeutic alliance with this process, based on active collaboration and genuine empathy, warmth and unconditional positive regard.

Introduction

All CBT should have clear goals and aims (Chapter 5). To achieve these, processes need to be followed in a structured way, both across therapy as a whole and within each session, so as to maximise the effectiveness of what is being done. In this chapter, the way in which the various phases of therapy – assessment, formulation, socialisation, intervention and relapse prevention – fit together will be explored. Sessional structure will also be discussed, looking at how each section can help maximise learning. Finally, this chapter will look at the concept of the collaborative therapeutic alliance in CBT, and how this can be incorporated into such a structured process.

Structure of Treatment in CBT

There are five main stages to cognitive behaviour therapy: assessment, formulation, socialisation, intervention and relapse prevention. As shown in Figure 7.1, these stages do not occur discretely, but instead each one builds on, and then refines, the stage preceding it.

Assessment and formulation are a symbiotic pairing, which aim to create a shared understanding between the therapist and patient of what the key problems are and how we can make sense of them within a cognitive behavioural framework. The very initial parts of assessing are quite open, as the therapist gathers enough general information about the problem to find a way to understand it – a vague formulation. As this continues, the initial formulation will indicate further assessment questions, further refining the formulation in a cyclical pattern. Throughout this assessment and formulation process, information is directly shared with the patient, both to aid their understanding, and to allow for any correction, until an agreed picture has been developed. For more information on this, including a step-by-step breakdown of the process, see Chapter 8.

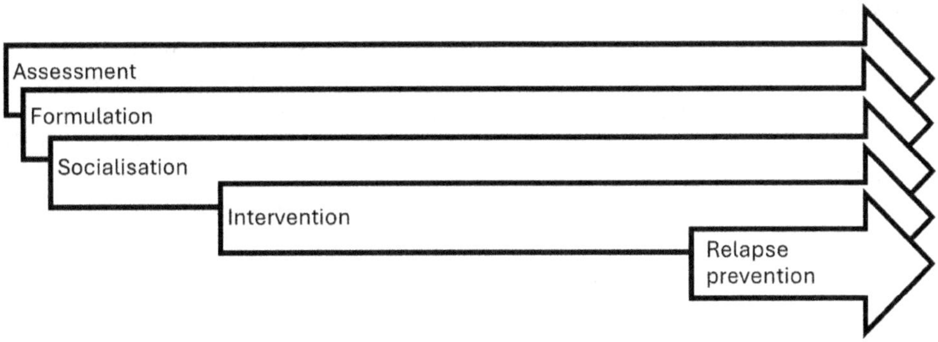

Figure 7.1 The stages of CBT.

Socialisation is an often poorly defined concept, though some key features have been more recently clarified [1]. As with formulation, socialisation to the general model of CBT starts very early on. Even in the initial assessment session, CBT therapists will aim to socialise the patient by doing things such as setting a shared agenda, asking questions that highlight the role of key cognitions and behaviours and devising appropriate homework tasks. Formulation is also a key feature of socialisation, as the patient and therapist sharing an agreed understanding of the problem is needed for any agreement in how to proceed. Finally, socialisation involves exploring what this model implies for making change. Within this, the therapist will generally need to supply psychoeducational information, or use a process such as Theory A/Theory B, to allow the patient to make sense of the processes in therapy, and the interventions to be used.

Once the patient is on board with the rationale for treatment, therapy can move into the intervention stage. This is where active change will really get started, helping to break the dysfunctional cycles occurring, and create new and more adaptive patterns of thoughts and behaviour. Typically, interventions follow a pattern, starting with more behavioural change, and then moving to ever increasingly central and long-held cognitions, often finishing with core beliefs. Throughout this, more information will come to light, adding depth and breadth to the shared formulation. A summary of the key techniques used in socialisation and intervention has already been given in Chapter 6, with further details of how these can be applied to a range of specific mental health disorders given in Part III.

The final stage of any CBT is to ensure that the changes made can be continued in the future, which is known as relapse prevention. As shown in Figure 7.1, the building blocks for this stage should begin at assessment, where the patient is made aware of the time limited nature of the therapy, and the concept of becoming their own therapist is explored [2]. Throughout therapy, the focus on active collaboration and following a shared understanding will have ensured that the patient not only makes change but understand how they have done so. In the relapse prevention stage, this learning is consolidated, and the pair explore how it can be applied moving forwards. Future obstacles and recurring stressors are considered, and a plan is generally made to both work through these problems and keep moving forwards to new goals and possibilities.

Sessional Structure

The structure within each session is considered key in CBT [3]. It allows for each session to cover the essential areas in promoting change, namely those of reviewing past change, considering or actively making new change, and planning future change. It is also pivotal to ensuring that the overall structure above can be achieved, and that therapy can focus on the right topics in the right order. While there can be some debate in CBT about the exact correct ordering of a session, the most commonly used structure is as follows:

- Mood check
- Summary of last session and feedback
- Setting an agenda
- Review of past homework
- Sessional work
- Summary and feedback
- Setting new homework

Let's now explore each of these sections in turn.

Mood check: This is the one of two areas of the session that generally occurs prior to setting an agenda. It involves gathering a brief summary of how the patient has been feeling over the past week, how their target problems have fluctuated, and any major events connected to these two concepts. Typical questions that can be used to initiate a mood check could be:

'How have you been since our last session?'

'How has your mood been over the past week?'

'Have there been any (major) ups or downs in the last week?'

'How has your [agreed descriptor of problem] been since we last spoke?'

It may be noted by some readers that these questions become increasingly closed and targeted as the list progresses. The choice of which question to use depends a lot on the patient and the process of therapy to date. A highly focussed patient, who holds a clear understanding of the role and limitations of therapy, and who is confident about what is relevant to treating their specific difficulties, will generally give highly relevant information when asked the first question. However, for those more anxious or unclear about what could be relevant, or less focussed in general, the latter questions may offer more structure and thus keep this part of the session on track. In all cases, the therapist should be flexible to the situation presented; offering direction to the conversation while remaining curious and open to material that they may not have expected but that nonetheless is important.

Some therapists do choose to do the mood check after agenda setting, in order to avoid extended conversations prior to making a shared agreement on how to spend the session. However, there are a number of advantages to doing it first. Knowing the patient's emotional state allows the therapist to gauge how quickly to move in the session ahead; a highly distressed patient is unlikely to be able to manage as much as one who is more positive and relaxed. If major events have occurred in the week, it may be that the session should focus upon these, either using the planned strategies but tailored to that content, or by changing the plan for the session entirely. In rare scenarios, it may even be better to cancel or reschedule the session, so as to allow the patient to manage a crisis pragmatically.

Summary of last session and feedback: The other half of the pre-agenda items is to explore what was covered in the preceding session, as well as some brief feedback on how this has since been reflected upon. Ideally, the patient should be given the lead with this, through questions such as:

'What do you remember from our last session?'

'What were the key points from last session?'

Any major gaps should then be filled in, especially in terms of key learning points, and the therapist should build a picture of how well the concepts overall have been understood and implemented. This allows for the next section – agenda setting – to be framed by the work to date.

Setting an agenda: Armed with the information from the mood check and the summary and feedback from the last session, as well as knowledge of the protocol being followed, the therapist should then collaboratively set an agenda for the remainder of the session. The purpose of this is to ensure that the session is spent doing things that both the patient and therapist value, and which will help with changing the problem.

Where possible, it is helpful to start agenda setting with the patient's perspective:

'What would you like us to focus on today?'

'What aspect of [agreed descriptor of problem] would you like us to work on today?'

'Given what we've discussed so far, what would be helpful for us to focus on today?'

'You've mentioned [list of events from mood check, and key point from last session]. Would it be helpful for us to explore any of these today, or is there something else that you would rather we looked at?'

'As discussed, so far we've been working on [most recent interventions(s)]. Would it be helpful for us to keep focussing on that, or do you feel ready to move onto the next phase?'

Again, these questions become more directive as the list goes on, but all give choice to the patient, and all encourage the patient to be an active participant. Importantly, they all emphasise the role of the patient as the expert in their own problem; while the therapist knows what interventions or strategies are important, only the patient will know the specific areas that have been most problematic over the previous week, and thus what areas could be most powerfully worked on in the session. In comparison, questions such as 'Is there anything you would like to add to the agenda?' imply that the patient can happily take no role in the agenda setting if they choose; that the therapist is the only expert needed. To many patients, it can even suggest that it is better if they do not provide material or a focus to the session, and so force them into a passive role.

Following the inclusion of the patient's preferred focus, the therapist can then add all the other standard items to the agenda that the patient didn't bring up themselves (past homework review, summary and feedback, new homework setting). If there is insufficient material from the patient, they may also add sessional work, though this should be done with genuine buy-in from the patient, by using sufficient rationale to explain why this work may be helpful.

Review of past homework: Reviewing how the patient has done with the last session's homework tasks serves a number of important functions. First, the act of asking about the homework, in and of itself, can serve as a powerful reinforcer to the patient to attempt the

Table 7.1 Examples of homework issues, and what might be driving them

Issue	Possible new information to be considered
Forgot the homework	Is the problem/therapy something that is less important than previously understood? Alternatively, is it something the patient actively avoids thinking about due to the distress it causes?
No time/too busy	What does the patient believe about the importance of their mental wellbeing versus other priorities? How beneficial to their wellbeing did they expect the homework to be?
Kept thinking about doing the homework, and putting it off	How did thinking about the homework make them feel? Is this situation/activity a more powerful trigger than realised? What new thoughts arose when considering this activity? How beneficial to their wellbeing did they expect the homework to be?
Started the homework, and became unexpectedly distressed/ stayed distressed longer than expected	What cognitions/images arose as they were doing the homework? What strategies were they using (overt and covert) to manage the situation? Were there any aspects to the situation that were more distressing than realised?

task. Given the anxiety-provoking nature of many homework tasks, anything that the therapist can do to help the patient engage is likely to be helpful.

The homework review also provides an opportunity to manage any issues that arose. These issues can be barriers that prevented or limited homework engagement, but can also involve times where the patient has attempted the homework and it has not gone as expected. The reaction of the therapist at these points is key. Following a scientist-practitioner approach, the therapist should explore what happened in detail, treating the situation empathically, but also as useful new information. Given that the pair had previously thought the homework would be manageable, and that it would go as expected, any issues must mean that something unknown has come to light. Often, this unknown concept will be part of what is maintaining the problem as a whole, and so discussing it, and seeing how it fits with the wider formulation, will be key to longer term changes. See Table 7.1 for some examples of homework issues, and what might be driving them.

Alternatively, the homework may have gone well. In this case, reviewing is equally important, to consider what new information has been uncovered about the solution to the problem. Does their anxiety reduce when they confront a trigger? Have they discovered a new way of understanding a situation or cycle? In each case, making this learning explicit, and helping the patient to connect this to the problem as broadly as possible, will maximise the benefit.

Sessional work: Once the therapist and patient have fully explored all the learning to date, new learning can begin. The focus of this will have been agreed during the agenda setting, with the patient providing the specific material regarding the problem, and the therapist considering and exploring the various intervention available to help with this (see Chapter 6). Each specific model and protocol will have its own guidelines on what might be most useful, including some whole session plans where appropriate.

A general guiding principle here is to consider what key change the sessional work is trying to achieve; what aspect of the problem from the formulation will the patient hopefully see differently by the end of the session? The tools and interventions can then be picked with this in mind, rather than seeing said interventions as the purpose in and of themselves.

Summary and feedback: After the sessional work is complete, it can be helpful to pause and consider the learning from the session as a whole. The therapist may want to summarise any new learning they themselves made about how the problem works, to ensure their understanding is the same as the patient's. More important though is asking the patient to feed back on what they have learnt. Suitable questions include:

'What key things have you taken from today's session?'

'What's changed for you today in how you view [the problem]?'

This key learning will be essential in the final part of the session, and so it is important to summarise from the patient's perspective, as otherwise homework setting is likely to go badly.

This key learning will be essential in the final part of the session, and so it is important to summarise from the patient's perspective, as otherwise homework setting is likely to go badly.

Finally, it can also be helpful to get feedback on how the patient found the session – which aspects they found most helpful, or how it felt emotionally. This can help refine the therapist's choices for future sessions and gives an opportunity to clear up any misunderstandings about the process.

Setting new homework: The use of homework in CBT is well established, with numerous studies showing the positive impact that homework compliance has on the overall efficacy of the therapy [4,5,6,7,8]. As such, homework setting is a key part of any therapy session and should be given enough time to allow for thorough exploration and planning.

Any homework set for the patient should be meaningfully linked to the recently summarised key learning from the therapy session. Depending on what this session has covered, and how it has covered it, the homework setting section might be simply a summary of the plans already made during homework review and sessional work. Alternatively, it can involve coming up with brand new ideas based on applying the cognitive shift that has occurred in the session to their life as a whole. Possible questions to encourage new homework tasks include:

'Where would it be useful to apply [key learning] in your life over the next week?'

'What could you do differently this week as a result of [key learning]?'

'How could you test out if [new possible belief] is true in other situations?'

While patients are generally the best people to devise good homework tasks, sometimes it can be too big a leap to come up with a suitable option, especially at the earlier stages of therapy. In these cases, tentative suggestions from the therapist can be appropriate. In either case, the key to the homework being a success is in checking that the patient has a clear rationale for doing the task. Possible ways to explore this are:

'What would be helpful for you about [doing homework task] in and of itself?'

'What would you hope to gain from [doing homework task]?'

'If [the homework task] does result in [hoped for outcome], what would that tell you? And how would that be helpful more widely?'

It is important to then follow up on the answers to these questions if the patient doesn't see a clear value – homework takes effort, so there needs to be a clear reward.

It's likewise important to ensure there are no barriers that will impede them from carrying out the task. Useful troubleshooting questions include:

'What might get in the way of [doing homework task] this week?'

'Is there anything that could happen which would stop you from [doing homework task]?'

'How could we adapt the plan to make it more manageable at this point?'

Finally, once the what's of the homework have been firmly decided upon, it is important to explore the rest of the Ws – where, when and with who will they do these tasks, and how will they record what happens. By making the plan as concrete as possible, we give the patient the best chance of success, and help reduce any procrastination or avoidance which could hold back their progress.

Therapeutic Alliance in CBT

Talk of structure can make CBT appear dismissive of the therapeutic alliance. However, as explored in the examples and details above, CBT is similarly focussed on collaboration, with an active and equal partnership between the therapist and the patient. This partnership ideally built on the firm belief that the patient is the expert in their problem, and the therapist is the expert in CBT [9]. If taken to heart, this concept should shape many of the questions we ask. For example, when asking a patient about new homework tasks, the therapist will likely know whether a more active or information gathering approach is likely to help (because that is a CBT expertise concept). However, the patient is the one who knows when this cycle occurs for them, and the situations where it most holds them back (because they are the expert in their problem). Only by combining these two pieces of information can we come up with the best homework task.

Another key part of the therapeutic alliance is the interpersonal style of the therapist. As described in the Manual of the Revised Cognitive Therapy Scale therapists are encouraged to show the core conditions of 'warmth, genuineness, empathy and understanding' [10]. While there are many good reasons for showing such traits [11], an additional reason in CBT is that they should flow somewhat intrinsically from our shared understanding of the patient's problem. Empathy, for example, is easier to feel when the key cognitions have been uncovered; almost by definition, these beliefs would provoke similar emotions in us all. Likewise, warmth and acceptance are natural responses to uncovering vicious cycles that we could all so easily fall into. For this reason, CBT trainees are often encouraged to use self-practice/self-reflection exercises during their training year to help connect with this genuine sense of understanding and empathy [12,13] – see Chapter 32 for more information on this.

Concluding Remarks

As discussed above, CBT is a collaborative process through which the patient and therapist work together towards defined goals. The structure of CBT as a whole helps to build this therapeutic alliance and shared understanding of the problem and its solution. The structure within each session then allows for optimal learning and development, ensuring time is spent on key areas based on the combination of what both the therapist can patient know to be important.

Further Reading

Dobson DJ, Dobson, KS. In-session structure and collaborative empiricism. *Cogn Behav Pract.* 2013;**20**(4):410–418.

References

1. Roos J, Wearden A. What do we mean by 'socialization to the model'? A Delphi study. *Behav Cogn Psychother.* 2009;**37**(3):341–345.
2. Beck JS, Beck AT. *Cognitive Behavior Therapy: Basics and Beyond.* 3rd ed. New York: Guilford Press; 2020.
3. Dobson DJ, Dobson KS. In-session structure and collaborative empiricism. *Cogn Behav Pract.* 2013;**20**(4):410–418.
4. Persons JB, Burns DD, Perloff JM. Predictors of dropout and outcome in cognitive therapy for depression in a private practice setting. *Cogn Ther Res.* 1988;**12**(6):557–575.
5. Burns DD, Nolen-Hoeksema S. Coping styles, homework compliance, and the effectiveness of cognitive-behavioral therapy. *J Consult Clin Psychol.* 1991;**59**(2): 305–311.
6. Burns DD, Nolen-Hoeksema S. Therapeutic empathy and recovery from depression in cognitive-behavioral therapy: A structural equation model. *J Consult Clin Psychol.* 1992;**60**(3):441–449.
7. Edelman RE, Chambless DL. Compliance during sessions and homework in exposure-based treatment of agoraphobia. *Behav Res Ther.* 1993;**31**(8):767–773.
8. Addis ME, Jacobson NS. A closer look at the treatment rationale and homework compliance in cognitive-behavioral therapy for depression. *Cogn Ther Res.* 2000;**24**(3):313–326.
9. Beck AT, Emery G, Greenberg RL. *Anxiety Disorders & Phobias.* New York: Basic Books; 1985.
10. James I, Blackburn I, Reichelt F. *Manual of the revised cognitive therapy scale.* Unpublished Manuscript Newcastle Cognitive Behaviour Therapy Centre, Newcastle 2001.
11. Rogers CR. The necessary and sufficient conditions of therapeutic personality change. *J Consult Psychol.* 1957;**21**(2):95–103.
12. Bennett-Levy J, Lee NK. Self-practice and self-reflection in cognitive behaviour therapy training: What factors influence trainees' engagement and experience of benefit? *Behav Cogn Psychother.* 2014;**42**(1):48–64.
13. Bennett-Levy J, Thwaites R, Haarhoff B, Perry H. *Experiencing CBT from the Inside Out: A Self-Practice/Self-Reflection Workbook for Therapists.* New York: Guilford Publications; 2014.

Chapter 8

Psychological Assessment, Formulation and Intervention in CBT

In this chapter we will help you to be able to:

- Explain the six key questions that are answered by a good formulation.
- Consider the purpose of formulation in shaping assessments and intervention.
- Create effective and idiosyncratic formulations and treatment plans for your own patients.

Introduction

As explored in Chapter 7, CBT follows the general structure of moving from assessment, to formulation and then to intervention. Said process is not linear, but instead each part feeds back into the others. This chapter will explore this concept of formulation as a link between assessment and intervention, as well as examining the six key questions that formulation aims to answer.

Formulation

Formulations are both a description and an explanation of a patient's difficulties, often shown pictorially. They are how therapists make sense of a patient's difficulties, so that we can help them to change. Breaking this down, formulations serve a number of important roles, as first described by Persons [1]:

(1) To create a problem list. When a patient first attends therapy, they will have many unpleasant and unwanted symptoms, which can feel overwhelming and inexhaustible. One of the very first roles a therapist can take is to help define this all-consuming experience into a finite list of problems, which therapy can then hope to tackle.

For example, a patient called Jenny described feeling overwhelmed by a black cloud of depression, which seemed to be touching every area of her life. She also described numerous physiological symptoms. The problem list that came from this was as shown in Table 8.1.

(2) To describe underlying psychological mechanism – key beliefs. While it is helpful to create a finite list of problems, the patient could still feel as though there is something fundamentally wrong with them, to have so many seemingly unrelated issues. A problem list also doesn't help them (or the therapist) to know how to change the problems. For example, with Jenny, it would be impossible for the therapist to work with her directly on 'sadness', and solutions aiming purely at giving her more energy would only be a short-term fix.

As such, the next role of a formulation is to find an underlying cause; a mechanism for why they keep feeling the way they feel and doing the things they do. In CBT, this

Table 8.1 Problem list

Jenny's problem list
Sadness
Hopelessness
Anxiety
Unable to enjoy others being happy
Unable to handle criticism
Tearfulness
Tired/no energy
Sense of always being rejected

mechanism is usually going to focus on their underlying beliefs – one (or a few) messages that the patient has confidence in and thus lives their life around – and the behaviours they engage in as a result of these beliefs (motivated behaviours) [2].

In Jenny's case, the underlying mechanism centred around her belief that 'I'm unlovable as I am' and subsequently 'other will always end up rejecting me'. This led to several behaviours aiming to either make herself more loveable, or to avoid experiencing being rejected. To avoid experiencing being rejected, she stopped going to social engagements, such as after-work drinks or dinner parties with her friends. To make herself worthier of love, she worked excessively long hours, as she felt that being a success in her career would make her worthier of love. She would also ruminate over why she had been rejected in the past, to try and find ways of avoiding this in future and, spend many hours on Facebook looking at others' happier lives. She tried to exercise excessively and starve herself, so that she could lose weight and be more attractive. In the light of her beliefs, these behaviours all make sense, though they may not actually be helpful, as discussed below (Figure 8.1).

(3) To explain how the key beliefs cause and maintain the list of problems. This set of beliefs and behaviours can then be linked to the original problem list, to explain how it all fits together. By explaining how the underlying mechanism can cause the problems, the formulation turns a list of disparate and inexplicable symptoms into a single connected and manageable problem. It gives the patient an explanation for why they are having all these different symptoms, and how it all fits together. It gives the therapist a plan for action, as knowing how the problems are maintained can allow them to pick the right interventions to change this [3].

Let's consider how Jenny's mechanism can make sense of her problems. Her belief that she is unlovable innately links to feeling sad and tearful, and the belief that others will always reject her leads to feeling either hopeless or anxious, depending on whether she thinks rejection is imminent. When feeling sad, anxious and hopeless, these beliefs then feel truer. Her mind filters information via these beliefs, resulting selectively remembering and noticing occasions where she is rejected, and perceiving ambiguous situations as rejection. This builds the evidence for these beliefs, strengthening them further.

The behaviours caused by her beliefs link the rest of the problems. By avoiding social situations, ruminating on her perceived failings and spending time on Facebook comparing her life to others, she is reducing the opportunities to feel happiness, increasing opportunities to see others being happier than her, and increasing her belief that she is being rejected

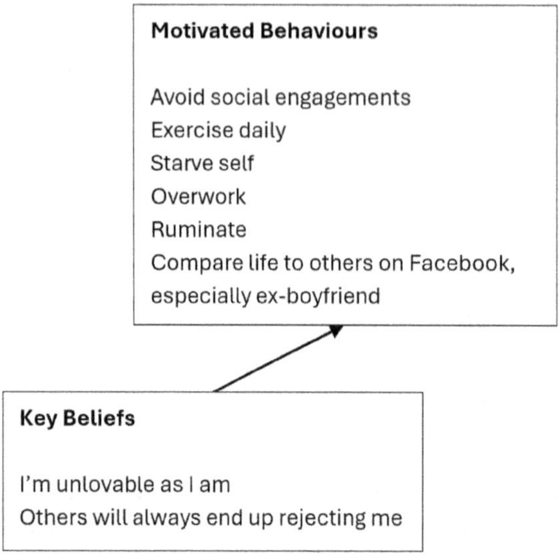

Figure 8.1 Describing Jenny's underlying mechanism.

and thus will be rejected in future. By overworking, exercising to excess and starving herself, she will innately feel tired. She will also remove any opportunity to see if she is lovable as she is, and so even positive experiences become evidence that she is not enough. They also ensure that any criticism at work will trigger the problem, as it has occurred despite her best efforts.

It is important to note the three sets of connections. First, the belief itself causes the motivated behaviours and many of the other symptoms. Second, the behaviours can cause further symptoms, and strengthen those caused by the belief, as well as making trigger situations more likely or more problematic. Finally, both the symptoms and behaviours strengthen the original belief, ensuring that the cycle continues.

This can seem quite complicated, but by finding and exploring these links, the therapist can help the patient to understand their difficulties fully and set the stage for effective and collaborative treatment (Figure 8.2).

(4) To identify precipitants. As well as understanding why this list of problems are continuing to happen, it can also be helpful to consider what events and environments caused the problem to present itself. For many patients, it can seem as though the problem came out of the blue, or that it was a massive overreaction to the events that occurred. This can lead to fear about the future ('what's to stop it happening again?') and self-blame ('I should be over this, I'm too emotional'). When the formulation has determined the central mechanism, it can then make predictions about what kind of event would cause the problems to start and make sense of why those events were experienced so negatively.

For Jenny, the experience of depression began when she discovered that her partner was leaving her for another woman, with whom he had been cheating on her. Many of her friends told her that it was his loss, and that she shouldn't let it get to her, and so she had become quite self-critical of what she saw as an extreme emotional and behavioural reaction to the ending of a fairly new relationship.

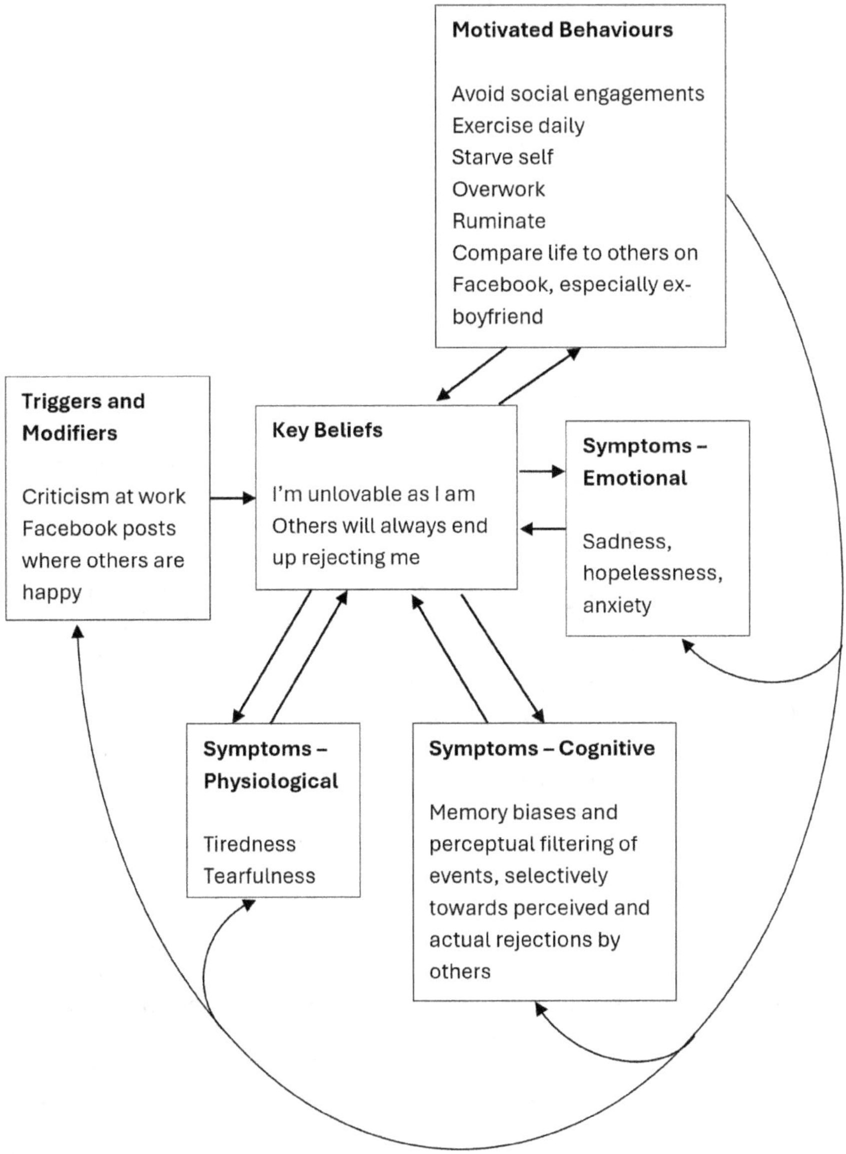

Figure 8.2 Explaining the links between Jenny's problems and the key beliefs.

On discussion of her beliefs 'I am unlovable as I am' and 'others will always end up rejecting me', this reaction makes more sense – it was not the break-up itself that caused the depression, but her interpretation of this (Figure 8.3).

(5) To identify origins of the beliefs in early life. So far, the formulation has linked the precipitating scenario to the activation of the underlying mechanism. But where did the underlying mechanism come from? What pre-existing beliefs and rules for living does

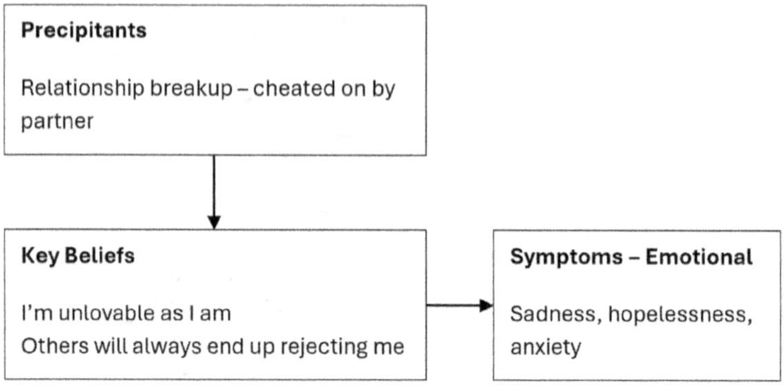

Figure 8.3 Jenny's precipitant added.

the patient have, and why does this patient have them? Unless these questions are answered, the patient may be left with only one of two choices – either they have these beliefs because they are true, or because they are crazy. Neither of these explanations are particularly comforting!

Formulations aim to offer an alternative answer to these questions, by looking at what the patient experienced far prior to any problems developing. Specifically, the formulation will connect the underlying beliefs to early experiences that would quite reasonably have led to these beliefs being formed, as well as long-term maintaining behaviours that have reinforced these rules over time. For the therapist, this offers another possible area of intervention, as re-evaluating the meaning of these early experiences, and adjusting these unhelpful behaviours, may be necessary to shift the current beliefs. For the patient, this offers an alternative, and far more hopeful, explanation as to why they have the beliefs at all.

Coming back to Jenny, her original explanation of her difficulties was that she truly was unlovable and doomed to be rejected; she felt that her beliefs accurately described her reality. On discussion, she realised that she had held the belief that she was not naturally lovable for as long as she could remember, and that she would only be worthy of love by doing things for others and putting effort in to hide her inadequacies. She had also believed that she should be grateful for any love offered. This had resulted in behaviours of saying yes to any demands made of her, over-preparing and working overtime, and spending lots of effort on her appearance, all so she could make herself lovable. It had also meant that she would not initiate relationships of any kind, but would form relationships with anyone who wanted to.

While these behaviours had 'worked' in relation to her having a partner and so feeling lovable, she had not felt depressed. However, it meant that she was highly susceptible to becoming depressed if love was withdrawn. These behaviours also kept these beliefs alive, as she never experienced being loved for who she was, and never discovered if she could be selective in who to have relationships with.

Going further, the therapist and Jenny also considered what had caused these beliefs in the first place. They realised that the first experience Jenny had of rejection was her father leaving when she was four years old. While logically, this shows nothing about Jenny's actual lovability as a person, it was how her childhood brain had interpreted his decision.

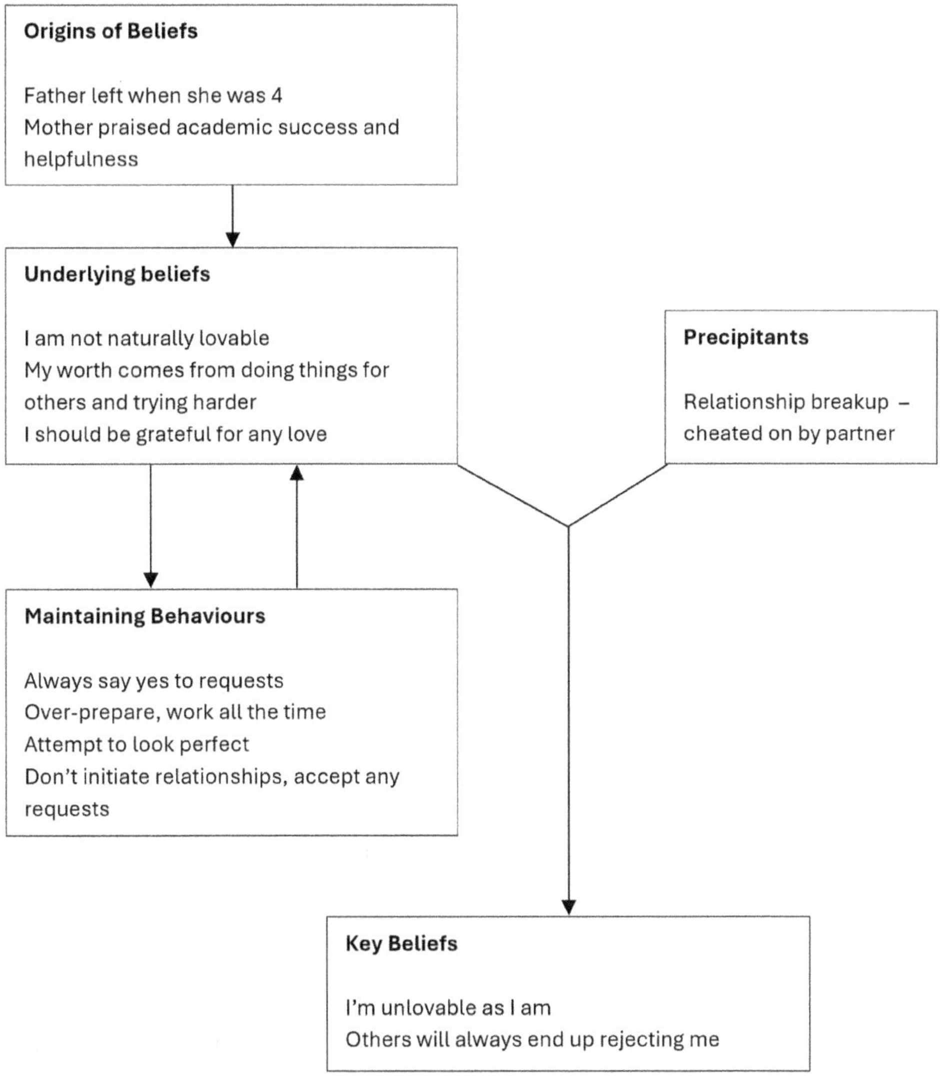

Figure 8.4 Links between Jenny's long-term, general assumptions and beliefs with her maintaining behaviours and early experiences.

Following this, Jenny's main experiences of love came from her mother, who she noted would praise her and show affection when she was academically successful, and when she was helpful around the house. Again, while proving nothing about Jenny's actual lovability, it is easy to see how this could have been understood by a child as meaning that these working hard and doing things for others were her only worth (Figure 8.4).

(6) Predict any obstacles to treatment. The final role of a formulation is to help spot any potential obstacles that might prevent therapy from being effective (Figure 8.5). The relationship between the therapist and the patient is likely to be vulnerable to the same

Figure 8.5 Potential obstacles for Jenny's treatment.

rules and behaviours that the patient applies to the rest of their relationships, and the tasks of therapy may well be approached just like any other task in the patient's life [4].

For Jenny, the formulation gives clues as to how she will approach homework tasks, requests and suggestions by the therapist, and attendance at sessions. Given her maintaining behaviour of over-preparing, she may well spend far longer on homework tasks than is needed, using time and energy to fill in diaries 'perfectly', and thus making the tasks more effortful and less rewarding than they could be otherwise. Given her tendency to say yes, she may not acknowledge when the therapist's requests seem too difficult, or where the therapist has missed the point. Given her fear of being rejected, she may skip sessions if her homework hasn't gone to plan, or if she isn't making the overall progress she expects the therapist to want. Not only are these innately problematic behaviours, but they will also continue to reinforce the patient's beliefs regarding being rejected and unlovable.

Putting this altogether gives a comprehensive picture of the problem's development and maintenance, explaining all the relevant aspects in a meaningful way (Figure 8.6).

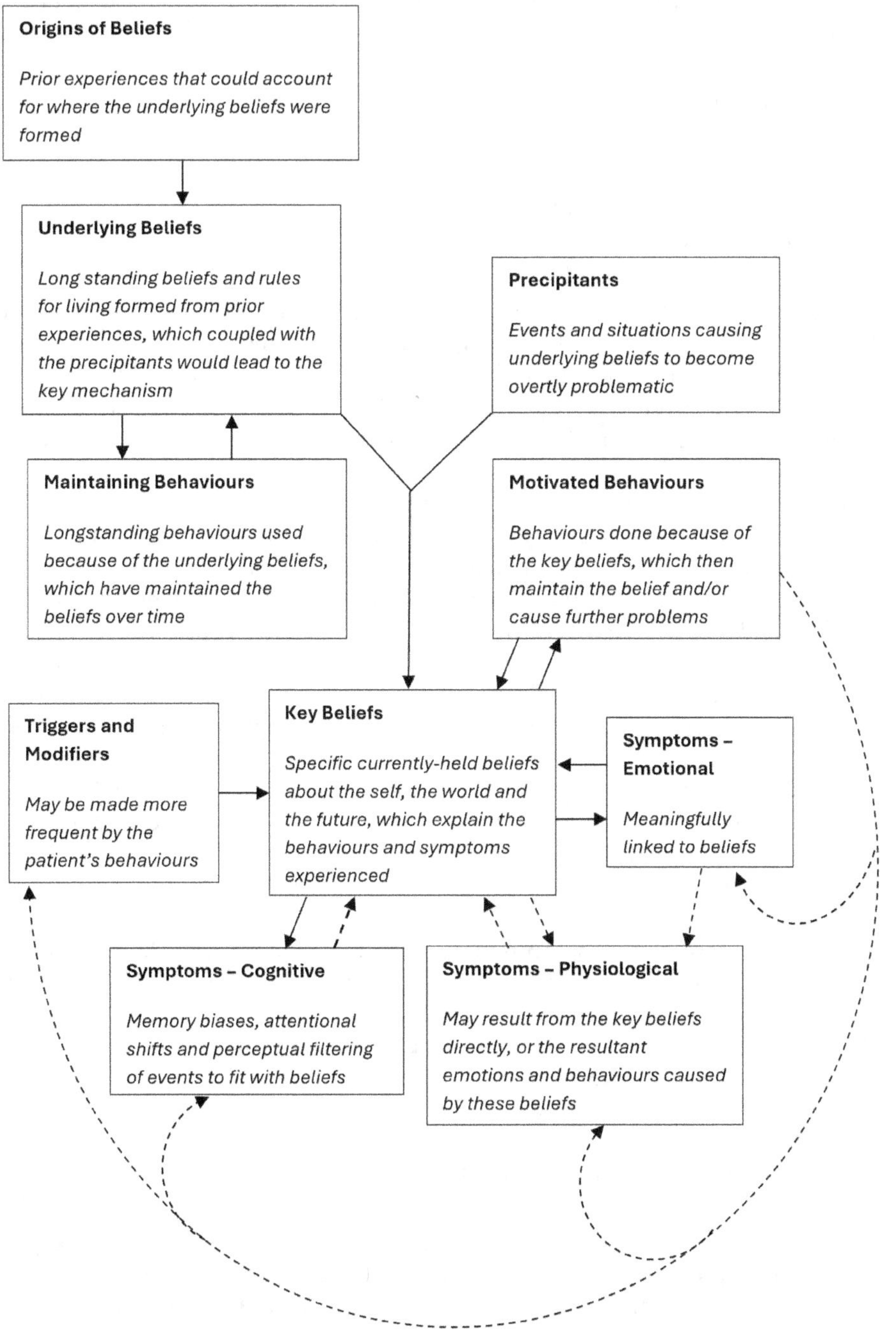

Figure 8.6 Complete generic formulation. Solid arrows are likely to appear in all cognitive formulations, while dotted arrows are possible additional links, but may not be relevant in all cases.

As shown earlier, these sections do not have to all be drawn as one, but instead can be constructed role by role. In simple terms, a formulation can be thought of as answering six key questions:

- 'What are the problems?'
- 'What is causing the problems?'
- 'How is this causing the problems?'
- 'What made the problems happen at that point?'
- 'What made the problems happen to them?' and
- 'What might get in the way of fixing the problems?'

This is a tall order, but hopefully it makes sense of why the formulation is so important in CBT, and the range of answers it can give to patient and therapist alike.

It also helps us answer the question of 'how much of the formulation should we share?' Not every patient will be interested, or helped, in having all six answers. For problems that started in early childhood, the question of 'why the problem started then' may be less important than 'why it happened to them'. Conversely, very specific problems starting later in life after a major trauma may not lead to the patient questioning what the early vulnerabilities were.

The formulation above is a general way of conceptualising the patient's difficulties, broad enough to cover any type of problem where CBT could help. However, there are also many other formulation templates available, specific to a given treatment protocol. These will be described in later chapters, in relation to the protocol they sit with.

The benefit of these more targeted formulations is that they are focussed specifically on the likely mechanisms that would drive each given disorder. They each propose specific types of underlying and or key beliefs to be uncovered, and tightly define how each of the other aspects of the issue will influence (and be influenced by) these beliefs. They will include only the linking arrows relevant to that problem. They may also contain additional features that do not apply in most disorders. In a sense, they are cheat sheets for creating the best possible formulation for that given problem.

On the other hand, protocol-specific formulations can make our view of an issue overly narrow. Many such formulations only answer some of the questions above, covering either how the problem developed or how it is maintained, but not both. Even those that cover all areas will only do so for the aspects of the patient's difficulties that fit the disorder in question – and few patients have problems that fit so neatly. Picking the best option means juggling these different considerations and weighing up what will best help you and your patient to understand their experiences.

Assessment

So, how do we gather the information needed to formulate?

When assessing a patient, many therapists will start by gathering a general problem list, using an initial broad open question such as 'what are the main problems you are experiencing?' and 'can you tell me a little bit more about [repeat problem back]?' Once a general picture of the current problems has been uncovered, the therapist will attempt to determine which diagnosis would best fit with these, by asking further questions to rule options in and out. Therapists generally work out what questions to ask based on their knowledge of the criteria described either in the American Psychological Association's Diagnostic and Statistical Manual (DSM) [5] or in the World Health Organization's International Classification of Diseases (ICD) [6]. Alternatively, they may use a more structured set of questions to both rule in and rule out possible disorders – if following the most recent DSM for example, the likely tool would be the Structure Clinical Interview for DSM-5 (SCID-5) [7].

Regardless of how the diagnosis is determined, the main purpose of doing so is to help pin down the most important aspects for assessment, formulation and treatment [4]. As will be discussed in later chapters, the each disorder has its own protocol or selection of protocols by which the problem can be treated, with specific interventions that have been shown to help, and types of cognitions specific to the disorder [8].

Coming back to Jenny, the initial problem list matched with one or more of several possible disorders, depending on what else was found to be true. The key possible diagnoses considered by the therapist were major depressive disorder (MDD), social anxiety disorder (SAD) and generalised anxiety disorder (GAD), as at least some symptoms of each of these appeared to be present, as defined by the therapist's preferred diagnostic manual, the DSM-5.

Regarding SAD, the therapist asked about the reasons for avoiding social situations, as one of the criteria required for this diagnosis is that 'the individual fears that he or she will act in a way (or show anxiety symptoms) that will be embarrassing and humiliating' [5]. In Jenny's case, there were no predictions regarding behaving in an embarrassing or humiliating manner, and she did not expect to appear overly anxious. Her prediction of being rejected were related to her belief that she was innately not good enough and had an unlovable personality, which she felt was true even when alone. As such, the therapist ruled this diagnosis out.

To likewise rule out GAD, the therapist asked about any experiences of worry. This was to determine whether Jenny was experiencing 'excessive anxiety and worry' and whether she was finding it 'difficult to control the worry', both essential criteria of GAD [5]. While Jenny initially described 'overthinking things' it was determined that this was in the context of rumination regarding past rejection, and not commonly future focussed. Any occasional worry was limited specifically to the concept of her failing to meet her own expectations and then being rejected.

To then confirm that MDD was the correct diagnosis, the therapist enquired about any remaining diagnostic symptoms, beyond those that Jenny had already described. By working through these, the therapist determined that Jenny was experiencing both of the two key criteria of a 'depressed mood' and a 'markedly diminished interest or pleasure in . . . almost all . . . activities' and that both of these symptoms were occurring 'most of the day, nearly every day' [5]. She was further experiencing fatigue, reduced appetite, feelings of worthlessness, a diminished ability to concentrate and recurrent thoughts of death (though without any current intent or plans to commit suicide). Jenny explicitly stated that she did not have any psychomotor retardation or agitation, nor any difficulties with insomnia or hypersomnia, but nonetheless did meet criteria for MDD due to the other seven criteria being present.

Of course, not all patients will fit so neatly into a single disorder. Many individuals only come to therapy when secondary problems arise, at which point they will fit two diagnoses. Others may not fit completely with any diagnosis at all. In either of these cases, the therapist may need to choose between following the best fit available for the key problems, choosing multiple options and attempting to marry the resultant formulations or not choosing any specific path. There are also some models for therapy that explicitly focus on transdiagnostic traits (such as perfectionism or low self-esteem) which the therapist may choose to use instead, if these traits appear to be a clearer explanation of the main issues than any single diagnosis.

Once the therapist has decided on a best fit (be that a single diagnosis, multiple diagnoses, a transdiagnostic trait or to use no disorder-specific view), they will then aim to understand the patient's idiosyncratic experiences, to determine specifically for this patient what the exact key beliefs are, which specific behaviours follow from this, and precisely how these result in the symptoms being experienced, as well as the beliefs being maintained. The therapist will modify the particular questions asked on the basis of the basic template they are considering, but it is important to remain open to the idea that the patient may not fit as expected, and allow for off-template information as well.

To ensure detailed information, and to get a clear sense of exactly how things fit together, it is often helpful to ask the patient about a specific, recent, typical example of the problem occurring. The therapist explores this by asking questions around a cycle. Generally, they will start by querying what external or internal stimulus initiated the problem, and then ask what thoughts this triggered. From here, they can follow the various other paths that the problem may have taken (to emotions, behaviours and/or other symptoms). With each question, the therapist is gathering another section of the formulation, while at the same, they are beginning to help the patient see how each symptom links to the next. Once the cycle is complete, further information can be gathered to see what occurs in other scenarios.

Further areas of the assessment will cover the patient's history, past episodes and treatment the patient has received, any past or current risk issues, other background information about the patient as a whole and goals for treatment, before ending with a shared exploration of how treatment might be able to help. In each of these areas, the potential avenues to explore are almost limitless, and thus the therapist needs to consider what information is most important for the case in question.

The patient's history is explored primarily in terms of understanding where and how the problem developed. Possible areas to explore include early family life, school, romantic and platonic relationships, major life transitions, their physical health history, any traumas that have occurred and their career. While it is often helpful to explore each of these areas at least briefly, knowing which of these to explore in more detail requires first having a working hypothesis as to the main core beliefs driving the patient's problems. For example, with Jenny, the therapist had a working concept that the underlying beliefs were:

- 'I am not naturally lovable'
- 'My worth comes from doing things for others and trying harder'
- 'I should be grateful for any love'

By asking Jenny when she had first experienced being rejected, and whether anyone had ever praised her as a child for being helpful or trying hard/succeeding, the therapist was able to quickly home in on the relevant early experiences.

Intervention

In CBT, intervention leads on almost innately from the formulation we have created. In most cases, interventions will initially address maintaining processes within the problem, often via changing key maintaining behaviours and challenging the patient's situational thinking. Following this, therapy may move on to exploring and modifying the underlying thinking processes and beliefs that made the patient susceptible to this problem. This helps to prevent the problem recurring in the future, when the patient encounters other possible critical incidents. For each of the protocols explored in the following chapters, there are a set of recommended interventions that will target each aspect of the disorder specific formulation. The general patterns of which intervention fits with each problematic process is shown in Figure 8.7.

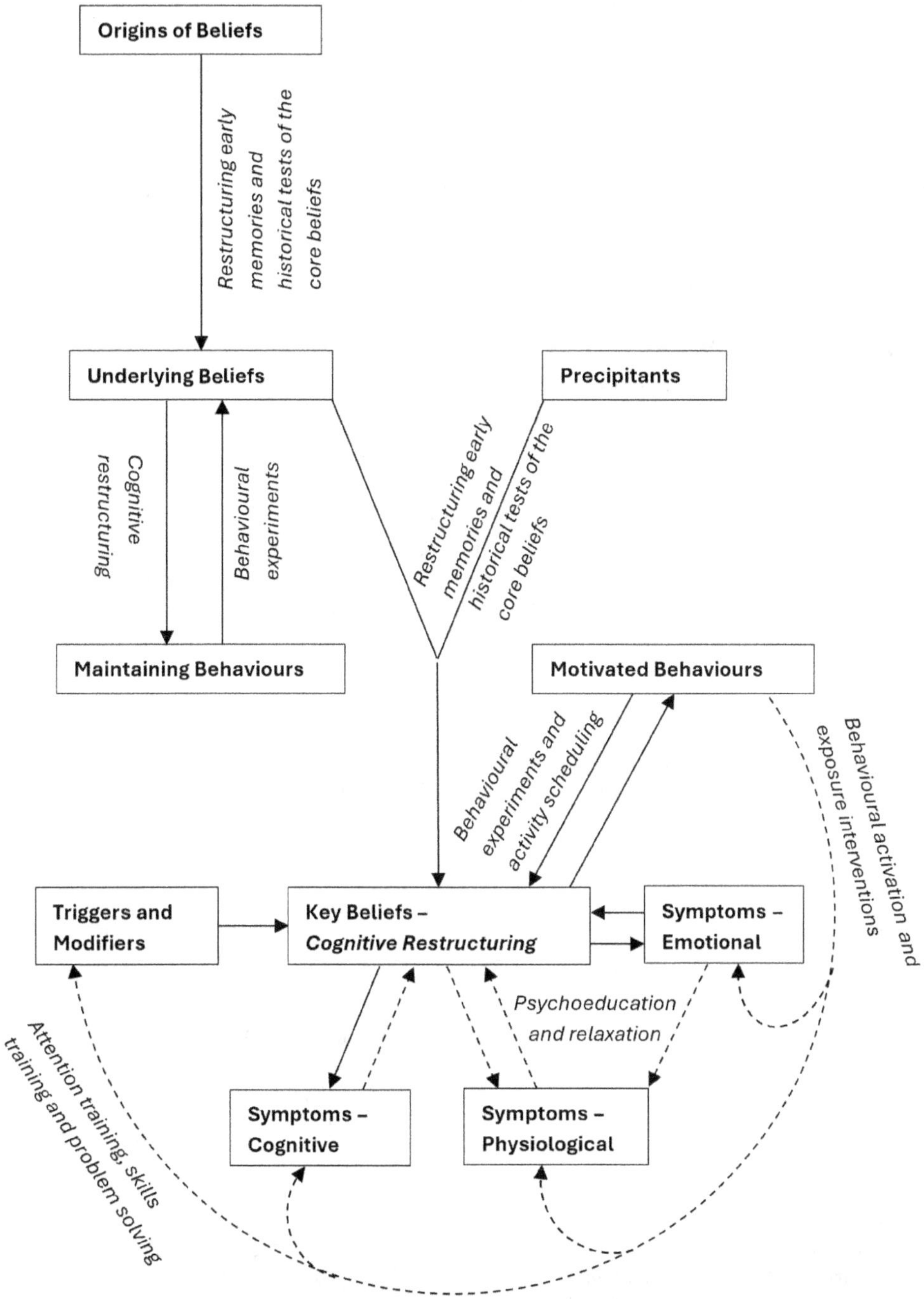

Figure 8.7 Generic formulation, with recommendations of which of the Chapter 6 interventions that could be best applied to each area.

It is important to remember that each intervention is simply a general tool which the therapist is using to disrupt a specific problematic cycle. As such, all interventions need to be applied flexibly and directed at the specific material of the patient in question. Following each application of each intervention, the therapist can consider what new information this disruption has provided, and reassess and/or reformulate as needed.

The therapist also needs to consider whether the patient will need to use the same intervention repeatedly to interrupt lots of similar cycles, or as a one-off. If the former, it will be important that the patient understands how the intervention is applied, and the steps involved. If the latter, excessive psychoeducation may simply delay therapy. For further details on each of the specific interventions in Figure 8.7, please see Chapter 6.

Concluding Remarks

Formulation lies at the heart of CBT, helping to guide assessment and then informing all of the choices made within treatment. Formulation aims to answer six main questions, which between them should help the patient and therapist to form a complete picture of the problem in question, as well as a path forward and possible obstacles ahead. While there are some key features common to all CBT formulations, other important links are specific to particular disorders, and so assessing which model will best fit is often the first task a therapist will undertake. Treatment then flows on from this shared picture; however further assessment and reformulation will keep occurring as additional details come to light, which may in turn impact the next steps.

Further Reading

Persons JB. *Cognitive Therapy in Practice: A Case Formulation Approach* [Internet]. New York: Norton; 1989. https://books.google.co.uk/books?id=UJOTQgAACAAJ.

References

1. Persons JB. *Cognitive Therapy in Practice: A Case Formulation Approach* [Internet]. New York: Norton; 1989. https://books.google.co.uk/books?id=UJOTQgAACAAJ.
2. Beck AT. Thinking and depression: II. Theory and therapy. *Arch Gen Psychiatry*. 1964;**10**(6):561–571.
3. Kuyken W. Evidence-based case formulation: Is the emperor clothed? In: N Tarrier (ed), *Case Formulation in Cognitive Behaviour Therapy* (pp. 12–35). Abingdon: Routledge; 2006.
4. Persons JB. *The Case Formulation Approach to Cognitive-Behavior Therapy*. New York: Guilford Press; 2008.
5. American Psychiatric Association. *Diagnostic and Statistical Manual of Mental Disorders: DSM-5*. Washington, DC: American Psychiatric Association;2013.
6. World Health Organization. *International Classification of Diseases*, 11th Revision (ICD-11). World Health Organization; 2019.
7. First, MB, Williams, JBW, Karg RS, Spitzer RL. *Structured Clinical Interview for DSM-5® Disorders – Clinician Version*. Abridged ed. Arlington, VA: American Psychiatric Association Publishing; 2016.
8. Beck AT. *Cognitive Therapy and the Emotional Disorders*. International Universities Press; 1976.

Chapter 9

Adaptations of the Original Model of Cognitive Behavioural Therapy

In this chapter we will help you to be able to:

- Describe the evolution of disorder specific CBT protocols.
- Explain the value of using a disorder specific protocol over a generic CBT approach.
- Consider the relative efficacy of CBT in different populations.
- Choose whether CBT is appropriate for your patient, and if so, which adaptation of CBT would be most helpful.

Introduction

Beckian Cognitive Therapy was originally devised specifically for depression [1], while early behavioural models focus on the acquisition and management of fear [2,3]. However, the underlying concepts – that it is our thoughts and behaviours which drive how we feel in situations – applies to all motivated behavioural and emotional difficulties. Since the early days of behavioural and cognitive therapy, there has been an explosion of more tailored approaches, based on increasingly specific theories as to why different disorders occur and are maintained, following the underlying concepts of CBT.

Following the development of a theory, protocols for each new problem get theorised and tested. CBT as a treatment approach lends itself well to standardisation and thus testing via RCTs, resulting in an ever-expanding evidence base. This chapter will explore this development from basic behavioural and cognitive roots to our current wealth of treatment options, and the options for making sense of the current evidence base as it grows.

Evolution of Disorder-Specific CBT Protocols

The earliest treatment approaches that would now be considered in the CBT umbrella were the behavioural approaches in the 1950s–1970s, based largely on the concepts of two-stage acquisition of fear [2] and reciprocal inhibition processes [3]. This was highly effective for disorders such as specific phobias, but limited for disorders such as agoraphobia with panic disorder [4] or Social Anxiety Disorder [5,6]. As the newly popular cognitive rationale for depression was showing success in a disorder where behavioural approaches had thus far failed, there were attempts made to apply it to the more treatment-resistant anxiety-based problems. A cognitive theory of panic disorder was devised [7] which considered the specific cognitive bases for the disorder (a catastrophic misinterpretation of specific bodily symptoms). This was then elaborated to consider the impact of safety behaviours [8,9] in maintaining the catastrophic misinterpretations, resulting in a cognitive-behavioural explanation of panic disorder. Similar processes were followed to create explanatory models of social anxiety disorder [10], OCD and illness anxiety disorder [11] and PTSD [12], all to good effect.

Within each disorder, evidence was sought initially for the underlying theory itself, then for the efficacy of specific interventions on specific symptoms, followed by clinical treatment studies and randomised control trials, and then finally implementation studies and meta-analyses. Recovery rates in some of these early RCTs were phenomenal – disorders which had been seen as treatment-resistant by early behavioural means started reaching recovery rates above 80% (e.g. Panic Disorder [13]). Moreover, trials showed that these approaches not only work, but are more powerful than a generic exposure approach [14], showing the importance of targeted models on patient recovery.

Following this, further cognitive themes were considered for other disorders, such as the overvaluation of weight and body shape and of controlling these in eating disorders [15], and the fear-avoidance beliefs in chronic pain [16]. Again, a process of testing would be followed to build evidence for the approach, with each protocol and disorder aiming for the end goal of robust real-world recovery or improvement for a significant proportion of patients.

Transdiagnostic CBT

The explosion of different approaches has been helpful in enhancing recovery rates, but problematic in terms of training therapists; it takes more time to become skilled in them all, and it is difficult to maintain that skill when caseloads vary. Diagnostic CBT can also be problematic when patients are co-morbid – while treating the primary disorder can help with secondary issues, overall recovery tends to drop.

A more recent development in CBT has thus been the creation of transdiagnostic approaches, which focus on shared common themes and ways to work with patients that can be effective for a wider number of patients. These range from protocols aiming at being applicable to all patients, such as Barlow's Unified Protocol [17] and Haye's Acceptance and Commitment Therapy [18], to those more selectively focussed on a specific transdiagnostic cognitive theme such as low self-esteem [19] or perfectionism [20]. These approaches have shown promise in matching the efficacy rates of the disorder-specific protocols, though further work is needed to evidence this sufficiently.

Efficacy Data for CBT for Specific Disorders

CBT is one of the most rigorously tested therapies in the world, with RCTs, implementation studies, and meta-analyses of its efficacy with many different disorders and issues. Reviews of these meta-analyses have now been carried out to bring this information together, first in 2006 [21] and again by Hoffman et al. in 2012 [22]. A summary of this latter review is given in Table 9.1, along with notes regarding key meta-analyses for each disorder since its publication.

Overall, there is significant evidence of the efficacy of CBT for mood disorders, anxiety disorders (including the now diagnostically separated Obsessive-Compulsive and Related Disorders (OCRD), somatic-symptoms disorders and PTSD), eating disorders, anger control problems and general stress issues, with ever-emerging evidence for most of the rest of

Table 9.1 Summary of Hoffman et al., 2012 across disorders, and subsequent developments

Disorder	Summary of efficacy as per Hoffman et al., 2012 [22]	Notable meta-analyses since 2012
Anger and aggression	Medium to large effect sizes	Henwood et al., 2015 [23] Fernandez et al., 2018 [24]
OCD, Body Dysmorphic Disorder & Illness Anxiety Disorder	Medium to large effect sizes	Öst et al., 2015 [25]
Bipolar Disorder	Small to medium overall effect sizes	Chiang et al., 2017 [26]
Chronic pain and fatigue	Small to medium effect sizes. Medium effects sizes in chronic fatigue syndrome and fibromyalgia	Khoo et al., 2019 [27]
Criminal behaviours	Small to medium effect sizes in reducing recidivism	
Anxiety disorders	Small to medium effect sizes, no evidence of superiority of CBT to other psychotherapies Large effect size for CBT and Pharmacotherapy combination CBT for Panic Disorder, GAD, Social Anxiety Disorders produce large effect sizes	Bhattacharya et al., 2023 [28] Bandelow et al., 2015 [29] Cuijpers et al., 2016 [30]
Depression and dysthymia	Small to medium effect sizes, some evidence of superiority of CBT to other psychotherapies	Cuijpers et al., 2023 [31] Fukomori et al., 2024 [32]
Distress due to medical conditions	Lack of evidence for most disorders. Small to medium effects in cancer and HIV	Scott et al., 2023 [33]
Eating disorders	Lack of evidence for some disorders. Medium effect sizes for bulimia and binge eating disorder	Linardon et al., 2017 [34]
General stress	Large effects sizes	
Insomnia	Medium to large effect sizes for chronic insomnia Small to medium effect sizes on daytime effects of insomnia Small effect sizes for insomnia interventions implemented in primary care	Chronic Insomnia – Trauer et al., 2015 [35] Daytime symptoms of Insomnia – Benz et al., 2020 [36] Primary care and community settings – Cheung et al., 2019 [37]
Pregnancy conditions and female hormonal conditions	Medium effect sizes for post-natal depression and pre-menstrual syndrome	Li et al., 2022 [38]

Table 9.1 (cont.)

Disorder	Summary of efficacy as per Hoffman et al., 2012 [22]	Notable meta-analyses since 2012
Personality disorders	Limited evidence of efficacy in some disorders	BPD – Crotty et al., 2024 [39]
Schizophrenia and other psychotic disorders	Small to medium effect sizes on positive symptoms and secondary outcomes	Bighelli et al., 2018 [40] Jauhar et al., 2014 [41]
Substance Use Disorder and Addiction	Small to medium effect sizes, though highly effective with nicotine and cannabis dependence	Magill et al., 2019 [42]

the disorders and problems listed in Table 9.1. Even where effect sizes are low, very few studies show inferiority of CBT to alternative approaches, and in a recent meta-review of such reviews, CBT was consistently shown to modestly improve health related quality of life for at least 12 months across a wide range of underlying conditions [43]. Given the developments over the past 50 years, it may well be that efficacy can be further raised as even better models are developed.

Choosing the Right Approach

For any given patient, there is now a wealth of options regarding possible treatments, each with a range of studies exploring its effectiveness. This can be overwhelming when trying to work out what could be best, especially given the differing ways in which effectiveness is measured, making direct comparisons difficult.

Worldwide, there are a number of organisations that have attempted to make sense of this information, to provide guidelines on optimal treatment choices for various populations. Some, such as the World Health Organization (WHO), and the UK's National Institute for Health and Care Excellence (NICE) cover guidance for healthcare as a whole, while others, such as the American Psychological Association (APA) in the US, and Centre for Outcomes Research and Effectiveness (CORE) in England, focus specifically on mental health and psychology. Below is a brief description of each body and the recommendations they provide, to help when looking for the right type of guidance.

WHO: This global organisation makes recommendations on wide range of health and related topics, including those relating to mental health. Their mental health related guidelines tend to focus on situational groups rather than diagnostic groups, for example 'WHO: Guidelines for the management of conditions that are specifically related to stress' [44] and 'WHO, Regional Office for Europe: Mental Health Promotion and Mental Health Care in Refugees and Migrants' [45]. As such, they may not be the first option for determining whether CBT is appropriate for a disorder, but can ensure therapy is offered in a context-appropriate way.

NICE: This UK-based organisation provides guidance regarding all areas of health and social care, to inform and guide the practice of the UK's National Health Service

(NHS). For each disorder where psychological treatments are indicated, their guidelines will include information on whether a CBT approach is first choice, second choice or not recommended for various disorders, based on the cost effectiveness of the approach for the NHS. Guidelines will further recommend specific key ingredients to CBT where evidence exists (e.g. must include Exposure and Response Prevention (ERP) for OCD), though they often do not go so far as to define specific protocols, other than as examples.

APA: This is an organisation based in the US, who focus on all forms on psychology, and aim to 'promote the advancement, communication, and application of psychological science and knowledge to benefit society and improve lives' [46]. Their CBT-focussed guidelines primarily explore whether a CBT approach is first choice, second choice, or not recommended for various disorders. These guidelines also separate out, where possible, the evidence for CT, CBT and BT, with some guidelines of what each should look like for each disorder, though they do not generally make recommendations about specific protocols for each disorder.

Roth and Pilling (CORE): As NICE guidance built up for the use of CBT in multiple conditions, there was increasing pressure on the NHS to train up CBT therapists to provide this. In order to ensure these therapists were trained appropriately, key competencies for CBT therapists were determined by Roth and Pilling at CORE, to aid with therapist education [47]. Part of this was determining which disorder-specific skills were needed, connected to most effective protocols. This competency framework remains a useful resource in considering possible protocols, though it needs updating to account for the evidence collated since 2007.

BABCP: This is the leading CBT organisation in the UK, and provides curriculum guidance for all courses being accredited with them. Within this, they provide guidance on what protocols should be taught for each disorder (and also which disorders are suitable to focus upon). This was initially based on the Roth and Pilling competencies framework described above, but has been updated in 2021 based on subsequent evidence [48].

Reviewing the recommendations made by each body can be a helpful starting point in considering what might be suitable for any given patient. However ideally it would then be considered how that information connects to the patient in particular, and the available options for treatment. To assist with this, each of the following chapters will include a comparison of the most commonly used protocols for each disorder, to allow therapists to consider not just which are the best protocols in general, but what might work best for each patient in each context.

Concluding Remarks

CBT has evolved from its separate behavioural and cognitive roots, and in doing so has become more effective. While it is not yet been made an effective therapy for every emotional and behavioural difficulty that it might wish to treat, research continues into how to best formulate and treat an ever-widening range of difficulties. For therapists wishing to offer the best possible care to their patients, it is important to keep abreast of the evidence base as it develops, by utilising the guidance provided by various national and international organisations.

Further Reading

Hofmann SG, Asnaani A, Vonk IJ, Sawyer AT, Fang A. The efficacy of cognitive behavioral therapy: A review of meta-analyses. *Cogn Ther Res.* 2012;**36**:427–440.

Roth AD, Pilling S. A competence framework for the supervision of psychological therapies. www.ucl.ac.uk/clinical-psychology/CORE/supervision_framework.htm.

References

1. Beck AT. Thinking and depression: II. Theory and therapy. *Arch Gen Psychiatry.* 1964;**10**(6):561–571.
2. Mowrer OH. On the dual nature of learning: A re-interpretation of 'conditioning' and 'problem-solving'. *Harv Educ Rev.* 1947;**17**:102–148.
3. Wolpe J. *Psychotherapy by Reciprocal Inhibition.* Stanford: Stanford University Press; 1958.
4. Michelson L, Mavissakalian M, Marchione K. Cognitive and behavioral treatments of agoraphobia: Clinical, behavioral, and psychophysiological outcomes. *J Consult Clin Psychol.* 1985;**53**(6):913–925.
5. Butler G, Cullington A, Munby M, Amies P, Gelder M. Exposure and anxiety management in the treatment of social phobia. *J Consult Clin Psychol.* 1984;**52**(4):642–650.
6. Butler G. Exposure as a treatment for social phobia: Some instructive difficulties. *Behav Res Ther.* 1985;**23**(6):651–657.
7. Clark DM. A cognitive approach to panic. *Behav Res Ther.* 1986;**24**(4):461–470.
8. Salkovskis PM. The importance of behaviour in the maintenance of anxiety and panic: A cognitive account. *Behav Cogn Psychother.* 1991;**19**(1):6–19.
9. Salkovskis PM. Phenomenology, assessment and the cognitive model of panic. In: Rachman S, Maser JD (Eds.) *Panic: Psychological Perspectives* [Internet]. Hillsdale, NJ: L. Erlbaum Associates; 1988. https://books.google.co.uk/books?id=LhFsAAAAMAAJ.
10. Clark DM, Wells A. A cognitive model of social phobia. In: Heimberg RG, Liebowitz MR, Hope DA, Schneier FR (Eds.) *Social Phobia: Diagnosis, Assessment, and Treatment* [Internet]. New York: Guilford Publications; 1995. p. 69–93. https://books.google.co.uk/books?id=rXrekuSy2bsC.
11. Salkovskis PM. Cognitive approaches to health anxiety and obsessional problems: Some unique features and how this affects treatment. In: *World Congress of Behavioural and Cognitive Therapies*, Copenhagen, Denmark. 1995.
12. Ehlers A, Clark DM. A cognitive model of posttraumatic stress disorder. *Behav Res Ther.* 2000;**38**(4):319–345.
13. Clark DM, Salkovskis PM, Hackmann A, Middleton H, Anastasiades P, Gelder M. A comparison of cognitive therapy, applied relaxation and imipramine in the treatment of panic disorder. *Br J Psychiatry.* 1994;**164**(6):759–769.
14. Salkovskis PM, Hackmann A, Wells A, Gelder MG, Clark DM. Belief disconfirmation versus habituation approaches to situational exposure in panic disorder with agoraphobia: A pilot study. *Behav Res Ther.* 2007;**45**(5):877–885.
15. Fairburn CG. *Cognitive Behavior Therapy and Eating Disorders.* New York: Guilford Press; 2008.
16. Vlaeyen JW, Linton SJ. Fear-avoidance and its consequences in chronic musculoskeletal pain: A state of the art. *Pain.* 2000;**85**(3):317–332.
17. Barlow DH, Farchione TJ, Fairholme CP, Ellard KK, Boisseau CL, Allen LB, et al. *Unified Protocol for Transdiagnostic*

Treatment of Emotional Disorders: Therapist Guide. New York: Oxford University Press; 2011.

18. Hayes SC. Acceptance and commitment therapy, relational frame theory, and the third wave of behavioral and cognitive therapies. *Behav Ther*. 2004;**35**(4):639–665.
19. Fennell MJV. Low self-esteem: A cognitive perspective. *Behav Cogn Psychother*. 1997;**25**(1):1–26.
20. Egan SJ, Wade TD, Shafran R, Antony MM. *Cognitive-Behavioral Treatment of Perfectionism* [Internet]. New York: Guilford Publications; 2016. https://books.google.co.uk/books?id=jpmCCwAAQBAJ.
21. Butler AC, Chapman JE, Forman EM, Beck AT. The empirical status of cognitive-behavioral therapy: A review of meta-analyses. *Clin Psychol Rev*. 2006;**26**(1):17–31.
22. Hofmann SG, Asnaani A, Vonk IJ, Sawyer AT, Fang A. The efficacy of cognitive behavioral therapy: A review of meta-analyses. *Cogn Ther Res*. 2012;**36**:427–440.
23. Henwood KS, Chou S, Browne KD. A systematic review and meta-analysis on the effectiveness of CBT informed anger management. *Aggress Violent Behav*. 2015;**25**:280–292.
24. Fernandez E, Malvaso C, Day A, Guharajan D. 21st century cognitive behavioural therapy for anger: A systematic review of research design, methodology and outcome. *Behav Cogn Psychother*. 2018;**46**(4):385–404.
25. Öst LG, Havnen A, Hansen B, Kvale G. Cognitive behavioral treatments of obsessive–compulsive disorder: A systematic review and meta-analysis of studies published 1993–2014. *Clin Psychol Rev*. 2015;**40**:156–169.
26. Chiang KJ, Tsai JC, Liu D, Lin CH, Chiu HL, Chou KR. Efficacy of cognitive-behavioral therapy in patients with bipolar disorder: A metaanalysis of randomized controlled trials. *PLoS ONE*. 2017;**12**(5).
27. Khoo EL, Small R, Cheng W, Hatchard T, Glynn B, Rice DB, et al. Comparative evaluation of group-based mindfulness-based stress reduction and cognitive behavioural therapy for the treatment and management of chronic pain: A systematic review and network meta-analysis. *BMJ Ment Health*. 2019;**22**(1):26–35.
28. Bhattacharya S, Goicoechea C, Heshmati S, Carpenter JK, Hofmann SG. Efficacy of cognitive behavioral therapy for anxiety-related disorders: A meta-analysis of recent literature. *Curr Psychiatry Rep*. 2023;**25**(1):19–30.
29. Bandelow B, Reitt M, Röver C, Michaelis S, Görlich Y, Wedekind D. Efficacy of treatments for anxiety disorders: A meta-analysis. *Int Clin Psychopharmacol*. 2015;**30**(4):183–192.
30. Cuijpers P, Gentili C, Banos RM, Garcia-Campayo J, Botella C, Cristea IA. Relative effects of cognitive and behavioral therapies on generalized anxiety disorder, social anxiety disorder and panic disorder: A meta-analysis. *J Anxiety Disord*. 2016;**43**:79–89.
31. Cuijpers P, Miguel C, Harrer M, Plessen CY, Ciharova M, Ebert D, et al. Cognitive behavior therapy vs. control conditions, other psychotherapies, pharmacotherapies and combined treatment for depression: A comprehensive meta-analysis including 409 trials with 52,702 patients. *World Psychiatry*. 2023;**22**(1):105–115.
32. Fukumori M, Kikuchi T, Zhou Y, Hattori S, Kudo T. Network meta-analysis of the effectiveness of psychotherapies with or without medication for treating adult depression. *Acta Neuropsychiatr*. 2024;**36**(6):423–437.
33. Scott AJ, Bisby MA, Heriseanu AI, Salameh Y, Karin E, Fogliati R, et al. Cognitive behavioral therapies for depression and anxiety in people with chronic disease: A systematic review and meta-analysis. *Clin Psychol Rev*. 2023;**106**:102353.
34. Linardon J, Wade TD, de la Piedad Garcia X, Brennan L. The efficacy of

cognitive-behavioral therapy for eating disorders: A systematic review and meta-analysis. *J Consult Clin Psychol.* 2017;**85**(11):1080–1094.

35. Trauer JM, Qian MY, Doyle JS, Rajaratnam SMW, Cunnington D. Cognitive behavioral therapy for chronic insomnia. *Ann Intern Med.* 2015;**163**(3):191–204.

36. Benz F, Knoop T, Ballesio A, Bacaro V, Johann AF, Rücker G, et al. The efficacy of cognitive and behavior therapies for insomnia on daytime symptoms: A systematic review and network meta-analysis. *Clin Psychol Rev.* 2020;**80**:101873.

37. Cheung JMY, Jarrin DC, Ballot O, Bharwani AA, Morin CM. A systematic review of cognitive behavioral therapy for insomnia implemented in primary care and community settings. *Sleep Med Rev.* 2019;**44**:23–36.

38. Li X, Laplante DP, Paquin V, Lafortune S, Elgbeili G, King S. Effectiveness of cognitive behavioral therapy for perinatal maternal depression, anxiety and stress: A systematic review and meta-analysis of randomized controlled trials. *Clin Psychol Rev.* 2022;**92**:102129.

39. Crotty K, Viswanathan M, Kennedy S, Edlund MJ, Ali R, Siddiqui M, et al. Psychotherapies for the treatment of borderline personality disorder: A systematic review. *J Consult Clin Psychol.* 2024;**92**(5):275–295.

40. Bighelli I, Huhn M, Schneider-Thoma J, Krause M, Reitmeir C, Wallis S, et al. Response rates in patients with schizophrenia and positive symptoms receiving cognitive behavioural therapy: A systematic review and single-group meta-analysis. *BMC Psychiatry.* 2018;**18**(1):380.

41. Jauhar S, McKenna PJ, Radua J, Fung E, Salvador R, Laws KR. Cognitive–behavioural therapy for the symptoms of schizophrenia: Systematic review and meta-analysis with examination of potential bias. *Br J Psychiatry.* 2014;**204**(1):20–29.

42. Magill M, Ray L, Kiluk B, Hoadley A, Bernstein M, Tonigan JS, et al. A meta-analysis of cognitive-behavioral therapy for alcohol or other drug use disorders: Treatment efficacy by contrast condition. *J Consult Clin Psychol.* 2019;**87**(12):1093–1105.

43. Fordham B, Sugavanam T, Edwards K, Stallard P, Howard R, Nair R das, et al. The evidence for cognitive behavioural therapy in any condition, population or context: A meta-review of systematic reviews and panoramic meta-analysis. *Psychol Med.* 2021;**51**(1):21–29.

44. World Health Organization. *Guidelines for the Management of Conditions that Are Specifically Related to Stress* [Internet]. World Health Organization; 2013. https://apps.who.int/iris/handle/10665/85119.

45. World Health Organization. Regional Office for Europe. *Mental Health Promotion and Mental Health Care in Refugees and Migrants: Policy Brief* [Internet]. World Health Organization. Regional Office for Europe; 2018. Report No.: WHO/EURO:2018–3138–42896–59848. https://apps.who.int/iris/handle/10665/345918.

46. American Psychological Association. *Impact: APA and APA Services*, Inc. strategic plan. 2019;**1**:2020.

47. Roth A, Pilling S. *The CBT Competencies Framework for Depression and Anxiety Disorders.* Lond UK Cent Outcome Res Eval. 2007.

48. Hool N, Bennett R, Corrie S, Cox A, Curran J, French S, et al. *BABCP Core Curriculum* [Internet]. Bury: British Association for Behavioural & Cognitive Psychotherapies; 2021. https://babcp.com/Core-Curriculum.

Chapter 10

Anxiety Disorders

In this chapter we will help you to be able to:

- Describe the development of CBT approaches for anxiety disorders.
- Explain how the four key factors influence the level of perceived threat from a cognitive perspective.
- Consider the comparative purposes of habituation, cognitive restructuring and behavioural experiments in treating anxiety disorders.

Introduction

Anxiety disorders are one of the areas where CBT has its greatest efficacy, and there are numerous specific protocols for helping individuals to overcome their problematic anxiety with a range of tailored techniques. NICE guidelines for panic disorder, generalised anxiety disorder [1] and social anxiety disorder [2] all recommend CBT as a high-intensity psychological approach of choice. This chapter will briefly introduce the key underlying concepts regarding anxiety disorders, including exposure for habituation, the threat equation and cognitive change methods and behavioural experiments for the purpose of belief disconfirmation.

Applying Behavioural Theory to Anxiety Disorders: Exposure for Habituation

The first question in understanding a disorder behaviourally is to ask what behaviours maintain the difficulty, and how. In anxiety disorders, the key behavioural answer is that of Mowrer's two-factor model of fear acquisition [3,4]. The first factor in the theory is that fear is initially developed through classical conditioning, where the to-be-feared stimulus is paired with a naturally aversive stimulus. This could be an animal being paired with pain, due to being bitten or stung, for example. As a result the initially benign stimulus of an animal is associated with the fear-inducing pain, and so the animal becomes fear-inducing in itself. The second factor is then the impact of avoidance and escape in response to this stimulus. Via operant conditioning, the behaviour of escaping or avoiding the feared stimulus is negatively reinforced because it reduces the fear being experienced. However, by escaping or avoiding, the individual's connection of a fear reaction to the object cannot lessen, as no new association of the stimulus with a benign outcome can occur – they never experience the animal without the bite or sting.

As such, behavioural treatment needs to break both of these sets of conditioning. The patient needs to be exposed to the feared stimulus without fear-inducing things occurring, and needs to stay there in order to break the link between the urge to escape and the fear reducing. The initial version of this process was known as systemic desensitisation, or reciprocal inhibition, and it supplemented exposing the individual to a hierarchy of their increasingly feared stimuli with relaxation techniques to actively inhibit the fear response [5]. However, subsequent studies determined that only the first half of this process – the graded exposure – was needed [6,7].

Commonly, exposure is done in a **graded** way, starting with versions of the feared stimulus that cause lower amounts of fear, so that the associations can be broken bit by bit [8,9,10]. Each time the individual is exposed and doesn't escape, the links between the stimulus, fear, and avoidance will be reduced, and **repeated** exposure experiences will then cause less fear, less of an urge to escape, and become tolerable more quickly. To ensure the urge to escape is extinguished as well the classically conditioned fear, exposure needs to be **prolonged**, lasting long enough for the patient to experience a reduction in fear despite not escaping [11,12]. To ensure the patient's mind is able to take in the learning and make the new connections, all of this needs to be done with the patient's full awareness, and so needs to occur **without distraction** [13,14].

Initial approaches based on this behavioural approach focussed strongly on habituating to the trigger stimulus, often recommending concepts such as staying until the anxiety had dropped by half. More recently the focus has shifted to a slightly more cognitive perspective, where the patient is asked to remain until they have learnt they can cope – that they do not need to escape to manage the fear, and that the stimulus itself is not dangerous [8,9,10,14].

Applying Cognitive Theory to Anxiety Disorders: Cognitive Change Methods

A different approach to understanding anxiety and fear is via the cognitive model. In this, the key driver to fear is seen as the predictions the individual is making about what will happen, either sometime in the future (anxiety) or imminently (fear and panic). Initially proposed by Beck, the cognitive model suggests that there are four main factors that affect how anxiety-provoking a concept is [15]. The first is how **awful** the outcome would be – from mildly inconvenient to life-ending. The second is how **likely** the outcome seems – from a one in a million chance to all-but-certain. The last two are how well the individual thinks that they would **cope** if the outcome occurred, and whether others would be willing and able to **rescue** them. The association of these four factors can be described verbally, or shown via the anxiety equation [16], as in Equation 10.1.

$$Level\ of\ threat = \frac{(Likelihood\ of\ event \times Awfulness\ of\ event)}{(coping + rescue)}$$

Equation 10.1 the anxiety equation

Applying this equation, high levels of fear come from the outcome being both awful and likely, and where the individual thinks both that they won't cope nor will others help them. Meanwhile lower levels of fear come from thinking that a situation either isn't likely, or wouldn't be that awful, and is further reduced by believing either that they could cope themselves, or that others would help them.

This equation holds the key both to understanding why individuals fear outcomes, and how to reduce this fear. Cognitive techniques can be applied to each of these four factors – we can explore the likelihood of outcomes, we can discuss what less awful options may be more likely. We can consider what would make an outcome awful, and evaluate the underlying rules that the individual holds about themselves and the world to find less awful interpretations. We can work through – verbally or via imagery – how the worst-case scenarios would play out, and discuss what the individual could do to cope, and how others might engage in rescue. Through this, each feature of the anxiety equation can be tackled as needed, to bring the overall threat level down.

Reapplying Cognitive Theory to Anxiety Disorders: Behavioural Experiments for Belief Disconfirmation

Using the tools above, there are three options for applying CBT to anxiety disorders – a purely behavioural exposure-based approach, a purely cognitive approach or a combination where cognitive techniques and behaviour therapy are combined, explaining the two separate but complimentary rationales at the same time.

An more integrated model was proposed by Clark and Salkovskis, whereby the role of escape, avoidance and other anxiety related behaviours were reconceptualised within a Beckian cognitive paradigm [17,18]. In this model, as above, anxiety is caused by cognitions about a perceived threat. As a result of this perceived threat, the patient may try to escape or avoid, and may also take a range of other actions, not purely to reduce anxiety, but in order to prevent the potential threat occurring – they seek safety. These 'safety-seeking' behaviours (later known as safety behaviours) are proposed to be what causes the perception of having just escaped danger and will cause this even if complete avoidance and escape are impossible. As a result, the patient will continue to fear the trigger, because they will continue to believe that the perceived threat would have occurred had they not used their behaviours.

Following this model, therapy takes the anxiety equation above, and then makes sense of behaviours not through a separate model, but by unpicking how each behaviour could be reinforcing the perceived threat. This could either by preventing the prediction from being disconfirmed, or by seeming to actively confirm it (such as in the case of social anxiety disorder, where some safety seeking behaviours can even cause the patient's feared outcomes to happen – see Chapter 13 for details). This can be drawn using the vicious flower model [16,17], as shown in Figure 10.1.

Taking specific predictions and behaviours from this model, therapy can use both cognitive techniques and behavioural experiments to test out the validity of the perceived threat. While these experiments generally involve exposure to the feared stimulus just as in the behavioural approach above, the focus is on disconfirming specific predictions rather than on reducing the anxiety itself or learning that they 'can cope'. As such, the dropping of meaningfully linked safety behaviours is just as important as remaining in the situation, and the duration of the exposure is based on the time that is needed to know that the feared outcome didn't occur. While this difference can seem pedantic, it has been shown to make significant difference to treatment efficacy, especially in conditions such as panic disorder [19].

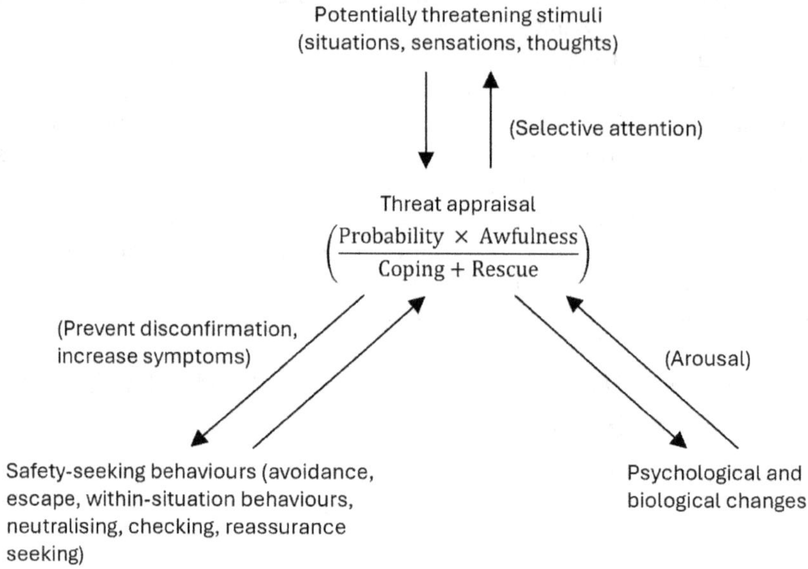

Figure 10.1 The vicious flower model, reproduced with permission from Salkovskis et al., 1988 [16].

Concluding Remarks

Anxiety disorders are characterised unsurprisingly by anxiety, along with predictions of threat and attempts to avoid, escape, and keep oneself safe. Treatment focusses on changing these via exposure, cognitive change methods, and behavioural experiments. Specific protocols focus respectively on habituation or belief disconfirmation as their primary focus, and the subsequent chapters will detail how each of these types of approaches can be applied to specific presentations of anxiety.

Further Reading

Marks I. Behavioral treatments of phobic and obsessive-compulsive disorders: A critical appraisal. In: Michel Hersen, Peter Michael Miller, Richard Morton Eisler (eds), *Progress in Behavior Modification, Volume 1* (pp. 65–158). New York: Academic Press, Inc; 1975.

Clark DM. Cognitive therapy for anxiety. *Behav Cogn Psychother*. 1986;**14**(4):283–294.

Salkovskis PM. The importance of behaviour in the maintenance of anxiety and panic: A cognitive account. *Behav Cogn Psychother*. 1991;**19**(1):6–19.

References

1. National Institute for Health and Care Excellence. Generalised anxiety disorder and panic disorder in adults: management [Internet]. 2020 Jun p. 47. Report No.: CG113. www.nice.org.uk/guidance/cg113/resources/generalised-anxiety-disorder-and-panic-disorder-in-adults-management-pdf-35109387756997.

2. National Institute for Health and Care Excellence. Social anxiety disorder: recognition, assessment and treatment [Internet]. 2013 May p. 39. Report No.: CG159. www.nice.org.uk/guidance/cg159/resources/social-anxiety-disorder-recognition-assessment-and-treatment-pdf-35109639699397.
3. Mowrer OH. Two-factor learning theory: Summary and comment. *Psychol Rev.* 1951;**58**(5):350–354.
4. Mowrer OH. *Learning Theory and Behavior.* New York: Wiley; 1960.
5. Wolpe J. *Psychotherapy by reciprocal inhibition.* Stanford: University Press; 1958.
6. Gillan P, Rachman SJ. An experimental investigation of desensitization in phobic patients. *Br J Psychiatry.* 1974;**124**(581):392–401.
7. Marks I. Behavioral treatments of phobic and obsessive-compulsive disorders: A critical appraisal. In: Michel Hersen, Peter Michael Miller, Richard Morton Eisler (eds), *Progress in Behavior Modification, Volume 1* (pp. 65–158). New York: Academic Press; 1975.
8. Craske MG, Barlow DH. *Mastery of your Anxiety and Panic: Therapist Guide.* 4th ed. New York: Oxford University Press; 2007.
9. Hope DA, Heimberg RG, Turk CL. *Managing Social Anxiety, Therapist Guide: A Cognitive-Behavioral Therapy Approach.* Oxford: Oxford University Press; 2006.
10. Craske MG, Antony MM, Barlow DH. *Mastering Your Fears and Phobias: Therapist Guide.* New Yorl: Oxford University Press; 2006.
11. Stern R, Marks I. Brief and prolonged flooding: A comparison in agoraphobic patients. *Arch Gen Psychiatry.* 1973;**28**(2):270–276.
12. Mathews AM, Gelder MG, Johnston DW. *Agoraphobia, Nature and Treatment.* New York: Guilford Press; 1981.
13. Grayson JB, Foa EB, Steketee G. Habituation during exposure treatment: Distraction vs attention-focusing. *Behav Res Ther.* 1982;**20**(4):323–328.
14. Craske MG, Kircanski K, Zelikowsky M, Mystkowski J, Chowdhury N, Baker A. Optimizing inhibitory learning during exposure therapy. *Behav Res Ther.* 2008;**46**(1):5–27.
15. Beck AT, Emery G, Greenberg RL. *Anxiety Disorders & Phobias.* New York: Basic Books; 1985.
16. Salkovskis PM, Forrester E, Richards C. Cognitive–behavioural approach to understanding obsessional thinking. *Br J Psychiatry.* 1998;**173**(S35):53–63.
17. Clark DM. Cognitive therapy for anxiety. *Behav Cogn Psychother.* 1986;**14**(4):283–294.
18. Salkovskis PM. The importance of behaviour in the maintenance of anxiety and panic: A cognitive account. *Behav Cogn Psychother.* 1991;**19**(1):6–19.
19. Salkovskis PM, Hackmann A, Wells A, Gelder MG, Clark DM. Belief disconfirmation versus habituation approaches to situational exposure in panic disorder with agoraphobia: A pilot study. *Behav Res Ther.* 2007;**45**(5):877–885.

Chapter 11

Specific Phobias

In this chapter we will help you to be able to:

- Describe what Specific Phobia is and how it typically presents and discuss the maintaining role of avoidance.
- Describe and use evidence-based CBT for Specific Phobia.
- Describe the elements of a CBT approach to managing Specific Phobias.

Introduction

Specific phobias are amongst the commonest type of anxiety disorder experienced by people [1]. It is very common for people to experience fears such as heights, spiders and flying, amongst many others. Perhaps we may all fear something to an extent but these fears, however much we experience them or feel embarrassed by their impact on us, do not interfere with the quality of our lives in the way that someone with a specific phobia experiences it. One may think therefore of fears as existing on a continuum with specific phobias existing at the end of the continuum. Fears associated with phobias are disproportionate to the actual risk of the occurrence of the feared-object or event and can be very impactful. As one makes sense of actions and of feelings, CBT is a good type of therapy for use with people with phobias.

Treatment of phobia within CBT has a long history and work by pioneers like Wolpe and much later Isaac Marks [2] established that psychological understandings, treatment models and interventions, such as systematic desensitisation (exposure), could successfully treat anxiety disorders. The idea that psychological therapy was an efficacious treatment approach, *on its own*, for anxiety disorders facilitated the development of research and innovation that inspired an evidence-based cognitive and behavioural approach to common mental health conditions.

Phobias are commonly characterised into four main categories or types [1] as follows:

Animals, e.g. dogs, snakes, rodents, etc.

Situational, e.g. enclosed/small spaces, flying, etc.

Natural environment e.g. fear of heights, water, etc.

Blood and injury, e.g. blood, vomit, etc.

There are so many phobias there is no official list of phobias but there are many websites that list names for the phobias. The reality of living with a phobia is impactful and individuals usually have to make accommodations within their lives and lifestyles that often function to help the person cope with their fears, but this also functions to maintain their level of this anxiety disorder. While in some instances it may be possible to identify an antecedent to the development of a phobia such as being bitten by a dog when young, and consequently experiencing distress and fear around dogs as an adult, the maintenance factors of avoidance and disproportionate thoughts about risk are more important for clinicians to take account of when treatment-planning.

Common criteria such as DSM-5 characterise phobias as intense, marked fears about specific objects or situations that provoke immediate anxiety when an individual is confronted with the fear object and the fear are disproportionate to the specific risk or danger of exposure. Distress/fear only occurs in the presence of the feared-object or situation and as such, the feared-object or situation is actively avoided. The fear usually must last for at least six months for diagnosis [1]. This description provides a good outline to allow a CBT therapist to consider how a treatment plan could be developed with the individual once they have decided to seek treatment. Without active treatment, specific phobias are very unlikely to spontaneously resolve and can become a life-long condition. Often due to the covert nature of avoidance of phobic objects, even close family members may not know a person has a life-impacting phobia. As a result, the person either does not seek help, or is not encouraged to address anxious symptoms.

As an example of this phenomenon, Mrs Green, presented for help with emetophobia (vomit phobia) after living with this condition for more than six decades. At the age of 69 years she decided that now was the time to overcome her fear. She had two adult sons, and three grandchildren, none of whom knew that she had a phobia of vomiting and this was so impactful she took evasive actions to avoid ever getting sick. When her family was young all family holidays were self-catering in their own caravans and Mrs Green never ate out at restaurants or fast-food outlets for fear of contracting food-poisoning and hence vomiting. She was also fearful of being sea-sick (the original source of her vomiting episode when she was a child aged nine years old) so avoided travel by ferry or boat therefore Mrs Green had never travelled far and never gone abroad. Treatment was approached consistent with practice literature [3] and Mrs Green engaged in treatment very well and through a simple process of some psychoeducation about anxiety, phobias and about risks associated with vomiting (she feared she would choke), and a review of how vomiting may have a useful function and how actively trying to prevent oneself from vomiting is not adaptive and not usually possible [3], she was able to agree to challenge her phobia. As Mrs Green was very well motivated and she was able to articulate her cognitions around feared consequences of vomiting and her overall general level of anxiety was low these factors may also have contributed to treatment success in this case [4].Treatment consisted of imaginal and in-vivo (real-life) exposure to a co-constructed hierarchy of feared-situations (see also [3]). We started out by helping her become more accustomed to talking and thinking about vomit and vomiting. We then moved onto looking at training videos of people who were mimicking vomiting and then to still and moving images of people vomiting and then on to behavioural experiments in which she exposed herself to situations she had previously avoided such as eating in restaurants, eating at fast-food venues, using the toilet at friends' houses and drinking some wine without a meal, and so on. We talked about the types of images and thoughts she habitually experienced before and after each step on the hierarchy of feared situations and we addressed safety-seeking behaviours. As we started treatment, Mrs Green decided to discuss her phobia with her husband (and then with her sons) and his support was recruited in ongoing behavioural experiments. Using graded exposure and systematic desensitisation she was able to overcome her phobia after about six sessions of therapy. At the end of treatment she was eating out in a range of food places and had been able to join friends on a boating trip. At discharge she had successfully managed a trip to London and was planning on a trip abroad.

Principles of Psychological Treatment for Specific Phobia

In general the main principle of a CBT approach to helping a person overcome a specific must include graded exposure [3,5] as a major component and ideally graded exposure consists of the therapist and client co-constructing a graded hierarchy of feared stimulus/situations/objects that are systematically approached in a way that provokes fear but is within manageable levels that the client can cope with. Exposure can be in-vivo in which case the person actually confronts the feared stimulus in real-life and in real-time, or it can be in-vitro or imagined exposure. In many cases a combination of in-vivo and imaginal exposure can be successful with clients and based on the context, while in-vivo exposure is most efficacious imaginal exposure is also an effective technique. Most graded exposure tasks/steps are completed as agreed homework tasks. Imagined exposure allows the client to break the feared stimulus into manageable steps that can be approached via a graded hierarchy of fears. In-vivo exposure is very powerful and if the client can be observed by a therapist they can ask their client what their cognitions are before, during and after exposure to a feared stimulus. An example of this may be a client with a fear of dogs who at the final step on their graded exposure agrees to meet and pet a dog in the clinic. Imaginal exposure requires the client and therapist to work together within sessions to maximise the benefit of approaching a feared stimulus.

The principles of exposure are that it must be ***graded*** (gradually the person approaches the feared stimulus, usually via a graded hierarchy), ***focussed,*** (the client should not use distraction techniques), ***repeated*** with good frequency (the client should seek to generalise the learning by repeating exposure with variations of types of feared stimulus e.g. if the fear is of dogs the person could repeat exposure by meeting more than one dog) and *prolonged* (for the person to habituate to the fear they should approach the feared stimulus with sufficient exposure time). While graded exposure most often will be used as part of a CBT approach to managing anxiety, Ost and colleagues [6] have demonstrated that single-sessions exposure may offer an alternative approach to overcoming specific phobias.

As graded exposure takes place, most commonly as part of a CBT treatment approach, cognitive elements of treatment for specific phobias will include developing a formulation with client so they can contextualise their understanding of how the fear has its impact on them, and engaging in cognitive restructuring challenging negative thoughts about feared consequences and challenging negative self-attributions. A formulation should include a discussion of safety seeking behaviours the client has used in the past when confronted with a feared stimulus [3]. Safety seeking in exposure can be overt, for example, the client seeks reassurance, or they limit their direct exposure to the stimulus, or it can be covert, for example, the client distracts themselves by thinking of something else. Therapists should look out for clients who seek reassurance about ability to cope with exposure or who seek to put off the next step in the graded hierarchy as these can be safety seeking attempts. It can be a good idea to discuss how and when the client will use imaginal exposure within the session before they use it as a homework task and they can be helped to identify and resist the use of safety-seeking behaviours and thoughts. Another important component of treatment is psychoeducation and this very often an important precursor to the client completing their hierarchy of feared stimulus/situations and then taking the first steps towards graded exposure. Standard cognitive restructuring is very helpful for clients in order to challenge any anxiety they hold about confronting fears. This is especially so as fears have often been maintained because the client has disproportionately over-estimated the sense of catastrophic outcome of being confronted by the feared stimulus and simultaneously underestimated their ability to manage how to deal with their fears.

Graded Hierarchy

Co-constructing a graded hierarchy within treatment should start very early within treatment. It is never too late to start talking to the client openly and honestly about how CBT for specific phobias works. It is a good idea at the point of assessment to briefly outline the steps of treatment and that avoidance only maintains fear and undermines the client's sense of being able to cope. It can be a helpful action on the part of the therapist to point out that efficacy for CBT for phobias are very good with respect to treatments of anxiety disorders. It is also important to remind the client that a graded approach to phobias leaves them in control of how fast they approach their fears and treatment emphasises that a graded exposure means not being out of their comfort zone in terms of emotional arousal.

Graded hierarches usually involve asking the client to work with you to create a list of objects/stimuli or situations that provoke an anxious response and can be measured on an increasing scale of fear. The graded hierarchy can consist of as many steps as the client wishes and usually is ranked on an increasing scale, commonly from 0–100/0–10 where 0 means the object/stimulus contains no fear for the client and 100 or 10 is maximal fear. Starting with the lowest manageable point on the graded hierarchy is a good idea. Therapists must be careful that clients who feel enthused by the approach as it is explained to them may wish to start too high on the graded hierarchy. It is always better to start low and go slow, as paradoxically this is the fastest way to overcome a phobia. Sometimes as clients move up the graded hierarchy the steps can seem more daunting and in this instance interim steps can be added as necessary but the client can be reminded that they have confronted their fears in getting along the graded hierarchy and avoidance only undermines their developing sense of achievement.

Using Graded Hierarchy as a Case Example

An example of a client who worked through a graded hierarchy is Miss Power, 71, who has been referred by her GP for 'anxiety management'. Her GP mentions that Miss Power has a great fear of enclosed spaces such as lifts or airplanes and has been seeing a hypnotherapist but without success. At assessment Miss Power completes a Beck Depression Inventory (BDI) and Beck Anxiety Inventory (BAI) and records a score of 38 and 16 respectively (by the end of treatment these had reduced to 5 and 8). She is afraid of going into lifts for fear of suffocation and avoids going on double-decker buses for any prolonged period of time when their doors are closed. In this scenario, she goes upstairs as she believes, 'It is cooler and airier.'

These anxiety symptoms have been present for a number of years and have had a significant impact on her life as she no longer goes on holidays, whereas in the past she was an adventurous traveller. Miss Power told her therapist that in a previous recent attempt

Table 11.1 Graded Hierarchy for situational phobia

Steps	Rating of severity, fear level/100
Going on buses for more than two stops,	30
Going on buses and not going upstairs	40
Taking large elevators up one floor in department stores (outside of busy times)	45
Taking large elevators up one floor in department stores (at busy times)	50
Taking small elevators up one floor in department stores (outside of busy times)	60
Taking small elevators up more than one floor in department stores (outside of busy times)	70
Taking smallest elevators in department stores	80
Going on trains that often stop in tunnels before arriving at busy main station platforms	85
Going on express inter-city coaches with sealed windows	90
Going on express inter-city coaches with sealed windows at busy times	95
Taking a boat trip	100

to overcome her anxiety and before seeking CBT help, she had bought an airline ticket to visit a family friend overseas but unfortunately had cancelled at last minute and lost all her deposit. As Miss Power had tried many different treatments to no avail, at the start of treatment, she commented, 'I am concerned that I cannot see how I will ever be able to face these situations.'

Over time using a simple graded hierarchy of feared situations, Miss Power was able to overcome feared situations gradually and to generalise gains beyond her initial goals.

Table 11.1 shows an example of graded hierarchy co-created with Miss Powers.

During the follow-up phase, the therapist and Miss Power talked about how she might maintain her progress and how she could continue to use the principles of graded exposure by herself after discharge by relying on her new knowledge about anxiety symptoms and remind herself about how she had overcome previous situations she thought were beyond her in order to progress further along to her goals.

At the end of treatment, while Miss Power did not consider herself fully 'cured' of her phobic anxiety she was aware of how far she had come so when discussing her post-treatment plans, she talked about taking a small trip to Europe but the thought of traveling alone was anxiety-provoking, 'I might just disappear from sight. I might just disappear from the planet. I'm alone in the world. I don't belong to anybody.' At the end session as the therapist worked with Miss Power to help her make notes on what she had gained from therapy, she joked at the time she might just take that flight to visit her friend!

As it turned out Miss Power did consolidate her gains from therapy and from within her own psychological resources she was able to travel independently to the destination she had planned but had failed to achieve just prior to starting CBT treatment. Once there she sent a postcard her to therapist that simply said, 'I thought you might like to know that I actually got here and having a lovely time with my friend.'

For someone unable to tolerate traveling on bus for more than two stops initially to be able to tolerate taking a flight by herself this was a very significant achievement and as such should stand as a reminder that our clients can achieve much more than we sometimes might envisage.

Conclusion and Summary

Psychological treatment of the phobic disorders has a long and efficacious history within CBT and BT. The condition may be very commonly treated at a lower level within many UK NHS talking treatment centres but treating phobias in a collaborative, empowering and effective way demands skill, knowledge and competence on the part of CBT therapists and to think otherwise is likely to lead to a poorer outcome. To ask someone to willingly and directly confront something that immediately and automatically generates a very strong fear reaction requires a skilled therapist working to engage a client and to do so collaboratively should not be underestimated. The phobic disorders share many conceptual similarities with CBT models of anxiety disorders but have their own particular features and require strong individualisation of treatment planning.

Further Reading

Marks I, Horder J. Phobias and their management. *BMJ.* 1987:295.

Wolitzky-Taylor K, Horowitz JD, Powers MB, Telch MJ. Psychological approaches in the treatment of specific phobias: A meta-analysis. *Clin Psychol Rev.* 2008; **28**(6):1021–1037.

Zlomke K, Davis T. One-session treatment of specific phobias: A detailed description and review of treatment efficacy. *Behav Ther.* 2008;**39**:207–223.

References

1. Burkauskas J, Fineberg NA, Enara A, Cirnigliaro G., Drummopmd LM. Specific phobias, in D Kingdon, P Rowlands, G Stein (Eds.), *Seminars in General Adult Psychiatry* (pp. 324 – 333) Cambridge: CUP; 2024. https://doi.org/10.1017/9781911623861.016.
2. Marks IM. Reduction of fear: Towards a unifying theory. *Canadian Psychiatric Association Journal.* 1973;**18**(1):9–12. https://doi.org/10.1177/070674377301800103.
3. Veale D. Cognitive behaviour therapy for a specific phobia of vomiting. *The Cogn Behav Ther.* 2009;**2**:272–288.
4. Böhnlein J, Altegoer L, Muck NK, Roesmann K, Redlich R, Dannlowski U, Leehr EJ. Factors influencing the success of exposure therapy for specific phobia: A systematic review. *Neurosci Biobehav Rev.* 2020;**108**:796–820.
5. Papworth M. Graded exposure therapy, in P Farrand (Ed.), *Low Intensity CBT Skills and Interventions* (pp. 211–224). 2nd ed. London: Sage; 2025.
6. Odgers K, Kershaw KA, Li SH, Graham BM. The relative efficacy and efficiency of single- and multi-session exposure therapies for specific phobia: A meta-analysis. *Behav Res Ther.* 2022;**15**:104203.

Chapter 12

Panic Disorder

In this chapter we will help you to be able to:

- Explain what panic disorder is and how it typically presents, including unexpected panic attacks, and subsequent fear and attempted avoidance of further attacks.
- Describe and use evidence-based CBT protocols for panic disorder.
- Choose and use appropriate formulation models for CBT for panic disorder.
- Describe the importance of using exposure to panic symptoms in any treatment plan.
- Develop a treatment plan for CBT for panic disorder, using appropriate measures.
- Take account of comorbidity in managing CBT for panic disorder.

Introduction

Panic as an emotion, panic attacks and panic disorder all have their place in the work of a CBT therapist. However, only in the last of these are the sensations of panic also the trigger for further panic, creating a vicious cycle of misinterpretation, safety seeking behaviours and fear, which can seem to come from nowhere. This chapter will explore the nature of panic disorder, how it is diagnosed and its aetiology in the general population. It will then go on to consider how panic disorder is understood from a CBT perspective, and describe the two main models most commonly used with panic disorder.

What Is Panic Disorder?

To define panic disorder, one must first define a panic attack, which the DSM [37, p. 242] states is an abrupt surge of intense fear or intense discomfort that reaches a peak within minutes, and during which time four (or more) of the following symptoms occur:

- Palpitations, pounding heart, or accelerated heart rate.
- Sweating.
- Trembling or shaking.
- Sensations of shortness of breath or smothering.
- Feelings of choking.
- Chest pain or discomfort.
- Nausea or abdominal distress.
- Feeling dizzy, unsteady, light-headed, or faint.
- Chills or heat sensations.

- Paresthesias (numbness or tingling sensations).
- Derealization (feelings of unreality) or depersonalization (being detached from oneself).
- Fear of losing control or 'going crazy'.
- Fear of dying.

In and of themselves, panic attacks occur in any number of disorders, normally triggered by known internal or external fear cues. The first criterion of panic disorder is that the individual has experienced 'recurrent, unexpected panic attacks' – that is, at least two such events where it was not pre-empted by a known fear trigger. The second criterion is that the individual fears further such attacks, and/or changes their behaviour to avoid them. Thus, the key feature of panic disorder is not so much the emotion of panic, or even the presence of panic attacks, as it is the unexpected and unpredictable nature of the panic attacks, the fear of the panic and the catastrophic meaning given to it. This is important when determining how to treat a patient, as many individuals may experience and dislike panic attacks, but only those where the panic attacks are being maintained by a panic disorder cycle will benefit from the approaches below.

Surveys with university populations [1,2] indicate that more than 25% of the overall population may experience an occasional panic attack sometime in a given year, with between 13% and 22% in the last month. Panic disorder, however, has been found to have a 12-month prevalence of 2.7% [3], rising to 4.7% over a person's lifetime [4]. As such, differentiating between a panic attack and the complete disorder is important, as the former is common in many non-panic disorder patients and so should not be seen as good evidence of the latter. It is twice as common in women as men [5] and typically has an age of onset between 16–40 years of age [4].

A common comorbidity in panic disorder is agoraphobia [6], and indeed in earlier versions of the DSM agoraphobia was a specifier for panic disorder, and so seen as part of the same disorder for a subset of patients. Helpfully, this means that both agoraphobic and non-agoraphobic presentations of panic disorder are fully accounted for in the key treatment approaches below.

Assessing for panic disorder can be aided by the use of specific measures. The Panic Disorder Severity Scale [7] is a useful 7-item scale, which can be a useful way to quickly explore all the different diagnostic aspects of Panic Disorder and then monitor them weekly over treatment. A cut-off of 8 is generally recommended for considering a case as having clinically meaningful panic disorder, though this should not replace clinical assessment [8]. For many patients it is also useful to use the Mobility Inventory [9,10] to assess and monitor any related agoraphobia, especially as this measure differentiates between avoidance when accompanied and alone. Further measures that can be useful on assessment are the Agoraphobic Cognitions Questionnaire – modified, and the Panic Safety Seeking Behaviours Questionnaire [11], which help to identify the patient's cognitions and safety seeking behaviours specific to panic disorder, some of which the patient may otherwise fail to mention.

Panic Disorder Treatment

Early theories of panic disorder were based on the idea that it was a neurochemical condition [12,13]; a biological disorder distinct from the other more psychologically driven anxiety disorders. There were a range of specific theories about the nature of the underlying cause, including mitral valve prolapse [14,15], vestibular abnormalities [16,17] or a misfiring suffocation alarm [18]. It was noted that panic attacks are helped by different medication than other anxiety symptoms [19,20] which further supported the idea that panic attacks were qualitatively different from high anxiety, and so possibly due to a biological rather than psychological cause, though other studies did contest this [21]. Prior to the specific cognitive theories of panic disorder, any cognitive-behavioural treatment was based on exposure for the agoraphobia that commonly accompanied panic [22], with the panic attacks being treated pharmacologically, but unlike with specific phobias such as of animals, this treatment was not initially promising [22].

Craske and Barlow theorised that panic disorder was caused by an interplay of four key things: a biological sensitivity to negative emotions (which would fit with the earlier biological theories), a belief that anxiety is harmful, a fear of bodily sensations and an increased awareness of such bodily sensations. As such, they theorised that treatment would need to tackle both the fear of sensations (through exposure to the sensations themselves) and a change in beliefs (through cognitive restructuring). In testing this, they compared a range of options for treating panic disorder – progressive muscle relaxation plus exposure, cognitive therapy plus exposure and breathing retraining, or a combination of them all [23]. All showed some improvement over those on a waitlist, but only the cognitive therapy plus exposure resulted in high proportions of panic-free patients at two-year follow-up [24].

Clark and Salkovskis focussed on a more specific cognitive model of catastrophic misinterpretations of symptoms as the maintaining mechanism in panic disorder, which acts directly by increasing the level of panic, and indirectly through the use of safety behaviours [25,26]. While very early versions of this model included a focus on breathing retraining, this was quickly dropped [27], and their approach now focusses on helping the patient to drop their catastrophic misinterpretations and build belief in a more benign explanation of their symptoms, via cognitive discussion techniques and a range of specific behavioural experiments.

Thus, the consensus is that treating panic disorder will focus on changing a patient's beliefs about their symptoms, their avoidance of panic sensations, and their resultant safety seeking behaviours and focus of attention, using a range of cognitive and behavioural tools.

Efficacy Data for CBT for Panic Disorder

To date, there have been more than 120 RCTs reviewing the efficacy of different versions and formats of CBT for Panic Disorder [28]. In a recent meta-analysis by Papola et al. [28] it was found that CBT, as well as what the paper defined as purely cognitive therapy or behavioural therapy, was statistical superior to treatment as usual, and appeared to have at least slight superiority to all other comparison treatment approaches, with the possible exception of short-term psychodynamic therapy. In line with this, NICE recommend CBT as the only psychological treatment of choice for panic disorder [29].

Picking a Protocol

As described above, there are a range of ways of conceptualising Panic Disorder, and so a range of possible ways to structure therapy. Currently, the most commonly used manualised approaches for treatment of Panic Disorder in the UK are:

- Clark and Salkovskis [30]

Or

- Craske and Barlow [31,32]

Each of these specific protocols has its strengths, and have a good evidence base for their efficacy, resulting in their inclusion in both the Roth and Pilling CBT Competencies [33] and the BABCP Core Curriculum [34]. See Table 12.1.

Both protocols will involve experiencing the symptoms related to panic, and exploring cognitions in one way or another. In picking between the protocols, it can be useful to consider the willingness of the patient to directly test their feared consequences regarding having a panic attack, versus their willingness to carry out repeated prolonged exposure with the aim of learning to tolerate panic.

Clark and Salkovskis

As explored above, this model posits that panic disorder is fundamentally driven by a catastrophic misinterpretation of bodily sensations, which are maintained in spite of the lack of catastrophe both due to enhanced internal focus and the use of safety behaviours. This is formulated early in treatment with the client, using the model in Figure 12.1, which can be drawn out with the client by exploring one of their recent experiences of a panic attack. Following this, treatment works by first providing an alternative explanation of the panic attacks being experienced (via Theory A/Theory B, see Chapter 6), and then by exploring each theory in turn, through a mixture of discussion techniques and behavioural experiments.

Discussion techniques may start with targeted psychoeducation, focussing on the key features of the fight or flight reaction that the patient misinterprets, or information about how the feared catastrophe actually occurs (what is needed in the body to faint, etc.). This psychoeducation is provided as part of a two-way discussion, checking in first on the patient's understanding of the issue, and adding in the needed details to ensure they have a full picture.

Another aspect of the discussion techniques is in reconsidering old information. This can include exploring the comparative frequency of episodes when alone and with others, or when they are able to focus on symptoms versus when they are distracted. In each case, the increased frequency makes better sense if the issue is one of anxiety about a feared catastrophe (Theory B) rather than the issue being the feared catastrophe itself (Theory A) and so this information can be added as evidence to support B.

Image modification may also be helpful if the patient has recurring distressing images associated with the panic attacks, and which they find distressing in themselves, independent of the attached verbal meaning. In these cases, it can be helpful to explore the image, determine what is particularly distressing about it, and then modify the image, either by helping the patient to imagine what would happen next, or by transforming parts of the image to make it less threatening.

Behavioural experiments have two key focuses in panic disorder. The first is recreating the panic sensations so as to show the benign cause of symptoms. The second focus is on showing that the symptoms also have a benign outcome, by again bringing on the symptoms and then abstaining from safety behaviours.

Experiments in the first category are generally performed without explaining the purpose to the client in advance. This is unusual in CBT, but is needed in these experiments

Table 12.1 A table comparing the Clark and Salkovskis and Craske and Barlow protocols for the treatment of Panic Disorder

Protocol	Clark and Salkovskis [30]	Craske and Barlow [31,32]
Theory of Panic Disorder	Catastrophic misinterpretations of symptoms maintain panic disorder, both increasing panic and sensations both directly, and indirectly through the use of safety behaviours.	Panic disorder is caused by an interplay of biological sensitivity to negative emotions, a belief that anxiety is harmful, a fear of bodily sensations, and an increased awareness of bodily sensations.
Aim of treatment	Identity catastrophic misinterpretations and helpful alternative interpretations of bodily sensations, and test out the validity of each by discussion and behavioural experiments	Reduction in fear through habituation, extinction, self-efficacy, emotional processing, and inhibitory learning, as well as learning that feared outcomes don't occur and fear can be tolerated
Recommended structure of therapy	5–15 sessions, each 1-hour duration, over 5–15 weeks Brief version – 6 sessions [35]	12 sessions, each 1-hour duration, over 12 weeks (or twice weekly to complete in 6 weeks)
Interventions used	• Theory A/B and targeted psychoeducation • Discussion techniques • Behavioural experiments	• Psychoeducation and monitoring, • Breathing and cognitive coping skills, • Exposure
Helpful when	Patient can be helped to be willing to explicitly test their catastrophic misinterpretations	Patient is familiar with and in favour of a hierarchy-based approach to confronting fears or is unwilling to attempt exposure without coping skills

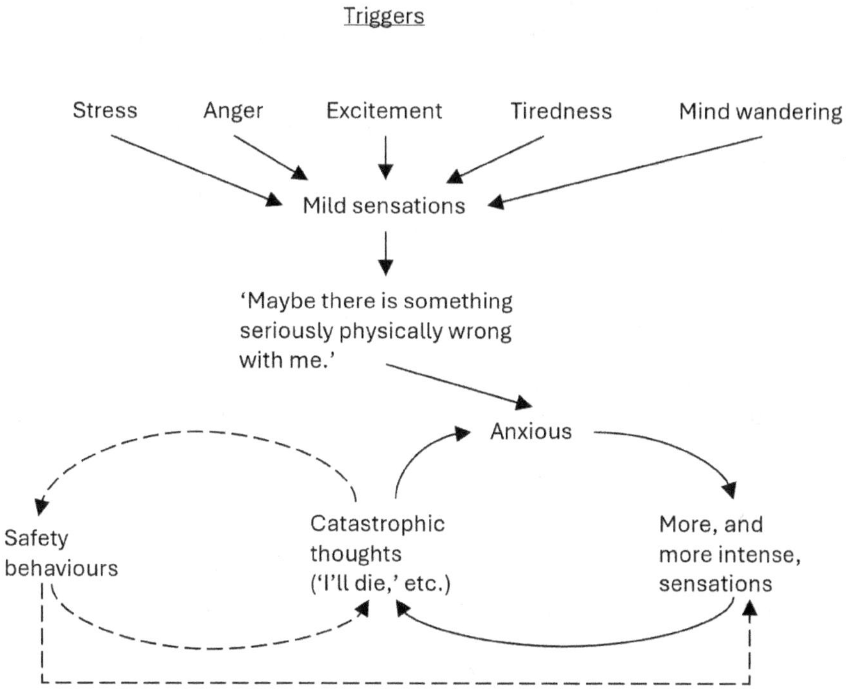

Figure 12.1 Clark and Salkovskis model of panic disorder, reproduced with permission from Guilford Press.

to allow them to work, as if the patient is told that the expectation is that the experiment will cause panic symptoms, they are likely to use safety behaviours and distraction to prevent this. As such, the experiments are generally described, and the patient asked to try them 'to see what happens', and then quickly terminated once the outcome is determined.

Examples of the first type of experiment include the paired associates test, where patients read lists of paired symptoms and feared outcomes (e.g. dizziness – fainting) and focus on the meaning of the pairings. Due to the link between thinking about feared outcomes and panic symptoms, this often brings on panic symptoms similar to a natural panic attack, which can be used to help the patient buy in to the idea that their thoughts about feared outcomes are what bring on the attacks in everyday life. This experiment can be done formally, as above, or can occur naturalistically during early sessions, when the act of the patient describing their experiences of panic and what they fear could happen may bring on an attack. As such, therapists are alert for this, and help the patient through Socratic questioning to notice this.

Other key experiments involve bringing on feared sensations through hyperventilation, sudden exercise, focussing attention on naturally occurring symptoms, or using the patient's own safety behaviours. A classic example of this last one is by having the patient demonstrate the way they attempt to 'breathe deeply' during a panic attack – a very common safety behaviour. The therapist and patient can then keep doing this together, to determine what impact it has on them while calm – the naïve expectation being that it will make us feel even calmer. Instead, deep breathing mimics hyperventilating in that it causes the body to feel more tense, and can make us dizzy and give a racing heart and tingling extremities. As soon as this is noticed, the experiment can stop, and the true impact of the safety behaviours can be discussed. Commonly, patients can ask at this point if there is a better way to try and breathe during attacks, and therapists can be tempted to teach breathing techniques. However, this model recommends that during subsequent attacks, any attempt at controlling breathing will likely result in hyperventilating, and will also cause unhelpful focus on breathing and symptoms, as well as reinforce the central concept that one needs to control breathing to survive. As such, therapists should instead help the patient make these links, and decide to drop the safety behaviour altogether, to see what happens when they simply let the symptoms happen.

This is a helpful entry point to the second type of experiment, where patients are encouraged (with full understanding of the plan) to bring on their feared symptoms, and then choose to drop their safety behaviours, in order to determine whether their feared outcomes actually occur. This type of experiment is obviously very anxiety provoking, which is why the experiments and discussion techniques above are needed to first loosen the belief in Theory A, and build hope that it could be possible to do this and have no catastrophe occur. Examples of how symptoms can be induced within the therapy office include excessive over-breathing, high intensity exercise and trying to go mad. In each case, the therapist elicits a prediction of what the patient fears and the safety behaviours they would normally use to prevent this fear from occurring, and then supports the patient to agree to engage in the planned experiment without using the safety behaviours. Ideally this is done in session, so that the patient can be encouraged and supported, and so that other automatic safety behaviours can be spotted, explored and dropped.

For those with external panic triggers, such as those with agoraphobia, experiments can then broaden to planned exposure to these cues, again while dropping the safety behaviours to determine what occurs. This can be used to test both whether the internal catastrophe occurs (passing out, choking, going mad) and whether others notice or react as feared. If the patient also fears how people will react if the feared outcome were to occur – such as fearing that were they to pass out, people would either panic themselves or leave them there indefinitely – the therapist can role play this in public, so the patient can see firsthand how others actually react. These disconfirming experiments are described in more detail in the next chapter on Social Anxiety Disorder.

As an example, Clint (Figure 12.2) had begun experiencing panic attacks suddenly while driving his truck six months ago, and had continued experiencing them in a range of situations ever since. The specific example drawn out was from going to a baseball game at the weekend, which had previously not been a known trigger. As in his initial attack, his key cognition was that he was going to pass out, which was especially panic-inducing due to the high bleachers he was sat in.

Clint's theory A/B focussed on the theories of 'I am going to pass out' versus 'I am overly concerned about bodily symptoms such as breathlessness'. Initially, Clint had been sceptical of this as a possibility, but he quickly realised that his knowledge about how and when people pass out was based almost exclusively on films and TV shows, and one experience where he had believed he had passed out, but that on closer discussion had not. This was contrasted against new information about what causes passing out, and his own repeated experiences of feeling lightheaded but then not passing out, sometimes even when he had done nothing to prevent it, but had simply been distracted.

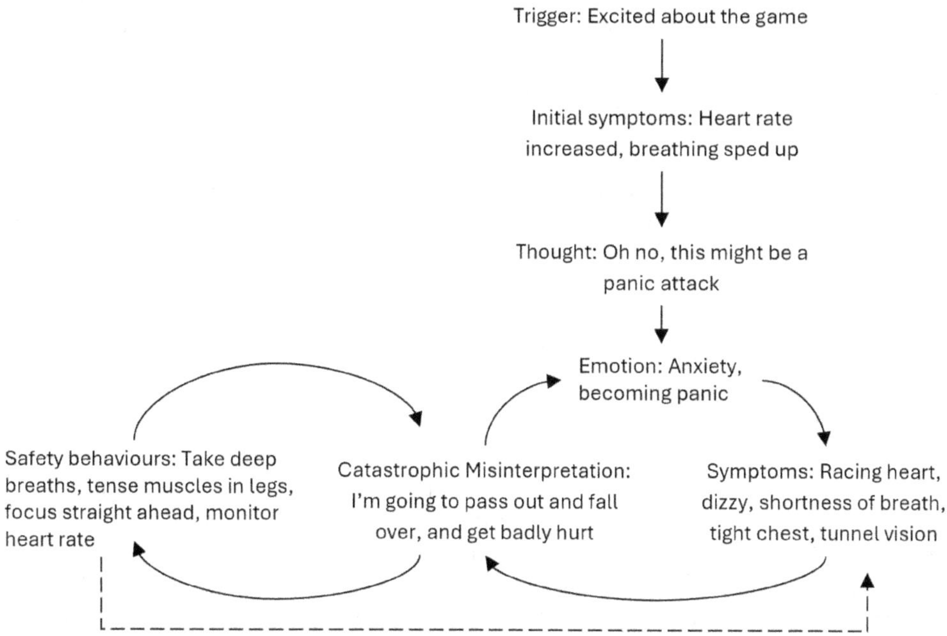

Figure 12.2 Clint's example cycle, adapted from Clark and Salkovskis model of panic disorder, reproduced with permission from Guilford Press.

Therapy quickly moved onto initial experiments, including reviewing what Clint noticed when he recreated his safety behaviour of deep breathing while calm. The speed at which this brought on feelings of dizziness and being out of breath was a powerful piece of evidence in favour of Theory B. Socratic discussion was used to explore how to incorporate this knowledge into how Clint could respond in future panic inducing situations or spontaneous attacks, and Clint decided that the best course of action would be to stop trying to control his breathing at all.

Sessions then focussed on actively bringing on dizziness and shortness of breath, while dropping all other safety behaviours. This included hyperventilating, running up and down stairs and spinning in a circle, each time dropping any attempt to control the anxiety caused, and eventually actively trying to increase the chances of falling over, by leaning forwards and standing on tip toes. Clint became increasingly confident that, no matter which panic symptoms he was experiencing, his body remained conscious, and he didn't pass out or fall over. He also noted which of his additional safety behaviours, such as tensing his legs and hands, had actually been making the panic symptoms worse, further reinforcing the idea that trying to control panic was counterproductive, and that worsening panic symptoms are commonly a product of our own behaviours, not a physical catastrophe.

Following this, targeted experiments were set up to test what happened when he drove without safety behaviours. Due to his concern about putting others at risk, this was initially carried out in an empty car park, before being replicated on the road, and eventually with his wife in the passenger seat. He also carried out experiments where he brought on sensations while going up and down stairs, and sitting at the top of a baseball stadium, to confirm that no matter how panicky he got, his body didn't respond by passing out.

Clint wasn't worried about the reactions of others during panic attacks, and had found his fearful images quickly resolved once he knew more about how passing out worked, and so these features of the protocol were not needed. As such, the therapy finished with relapse prevention at this point, helping Clint to summarise his key learning from the therapy, and consider how he should approach future situations where passing out would be particularly problematic. Clint stated that he had actually agreed to go to a bachelor party that involved a tree-top rope course, and so they explored how specifically to manage this as another experiment, and what safety behaviours to look out for and drop, as an example of how to do this more generally.

Craske and Barlow

Treatment within this protocol follows four main stages: psychoeducation and monitoring, coping skills, exposure and relapse prevention.

Psychoeducation starts around the model shown in Figure 12.3, in terms of the various vulnerabilities and experiences that lead to panic disorder, in contrast to the often-believed causes of a health issue or chemical imbalance. This then leads into an overall explanation of the treatment, which will focus on changing the beliefs and behaviours around panic attacks and their triggers. Next, the concept of the panic cycle is explained, where thoughts, physiology, emotions and behaviours are all interconnected. There is no single model used to connect these in this protocol, but the chain of what the patient notices can be

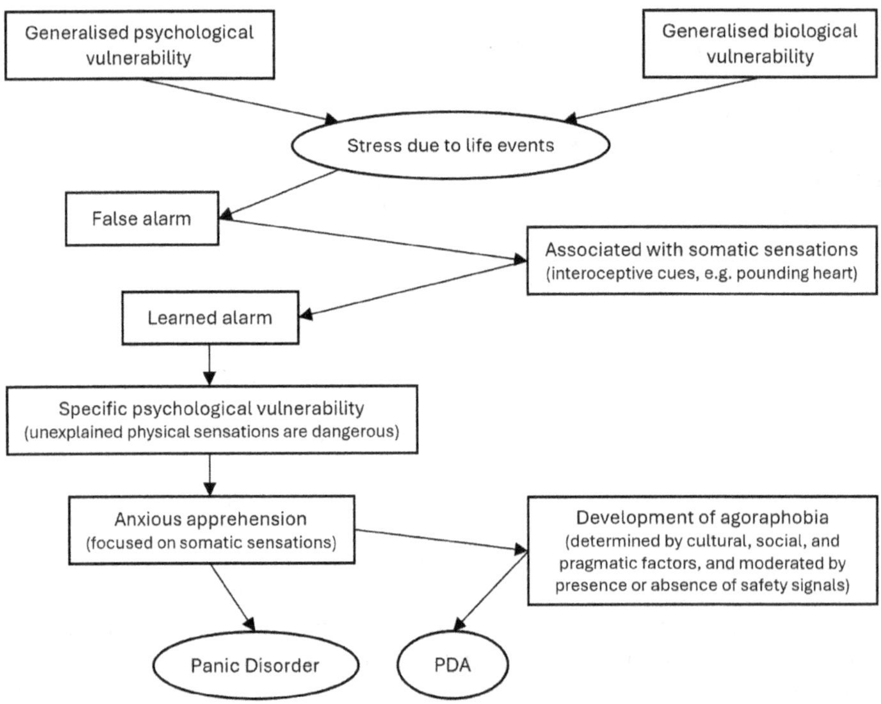

Figure 12.3 Model of the aetiology of panic disorder and agoraphobia, reproduced with permission from Oxford University Press.

drawn either as a cycle or a straight line. Finally, the concept of the fight or flight reaction, and the concept that a panic attack is a fear of one's own physical sensations that is then reinforced by the fight or flight reaction, is explored.

Meanwhile monitoring, which should start from the first session, involves both a daily mood diary and a panic attack record. The daily mood diary rates average depression, anxiety, and worry about panic, and is used to monitor how these change over the course of therapy. The panic attack record is used each time the person has a panic attack, and notes all the relevant features: triggers, whether it was expected, symptoms, cognitions and behaviours, as well as rating the maximum level of fear.

The next step of therapy is creating a hierarchy of avoided situations. Patients are asked to review a list of commonly avoided situations, as well as adding any idiosyncratic ones they have realised due to their panic records. They then consider a set of key modifiers – distance from their home or a safe place, distance from a means of escape, the time of day and/or day of the week, how busy the place is and whether they have anyone specific with them. Using these modifiers they can be assisted to create a hierarchy of feared situations that ideally range from very mild anxiety to 10 out of 10. Patients are also asked to create a list of all safety behaviours they have previously relied on in these situations, as these will need to be dropped to allow for exposure to work.

Before exposure commences, patients are taught two further skills. The first of these are breathing skills. To start this, the patient and/or the therapist purposefully hyperventilate, to show the impact of breathing like this on the body. Patients are then taught how to use various specific breathing skills. The first of these is diaphragmatic breathing, which involves expanding their stomach as they breathe in, minimising the amount the chest moves, and focussing mindfully on their breaths. The next is slowed breathing, where each inhale and exhale are timed to be about two seconds, and with a one second pause after each breath in and each breath out. Each of these needs to be practised at least twice daily for 10 minutes each time, and done to start with when the patient feels calm, ideally practicing each type for a week before moving on. Once this has been learnt in calm settings, the third stage is applying both the speed and use of the diaphragm when the patient starts to feel anxious.

The second skill is cognitive restructuring. Patients are taught to use downward arrow questioning such as 'what was the worst that could happen' and 'what would that mean' to pin down their predictions and conclusions about the dangers during their panic attacks and in their agoraphobic situations. They are taught the thinking errors of jumping to conclusions and awfulising. In response to jumping to conclusions, they are then taught to challenge the thoughts by looking at the empirical data, the impact of past avoidance on missing data, the realistic likelihood of the outcome, and the alternative possible outcomes. They are also taught about the thinking error of awfulising, and helped to consider if the feared outcome it is as unbearable and awful as believed, by focussing on how they would cope if it did happen.

With these skills in hand, the patient now starts working through their hierarchy. For each item, they start by considering what end goal needs to be reached to disprove their feared outcomes. They can then work up to this end goal, or decide to try it from the start, in either case dropping their safety behaviours and practising at least three times a week. While they are carrying out the exposure, they can use the cognitive restructuring answers to remind themselves of how unlikely their fears are and how they would cope, and use their breathing skills to interrupt the panic cycle.

Often, the patient will experience some partial panic symptoms naturally during the course of exposure, but if not, they can then be asked to repeat exposure exercises while deliberately provoking symptoms. In addition to this paired situational exposure, the patient can also be supported to bring on symptoms through pure symptom induction, using a range of standard techniques (such as hyperventilating, spinning or running on the spot). These can then be turned into their own hierarchy, and worked on in the same way as the situation hierarchy, to learn at a gut level that these symptoms are not harmful and can be coped with. Following the standard exercises, patients are encouraged to allow symptoms to occur by exposing themselves to everyday triggers, such as caffeine, exercise and being in hot places. This is particularly emphasised in the most recent editions of the manual, which stresses the importance of inhibitory learning and the need to experience the previously feared sensations in a wide range of contexts so as to learn the new benign meaning as broadly as possible.

Finally, relapse prevention focusses on reviewing the progress made to date, and considering what further practice will be needed of each of the four areas – breathing skills, cognitive work, in vivo exposure and symptom exposure. To aid with motivation, it can be helpful to review and determine long-term goals that the patient can work towards having overcome their panic and any connected agoraphobia.

As an example, Bhavna was extremely worried when she first started having panic attacks, both about the panic attacks themselves, and about what they meant about her neurologically. She knew her aunt had been diagnosed with panic disorder and agoraphobia and had been housebound for many years, and did not want to 'end up like her'. The therapist discussed this with her, exploring the idea that there are biological vulnerabilities that can make someone more predisposed to negative emotions, but that this needs to be coupled with learned psychological factors – both general and specific – to result in panic disorder, and that those learned factors can be changed. They explored how her experiences and learning about her aunt's difficulties may have led to her general beliefs that anxiety is dangerous and damaging, and to pay more attention to her own signs of anxiety than others might. Bhavna found this made a lot of sense, and helped her to marry the ideas that she could have a family history of panic disorder with the hope that it could be successfully treated through psychological approaches, and didn't mean that she was doomed to a lifelong struggle with mental health. She found the statistics in the workbook particularly reassuring, that 70–90% of people are free of panic by the end of the programme, and that this can last for years.

Bhavna agreed to start monitoring her mood and panic attacks from this point, using the records. She initially expected that most would have no apparent triggers, but was quickly surprised to realise that feeling out of breath and being in larger groups were recurring features of her records. Most of the symptoms and thoughts she had were as she'd expected, but she was surprised by how often dizziness played a part, and that she used sitting down and monitoring her heartbeat as a safety behaviour in almost all situations. In terms of her mood, she noticed a trend towards greater anxiety and worry about panicking on Fridays, prior to attending her mosque, but also an improvement in her depression rating on those days and the day after. This highlighted to her how much she valued being able to go to weekly prayers, and the importance of overcoming her anxieties around breathlessness and large groups to support her in being able to be fully present.

Bhavna had little prior knowledge of the fight or flight reaction, and had never considered anxiety in any kind of positive light, and so she found the information on the

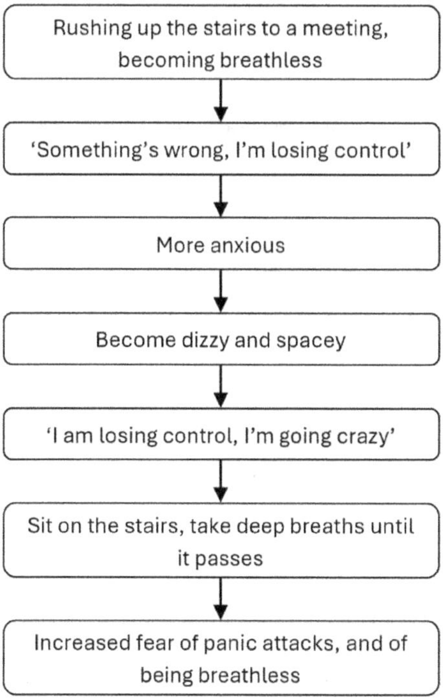

Figure 12.4 Bhavna's panic chain.

Yerkes-Dodson law surprising and enlightening. Using an example from her records, she mapped out how rushing up some steps, leading to breathlessness, had ended up with a panic attack around going crazy and increased fear about being dizzy, as shown in Figure 12.4.

She could see how her symptoms of breathlessness and dizziness fitted with the fight or flight reaction, though she noted that it still very much felt like she was losing control and going crazy, and the therapist reassured her that they would continue to look at this over treatment.

Using Bhavna's prior knowledge of her experiences along with her panic records, a hierarchy was created, as shown in Table 12.2. This included both situations she attended with anxiety, such as the mosque and being home alone, and those she avoided, such as the elevators at work and busy shopping centres. The time of day played a big part in how anxiety provoking various situations would be for her, as would being accompanied by her sister and/or mother.

Her key safety behaviours were asking her mother and sister for reassurance, keeping her mobile phone in her hand, checking exit routes and tightly gripping her other hand, using the pain of her nails in her palm to distract herself.

Bhavna found the breathing section initially stressful, as while the over-breathing exercise caused a lot of the symptoms she was anxious about, the diaphragmatic and slowed breathing did not remove all such symptoms, and made her uncomfortably aware of feeling short of breath at points. However, with repeated practice this subsided, and added evidence to the concept that feeling short of breath wasn't dangerous and that physical symptoms

Table 12.2 Bhavna's exposure hierarchy, adapted from *Mastery of Your Anxiety and Panic: Workbook* (4th ed.), Barlow and Craske [36], with permission from Oxford University Press.

Agoraphobia hierarchy	
Situation	**Anxiety and/or avoidance (0–10)**
Going to a busy shopping centre alone on a Saturday	10
Going to the mosque alone	9
Taking the elevator at work when it's full	8
Going to a shopping centre with sister when not too busy	7
Going to the mosque with sister and mum	6
Taking the elevator at work alone	5
Being home alone in the evening	4
Being home alone during the day	3

may be more about what she was thinking and doing, than anything actually being wrong in her body.

This blended well with the work done on thinking skills generally. Bhavna's key cognitions were 'I will panic if I go there', 'I will lose control', 'I will go crazy' and 'everyone will see that I'm panicking, think I'm insane and reject me'. For the thoughts about losing control and going crazy, she found reviewing the times where this had felt most overwhelming in the past, and yet she had not gone crazy, especially helpful. In terms of others seeing and rejecting her, this was broken down into parts. First off, they considered how often she had felt highly panicky, and how often others had noticed anything. Then, what it actually was that others had noticed – in almost all cases it had been her safety behaviours that had alerted people to her panic, and no one had ever actually called her insane. Lastly, they explored how she could cope in the future if someone did tell her she was insane and reject her, as she had seen happen to her aunt. They explored stating that she was just feeling a bit breathless and dizzy, but it would pass, and that they didn't need to worry. She felt that saying this, rather than calling it a panic attack, would be better understood by those around her, and so would better help her to cope without embarrassment.

Bhavna now moved on to her exposure, taking some scenarios in a single leap, and others step by step. She found it helpful to remind herself that feeling anxious and going crazy were not same, and to use her breathing techniques briefly as and when panic started to build to prove that the cycle was controllable. Pure symptom induction focussed on over-breathing and staring at herself in a mirror to maximise new learning that symptoms are not a sign of madness, and can be experienced without responding. She then went on to use staring at oneself in a mirror during and just before some latter exposure exercises (including going to a shopping centre) to fully prove to herself that others don't actually notice internal sensations, and that she can have symptoms even in these situations without danger.

By the end of therapy, Bhavna was pleased to consider herself part of the 70–90% who were panic attack-free, having not had a full panic attack in four weeks, and having only had minor symptoms in her most anxiety-provoking situations. Looking longer term, she set new goals of flying to visit family overseas, and also wanted to prepare for her sister's wedding, which was set for three months' time. She knew she would need to be in a lot of larger groups, and would receive a lot of scrutiny from other guests, and would not want to rely on any reassurance from her mother or sister. As such, she focussed her plans for the next three months on greater exposure to larger groups, actively allowing herself to be more central in events so as to reinforce how quickly symptoms remit and how little people notice.

Concluding Remarks

While panic attacks are a common reaction in many psychological disorders, panic disorder is a specific difficulty whereby the fear of panic attacks creates a vicious cycle of avoidance and further attacks. Treatment focusses on challenging the beliefs an individual has about their panic attacks, and exposing them to panic symptoms as well as avoided situations, to help them learn the true causes of their symptoms, and to discover that panic attacks, while unpleasant, are benign. The use of breathing techniques and hierarchies are two of the things that separate the currently recommended approaches, but in both cases cognitive techniques and interoceptive exposure are key.

Further Reading

Clark DM, Salkovskis PM. Panic disorder. K Hawton, PM Salkovskis, J Kirk, DM Clark (Eds.), *Cognitive Behaviour Therapy: A Practical Guide* [Internet]. 2009 [accessed 21 November 2024]; https://oxcadatresources.com/wp-content/uploads/2018/06/Cognitive-Therapy-for-Panic-Disorder_IAPT-Manual.pdf.

Craske MG, Barlow DH. *Mastery of Your Anxiety and Panic: Therapist Guide*. 4th ed. New York: Oxford University Press; 2007.

References

1. Brown TA, Cash TF. The phenomenon of nonclinical panic: Parameters of panic, fear, and avoidance. *J Anxiety Disord.* 1990;**4**(1):15–29.
2. Norton GR, Dorward J, Cox BJ. Factors associated with panic attacks in nonclinical subjects. *Behav Ther.* 1986;**17**(3):239–252.
3. Kessler RC, Chiu WT, Demler O, Walters EE. Prevalence, severity, and comorbidity of 12-Month DSM-IV disorders in the national comorbidity survey replication. *Arch Gen Psychiatry.* 2005;**62**(6):617–627.
4. Kessler RC, Berglund P, Demler O, Jin R, Merikangas KR, Walters EE. Lifetime prevalence and age-of-onset distributions of DSM-IV disorders in the national comorbidity survey replication. *Arch Gen Psychiatry.* 2005;**62**(6):593–602.
5. Eaton WW, Kessler RC, Wittchen HU, Magee WJ. Panic and panic disorder in the United States. *Am J Psychiatry.* 1994;**151**(3):413–420.
6. Kessler RC, Chiu WT, Jin R, Ruscio AM, Shear K, Walters EE. The epidemiology of panic attacks, panic disorder, and agoraphobia in the national comorbidity survey replication. *Arch Gen Psychiatry.* 2006;**63**(4):415–424.
7. Shear MK, Brown TA, Barlow DH, Money R, Sholomskas DE, Woods SW, et al. Multicenter collaborative panic disorder severity scale. *Am J Psychiatry.* 1997;**154**(11):1571–1575.

8. Shear MK, Rucci P, Williams J, Frank E, Grochocinski V, Vander Bilt J, et al. Reliability and validity of the panic disorder severity scale: Replication and extension. *J Psychiatr Res*. 2001;**35**(5):293–296.
9. Chambless DL, Caputo GC, Jasin SE, Gracely EJ, Williams C. The mobility inventory for agoraphobia. *Behav Res Ther*. 1985;**23**(1):35–44.
10. Chambless DL, Sharpless BA, Rodriguez D, McCarthy KS, Milrod BL, Khalsa SR, et al. Psychometric properties of the mobility inventory for agoraphobia: Convergent, discriminant, and criterion-related validity. *Behav Ther*. 2011;**42**(4):689–699.
11. OxCADAT Resources [Internet]. 2018 [accessed 11 January 2025]. OxCADAT Resources for cognitive therapy for PTSD, social anxiety disorder and panic disorder. Panic Disorder Questionnaires and Therapy Materials. https://oxcadatresources.com/panic-disorder-questionnaires-and-therapy-materials/.
12. Charney DS, Heninger GR, Breier A. Noradrenergic function in panic anxiety: Effects of yohimbine in healthy subjects and patients with agoraphobia and panic disorder. *Arch Gen Psychiatry*. 1984;**41**(8):751–763.
13. Sheehan DV. Should not panic disorders be classified as panic disorders, with or without agoraphobia, rather than agoraphobia, with or without panic attacks (as in DSM-III)? *J Clin Psychopharmacol*. 1982;**2**(6):18s.
14. Venkatesh A, Pauls DL, Crowe R, Noyes R, Van Valkenburg C, Martins JB, et al. Mitral valve prolapse in anxiety neurosis (panic disorder). *Am Heart J*. 1980;**100**(3):302–305.
15. Pariser SF, Pinta ER, Jones BA. Mitral valve prolapse syndrome and anxiety neurosis/panic disorder. *Am J Psychiatry*. 1978;**135**(2):246–247.
16. Jacob RG. Panic disorder and the vestibular system. *Psychiatr Clin North Am*. 1988;**11**(2):361–374.
17. Jacob RG, Møller MB, Turner SM, Wall C. Otoneurological examination in panic disorder and agoraphobia wih panic attacks: A pilot study. *Am J Psychiatry*. 1985;**142**(6):715–720.
18. Klein DF. False suffocation alarms, spontaneous panics, and related conditions: An integrative hypothesis. *Arch Gen Psychiatry*. 1993;**50**(4):306–317.
19. Klein DF. Delineation of two drug-responsive anxiety syndromes. *Psychopharmacologia*. 1964;**5**(6):397–408.
20. Klein E, Metz L. Differential drug response of panic and agoraphobic avoidance in a case of panic disorder. *Acta Psychiatr Scand*. 1990;**82**(1):86–87.
21. Chouinard G, Annable L, Fontaine R, Solyom L. Alprazolam in the treatment of generalized anxiety and panic disorders: A double-blind placebo-controlled study. *Psychopharmacology (Berl)*. 1982;**77**(3):229–233.
22. Marks I, Gelder M. A controlled retrospective study of behaviour therapy in phobic patients. *Br J Psychiatry*. 1965;**111**(476):561–573.
23. Barlow DH, Craske MG, Cerny JA, Klosko JS. Behavioral treatment of panic disorder. *Behav Ther*. 1989;**20**(2):261–282.
24. Craske MG, Brown TA, Barlow DH. Behavioral treatment of panic disorder: A two-year follow-up. *Behav Ther*. 1991;**22**(3):289–304.
25. Clark DM. A cognitive approach to panic. *Behav Res Ther*. 1986;**24**(4):461–470.
26. Salkovskis PM. Phenomenology, assessment and the cognitive model of panic. In: S Rachman, JD Maser (Eds.), *Panic: Psychological Perspectives* [Internet]. Hillsdale, NJ: L. Erlbaum Associates; 1988. https://books.google.co.uk/books?id=LhFsAAAAMAAJ.
27. Clark DM, Salkovskis PM, Hackmann A, Middleton H, Anastasiades P, Gelder M. A comparison of cognitive therapy, applied relaxation and imipramine in the treatment of panic disorder. *Br J Psychiatry*. 1994;**164**(6):759–769.
28. Papola D, Ostuzzi G, Tedeschi F, Gastaldon C, Purgato M, Giovane CD, et al. Comparative efficacy and acceptability of psychotherapies for panic disorder with or

without agoraphobia: systematic review and network meta-analysis of randomised controlled trials. *Br J Psychiatry.* 2022;**221**(3):507–519.

29. National Institute for Health and Care Excellence. Generalised anxiety disorder and panic disorder in adults: management [Internet]. 2020, p. 47. Report No.: CG113. www.nice.org.uk/guidance/cg113/resources/generalised-anxiety-disorder-and-panic-disorder-in-adults-management-pdf-35109387756997.
30. Clark DM, Salkovskis PM. Panic disorder. K Hawton, PM Salkovskis, J Kirk, DM Clark (Eds.), *Cognitive Behaviour Therapy: A Practical Guide* [Internet]. 2009 [accessed 24 November 2024]; https://oxcadatresources.com/wp-content/uploads/2018/06/Cognitive-Therapy-for-Panic-Disorder_IAPT-Manual.pdf.
31. Craske MG, Barlow DH. *Mastery of Your Anxiety and Panic: Therapist Guide.* 4th ed. New York: Oxford University Press; 2007.
32. Craske MG, Barlow DH. *Mastery of Your Anxiety and Panic: Therapist Guide.* 5th ed. Oxford: Oxford University Press; 2022.
33. Roth A, Pilling S. The CBT competencies framework for depression and anxiety disorders. *Lond UK Cent Outcome Res Eval.* 2007.
34. Hool N, Bennett R, Corrie S, Cox A, Curran J, French S, et al. *BABCP Core Curriculum* [Internet]. Bury: British Association for Behavioural & Cognitive Psychotherapies; 2021 p. 27. https://babcp.com/Core-Curriculum.
35. Clark DM, Salkovskis PM, Hackmann A, Wells A, Ludgate J, Gelder M. Brief cognitive therapy for panic disorder: A randomized controlled trial. *J Consult Clin Psychol.* 1999;**67**(4):583–589.
36. Barlow DH, Craske MG. *Mastery of Your Anxiety and Panic: Workbook.* 4th ed. New York; Oxford University Press; 2007.
37. American Psychiatric Association. *Diagnostic and Statistical Manual of Mental Disorders,* Fifth Edition, Text Revision. Washington, DC, American Psychiatric Association, 2022.

Chapter 13

Social Anxiety Disorder

with Rachel Handley

In this chapter we will help you to be able to:

- Explain what Social Anxiety Disorder is and how it typically presents, including distorted mental representations and selective focus of attention.
- Describe and use evidence-based CBT protocols for Social Anxiety Disorder.
- Choose and use appropriate formulation models for CBT for Social Anxiety Disorder.
- Describe the importance of using exposure to social situations in any treatment plan.
- Develop a treatment plan for CBT for Social Anxiety Disorder, using appropriate measures.
- Take account of comorbidity in managing CBT for Social Anxiety Disorder.

Introduction

Initially considered as part of the range of specific phobias, Social Anxiety Disorder has been the subject of intense scientific interest since the mid-1980s. The central conundrum of Social Anxiety Disorder – that of understanding how individuals can remain fearful of situations that are experienced so frequently – has led to a range of interesting theories and studies. At present, there are two main models of social anxiety that attempt to explain how the problem maintains itself, each with a substantial evidence base and well-established treatment protocol.

This chapter will start by defining what Social Anxiety Disorder is, including its diagnostic criteria and key features. We will then explore how our understanding Social Anxiety Disorder has developed, before looking at the current models for treatment and how these might be applied to specific cases.

What Is Social Anxiety Disorder?

Social Anxiety Disorder (then known as Social Phobia) was first classified as a distinct disorder in the Third Edition of the Diagnostic and Statistical Manual (DSM-III) [1] following proposals that it may be qualitatively different from other phobias [2,3]. Since this time, the definition of Social Anxiety Disorder has been successively refined, leading to its current criteria in the Fifth Edition of the DSM [4].

The first two of these is that the individual experiences 'marked fear or anxiety about one or more social situations in which the individual is exposed to possible scrutiny by others' when they fear they 'will act in a way or show anxiety symptoms that will be negatively evaluated'. This is a helpfully cognitive set of criteria, as it's the precise content of the patient's predictions that define if this is social anxiety. Only if the patient fears being negatively evaluated, and if the expected negative evaluation is focussed on the way they act or anxiety symptoms being noticed, can this be social anxiety disorder. This helps separate out these patients from those with other anxiety disorders, whose fears may be on being rejected for other reasons, or on wider concerns about what might happen at a social event.

The following three criteria are that the relevant social situations 'almost always provoke fear or anxiety' and 'are avoided or endured with intense fear or anxiety', which is 'out of proportion to the actual threat posed'. Again, this helps to separate out social anxiety from other disorders regarding social situations, in that the fear doesn't dissipate during the event or move onto a new focus. From a cognitive perspective, we would assume that this is because the individuals do not believe that their feared outcomes are unfounded – for the socially anxious patient, at least some of their expectations either do come true, or are at risk of coming true, throughout the social event. As the fear is out of proportion, it must be that there is a mismatch somewhere, between the patient's beliefs about the situation, and reality.

The sixth criterion is that the problem persists for at least six months, and indeed the average course is much longer than this. While social anxiety disorder (unlike specific phobias) rarely starts in early childhood [5,6], it is more commonly precipitated in adolescence, with a median age of onset of 13 years old [7]. It has been suggested that this may be due to the change in key attachment figures at this point in a person's development, from parents to peers, which brings with it far more ambiguity in social cues, and greater risk of rejection [8]. In any case, once Social Anxiety has developed it shows relatively low levels of remittance [9] even in comparison to fairly persistent disorders such as Generalised Anxiety Disorder, explaining the significant adult population seeking treatment.

There are two main measures commonly used to assess and monitor the key symptoms of Social Anxiety Disorder: the Social Phobia Inventory (SPIN) [10] and the Liebowitz Social Anxiety Scale (LSAS) [11,12]. The SPIN is a 17-item measure that can be used weekly, and covers a range of symptoms and situations that the individual may find anxiety provoking or distressing. The LSAS is a 24-item scale that assesses a wider range of possibly avoided situations, and separately rates the individual's fear of the situation and their avoidance. Further measures that can be helpful at initial assessment and review are the Social Cognitions Questionnaire [13], the Social Behaviour Questionnaire and the Social Attitudes Questionnaire, which respectively assess for the possible cognitions, safety behaviours and underlying attitudes that are commonly found in Social Anxiety Disorder [14], and which successful treatment should help to reduce.

Social Anxiety Treatment

As described above, social anxiety disorder involves a persistent and disproportionate fear or anxiety of events where a person might be negatively evaluated due to how they perform or due to noticeable anxiety symptoms. However, this creates a conundrum; given that social interaction is ubiquitous in everyday life, how do people continue to fear social situations despite being constantly exposed?

This question led to various suggestions being made; perhaps the feared outcomes are occurring, due to the impact of anxiety on the social performance of the patient [15], or due to genuine social skills deficits [16]. Alternatively, the difference could be cognitive; those with social anxiety may selectively recall negative feedback [17], and negatively appraise their performance even if it was not objectively problematic [18,19]. It was also theorised that there may be evolutionary priming towards social fears, due to the cost of missing threat cues in social situations in the past (and so being cast out from the group) [20], and that social anxiety behaviours may have been a way of avoiding challenging the dominant group members unnecessarily [21].

Bringing these theories together, Clark and Wells proposed that social anxiety is maintained by safety-seeking behaviours and an internal focus of attention. Together these both prevent disconfirmation of the feared negative evaluation (e.g. through avoidance of the particular feared social interactions or hiding anxiety symptoms) and provide further evidence to support the fears, as interoceptive information (e.g. about anxiety symptoms) is interpreted as confirming the individual's beliefs about how they must be coming across negatively to others. For example, on sitting down to dinner in a restaurant with friends, an individual who fears such social events might experience the activation of unhelpful and inaccurate assumptions about the level of social 'performance' required. They may assume that all conversation at the dinner table needs to be charming, witty and full of interesting anecdotes. They may assume that it is their responsibility to make sure conversation does not falter and that those around them are entertained. The person might understandably fear that they will fall short of such high standards, that they may not have anything witty or interesting to say and that they will stammer and trip over their words, and that this will betray their anxiety and those around them will consider them to be boring and pathetic. The person may then work hard to avoid others drawing these conclusions and potentially rejecting them. They may rehearse topics of conversation in their heads, run through anecdotes in their minds before sharing them out loud and speak quickly or quietly to avoid drawing too much attention to themselves. Whilst rehearsing their planned conversation the individual is focussed internally and unable to focus fully on the interaction around them. They imagine themselves as coming across as mousy and quiet, like a tiny little person barely able to peak over the table at their friends, and become increasingly self-conscious. They become more and more aware of anxiety symptoms in their body and a lump steadily forming in their throat which in turn makes them certain they will be unable to get their words out when they do finally pluck up the courage to speak. The image in their heads and the heightened awareness of what is going on in their body make them feel certain that others will judge them as boring and pathetic. When they do attempt to join the conversation they find that the conversation has moved on from the topic that they had been rehearsing in their mind and they double down on their efforts to think of something, anything interesting to say becoming more and more self-conscious and self-focussed. When the person leaves the situation their memories are not of how the event really went, of friends laughing together around a table, swapping some interesting, some mundane, some serious and some silly chat, but rather of the mousy, quiet person they pictured in their head and their perceived failure to meet their own high standards for social performance.

Following this, an alternative model was proposed by Rapee and Heimberg [22]. Similarly to Clark and Wells, they propose that individuals with social anxiety have a representation of how they are coming across in social situations, and how the audience will expect them to come across, and will over-value coming across well. In this model, the representation is built from all cues and information that a person can monitor – their facial expressions, posture, actions and any internal feelings that may manifest in outward appearance (for example, feeling hot equalling sweating). This is combined with other data (memories and external cues) to give a distorted self-image. Said image isn't how the patient generally views themselves, but is what they think the audience is perceiving. Historical information – including negative comments that others have previously said to them, memories of how they appeared in the past from mirrors and photographs and prior negative experiences – provides the base image onto which all current information from various internal and external cues is added.

Furthermore, in this model the individual assumes that others are and will be inherently critical, and so likely to negatively evaluate them. As such, this model proposes that those with social anxiety will split their attention between the internal cues, and negative external cues, such as people seeming disinterested. Due to the difference in how they think they should be coming across compared to how they think they are being perceived, they predict negative evaluation and future social danger or loss, and so become anxious. That anxiety leads to further cognitive, behavioural and physiological responses, which impair social performance and lead to more negative internal and external cues.

One key difference between these theories is in the proposed behaviour of socially anxious individuals towards negative cues from others in their feared situations; Hope and Heimberg propose that these individuals selectively attend towards such cues, while Clark and Wells propose that they selectively attend away. In an attempt to determine this, various studies have been conducted exploring where such individuals appeared to focus their attention, measured by recording how quickly they noted a target item subsequently placed in the same location [23,24,25]. These studies found, as both theories would assume, that social phobics react faster than average when the target item appears after a negative social word, mirroring the selective attention towards their own negative social evaluations [24]. The studies also found that such individuals, when in a socially anxious state reacted slower than average when the target appeared where a negative face had been, suggesting that their attention was not in that spot, and has actively attended away from the negative face [25]. While this would appear to support the theory proposed by Clark and Wells, it could also be taken that they had first attended, and then actively looked away – that they attend to negative external cues but only transiently.

Efficacy Data for CBT for Social Anxiety Disorder

In a major meta-analysis of psychological and pharmacological interventions for Social Anxiety Disorder it was found that individual CBT had the highest efficacy of all the psychological models reviewed [26]. This study reviewed data from 15 trials involving individual CBT, and 28 trials involving group CBT (the next most effective psychological intervention). In line with this, England's NICE guidance is to offer individual CBT as the first choice treatment intervention [27].

In considering the components within each treatment, one interesting study to bear in mind is that of Warnock-Parkes et al., which looked specifically at the impact of a session focussed on video-feedback, compared to control periods of therapy [28]. This study found that, when conducted following the guidance given in the paper, this particular intervention can have a significant impact, justifying its early inclusion in Clark's protocol.

Co-morbidity and Treatment

Social anxiety disorder is one where there is frequent comorbidity with other disorders, especially depression, other anxiety disorders and drug and alcohol abuse [29,30]. In such cases, social anxiety disorder is often found to begin prior to comorbidities, especially in depression, where social anxiety has the earlier onset in three quarters of cases [31]. Social anxiety disorder also correlates significantly with having experienced early socially traumatic events [32].

When considering how this should impact treatment, one suggestion is to focus on the functional linkage of the disorders: does one stem from managing the cognitions or symptoms of the other, or are they independent [8]? They additionally recommend considering the historical patterns of the disorders: which one had first onset, does one precede the other in changes in severity and does one of the disorders remain even when the other is in remission, as all of these would be indicators of the likely primary issue? Generally, if depression is secondary, then it may be better to treat the social anxiety disorder first, as this has better treatment outcomes of the two [8].

It is also important to distinguish between social anxiety and two similar issues – shyness and avoidant personality disorder. In particular, while shyness can be seen as a problem to some people, and does correlate with a number of Axis I disorders [33], it does not result in significant negative impact on functioning outside of the normal range [34] and so is not an appropriate thing to pathologise or treat in itself.

Picking a Protocol

As described above, there are a range of ways of conceptualising Social Anxiety Disorder, and so a range of possible ways to structure therapy. Currently, the most commonly used manualised approaches for treatment of Social Anxiety Disorder in the UK are based on:

- Clark's (2001) 'A Cognitive Perspective on Social Phobia' [35], (most recently elaborated in the 2018 CT-SAD-A manual [8]) and
- Hope, Heimberg and Turk's (2006) '*Managing Social Anxiety: A Cognitive-Behavioral Therapy Approach, Therapist Guide*' [36] (currently on its third edition in 2019 [37]).

Each of these specific protocols has its strengths, and have a good evidence base for their efficacy. Both models formulate the condition as involving a number of processes to maintain itself, as unlike in many other anxiety disorders, the phobic object itself (the audience) is affected by the individual's reactions. A key difference between the models is in the patient's expected focus of attention – while Clark's model predicts that this will be primarily internal during social situations, Heimberg's model assumes more of a split between the internal and scanning for negative external cues. See Table 13.1.

As always, it is important to remember that these protocols have more to unite them than divide, and thus picking exactly how to work with your patient is mostly about considering which feels like the best fit for them. Both models focus on negative appraisals before, during and after social situations, and both protocols include the use of both cognitive work and exposure to feared situations. As such, when picking how to approach your case, it can be useful to consider whether the patient describes a predominantly inward focus of attention, or a mix of this and scanning for negative external cues.

Table 13.1 A table comparing the Clark and Hope, Heimberg and Turk protocols for the treatment of Social Anxiety Disorder

Protocol	Clark (2001) [35]	Hope, Heimberg and Turk (2006) [36]
Theory of Social Anxiety Disorder	Individuals with SAD are likely to have excessively high standards for social performance, conditional beliefs about the social evaluation caused by suboptimal performance, and negative core beliefs about the self that are triggered in social situations. Social anxiety is then maintained by various cycles: 1) Being anxious causes anxiety symptoms, which leads to further perceived danger 2) Focussing attention of sensations and cognitions prevent accurate processing of benign social information 3) Threat appraisals cause safety behaviours, which worsen social performance, and/or cause further physical sensations.	Individuals with SAD highly value positive appraisal but expect others to be inherently critical. In social situations, they focus on their mental representation of how they are coming across and perceived threat from the environment, as well as internal cues. They then compare their perceived performance against their perception of the audience's expectations, and so assume they are being judged. This leads to anxiety, which in turn leads to a range of exacerbating thoughts, behaviours and sensations.
Aim of treatment	Treatment aims to: • Help patients determine that their internal focus and safety behaviours impair their social performance. • Correct their negative self-image • Correct their predictions about negative evaluation from others • Modify their underlying conditional and core beliefs	Treatment aims to: • Shift attentional focus • Restructure cognitions regarding how the audience appraises the individual • Gain feedback on actual performance • Ensure dropping of maladaptive behaviours
Recent updates	Working on socially traumatic memories, and specialised protocol for adolescents	Focussing on values
Recommended structure of therapy	Up to 14 sessions, each 90 minutes duration, over 18 weeks	15 sessions, each 60 minutes duration, plus 1x90 minute exposure session, over 16–20 weeks
Interventions used	• Behavioural experiments, including specified set of experiments	• Fear and avoidance hierarchy • Cognitive restructuring including thinking biases

Table 13.1 (cont.)

Protocol	Clark (2001) [35]	Hope, Heimberg and Turk (2006) [36]
	• Video-feedback • Attention training • Surveys • Cognitive discussion techniques • Modifying Images	• Exposure • Further ad hoc tools for challenging cognitions • Core belief work
Helpful when	Focus of attention is primarily inward, and where the individual can verbalise what negative concept they fear others noticing about them	Focus of attention is shared between internal and negative external cues, and when key misappraisals are either global views of the self or excessive standards of others and the expectation of others to be generally critical

Clark

As mentioned, the Clark and Wells model of social anxiety (see Figure 13.1) proposes that in social situations perceived as threatening, the socially anxious individual experiences the activation of unhelpful assumptions or rules about social performance. They believe that their own social performance will violate these rules and that they will be judged negatively by others. The socially anxious individual will therefore engage in safety seeking behaviours to prevent these negative judgements. Safety-seeking behaviours may include avoiding the social situation altogether, avoiding aspects of the situation, attempting to hide themselves or hide or control their anxiety symptoms, monitoring their performance and effortfully attempting to enhance performance. These safety-seeking behaviours prevent the person from disconfirming their fears about how they will be judged by others, can contaminate the social interaction (negatively impacting social 'performance') and further serve to focus the individual's attention on themselves. When focussed on themselves they become aware of interoceptive information that is taken as evidence that they are likely to be coming across negatively and of impending judgement by others. It is often the case that they have a distorted and inaccurate mental image of how they are coming across to others which is processed as further evidence of appearing negatively to others and so the social anxiety cycle is maintained.

Building on this model, the treatment of Social Anxiety aims to disconfirm the feared perceptions of how others judge them. This is facilitated by the key steps in the treatment. First, the patient and therapist collaborate to draw out an idiosyncratic version of the social anxiety formulation based on a recent, typical experience of anxiety. Typically the patient is then encouraged to experiment with dropping safety-seeking behaviours and focussing externally whilst engaging in a social interaction in the therapy session with an external volunteer, for example, a short conversation on a pre-determined topic. This interaction is then repeated, but this time the patient is encouraged to re-engage in their safety-seeking behaviours and self-focussed attention. The patient rates anxiety, self-consciousness, and the likelihood of their

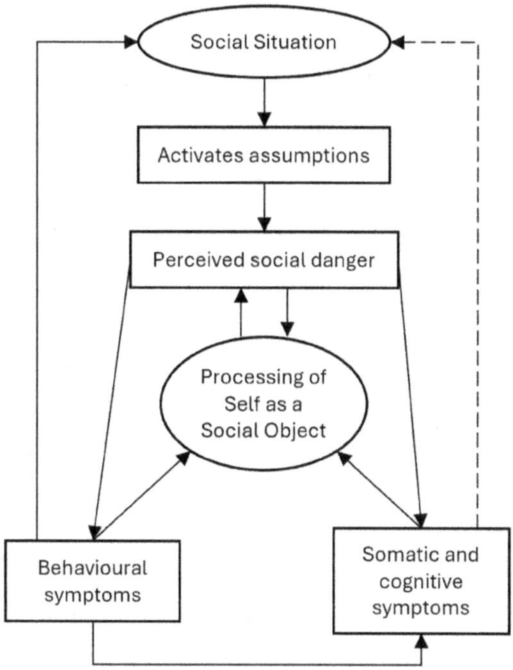

Figure 13.1 Clark and Wells 1995 model, reproduced with permission from Guilford Press.

feared social outcomes and evaluations having taken place. They compare these ratings across conditions. The patient is then invited to view both interactions on a video recording that has been made of the experiments, again rating the identified predictions both before and after viewing and comparing these. Finally, the patient is provided with feedback from the volunteer who has rated the same items with respect to how the patient has come across. Therapist and patient then review the 'data' from all these ratings together and the therapist uses Socratic dialogue to draw out key learning points. The patient typically discovers that they anticipate that they will come across more negatively in the conversations than they feel they have done afterwards. They typically learn that they feel more anxious and self-conscious when they are self-focussed and using their safety-seeking behaviours than when they focus externally and also that they feel they have come across better in the latter scenario. When they view the video they typically also learn that they judge themselves more harshly than they appear on screen. Finally, on reviewing the honest feedback of the volunteer, they typically learn that other people judge them much less harshly than they judge themselves.

The rest of the therapy largely builds on and extends the learning from this key experiment. Patients collaboratively agree further behavioural experiments to be carried out within sessions and importantly in their everyday life that test out their social concerns. Experiments include those testing the occurrence and observability of their anxiety symptoms and behaviours, and those testing outcomes if these symptoms and behaviours are present (often deliberately exaggerated) and observed. Typical learning from the former is that symptoms are not noticeable or obvious to others, and from the latter, that the feared catastrophe, such as social rejection or harsh personal judgement, does not occur. In essence, the patient learns that they are socially acceptable, just as they are, without attempting to conceal or control their symptoms and behaviours.

Therapy may also include attention training components, where the patient is taught to recognise their internal focus of attention and to switch to an external focus of attention. This is usually practised initially in non-social situations (such as paying attention to sights, sounds or sensory details in the environment) and then in social interactions such as conversations with others. Where individuals become aware of self-imagery in social situations that is linked to early negative social experiences, for example childhood bullying, the therapy may also include re-scripting of these early memories. As with all CBT approaches, therapy also includes a 'blueprint' or drawing together of learning in therapy to enable the patient to take learning forward and as a tool for relapse prevention.

As an example, Cathy was a successful young professional who sought treatment of social anxiety as she found it was increasingly interfering with her ability to engage in meetings and presentations at work that were essential for her role and career progression. Cathy and her therapist worked together to formulate a recent example when this had been problematic for her (see Figure 13.2), to understand the thoughts, behaviours and attentional processes that were maintaining this and added to this from other similar social situations. They discovered together that when Cathy was in these situations, particularly with senior colleagues present, she was concerned that she would blush and stammer, that her colleagues would notice this and judge her to be incompetent, weak and childish. This was understandably very anxiety provoking so, in order to stop these judgements being made, Cathy was working hard to prevent and cover-up blushing and stammering and where possible to avoid being observed in these situations in the first place. Cathy would often make excuses for meetings, suggest that colleagues present work they had co-produced or keep her contributions to the bare minimum to avoid others being focussed on her. She would try and avoid attention by sitting at the edge of the room at meetings, keeping her head down and avoiding eye-contact. When she could not avoid speaking up at meetings or doing presentations Cathy would script and rehearse everything she planned to say extensively and run it through in her head to practise sounding fluent and coherent. Cathy wore her hair down and thick foundation to try and conceal blushing on her face and she always wore high-necked jumpers and shirts at work as she was particularly conscious of blushing on her chest which she felt was the most observable symptom of her anxiety. When asked where her attention was focussed in these moments when she was looking down, avoiding eye-contact and rehearsing her contribution to meetings, Cathy realised that she was very much focussed on herself and how she was feeling internally. She was able to identify an image she had of herself in these moments as small, almost childlike, stuttering helplessly and repeatedly and looking deeply red and blotchy all over her face and chest. This image increased her sense of herself as coming across as weak and incompetent and made her even more anxious. She realised that as her anxiety built she became very aware of her cheeks and chest 'burning', a dry mouth and a lump in her throat. These physical symptoms further grabbed her attention which was firmly focussed on herself within the situations she feared and made her feel even more self-conscious and aware of her internal negative self-image. She felt even more convinced that her blushing must be painfully obvious to all and that she would not be able to get her words out, further confirming her fears that she would be negatively judged.

In order to demonstrate these processes more clearly in action and how her problems were being maintained, the therapist agreed with Cathy that a 'stooge' (a person external to the patient-therapist dyad) could come and have a conversation with Cathy. As Cathy was not generally anxious about brief social conversations outside of the workplace, the therapist and

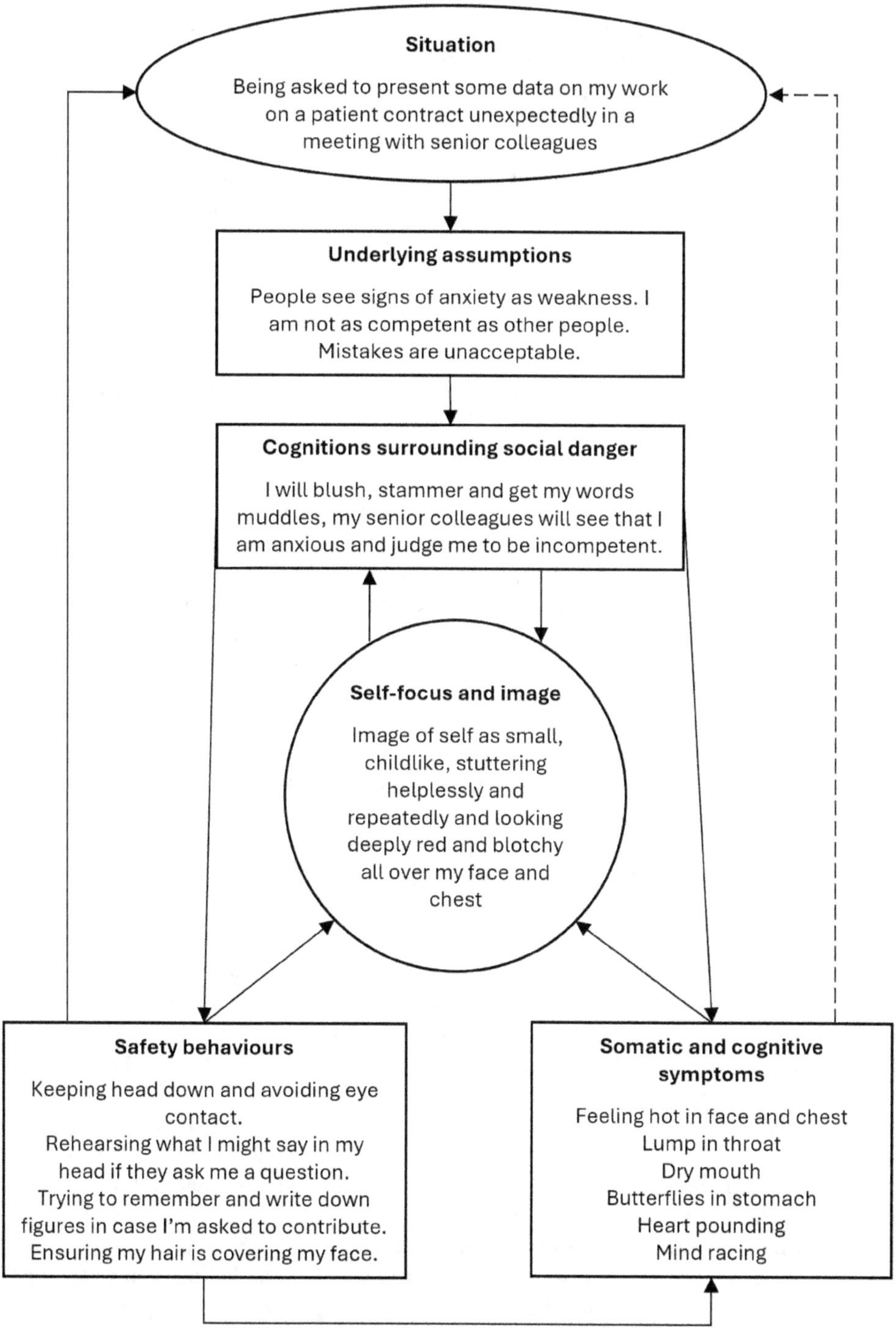

Figure 13.2 Example of model for Cathy, adapted from Clark and Wells 1995 model, reproduced with permission from Guilford Press.

Cathy agreed that she would instead do a three-minute presentation of an area of her work to the stooge. Cathy rated how anxious she felt she would be, how self-conscious, how observable her blushing and stammering would be and how much the person would judge her to be weak and incompetent. She then completed the presentation whilst engaging in her safety-seeking behaviours, focussing particularly on rehearsing everything she was about to say in her head and avoiding eye-contact with the stooge. After the conversation, Cathy rated again the items she had rated before the experiment and agreed to do another brief presentation to the same person, but this time, in as best she could, dropping her safety-seeking behaviours. To keep this as simple as possible, the therapist encouraged Cathy to try and just say whatever came into her head (without rehearsing it) and to make more eye contact. Ratings of the same items were taken once again before and after the presentation.

Cathy found this experience challenging but really helpful as she was able to see that she felt less anxious and that she performed better when she was not engaging in her safety behaviours and self-focus. She viewed a recording of the conversations and was quite struck by how different she looked to the image she had in her head. Whilst she was still inclined to think she came across as rather less confident than she would like and noticed her anxiety symptoms, they were not nearly as clearly observable as she predicted and, in fact, she thought she did ok overall. When she went through feedback from the person to whom she had presented with her therapist she was really surprised to find that they hadn't noticed her stammer or blush at all and found her presentation professional, informative and interesting and that the idea that she was weak or incompetent hadn't occurred to them at all.

Over the next few sessions Cathy engaged in further behavioural experiments, first presenting to more people and simulating meeting situations where she had to speak spontaneously, and then deliberately exaggerating her stammering and blushing using make-up. Throughout these experiments Cathy was encouraged to drop her safety behaviours and to focus externally. The therapist worked with Cathy to do a short session of attention training to help with this; first practising attending to external non-social stimuli (such as sounds and colours) and switching back and forth to an internal, self-conscious focus of attention and then applying this more in social interactions. She made many adjustments such as wearing tops that exposed the blushing on her chest, tying her hair back and reducing the make-up she usually wore to cover her blushing. In parallel, Cathy and her therapist planned behavioural experiments for her to conduct between sessions in her workplace and beyond, turning every meeting and workplace gathering into an opportunity to test out her fears. In these experiments, Cathy consistently discovered that people did not judge her as she feared. The within session experiments were helpful as she was able to gain direct feedback from 'stooges'. In exaggerating the symptoms she was able to see that people generally really didn't notice things she thought were entirely unmissable and even when they did they didn't use the criteria she thought to judge others. She worked with her therapist to make predictions about how she would know if her colleagues judged her to be weak or incompetent without directly asking them. These included directly contradicting or ignoring her contributions to meetings, putting her down or deliberately excluding her from other work projects. Again, Cathy found that not only did these not occur, but that the more she spoke up and responded 'in the moment', the more work she was entrusted with and the more her opinion was sought.

Later in therapy Cathy suffered a setback when she went to visit her parents and her mother suggested that Cathy might not want to wear a particular outfit to a family wedding they were attending as 'it will show that awful blotchy redness on your chest and people will think it very odd'. In session, Cathy and her therapist were able to identify how this triggered her assumptions about social performance and how, indeed, her mother's comments over the years in similar situations had probably contributed to the formation of her rules and standards about social performance. She recalled a particular occasion when she was very young when her parents had had friends in for an evening and she had been invited down in her nightdress to say goodnight at bedtime and she had felt very embarrassed and awkward. She recalled that she was blushing on her face and chest and that her siblings had laughed at this and her mother had ushered her out of the room in an embarrassed and concerned manner. She realised that this memory mirrored many aspects of the image she had of herself currently in social situations. She also realised that her mother also very likely had social anxiety and was particularly anxious about her own blushing. The therapist and Cathy worked together to identify the thoughts and feelings she had in that situation (I've let my parents down, I'm an embarrassment, I should not be seen by grown-ups . . .) and to generate more accurate and helpful alternatives (there was nothing wrong with how I appeared, kids will laugh at anything slightly different and my siblings were actually poking fun at my nightdress, my Mum was just anxious that I felt uncomfortable and had her own worries about blushing which other people don't share) and to update the memory in imagery. She chose to 're-enter' the memory herself as an adult and tell young Cathy that she was ok, she didn't need to leave, she just needed a little encouragement and that with time she would learn that her blushing wasn't something to worry about but something that people don't notice and many actually find endearing. She was able to tell herself that she would grow up to be successful at work and find that she could talk to people and groups of people in the workplace with confidence. She was even able to tell her mother not to worry, that Cathy was OK and that she should just notice how sweet she looked and give her a big cuddle.

Following this session Cathy was able to continue with her behavioural experiments until she had met all her therapy goals, bar a few big presentations at work that she had planned for the coming months in line with their work schedule. She and her therapist made a blueprint including this as a plan, along with all that she had learned about social anxiety and in particular the importance of testing things out, dropping her safety behaviours and externally focussing her attention. She was able to say at the end of therapy, 'it is ok to be me, I come across as competent and even confident at work when I am just myself'.

Hope, Heimberg and Turk

As explored above, the protocol is based on the theory that individuals with social anxiety build a negative mental representation of themselves in social situations due to both internal and external cues, which they then compare to their representation of what the audience will be expecting, and as such predict judgement and negative social consequences. This leads to anxiety, and resultant negative behaviours, sensations and cognitive symptoms of anxiety, leading in turn to further negative internal cues and negative external cues from the audience. A full picture of this formulation is shown in Figure 13.3; however, it is not recommended to use this model directly with patients, as it can be overly complicated to use in a collaborative manner, and so an ABC cycle is used instead.

Following this model, the treatment approach brings together psycho-education, graded exposure and cognitive restructuring regarding social fears in a step-by-step approach. Sessions one to three (or fewer, if the patient is able to work through this material more quickly) focus on explaining what a diagnosis of social anxiety means, and how thoughts, behaviours and feelings interact to maintain social anxiety, with a focus on how the

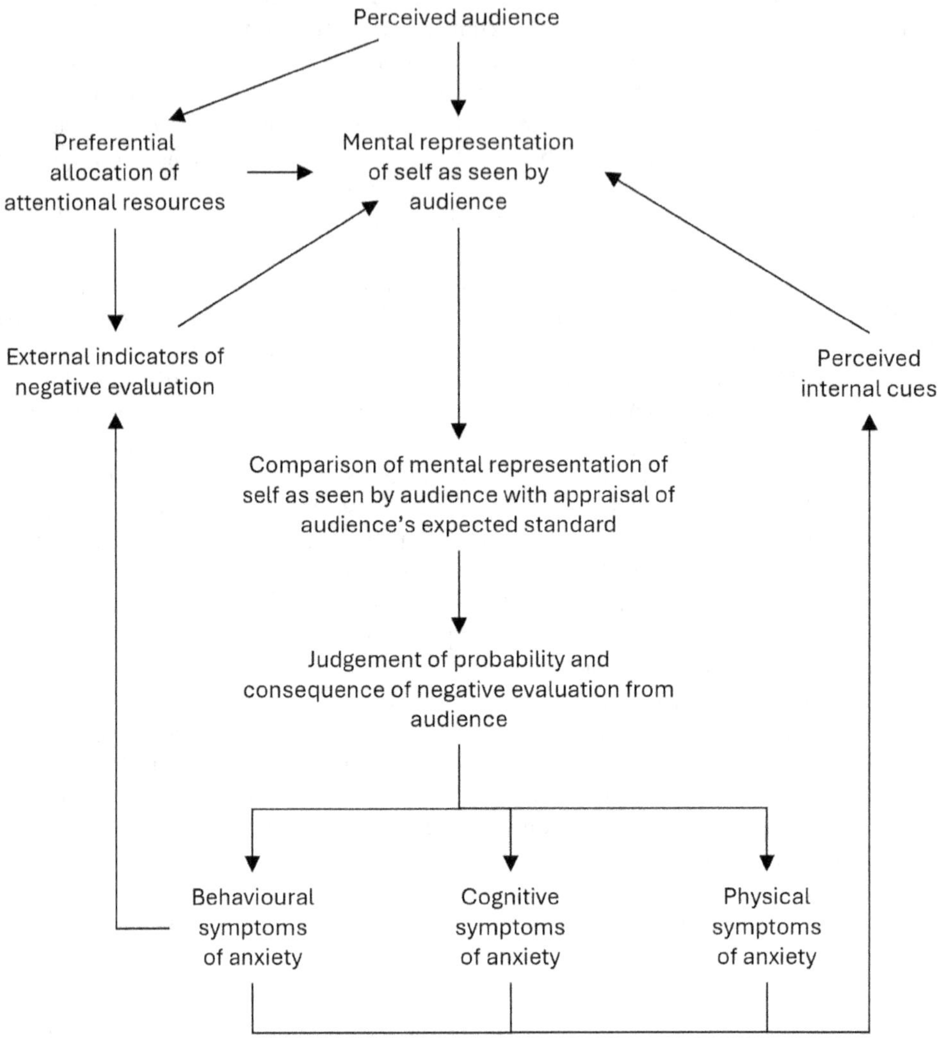

Figure 13.3 Hope, Heimberg and Turk (2006) model, reproduced with permission from Elsevier.

cognitions will initiate the cycle, and how the behaviour of avoidance will initially help, but over the long term will maintain and exacerbate the cycle.

The next session is devoted to creating a hierarchy of social fears. This starts with brainstorming possible social situations that can cause anxiety for the patient, aiming for a wide range of situations, but ensuring all are relevant in terms of creating social anxiety. To further widen the range, the therapist should then explore modifiers, which make the various situations more or less anxiety provoking, such as how many people will be there, or their ages. The therapist and patient will then create a Subjective Units of Distress Scale (SUDS), with anchor points of social situations that have caused 0%, 25%, 50%, 75% and 100% anxiety. Using this, the patient will rate each of the situations, both against their SUDS, and on a 0–100 avoidance scale. Using both of these ratings together, the final hierarchy can be devised, going from least anxiety-provoking situations up to most anxiety-provoking situations, and using the avoidance ratings to order those situations that cause the same level of anxiety. The hierarchy doesn't have to include all possible situations, but should contain a good range of situations of differing SUDS that the patient will have the opportunity to confront in their everyday life. This process not only provides a structure for future therapy work, but also helps the therapist to understand precisely what makes various situations anxiety provoking for the patient, and sets goals regarding the situations that the patient would like to confront without anxiety. As therapy continues, it can also be used to track progress, showing how far the patient's anxiety has reduced, and how much more able they are to approach avoided situations.

Prior to engaging in exposure, treatment moves onto the concept of cognitive restructuring, teaching patients to both identify and challenge their negative automatic thoughts (NATs) regarding social situations. This protocol lists a number of specific thinking errors that can occur in social anxiety, many of which split into self-based thoughts (those the person believes about themselves) and other-based thoughts (what they believe others will notice or think about them). These are:

- 'self-labelling' (I'm weird)
- 'other-labelling' (they'll think I'm weird)
- 'visible signs' (I will shake)
- 'other visible signs' (he will see me shake)
- 'self-social norms' (it is unacceptable to pause too long)
- 'other social norms' (they'll think I'm rude if I do that), [non-visible]
- 'symptoms' (my mind will race)
- 'past memories' (I always mess up those kinds of conversations)
- 'performance' (I won't be interesting enough)
- 'negative outcome' (people won't speak to me) and
- 'avoidance' (I should just leave) [38]

Treatment now moves onto exposure, and so the next session will be scheduled to last 90 minutes rather than the usual 60, to ensure there is enough time to fully experience the benefits. Ideally a situation causing 40–50% SUDS will be used, and one that can be role-played in the session with minimal acting – for example having a casual conversation with an acquaintance. The session will start with identifying the related NATs attached to the chosen situation, and challenging some (ideally those relating to the expected performance outcomes for this first exposure), creating a more rational response for the patient to remind themselves of during the exposure. The therapist will also help the patient set a clear behavioural goal for the exposure, such as to stay in the situation until the therapist ends it, or to say at least four things.

Exposure is then started, with the therapist getting the patient to rate their anxiety each minute, again using the SUDS, and then repeat their rational response. Other than these ratings and response repetitions, the therapist and patient should both focus on acting as though the situation is the actual concept from the hierarchy. Ideally the exposure continues until the patient has achieved their behavioural goals, and is ended at a point where they are fully engaged and focussed on the role-play.

After the exposure, the therapist leads a debrief, focussing on whether the behavioural goals were achieved, first from the patient's perspective, and then their own. Where there are major problematic safety behaviours undermining the patient's performance, one of these might be discussed each time, to consider the impact and explore whether repeating the exposure with additional behavioural goals around acting opposite to those safety behaviours. During debrief the therapist will also explore the NATs from prior to the exposure, and the rational response, to note any change in belief in the fears due to the exposure experience. If there is no change, then the reasons that the exposure was unable to achieve this can be explored, to refine future exposure plans. It is also useful to look for any new NATs that the exposure produced, so these can also be restructured. Finally, the SUDS ratings can be reviewed, to note either how anxiety dropped at points or over time, or how the patient met their behavioural goals in spite of the anxiety. If anxiety spiked at any point, this can be explored to better understand their difficulties as a whole, and create new exposure ideas or behavioural goals. Once all the reviews have been carried out, a summarising take home message can be created, to ensure the new information is taken on.

Further exposure sessions will follow a similar pattern to that above, and generally four to six such sessions are recommended. While some exposure exercises may involve leaving the therapy office to try things out in crowded situations or with strangers, it is recommended that the majority are done as in-office role plays, so that the specific fears and reactions the patient predicts can be tested out. To generalise the learning to the real world, homework can involve repeating the exercises in the actual situations from the hierarchy. Further cognitive restructuring, including working on core beliefs, is weaved in as needed, and final exposures may be based on testing out alternative core beliefs rather than purely working on the original hierarchy. Further psychoeducation and exposure exercises are also focussed specifically around conversation fears and public speaking fears, as these are common in many patients. Treatment is then finished off via relapse prevention work, focussing on setting specific further exposure goals, so that the patient is motivated not to stop making progress.

An example of this approach was taken with Henry, who struggled with social events such as parties, group dinners and evenings at the pub. He believed he was generally bad at these situations, and that others expected him to be funny and interesting, or he shouldn't be there. In such situations, he would rehearse what to say and focus intently on how others reacted when he spoke, looking for signs that they were bored or finding him lacking – such as someone interjecting or turning away. At the first signal of this, he would retreat into himself, trailing off and avoiding further conversation, often ruminating intently about how he had failed and what they were all thinking of him, and how he would be dropped from future social groups. Increasingly, Henry had limited his engagement in such events, only going if it was planned to be with a trusted small group, and then leaving if others came. He was also minimising time spent at 'essential' parties, such as major work social evenings, as well as drinking more than he would otherwise like on pub events, which then resulted in morning-after shame. He was not generally a heavy drinker, and as his attendance at social events was reduced at the time of assessment to only once every few weeks, his overall drinking was significantly below cut offs, though was clearly nonetheless having a negative impact on how he felt about himself. Henry came to therapy as his best friend had recently gotten engaged and he had been asked to be best man, and the idea of giving the speech had made him say he wasn't sure. Interestingly, Henry found one-on-one situations much less problematic, which in part he attributed to being able to monitor how he was being received better, and knowing that the person was interested as they had asked the question.

Early sessions explored the concept of Social Anxiety, and how this fitted with Henry's experiences and beliefs. Following this, an ABC cycle was created, focussing on the process of being at a recent social event at the pub where someone spoke over him, and Henry then thinking he was being boring, and so feeling anxious. How this then led to him stopping talking and withdrawing into a corner, ruminating and feeling awkward and tense. While in the short term, this made him feel less overtly scrutinised, and less at risk of humiliation, it also meant that the conversation moved on without him, and maintained his belief that he is boring. The therapist explored how typical this was for Henry, and he agreed this was a common occurrence for him, having a significant negative impact on his life. They then explored how this pattern of avoidance when he felt anxious meant that the anxiety would likely come back each time, that more and more situations were becoming anxiety-provoking, and he never found out what would happen to the anxiety if he remained. Over the following week, Henry was encouraged to draw out more cycles of other common situations where he felt anxious and avoided, to spot the thoughts and behaviours that were central to the issue. On reviewing these, the therapist helped Henry to further his understanding of the short term versus long term impacts of his avoidance. They also explored where his social anxiety had stemmed from, and where he had started learning his current rules and beliefs. Henry remembered particular times at school where he had been called dull, and his mother's comments that he shouldn't bore people, and no one liked someone who droned on and on. The therapist gently helped Henry consider where his mother's comments may have been coming from, and Henry realised that his mother had similar issues with social anxiety as he did. The therapist explored how this connected to the idea that there can be a genetic predisposition to becoming socially anxious, which can then be activated by certain experiences, which Henry found helpful, as he'd previously assumed that it was a lack of social skills that he had inherited.

Following this, the therapist and Henry devised a hierarchy of his feared situations, from chatting at lunch with his colleagues, to the proposed wedding speech. After creating anchor points, the situations were rated for SUDS and avoidance, and then ordered, as shown in Table 13.2.

Coming back to the idea of predisposition and prior experiences, therapy next focussed on the cognitions Henry had developed over time. The therapist started by explaining the concept that we all develop different ways of viewing the world, and our genetics and experiences can

Table 13.2 Henry's hierarchy of fear

Situation	SUDS	Avoidance
Giving a toast as best man	100	100
Go to work Christmas Party, chat with whoever is sat with, talk to at least 10 people	95	80
Go on work night out, answer questions and join in conversations	90	90
Hosting dinner party with work group, speak at least 5 times	85	75
Going to dinner party with work group, actively tell a story about what's being discussed without preparing	80	60
Go to pub with friends and other less well-known people and talk at least 5 times	75	80
Go to the pub with friends without excessive drinking and talk at least 5 times	60	50
Chat with colleagues at work over lunch, say at least 3 things	50	25

lead us to view social situations with 'Amber Glasses', where the world is tinted towards danger and threat. This then leads to automatic thoughts (ATs) in social situations, which fit with this tinting, and which tend to be accepted as fact. On exploring Henry's ATs, he was quick to notice his cognition of 'I'm boring' and 'others will think I'm boring', and on gentle questioning realised the related concerns of 'I'll say too much, talk for too long', 'I'll make a bad impression' and 'people won't want to speak to me again, will hope I'm not invited'. The therapist and Henry explored the thinking styles there each related to, respectively Self Labelling, Other Labelling, Self-Social Norms, Performance and Negative Outcome.

Using disputing questions, Henry was helped to evaluate these thoughts, and then come up with more rational responses. These included 'My friends may find me interesting', 'people keep inviting me, so they might enjoy speaking to me', 'speaking about a topic I'm passionate about doesn't mean I'm droning on', 'I only have to say things that are relevant, I don't have to be utterly fascinating'. While Henry did not initially believe these new thoughts 100%, he could see how acknowledging them as possible truths would make socialising easier and less anxiety-provoking, and so would be worth trying out.

The first exposure task was based on the concept of chatting to colleagues at work, and the therapist invited two other people as agreed with Henry to play additional colleagues. The specific scenario to be trialled was answering the question 'what did you do over the weekend?', which Henry often feared and would generally answer with 'not much'. Before starting the role play, the therapist and Henry briefly explored his key ATs regarding the scenario – that he would have nothing to say, that he would forget what he was saying and freeze and that the others would find him boring. The therapist focussed in on the concept of having nothing to say, and they brainstormed what options there were. She also explored the expected reactions of others if he did freeze or forget where he was, which he feared would include laughing at him or rolling their eyes.

To ensure the task was clearly defined, the therapist and Henry set clear goals of 'staying in the situation until the therapist ends it' and 'describing at least two activities I had done'. The additional role players then came in, and the therapist took an initial SUDS rating and then started the role play by asking what Henry had done over the weekend. Henry answered, briefly noting two activities (cooking and watching a football match) with limited elaboration. One of the stooges then mentioned they had watched the same match, and asked what he'd thought of the referee's decision. Henry was able to answer more fully at this point, after which the stooge gave their thoughts on the match and then the therapist stopped the role play. Throughout, the therapist had taken two other quick SUDs ratings, each of which Henry had put at lower than the start.

Asking how the role play had gone, Henry initially answered that he had been dull, describing boring activities that everyone does at the weekend. The therapist then explored first if Henry had managed his behavioural goal, and if this was different from how he does usually. Henry acknowledged that he had achieved this, and stated that his answers had probably been less boring that saying, 'not much'. The therapist reviewed if he had frozen, or forgotten what to say, and explored what he made of the stooge having watched the same match. Henry noted that the unplanned response he had given there was longer and together they reviewed the evidence from the others suggesting that while he'd spoken for longer, he hadn't appeared to have bored them. They also explored the reducing SUDs scores, and how the conversation had felt easier as he had continued. This was compared to his usual lunchtime experience, where he would feel less anxious to start once the conversation moved away from him, but then increasingly embarrassed as others successfully answered the question. His take home message, that he can answer the question of what he'd done over the weekend and that he may feel less anxious if he does overall, was worked on for homework, with him trying out answering this and similar questions at lunch with his real colleagues.

Five of the next seven sessions were likewise spent on role play exposures, covering increasingly complex and challenging situations, including telling stories, discussing politics and work dynamics, and answering personal questions about his life. These role plays were then used to promote changed interactions in vivo as homework, and then explored in the following sessions. Henry realised he had a tendency to try and turn every story into a joke, and so some exposures were repeated without finishing on a punchline, to see if he could have acceptable interactions if he was not always funny. Homework also involved putting himself in more potential social situations, by accepting more invitations out, and having lunch with colleagues each day rather than running errands. He was also supported to join the local football team, both because this was an interest of his, and to increase the number and frequency of opportunities to try out his new ways of being.

Two sessions in particular were focussed on the upcoming best man's speech, which Henry had decided to agree to undertake. Role plays were set up to helpfully replicate the situation, including him having pre-prepared notes, and a varying level of heckling and positive and negative audience responses, to feel more confident with giving the whole speech regardless of the reactions of the audience. The audience itself was mostly made up of the therapist and then empty chairs and a camera, though the final role play included a few additional audience members to consolidate the learning with new attendees.

Cognitive restructuring continued throughout these sessions, working from the concrete predictions to what others would be thinking and the reasons for their behaviour, down to Henry's central beliefs about him being boring and others being critical and judgemental. Two useful specific exercises were using a pie chart to re-examine all the reasons someone might interrupt him talking other than because they were bored, and creating a continuum of awfulness of occurrences, to determine how bad it would be if no one laughs at any given joke in a speech. This restructuring was weaved around the exposure exercises, and helped Henry to take bigger risks, and to continue in social situations when his feared initial concerns (being interrupted, not getting a big laugh) occasionally occurred, as they would for most people.

In the final sessions, the fear and avoidance hierarchy was re-rated, and Henry was surprised at how far items had come down on both scales. The feared wedding was still six weeks away at the point of completing the main therapy, and so the final two booster sessions were planned either side of this, to support him in carrying out the task, and then consolidating the learning from it. Said learning was surprisingly vivid – having practised giving speeches to role players, Henry had assumed that in reality things wouldn't go so well. Instead, when giving a speech to those who knew him and who were deeply connected to the subject matter, and who were generally happy and relaxed, the response was better than he could ever have hoped. His main takeaway was a powerful sense that audiences could actually be supportive and beneficent, reinforced by a photograph from the wedding of him speaking and his friend and friend's mother laughing deeply. While he knew not every joke had landed perfectly, he felt able to focus on the overall positives, and was proud at having completed a role he had thought he would never manage. He and the therapist explored how this could continue, with other, albeit smaller, opportunities for public speaking, so that he could maintain his sense that speaking socially was not as dangerous as he had always feared.

Concluding Remarks

Social Anxiety Disorder is a disorder characterised by a threat-based focus of attention, which as a result maintains a sense of anxiety despite frequent exposure to the feared stimuli. This is then further worsened by the use of safety behaviours, which both prevent disconfirmation of the feared outcomes, and impair social performance. Two different protocols for working with Social Anxiety Disorder have been thoroughly tested and shown to be effective, which differ primarily on their focus on an internal focus of attention or a split focus between this and external negative threat cues. In either case, treatment seeks to change focus of attention and problematic social cognitions, and encourage exposure without the use of safety behaviours.

Further Reading

Clark DM and Wells A. A cognitive model of social phobia. In: R. G. Heimberg, M. R. Liebowitz, D. A. Hope, F. R. Schneier (Eds.), *Social phobia: Diagnosis, assessment, and treatment.* (pp. 69–93). The Guilford Press; 1995.

Clark DM. Cognitive perspective on social phobia. In: Crozier WR, Alden LE (Eds.), *International Handbook of Social Anxiety: Concepts, Research, and Interventions Relating to the Self and Shyness* (pp. 405–430). New York: Wiley; 2001.

Hope DA, Heimberg RG, Turk CL. *Managing Social Anxiety, Therapist Guide: A Cognitive-Behavioral Therapy Approach*, 3rd Ed. Oxford: Oxford University Press; 2019.

References

1. American Psychiatric Association Staff. *Diagnostic and Statistical Manual of Mental Disorders (DSM-III).* Washington, DC: American Psychiatric Publishing; 1980.
2. Marks IM. The classification of phobic disorders. Br J Psychiatry. 1970;**116**(533):377–386.
3. Marks I, Gelder M. A controlled retrospective study of behaviour therapy in phobic patients. Br J Psychiatry. 1965;**111**(476):561–573.
4. American Psychiatric Association. *Diagnostic and Statistical Manual of Mental Disorders: DSM-5.* Washington, DC: American Psychiatric Association; 2013.
5. Wittchen HU, Stein MB, Kessler RC. Social fears and social phobia in a community sample of adolescents and young adults: Prevalence, risk factors and co-morbidity. Psychol Med. 1999;**29**(2):309–323.
6. Marks IM, Gelder M. Different ages of onset in varieties of phobia. Am J Psychiatry. 1966;**123**(2):218–221.
7. Kessler RC, Berglund P, Demler O, Jin R, Merikangas KR, Walters EE. Lifetime prevalence and age-of-onset distributions of DSM-IV disorders in the national comorbidity survey replication. Arch Gen Psychiatry. 2005;**62**(6):593–602.
8. Leigh E, Clark DM. Cognitive Therapy for Social Anxiety Disorder in Adolescents [Internet]. 2018. https://oxcadatresources.com/wp-content/uploads/2018/11/CT-SAD-A-MANUAL.pdf.
9. Bruce SE, Yonkers KA, Otto MW, Eisen JL, Weisberg RB, Pagano M, et al. Influence of psychiatric comorbidity on recovery and recurrence in generalized anxiety disorder, social phobia, and panic disorder: A 12-year prospective study. Am J Psychiatry. 2005;**162**(6):1179–1187.
10. Connor KM, Davidson JR, Churchill LE, Sherwood A, Foa E, Weisler RH.

Psychometric properties of the Social Phobia Inventory (SPIN): New self-rating scale. Br J Psychiatry J Ment Sci. 2000;**176**:379–386.

11. Liebowitz MR. Social phobia. In: Klein DF (ed.), *Anxiety: Modern Problems in Pharmacopsychiatry* (pp. 141–73). [Internet]. Basel: Karger; 1987 [accessed 11 January 2025]. (Modern Trends in Psychiatry; vol. 22). https://karger.com/books/book/1802/chapter/5676378/Social-Phobia.
12. Rytwinski NK, Fresco DM, Heimberg RG, Coles ME, Liebowitz MR, Cissell S, et al. Screening for social anxiety disorder with the self-report version of the Liebowitz Social Anxiety Scale. Depress Anxiety. 2009;**26**(1):34–38.
13. Wells A, Stopa L, Clark D. The social cognitions questionnaire. Unpublished, Department of Psychiatry, University of Oxford, Warneford Hospital, Oxford, UK. 1993;
14. OxCADAT Resources [Internet]. 2018 [accessed 11 January 2025]. OxCADAT Resources for cognitive therapy for PTSD, social anxiety disorder and panic disorder. Social Anxiety Disorder Questionnaires and Therapy Materials. https://oxcadatresources.com/questionnaires/.
15. Wolpe J, Lazarus AA. *Behavior Therapy Techniques: A Guide to the Treatment of Neuroses* [Internet]. Oxford: Pergamon Press; 1966. https://books.google.co.uk/books?id=wQZsAAAAMAAJ.
16. Arkowitz H, Lichtenstein E, McGovern K, Hines P. The behavioral assessment of social competence in males. Behav Ther. 1975;**6**(1):3–13.
17. O'Banion K, Arkowitz H. Social anxiety and selective memory for affective information about the self. Soc Behav Personal Int J. 1977;**5**(2):321–328.
18. Hartman LM. A metacognitive model of social anxiety: Implications for treatment. Clin Psychol Rev. 1983;**3**(4):435–456.
19. Hartman LM. Cognitive components of social anxiety. J Clin Psychol. 1984;**40**(1):137–139.
20. ÖHman A. Face the beast and fear the face: Animal and social fears as prototypes for evolutionary analyses of emotion. Psychophysiology. 1986;**23**(2):123–145.
21. Trower P, Gilbert P. New theoretical conceptions of social anxiety and social phobia. Clin Psychol Rev. 1989;**9**(1):19–35.
22. Rapee RM, Heimberg RG. A cognitive-behavioral model of anxiety in social phobia. Behav Res Ther. 1997;**35**(8):741–756.
23. MacLeod C, Mathews A. Anxiety and the allocation of attention to threat. Q J Exp Psychol. 1988;**40**(4):653–670.
24. Mogg K, Mathews A, Eysenck M. Attentional bias to threat in clinical anxiety states. Cogn Emot. 1992;**6**(2):149–159.
25. Mansell W, Clark DM, Ehlers A, Chen YP. Social anxiety and attention away from emotional faces. Cogn Emot. 1999;**13**(6):673–690.
26. Mayo-Wilson E, Dias S, Mavranezouli I, Kew K, Clark DM, Ades AE, et al. Psychological and pharmacological interventions for social anxiety disorder in adults: a systematic review and network meta-analysis. Lancet Psychiatry. 2014;**1**(5):368–376.
27. National Institute for Health and Care Excellence. Social anxiety disorder: recognition, assessment and treatment [Internet]. 2013, p. 39. Report No.: CG159. www.nice.org.uk/guidance/cg159/resources/social-anxiety-disorder-recognition-assessment-and-treatment-pdf-35109639699397.
28. Warnock-Parkes E, Wild J, Stott R, Grey N, Ehlers A, Clark DM. Seeing is believing: Using video feedback in cognitive therapy for social anxiety disorder. Cogn Behav Pract. 2017;**24**(2):245–255.
29. Ruscio AM, Brown TA, Chiu WT, Sareen J, Stein MB, Kessler RC. Social fears and social phobia in the United States: Results from the national comorbidity survey replication. Psychol Med. 2008;**38**(1):15–28.
30. Crome E, Grove R, Baillie AJ, Sunderland M, Teesson M, Slade T. DSM-

IV and DSM-5 social anxiety disorder in the Australian community. Aust N Z J Psychiatry. 2015;**49**(3):227–235.

31. Lecrubier Y. Comorbidity in social anxiety disorder: Impact on disease burden and management. J Clin Psychiatry. 1998;**59**(17):33–38.
32. Erwin BA, Heimberg RG, Marx BP, Franklin ME. Traumatic and socially stressful life events among persons with social anxiety disorder. J Anxiety Disord. 2006;**20**(7):896–914.
33. Heiser NA, Turner SM, Beidel DC. Shyness: relationship to social phobia and other psychiatric disorders. Behav Res Ther. 2003;**41**(2):209–221.
34. Turner SM, Beidel DC, Townsley RM. Social phobia: Relationship to shyness. Behav Res Ther. 1990;**28**(6):497–505.
35. Clark DM. Cognitive Perspective on Social Phobia. In: WR Crozier, LE Alden (Eds.), *International Handbook of Social Anxiety: Concepts, Research, and Interventions Relating to the Self and Shyness* (pp. 405–30). New York: Wiley; 2001.
36. Hope DA, Heimberg RG, Turk CL. *Managing Social Anxiety, Therapist Guide: A Cognitive-Behavioral Therapy Approach.* Oxford: Oxford University Press; 2006.
37. Hope DA, Heimberg RG, Turk CL. *Managing Social Anxiety, Therapist Guide: A Cognitive-Behavioral Therapy Approach*, 3rd ed. Oxford: Oxford University Press; 2019.
38. Hope DA, Burns JA, Hayes SA, Herbert JD, Warner MD. Automatic thoughts and cognitive restructuring in cognitive behavioral group therapy for social anxiety disorder. Cogn Ther Res. 2010;**34**(1):1–12.

Chapter 14

Generalised Anxiety Disorder

with Saevar Már Gústavsson

In this chapter we will help you to be able to:

- Understand what GAD is and how it typically presents.
- Describe and use evidence-based protocols for GAD.
- Choose and use appropriate formulation models for CBT for GAD.
- Understand why and how to use therapeutic techniques such as behavioural experiments, imaginal exposure, applied relaxation and cognitive restructuring when using CBT for GAD.
- Develop a treatment plan for CBT for GAD.
- Take account of comorbidity when treating GAD.

Introduction

Those suffering from generalised anxiety disorder (GAD) experience high levels of anxiety, either regularly or constantly to the extent that it interferes with daily functioning, causes distress and impairs quality of life. It is characterised by excessive worries about a number of different things, including school/work, family and friendships, finance, health and the future, that are perceived as intrusive and difficult to control [4].

Historically, GAD was referred to as 'free floating anxiety' (along with panic attacks) and was initially included in the DSM-III as a residual diagnosis, only to be used when no other anxiety or mood disorder could be applied [24]. In the DSM-III-R, excessive and unrealistic worry (later 'uncontrollable' in the DSM-IV) were made the cardinal symptoms GAD [2,3]. This addition, alongside the possibility of diagnosing primary GAD with co-morbidities, or as a secondary diagnosis, increased the diagnostic reliability of GAD considerably and it became a 'proper' mental health disorder warranting interest from clinician and researchers [5]. The term 'generalised anxiety disorder' has also been contested and other names for this diagnosis categories have been proposed, such as 'major worry disorder' reflecting the cardinal symptom of GAD [5].

In this chapter we will explore the clinical presentation of GAD, different empirically grounded and evidence-based treatment protocols for GAD, the effectiveness of CBT for GAD, the impact of co-morbidity on treatment and how to pick a protocol when treating GAD. There is an array of theories and treatment protocols for GAD and worry. Here we will only cover the treatment protocols included in the NICE guidelines and the BABCP core curriculum. As the meta-cognitive protocol for GAD [66] is not included in these guidelines this chapter will not cover meta-cognitive approaches despite studies indicating promising efficacy [50]. This is also the case for the cognitive model of worry (CMW) protocol by [40]. The CMW protocol builds on the Borkovec protocol (discussed later in this chapter) but incorporates insights from cognitive research, and importantly, the use of an idiosyncratic formulation of the patient's problem. For a review of theories and treatments of GAD, included and excluded from this chapter, see the review articles of Behar et al. [9] and Freeston [33].

What Is Generalised Anxiety Disorder?

As discussed above the cardinal symptoms of GAD are excessive worries about various day-to-day events and that these worries are often perceived as uncontrollable. The worries need to have been present for most days for the past six months and accompanied by at least three out of six additional symptoms (irritability, sleep difficulties, difficulty concentrating, muscle tension, feeling tired or exhausted and restlessness). A further DSM-5 criterion is that the 'disturbance is not by another mental disorder' reflecting the residual category of GAD since its inclusion in the DSM-III. GAD is the only anxiety disorder in the DSM that has no criteria for the focus of the threat or behavioural avoidance.

Worldwide prevalence is estimated at 3.7%, with higher prevalence (5.0%) in high-income countries, and twice as many females are diagnosed with GAD as compared to males [57]. The functional impairment of 'pure' GAD (no co-morbidities) is at least as severe as for major-depressive disorder (MDD), but help-seeking rates for people with GAD tend to be low until they have developed a co-morbid problem such as MDD, insomnia or somatic problems such as chronic headaches or irritable bowel syndrome [41,73]. Frustratingly, most people with GAD do not receive a proper assessment or treatment [52,54,68], and more receive pharmacotherapy compared to psychotherapy [54]. Furthermore, research on GAD has lagged behind research on other anxiety disorders and remains an understudied problem [29].

People diagnosed with GAD worry about the same subjectively important things as other people. Broadly, these worry themes are work/school, family, friends, finances and future prospects. As such, GAD could be seen as simply an amplification of 'everyday' anxiety. However, more detailed analysis of the thoughts that accompany increases in anxiety for GAD patients indicates a more complex picture. Breitholtz et al. [17] categorised the anxious thoughts that GAD patients had reported in their 'thought diaries'. In that study around 45% of the anxious thoughts fell into the categories of (i) thoughts about interpersonal matters, (ii) thoughts about personal competence, (iii) thoughts about acceptance and (iv) thoughts about the welfare of loved ones. Another study by the same research group [18] reported that for 37% of the GAD participants thoughts about 'inability to cope' were ranked as the most important thoughts in relation to their anxiety problem, that is, the content of the anxious thoughts had something to do with the consequences of not being able to cope with a problem or situation. These findings are in line with the cognitive theory of GAD put forward by Beck et al. [8], and further elaborated by Clark [21,22], where they highlight the presence of unhelpful beliefs and assumptions about acceptance, competence responsibility, control, and the consequences of failure.

GAD Treatment

Therapy for GAD typically involves some combination of helping the sufferer to mitigate the impact of their anxiety and/or reducing factors believed to be driving the components of general anxiety. These approaches all draw upon Lang's [45] observation that 'anxiety is not a lump'; that is, it is composed of multiple components, typically described as physiological, behavioural, cognitive and emotional. These components are defined as 'loosely coupled', meaning that changes are linked but not entirely correlated. All treatment approaches for GAD acknowledge this to a greater or lesser degree, and typically focus on different systems. What follows is a discussion of the theoretical framework behind each treatment protocol included in the NICE guidelines for GAD.

Applied Relaxation

In the 1970s and early–mid 1980s several behavioural approaches were developed to target chronic, high arousal anxiety experienced by patients with free-floating anxiety (later GAD and PD). The most researched behavioural treatments applied to GAD are applied relaxation (AR; [53]) and progressive relaxation training (PR; [10,11,12]). Neither of these treatments were specifically developed for GAD and are therefore not based on a specific theory on GAD but on anxiety (phobic and non-phobic) in general. When AR was developed it put more focus on applying the relaxation skills in real life situations compared to PR. However, the application of these skills in day-to-day situation was later include in PR [11,12]. Both AR and PR are based on progressive muscle relaxation as developed by Edmund Jacobsson [42] and later refined by Joseph Wolpe [70]. The ultimate goal of these treatments is to teach the client to detect early signs of anxiety (such as somatic signs or the initiation of worry), apply relaxation techniques when anxiety is detected and, importantly, to approach the anxiety provoking situation or to not escape from the situation but remember they can cope with the anxiety to create opportunities for extinction of anxiety [12,53].

The Avoidance Model of Worry (AMW)

The AMW has been the most influential model of worry and GAD. The work by Tom Borkovec and his collaborators is still guiding theoretical and clinical developments in the field. The most important insight of the AMW is the conceptualisation of worry as a 'chain of thoughts and images, negatively affect-laden and relatively uncontrollable' [14] that are manifested in the form of 'What if . . . ?' questions, anticipating potential future. As such, worry is an attempt to identify potential future threats or problems and ways to deal with them [13,27,46]. Building on the behavioural account of anxiety the AMW is grounded in the two-process model of anxiety [47] and the emotional processing model [32]. The AMW conceptualises worry as a cognitive avoidance that is negatively reinforced via avoidance of anxious arousal and distressing images and by the non-occurrence of perceived threat [9,13]. The avoidance of these internal states prevents the activation of the 'fear structure' which contains 'propositions about stimuli, response and their meaning' [32, p. 27]. If the fear structure is not activated the meaning cannot be changed, that is to say, extinction does not occur [32]. The AMW also highlights the role of positive beliefs about worry which motived the use of worry as a coping strategy and these beliefs are then negatively, and positively, reinforced by the non-occurrence of the perceived threat and finding a solution to the problem. Borkovec et al. [13] hypothesised that the formation of these positive beliefs about worry might be attributed to experiences of inhibited somatic arousal caused by the act of worrying. The worrier might thus learn that 'worry prepares me for a catastrophe'.

As the AMW conceptualises worry as a cognitive avoidance which interferes with exposure to the fear structure, the key therapeutic implications of the AMW for GAD are therefore exposure and response prevention (ERP) and imaginal exposure. This includes the scheduling of a 'worry time' or a 'worry-free zone', worry outcome monitoring, applied relaxation and self-control desensitisation [12,13,15]. Furthermore, the group behind the AMW also highlights the role of cognitive therapy methods as described by Beck et al. [8] to help patients to re-evaluate their anxious predictions about the future and to focus on the present moment [13]. These cognitive restructuring skills are applied during imaginal exposure to replace the threatening image with one which is more realistic and includes the deployment of learned coping skills. In this aspect the clinical implications of the AMW for GAD is a multiple component therapy based on behavioural principles with the addition of generic cognitive therapy methods.

Later developments of the AMW have focussed on the role attachment issues, interpersonal issues and previous trauma the development and maintenance of GAD [48,62].

Mastery of Your Anxiety and Worry (MAW)

The MAW protocol has been published as a therapist guide [72] with an accompanying patients' workbook [23]. The MAW conceptualises GAD as an interaction between the tendencies to be hypervigilant and to catastrophise with inability to terminate bouts of worry which is caused by the avoidant function of worry [72, p. 27]. This model incorporates the AMW definition of worry as an avoidance of distressing images and arousal. The non-occurrence of emotional processing maintains states of high anxiety which then leads to problem-solving difficulties and more worry topics. As such, the MAW is heavily influenced by the emotional processing model of anxiety [32] and Borkovec's original description of worry as an avoidance behaviour.

As the AMW, the MAW combines behavioural and cognitive interventions. The key targets in the MAW protocol are perceived lack of safety, lack of predictability and lack of controllability over anxiety. These targets are addressed by (1) psychoeducation and cognitive restructuring, (2) applied relaxation, (3) imagery exposure and (4) in-vivo exposure. Psychoeducation and cognitive restructuring are used to address perceived lack of safety and predictability, relaxation for perceived uncontrollability of anxiety and imaginal and in vivo exposure for all targets. Importantly, cognitive restructuring and the application of relaxation techniques are taught prior to exposure and response prevention exercises to increase approach behaviours.

The Intolerance of Uncertainty Model (IUM) of Worry and GAD

As evident by the name the IUM maintains that negative beliefs and assumptions about uncertainty are key factors in the development and maintenance of GAD and are understood as a 'dispositional characteristic' for GAD [28,30]. The original IUM identifies three other components that are involved in the maintenance of GAD: (1) positive beliefs about worry, (2) negative problem orientation and (3) cognitive avoidance. The IUM does not include any techniques to address the somatic symptoms of anxiety and worry as the AMW and MAW protocols as somatic symptoms are seen as the result of chronic worrying.

The IUM conceptualises positive beliefs about worry in similar fashion as the AMW. However, a later conceptualisation of this construct includes five types of positive beliefs. Positive beliefs about worry are activated by the detection of uncertainty, that is, worry is seen as a helpful way to generate a solution to a problem or a threat. The use of worry leads to increase in anxiety, negative problem orientation ('I won't be able to handle this problem') and cognitive avoidance. Negative problem orientation maintains the worry by preventing the use of helpful coping skills. Cognitive avoidance in the IUM encompasses other behaviours than worry, such as active thought suppression or the replacement of worries with positive thoughts. According to the IUM cognitive avoidance strategies are thought the serve the function of dampening arousal and distressing images, and the creation and maintenance of negative beliefs about uncertainty.

Even though the IUM identifies and targets these four components, intolerance of uncertainty is thought to be the main therapeutic target [28]. The IUM treatment is composed of (1) psychoeducation and worry awareness training, (2) uncertainty recognition and in-vivo exposure to uncertainty inducing situations, (3) re-evaluation of positive beliefs about worry, (4) problem-solving training, (5) imaginal exposure and (6) relapse prevention.

A recent development of the IUM streamlines the treatment and changes the focus of in-vivo exposure to behavioural experiments using belief disconfirmation techniques [39]. Positive beliefs about worry, negative problem orientation and cognitive avoidance are dropped altogether and are not addressed in this updated version of the IU protocol.

Cognitive Therapy for GAD

Beck et al. [8] offered a conceptualisation of GAD based on the cognitive theory of emotional disorders [7]. According to Beck et al. [8] anxiety problems have at their heart exaggerated threat appraisals which are based on (1) an overestimation of perceived awfulness of threat (i.e. idiosyncratic meaning), (2) an overestimation of perceived probability of threat and (3) an underestimation of perceived abilities to cope and other rescue factors (such as if other people can help). The exaggerated threat beliefs are then maintained by safety-seeking behaviours that prevent their disconfirmations, selective attention towards threat and safety and physiological changes [58,61].

Beck et al. [8] proposed that GAD was not different from other anxiety disorders and had at its core exaggerated threat beliefs based on unhelpful beliefs and assumptions about themselves, other people and the world. We could expect to see beliefs such as 'I'm a failure'; 'others can't be trusted'; 'the world is unfair' with the theme of threat being the fear of failure and its consequences. David M. Clark [21] included further assumptions into the cognitive conceptualisations of GAD such as unhelpful assumptions about responsibility, acceptance and competence. Importantly, this cognitive theory of GAD focuses on an idiosyncratic threat belief and the maintenance factors that prevent its disconfirmation.

CT for GAD has seen little development since the work of Beck et al. [8] and Clark [21]. Butler et al. [20] developed a treatment protocol for CT for GAD and compared it with a behavioural therapy that included progressive muscle relaxation and graded exposure in a RCT with favourable results for the CT condition. This protocol was the first to include the use of behavioural experiments to manage 'subtle forms of avoidance' in GAD. However, this protocol developed by Butler et al. [20] has not been developed further despite its initial promise.

Recently, Gústavsson et al. [35,36] updated the original cognitive model of GAD, highlighting the role of faulty beliefs about responsibility and the role of worry as a safety-seeking behaviour in the maintenance of exaggerated threat beliefs. This updated model does not include thought challenging using automatic thought records but rather the utilisation of behavioural experiments to test out two competing views of the problem (Theory A versus Theory B).

As mentioned above, the cognitive model of GAD conceptualises worry as a safety-seeking strategy but not as an avoidance of distress as AMW does [35]. In this cognitive model worry is understood as a normal cognitive process which is in most cases helpful and, importantly, self-eliminating. Essentially worry consists of (1) a *scenario analysis* (What if . . . ?), (2) threat appraisal (the idiosyncratic meaning of the What if . . .) and (3) a *crisis response plan* (how to prevent or deal with the perceived threat). However, when the threat appraisal is exaggerated worry will be used as a *search for certainty of safety from harm* and thus becomes excessive, because: (1) as a safety-seeking behaviour it maintains exaggerated threat beliefs [58,61]; (2) it becomes over-practised or proceduralised resulting in the function of the behaviour being not immediately apparent to the person; and (3) it impacts the persons ability to function in daily activities. This is a key departure from the behavioural model of worry where it is seen as an avoidance of distress.

Efficacy Data for CBT for Generalised Anxiety Disorder

In the most recent meta-analysis by Cuijpers et al. [26] CBT for GAD was reported to have large effect size g = 0.80 (95% CI: 0.67–0.93) compared to waiting lists. However, analysis indicated a significant publication bias, and the adjusted effect size was g = 0.59 (95% CI: 0.44–0.75). According to Cuijpers et al. [26] the numbers needed to treat (NNT) of GAD for CBT is 2.23, indicating that to see one patient improve we need to treat two.

The National Institute for Clinical Excellence [49] recommends offering the patient a choice of either high-intensity therapy, either CBT (CT for GAD; IU-CBT for GAD or combination of CT and applied relaxation) or applied relaxation, or SSRI medications, if they have not responded adequately to low-intensity intervention or have a marked functional impairment. According to the NICE guidelines [49] CBT is neither inferior nor superior to applied relaxation but there it is also stated that CBT has more robust clinical evidence than applied relaxation. Limited head-to-head comparisons between these different GAD protocols have been conducted and therefore little can be said about their relative efficacy. Furthermore, to this date no RCTs comparing the relative effectiveness of CBT vs medications (such as SSRIs) have been conducted. Therefore, no guidelines exist to match patients to CBT, medication or combined treatment.

Co-morbidity and Treatment

In clinical samples it is the rule rather than the exception that those diagnosed with GAD also meet criteria for other mental disorders, where co-morbidity has been estimated around 90% [44,56]. However, in population samples the co-morbidity of GAD with other mental disorders is not greater than for other anxiety disorders [43] and the most common co-morbidity for patients with GAD is MDD. For patients with co-morbid GAD and MDD, GAD is often the temporarily primary disorder, highlighting the impact of GAD on the patients functioning and well-being if the problem is left untreated [44]. Specific phobias, social anxiety disorder and panic disorder are also common co-morbidities [19,74].

While GAD patients are frequent users of primary health care, they are unlikely to seek treatment for their anxiety, and when they turn to primary health care, they are more likely to seek treatment for pain, stomach complaints or sleep difficulties [51,52,69].

The bottom line is that co-morbidity is the rule rather than exception for treatment seeking adults with GAD. In the face of co-morbidity treatment planning should take into account (1) whether the disorders are functionally linked, (2) first onset of each problem, (3) what problem has been the most persistent and (4) what problem is currently causing the greatest functional impairment. If MDD is currently primary it is important to assess whether avoidance and procrastination due to anxiety and worry is a causal factor in the MDD symptoms or if MDD has become a problem on its own.

In the case of comorbid social anxiety (a common presentation), assess whether the most impairing worries centre around performance in social situations and being negatively judged as a result. If yes, have a conversation with the patient about whether treating the social worries using established CBT protocols for social anxiety should take priority. If social anxiety is the secondary problem treatment should focus on GAD symptoms. However, if it becomes apparent during therapy that social anxiety is an important part of the presentation, we recommend based on our clinical experience, to incorporate behavioural experiments specifically designed to address self-focussed attention and safety-seeking behaviours in social situations, that is, the stooge and video feedback experiments [64]. As behavioural experiments have been found to lead to greater symptom reductions compared to in vivo exposure for social anxiety [67], we can safely assume the same for social worries in the context of GAD.

As mentioned above, people with GAD often have comorbid somatic problems or persistent physical symptoms (PPS), such as irritable bowel syndrome or fibromyalgia. No guidance exists on best-practice treatment in the case of GAD and comorbid PPS. The implications of the presence of PPS in symptoms when treating GAD is probably the use of a thorough case formulation that accounts for the interaction between the PPS and GAD symptoms. The case formulation could for example highlight what worries are excessive and need to be dealt with using CBT techniques and what worries are realistic, that is, they are about actual problems with real implications, such as increase in sick days due to PPS symptoms and the financial difficulties this can cause. These worries about actual problems can only addressed by finding practical solutions and other coping strategies such as applied relaxation.

Picking a Protocol

With this plethora of GAD protocols therapists can understandably feel daunted by the task to select which protocol to use in general and what best fits the patient's needs (see Table 14.1 for an overview of protocols included in the NICE guidelines). When picking a protocol, you need to consider both the therapist training (his experience and what therapy modality he is most familiar with) and the patient's preference. Even though relatively as efficacious, more theoretical research has been conducted on the AMW, the MAW and the IUM compared to the AR and CT for GAD. The different protocols have many commonalities but to a different extent. The AMW and the MAW are perhaps the most similar and the AR is their close relative in the behavioural family. Both the IUM and CT for GAD are members of the cognitive family and focus on changing unhelpful beliefs and do not address the somatic anxiety directly. The IUM initially espoused the use of

Table 14.1 Description of CBT protocols for GAD

Protocol	Öst [53]; Bernstein & Borkovec [10]	Borkovec & Costello [12]	Zinbarg et al. [72]	Dugas & Robichaud [28]; Robichaud et al. [55]	Beck et al. [8]; Butler et al. [20]
Theory of Generalised Anxiety Disorder	Based on a general theory of anxiety and not specifically applied to GAD	GAD caused by cognitive biases and inadequate coping responses, and the use worry as a cognitive avoidance behaviour that prevents exposure to the feared stimuli	GAD caused by hypervigilance and cognitive biases, and the use of worry as a cognitive avoidance strategy, preventing exposure to the feared stimuli	GAD cause by negative beliefs about uncertainty, positive beliefs about worry, negative problem orientation and cognitive avoidance	GAD caused by negative beliefs about self, the world, and others. Safety-seeking behaviours prevent the disconfirmation of faulty threat beliefs
Aim of treatment	To learn that anxiety in daily life can by coped with using relaxation techniques	Reduce cognitive biases and physiological arousal, and exposure to the feared stimuli to allow for emotional processing	Reduce cognitive biases and physiological arousal, and exposure to the feared stimuli to allow for emotional processing	Change unhelpful beliefs about uncertainty and find more flexible ways to respond to felt uncertainty	Change unhelpful beliefs about self, others and the world and find more flexible ways to respond to challenging situations
Recent updates				Hebert & Dugas [39]; Dugas et al. [31]	Gústavsson et al. [35,36]
Recommended structure of therapy	12 sessions, each 60 min	12–15 sessions, each 60 –90 min	12 sessions each 60 min	12–20 sessions, each 60 –90 min	12–15 sessions, each 60 to 90 min
Interventions used	Anxiety cue monitoring, progressive muscle relaxation, and applied relaxation	Worry time or a worry-free zone worry outcome monitoring applied relaxation self-control desensitisation cognitive restructuring	Worry awareness training Cognitive restructuring applied relaxation imaginal exposure and in vivo exposure	Worry awareness training in vivo exposure or behavioural experiments cognitive restructuring, problem-solving training imaginal exposure	Case formulation Theory A/B Cognitive restructuring Belief disconfirmation via behavioural experiments Attention training
Helpful when	Patient finds it difficult to access thoughts and/or is most bothered by somatic symptoms of anxiety	Patient is bothered by cognitive and somatic symptoms of anxiety	Patient is bothered by cognitive and somatic symptoms of anxiety	Patient describes a tendency to be intolerant of any amount of uncertainty	Patient describes range of unhelpful beliefs and assumptions about self, others, and world

in vivo exposure but a recent update on the model advocates dropping in-vivo exposure for belief disconfirmation exercises (i.e. behavioural experiments). This development means that in practice and theory, the IUM and CT for GAD are in many ways compatible, but the key difference is the assumption of what kind of beliefs need to be addressed in therapy. In this section we cover these protocols in more details using case examples and how each treatment modality can be used in practice.

The AR Protocol

As discussed above the AR protocol is not based on a model of GAD but a general theory of anxiety. Essentially, the AR protocol builds on extinction theories of anxiety where the goal of treatment is to approach the anxiety provoking situation and stay in it until anxiety decreases. Therefore, treatment teaches how to apply relaxation techniques in an anxiety provoking situation which should ultimately lead to habituation of the anxious response.

Case Example: Tom

Tom was a 45-year-old man, father of two and recently divorced. He had been having difficulties with his mental health for many years and last year he was on a sick leave for six months due his anxiety and chronic pain problem where he participated in a work rehabilitation. Now he had returned to his job but only working four days a week as he felt he was not able to carry on full time despite his rehabilitation. His main complaints were constant tension, always feeling alert which made his pain problem worse. He reported that this affected his sleep greatly and that he was exhausted at the end of the day, not able to do anything more than getting home, cooking dinner and staying home watching TV.

The first session in AR was devoted to discussing the rationale for AR and conceptualising Tom's goals for treatment. Tom had three goals: (1) be able to fall asleep in less than one hour, (2) decrease exhaustion and (3) engage more in enjoyable activities.

The rationale for AR is to learn to spot early signs of anxiety and apply relaxation skills as a response, whether in a difficult situation or at home. In the first session Tom reported that he notices physical symptoms as soon as he wakes up in the morning. When transporting to work his symptoms would decrease but increase again when he met with his colleagues at work.

Progressive relaxation training was introduced in sessions 2 and 3. In the first session the muscle groups in the hands, arms, face, neck and shoulders were used for relaxation training. In the next session muscle groups in the rest of the body were included as well. The therapist guided Tom through the relaxation procedures, making sure he was doing everything correctly by monitoring and checking in on him throughout the session. Tom's home assignment after sessions 1 and 2 was to practice the relaxation skills for 15–20 minutes twice a day, record when each exercise took place and measure the degree of relaxation achieved (0–100).

The aim of session 4 was to decrease the time needed to achieve a relaxed state from 15–20 minutes down to 5–7 minutes. This was done by excluding the tensing part and only use release of the muscle groups. Tom found it difficult to only use the release technique to achieve relaxation in his neck and shoulders. To achieve the desired state of relaxation the therapist asked Tom to use both tense and release for these muscle groups which helped. Because Tom experienced difficulties with using only release for his neck and shoulders it was decided to have another session focussing on using only release. Tom's homework after sessions 4 and 5 was to practice release only twice per day and record how long it took to achieve a relaxed state.

Cue-controlled relaxation was introduced in session 6. Here Tom was instructed by the therapist to use the release technique to induce a relaxed state. Then the therapist helped Tom to use his breathing as a cue for relaxation by saying 'inhale' just before inhalation and 'relax' at exhalation. The therapist continued this for several breaths and then Tom did this on his own by thinking inhale and relax when breathing. This training was continued for session 7 and Tom would practice this at home twice per day between sessions. In session 7 Tom could achieve a state of relaxed in the expected 2–3 minutes.

In sessions 8 and 9 Tom practised using his relaxation skills in other settings than sitting in a comfortable chair with his eyes closed. At first, he practised his relaxation skills with his eyes open and moving different part of his bod and applying release only when he found tension. Then he progressed to sitting at a desk, while writing on a keyboard. In next session the same exercises were conducted while Tom was standing and walking. After session 9 Tom was able to apply his relaxation skills at home and reach a state of relaxation in 60–90 seconds.

Next up was the rapid relaxation phase where the goal was to apply the relaxation skills in non-stressful situations and reduce the time needed to relax down to 20–30 seconds. The session was devoted to identifying cues in Tom's surroundings at which he would relax. At home Tom was to relax 15–20 times a day using the identified cues using the cue-controlled relaxation technique.

Now was time for Tom to practice his relaxation skills in anxiety provoking situations. The main triggers for Tom's anxiety and worries were (1) deadlines at work, (2) communication with his ex-partner, (3) thinking about the welfare of his son and daughter and (4) going to sleep. An in-session exposure was conducted where Tom, sitting at a desk, imagined himself receiving a reminder for a deadline at work and when he felt the anxiety increasing to apply his relaxation skills. Homework for next session was to apply the relaxation skills at work, when communicating with ex-partner, thinking about his kids and going to sleep. Tom was gently reminded to show himself patience as he would most likely experience difficulties at first, but with further practice, he would find that he could successfully apply his relaxation skills and control his anxiety reactions.

In the next session (session 12) the homework was reviewed, and problems were identified and resolved. Tom reported that he found it quite easy to use his skills when falling asleep and at work but found it more challenging when it came to his ex-partner and kids. He found that the improved sleep and ability to be relaxed during work had a significant impact on his fatigue throughout the day and he would not come home after work feeling exhausted. Two follow-up sessions were scheduled to help Tom with problems that might come up.

The Borkovec Protocol

The AMW suggests possible etiological factors for the development of GAD such as (1) poor interpersonal skills, (2) stressful lifetime events and (3) insecure attachment styles [13,62]. These factors are thought to contribute to tendencies to view the world as dangerous and underestimate one's coping abilities. The tendency to make exaggerated threat appraisals leads to excessive anxiety which triggers the ineffective deployment of worry as a cognitive avoidance behaviour. Worry actively supresses the somatic response of anxiety and periodic

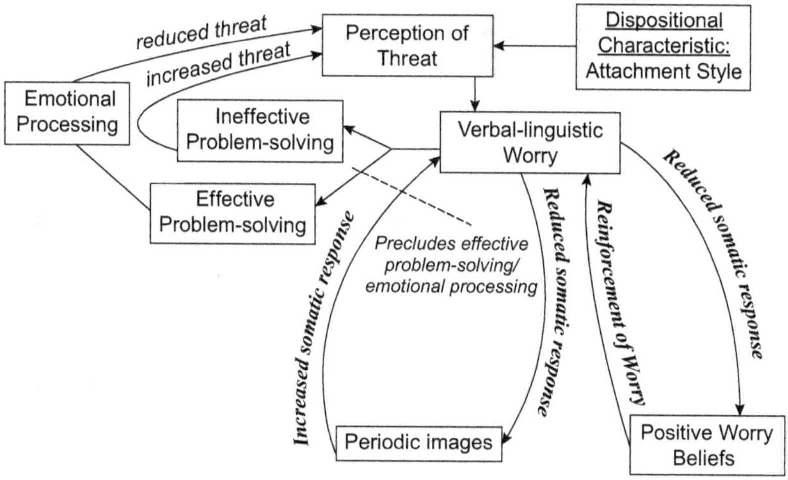

Figure 14.1 The avoidance model of worry and GAD, reproduced with permission from Elsevier.

threatening images and adaptive emotional processing of threat stimuli does not take place. The aim of treatment is to facilitate successful emotional processing by (1) reducing the use of worry as a response to anxious arousal and threating imagery and (2) increasing approach seeking behaviours. A visualisation of this is shown in Figure 14.1, which can be used to formulate GAD within this model.

The AMW led to the development of a multimodal treatment package for GAD [12]. The protocol developed by Tom Borkovec and his collaborators at Penn State University is a multimodal treatment combining cognitive and behavioural techniques [16]. It consists of (1) awareness and self-monitoring, (2) applied relaxation, (3) cognitive restructuring and (4) imagery rehearsal of coping strategies. Three additional intervention methods can also be applied: (1) stimulus control of worry, (2) imagery or in-vivo exposure and (3) behavioural activation.

It is difficult to find precise instruction on how many sessions are devoted to each module. However, from Borkovec and Costello [12] it can be inferred that the first three sessions are devoted to self-monitoring and relaxation training. Importantly, in this multimodal package the AR training is not as extensive as when AR is delivered on its own. Here less time is spent on early cue detection and ways of relaxing. In session 4, imagery rehearsal of coping strategies using self-control desensitisation is introduced where relaxation techniques are used in response external and internal anxiety cues. Cognitive therapy methods are introduced in session 5. These methods involve identifying cognitive biases, finding alternative less-threatening perspectives and 'behavioural testing of beliefs' [12], including positive beliefs about worry. For the remainder of the treatment, imagery coping strategies and cognitive therapy are covered in all sessions but only 10–15 minutes are devoted to the cognitive therapy techniques. Here, these cognitive therapy techniques are mainly meant to develop coping strategies to be used when performing self-control desensitisation exercises.

As mentioned above three additional interventions have been suggested by Borkovec [16]. Exposure techniques should be used when it is possible to identify specific internal or external triggers. Behavioural activation can be used especially when depression is co-morbid to GAD. However, the principles of behavioural activation can readily be applied in all modules of treatment both to increase time spent doing enjoyable activities and as well to assist with present moment focus [16].

Stimulus control of worry aims to limit the stimulus condition for which worry occurs and thus reduce the time spent worrying and provides more opportunities for successful emotional processing. Here it is important to introduce and teach behaviours and activities that are incompatible with worrying, such as relaxation or active engagement in an enjoyable activity. Stimulus control of worry consists of (1) learning to identify and monitor worrisome thoughts, (2) establish a worry-free period (e.g. 30 minutes) at the same time and location every day, (3) when you catch yourself worrying, postpone the worry and move your attention to what is in front of you and (4) use the worry period to go through all of the postponed worries and use problem-solving or cognitive restructuring methods to deal with the worries. Alternative stimulus control method is to establish a worry-free zone (a place or activity or both). When in these 'zones' all worries are postponed until later time and gradually these worry-free zones are made to encompass more activities and longer time periods.

Case Example: Irina

Irina was a 68-year-old woman and was living with her husband. She had three grown up children and six grandchildren. She stopped working one year ago but she had worked as an office manager most her of her work life. Initially, her husband had contacted their GP because Irina had been unable to leave the bed for over a week due to low mood. The GP prescribed SSRIs and a short-term dosage of benzodiazepine. When she presented for therapy, her low mood had improved, and her main complaints were never being able to relax, expecting the worst and being irritable.

Irina reported that she frequently worried about the welfare and safety of her daughters and grandchildren. She would wake up early in the morning and begin to worry about what she would need to do that day to help her daughters with the day-to-day activities. Importantly, she avoided planning something for herself just in case something would come up with her grandchildren and her help was needed. Irina felt she was constantly on edge and would often 'snap' at her husband if he said that she should not worry so much and do more for herself. This caused Irina further worries about the status of her marriage and whether she would spend the best years of her life alone and depressed.

In the first three sessions worry awareness monitoring was introduced along with applied relaxation exercises (as described in the AR protocol). Session 4 introduced self-control desensitisation techniques combining the use of imagery exposure and applied relaxation. Instead of actual exposure to a threatening image Irina was supposed to achieve a relaxed state before exposing herself to the threating image. As soon she experienced increase in anxiety she was instructed to use her relaxation skills.

Traditional cognitive restructuring techniques were introduced in session 5. In this session the self-control desensitisation exercises were continued but included the use of cognitive restructuring techniques as well as applied relaxation. At this time Irina was using the worry-free zone technique between sessions, where she would postpone paying attention to her worries during particular activities throughout the day: (1) during her morning routine and (2) when doing pleasurable activities (such as spending time with grandchildren or meeting with friends). To help Irina with moving her attention from the worries and to what was going on around her, principles of behavioural activation were applied to increase engagement in enjoyable activities (such as reading a book, walking and organising meetings with friends).

In-vivo exposure was used to help Irina with her worries about her grandchildren getting injured when she was watching them. Irina reported that when she went with her youngest grandchild (six years old) to the playground she would not allow him to use the swings. Every time they visited the playground Irina would have an image of her grandchild falling from the swings and hurting himself badly. She found this image terrible and was unwilling to take the chance of this happening however unlikely. Prior to the exposure exercise Irina was to go to the playground by herself and observe other kids, and their caregivers, using the swings. When Irina was doing this preparation exercise, she witnessed a child falling from the swing from a considerable hight, but the child was able to manoeuvre in the air and control its fall and had only minor injuries. This was a lucky accident (not for the kid perhaps) because Irena saw that even thought it was an actual possibility that her grandchild might fall from the swings under her watch, her image of what would happen was unlikely. So, the in-vivo exposure involved Irina taking her grandchild to the playground and allowing her to go on the swings. During this exercise, Irina was supposed to stay with the threatening image and not engage in avoidance strategies.

During the end of therapy Irina reported that she was engaging in more pleasurable activities and was more able to enjoy spending time with her grandchildren. She had learned that she could not prevent her grandchildren from getting hurt from time to time and that actually her daughters were more than capable to come up with solutions with their day-to-day hassles than she had previously thought. Importantly, she was now having more quality moments with her husband and felt her marriage was in a better place than prior to therapy.

The MAW Protocol

The theoretical foundations of the MAW for GAD protocol are laid out in Barlow [6] and Zinbarg [71]. Here GAD is thought be a state that is the result of an interaction between biological vulnerabilities (neuroticism) and psychological vulnerabilities (cognitive and attentional biases) with life events (stress). The tendency to experience often anxious arousal and interpret ambiguous stimuli as threatening is thought to make the person vulnerable to becoming stuck in a state of chronic anxiety after experiencing a prolonged stress or stressful live events.

The conceptualisation of GAD in the MAW protocol posits that anxiety is triggered by an automatic threatening image which is based on cognitive biases (e.g. catastrophising). Worry then is an anxious response and has an avoidant function where it both supresses the threatening image, leading to inhibited physiological arousal, and distraction from the image which hinders emotional processing. This results in a non-remitting worry where the person is unable to end the worry bout. Chronic anxiety then leads to physical tension, poor concentration (due to heightened self-focus) and impaired performance.

The MAW treatment protocol by Zinbarg et al. [72] comes with a highly structured patient workbook and aims to decrease cognitive biases, physiological arousal and avoidance behaviours that are thought to maintain perceptions of lack of safety, unpredictability and uncontrollability. As its theoretical underpinnings are based on the emotional processing theory of anxiety [32] and the avoidance theory of worry [16] imagery and in-vivo exposure with response prevention are the most important therapeutic techniques. Here, the MAW differs from the AMW where the latter emphasises the replacement of a threating image during imaginal exposure with a 'coping image' developed with cognitive discussion methods, but the former does not. Both imagery and in-vivo exposure are presented in a graded manner and patients are encouraged to not distract themselves from the imagery, or leave the situation, until the anxiety has begun to decline to allow for a full emotional processing.

The protocol consists of 4 treatment modules that are traditionally covered in 12 sessions, with the 8 weekly sessions, followed with 4 bi-weekly sessions. The treatment modules are: (1) psychoeducation and cognitive restructuring, (2) applied relaxation, (3) imagery exposure and (4) in-vivo exposure. In the patient workbook problem-solving and time management techniques are also introduced and these can be incorporated in sessions when applicable. Psychoeducation and cognitive restructuring are used to address perceived lack of safety and predictability, relaxation for perceived uncontrollability of anxiety and imaginal and in-vivo exposure for all targets. Importantly, cognitive restructuring and the application of relaxation techniques are taught prior to exposure and response prevention exercises to increase approach behaviours. The MAW therapist guide recommends a general structure of each therapy session: (1) check in from last session and review of homework, (2) agenda-setting, (3) discussion and review of treatment targets and procedures, (4) negotiation of homework and (5) session summary and feedback.

Although highly structured, the MAW offers flexibility to adapt the treatment to the patient's presentation. Such as when a patient is in a highly stressful environment and is mainly bothered by physical symptoms more focus on problem-solving and applied relaxation is warranted. Outcome studies for the MAW treatment have mainly been conducted with older people, but there is no reason to believe that the MAW works is less efficacious for people of working age.

Case Example: Jakup

Jakup was a 27-year-old man, living with his girlfriend who was expecting their second child, but their first child had died during pregnancy. He was studying computer science at a university when he presented for treatment. During his early twenties he dropped out of high school and was working in several service jobs which he did not enjoy. He had a long history of mental health problems and was diagnosed with GAD and recurrent MDD during assessment. Previously he had a successful treatment for MDD, and he now had much better control over his depressive symptoms. However, he had never been able to overcome his tendency to always expect the worst, which was having a big impact on him, especially now as his girlfriend was pregnant for the second time.

In Jakup's first session he was provided with psychoeducation about GAD, what to expect from therapy, the general spirit which therapy is conducted in and the idea of increasing awareness of anxiety, worry and anxious behaviours. Using Socratic questioning, Jakup and his therapist were able to identify how his worries were interfering with his daily life and what would change if he would worry less: (1) to spend more time with friends and family, (2) to fall more quickly to sleep, (3) to be more involved in preparations for his child's birth. For homework, Jakup was to begin self-monitoring of his anxious thoughts, anxious behaviours and triggering events using the accompanying self-monitoring form in the workbook.

The second session (corresponding to chapter 3 in the workbook) was devoted to more specific psychoeducation about the function of anxiety and its three components: physiological (central and autonomic nervous system arousal), cognitive (thoughts, beliefs and images about perceived danger and uncontrollability) and behavioural (avoidance, checking, safety behaviours). Furthermore, each component's role in the activation of anxiety was discussed, and specifically how the interaction between served to maintain the vicious worry cycle.

The third session (chapter 4 in the workbook) begun with review of the homework and what Jakup had learned about his anxiety problem. This session introduced more detailed discussion about GAD and the maintenance factors to be targeted in treatment: (1) excessive anxiety interfering with performance, (2) attentional biases, (3) worry 'chaining', (4) the role of automatic thoughts, (5) beliefs about worry and (6) avoidance and distraction strategies. This discussion laid down the plan for the subsequent modules, starting with applied relaxation in session four.

Session five introduced progressive muscle relaxation. Guidelines for doing applied relaxation were provided in the client workbook (chapter 5). The homework assigned to Jakup after this session was to practice progressive muscle relaxation (using the eight muscle groups) at least twice per day using the guidelines in the client workbook.

In the next two sessions cognitive restructuring methods (chapters 6 and 7 in the workbook) to decrease the tendency to overestimate the likelihood and awfulness of perceived threat were introduced. In these sessions it was identified that Jakup engaged in various safety-seeking behaviours that served to reinforce his assumptions that he would not be able to cope with difficulties and that he was a burden on other people. Between sessions Jakup used worksheets from the client workbook to practice finding alternative thoughts to his worries and more realistic ways to dealing with the most likely outcome of his worries.

Next steps in the treatment were imagery and in vivo exposure (chapters 8 and 9 in the workbook). In imagery exposure it is important that the patient allows himself to think about the most feared catastrophe for emotional processing to take place. Before imagery exposure takes place, it is important to use the downward arrow technique to establish the meaning of the feared catastrophe. Graded exposure is recommended to increase motivation for engaging in this exercise. It is helpful to make an audio record of the exposure scenario for the client to listen to between session to aid with exposure at home.

The rationale for in-vivo exposure is that for habituation to take place all avoidance behaviours need to be prevented for emotional processing to take place. Jakup was often engaging in subtle safety-seeking behaviours, such as seeking reassurance, making plans how to deal with feared outcomes before entering a situation and being careful of not offending people. He developed an exposure hierarchy with his therapist. At the top of the hierarchy was to take a stand with his own interest and needs in his relationship with friends and family. Imaginal and in-vivo exposure continued for five sessions. At the end of treatment Jakup found that he was now looking more forward to the birth of his child and was already spending more time with friends and family. And most importantly, was now taking better care of himself which had a good impact on the relationship with his girlfriend.

The IUS Protocol

The theory behind the IUS protocol is that negative beliefs about uncertainty and its consequences are the key mechanism behind GAD and worry [28]. As described in Dugas and Robichaud [28], the development of the IUS protocol stemmed from research evidence and clinical experience: namely that many patients with GAD did not get better with AR or traditional cognitive methods such as re-evaluation of perceived likelihood and cost of threat. They observed that clients with GAD 'seem to require absolute certainty that either a given event will not occur or that they will be able to deal with it should it take place' [28, p. 25] and from this observation developed the hypothesis that GAD is caused by intolerance of uncertainty. Even though the authors of the IUS model identify it as a cognitive model it draws from the emotional processing theory of fear [32] and Tom Borkovec's conceptualisation of worry as a cognitive avoidance strategy. Further components of the model are (1) positive beliefs about worry, (2) negative-problem orientation and (3) cognitive avoidance, as shown in Figure 14.2.

The IUS protocol differs both from the AMW and the MAW protocols as it does not include techniques such as relaxation or cost/likelihood re-evaluation. However, cognitive restructuring is used to reduce positive beliefs about worry. The focus of the treatment is on excessive worry and intolerance of uncertainty where the main goal is to help the patient to become more tolerant to, and more flexible in his response to uncertainty which should reduce the excessive worry. The protocol is made up of six treatment modules covering 12 to 20 sessions: (1) psychoeducation and worry awareness training, (2) uncertainty recognition and uncertainty exposure, (3) re-evaluation of the usefulness of worry, (4) problem-solving training, (5) imaginal exposure and (6) relapse-prevention. There are no guidelines about how many sessions should be devoted to each module and it is up to the therapist to assess how many sessions are needed on each module. However, the protocol explicitly states that

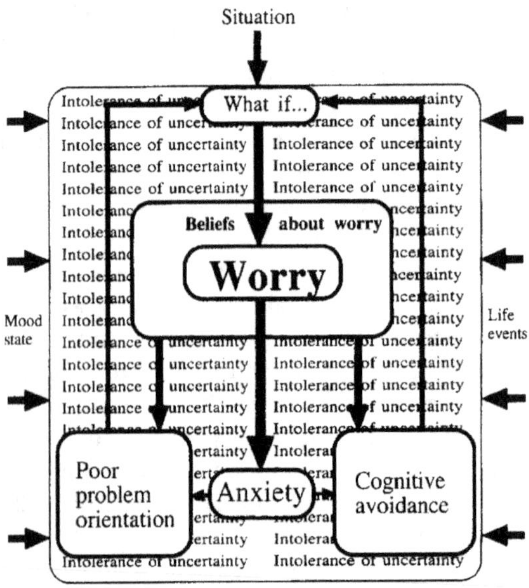

Figure 14.2 IUS model, reproduced from Dugas et al. [30] with permission from Elsevier.

intolerance of uncertainty is the mechanism behind the problem and therefore most of therapy should focus on improving cognitive and behavioural flexibility to felt uncertainty.

As discussed above, the IUS model has changed significantly since the publication of the original manual by Dugas and Robichaud [28]. The original protocol is included in the NICE guidelines, but the later developments are not.

In the updated model and protocol, negative beliefs about intolerance of uncertainty are purported to lead to catastrophic misinterpretation of uncertainty which triggers safety-seeking behaviours such as excessive reassurance seeking or overpreparation [31,39,55]. Importantly, this refined IUM also breaks from the behavioural account of worry as an avoidance of distress and conceptualises worry as a safety-seeking behaviour with the aim of decreasing felt uncertainty [31].

Case Example: Samantha

Samantha was a 29-year-old woman, living with her husband. She recently graduated as a primary school teacher and was starting her first role as a teacher. When she presented for treatment, she had been taking SSRIs for more than three years and had also prescribed benzodiazepine which she reported taking every other day when feeling extra stressed. She was diagnosed with ADHD as a child and was taking medication for that which she reported to be helpful. In the past she had seen four different therapists due to her anxiety problem and diagnosed with GAD. She had once completed a full round of treatment, but which was ultimately unsuccessful. Her motivation to seek treatment now was driven by her excessive worries about being unfit to be a teacher.

In Samantha's first treatment session she was given information about CBT and what she could expect in therapy. In the second session psychoeducation about GAD was provided and the intolerance of uncertainty model was introduced. The intolerance of uncertainty model was presented bit by bit during the first sessions. Worry awareness training was introduced in session 1 and Samantha was given the task to monitor her worries between sessions. The goal of this task is to gather information about (1) the patients worry 'themes', (2) how much time is spent worrying during the day and (3) help the patient see that worries can be about current or hypothetical situations and involves future threat.

What Samantha discovered in this exercise that she did in fact worry about more topics than just her performance in her future role as a teacher such as the status of her marriage, whether she would have any accidents and be a good mother in the future. The discovery of more worry topics initially made Samantha hopeless about ever getting better. However, her therapist reminded her that all these different worry topics were driven by the same underlying processes. Which meant that in treatment they would try and change the common underlying process behind all worry topics but not deal with each topic individually.

Next module introduced intolerance of uncertainty to the formulation. To describe intolerance of uncertainty the therapists used the allergy analogy. When people are intolerant of uncertainty, any amount of uncertainty will trigger their worry and anxiety. Just as when people with an allergy to dogs will get allergic reactions even when they are not around a dog but a person who was around dogs. In the same way, intolerance of uncertainty makes even the slightest amount of uncertainty being perceived as dangerous result in anxiety and worry.

Samantha held some unhelpful beliefs about uncertainty such as 'Uncertainty makes me unable to be productive'; 'Uncertainty should be avoided'. Samantha's intolerance of uncertainty led to various strategies with the aim of avoiding or eliminating any source of uncertainty. In relation to her work, she would check repeatedly and do things again to make sure she did everything correctly and gather all information possible before doing something such as creating a curriculum. She would repeatedly seek reassurance that her husband was not cross with her, procrastinating talking with him about trying to have a child, try to picture how things would go and what she needed to do to make everything go as planned and read texts messages and emails repeatedly before pressing send.

These beliefs were put to the test using behavioural experiments to challenge catastrophic misinterpretation of uncertainty (note that in the original IU protocol graded exposure is recommended). One of the experiments that Samantha found most difficult, but helpful in the long run, was to go to a restaurant with her husband without (1) checking on the menu beforehand, (2) looking at pictures of the place to imagine how it would be and (3) seeking information from other people of how the place was and what to expect. Her predictions were: 'I will be too anxious to decide what to have' (90%), 'I won't be able to enjoy myself' (90%), 'I will disappoint my husband' (95%). To help with the experiment Samantha was to try to put her attention outwards and be curious about what other people were doing around her. To Samantha's surprise she found that even though anxious she had a better time than expected, and importantly, she was not as preoccupied with the prospect of going out to dinner throughout the day.

Over the course of therapy Samantha would engage in more behavioural experiments with the aim to test her unhelpful beliefs about uncertainty and find new ways to engage with her duties in life despite their inherent uncertainty.

While making good progress in terms of tolerating uncertainty more successfully Samantha continued to catch herself worrying about number of things. She said that she understood it intellectually that she did not need to worry but nevertheless, in moments of uncertainty, she felt that it was better to worry than not. At this point in therapy the term positive beliefs about worry were introduced. Samantha reported that she believed that to worry shows that she cares, and to not worry equals imprudence. This worry belief was challenged using cognitive restructuring methods and with a survey. Samantha and her therapist collaborated to design a series of questions pertaining to these specific beliefs. For example, whether people thought that you can be a good and caring person if you are not spending time worrying about the welfare of other people.

To improve Samantha's problem orientation the idea that every time we caught ourselves worrying, we could replace that worry with a problem statement was introduced. This means substituting the 'What if … ?' thought and subsequent ruminative worry with a problem-statement that is less negative and more manageable than the catastrophe at the heart of the worry. This strategy applies to the worries that are about a current problem, which the patient can respond to. Samantha held the belief that she could not cope with problems and that she was bad at problem-solving. This meant that every time she was confronted with a problem, she was unsure about her abilities to resolve the problem and this uncertainty triggered her negative beliefs about uncertainty and thus fuelled the worry bout. To test these beliefs Samantha helped to identify if her worries were about an actual problem, and if yes, to reframe them as a problem statement and to generate possible problem solutions and apply them instead of engaging in worry and unhelpful ways to manage uncertainty.

In the next module Samantha was helped to expose herself to threatening images. Imaginal exposure is used to help with worries about hypothetical scenarios where problem-solving does not help. In this module the goal is to expose oneself to a threatening image and dropping cognitive avoidance strategies such as distraction. First, the effect of avoidance and neutralisation on anxiety is discussed (i.e. makes thoughts more intrusive), and then, the third option of facing fears is introduced, illustrated with an extinction curve. The preparation for imaginal exposure involves four components: (1) identifying the exposure theme using the arrow down technique, (2) preparing a draft of the exposure scenario, (3) finalising the scenario and (4) recording the scenario to be used for repeated exposure.

Samantha chose to work with her worries about failing as a mother in this module. The downward arrow technique was used to identify the fear belief underlying her initial worry. Underneath she feared that her husband and future children would reject her, and she would live an empty and meaningless life.

Then Samantha drafted an exposure scenario. When writing the scenario Samantha was instructed to write it (1) in first person, (2) in present tense, (3) using vivid descriptions and (4) excluding any avoidance or neutralisation. Furthermore, to describe the situation or context, how she would react to the situation and, importantly, what it would mean to her ('I will be rejected'). In the next session the scenario was revised to make sure no neutralisations were included in the description which would hinder functional exposure. The next step was for Samantha to record herself reading the exposure scenario. The first exposure was conducted in session where Samantha listened to the audio record. Subsequently, Samantha was given the homework to listen to the record at least once per day, with the goal to feel increased anxiety followed by its return to baseline levels to allow for emotional processing of her core fear. During the exposure module Samantha reported that she had learned her avoidance of thinking about her core fear had increased her sense that the worst outcome was the most likely. But, afterwards, she was more able to dismiss these worries as far-fetched and look at all the clues in her life that she was doing a good job and was a caring person.

In the last two sessions the work was focussed on relapse prevention. Samantha reported that she had found the problem-solving training the most practical thing she learned during treatment and that she would be able to use it on daily basis. Furthermore, that she thought to continue facing the uncertainty of life would be a key thing for here to increase her recovery. During the last sessions Samantha said that even though she knew that being a parent involved facing many uncertainties she was now looking forward to being a mother but not terrified of it as before treatment.

The CT Protocol

CT for GAD is based on the cognitive theory of emotional disorders [8,22,58,61] which states that when people experience anxiety they *believe* that they are threatened with a social or physical harm. Here, the persons interpretations of what is happening to them is the key, that is, what the situation or what is happening *means* to them. The intensity of the threat appraisal is based on a synergistic interaction between the perceived awfulness of the threat (the idiosyncratic *meaning* of the threat), perceived likelihood of the threat (which is increased by the perceived awfulness) and perceived coping/rescue factors. The exaggerated threat appraisal triggers belief-maintaining responses: safety-seeking behaviours, physiological changes and changes in attention (such as selective attention towards threat). Here safety-seeking behaviours play a key role. These behaviours are meaningfully linked to the threat beliefs. They are meant to explicitly deal with the perceived threat in some way or another but ultimately maintain the problem because they prevent the opportunity to test the validity of exaggerated threat beliefs.

CT for GAD begins with psychoeducation and socialisation to the cognitive theory of GAD. In the first session an idiosyncratic formulation is developed highlighting the role of exaggerated threat beliefs and the factors that prevent their disconfirmation. This is considered a first version of the formulation and will be updated as needed throughout as therapy proceeds. Interestingly, CT is the only treatment for GAD which explicitly identifies case formulation as a key therapeutic technique.

In the second session the patient is thought to use automatic thought records to identify their anxious thoughts and develop alternative thoughts. Importantly, the information generated using the thought records are used to guide behavioural experiments where the threat beliefs are tested by doing things differently, such as dropping safety-seeking behaviours. Behavioural experiments, both within and between sessions, are introduced in session three and used continuously throughout therapy. In session six the role of conditional beliefs is discussed, and these beliefs then identified and tested in behavioural experiments. Based on the Butler et al. [20] protocol it is expected that treatment will go on for twelve sessions with up three follow up sessions. CT for GAD assumes that for every patient, behind all the different worries (and the shifting focus of worry topics) is an idiosyncratic meaning-making structure that incorporates unhelpful beliefs and assumptions. Therefore, in CT for GAD the goal is to formulate what beliefs ties all the different worry topics together and then proceeds by working on the underlying beliefs assumptions instead of dealing individually with each worry topic [20].

Recent developments on the cognitive theory of GAD

Gústavsson et al. [35,36] updated the cognitive theory of GAD based on developments in the cognitive theory of anxiety disorders that precede the Butler [20] protocol. Most importantly, Gústavsson [35,36] highlights the role of various safety-seeking behaviours in the maintenance of threat beliefs in GAD, such as excessive reassurance seeking, worry as an excessive search for safety and hypervigilance. Here excessive worry is seen as a thwarted problem-solving process [27] as opposed to being fundamentally pathological. Furthermore, in this updated account of GAD unhelpful beliefs about responsibility ('It is my responsibility to make sure everyone is happy and safe'; 'It is important that I am careful to make sure that I don't upset other people') are thought play an important role. Gústavsson et al. [35] explicitly hypothesise that the 'theme of threat beliefs in GAD can be conceptualised as a tendency to understand the outcome of external everyday situations such as making the cake for your child's birthday party, taking exams, or the well-being of your family and friends, in a way that you bear responsibility for the outcome and that you are accountable to others for the outcome' [36, p. 8].

The clinical implications of this updated version of the cognitive theory of GAD are mainly threefold: (1) more attention is paid to safety-seeking behaviours and consequently behavioural experiments, (2) excessive worry is conceptualised as over-practiced search for safety and (3) using the initial vicious-circle formulation, theory A (the understanding of the problem that the patient brings to therapy) and theory B (an alternative, less threatening view of the problem) are developed collaboratively by the patient and the therapist [61]. Therefore, an updated version of CT for GAD introduces (1) behavioural experiments where the effects of safety-seeking behaviours on anxiety and worry are tested, (2) behavioural experiments where safety-seeking behaviours are dropped for belief-disconfirmation, (3) attention training where shifting focus externally is encouraged to aid with behavioural experiments and as well as to test the felt uncontrollability of worries and (4) beliefs and assumptions about responsibility are tested via series of behavioural experiments. The key therapeutic models of the updated CT for GAD are as follows: (1) psychoeducation about GAD and anxiety/socialisation to CBT; (2) formulation based on a shared understanding of the problem (theory A/B); (3) increasing awareness about anxiety and worry; (4) attention training to increase externally focussed attention and engagement; (5) testing the felt uncontrollability of worries; (6) testing threat beliefs and core beliefs with behavioural experiments; (7) collecting information to affirm the shared understanding.

Case Example: Tosh

Tosh was a 35-year-old woman, who lived with her husband and two daughters (9 and 4 years old). She used to work in retail business, in a senior position, but had not worked since the birth of her older daughter due to birth related complications which exacerbated her chronic pain problem leaving her unable to carry on working out of her home. Previously, she had had successful treatment for an eating disorder and post-traumatic stress disorder, but her anxieties and worries remained intact. She had now been referred to psychological treatment by her GP which was concerned about her mental health due to the chronic pain problem. Initially she was quite hesitant accepting that she had an anxiety problem and ambivalent about committing to treatment. In all, Tosh had 14 therapy sessions with two booster sessions.

The first session was mainly devoted to psychoeducation about GAD and socialisation to CBT. In this session Tosh voiced here ambivalence to committing to treatment. She said that she could not imagine herself not worrying and that she would be unable to change her thoughts as she has been like this all her life. Furthermore, when discussing the impact of her pain problem on her daily life Tosh said that it was 'not an option to give up – I have to keep on going, can´t complain and just power through'. Here the therapist gently reminded her that the goal of therapy was not to stop worry altogether or become 'lazy' or 'uncaring' person, but instead, finding ways to take back control from the worries. As well as to do the things that are important to her (be a good caring mother, spouse and a friend) without feeling overwhelmed.

In the following session the goal was to develop a formulation of Tosh´s anxiety problem (and its interaction with her chronic pain problem) in a collaborative manner. A vicious flower formulation was sketched using a recent worry bout that was typical for her problem (see Figure 14.3).

We also examined specifically the effect of the safety-seeking behaviours on her chronic pain problem. Even though Tosh was hesitant to discuss this she acknowledged that when she was trying to do everything and not giving her any slack, this resulted in increased fatigue and pain, exhaustion and poor sleep due to intense pain. And that her feeling exhausted also fed back to her anxious thoughts making them more believable.

During further discussion about the vicious flower several conditional beliefs were identified: If something goes wrong it is my fault and would prove to myself and others that I am faulty, hopeless, and inadequate; to protect myself everything I do has to be 100% (no less is acceptable); I can never show any signs of weakness and must never, ever give up.

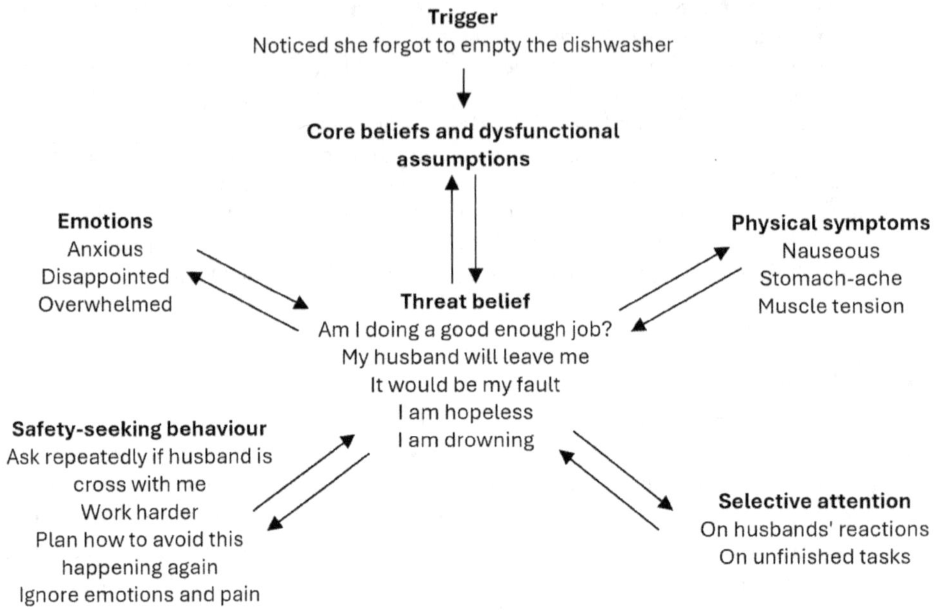

Figure 14.3 Formulation of Tosh's worry problem.

In sessions 3 and 4, theory A and B were developed (see Table 14.2). Tosh felt she could understand theory B intellectually but voiced concerns that she would ever be able to really believe it, because she had believed theory A for as long as she could remember, and that it had become automatic in her daily life. Furthermore, she could see how theory B was more aligned with her goals of being a good and caring mother because it would allow her to relax, be more present minded and, importantly, allow her to manage her pain problem more adaptively. Here it was highlighted that moving on, treatment would focus on testing out these theories to see which predicted best how the world really works [61,63]. Importantly, theory A and B were used to figure out what learning experience (behavioural experiments) would be helpful for Tosh to learn something new about her anxiety problem and new ways to deal with it.

Because excessive worry and other safety-seeking behaviours are often highly proceduralised in GAD it is important to help patients decrease their automaticity. After session 4, where theory A and B were developed, Tosh got the homework assignment to write down her worries three times during each day: (1) after her daughters had gone to school and she was alone at home, (2) just before she picked them up in the afternoon and (3) after they fell asleep. A further part of this assignment was that Tosh was supposed to (1) ask herself whether the perceived threat underlying every worry topic matched with theory A, and (2) what safety-seeking behaviours she engaged in for each worry topic.

In session 5 attention training was introduced, first with thought-suppression exercises [65] and then systematic training in externally focussed, non-evaluative attention in the same fashion as is done in CT for social anxiety disorder. The rationale for attention training in GAD is to help patients experience a sense of control over their attention and worries as well to assist with later behavioural experiments where it is

Table 14.2 Two ways to look at the world: Tosh´s theory A and theory B

Theory A	Theory B
The problem is that I AM a faulty, hopeless, and inadequate as a person. If I make mistakes, fail at something, or do not excel. other people will see my true self, judge me in a negative way and abandon me. Therefore, I must do everything perfectly, never make mistakes, be careful of how I behave and what I say, be constantly alert and mindful of what needs to be done, repeatedly check and seek reassurance to try to be absolutely certain that I have not failed and disappointed other people or caused them any harm.	The problem is that I FEEL LIKE I am a faulty, hopeless, and inadequate as a person because of the unfair things that have happened to me. This makes feel responsible for everything that can go wrong and that I need to 100% certain that I am not failing other people. This strategy really helped me when I was living in a hostile environment. Unfortunately, today, my attempts to reach certainty by making myself worry, repeatedly seeking reassurance, watch my behaviour, and being alert all the time reinforces my sense of uncertainty and threat which exacerbates my anxiety (and my pain problem).

essential to collect information about what really happened as opposed to what 'I felt was happening' [36]. With attention training Tosh was able to see that she did not need to supress intrusive thoughts but could instead become aware of them and try to focus her attention to something else in her environment.

The remaining sessions focussed on testing out Theory A and B with various behavioural experiments and information gathering. One of the first experiments was to not ignore emotions and physical symptoms but to be mindful of them and try to manage them (such as pausing, laying down, play with daughters and focus externally) instead of pushing on. Tosh found this experiment difficult to do so we designed an A-B-A experimental design. On day one Tosh would behave as theory A was true and on day two, she would behave as theory B was true and so forth. Here we wanted to test the effects of these safety-seeking behaviours on her anxious symptoms. What Tosh found out is that her anxiety was as high in both conditions but when she behaved according to theory B, she felt less overwhelmed and disappointed because (1) she was able to take a much-needed rest and (2) spent more time with her daughters which is the most important thing to her.

Importantly, the case formulation provided Tosh with motivation to engage in experiments which she found difficult. The formulation helped her to see that even though she often felt that the safety-seeking behaviours were helpful they also made her pain problem unbearable which in turn made her worries worse.

Other behavioural experiments involved using surveys to gather information about other people's attitudes, substituting reassurance seeking with support seeking [37,38] sharing responsibilities for house chores with husband, not doing everything at 100% (or higher) but do what was realistic for her due to her pain problem, acknowledging to herself when she was in too much pain or fatigued, discussing her illness with people close to her and giver herself the time to engage in her hobbies. All these experiments were devised to test whether theory A or B fitted the world better. Tosh was able to learn that her worst fears of people abandoning her if she would make mistakes or fail at something were exaggerated. What she found that most of the people closest to her had found it uncomfortable how she was always on top of things and went out of her way to make sure that everyone was OK, and importantly, that they, in general, found her to be among the most caring and kind people they knew. Furthermore, she was able to give her the time she needed to manage her pain problem more successfully which helped her to live the life she wanted to have.

Conclusion

GAD is a chronic, impairing mental health problem that is systematically understudied, is often undetected in health care settings and many therapists find difficult to treat. GAD can be difficult to treat but by combining case formulation with the flexible use of evidence-based protocols every patient is given the chance to gain recovery from their anxiety problem.

Multiple models and treatment protocols for GAD have been developed and it is safe to state that it is almost impossible for clinicians to keep up with all the latest developments in the GAD literature. However, the treatment protocols recommended by the NICE guidelines and the BABCP core curriculum, overlap both in theory and practice which makes it possible for CBT therapists to acquire competence in all of them. It is important that CBT therapists are equipped with good understanding of behavioural and cognitive theories of anxiety disorders to be apple to make clinical decisions on what procedures to use when working with GAD.

The key differences between the available protocols are (1) the use of habituation versus belief disconfirmation techniques and (2) the use of behavioural techniques explicitly to decrease physical symptoms or the use of reduction in anxiety in general through reversing maintenance factors of unhelpful beliefs. In the former category consists of the AR, the AMW and MAW protocols but the IUS and the CT protocols under the latter.

There are still considerable developments taking place in CBT for GAD. The CMW protocol [40], which was excluded for detailed discussion in this chapter, builds on the AMW protocol and has shown promising results in clinical settings [40]. The meta-cognitive model as well has been shown to efficacious in several RCT's, both within research [50] and clinical settings [1]. We can expect that these protocols will be included in the NICE guidelines and the BABCP curriculum in the near future. Furthermore, the IUS and the CT protocols have been revised to include key empirically based psychological interventions such as belief disconfirmation experiments and attention training [35,36,39]. Even though not part of the NICE recommended protocols, the revisions for both these protocols are based on empirically grounded interventions and strong theoretical grounds and are therefore applicable to be used clinically [59].

As therapist, we should in general adopt the mindset of seeing the glass as half-full but not half empty [34], especially when working with people with chronic problems and that have not gained from previous therapy. Furthermore, clinical practice should be guided by the scientist-practitioner model where clinical practice is informed by outcome studies, but importantly, also by empirically grounded interventions that are known to reverse key psychological maintenance factors [59] such as belief disconfirmation experiments [60,67]. It is our hope that this chapter will help you with your work with patients that are battling with GAD and spark some enthusiasm to improve the care that this group receives in the spirit of the scientist-practitioner model.

Further Reading

Beck AT, Emery G, Greenberg RL. *Anxiety Disorders and Phobias: A Cognitive Perspective.* New York: Basic Books; 1985.

Borkovec TD. Applied relaxation and cognitive therapy for pathological worry and generalized anxiety disorder. In GCL Davey, A Wells (Eds.), *Worry and Its Psychological Disorders: Theory, Assessment and Treatment* (pp. 273–288). Chichester: Wiley Publishing;2006.

Foa EB, Kozak MJ. Emotional processing of fear: Exposure to corrective information. *Psychology Bulletin*, 1986;***99***(1):20–35.

Öst LG. Applied relaxation: Description of a coping technique and review of controlled studies. *Behaviour Research and Therapy*, 1987;***25***(5):397–409. https://doi.org/10.1016/0005-7967(87)90017-9.

Robichaud M, Koerner N, Dugas MJ. *Cognitive-Behavioral Treatment for Generalized Anxiety Disorder: From Science to Practice.* 2nd ed. New York: Routledge; 2019.

Salkovskis PM. The cognitive approach to anxiety: Threat beliefs, safety-seeking behaviour, and the special case of health anxiety and obsessions. In PM Salkovskis (Ed.), *Frontiers of Cognitive Therapy* (pp. 48–75). New York: Guilford; 1996.

Sibrava N, Borkovec TD. The cognitive avoidance theory of worry. In GCL Davey, A Wells (Eds.), *Worry and Its Psychological Disorders: Theory, Assessment and Treatment* (pp. 217–237). Chichester: Wiley Publishing; 2006.

Zinbarg RE, Craske MG, Barlow DH. *Mastery of Your Anxiety and Worry (Therapist Guide).* 2nd ed. Oxford: Oxford University Press; 2006.

References

1. Af Winklerfelt Hammarberg S, Toth-Pal E, Jansson-Fröjmark M, Lundgren T, Westman J, Bohman B. Intolerance-of-uncertainty therapy versus metacognitive therapy for generalized anxiety disorder in primary health care: A randomized controlled pilot trial. *PloS One*, 2023;***18***(6):e0287171. https://doi.org/10.1371/journal.pone.0287171.
2. American Psychiatric Association. *Diagnostic and Statistical Manual of Mental Disorders* 3rd ed. rev. Washington, DC: American Psychiatric Association; 1987.
3. American Psychiatric Association. *Diagnostic and Statistical Manual of Mental Disorders* 4th ed. Washington, DC: American Psychiatric Association; 1994.
4. American Psychiatric Association. *Diagnostic and Statistical Manual of Mental Disorders* 5th ed. Washington, DC: Author. American Psychiatric Association; 2013.
5. Andrews G, Hobbs MJ, Borkovec TD, Beesdo K, Craske MG, Heimberg, RG et al. Generalized worry disorder: A review of DSM-IV generalized anxiety disorder and options for DSM-V. *Depression and Anxiety*, 2010;***27***(2):134–147. https://doi.org/10.1002/da.20658.
6. Barlow DH. *Anxiety and Its Disorders: The Nature and Treatment of Anxiety and Panic.* New York: Guilford Press; 2004.
7. Beck AT. *Cognitive Therapy and the Emotional Disorders.* Harmondsworth: Penguin; 1976.
8. Beck AT, Emery G, Greenberg RL. *Anxiety Disorders and Phobias: A Cognitive Perspective.* New York: Basic Books; 1985.
9. Behar E, DiMarco ID, Hekler EB, Mohlman J, Staples AM. Current theoretical models of generalised anxiety disorder (GAD): Conceptual review and treatment implications. *Journal of Anxiety Disorders*, 2009;***23***(8):1011–1023. https://doi.org/10.1016/j.janxdis.2009.07.006.

10. Bernstein DA, Borkovec TD. *Progressive Relaxation Training: A Manual for the Helping Professions*. Illinois: Research Press; 1973.

11. Bernstein, DA, Borkovec TD, Hazlett-Stevens H. *New Directions in Progressive Relaxation Training: A Guidebook for Helping Professionals*. Westport: Praeger Publishers; 2000.

12. Borkovec TD, Costello E. Efficacy of applied relaxation and cognitive-behavioral therapy in the treatment of generalized anxiety disorder. *Journal of Consulting and Clinical Psychology*, 1993;***61***(4):611–619. https://doi.org/10.1037/0022-006X.61.4.611.

13. Borkovec TD, Alcaine O, Behar E. Avoidance theory of worry and generalised anxiety disorder. In RG Heimberg, CL Turk, DS Mennin (Eds.), *Generalised Anxiety Disorder: Advances in Research and Practice* (pp. 77–108). New York: Guilford Press; 2004.

14. Borkovec TD, Robinson E, Pruzinsky T, DePree JA. Preliminary exploration of worry: Some characteristics and processes. *Behaviour Research and Therapy*, ***21***(1), 9–16. https://doi.org/10.1016/0005-7967(83)90121-3.

15. Borkovec TD, Newman MG. Worry and generalized anxiety disorder. In AS Bellack, M Hersen (Series Eds.), P Salkovskis (Vol. Ed.), *Comprehensive Clinical Psychology: Vol. 6. Adults: Clinical Formulation and Treatment* (pp. 439–459). London: Pergamon Press; 1998.

16. Borkovec TD. Applied relaxation and cognitive therapy for pathological worry and generalized anxiety disorder. In GCL Davey, A Wells (Eds.), *Worry and Its Psychological Disorders: Theory, Assessment and Treatment* (pp. 273–288). Chichester: Wiley Publishing; 2006.

17. Breitholtz E, Johansson B, Öst LG. Cognitions in generalised anxiety disorder and panic disorder patients: A prospective approach. *Behaviour Research and Therapy*, 1999; ***37***(6):533–544. https://doi.org/10.1016/S0005-7967(98)00147-8.

18. Breitholtz E, Westling BE, Öst LG. Cognitions in generalised anxiety disorder and panic disorder patients. *Journal of Anxiety Disorders*, 1998;***12***(6):567–577. https://doi.org/10.1016/S0887-6185(98)00034-6.

19. Brown TA, Campbell LA, Lehman CL, Grisham JR, Mancill RB. Current and lifetime comorbidity of the DSM-IV anxiety and mood disorders in a large clinical sample. *Journal of Abnormal Psychology*, 2001;***110***(4):585–599. https://doi.org/10.1037/0021-843X.110.4.585.

20. Butler G, Fennell M, Robson P, Gelder M. Comparison of behavior therapy and cognitive behavior therapy in the treatment of generalised anxiety disorder. *Journal of Consulting and Clinical Psychology*, 1991;***59***(1):167–175. https://doi.org/10.1037/0022-006x.59.1.167.

21. Clark DM. Anxiety states: Panic and generalised anxiety. In K Hawton, PM Salkovskis, J Kirk, DM Clark (Eds.), *Cognitive Behaviour Therapy for Psychiatric Problems: A Practical Guide* (pp. 52–96). Oxford: Oxford University Press; 1989.

22. Clark DM. Cognitive therapy for anxiety. *Behavioural and Cognitive Psychotherapy*, 1986;***14***(4):283–294.

23. Craske MG, Barlow DH. *Mastery of Your Anxiety and Worry*. Oxford: Oxford University Press; 2006.

24. Crocq MA. The history of generalised anxiety disorder as a diagnostic category. *Dialogues in Clinical Neuroscience*, 2017; ***19***(2):107–115. https://doi.org/10.4324/9781315079097-30.

25. Cuijpers P, Sijbrandij M, Koole S, Huibers M, Berking M, Andersson G. Psychological treatment of generalised anxiety disorder: A meta-analysis. *Clinical Psychology Review*, 2014;***34***(2):130–140. https://doi.org/10.1016/j.cpr.2014.01.002.

26. Cuijpers P, Gentili C, Banos RM, Garcia-Campayo J, Botella C, Cristea IA. Relative effects of cognitive and behavioral therapies on generalized anxiety disorder, social anxiety disorder and panic disorder: A meta-analysis. *Journal of Anxiety Disorders*. 2016;**43**:79–89.

27. Davey GCL. Pathological worrying as exacerbated problem-solving. In GCL Davey, F Tallis (Eds.), *Worrying: Perspectives on Theory, Assessment, and Treatment* (pp. 35–59). Chichester: John Wiley & Sons; 1994.

28. Dugas M, Robichaud M. *Cognitive-Behavioural Treatment for Generalised Anxiety Disorder: From Science to Practice.* Routledge;2007.

29. Dugas MJ, Anderson KG, Deschenes SS, Donegan E. Generalized anxiety disorder publications: Where do we stand a decade later? *Journal of Anxiety Disorders*, 2010; ***24*** (7):780–784. https://doi.org/10.1016/j.janxdis.2010.05.012.

30. Dugas MJ, Gagnon F, Ladouceur R, Freeston MH. Generalized anxiety disorder: A preliminary test of a conceptual model. *Behaviour Research and Therapy*,1998; ***36***(2):215–226. https://doi.org/10.1016/S0005-7967(97)00070-3.

31. Dugas MJ, Sexton KA, Hebert EA, Bouchard S, Gouin J-P, Shafran R. Behavioral experiments for intolerance of uncertainty: A randomized clinical trial for adults with generalized anxiety isorder. *Behavior Therapy*. 2022;53(6):1147–1160. https://doi.org/10.1016/j.beth.2022.05.003.

32. Foa EB, Kozak MJ. Emotional processing of fear: Exposure to corrective information. *Psychology Bulletin*, 1986;***99***(1):20–35.

33. Freeston MH. What if we have too many models of worry and GAD? *Behavioural and Cognitive Psychotherapy*, 2023:1–20. https://doi.org/10.1017/s1352465822000649.

34. Geschwind, N., & Dunn, B. D. The glass half-full or half-empty: A within-subject comparison of solution-focused versus problem-focused client descriptions on therapist emotions and hope for treatment. *Behavioural and Cognitive Psychotherapy*, 2023:1–6. https://doi.org/10.1017/s135246582300022x.

35. Gústavsson SM, Salkovskis PM, Sigurðsson JF. Cognitive analysis of specific threat beliefs and safety-seeking behaviours in generalised anxiety disorder: Revisiting the cognitive theory of anxiety disorders. *Behavioural and Cognitive Psychotherapy*, 2021:1–14. https://doi.org/10.1017/S135246582100014X.

36. Gústavsson SM, Salkovskis PM, Sigurðsson JF. (2022). Revised Beckian cognitive therapy for generalised anxiety disorder. *Cognitive Behaviour Therapist*, ***15***. https://doi.org/10.1017/S1754470X22000563.

37. Halldorsson B, Salkovskis PM. Why do people with OCD and health anxiety seek reassurance excessively? An investigation of differences and similarities in function. *Cognitive Therapy and Research*, 2017;***41*** (4):619–631. https://doi.org/10.1007/s10608-016-9826-5.

38. Halldorsson B, Salkovskis PM. Reassurance and its alternatives: Overview and cognitive behavioural conceptualisation. *Journal of Obsessive-Compulsive and Related Disorders*, (2023);*36*:100783. https://doi.org/10.1016/j.jocrd.2023.100783.

39. Hebert EA, Dugas MJ. Behavioral experiments for intolerance of uncertainty: Challenging the unknown in the treatment of generalized anxiety disorder. *Cognitive and Behavioral Practice*, 2019;***26*** (2):421–436. https://doi.org/10.1016/j.cbpra.2018.07.007.

40. Hirsch CR, Beale S, Grey N, Liness S. Approaching cognitive behavior therapy For generalized anxiety disorder from a cognitive process perspective. *Frontiers in Psychiatry*, 2019;***10***(November):1–14. https://doi.org/10.3389/fpsyt.2019.00796.

41. Hoffman DL, Dukes EM, Wittchen HU. Human and economic burden of generalised anxiety disorder. *Depression and Anxiety*, 2008;***25***:72–90. https://doi.org/10.1002/da.

42. Jacobson E. *Progressive Relaxation.* Chicago: University of Chicago Press; 1938.

43. Kessler RC. The epidemiology of pure and comorbid generalized anxiety disorder: A review and evaluation of recent research. *Acta Psychiatrica Scandinavica, Supplement*, 2000;***102***(406):7–13. https://doi.org/10.1111/j.0065-1591.2000.acp29-02.x.

44. Kessler R, Keller M, Wittchen HU. Epidemiology of generalized anxiety disorder. *Psychiatric Clinics of North America*, 2001;***24***(1):19–39.

45. Lang PJ. Fear reduction and fear behavior: Problems in treating a construct. In JM Shlien (Ed.), *Research in Psychotherapy* (Vol. **3**, pp. 90–102). American Psychological Association; 1968.

46. Mathews A. Why worry? The cognitive function of anxiety. *Behaviour Research and Therapy*, 1990:***28***(6):455–468. https://doi.org/10.1016/0005-7967(90)90132-3.

47. Mowrer OH. On the dual nature of learning: A re-interpretation of 'conditioning' and 'problem solving'. *Harvard Educational Review*, 1947;**17**:102–148.

48. Newman MG, Castonguay LG, Borkovec TD, Fisher AJ, Boswell F, Szkodny LE, Nordberg SS. A randomized controlled trial of cognitive-behavioral therapy from emotion-focused and interpersonal therapies. *Journal of Consulting and Clinical Psychology*, 2011;***79***(2):171–181. https://doi.org/10.1037/a0022489.A.

49. NICE. *Common Mental Health Disorders: Identification and Pathways to Care. Clinical Guideline 123*. London, UK: National Institute for Health and Clinical Excellence; 2011. www.nice.org.uk.

50. Normann N, Van Emmerik AAP, Morina N. The efficacy of metacognitive therapy for anxiety and depression: A meta-analytic review. *Depression and Anxiety*, 2014;***31***(5): 402–411. https://doi.org/10.1002/da.22273.

51. Olfson M, Gameroff MJ. Generalized anxiety disorder, somatic pain and health care costs. *General Hospital Psychiatry*, 2007;***29***(4):310–316.

52. Olssøn I, Mykletun A, Dahl AA. Recognition and treatment recommendations for generalized anxiety disorder and major depressive episode: A cross-sectional study among general practitioners in Norway. *Primary Care Companion to the Journal of Clinical Psychiatry*, 2006;***8***(6):340–347. https://doi.org/10.4088/pcc.v08n0604.

53. Öst LG. Applied relaxation: Description of a coping technique and review of controlled studies. *Behaviour Research and Therapy*, 1987;***25***(5):397–409. https://doi.org/10.1016/0005-7967(87)90017-9.

54. Roberge P, Normand-Lauzière F, Raymond I, Luc M, Tanguay-Bernard MM, Duhoux A et al. Generalized anxiety disorder in primary care: Mental health services use and treatment adequacy. *BMC Family Practice*, 2015;***16***(1):19–21. https://doi.org/10.1186/s12875-015-0358-y.

55. Robichaud M, Koerner N, Dugas MJ. *Cognitive-Behavioral Treatment for Generalized Anxiety Disorder: From Science to Practice* 2nd ed. New York: Routledge; 2019.

56. Ruscio AM, Chiu WT, Roy-Byrne P, Stang PE, Stein DJ, Wittchen HU, Kessler RC. Broadening the definition of generalized anxiety disorder: Effects on prevalence and associations with other disorders in the National Comorbidity Survey Replication. *Journal of Anxiety Disorders*, 2007;***21***(5):662–676.

57. Ruscio AM, Hallion LS, Lim CCW, Aguilar-Gaxiola S, Al-Hamzawi A, Alonso J et al. Cross-sectional comparison of the epidemiology of DSM-5 generalized anxiety disorder across the globe. *JAMA Psychiatry*, 2017;***74***(5):465–475. https://doi.org/10.1001/jamapsychiatry.2017.0056.

58. Salkovskis PM. The importance of behaviour in the maintenance of anxiety and panic: A cognitive account. *Behavioural Psychotherapy*, 1991;***19***(1):6–19. https://doi.org/10.1017/S0141347300011472.

59. Salkovskis PM. Empirically grounded clinical interventions: Cognitive-behavioural therapy progresses through a multi-dimensional approach to clinical science. *Behavioural and Cognitive Psychotherapy*, 2002;***30***(1):3–9. https://doi.org/10.1017/s1352465802001029.

60. Salkovskis PM, Hackmann A, Wells A, Gelder MG, Clark DM. Belief disconfirmation versus habituation approaches to situational exposure in panic disorder with agoraphobia: A pilot study.

Behaviour Research and Therapy, 2007;***45***(5):877–885. https://doi.org/10.1016/j.brat.2006.02.008.

61. Salkovskis PM. The cognitive approach to anxiety: Threat beliefs, safety-seeking behaviour, and the special case of health anxiety and obsessions. In PM Salkovskis, (Ed.), *Frontiers of Cognitive Therapy* (pp. 48–75). New York: Guilford; 1996.

62. Sibrava N, Borkovec TD. The cognitive avoidance theory of worry. In GCL Davey, A Wells (Eds.), *Worry and Its Psychological Disorders: Theory, Assessment and Treatment* (pp. 217–237). Chichester: Wiley Publishing; 2006.

63. Sighvatsson MB, Salkovskis PM, Sigurdsson E, Valdimarsdottir HB, Thorsdottir F, Sigurdsson JF. Evaluation of mechanism of change in transdiagnostic cognitive behaviour therapy using single case experimental design. *Journal of Behavior Therapy and Experimental Psychiatry*, 2021;***71***:101634. https://doi.org/10.1016/j.jbtep.2020.101634.

64. Warnock-Parkes E, Wild J, Stott R, Grey N, Ehlers A, Clark, DM. Seeing is believing: Using video feedback in cognitive therapy for social anxiety disorder. *Cognitive and Behavioral Practice*, 2017;***24***(2):245–255. https://doi.org/10.1016/j.cbpra.2016.03.007.

65. Wegner DM, Schneider DJ, Carter SR, White TL. Paradoxical effects of thought suppression. *Journal of Personality and Social Psychology*, 1987;**53**(1):5–13. https://doi.org/10.1037/0022-3514.53.1.5.

66. Wells A. A metacognitive model and therapy for generalized anxiety disorder. *Clinical Psychology and Psychotherapy*, 1999;**6**:86–95.

67. Wells A, Clark DM, Salkovskis P, Ludgate J, Hackmann A, Gelder M. Social phobia: The role of in-situation safety behaviors in maintaining anxiety and negative beliefs. *Behavior Therapy*, 1995;***47***(5):669–674. https://doi.org/10.1016/j.beth.2016.08.010.

68. Wittchen HU. Generalized anxiety disorder: Prevalence, burden, and cost to society. *Depression and Anxiety*, 2002;***16***(4):162–171. https://doi.org/10.1002/da.10065.

69. Wittchen HU, Hoyer J. Generalized anxiety disorder: Nature and course. *Journal of Clinical Psychiatry*, 2001:***62***:15–21.

70. Wolpe J. *Psychotherapy by Reciprocal Inhibition*. Stanford: Stanford University Press; 1958.

71. Zinbarg RE. Concordance and synchrony in measures of anxiety and panic reconsidered: A hierarchical model of anxiety and panic. *Behavior Therapy*, 1998:***29***(2):301–323. https://doi.org/10.1016/S0005-7894(98)80009-9.

72. Zinbarg RE, Craske MG, Barlow DH. *Mastery of Your Anxiety and Worry (Therapist Guide)*. 2nd ed. Oxford: Oxford University Press; 2006.

73. Revicki DA, Travers K, Wyrwich KW, Svedsäter H, Locklear J, Mattera MS, et al. Humanistic and economic burden of generalized anxiety disorder in North America and Europe. *Journal of Affective Disorders*, 2012:***140***(2):103–112.

74. Carter RM, Wittchen HU, Pfister H, Kessler RC. One-year prevalence of subthreshold and threshold DSM-IV generalized anxiety disorder in a nationally representative sample. *Depression and Anxiety*, 2001;***13***(2):78–88.

Chapter 15

Obsessive Compulsive or Related Disorders

In this chapter we will help you to be able to:

- Describe the impact of preoccupation, a sense of responsibility and locus of control in these disorders.
- Explain how anxiety disorder interventions were further modified to better aid these presentations.

Introduction

Outside of the core anxiety disorders, there are a number of other diagnoses where anxiety plays a key role, as well as other strong emotions – particularly disgust, shame and guilt. A unifying feature of these disorders is the role of preoccupation with a feared concept, along with a sense of responsibility and personal control. While the DSM-5TR [1] has these disorders of preoccupation across multiple categories, the ICD-11 [2] brings them all under the category of Obsessive Compulsive or Related Disorders (OCRD). This represents a shift from earlier classification systems, and highlights the increasing awareness in the field of the central role of preoccupation and repetitive behaviours in these difficulties [3]. Treatment for these disorders is thus focussed on changing the repetitive behaviours and helping the patient to let go of their preoccupation.

Applying Behavioural Theory to OCRD: Exposure and Response Prevention

OCRD are united by distress that is managed through the use of repetitive response behaviours, rather than solely through avoidance and escape. This makes sense, given that the triggers of the distress are often internal – an intrusive thought, a mental self-image or a physical sensation – none of which can be avoided or escaped. As such, exposure alone would simply result in an increase in their repetitive behaviours, and a subsequent reinforcement of the primary issue.

To combat this, exposure with response prevention is needed – where the patient is exposed to their feared trigger, and at the same time encouraged to drop their responses. In doing this, the patient can experience their distress reducing, and their feared outcomes not occurring, without using their repetitive behaviours, and so the link between the preoccupation and the responses is broken. In practice, this could involve the patient with contamination OCD touching 'contaminated' items without washing or keeping a mental track of where they've touched. Likewise, the patient with health anxiety could expose themselves to videos about their feared disease, without body scanning, googling symptoms or asking for reassurance.

As in anxiety disorders, such exposure work can be done in two different ways – focussing on the distress tolerance, or focussing on disconfirming the beliefs of what would happen if the patient exposed themselves and doesn't use their response behaviours. In the former, exposure hierarchies with responses to be prevented can be used to make a plan for the bulk of the work. In the latter, theory A/B is particularly useful as such a guide, especially as it is often impossible to truly disprove various feared beliefs, but it can be possible to build evidence for an alternative explanation – that the patient's symptoms and distress is being caused by preoccupation.

Concluding Remarks

OCRD are conditions where the key driver of distress is an enduring preoccupation with a feared outcome, which is managed through the use of repetitive behaviours. Treatment for these disorders is centred around exposure with response prevention, to break the link between the use of responses and the distress otherwise experienced.

References

1. American Psychiatric Association, ed. (2022). *Diagnostic and Statistical Manual of Mental Disorders: DSM-5-TR*. 5th ed., text revision. Washington, DC: American Psychiatric Association Publishing.
2. World Health Organization. (2019). *International Classification of Diseases*. 11th Revision (ICD-11). World Health Organization.
3. van den Heuvel, O. A., Veale, D., & Stein, D. J. (2014). Hypochondriasis: Considerations for ICD-11. *Rev Bras Psiquiatr*, 36(Suppl 1), 21–27.

Chapter 16

Obsessive Compulsive Disorder

In this chapter we will help you to be able to:

- Explain what OCD is and how it typically presents.
- Describe and use evidence-based CBT protocols for OCD.
- Choose and use appropriate formulation models for CBT for OCD.
- Describe the importance of using exposure and response prevention and/or behavioural experiments in any treatment plan.
- Develop a treatment plan for CBT for OCD, using appropriate measures.
- Take account of comorbidity in managing CBT for OCD.

Introduction

Obsessive compulsive disorder (OCD) is characterised by the presence of obsessions and compulsions, which are often time consuming and cause significant impairment in the individual's life. Historically, OCD was considered a treatment resistant condition, with various treatment approaches – including early implementations of CBT – failing to change the problem or provide relief. However, since the 1980s, targeted CBT approaches to this problem have been developed and refined, largely focussing around the novel concepts of exposure with response prevention (ERP) and behavioural experiments. These newer approaches have been found to be highly effective, resulting in CBT being the only psychological treatment of choice for OCD, as recommended by NICE guidelines [1].

This chapter will explore the unique nature of OCD and the development of CBT treatment approaches to work with this disorder. We will then go into greater detail about the three most efficacious and commonly used protocols in current UK practice, namely those of Kozak and Foa [2], Wilhelm and Steketee [3] and Salkovskis et al. [4,5].

What Is OCD?

To be diagnosed with OCD via the DSM-5, an individual must be experiencing obsessions and/or compulsions. Obsessions can be thoughts, images or urges, which occur repeatedly and stay with the individual. To be considered an obsession, these thoughts, urges or images must at times be both intrusive and unwelcome, and as such will be distressing in some way. Compulsions meanwhile are repetitive behaviours that the person will carry out either in response to the obsession or according to specific rules. These compulsive behaviours can either be overt (such as hand washing) or covert (mental behaviours such as praying or counting) and are done to either reduce feelings of distress or to somehow prevent something bad from happening.

Further criteria dictate that these obsessions and/or compulsions must be emotionally distressing, functionally impairing, or be time consuming, which is defined as taking at least one hour per day. In reality, most individuals with OCD lose far more time than this to their condition. OCD is also a persistent condition; the typical age of onset is between 15 and 20 years old [6] but individuals take an average of 11 years to access treatment after first meeting diagnostic criteria [7], and few spontaneously recover without this support. Given this, it is unsurprising that OCD was one of the top 10 leading causes of disability in 1990 [8], as measured by years lived with a disability.

Both obsessions and compulsions are idiosyncratic in their detail, but there are common themes to be found, as listed below:

- Contamination obsessions, leading to compulsive cleaning and washing.
- Obsessions regarding harm to self or others, leading to compulsive checking.
- Taboo obsessions (religious, sexual or aggressive) leading to range of compulsive responses.
- Symmetry obsessions leading to compulsive ordering and counting.

Individuals will frequently fit into more than one of these subtypes; these are useful ways of seeing patterns of thought and behaviour, not discrete disorders.

Obsessions tend to become linked with specific situations, or triggers. For example, a person who fears being contaminated by faeces is far more likely to have this thought intrude when entering a public bathroom. As these intrusions cause distress, it is unsurprising that individuals with OCD may start to avoid these situations. At other times, the intrusions will occur out of the blue. When intrusions do occur (either due to unavoidable exposure to the trigger situations, or spontaneously) the person will then use their compulsions to cope.

OCD commonly occurs alongside a range of other psychological disorders, and so assessing for comorbidity is key. In particular, specific phobias, social anxiety disorder and depression have high rates of comorbidity in those with OCD [9], and so potential symptoms of these should be explored fully.

There are many useful measures in OCD for aiding with assessment and ongoing monitoring and evaluation. The Obsessive Compulsive Inventory (OCI) is a 42-item scale, which covers seven main concepts within OCD: washing, checking, doubting, ordering, obsessing, hoarding and mental neutralising [10]. A shorter version, the Obsessive Compulsive Inventory – Revised, has only 18 items, yet covers all of the above concepts apart from doubting [11], and so may be more appropriate if the patient would struggle with a longer measure and where obsessive doubting isn't a key issue. Alternatively, the Yale-Brown Obsessive Compulsive Scale (YBOCS) is a 10-item scale rated by the clinician, which looks at obsessions and compulsions as overall concepts, looking at the time spent, interference caused, distress associated, resistance against and control over each [12]. In addition to these, the Responsibility Attitudes Scale (RAS), is a 26-item measure that explores how strongly the patient endorses a range of underlying attitudes surrounding personal responsibility for harm and associated concepts, which may underlie their presenting OCD symptoms [13].

OCD Treatment

Prior to the proposal of specific theories of OCD, CBT treatment was based on generic cognitive principles and habituation/desensitisation concepts, as was being used in the treatment of depression and various anxiety disorders. However, while these approaches helped in these other conditions, with OCD they were found to be largely ineffective. So too were alternative theories based on psychodynamic models [14] or psychoanalysis [15].

The initial behavioural theory of anxiety disorders – based on Mowrer's two-stage acquisition of fear [16] – was then applied to OCD by Rachman [17]. Stage one of this is that the neutral event is associated with fear due to immediate pairing with an aversive stimulus; in OCD this is a benign obsessional thought and/or an external-but-neutral trigger being paired with some traumatic or aversive event. Stage two is that the individual's safety-seeking behaviours (in OCD these would be avoidance and the use of rituals) are negatively reinforced because they result in a reduction of fear or discomfort. This two-stage theory explains one of the key differences between OCD and other anxiety disorders; that of the existence of complex rituals in OCD. In a phobia, for example, simple strategies of avoidance and escape can generally be employed, as the feared stimuli are external. Meanwhile, OCD sufferers use rituals as well, as some (even most) of the feared stimuli are internal, in the forms of obsessional thoughts and intrusions, and these cannot be avoided or escaped.

The first OCD-specific protocols took this theory and considered how treatment of phobias could be adapted. Pure exposure was modified into a novel process called exposure and response prevention [18, 19, 20] which allowed for habituation to both internal and external triggers by removing both the avoidance and the use of rituals. This approach showed great promise, and studies confirmed that the combination of exposure and prevention of responses was more effective at changing anxiety levels than either component alone [21].

Over time, the ERP method has been refined and elaborated, with modern versions (e.g. 2) generally including some discussion of cognitive aspects, such as the importance of risk-taking, the cost of avoidance and ritualising and the futility of attempts to obtain fail-safe guarantees. However, these cognitive aspects are described as a means to encouraging the behavioural end goal; habituation-focussed ERP remains the primary aspect of the treatment.

However, while these behavioural approaches based on Rachman's theory appeared to be effective, there were some patients that didn't improve with pure ERP. As such, the next step was to re-examine each part of the two-stage theory through experimental studies and patient interviews, to see if there might be more to the problem. To prove second part of the theory – that of the maintenance of the problem due to negative reinforcement of rituals – researchers explored what happened to anxiety levels when they were employed. As expected, the use of rituals did indeed reduce anxiety in most OCD-sufferers [22,23,24] and so would be negatively reinforced whenever used.

Meanwhile the concept of fear acquisition due to traumatic pairing did not seem to be as clearly verifiable. Most patients describe having no such explicit pairing, no clear trauma on which they can pin their acquisition of fear. In addition, the specific neutral stimuli that are problematic for any given individual generally has social and cultural relevance, as well as a connection to their personally held values, which does not make sense if the cause was purely a chance pairing. Importantly, this differs from phobias, where the fears are less connected to a threat to the individual's values. The search thus continued for the reason why OCD begins, why the fear is acquired.

Meanwhile Salkovskis explored a more cognitive approach, with a strong focus on responsibility for harm. 'OCD would occur if intrusive cognitions were interpreted as an indication that the person may be, may have been, or may come to be, responsible for harm or its prevention' [4]. Key to the level of threat of this appraisal are two things: how likely the outcome is, and how awful the individual would find this outcome. OCD differs from other anxiety disorders thus because it is not just the content of the intrusions that appear dangerous, but that meaning is applied to having had the intrusive thought itself. As such treatment again focuses on exposure with response prevention, but with a primary rationale of disconfirming key cognitions, rather than habituation. Treatment also has significantly more cognitive discussion techniques involved and weaved throughout, and the whole of treatment is framed within the concept of there being two theories for the issue – one of threat versus one of preoccupation. Key themes are that obsessions/intrusions signal threat, that the patient is overly responsible regarding the threat, and that the threat can be in some way controlled via compulsions. Thus, while Foa says difference between obsessions and compulsions is whether they cause or reduce distress, Salkovskis says difference is whether they make patient aware of danger that they are responsible for preventing or causing, or are intended to prevent or neutralise the danger and thus reduce their responsibility for its occurrence. Thus, reduction in anxiety is seen by Salkovskis as a secondary aim, or indeed at times not an aim at all.

The final commonly used approach is that of Willhelm and Steketee. Steketee had originally focussed behaviourally, working with Foa on ERP protocols [25]. However, as discussed in her later works [3], her team began to question the need for prolonged exposure, which they were finding caused significant drop-out due to its time intensive and distressing nature. As such, they looked more widely at the possible belief domains causing and maintaining OCD, through the Obsessive Compulsive Cognition Working Group [26]. In this, the main domains that were found were the importance and control of thoughts, the need for certainty and perfectionism, and concepts of threat and/or responsibility. The treatment that follows from this model is thus a largely cognitive one, looking at each of the above domains (as well as fears of positive experiences and fears of the consequences of feeling anxiety), and using both cognitive restructuring and behavioural experiment techniques. Unlike Salkovskis' protocol, the range of cognitive domains is broader, which may allow it to be fitted to a wider population, but on the other hand results in the recommendation for a larger number of treatment sessions.

Thus, the consensus is that treating OCD will focus on breaking the connections between the patient's intrusions, feared consequences and compulsive behaviours, using tools such as exposure with response prevention, behavioural experiments and cognitive discussion techniques focussed on their interpretations of the intrusions, rather than the intrusions themselves.

Efficacy Data for CBT for OCD

There have been many RCTs reviewing the efficacy of CBT for OCD. In a recent meta-analysis by [27] it was found that cognitive behavioural approaches such as those described above result in significantly greater effect size than either placebo or medications such as SSRIs. Moreover, it was found that the addition of medication did not significantly enhance outcomes for those undertaking CBT, and thus CBT alone is an appropriate intervention.

On the strength of such studies, the National Institute for Clinical Excellence [1] have recommended CBT as the treatment of choice for OCD, alongside SSRIs or clomipramine for those with more significant functional impairment. Due to the rapid research developments in OCD, these guidelines are currently under review, and future updates are likely to widen the therapeutic recommendations to account for the growing evidence-based range of options.

Picking a Protocol

As described above, there are a range of ways to conceptualise OCD, each with their own recommendations on how to structure therapy. Currently, the most commonly used manualised approaches for treatment of OCD in the UK are:

- Kozak and Foa's (2004) guide *Mastery of Obsessive-Compulsive Disorder: A Cognitive Behavioural Therapy Approach* [2]
- Wilhelm and Steketee's (2006) guide *Cognitive Therapy for Obsessive Compulsive Disorder: A Guide for Professionals* [3]

Or

- Bream, Challacombe, Palmer and Salkovskis's (2017) guide *Cognitive Behaviour Therapy for OCD* [4]

Each of these specific protocols has its strengths, and all three have a good evidence base for their efficacy (Table 16.1). Overall, the broadest evidence base has been found for Foa's behavioural ERP approach, however, in studies at least equal effect sizes were found using Salkovskis' approach without a need for prolonged exposure, and with slightly greater improvement on anxiety and irrational beliefs in general [28]. Salkovskis' protocol however requires explicit predictions regarding outcome of ritual prevention – as such, for those who cannot access these, or who focus almost exclusively on inability to tolerate emotions, it may be less helpful. However, if there are protocol-suitable cognitions that can be accessed, this may be a faster approach [29]. Steketee's protocol covers a wider range of cognitions, and can be especially helpful for those with entirely mental ritualising (covert rituals).

Cognitive models in general appear to show a wider acceptability to patients, and appear to have a lower dropout rates than ERP [27,30], however, without ERP these models do not meet the requirements for a NICE recommended initial treatment option [1]. Last, one consideration may be that Salkovskis' model is the most amenable to the standard model of therapy planning – 12 weekly hour-long sessions.

As always, it is important to remember that these protocols have more to unite them than divide, and thus picking exactly how to work with your patient is mostly about considering which feels like the best fit for them. In particular, it can be useful to consider what underlying way of viewing OCD best fits with what your patient is describing, and what appears to be most driving their urge to ritualise. A summary of what each protocol entails, and an example of it in practice, will now be explored.

Foa and Kozak Protocol

As previously discussed, the key concept behind the behavioural approach is that obsessions and intrusions cause distress, because they have become linked to distress at some point, and then compulsions are used to reduce or prevent distress (as avoidance alone cannot, due to unpredictability of obsessional thoughts). Furthermore, people with OCD assume there is

Table 16.1 Comparison of three key CBT protocols for OCD

Protocol	Foa and Kozak (2004) [2]	Salkovskis (2017) [4]	Steketee (2006) [3]
Theory of OCD	OCD caused by aims to prevent distress by avoidance of stimuli and then reduce distress by rituals	OCD caused by beliefs that intrusions mean patient is responsible for harm, and compulsions reduce that responsibility or risk of harm.	OCD caused by beliefs across eight domains – over-importance of thoughts and control of thoughts, overestimation of danger and responsibility, and desire for certainty and perfectionism. These combined make intrusive thoughts unacceptable, leading to attempts to suppress which then cause more intrusions.
Aim of treatment	Reduce distress caused by obsessions and reduce urge to ritualise.	Change beliefs regarding responsibility for harm so as to remove need to ritualise and avoid.	Change beliefs across domains above, dependent upon patient, to thus reduce distress and behaviours.
Recommended structure of therapy	15 sessions, each 90–120 minutes duration, over 3 weeks, followed by 8–10 weekly sessions.	12 sessions (not including follow ups), each 60 minutes duration, over 12+ weeks (later sessions spaced out).	18–22 sessions, each 50–60 minutes duration, over 20–24 weeks.
Interventions used	• Informal cognitive discussion techniques (re overestimation of threat and cost benefit of treatment) • ERP (habituation focus)	• Theory A/B • Behavioural experiments, including ERP (belief disconfirmation focus) • Further cognitive discussion techniques	• Thought records • Cognitive restructuring – wide range of transdiagnostic techniques to be applied depending on the key domains causing issues
Helpful when	Patient is describing need to use behaviours primarily due to distress intolerance.	Patient is describing need to use behaviours primarily to prevent harm or reduce responsibility.	Patient describing range of beliefs regarding value of compulsive behaviours, or in patients predominantly using mental rituals and neutralising strategies. NOTE: As this protocol does not involve ERP, it is not currently recommended by NICE guidelines (2005) excepting in cases of poor response to initial treatment.

threat unless they have evidence of safety, rather than assuming safety unless there is evidence of threat. The proposed intervention is thus a combination of exposure to reduce obsessional distress, and response prevention to reduce the urge to ritualise. While it may be explored with patients that doing this will weaken their beliefs in the consequences of exposure without ritualising, there is no explicit cognitive rationale for the process – the focus is on the reduction distress caused by obsessions and distress caused by not engaging with compulsions that will occur through habituation.

Therapy starts with creating a shared understanding of the problem in order to create a plan for exposure-based treatment, and then persuading the patient to use the plan. The first task is thus to identify objects, situations, thoughts, images, impulses and bodily sensations that cause the patient distress. The therapist will also probe for any disastrous consequences that could occur if not prevented, so as to ensure exposure directly provokes and thus confronts these fears. Following this, the therapist and patient explore the avoidance patterns and rituals that have been used to cope until now. It is important in this that the therapist helps the patient to understand and identify these themselves, rather than taking too much of a lead on it. This way the patient can play a part in spotting new or unmentioned ones during the active exposure phase, and either stop them spontaneously, or let the therapist know so they can take it into account.

Contrary to other approaches, this model recommends the use of didactic psychoeducation, explaining that the aim of ERP is to weaken the connections between the feared situations and feeling distress, and to weaken the association between using rituals and feeling relieved. Psychoeducation should also cover the secondary impact this will have on beliefs about the risks of outcomes occurring and on beliefs about anxiety. With a shared understanding of the problem and the rationale, the therapist and patient can then build an exposure hierarchy, of between 10 and 20 situations, which should cover all the main difficulties the patient avoids or finds distressing.

Exposure itself was originally proposed to then be carried out in daily therapy sessions for three weeks (though other schedules can be used). Ideally, the highest part of the hierarchy will be reached by day six, with further sessions then focussing on repetition and variations, so that by the end of the fifteenth session, all options have been covered comprehensively. Ideally all situations are confronted in vivo, though imaginal exposure can be used if the actual situation required would be disruptive to others (such as with certain religiously themed obsessions) or to maintain gains where repetition of in vivo would be problematic.

Case Example: Fatwa

Fatwa was a 23-year-old female living with her parents and two sisters. For as long as she could remember, she had been concerned about whether she was clean, and had used a mixture of avoidance and ritualised repetitive washing to manage this.

Problematic concerns about cleanliness and ritualised washing occurred in three major areas – showering and washing her hair, washing after using a bathroom, and washing dishes. In each case, the potential risk was different (insufficient washing after using a bathroom might lead to her becoming sick due to contamination by another's faecal matter, while careless showering might leave soap residue on her skin); however, in all cases, she predicted that there would be intense distress if she was unable to complete her washing to the point where she was certain it was complete. She had begun to avoid showering and

Box 16.1 Fatwa's hierarchy

1. touch office pens
2. touch office doorknobs
3. touch top/sides of soap dispenser
4. touch nozzle of soap dispenser
5. touch used dish sponge
6. put arms in lightly soapy water
7. touch office bathroom door
8. touch work bathroom door
9. put soapy flannel on leg
10. touch office toilet seat
11. touch work toilet seat
12. touch toilet paper with urine on it
13. touch excrement

housework whenever she felt overly stressed, and would only use the bathroom at home, as in all cases, the act of compulsively washing was itself distressing, due to how difficult it was to be certain she was clean. She had never discussed these difficulties with anyone, but her family had noticed her refusal to do housework and were asking more and more questions.

The therapist and Fatwa began sessions by exploring the various situations, sensations and intrusions that caused her distress and resulted in an urge to wash. They went through each of these, and explored what the feared outcome would be. Using this information, they drew up a detailed hierarchy of 13 scenarios that Fatwa could confront during therapy (see Box 16.1). The concept of imaginal exposure was considered, but as all Fatwa's feared situations could be actively and repeatedly confronted in vivo, it was agreed that imaginal work was unneeded.

Ritual prevention was then explored, to consider what behaviours, both overt and covert, the patient would need to prevent herself from engaging in during and around her exposure exercises. For Fatwa, these rituals were all variations around washing herself in an ordered and repetitive way, rinsing in multiples of three, and inspecting skin for sensations of cleanliness in order to determine if it was safe to stop. Initially, the very concept of preventing her rituals was alien to Fatwa, as she could not conceive that it was possible for her to simply choose to abstain from her ritualised washing. Exploration of occasions where her family members had interrupted her washing – resulting in her delaying the ritual until they had left – helped to loosen this belief. It was then discussed how washing could be reduced to only the very minimum needed for social acceptance. It was agreed that no washing of any kind would be used during the three-week period, excepting for a single 10-minute shower every three days. Fatwa was distressed by the concept of not washing her hands after using the bathroom, as she felt this was beyond what normal people would do. This was discussed both in terms of the aims of ERP being to change the distress and urge to ritualise, not simply to mimic others, and also in terms of the statistics on how many 'normal' people actual do not wash their hands after using the toilet. The therapist empathised with the difficulty of dropping rituals cold turkey, and having to cut out even most 'normal' washing, but repeated how key this was to ensuring that exposure was effective.

Active exposure work was then conducted over a three-week period, with daily 1.5–2-hour sessions. In the first session, Fatwa and the therapist confronted her first two hierarchy items, by touching various pens in the therapy office, and the various doorknobs in the building. She then rubbed their hands together in order to spread the perceived contamination, and ran her hands up her arms, over her phone and through her hair. This contamination spreading was repeated at least once every five minutes, with regular SUDs ratings being taken to monitor habituation. New items were added as the ratings came down, but with no new items in the final section of the session, so as to avoid exposure without habituation.

Sessions 2–5 then continued up the hierarchy, with each session repeating the new exposure from the session before, and then adding in another 1–2 situations as time allowed. Each time, the contamination spreading process from session one was repeated, to ensure that Fatwa was fully exposed, and recurring SUDs ratings taken to check habituation was occurring, and nothing was interfering with this process. Fatwa was also asked to monitor and express any further rituals she found herself engaging in. One such ritual that she noticed was tracking where the contamination was, in order to be able to monitor those areas until she next washed, and limit what they cross-contaminated. The therapist explored how this might be maintaining anxiety and limiting habituation, and Fatwa agreed to drop this and actively try to cross-contaminate without tracking.

As had been agreed from the start of the exposure period, session 6 involved confronting Fatwa's greatest fear, touching excrement. Prior to the session, the therapist had gone to a nearby park and found some dog poo, which was brought to the session in a plastic bag. The therapist and Fatwa each touched the excrement with their finger, and then went through the contamination spreading process. Fatwa then touched a tissue to the excrement, so she could repeat the exercise that evening and in the next session.

Session 7–15 involved repeating the exercises above, along with visiting a range of toilets, and visiting her home. During the home visit, Fatwa exposed herself to the actual sponge used for washing up after dinner, and the soaps and flannels used to shower with. Interestingly, for Fatwa, the once per three-day shower could itself be used as an exposure exercise, as it involved exposing herself to being covered in soap residue, and then not ritualistically removing it. As she was uncomfortable enlisting her family for support, she chose to schedule her showers for just before work, so she would be less tempted to go over the allotted time allowance.

Treatment concluded with exploration of how to move forwards into normal patterns of touching things and washing behaviour. As Fatwa's concerns included failing to remove soap after starting washing, it was helpful to bring washing frequency in line with cultural norms, and to mainly focus on keeping each episode of washing brief, without repetition of rinsing or checking for cleanliness. A list of potential future scenarios was devised that Fatwa might find challenging; they then considered how the approaches in therapy could be applied to confronting these scenarios without ritual.

The Salkovskis Protocol

This approach is based is the concept that OCD is caused by appraising intrusions as signalling a threat, by believing oneself to be overly responsible for said threat, and by connecting the use of compulsions to harm reduction (where actually the threat of said harm was never high to begin with). Within this, there are several key, common problematic beliefs:

- Thinking of an action is equivalent to its performance;
- Failing to prevent (or failing to try to prevent) harm to self or others is morally equivalent to causing the harm;
- Responsibility for harm is not lessened by any extenuating circumstances;
- Failing to ritualise in response to an idea about harm is the same as an intention to harm; and
- One should exercise control over one's thoughts.

Put together, such beliefs make intrusions highly threatening, and make rituals and behaviours in response to intrusions highly compelling. As such, more and more intrusions will occur, the patient will focus (even obsess) about them more and more, and will feel compelled to use rituals and other neutralising and unhelpful behaviours (compulsions) to feel safer, inadvertently making the problem worse.

This approach makes sense of both the development and maintenance of OCD, and encourages sharing this formulation with patients pictorially, as shown in Figure 16.1.

Starting with the central maintenance cycles, often termed a 'vicious flower', it is suggested that the central problem is not intrusions themselves, but the **meaning** that the patient attributes to these intrusions. Namely this will be of a serious risk of harm occurring, and a belief that one is excessively responsible for preventing this potential harm occurring. Due to this, the patient will try to manage this risk through a range of **counter-productive strategies**, such as trying to suppress the intrusions, or deciding upon a set of impossible criteria by which to define safety, as well as frank and subtle avoidance of perceived risks. They will also use various **neutralising** techniques, in order to try and increase certainty of safety or undo the risk caused by the intrusion. The patient's **attention** will shift towards evidence of threat and triggers for intrusions, and their **mood** will become anxious, depressed, guilty or disgusted.

Each of these changes then reinforce, maintain or prevent disconfirmation of the perceived meaning of the intrusions. The behavioural changes will either result in finding evidence for the feared risk's possibility, or will reinforce the concept that said behaviours were needed and in turn makes the sense of responsibility stronger. The shift in attention will find further evidence of threat, and the negative mood changes will make threat feel more significant through emotional reasoning. As such, the central meaning of the intrusions becomes more deeply believed over time. Moreover, these behavioural, attentional, emotional and cognitive shifts also directly affect the number of intrusions experienced and noticed, and so the entire cycle occurs ever more frequently.

Having made sense of how the problem worsens, and the central role of the individual's ascribed meaning to their intrusions, it can also be helpful to consider where the problem started. This model suggests that various early experiences, especially those involving excessive or absent responsibility, and/or significant actual or perceived harm, can result in generalised beliefs about the self, world and others, and also specifically about the concepts of personal responsibility and harm. Over time, or in reaction to specific critical incidents, these beliefs will impact how the patient reacts to otherwise benign intrusions, starting off the vicious flower above.

Following formulation, the therapist will then consider how the patient's current view of the problem (the central meaning within their vicious flower) compares to an alternative

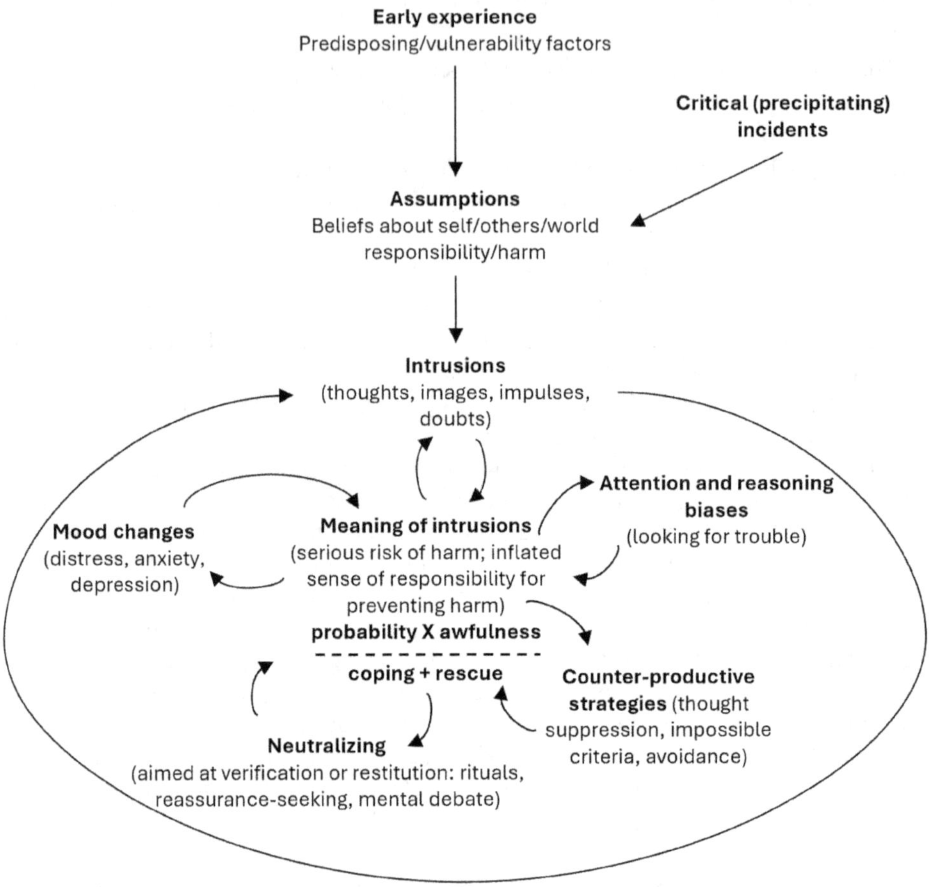

Figure 16.1 Salkovskis Formulation of OCD (from Bream et al., 2017, Cognitive model of OCD. Data from Paul M. Salkovskis, Obsessional-compulsive problems: A cognitive-behavioural analysis. *Behaviour Research and Therapy*, 23(5), 571–583, 1985).

explanation of their difficulties, suggested by the therapist. This approach is called theory A/ theory B. While theory A revolves around the problem being danger and the patient's responsibility to stop it, theory B is that the patient is oversensitive to, and thus overly worried about danger. Both theories need to be considered side by side, in terms of the evidence for them both, the behavioural implications if each is true, what each theory says about the patient as a person, and the impact of the patient's life if they follow each theory. By doing this, the patient is able to consider a credible alternative, and thus make a choice to try living as though this alternative theory is correct.

Once the patient has agreed to try out theory B, treatment itself will focus on the use of behavioural experiments, many involving exposure with response prevention, to confront their fears and build up evidence for the validity of theory B. Such experiments will include in-session work, such as a thought suppression experiment to determine the usefulness of suppressing intrusions, as well as real world exposure to the patient's feared stimuli. They can also include behaving opposite how theory A would suggest, known as an anti-OCD behaviour, to test out what happens if they drop all unneeded safety precautions. These can range from eating after touching toilets, to purposely leaving things switched on or unlocked, to actively trying to send oneself crazy. In doing so, the patient can gain confidence in how little active work they need to do to prevent disaster in future.

A hierarchy is not used in this protocol; instead experiments are devised based on what is meaningful and problematic to the patient. Experiments may build step by step, however; a patient may start by dropping their neutralising behaviours, and learn that their feared consequence does not occur, and then move onto an anti-OCD experiment to prove that this was not simply luck. Each subsequent experiment would start by noting what remaining beliefs are left, and what else the patient needs to discover.

Various cognitive techniques are also used, where a purely experimental approach may not fit. These include responsibility pies (to reassess fault for past or potential harm), surveys (to discover how others react and think, and the range of human experiences beyond the patient), continuums (to enhance flexibility in underlying beliefs) and general guided discovery.

Case Example: Simon

Simon was a 35-year-old man, who lived alone and worked in a warehouse. He came to therapy describing longstanding issues with 'awful thoughts' and that these caused him difficulties in being around women and children. He was initially unable to tell the therapist about the content of these thoughts, as he was convinced that the therapist would think there was something terribly wrong with him, and would have him arrested or sectioned.

Through careful exploration and normalisation, the therapist helped Simon to reveal that a number of these intrusive thoughts were that of assaulting the women around him. When these images popped into his mind, he would interpret them as meaning that he was secretly a violent, evil man, and that he might be about to lose control and hurt someone. In response, he would scan the room to check there were no potential weapons nearby, keep distance between himself and the woman in question, and put his hands in his pockets. He would mentally bring on images of taking his own life, which he did to ensure that any loss of control and subsequent violence would be directed at himself, rather than the innocents around him.

More generally, Simon arranged his life so as to minimise contact with women or children, and especially to minimise being alone with them. He had avoided promotions where there would need to be contact with female colleagues and did not date. He had some limited contact with his niece and nephew, but had refused to attend their birthday parties, or to babysit them.

The therapist began by exploring a recent example where Simon had felt distressed by such an intrusion, drawing out the interpretation Simon had made of this intrusion ('I'm going to lose control and hurt her'), and the various behaviours and emotional reactions this interpretation had provoked. They then explored how these behaviours and emotions had impacted his belief that he would have otherwise have 'lost control and hurt her', and on the frequency and vividness of subsequent intrusions.

They then reflected back on how this might have all started, considering Simon's early experiences with his mother and sister, and his memories of both being expected to be 'the man of the house' and of being told how dangerous and violent men can be, and how 'bad' his own father had been, who he had never met. In particular, he had a memory of pushing

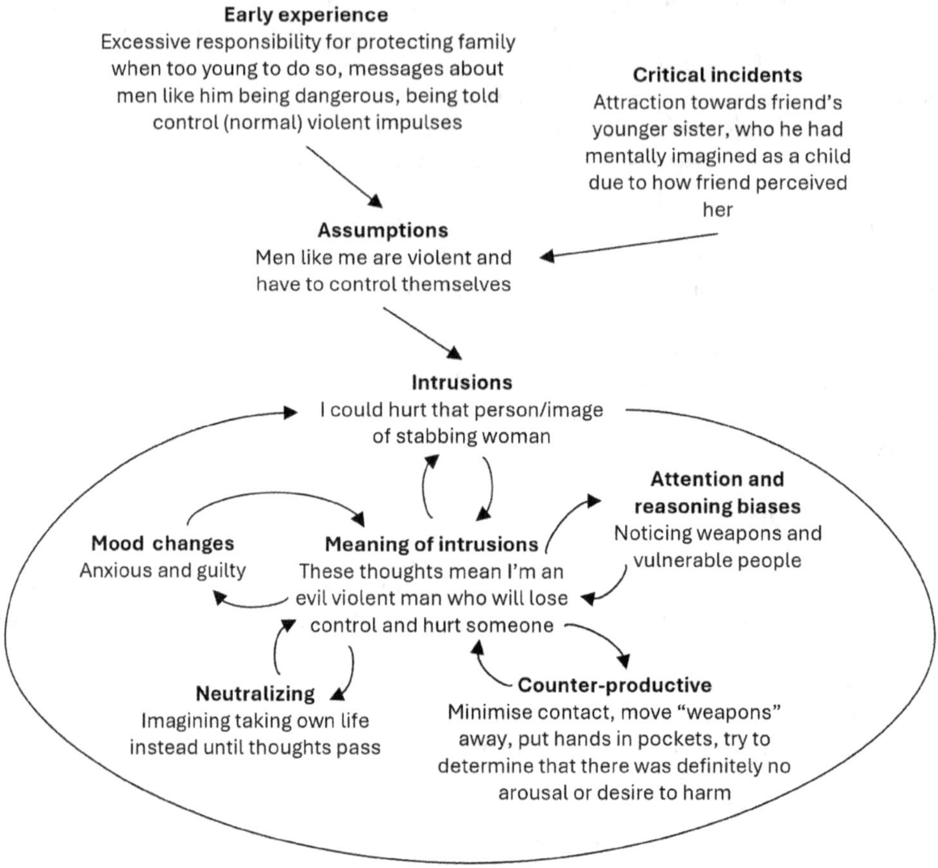

Figure 16.2 Simon's idiosyncratic model (adapted from Bream et al., 2017).

his older sister when they were just out of the bath, and his mother telling him to control himself. Later in therapy, he also disclosed a vivid memory of first meeting his friend's younger sister when he was in sixth form, and finding her attractive, and then being horrified at himself for this as she was 15 (he himself was only 17 at the time). In his mind, this had become proof that he was a paedophile and could not be trusted around anyone other than adult men.

The resultant formulation, developed over the course of therapy, is shown in Figure 16.2.

Following this, and the subsequent home project of drawing up vicious flowers for other such events over the week, the therapist and Simon explored two alternative theories of what might be maintaining his current experiences – Theory A and Theory B. Theory A was Simon's own theory to date, which he verbalised as 'the problem is that I am an evil, violent person, who will hurt women and children unless I constantly control myself, and who others would reject if they knew the truth'. Meanwhile, Theory B was proposed by the therapist as how the therapeutic model might explain things, and was stated as 'The problem is that I am a caring, non-violent person who is excessively worried about hurting others.'

The initial evidence for each was explored, leading to Simon concluding that there was a possibility either theory could be true, believing them 40:60, A:B. However, he acknowledged that when his intrusions were occurring and he felt more distressed, he would be likely to believe Theory A again more strongly. The therapist and Simon then discussed the implications of each theory, in terms of what Simon should do if it was true. For Theory A, a long list of safety seeking behaviours was drawn up, including avoiding potential victims, neutralising his thoughts, and keeping track of potential weapons. Meanwhile, for Theory B, Simon determined that he would need to engage with those he feared hurting, treat intrusive thoughts as meaningless and safe and allow himself to be in proximity to potential weapons freely. While the list for theory B seemed challenging, Simon could see how it would bring him closer to his long-term goals for life. In comparison, the list of behaviours for theory A seemed draining, limiting and time consuming.

The therapist and Simon then moved onto considering what each theory said about Simon as a person, and what it said about his future. As had already been noted in the earlier aspects, Theory B painted a far more promising picture, despite the apparent risks it might pose to try out. Finally, the therapist discussed with Simon which theory he wanted to choose to live by moving forwards, acknowledging the risks on both sides. While Theory B seemed extremely risky to consider, Simon agreed that he would like to try moving towards this.

Future sessions were subsequently focussed on auctioning this decision, taking the list of implications of Theory B one at a time and devising ways for Simon to test out what happened if he behaved in this way. One of the first such experiments revolved around treating his intrusive thoughts as safe. Simon acknowledged that there were a number of 'worse' intrusions that he had yet to disclose to the therapist, due to his Theory A prediction that she would reject him, or even call the police. This was then tackled as an experiment, and Simon was greatly surprised to learn that the therapist did not rush from the room as predicted when he disclosed intrusive images of rape and abusing a child, but instead normalised the intrusions as she had for his earlier ones.

Later experiments focussed on Simon interacting with women at work and social events, and re-engaging with his niece and nephew without neutralising or avoidance. While initially these experiments were devised with the help of the therapist, this was later left to Simon alone, so as to avoid the perceived safety signal of the therapist endorsing the experiment. Some sessions were also focussed on the underlying belief itself that having such thoughts was morally repugnant, and that it meant he was an evil, violent person. Socratic discussion of what reinforced this belief, and how else he could make judgments of his morality, helped him come to the alternative rule of 'my morality is based on what I do to others, and my desires, not things outside of my control such as intrusive thoughts'.

To consolidate his growing belief that he was not a danger to others, and that he did not need to control himself, some 'anti-OCD' experiments were devised, where Simon actively tried to lose control, such as by holding a potential weapon (some scissors) and trying to think himself into stabbing the therapist. While initial highly anxiety provoking for Simon, these sessions were important in giving Simon confidence that he truly could trust himself, as no matter how little he tried to control himself, he never became violent. This then made similar scenarios at work, where he needed to be opening boxes with scissors while female colleagues might be coming through, much more manageable.

Steketee Protocol

Steketee's model of OCD is based on the Obsessive Compulsive Cognition Working Group's findings regarding the main cognitive patterns in those with OCD, seeing these as the cause of both having more intrusions and of the interpretations made by the patient, which in turn lead to the emotions and problematic behaviours (see Figure 16.3 for how this can be formulated). As such, the protocol works to identify and then change beliefs across any and all of the eight cognitive areas, so as to change the patient's need to avoid and ritualise.

This treatment protocol is fairly open and flexible in its interventions, depending on the cognitive domains that are most relevant for the particular patient. As such, sessions 1–4 are focussed on assessment and psycho-education, in particular working out which of the belief domains are relevant for that patient. Sessions 5–20 are then spent implements the relevant treatment modules for each of the patients' identified idiosyncratic beliefs; typically 4–5 areas from the list will be chosen, with therapy spending 3–4 sessions on each area.

For any and all areas, it is generally helpful to use a downward arrow technique and Socratic questioning to better understand the thoughts and how they link, and to start

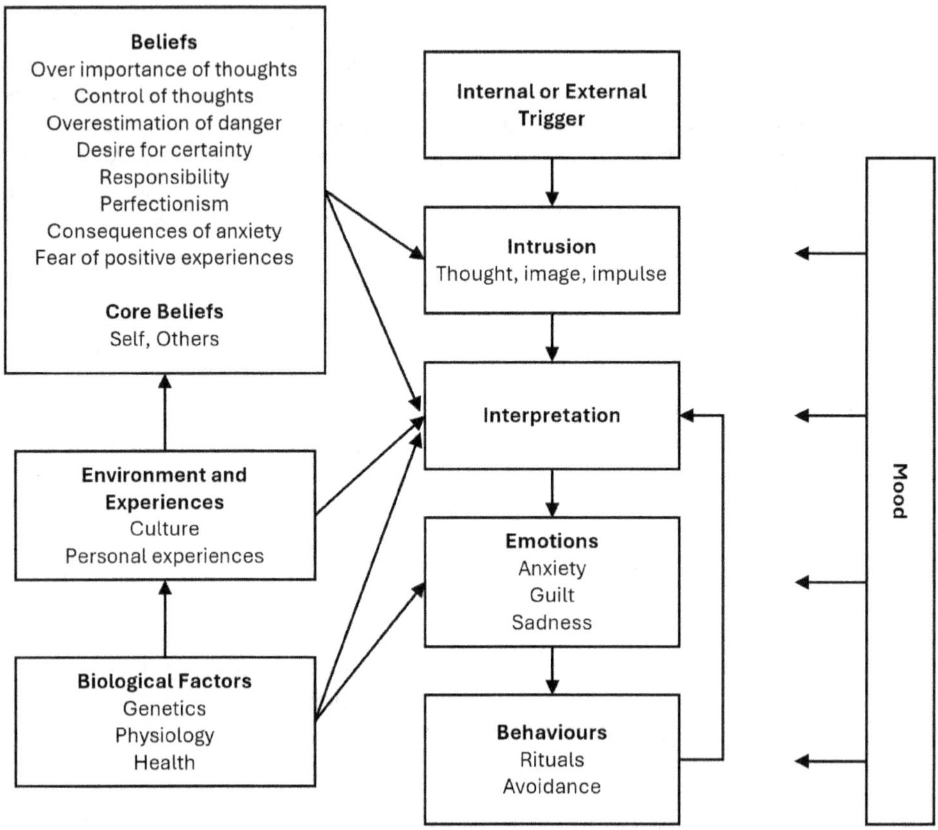

Figure 16.3 Steketee Formulation of OCD (from Wilhelm and Steketee, 2006, p. 213).

creating flexibility. In addition, each area has its own recommended focus. For over-importance of thoughts, therapy will cognitively explore the meaning the patient attaches to having had intrusions. Following this, therapy will challenge that

- having a thought means it's important,
- having a thought means one might act on it or it might magically happen, and
- having a thought makes one morally as bad as having done the action.

For control of thoughts, intervention starts by exploring the reasons for thinking that one should or indeed can control thoughts, and then will use a thought suppression experiment to test out these beliefs, before encouraging the patient to try out not controlling thoughts. For overestimation of danger, there are a number of options. The therapist and patient can calculate the likelihood of various danger steps that would be needed for the feared consequence to occur, and then multiply these to determine the probability of them all occurring. Alternatively, the pair can consult an expert to get actual danger information, for things where it might be difficult for estimations without specialist knowledge. They can also use a survey to help the patient realise how often others do the thing they fear doing, to determine how often others have so far avoided the danger without these precautions. Following these more exploratory approaches, it can be helpful to encourage the patient to conduct a behavioural experiment where they determine in practice what will happen if they drop a safety behaviour or compulsion, by trying it out and comparing to their prediction.

For desire for certainty, it can be helpful to explore the concept via a pros and cons list of aiming for certainty, to determine if this aim is truly worth all of the costs, especially in light of the probability of success. To help gauge what is a 'normal amount of certainty', especially about topics where the therapist wouldn't have a good reason to be an expert, it can be helpful to carry out a survey on how certain others are about the topic and how much they care that they are not more certain. To improve flexibility of thinking regarding certainty, an option is to use a continuum to look at what they need to be comparatively certain of and what is less important – for example if one is an air traffic controller, it's more important to be certain that a given runway is clear, compared to whether you have added exactly the right amount of sugar to a cup of tea.

For responsibility, one technique is to draw out a pair of pie charts – the first showing how much responsibility they instinctively feel they have for an outcome, and then another with all the possible factors accounted for and plotted leaving them until last, to determine what actual responsibility is left. Considering how the case would be argued in a court room can also help patients to see if they can truly prove their fault. As part of Socratic dialogue, it can be helpful to consider if they would apply the same standard were they the harmed one and another had been 'at fault', to reappraise the fairness of giving the responsibility based on the 'fault' in question. Additionally, as with certainty, a continuum technique can be used to help the patient see the value of a middle ground attitude for responsibility and a pros and cons list for over-responsibility can be created to see the costs involved.

For perfectionism, therapy can explore whether perfectionism would be a good rule to encourage others to have, such as whether they would wish a cherished loved one to take on the burden (the double standards technique). Again, it can be helpful to look at the pros and cons of perfectionism, including some quick maths on the time the patient has lost to perfectionism, and to create a continuum to explore how perfect things need to be in different situations. Following this, behavioural experiments can be used to test out the consequence of actually being imperfect – does anyone notice, do any bad outcomes occur at all, and if they do, are they an acceptable sacrifice to get back all the time taken to avoid imperfection.

For consequences of anxiety, it can be helpful to make 'extreme contrasts' of the patient's feared versus actual outcomes of anxiety, and review the past evidence to consider likelihood of each. Following this, the therapist and patient will devise behavioural experiments to see what actually happens when the patient does not try to prevent anxiety (for example, that they don't suddenly do much worse at things, that they don't go crazy and also that the anxiety drops without their active input). Either following this or prior, depending on how the patient feels about experimenting, the pros and cons of controlling anxiety can be reviewed and explored.

Last, in terms of the belief domain modules, is fear of positive experiences. A review of the evidence from the patient's life to date can allow the therapist and patient see if positive experiences have led to harm, or if acknowledging good has apparently jinxed it. So long as this does not show any clear links, the therapist can then suggest using behavioural experiments to try and actively cause jinxing, often initially directed at the therapist! If the patient's beliefs specifically focus on whether they deserve happiness, the pair can use a survey to determine if others think someone like them deserves to be happy, and they can also use the double-standard technique to consider if they think someone similar to them would deserve to get better, or if they would doom another to unending unhappiness. Finally, they can again use a pros and cons of allowing oneself to feel happy, given what they have learnt.

After each of the relevant modules above have been completed, it may be relevant to spend some sessions working on any identified core beliefs, via several of the tools above or from standard core belief work (as described in Chapter 20) – a core beliefs record, core belief filter (see below), continuum techniques, extreme contrasts, the double-standard technique, the courtroom technique, reframing the evidence and using historical testing of core belief. After this, all that remains is relapse prevention, which will generally be done over the final two sessions.

Case Example: Steve

Steve was the son of a minister, and had grown up in a religious household, with a fairly authoritarian set of parents. He came to therapy due to having intrusions regarding sacrilegious concepts, and which he perceives as extremely important, believing that having a sacrilegious thought means he is evil. Steve expresses thoughts such as 'I shouldn't have these thoughts', 'I'm going to become more and more evil over time', 'my true nature will be revealed' and 'just having the thought means I'm already evil'. Steve explains that the thoughts first started when he was 10. He remembers vividly being in church and having a 'silly' thought, and giggling, and his father looking angry at him, and how in that moment he felt like God was judging him.

Steve's father died when he was 21, and he is now 42. He described having been almost permanently single despite multiple attempted set-ups by his church group, which he puts down to the fact that he 'doesn't want to drag someone down with me'. Given how young his father was when he died, he is getting increasingly concerned about his own mortality, and thus increasingly concerned he will go to hell. His new minister's wife is a counsellor, and when he partially opened up to her about his fears, she recommended CBT to help.

For Steve's beliefs about the **over-importance of thoughts**, the therapist explored when the issue started, and how he had been interpreting the bible at that age regarding sections about thoughts (Sermon on the Mount). They then explored whether he had reviewed that section as an adult, which he hadn't, as he found the concept too scary. Following this, the pair explored Steve's wider understanding of God's attitude, which he stated was that God is kind and loving, and how that fitted in with his belief of being damned for intrusive thoughts. Given the discrepancy, Steve agreed to speak to the minister's wife as homework, to explore how she understands the sections of the bible that had concerned him, and whether God would want him to avoid things that seemed to cause the intrusions (such as prayer) given the value of prayer overall. In the following session, the pair explored the results. Steve had been amazed that not only did she suggest that those sections of the Bible were about known desires, not intrusions, but that it was better to ignore intrusions and refocus on God, than allow them to distract and distance him from God. This was then considered in terms of how that fitted with the model of what was going on for Steve, and generally with the concept of the importance or otherwise of thoughts.

From there therapy went onto concept of **trying to control thoughts**. Steve's normal techniques were to avoid activities like prayer unless he felt 'safe', to think through each word before 'praying it' to ensure it wasn't a swear word, and to repeat 'I love God' until he felt any danger had passed. His belief was that having these thoughts meant he was evil, and if he was good he would be able to stop them. To start challenging this, the therapist used a thought suppression experiment to show that trying to stop thoughts is what makes them happen more; Steve had never thought of a pink elephant in his life until the therapist told him not to! The therapist then asked Steve to alternate days where he would try and suppress thoughts about swearing at God during prayer (a common intrusion for him) followed by not suppressing the intrusions for the rest of the week, and keeping a loose track of how often the intrusion occurred every day. Unsurprisingly, the intrusions happened more on days where he tried to suppress, leading him naturally to want to stop any suppression attempts.

Steve wanted to **be certain** he hadn't sworn, so the therapist helped him to explore the pros and cons of this. Given the prior learning he had already done on thought suppression, he realised aiming for certainty wasn't reducing the chance of intrusions happening and thus the only advantage of certainty was a short-term reduction in anxiety. Meanwhile, the cost was his increased anxiety long-term, as well as lots of missed opportunity for prayer, and an enduring sense of disconnect from his prayer group and in church services when he was not engaging in group prayer because he was trying to be certain he was safe. He decided that being uncertain was scary but it would be worth it in order to focus on what mattered and allow him a sense of community. Steve added to this pros and cons over the following week, noting other areas and ways in which desiring certainty was disadvantageous. Steve also realised that mental reviewing of his praying to check he hadn't sworn didn't actually result in feeling more certain, so the therapist explored with him the pros and cons of giving the behaviour up. Lastly, they carried out a survey to determine how much of prayer other peoples remembered by the end of a service, and how bothered they were by whether they remembered it. Doing this helped Steve to normalise not remembering every second of his prayer, realising that this didn't mean he had sworn and them blanked it out, so he could trust it even if he was uncertain. This was added to by a group in the survey commenting they'd been distracted briefly by someone sneezing; the therapist and Steve explored how this suggests if one is not certain, then it is likely that nothing interesting or unusual happened.

Steve had rules about conducting spiritual behaviours **perfectly**, as God was perfect. Socratic discussion helped loosen the idea that God expected Steve to likewise be perfect, and Steve was reminded of some passages from the bible highlighting man's imperfection. The therapist also explored whether others were perfect, and how Steve himself reacted to other's imperfections (such as the minister mispronouncing a word in a sermon) as well as how the rest of the congregation reacted. Following this, they used a continuum to consider what situations required each level of correctness – it was more important to get the words right when leading prayer or praying aloud/singing as a group, as might be distracting to others, but even then, it was not essential, as Steve noted that the common reactions of those around him to mistakes made by others were people smiling or not noticing. The top items where Steve felt one had to be the most correct were if ever leading prayers for the nation, or singing for the Archbishop of Canterbury – as even then, if they were Christian Steve reasoned they would forgive him any errors, and God would see into his heart rather than judge him on his imperfect actions.

Later in therapy, they worked on the key core belief of 'I am irredeemably evil', moving towards the more balanced belief of 'I am fallible, but good enough in this imperfect world and loved by God in his mercy'. They explored his usual core belief filter, and how he ignored all evidence of being good in any way or situation, or being lovable and redeemable to God. They also explored how the bible defines good and evil and used the continuum technique to explore where he would fit; in this they together noted much of Steve's behaviour that was incompatible with being evil, and not fitting with biblical examples of irredeemably evil people. They then explored how Steve could reinforce his confidence that he was a generally good enough person. For Steve, it would be contrary to his religious beliefs to aim for 'I am a good person' as he believed all humans imperfect and fallible, and thus the aim was to see he was like other Christians and not irredeemable. Homework included keeping a list of rejected positive information, and accepted negative information, and later to add behaviours on the good–evil continuum to weigh up where he fell. Following this, relapse prevention helped Steve to summarise his key cognitive shifts, and the resultant changes in behaviour that he had made to reinforce that intrusions were not overly important, that he could generally trust that he wouldn't and hadn't sworn during prayer, and that he was good enough despite any imperfections. They considered longer-term goals, and Steve explored how to use the same tools and challenges to support him once he tried out dating again.

Concluding Remarks

Obsessive compulsive disorder can be a deeply disabling condition, where fear and a sense of responsibility for possible harm result in time consuming and life-interfering compulsions, as well as limits put on one's life through avoidance. Treatment focusses on changing this cycle via exposure to feared thoughts and situation and the dropping of behaviours used to prevent the feared harm, as well as exploration of the beliefs driving these behaviours. Specific protocols as such focus respectively on ERP or cognitive reappraisals with behavioural experiments, or a combination of the two.

Further Reading

Kozak MJ, Foa EB. *Mastery of Obsessive Compulsive Disorder: A Cognitive Behavioural Approach (Therapist Guide).* Oxford: Oxford University Press; 1997.

Wilhelm S, Steketee G. *Cognitive Therapy for Obsessive Compulsive Disorder: A Guide for Professionals.* Oakland: New Harbinger Publications; 2006.

Bream V, Challacombe F, Palmer A, Salkovskis P. *Cognitive Behaviour Therapy for Obsessive-Compulsive Disorder.* Oxford: Oxford University Press; 2017.

References

1. National Institute for Health and Care Excellence. Obsessive-compulsive disorder and body dysmorphic disorder: Treatment. Clinical Guidance [Internet]. NICE; 2005. Report No.: CG31. www.nice.org.uk/guidance/cg31.
2. Foa EB, Kozak MJ. *Mastery of Obsessive-Compulsive Disorder: A Cognitive-Behavioral Approach Therapist Guide* [Internet]. New York: Oxford University Press; 2004. https://books.google.co.uk/books?id=hX7w8A75BksC.
3. Wilhelm S, Steketee G. *Cognitive Therapy for Obsessive-Compulsive Disorder: A Guide for Professionals* [Internet]. Oakland: New Harbinger Publications; 2006. https://books.google.co.uk/books?id=zvJrAAAAMAAJ.
4. Bream V, Challacombe F, Palmer A, Salkovskis P. *Cognitive Behaviour Therapy for Obsessive-Compulsive Disorder.* Illustrated ed. Oxford: Oxford University Press; 2017.
5. Salkovskis PM. Obsessional-compulsive problems: A cognitive-behavioural analysis. Behav Res Ther. 1985;**23**(5):571–583.
6. Angst J, Gamma A, Endrass J, Goodwin R, Ajdacic V, Eich D, et al. Obsessive-compulsive severity spectrum in the community: prevalence, comorbidity, and course. Eur Arch Psychiatry Clin Neurosci. 2004;**254**(3):156–164.
7. Pinto A, Mancebo MC, Eisen JL, Pagano ME, Rasmussen SA. The Brown Longitudinal Obsessive Compulsive Study: Clinical features and symptoms of the sample at intake. J Clin Psychiatry. 2006;**67**(5):703–711.
8. Murray CJ, Lopez AD, World Health Organization. The global burden of disease: A comprehensive assessment of mortality and disability from diseases, injuries, and risk factors in 1990 and projected to 2020: Summary. Boston: Harvard University Press; 1996.
9. Ruscio AM, Stein DJ, Chiu WT, Kessler RC. The epidemiology of obsessive-compulsive disorder in the National Comorbidity Survey Replication. Mol Psychiatry. 2008;**15**(1):53–63.
10. Foa EB, Kozak MJ, Salkovskis PM, Coles ME, Amir N. The validation of a new obsessive–compulsive disorder scale: The Obsessive–Compulsive Inventory. Psychol Assess. 1998;**10**(3):206–214.
11. Foa EB, Huppert JD, Leiberg S, Langner R, Kichic R, Hajcak G, et al. The Obsessive-Compulsive Inventory: Development and validation of a short version. Psychol Assess. 2002;**14**(4):485–496.
12. Goodman WK, Price LH, Rasmussen SA, Mazure C, Fleischmann RL, Hill CL, et al. The Yale-Brown Obsessive Compulsive Scale: I. Development, use, and reliability. Arch Gen Psychiatry. 1989;**46**(11):1006–1011.
13. Salkovskis PM, Wroe AL, Gledhill A, Morrison N, Forrester E, Richards C, et al. Responsibility attitudes and interpretations are characteristic of obsessive compulsive disorder. Behav Res Ther. 2000;**38**(4):347–372.
14. Freud S. *The Complete Psychological Works of Sigmund Freud Vol.10: Two Case*

Histories (Little Hans and the 'Rat Man' [Internet]. London: Random House UK; 1955. https://books.google.co.uk/books?id=ANaozwEACAAJ.

15. Fenichel O. Neurotic acting out. Psychoanal Rev 1913–1957. 1945;**32**:197–206.
16. Mowrer OH. On the dual nature of learning: A re-interpretation of 'conditioning' and 'problem-solving'. Harv Educ Rev. 1947;**17**:102–148.
17. Rachman S. Obsessional ruminations. Behav Res Ther. 1971;**9**(3):229–235.
18. Meyer V, Levy R. Modification of behavior in obsessive-compulsive disorders. In Adams HE, Unikel IP, *Issues and Trends in Behavior Therapy* (pp. 77–136). Springfield: Charles C Thomas; 1973.
19. Marks I, Hodgson R, Rachman S. Treatment of chronic obsessive-compulsive neurosis by in-vivo exposure: A two-year follow-up and issues in treatment. Br J Psychiatry. 1975;**127**(4):349–364.
20. Foa EB, Goldstein A. Continuous exposure and complete response prevention in the treatment of obsessive-compulsive neurosis. Behav Ther. 1978;**9**(5):821–829.
21. Foa EB, Steketee G, Grayson JB, Turner RM, Latimer PR. Deliberate exposure and blocking of obsessive-compulsive rituals: Immediate and long-term effects. Behav Ther. 1984;**15**(5):450–472.
22. Hodgson RJ, Rachman S. The effects of contamination and washing in obsessional patients. Behav Res Ther. 1972;**10**(2):111–117.
23. Roper G, Rachman S, Hodgson R. An experiment on obsessional checking. Behav Res Ther. 1973;**11**(3):271–277.
24. Roper G, Rachman S. Obsessional-compulsive checking: experimental replication and development. Behav Res Ther. 1976;**14**(1):25–32.
25. Steketee G. *Treatment of Obsessive Compulsive Disorder* [Internet]. New York: Guilford Publications; 1993. https://books.google.co.uk/books?id=HZO_QgAACAAJ.
26. Obsessive Compulsive Cognitions Working Group. Cognitive assessment of obsessive-compulsive disorder. Behav Res Ther. 1997;**35**(7):667–681.
27. Öst LG, Havnen A, Hansen B, Kvale G. Cognitive behavioral treatments of obsessive–compulsive disorder: A systematic review and meta-analysis of studies published 1993–2014. Clin Psychol Rev. 2015;**40**:156–169.
28. Van Oppen P, De Haan E, Van Balkom AJLM, Spinhoven P, Hoogduin K, Van Dyck R. Cognitive therapy and exposure in vivo in the treatment of obsessive compulsive disorder. Behav Res Ther. 1995;**33**(4):379–390.
29. Salkovskis PM, Hackmann A, Wells A, Gelder MG, Clark DM. Belief disconfirmation versus habituation approaches to situational exposure in panic disorder with agoraphobia: A pilot study. Behav Res Ther. 2007;**45**(5):877–885.
30. Wilhelm S, Steketee G, Fama J, Golan E. A controlled trial investigating CT for OCD treatment outcome, acceptability and mechanisms of improvement. Symposium presented at the annual meeting of the Association for the Advancement of Behavior Therapy, Boston, MA (November 2003).

Chapter 17

Body Dysmorphic Disorder

In this chapter we will help you to be able to:

- Explain what BDD is and how it typically presents, including a preoccupation with either imagined or minor physical flaws, and the resultant safety behaviours to manage the feared impact of others perceiving this flaw.
- Describe and use Veale and Neziroglu's CBT protocol for BDD.
- Explain the importance of using mirror retraining in treatment.
- Develop a treatment plan for CBT for BDD, using appropriate measures.
- Take account of comorbidity in managing CBT for BDD, including that of depression, social anxiety and OCD.

Introduction

Body dysmorphic disorder is a disorder of preoccupation, focussed on perceived flaws in appearance that the patient believes are significant and problematic, but which others either don't notice or would perceive as minor. Descriptions of this presentation can be found in the relevant literature spanning more than a hundred years [1,2], but the disorder was not well understood, nor included in the early versions of international diagnostic manuals. Even after its addition in its own right in DSM-III-R [3], it has gained comparatively little attention from the research community [4], and is frequently overlooked diagnostically by clinicians [5,6]. This chapter will explore the diagnosis and presentation of BDD, including its most common comorbidities. It will then explore how CBT can be applied with this disorder and illustrate this with a typical case.

What Is BDD?

The most recent diagnostic criteria for BDD in the DSM-5TR centre on a preoccupation with perceived physical flaws 'that are not observable or appear slight to others' [7, p. 271], resulting in repetitive behaviours and/or mental strategies, as well as significant distress and/or impairment in functioning. The DSM-5TR also notes two sets of specifiers – one regarding level of insight, and the other noting the presence or absence of 'muscle dysmorphia', where the preoccupation includes a focus on not being muscular enough. While eating disorders and BDD can be co-morbid, the DSM states a key exclusion criterion is that the presentation cannot be better accounted for by a preoccupation with weight as part of an eating disorder.

A recent systematic review of BDD rates has suggested that internationally, BDD has a prevalence of 1.9% in the general population [8]. Onset is most commonly during adolescence, and builds from a subclinical concern into a persistent disorder for many years prior to treatment [9]. Within those diagnosed with BDD, the most common perceived flaws include skin, hair and nose, followed by stomach, teeth and weight [9].

The impact of BDD on the individual's life can be extensive. They are less likely to get married [10], more likely to consider and attempt suicide [11] and more likely to be unemployed, or have their work impacted by their difficulty [12]. As such, it is particularly concerning that BDD is so frequently missed in general mental health assessments [6]. Common reasons for this are that patients fear being judged for having such concerns, are embarrassed by the problem, and worry that their symptoms won't be understood [13]. However, it appears that this can be greatly improved by the use of brief screening measures, such as the Body Dysmorphic Disorder Questionnaire [14], or by routinely noting to new patients that appearance concerns can be a problem and asking if they have such worries about their appearance [15, p. 6].

When considering difficulties such as BDD, it is important to note that having distorted views of the self is actually the norm – those without BDD do not accurately view themselves either. Most people however have rose tinted glasses for themselves, and view themselves more favourably than reality would suggest or others would rate them [16]. This is the same as in eating disorders and depression – it is not just that those with the disorder see themselves negatively, but that they do not have the self-protective, overly-positive perception of themselves that is most common in the general population.

Body dysmorphic disorder has high levels of comorbidity, especially with depression, social anxiety disorder and OCD [17]. In terms of social anxiety disorder, the cognitive overlap is in the fear of judgement, and so clinicians will benefit from determining if the key feared judgment is focussed on how the patient looks, or how they perform socially/their anxiety symptoms. In terms of OCD, the two disorders share and over-valuing of internal images and an urge to repeat compulsive behaviours until it feels right. As such, comorbidity is defined by the intrusions and compulsions extending beyond the management of perceived flaws. In either case, it will be useful to determine which disorder is causing the greatest distress, and which started first, and then commit to working on this problem.

Efficacy Data for CBT for BDD

To date, there have been comparatively few RCTs reviewing the efficacy of CBT for BDD. In a recent meta-analysis by Phillipou et al. [4] it was found that all of the RCTs involving CBT for BDD showed some improvement of symptoms, though the magnitude of these changes were lower in the more recent studies than the earlier ones. Despite this limited evidence base, NICE guidelines still (as of April 2022) recommend CBT as the first treatment of choice for mild BDD, as one of two options for moderate BDD, and as part of a combined treatment for severe BDD [18].

BDD Treatment

The key protocol used with BDD is that of Veale and Neziroglu [15]. In this, the primary concepts are that individuals see themselves primarily as an unacceptable aesthetic object, believe that their appearance and how others view them physically is highly important, and that their physical imperfections mean that they are globally negative – unattractive, ugly, inferior and worthless [19]. Due to this, the model proposes that those with BDD focus excessively on the self as if from an observer perspective and use safety behaviours to manage the perceived risk – as found in social anxiety [20]. Such safety behaviours in BDD tend to fall into three categories – those used to restore, improve or change the flawed feature itself, those used to avoid, hide or distract away from other seeing the flawed feature and those used to check their appearance or how they are being viewed by others. In each case, there is also a cognitive version – trying to neutralise thoughts, avoid thinking about the flaw (distraction or thought suppression) and mentally review.

Treatment within this protocol starts with formulating the difficulty according to the model, generally using an idiosyncratic version of the diagram in Figure 17.1.

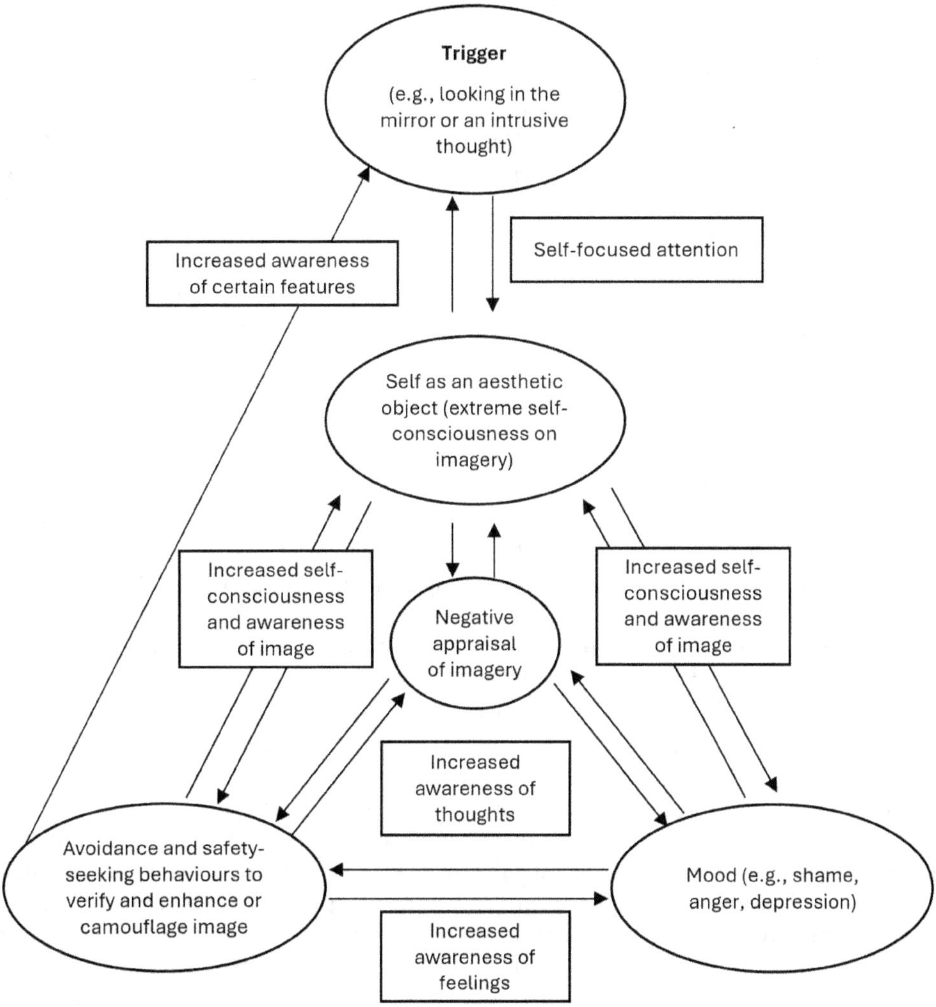

Figure 17.1 Veale and Neziroglu's model of Body Dysmorphic Disorder, 2010, reproduced with permission from Wiley-Blackwell.

Following this formulation of the problem as it currently stands, the second half of understanding the problem is using Theory A/Theory B – building an alternative explanation of the problem. Theory A in this case is some version of 'The problem is I'm ugly (because of X)' and Theory B is generally that 'The problem is that I'm preoccupied with an upsetting impression of how I look to others'.

Following these two processes of conceptualisation, treatment should work through a number of interventions to help the patient to break the key maintaining factors. A technique that is often used early in treatment is imagery rescripting, which aims to help reprocess old aversive memories connected to their problem both so that they feel more like a normal old memory, and have a less negative meaning attached to them, so that the patient can start to change how they feel about themselves as a whole. Imagery rescripting starts by finding and exploring the images the patient tends to have when they are feeling distressed about their appearance, and then exploring the meaning/interpretation behind the image. From here, the therapist will explore what early memories and experiences appear to be linked to these images, ideally asking the patient to relive the memory as in PTSD (see Chapter 19) to fully recall and evoke the details of the memory. From here, guided discovery can be used to explore and hopefully modify the attached meaning of the image, either by re-understanding the events from the past, or by separating them from the person as an adult. To then make this cognitive change more vivid, rescripting can be used, where the patient repeats the reliving aspect, but imagines their adult self (or another safe adult) showing the child what they now believe, either by arguing with the bullies or other unhelpful people in the memory, or by taking the younger self away and discussing it compassionately with them. Uniquely to BDD, it can be helpful within this section to ask how the compassionate adult views the younger self's appearance, as this can help the adult self to see themselves more compassionately. Finally, a third reliving of the memory occurs, back from the younger self's point of view but with the adult self intervening, where the younger self can add in any additional needs they have to feel safe and cared for.

Another early strategy is teaching the patient to shift their focus externally, to manage the tendencies in BDD to either focus on threat – both in terms of external threats, and on internal thoughts and images regarding the perceived flaw. This will begin with both skills training on how to focus more externally (see Chapter 13) and monitoring to know when they tend to focus internally or become hypervigilant and so need to actively refocus. For some patients, this will be sufficient for them to be able to reduce their threat-focus, while for others behavioural experiments showing the costs of internal or external threat focus will be useful to change the underlying beliefs. In either case, patients should then be encouraged to increasingly switch their attention to their overall tasks and environments whenever possible, moving from easier scenarios to doing this even when feeling under threat.

Another set of key maintaining features in BDD are covert mental strategies, including worry and rumination, self-attacking and reassurance, mental planning and mental checking. Once these have been identified, the therapist would explore the positive and negative beliefs about these strategies, before evaluating these to help the patient become more aware of the unintended consequences and costs, including setting up behavioural experiments to compare using them and not. Through this, the patient is likely to become aware that these are droppable and unhelpful strategies, and so be willing to try out alternatives. Such alternatives can then be explored, including problem solving, diffusion, becoming absorbed in activities or pleasurable images and activity scheduling.

As with the covert strategies, interventions are also needed to manage the overt behavioural strategies, including avoidance and safety behaviours. To do this, exposure to the feared situations without using the safety behaviours is set up, ideally as a behavioural experiment with clear predictions. As with other disorders such as OCD (see Chapter 16), SAD (see Chapter 13) and panic disorder (see Chapter 12) it can be helpful to actively do the opposite of what the fears would encourage, such as by using make-up and clothing to make the perceived flaw more obvious, to really be sure that no major catastrophe will occur, and that people are far less focussed on flaws in the patient than feared. Within these experiments, the therapist should be aware of the difference between unlikely feared catastrophes, and possible unhelpful outcomes, such as the reactions female patients may receive when they reduce their use of makeup. As such, setting objective and clear feared outcome, and exploring alternative meaning of more benign observations from others can be helpful.

Within this behavioural strategy work, there are specific guidelines to assess for and work with 'mirror-gazing' – that is, excessive use of mirrors to check how they look and somehow change it – and 'avoiding unsafe mirrors' – that is, attempting to avoid seeing their reflection in any mirrors they don't trust to be accurate. As with the other strategies above, both cognitive discussion techniques and behavioural experiments can be used to help the patient see these strategies as unhelpful. After this, specific guidelines can be provided to change their interaction with mirrors into something more helpful, as shown in Box 17.1.

In addition to using mirrors as described in Box 17.1, patients should be encouraged to monitor and reduce the frequency and/or duration of mirror usage.

Working with the patient's underlying appraisals is also an important feature of treatment. As in social anxiety disorder (see Chapter 13) video and/or photo feedback (or even

Box 17.1 Guidelines for helpful use of mirrors in BDD. Reproduced with permission from Veale and Neziroglu [15]

a) To use mirrors at a slight distance or ones that are large enough to reflect most of their body.
b) To deliberately focus attention on their reflection in the mirror rather than an internal impression of how they feel.
c) To use a mirror only for an agreed function (e.g. shaving, putting on make-up) for a limited period of time.
d) To use different mirrors and lights rather than sticking to ones they 'trust'.
e) To scan their body and focus attention on the whole of the face or body rather than a specific 'defect' or in any detail. As there is some evidence that healthy people focus attention on their features considered to be most attractive, this is an alternative strategy if preferred by the client.
f) To be non-evaluative about their appearance and to use detached mindfulness when there are intrusive thoughts about being ugly or defective.
g) Not to use mirrors that magnify their reflection.
h) Not to use ambiguous reflections (e.g. windows, the backs of CDs, cutlery, dusty or cracked mirrors).
i) Not to use a mirror when they feel the urge to check, but to delay the response and do other activities until the urge has subsided.

feedback via a face mask created of the patient) can be used to test out beliefs regarding objectively testable perceive flaws – such as the patient's face being a specific shade of red, or a body part being obviously asymmetrical. Beyond this, the focus for much of the early work regarding NATs is on distancing from their appraisals, rather than challenging them outright – seeing them as cognitions, noticing the thinking errors and seeing them as just thoughts that can be ignored. In terms of underlying assumptions and beliefs, the same initial strategy is also suggested, as for many patients, the changing of strategies above, and the resultant change on the patient's internal images, will modify the beliefs without the need for direct action. However, if these beliefs persist despite the behavioural work, then cognitive discussion techniques focussed on the pragmatic value of the beliefs, or using a cost/benefit analysis, can be added.

Three more specific cognitive change techniques that may also be used are Big I/Little I, reverse role-play and assertive defence of the self. Big I/Little I is a process for helping patients to see that their complete self – their Big I – is made up of many specific features and concepts – their Little I's – of which their 'flawed' body part is only one. By asking patients to write out all of the things that make them who they are – their experiences, preferences and physical features – they can see visually how small a part of them their perceived flaw actually is. Reverse role play, as in GAD [21], aims to help patients to change their beliefs about their flaw at gut level, by arguing against their beliefs and related cognitions. Finally, assertive defence of the self, as used in social anxiety [22,23] can be used to help patients to create, and then feel comfortable using, assertive responses to feared reactions from others, helping them to realise that even in this extreme feared scenario, they would be able to cope.

One treatment complication that can occur in BDD is the patient wanting to explore cosmetic surgery solutions to their appearance, either as well as or instead of CBT. Veale and Neziroglu would recommend using cost-benefit analysis to explore the risks and costs of surgery versus the benefits to one with BDD (as the evidence would suggest that for those with BDD, surgery can often be a net negative). If possible, it is preferable to encourage the patient to give up on the concept of surgery rather than only delaying it until after treatment, as they will likely be less motivated to fully engage in the treatment while having a backup in mind. Alternatively, if the patient is actively planning surgery, and is already convinced that the benefits are worth it, then therapy should be postponed until after the surgery.

Another treatment complication is comorbid depression, as BDD typically results in significant avoidance of otherwise enjoyable activities, and increased rumination even when doing activities that might otherwise be pleasant. BDD also has been shown to correlate with significantly higher rates of suicidal ideation and attempted suicide [11]. As such, it can be useful to screen for comorbid depression, and if relevant apply a behavioural activation approach (as described in Chapter 20), as this is the most parsimonious option for managing this at the same time as the BDD.

An example of this approach can be shown with Vardah, a 22-year-old Iraqi woman, currently living in university accommodation while studying for her undergraduate degree. She is a few years older than the rest of her classmates, due to having low A level grades, which resulted in her taking a year out, and then reapplying for a foundation year prior to her planned degree in biology. She has been struggling to make friends at university, and is quite low and isolated. She tells her doctor, and the therapist, that she finds social situations quite anxiety-provoking, but she is unclear about what specific fear she has regarding judgement from others. The therapist noted that on intake screening, Vardah had endorsed concerns regarding her appearance, specifically around her nose and chin. On exploring this further at assessment, Vardah expressed significant fears that her nose was huge and unsightly, and that her chin was protruding and overly pointy. The therapist couldn't see any such flaws in the moment, but was aware that the head covering being worn by the patient would somewhat limit the obviousness of such features in the chin if they were marked. The therapist explored what the feared consequences were of others seeing said flaws, and Vardah stated she believed that she would be rejected and would never find love, and also that she will have no friends, as they wouldn't want to be seen with her. To manage this risk, she would look at her flaws in her 'safe' mirror for up to an hour each morning, using makeup and head-covering to try and reduce visibility of chin and minimise the apparent size of her nose with contouring. During the day, she would sneak glances of self in any reflective surfaces to see if her chin and nose looked acceptable, and then ruminate on how big her nose looked and how pointy her chin was. Whenever others were around, she kept her head at 'safe' angles (tilted down so the nose protruded less and the chin was flattened into the neck), which the therapist realised she was also doing during the session.

The therapist explored how these beliefs had first come to Vardah, and how they had developed. Vardah described having initially believed herself pretty as a child, and remembers her father calling her his little flower. However, as she entered her teens, she started to become more self-conscious about her looks, especially when she begun to get acne. Her brothers would tease her about her appearance, and in particular would tell her that she looked like a witch due to her big, hooked nose and pointy chin. She remembers a day in her early teens where her mother was asking her what fancy dress she'd like for a party, and her brothers had all said she had to be a witch, and then her mother had laughed. Her mother had later apologised, and said that she didn't agree and that Vardah was pretty, but Vardah couldn't shake the belief that secretly everyone did think she looked like a witch. She acknowledged that this was when she had started wearing more concealing head scarves, and practising different make-up techniques to try and mask the things her brothers had focussed on. When she did this, her brothers seemed to pay less attention to her appearance, which she took as proof that she needed to conceal her flaws to be safe.

As usual, treatment began with an idiosyncratic formulation of Vardah, as shown in Figure 17.2. In this, Vardah could see how her safety behaviours made her more aware of her thoughts about being a 'repulsive witch' and caused her to have more intrusions about her appearance, as well as more self-conscious and focussed on her feared internal image. She also connected the image that came to mind, and the phrase 'ugly little witch' with her brothers mocking her, so this was added in.

Following formulation, Vardah and the therapist explored the concepts of Theory A/B. Theory A was 'the problem is that my nose and chin make me hideously ugly', while Theory B was 'the problem is that I'm preoccupied with an upsetting image of how I look'. Vardah's key takeaway from this exercise was that while she still felt fairly sure she was hideously ugly, she could also see that Theory B was true, and that continuing to live based on Theory A was unlikely to result in the life she want – one with close friendships and a romantic relationship – especially given the effect her current behaviours and focus were having on socialising and connecting with others. As such, she agreed to try testing out living as though Theory B was true, and set goals for treatment as follows: to be able to go to lectures without spending more than 30 minutes on appearance, to speak to people without trying to hide 'flaws', and to invite someone from class to do something socially, like go for a coffee.

Intervention work started with imagery rescripting of the 'fancy dress' memory. First, a discussion occurred resulting in re-understanding why her mother had laughed

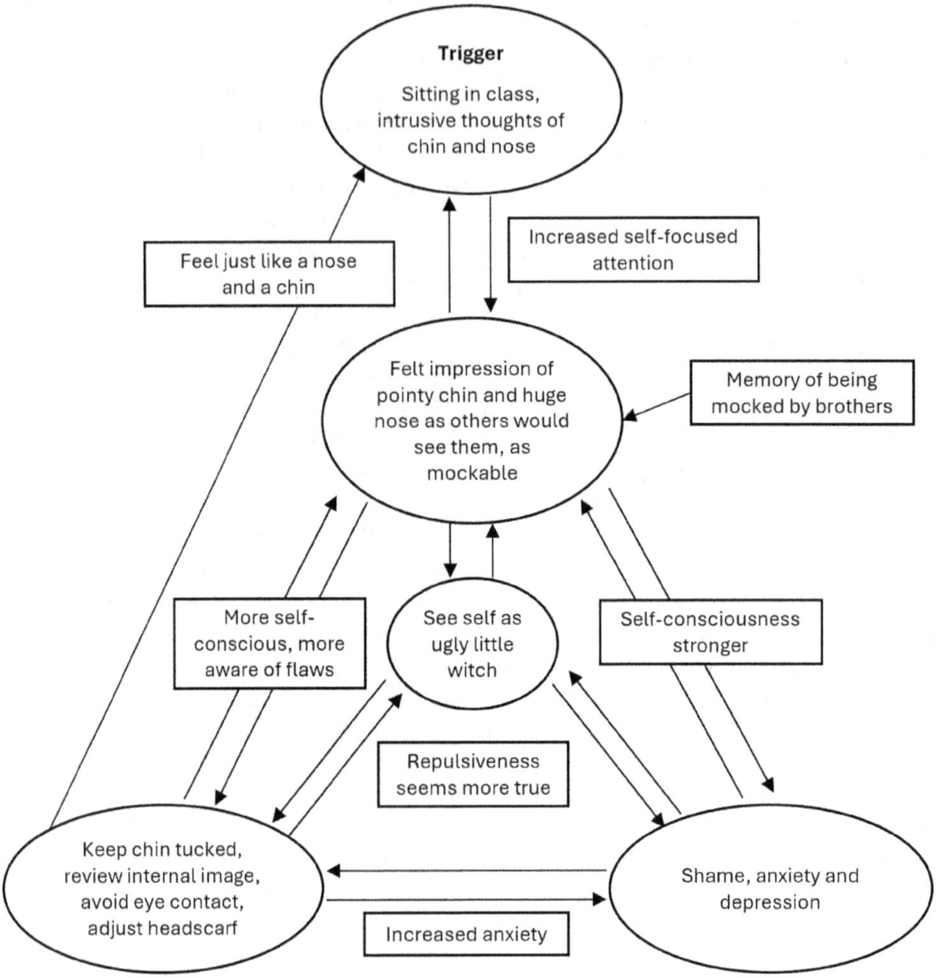

Figure 17.2 Vardah's version of Veale and Neziroglu's model of Body Dysmorphic Disorder, 2010, adapted with permission from Wiley-Blackwell.

(because her brothers had used a funny turn of phrase, not because the concept was true, as mother wouldn't have found it funny for her daughter to be hideous) and why her brothers had mocked her (they mocked each other a lot, and they noticed this phrase and focus upset her so kept using it). Following this new understanding of the events, Vardah chose to rescript using her adult self. She found that looking back at 11-year-old Vardah made her not see the flaws in the same way. Instead, she saw how excited she had initially looked to have a fancy dress outfit bought, and how the mocking had hurt her. Within the memory, adult Vardah told her mother that she needed to stop the brothers mocking her child self, as it was not just 'silly sibling stuff', and then told little Vardah she was taking her shopping for a princess outfit because she could dress as anyone she wanted, and didn't need to hide how she looked. On exploring from the child side, she noted that she also wanted her mother to apologise to her, and tell her she didn't look like a witch, which she could easily imagine her mother then doing, including giving her a hug.

As Vardah had quickly grasped the cost of internal focus, she was willing to learn and apply attention training as a skill. As a starting point, she found it easier to try to avoid having an internal focus, as she could see there was no value to focussing on the internal image and that it wouldn't change her appearance. What was harder was to shift her focus from potential external threat when she was thinking others were looking at her, as she felt that knowing if others were looking could mean she could ensure they saw her from the right angle. The therapist and Vardah spent time considering pros and cons of focus, and Vardah kept working on shifting this attention over several weeks. To further support this, the therapist and Vardah also explored the pros and cons of trying to hold a perfect angle, and experimented with dropping this safety behaviour altogether. To Vardah's surprise, this didn't seem to result in any negative reactions from others, but did make it easier to talk to people, as she came across less shy.

This opened up the conversation to exploring dropping more of her overt coping strategies, including avoiding eye contact and adjusting her headscarf. Initially trying these changes with comparatively trusted social contacts, Vardah increasingly let go of these behaviours in all situations, as she could see that they reinforced her threat focus and impaired socialising. Covert strategies were likewise explored, focussing on Vardah's tendency to ruminate after social situations about her nose and chin and how they were ruining her life. They noticed that this rumination made Vardah less motivated to socialise in the future, which in turn was making it harder for Vardah to make friends and reach her valued goals. They also noted that the content of the rumination – that her perceived flaws were irrevocably ruining her life – no longer felt as true, as her behavioural changes had resulted in more successful social experiences. Vardah agreed to try dropping rumination as a process, refocussing her attention on her current activities as she had learnt earlier.

Mirror gazing was the next therapeutic focus. The therapist and Vardah explored her reasons for mirror gazing, and the frequency and duration of this activity. The mirror use could be split into two for Vardah. First, her morning/leaving her room gazing, which would take up to two hours with a trusted mirror, and was focussed on trying to camouflage her flaws with her makeup and headscarf. Second, checks throughout the day in any available reflective surface or using her phone selfie camera, which were done with the hope that she would look better than expected and so feel less anxious. The latter belief was most easily challenged through an ABAB experiment, where Vardah checked at every urge on alternate days, and didn't check at all on the others. She quickly realised that her anxiety was actually worse on the checking days, and became aware of how frequently the image was just as bad as feared, if not worse. Vardah queried if this didn't mean that her fears must be accurate. The therapist re-explored with Vardah the concept that the image we see is based on both what is in front of us, *and* our own memories and internal images. They also explored the concept of cameras, and how different lenses create a different image, and how as such, there may be no one 'true' image of how a person looks.

Next the morning ritual was explored, focussing on the pros and cons of mirror gazing and camouflaging until she felt right. At this point, Vardah was given the list of suggested mirror retraining goals as shown in Box 17.1. The therapist and Vardah explored what a suitable amount of time would be for using the mirror to put on makeup and her headscarf, agreeing on an initial aim of 30 minutes, which was later shortened to 20 minutes with a focus on applying each part of her makeup with equal focus, rather than purely focussing on contouring her nose and jaw. Likewise, the therapist and Vardah explored how she viewed wearing a headscarf, and how she wanted to view it. Vardah realised that while she did believe in wearing a headscarf for religious reasons, she had increasingly lost sight of that, and had been wearing it more to camouflage her flaws. She recommitted to wearing her headscarf for its intended purpose, focussing only on whether it was covering her as her faith encouraged.

Throughout therapy, as Vardah had dropped her safety behaviours, and changed how she interacted socially, she had found herself talking to more people, and being included in more informal social events, such as getting a coffee after lectures. However, she still struggled with the idea that she was fundamentally flawed due to how she looked, and that people would never truly want to be her friend or partner. The therapist and Vardah countered this using Big I/Little I, exploring all of the many interests and experiences that made Vardah up as a whole, from her love of specific comedians, to her passion for microbiology, to her skills at cooking certain dishes. Emboldened by this, Vardah was encouraged to actively seek out new social opportunities, including joining the university comedy club as a helper and inviting some new friends round for a meal.

Reviewing therapy as a whole, Vardah was surprised that she had met, and even surpassed, all of her treatment goals. Her therapist helped her to explore how she could build on these successes to keep developing friendships, and they tentatively explored how Vardah could manage any new anxieties that could arise as and when she began dating.

Concluding Remarks

Body dysmorphic disorder is a disorder of preoccupation, focussed on a perceived physical flaw that causes significant distress and/or impairment in the person's life. It often has an early age of onset and tends to persist and build for many years prior to diagnosis, resulting in significant impairment in a range of areas of functioning. It has high rates of comorbidity, especially with depression, social anxiety, and OCD. Veale and Neziroglu's model conceptualises BDD as a difficulty characterised by a threat-based focus of attention and a range of covert and overt coping strategies, commonly including mirror gazing. Treatment aims to change these via the use of behavioural experiments, cognitive discussion techniques and specific skills development, including shifting attention and mirror retraining.

Further Reading

Veale D, Neziroglu FA. *Body Dysmorphic Disorder: A Treatment Manual*. Chichester: Wiley-Blackwell; 2010.

Phillips KA, Menard W, Fay C, Weisberg R. Demographic characteristics, phenomenology, comorbidity, and family history in 200 individuals with body dysmorphic disorder. Psychosomatics. 2005;**46**(4):317–325.

References

1. Morselli E. *La dismorfofobia e la tafefobia nei loro rapporti con le forme consimili di pazzia del dubbio (paranoia rudimentaria).* Naples: Tipografia della riforma medica; 1891.
2. Janet P. Les Obsessions Et la Psychasthenie. 1903.

3. American Psychiatric Association. *Diagnostic and Statistical Manual of Mental Disorders* (3rd ed. rev.) Washington, DC: 1987.

4. Phillipou A, Rossell SL, Wilding HE, Castle DJ. Randomised controlled trials of psychological & pharmacological treatments for body dysmorphic disorder: A systematic review. Psychiatry Res. 2016;**245**:179–185.

5. Grant JE, Kim SW, Eckert ED. Body dysmorphic disorder in patients with anorexia nervosa: Prevalence, clinical features, and delusionality of body image. Int J Eat Disord. 2002;**32**(3):291–300.

6. Singh AR, Veale D. Understanding and treating body dysmorphic disorder. Indian J Psychiatry. 2019;**61**(Suppl 1):S131–5.

7. American Psychiatric Association, editor. *Diagnostic and Statistical Manual of Mental Disorders: DSM-5-TR*. 5th ed., text revision. Washington, DC: American Psychiatric Association Publishing; 2022.

8. Veale D, Gledhill LJ, Christodoulou P, Hodsoll J. Body dysmorphic disorder in different settings: A systematic review and estimated weighted prevalence. Body Image. 2016;**18**:168–186.

9. Phillips KA, Menard W, Fay C, Weisberg R. Demographic characteristics, phenomenology, comorbidity, and family history in 200 individuals with body dysmorphic disorder. Psychosomatics. 2005;**46**(4):317–325.

10. Koran LM, Abujaoude E, Large MD, Serpe RT. The prevalence of body dysmorphic disorder in the United States adult population. CNS Spectr. 2008;**13**(4):316–322.

11. Rief W, Buhlmann U, Wilhelm S, Borkenhagen A, Brähler E. The prevalence of body dysmorphic disorder: A population-based survey. Psychol Med. 2006;**36**(6):877–885.

12. Didie ER, Menard W, Stern AP, Phillips KA. Occupational functioning and impairment in adults with body dysmorphic disorder. Compr Psychiatry. 2008;**49**(6):561–569.

13. Conroy M, Menard W, Fleming-Ives K, Modha P, Cerullo H, Phillips KA. Prevalence and clinical characteristics of body dysmorphic disorder in an adult inpatient setting. Gen Hosp Psychiatry. 2008;**30**(1):67–72.

14. Phillips K. Diagnostic instruments for body dysmorphic disorder. New research programs and abstracts. American Psychiatric Association 148th Annual Meeting, Miami. American Psychiatric Press; Washington, DC: 1995.

15. Veale D, Neziroglu FA. *Body Dysmorphic Disorder: A Treatment Manual.* Chichester: Wiley-Blackwell; 2010.

16. Jansen A, Smeets T, Martijn C, Nederkoorn C. I see what you see: The lack of a self-serving body-image bias in eating disorders. Br J Clin Psychol. 2006;**45**(1):123–135.

17. Gunstad J, Phillips KA. Axis I comorbidity in body dysmorphic disorder. Compr Psychiatry. 2003;**44**(4):270–276.

18. National Institute for Health and Care Excellence. Obsessive-compulsive disorder and body dysmorphic disorder: Treatment. Clinical Guidance [Internet]. NICE; 2005 Nov. Report No.: CG31. www.nice.org.uk/guidance/cg31.

19. Cooper M, Osman S. Metacognition in body dysmorphic disorder: A preliminary exploration. J Cogn Psychother. 2007;**21**(2):148–155.

20. Clark DM. Cognitive perspective on social phobia. In: WR Crozier, LE Alden (Eds.), *International Handbook of Social Anxiety: Concepts, Research, and Interventions Relating to the Self and Shyness* (pp. 405–430). New York: Wiley; 2001.

21. Dugas MR, Koerner N, Michel J. *Cognitive Behavioral Treatment for Generalized Anxiety Disorder: From Science to Practice.* 2nd ed. New York: Routledge; 2019.

22. Padesky CA. A more effective treatment focus for social phobia? Int Cogn Ther Newsl. 1997;**11**(1):1–3.

23. Leigh E, Clark DM. Cognitive Therapy for Social Anxiety Disorder in Adolescents [Internet]. 2018. Available from: https://oxcadatresources.com/wp-content/uploads/2018/11/CT-SAD-A-MANUAL.pdf

Chapter 18

Illness Anxiety Disorder

In this chapter we will help you to be able to:

- Explain what illness anxiety disorder (IAD) is and how it typically presents, including preoccupation with a serious illness and the resultant changes in attentional focus and safety behaviours.
- Describe and use Salkovskis, Warwick and Deale's CBT protocol for illness anxiety disorder.
- Develop a treatment plan for CBT for illness anxiety disorder, using appropriate measures.
- Take account of comorbidity in managing CBT for illness anxiety disorder, including depression and panic disorder.

Introduction

Illness anxiety disorder is a new term for a long-described condition [1], but one that has historically stumped therapists. Comparatively recent advances in disorder-specific CBT has changed this picture, with a clear model that can be followed and adapted based on the feared physical health condition(s). This chapter will describe both the history and the current status of what was historically called Hypochondriasis, along with a recommended treatment approach based on this new understanding of the disorders underlying mechanisms, many of which are shared with either OCD or panic disorder.

What Is Illness Anxiety Disorder?

As per the most recent edition of the DSM [2], IAD is defined by an enduring 'preoccupation with having or acquiring a serious illness' despite mild or no somatic symptoms, and a general anxiety about their health, resulting in health-related safety behaviours and/or avoidance.

A diagnostic feature that has been removed in DSM-5 was that of the difficulty persisting despite medical reassurance [3,4]. It is helpful to have had this requirement dropped, so as to ensure patients are not excluded due to having not had medical reassurance available. Nonetheless, this is an interesting feature of IAD, as it marks a noticeable difference to the reactions of others when given medical reassurance, who are likely to remain reassured for a prolonged period, whereas those with IAD can become anxious again in as little as 24 hours [5]. Additionally, to meet the diagnostic criteria for IAD, the patient must have either no somatic symptoms, or only ones that are 'mild in intensity' [4] – otherwise, they are likely better accounted for with the diagnosis somatic symptom disorder (SSD). This divide is subject to some debate, with several stating that the division of those with high health anxiety based on their level of somatic symptoms doesn't make diagnostic sense, as there is more to unify these groups than there is the various sub-groups within SSD [6,7].

Until the 1980s, IAD, or hypochondriasis as it was known at the time, was a very poorly understood condition, with minimal treatment options [8,9] and no clear CBT understanding of how the problem developed or was maintained. Often assumed to be secondary to depression, it was commonly not seen as the target for clinical work, and indeed the disorder has high levels of comorbidity with both depression and panic disorder [9]. However, IAD has a significant impact on the lives of those living with it. Most surprisingly, despite the aim in IAD to be alert for and so treat serious illnesses early, it has been shown to correlate to higher all-cause mortality rates compared to healthy controls [10], in part due to a fourfold increase in suicide in this group, as well as potentially the impact on the body of chronic stress.

Now seen as separate from both depression and anxiety disorders, health anxiety is still a difficult disorder to classify and name. While in the DSM-5 and DSM-5TR it falls within the somatic symptom and related disorders and is called illness anxiety disorder [2,4], in ICD-11 the term hypochondriasis is still used, and the disorder has been moved into the obsessive compulsive and related disorders, as we have chosen to follow here [11].

Due to the changing definitions of this condition – from hypochondriasis in DSM-IV [3], to various proposed concepts of health anxiety [12,13], to the most recent set of criteria of IAD in DSM-5 [4] – there have likewise been varying estimates of its prevalence, both in medical settings (e.g. 7% [14], 3% [15]) and in the general population (3.4% [13], 0.4–1% [15]), and a difficulty in determining whether this is increasing over time. One interesting study did find a way to explore this, by looking at scores on one specific measure (the Illness Attitudes Scale), and had found that clinically significant health anxiety in students had almost doubled in the past 30 years [16]. As such, it may be that supporting and treating patients with IAD will become an ever-more significant part of a CBT therapist's caseload.

A different measure that can be useful in assessing IAD is the Health Anxiety Inventory [17]. This 18-item measure looks at the individual's preoccupation and awareness of symptoms, thoughts of illness and beliefs about the negative consequences of a serious illness. It can be used weekly as an ongoing monitoring tool, and is generally considered to have a cut-off of 18 for clinical caseness, though there is some disagreement as to whether this is the best number to use [18,19,20].

Efficacy Data for CBT for Illness Anxiety Disorder

To date, there have been more than 15 RCTs reviewing the efficacy of CBT for IAD. In a recent meta-analysis by Cooper et al. [21] it was found that CBT has a substantial effect size on symptoms of IAD compared to treatment as usual or wait list. Interestingly, this was found to be true whether those with diagnosed physical health conditions were included or excluded, suggesting that therapists considering this approach do not need exclude those with comorbid physical health conditions. Currently, there are no NICE or APA guidelines specifically related to IAD or hypochondriasis, though there continue to be calls for this [22].

IAD Treatment

The treatment put forward by Salkovksis, Warwick and Deale [23] is carried out over up to 16 sessions, ideally within a 4-month window. It is based on previously described models for panic disorder ([24] see Chapter 12) and OCD ([25] see Chapter 16), with a central focus upon reattribution of the patient's difficulties via Theory A/Theory B (see Chapter 6).

The central premise to this model is that IAD is driven by a consistent bias towards misinterpreting benign or ambiguous bodily changes and sensations, such as pain, rashes and swelling, as meaning that they have a serious health condition that will need rapid medical intervention to prevent death or major disability. Such misinterpretations then endure, and result in a range of safety-seeking behaviours and selective attention, as well as physiological and emotional changes, which in turn can worsen the experience of the symptoms, provide more ambiguous and potentially threatening information and reinforce the belief that there is something seriously wrong. This can be explained idiosyncratically with clients via a vicious flower model, as in Figure 18.1.

Following the creation of an idiosyncratic version of this model, patients are supported to consider the less threatening alternative view of their problems as one of a fear of, or preoccupation with, a serious illness, rather than having the illness. Given the aforementioned difficulties with believing that they don't have a serious illness through medical reassurance and testing, this alternative approach of focussing on what better accounts for their overall experiences is especially useful in IAD.

Treatment then focusses on an interweaving of discussion techniques and behavioural experiments, helping the patient to shift constituent beliefs regarding health, medical professionals and procedures, safety seeking behaviours, the meaning of symptoms and the concept of dying. Early homework tasks may also include monitoring, to help gather information during periods of stress regarding triggers, avoidance, cognitions and safety seeking behaviours, and the impact of these things in terms of effort, time and emotional distress, on a typical week.

A difficulty in treating IAD is that of the patient's tendency to overlook non-serious and benign causes of symptoms. Managing this is important, and generally requires helping the patient to re-evaluate the comparative likelihood of their feared outcomes and more common conditions and causes. One way to do this is via a pie chart technique, similar to

Figure 18.1 Maintenance formulation of Illness Anxiety Disorder, reproduced with permission from Oxford University Press.

the responsibility pie chart in OCD, where the possible causes that could be 'responsible' for the symptoms are listed, with the feared illness first, and then the percentage likelihood of each is charted, starting at the bottom of the list. Alternatively, the inverted pyramid can be used, where progressively smaller bars are drawn to represent the number of patients experiencing a symptom, sustaining the symptom, seeing a doctor, needing tests, needing treatment and failing to respond to treatment. This can show the comparative likelihood of the various feared outcomes, compared to the many, many, people who have the initial symptom but do not need medical intervention. However, in either case, and when applying general cognitive reattribution techniques, the therapist should be careful to avoid reinforcing the underlying belief that symptoms need to be explained, and that all symptoms should be reattributed to a known condition. Doing so leaves the client more prone to future relapse, when new symptoms appear for which they do not have as many known explanations, and reinforces the tendency to attend to symptoms and obsess over causes.

As in most of the disorders of Chapters 10–18, behavioural experiments can be a major aspect of treatment. Specific experiments that can be helpful in IAD include selective attention and testing catastrophic prediction experiments, as in panic disorder, and ABAB experiments where safety-seeking behaviours are alternately enhanced and dropped to see the comparative effects they have on anxiety, symptoms and strength of belief. Experiments can also be carried out to determine the impact of specific key maintaining features, namely the impact of worrying and rumination, and of reassurance seeking and medical consultations. In each case, after the behaviour has been explored, pros and cons of the behaviour determined and a behavioural experiment carried out, it is helpful to agree new guidelines with the client on how they will handle this. For example, worry and rumination can be limited to a set period of worry time (see Chapter 14) or phased out altogether, reassurance can be replaced with agreed supportive reactions from loved ones, and medical consultations can be postponed following expectations of symptom remission if not serious.

Underlying belief work requires first identifying the key beliefs that have made the patient predisposed to IAD, and then exploring and modifying these one by one. Gaining a full understanding of what beliefs the patient holds can be tricky in IAD, but is often assisted by probing for and then exploring images the patient holds [26]. These beliefs can include general concepts such as 'all symptoms need a clear explanation', and 'medical tests are the only way to rule out a serious illness' as well as more self-referent ideas such as 'I have a weak heart', 'bad things always happen to me', 'I deserve punishment' and 'thinking positively will tempt fate'. Depending on the belief, it may be more suited to further behavioural experiments, or further cognitive discussion techniques, including logical, empirical and pragmatic evaluation.

As an example of this, Serg was a married man in his late thirties, who was deeply preoccupied by the concept that he may have or develop cancer, and then eventually die of this. To reduce the risk of this Serg would engage in a number of long-standing health behaviours. This included keeping his weight to a healthy level and following quite restrictive food choices, due to suggested links of various eating habits with cancer. He also had a complex relationship with exercise, as he wanted to do lots of exercise, and would go for walks and gentle cycle rides multiple times a week to stay healthy, but he had quit his football team as the sweating and racing heart it would provoke was too distracting and anxiety provoking, and he felt he was simply letting down the team. Another daily experience was of scanning his body in the shower each morning, both during the shower and

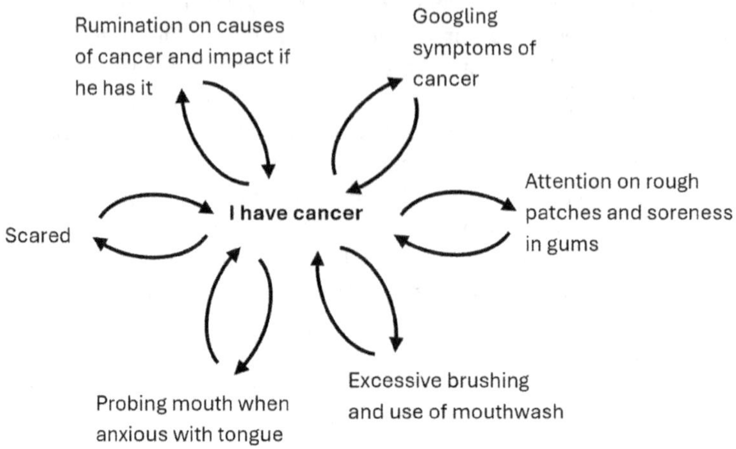

Figure 18.2 Example of a maintenance formulation of illness anxiety disorder for Serg, adapted and reproduced with permission from Oxford University Press.

when drying off. This could result in delaying getting up, because he was dreading what he might find, and he then would rush because he was running late, but then ruminate over whether he had missed something. Serg came to therapy after a bowel cancer scare, where excessive wiping had resulted in micro-tears, resulting in apparent blood in the stool, and then multiple tests with a GP. On discussion, Serg and the therapist determined that the main impacts of the IAD on his life were the limitations due to the need to rigidly follow a healthy lifestyle, the avoidance of previously valued activities due to symptom induction and the inability to follow through on his desire to have a child, which he felt unable to action due to the belief that he would not be around to be a father.

Therapy began with the creation of an idiosyncratic example of the vicious flower, focussing on a new fear regarding having gum cancer (see Figure 18.2), based on symptoms of tooth ache, rough patches of skin in the mouth and some mild bleeding from the gums. As shown, this fear resulted in him brushing his teeth repeatedly and then scanning and probing for signs of bleeding or rough patches across the course of the day. He also described googling symptoms of gum cancer, and then repeatedly using mouthwash between brushing, as one article had suggested a possible link between gum disease and cancer. The therapist explored with him the possible impact of teeth brushing, excessive mouthwash use and probing the gums, on his bodily symptoms, and he could see how this may exacerbate them. They also explored the impact of googling 'symptoms of gum cancer' on his belief that he had gum cancer, and on his selective attention towards relevant symptoms. As homework, Serg was asked to complete further vicious flowers, on other examples of feared illnesses.

From this, Serg and the therapist created his version of Theory A/Theory B, based on the competing theories of 'The problem is I have cancer' and 'The problem is that I am highly preoccupied with the thought of having cancer'. While, at this point, the evidence on each side meant that he couldn't know which Theory was more likely to be true, the impact of living on the basis of Theory A was extremely negative to him when laid out in black and white, especially the concept that he would likely never feel able to have children with his wife. As a result, he was highly motivated to test out Theory B living, to see if he could build more evidence for this over therapy and so build his confidence that it was true.

Living by Theory B was operationalised step by step, initially focussing on the specific current fear of gum cancer. Serg could see how the rigorous teeth brushing and excessive use of mouthwash would worsen dry skin and bleeding, and a brief focus of attention experiment illuminated the impact of paying attention to his mouth on how the symptoms felt. The pros and cons of these behaviours, versus dropping them all for a week, were explored, including the risk of waiting versus the value of removing any self-caused symptoms. Serg agreed to then try dropping all mouth probing, refocus his attention and brush his teeth only twice a day for two minutes for a week, to see what happened to his sensations, anxiety and beliefs about gum cancer.

Having found that the severity of the symptoms he experienced, the level of anxiety and preoccupation and the belief in having cancer all diminished as he followed Theory B, Serg was further motivated to apply this in other ways. The next session focussed on his other scanning and probing behaviours, comparing this to NHS guidelines and exploring how he could shower differently to reduce the temptation to probe. Serg and the therapist created some guidelines for him to follow, based on the NHS guidelines, but also highlighting the importance of checking based on a plan, and not in response to anxiety or thoughts about health.

The following sessions Serg asked to discuss reassurance seeking, as his wife had commented that this had worsened over the previous two weeks, often focussed on questioning whether it was irresponsible to ignore a possible health issue. The experience of reassurance seeking was explored, and how this had sometimes made him feel better for short periods of time, but could also strain the relationship, or make him feel worse, depending on her reaction. They then discussed the practicalities of how he could notice he was about to reassurance seek, and what he could say instead, to maximise the chance of empathy and support, rather than reassurance or an argument. While Serg felt that it should be predominantly his responsibility to avoid asking for reassurance, he also agreed to explicitly discuss this with his wife, so that she knew he was trying to break out of the cycle and would herself have her own planned response. The therapist and Serg discussed what this might look like, and briefly role played him starting the conversation.

Therapy then focussed on medical reassurance, both in terms of going to a doctor, and asking 'Dr Google'. A reverse pyramid was used to show how common a fleeting symptom could be, versus one that might warrant medical assessment, and some guidelines were drawn up regarding when it would be helpful to book to see the GP, with the deal to put any 'if still symptomatic call now' reminders on his phone, and then drop attention on the symptom in question until this point. The idea of this is that most symptoms will pass naturally if not probed, scanned and reinforced, and those that persist are more likely to be those that will benefit from some medical intervention. In terms of googling symptoms, it was agreed that this was generally not needed or helpful, and so for Serg, it would be better to follow the medical appointment plan and resist the urge to try and self-diagnose at all.

Tolerating self-induced physical sensations then became the focus, so as to allow Serg to go back to football, as the new season was about to start. Symptom induction was carried out in session, by having Serg run vigorously on the spot, and then his resultant safety behaviours were noted and explored. The alternative Theory B response was discussed, and Serg tried bringing on the symptoms again, but refocussing his attention on trying to get his knees up and seeing how fast he could go. He was surprised at how much attending to the symptoms had been exacerbating them, and how much choosing to ignore them made them feel more tolerable. Between sessions, it was agreed for Serg to go to the start of season practice and choose to act as though exercise-induced symptoms were not important.

Underlying belief work started with reviewing the key beliefs the patient had held at the start of therapy via reapplication of the Illness Attitudes Questionnaire. While some beliefs, such as 'bodily changes are always a sign that something is wrong' had changed markedly due to the earlier sessions, other beliefs about doctors and medical tests had remained, such as 'I or my doctor must be able to find an explanation for any physical symptom' and 'detailed tests are the only way to really rule out an illness'. This was explored initially via general Socratic dialogue, followed by exploring the pros and cons of following each rule, compared to an alternative more flexible rule such as 'some symptoms are normal fluctuations and so won't have a definitive explanation' and 'detailed tests can be helpful in some situations, but doctors can also rule things out by looking at the overall presentation, and detailed tests can in those situations be unhelpful'.

By the end of therapy, Serg was much less preoccupied by the concept of cancer and was finding it significantly easier to notice a symptom and then put it to one side and refocus on his day, which he regularly found resulted in the symptom subsiding. He took this as strong evidence for Theory B. The therapist and Serg explored that he may struggle in the future if he had a new symptom, and one that lasted longer than a few days, and so explored how to apply the tools from therapy to that scenario. Serg and his wife were also trying to get pregnant, and so relapse prevention explored how he could manage the health appointments and useful health information that could accompany this without over-preoccupation regarding his wife's health.

Concluding Remarks

No longer considered to be simply part of other conditions such as depression or anxiety disorders, IAD is now seen as a diagnosis in its own right, though questions remain about whether it is best characterised as part of the somatic symptom disorders or the obsessive compulsive and related disorders. As described above, effective treatment for this condition aligns strongly with that for OCD and panic disorder, using a vicious flower model, Theory A/Theory B, and then a mixture of cognitive discussion techniques and behavioural experiments involving exposure with response prevention.

Further Reading

Warwick HM, Salkovskis PM. Hypochondriasis. *Behav Res Ther.* 1990;**28**(2):105–117.

Salkovskis PM, Warwick H, Deale AC. Cognitive-behavioral treatment for severe and persistent health anxiety (hypochondriasis). *Brief Treat Crisis Interventions.* 2003;**3**(3):353–367.

References

1. Burton R. *The Anatomy of Melancholy: What It Is. With All the Kindes, Causes, Symptomes, Prognostickes, and Severall Cures of it.* Oxford: John Lichfield and James Short; 1621.
2. American Psychiatric Association. *Diagnostic and Statistical Manual of Mental Disorders: DSM-5-TR.* 5th ed., text revision. Washington, DC: American Psychiatric Association Publishing; 2022.

3. American Psychiatric Association. *Diagnostic and Statistical Manual of Mental Disorders: DSM-IV*. Washington, DC: American Psychiatric Association; 1994.
4. American Psychiatric Association. *Diagnostic and Statistical Manual of Mental Disorders: DSM-5*. Washington, DC: American Psychiatric Association; 2013.
5. Lucock MP, Morley S, White C, Peake MD. Responses of consecutive patients to reassurance after gastroscopy: Results of self administered questionnaire survey. BMJ. 1997;**315**(7108):572–575.
6. Bailer J, Kerstner T, Witthöft M, Diener C, Mier D, Rist F. Health anxiety and hypochondriasis in the light of DSM-5. Anxiety Stress Coping. 2016;**29**(2):219–239.
7. Newby JM, Hobbs MJ, Mahoney AEJ, Wong S (Kelvin), Andrews G. DSM-5 illness anxiety disorder and somatic symptom disorder: Comorbidity, correlates, and overlap with DSM-IV hypochondriasis. J Psychosom Res. 2017;**101**:31–37.
8. Gelder MG, Gath D, Mayou R. *Oxford Textbook of Psychiatry*. Oxford: Oxford University Press; 1983.
9. Warwick HM, Salkovskis PM. Hypochondriasis.Behav Res Ther. 1990;**28**(2):105–117.
10. Mataix-Cols D, Isomura K, Sidorchuk A, Rautio D, Ivanov VZ, Rück C, et al. All-cause and cause-specific mortality among individuals with hypochondriasis. JAMA Psychiatry. 2024;**81**(3):284–291.
11. World Health Organization. *International Classification of Diseases*, 11th revision (ICD-11). World Health Organization; 2019.
12. Fink P, Ørnbøl E, Toft T, Sparle KC, Frostholm L, Olesen F. A new, empirically established hypochondriasis diagnosis. Am J Psychiatry. 2004;**161**(9):1680–1691.
13. Sunderland M, Newby JM, Andrews G. Health anxiety in Australia: Prevalence, comorbidity, disability and service use. Br J Psychiatry. 2013;**202**(1):56–61.
14. Pandey S, Parikh M, Brahmbhatt M, Vankar GK. Clinical study of illness anxiety disorder in medical outpatients. Arch Psychiatry Psychother. 2017;**4**:32–41.
15. Weck F, Richtberg S, Neng JMB. Epidemiology of hypochondriasis and health anxiety: Comparison of different diagnostic criteria. Curr Psychiatry Rev. 2014;**10**(1):14–23.
16. Kosic A, Lindholm P, Järvholm K, Hedman-Lagerlöf E, Axelsson E. Three decades of increase in health anxiety: Systematic review and meta-analysis of birth cohort changes in university student samples from 1985 to 2017. J Anxiety Disord. 2020;**71**:102208.
17. Salkovskis PM, Rimes KA, Warwick HM, Clark D. The Health Anxiety Inventory: Development and validation of scales for the measurement of health anxiety and hypochondriasis. Psychol Med. 2002;**32**(5):843–853.
18. Rode S, Salkovskis P, Dowd H, Hanna M. Health anxiety levels in chronic pain clinic attenders. J Psychosom Res. 2006;**60**(2):155–161.
19. The National Collaborating Centre for Mental Health. *The Improving Access to Psychological Therapies Manual*. Mental Health Policy Team, Operations and Information Directorate; 2018.
20. Alberts NM, Hadjistavropoulos HD, Jones SL, Sharpe D. The Short Health Anxiety Inventory: A systematic review and meta-analysis. J Anxiety Disord. 2013;**27**(1):68–78.
21. Cooper K, Gregory JD, Walker I, Lambe S, Salkovskis PM. Cognitive behaviour therapy for health anxiety: A systematic review and meta-analysis. Behav Cogn Psychother. 2017;**45**(2):110–123.
22. Bailey R. Why health anxiety needs NICE clinical guidelines. Lancet Psychiatry. 2024;**11**(3):164–165.
23. Salkovskis PM, Warwick H, Deale AC. Cognitive-Behavioral Treatment for Severe and Persistent Health Anxiety (Hypochondriasis). Brief Treat Crisis Interv [Internet]. 2003 [accessed

22 February 2024]; https://psycnet.apa.org/record/2003-10795-005.

24. Clark DM. A cognitive approach to panic. Behav Res Ther. 1986;**24**(4):461–470.
25. Salkovskis PM. Obsessional-compulsive problems: A cognitive-behavioural analysis. Behav Res Ther. 1985;**23**(5):571–583.
26. Wells A, Hackmann A. Imagery and core beliefs in health anxiety: Content and origins. Behav Cogn Psychother. 1993;**21**(3):265–273.

Chapter 19

Post-traumatic Stress Disorder (PTSD)

with Rachel Handley

In this chapter we will help you to be able to:

- Explain what PTSD is and how it typically presents, including the nature of trauma memories and associated re-experiencing.
- Describe and use evidence-based CBT protocols for PTSD.
- Choose and use appropriate formulation models for CBT for PTSD.
- Describe the importance of reprocessing in any treatment plan.
- Develop a treatment plan for CBT for PTSD, using appropriate measures.
- Take account of comorbidity in managing CBT for PTSD.

Introduction

The concept that individuals can be deeply and enduringly marked by trauma has been known and reported through the ages [1,2], but the concept of PTSD as a medical diagnosis is far more recent [3]. A disorder with strong features of anxiety, yet with a focus in the past; PTSD can seem a conundrum. This chapter will explore how PTSD is now defined, and the various ways in which it can be made sense of within CBT. The high levels of efficacy in CBT for PTSD will be reviewed, before each of the key modern protocols is discussed in turn.

Working with trauma is an emotionally challenging area, and like the work itself, this chapter will explore some difficult topics and examples. Please be compassionate to yourself when reading this section, and when doing this work, and ensure you have support networks in place to manage your own reactions.

What Is PTSD?

To define PTSD, the concept of a trauma must first be defined. The DSM5 defines a trauma as 'exposure to actual or threatened death, serious injury, or sexual violence' [4] while the ICD-11 describes it as 'exposure to an event or situation (either short- or long-lasting) of an extreme threatening or horrific nature' [5]. Traumas may be experienced directly by the patient, or witnessed, or they may learn of it happening to a loved one (or in the case of those whose work connects to traumas, being repeatedly exposed to the aftermath). What is key is that the event was experienced at some point as extremely threatening; in this sense, the word trauma is more specific when discussing PTSD than in everyday language.

Following such a trauma, PTSD can then develop, presenting as a range of symptoms, including re-experiencing, changes in mood, heightened arousal and reactivity and avoidance of reminders or the memory itself. Each of these symptoms in and of themselves are a common reaction to trauma, but PTSD is diagnosed when these persist for more than a month and cause significant distress or impact on functioning.

The DSM-5 and ICD-11 diagnostic criteria include three shared clusters of symptoms in the domains of (1) re-experiencing (e.g. intrusive, unwanted images of the trauma, flashbacks and nightmares related to the trauma), (2) avoidance (e.g. avoiding memories of the trauma or people or places associated with the trauma) and (3) hyperarousal and reactivity (e.g. startle reactions, hypervigilance for threat and difficulties sleeping or concentrating). The DSM-5 has an additional criterion of 'negative alterations in cognitions and mood' which includes persistent emotional states such as low mood or anger, gaps in memory of the trauma and 'persistent distorted cognitions' such as those concerning responsibility for the trauma or the consequences of the trauma. The DSM-5 requires at least one re-experiencing symptom and avoidance symptom and two or more negative alterations in cognitions and mood and hyperarousal symptoms. The ICD-11 require at least two symptoms of re-experiencing, avoidance and hyperarousal. In both classification systems the symptoms also need to be accompanied by an interference in normal functioning for the individual. The DSM-5 further stipulates sub-types of PTSD with or without dissociative symptoms and that PTSD may have delayed onset (at least six months after the trauma). Individuals with PTSD commonly present with comorbid psychological disorders, in particular depression, substance abuse and other anxiety disorders [6].

The ICD-11 has introduced an additional diagnosis of 'complex PTSD' (CPTSD) which includes all the usual symptoms of PTSD along with criteria relating to three additional areas, which are disturbances in the self of self, interpersonal processes and affect regulation. These presentations are often, but not always, seen when traumas have been repeated, prolonged and/or occurred in childhood.

Putting to one side the nuances of the different diagnostic classification systems, clinically, the cardinal feature of PTSD is re-experiencing. Traumatic memories are often described by patients as being experienced 'as if they are happening again'. Whilst this may be on a continuum from, at its most extreme, a dissociative flashback where the individual feels like they completely lose touch with the 'here and now', to a milder sense of being somewhat present within the traumatic events, the memories rarely feel like they are completely in the past. This is an important part of what fuels the sense of current threat in PTSD, drives the avoidance symptoms and perpetuates arousal and emotional reactions.

PTSD can develop after any relevant trauma, but most traumas do not result in PTSD as one would guess, given that studies have found around 60% of people have experienced a trauma in their life [7], yet only 8–14% of individuals ever develop PTSD [7,8,9]. Further, there appears to be significant variation in the likelihood of PTSD depending on the type of trauma experienced.

Point prevalence in both the UK and US have been found to be between 4–5% for PTSD [10,11], with prevalence higher amongst females and in particular younger females, and otherwise quite stable across much of the lifespan, declining in older age (after 75). In populations at higher risk of trauma exposure, much greater prevalence statistics have been noted (e.g. police [12]). Among those seeking treatment for PTSD in the USA the average time from onset was 4.5 years [10], although only around 50–60% reporting having experienced PTSD in both the UK and US also reported seeking or receiving treatment so it is reasonable to assume that a lot of PTSD goes untreated [10,11].

There are various measures that can be useful in the assessment, formulation and monitoring of PTSD. The PTSD Symptom Checklist (PCL-5) [13,14,15] is a 20-item self-report measure that assesses each of the symptoms of PTSD as defined in the DSM-5. It can be used every session to monitor change across symptoms, and to help decide targets for treatment within a session. It is generally considered to have a clinical cut-off of 32, with a change of 10 or more representing reliable improvement [16]. Alternatively, the International Trauma Questionnaire follows the diagnostic features from the ICD-11, and so contains items related to both PTSD and CPTSD, allowing for distinguishing between these on the basis of disturbances in self-organisation [17]. There are further process measures, such as the Post Traumatic Cognitions Inventory (original [18] or short [19]), the Response to Intrusions Questionnaire [19] and the Safety Behaviours Questionnaire [19], which help elaborate the specific thoughts and behaviours that the individual may be experiencing, and can support with formulation and treatment planning.

PTSD Treatment

One of the first theories explaining the presentation of PTSD, known as emotional processing theory, was devised by Edna Foa. She was already working with other anxiety-based presentations, and treating first phobias and later OCD using the process of graded exposure, allowing individuals to overcome their fear and learnt avoidance through habituation and emotional processing [20,21]. Foa proposed that in PTSD, as in other anxiety disorders, there are problematic fear constructs in the brain, containing representations of the feared thing (the phobic object in phobias, or things connected to the trauma in PTSD), along with fear responses, and unhelpful meanings about both [22,23]. As such, she proposed using the same treatment process with patients experiencing PTSD to dismantle these fear constructs, exposing them to both the benign triggers that elicit their fear, and to the memories of the trauma itself, so as to help them to overcome the fear and avoidance impacting their lives post-trauma, a treatment she has termed prolonged exposure therapy (PET) [24].

Resick's work initially followed similar lines, but she then began to explore the cognitive side of PTSD leading to the development of cognitive processing therapy (CPT). She noted during her work with rape victims in the 1980s that many of them did not seem to be experiencing fear as the primary emotion, so much as betrayal, shame and disgust [25]. As such, and in line with the work of Janoff-Bulman regarding the just world hypothesis and how trauma can shatter beliefs [26], and building on the ideas of Hollon and Garber regarding the ways beliefs can be impacted by events [27], she proposed a theory of PTSD in which the key symptoms are maintained through the trauma being either assimilated into prior beliefs or over-accommodated for [28,29]. What this means is that the events and meaning of the trauma is processed either by distorting the facts to make them fit pre-existing beliefs (assimilation), or by significantly changing beliefs to fit with the new information (over-accommodation). Over-accommodation results in both fear and other emotions depending on what new beliefs have been formed, and assimilation results in guilt and shame based on how the facts of the events have been distorted. This theory was supported by the previously mentioned research showing that different trauma types seem to have different rates of subsequent PTSD, as different types of trauma will be differently likely to violate an individual's core beliefs [7]. From this, Resick proposed and trialled therapy focussed primarily not on the trauma memory itself, but on the resulting meaning and sense-making of the trauma, and its impact on five main areas of broad cognition – safety, trust, power and control, esteem and intimacy [28,29]. Cognitive processing therapy was originally devised with rape victims in mind, but has since been broadened to other trauma types, where it also appears to have great validity [28,29,30]. While some written exposure was initially incorporated, further dismantling studies showed the validity of the therapy without this at all [31], and so in most recent treatment manuals this is optional.

Meanwhile, in the UK, the same research group who had been making sense of the anxiety in panic disorder and social anxiety through a cognitive behavioural lens, led by Anke Ehlers, attempted to make sense of PTSD – a disorder where anxiety is focussed on an event in the past. Building on both theoretical approaches from the USA [24,29], they proposed that PTSD is caused through the cognitive processing of events in a way that creates a sense of current threat, due to both what cognitions are formed and the nature of the memory itself [32]. PTSD is then maintained through the use of cognitive and behavioural strategies that the patient employs to attempt to reduce this sense of current threat, but which actually preserve and reinforce both their unhelpful appraisals and the problematic nature of the memory. In this model, the key cognitive focusses are on the trauma not feeling time limited, and on its future implications. The model encourages therapists to look for cognitions regarding the trauma itself, the resultant PTSD symptoms, the reactions of others since the trauma occurred and any external consequences of the trauma. The model also explores these in terms of five key emotional themes – anger, guilt, fear, shame and sadness – though there is no expectation that these will all relate to all patients. In the same initial paper, the proposed therapy is also laid out, trauma-focussed cognitive therapy (TF-CT), which includes both memory and in-vivo exposure with a belief disconfirmation focus, and various other cognitive and behavioural strategies to help the patient modify their maintaining strategies, elaborate and contextualise the memory, and modify unhelpful cognitions [32].

Thus, the consensus is that treating PTSD will focus on modifying the nature of the trauma memory, the individual's cognitive appraisals from the trauma and their associated changes in behaviour (predominantly avoidance), using tools such as exposure and/or behavioural experiments, direct memory work and cognitive restructuring. Due to the interconnected nature of these process and symptoms, the various models differ on whether they focus on cognitive, behavioural or a mixed approach, but all aim to result in an individual being able to have processed the memory and think about the event in a way that is more helpful, feeling less at current threat and more being able to live their life without avoidance of benign but associated stimuli.

Efficacy Data for CBT for PTSD

Despite the comparatively late recognition of PTSD as a disorder, there is a wealth of research into the efficacy of treating it, with more than 27 RCTs exploring the efficacy of CBT for in adults alone, as well as at least 33 studies reviewing its effectiveness in routine care settings [33]. In a recent meta-analysis of all psychological treatments for PTSD [34] it was found that CBT was a valid treatment for PTSD, with large effect sizes for PTSD symptom reduction. This was found to be true for exposure-based approaches (including PET), and for cognitive approaches (which in this analysis included both CPT and TF-CT), between which there appeared to be no significant difference in efficacy in terms of loss of PTSD diagnosis. In line with this, trauma-focussed CBT (including any of the three approaches above) is the first line treatment recommended for PTSD in recent NICE guidelines [35].

An interesting finding in the various trials on CBT for PTSD is what happens when treatment approaches are mixed. Both Resick's cognitive approach and Foa's behavioural approach have been trialled with and without the core component of the other – that is, trialling CPT with added exposure, and trialling PET with added cognitive techniques. In both cases, there was no benefit in adding the opposing techniques, and indeed the therapy was found to either have lower efficacy or higher drop-out rates as a result [31,36]. This in turn makes it somewhat surprising that TF-CBT appears to have such high efficacy. It warns against a mix-and-match approach to therapy as it would appear that following any single approach is likely to be more effective than switching or attempting to augment the process.

Picking a Protocol

As described above, there are a range of ways of conceptualising PTSD, and so a range of possible ways to structure therapy. Currently, the most commonly used manualised approaches for treatment of PTSD in the UK and USA are:

- Foa, Hembree and Rothbaum's guide *Prolonged Exposure Therapy for PTSD* [37]
- Resick, Monson and Chard's guide *Cognitive Processing Therapy for PTSD: A Comprehensive Manual* [30]

And

- Ehlers and Clark's paper 'A cognitive model of posttraumatic stress disorder' [32] (further illustrated at OxCADATResources.com)

Each of these specific protocols has its strengths, and all three have a good evidence base for their efficacy, as shown in Table 19.1.

Table 19.1 A summary of the protocols for the treatment of PTSD (Foa, Hembree and Rothbaum, Resick, Monson and Chard and Ehlers and Clark)

Protocol	Foa, Hembree and Rothbaum – PET [37]	Resick, Monson and Chard – CPT [30]	Ehlers and Clark – TF-CBT [32]
Theory of PTSD	PTSD is caused by a fear structure connecting a large number of stimulus elements to a meaning of danger, resulting in seeing the world as dangerous and themselves as unable to cope, followed by a failure to process the trauma memory due to avoidance.	PTSD is caused by patients experiencing events which violate their prior beliefs, including the Just World Hypothesis, resulting in assimilation and over-accommodation.	PTSD caused by nature of trauma memory and negative appraisals of the trauma and its sequelae resulting in sense of present threat, which is then maintained by behavioural and cognitive strategies aimed to reduce the threat in the short term.
Aim of treatment	Emotionally process the traumatic memory and	Cognitively reappraise the trauma 'stuck points'	Modify the negative appraisals, elaborate the trauma memory and

Table 19.1 (cont.)

Protocol	Foa, Hembree and Rothbaum – PET [37]	Resick, Monson and Chard – CPT [30]	Ehlers and Clark – TF-CBT [32]
	remove other avoidance behaviours.	across the themes of safety, trust, power/ control, esteem and intimacy.	improve stimulus discrimination, and modify the cognitive and behavioural maintenance strategies.
Recommended structure of therapy	10–15 sessions, each 90 minutes duration, over up to 15 weeks.	12+ sessions, each 50–60 duration, over 12+ weeks.	Up to 12 sessions, each 90 minutes for initial sessions, then 60 minutes for later sessions, over up to 13 weeks.
Interventions used	• Psychoeducation regarding common trauma reactions • Breathing retraining • Repeated, prolonged imaginal reliving of the trauma memory • In-vivo exposure to avoided situations and objects connected to the trauma via hierarchy	• Exploring the index trauma for stuck points • Cognitive Restructuring of stuck points using ABC, challenging questions and challenging beliefs worksheets • Psycho-education and restructuring based on themes of safety, trust, power/control, esteem and intimacy, followed by connected behavioural assignments	• Reclaiming life • Imaginal reliving, narrative writing, and or site visits for identifying hotspots and elaborating and contextualising memory • Cognitive restructuring of appraisals from the trauma, and updating the trauma memory • Cognitive restructuring and behavioural experiments to disconfirm other appraisals. • Stimulus discrimination • Imagery transformation techniques • Exploration of strategies and then dropping as a behavioural experiment.
Helpful when	Patient has difficulties accessing cognitions, and is highly avoidant of both the memory and situations due to fear.	Patient is unable or unwilling to engage in reliving, especially when this is due to high levels of guilt and shame.	Patients have clear appraisals of the trauma or its sequelae, as well as maladaptive behaviours associated with their PTSD. As this model covers both the behavioural and cognitive aspects, it is of use in most cases.

While these approaches run the spectrum from mostly behavioural to mostly cognitive, they do have many similarities, and will impact much of the same symptoms, and so picking exactly how to work with your client is mostly about considering which is the best fit for them. In particular, it can be useful to consider the patient's comparative focus on fear and memory avoidance, versus cognitive misappraisal and shame. It is also useful to consider if the patient has at least some access to the memory of the trauma (which can be limited or absence if there was significant drug or alcohol involvement or head injury) and how able they are to access and verbalise their cognitions.

Foa and Rothbaum

As briefly mentioned above, this model is based on the underlying concept of emotional processing theory, where anxiety disorders are caused by pathological fear constructs, which include problematic connections between concepts which don't match how the world works, benign stimuli triggering avoidance and fear, benign stimuli being connected to meanings of threat, and as such excessively triggered threat responses occurring in ways that reduce functioning [22]. In PTSD, this presents as a large fear construct made up of representations of many benign stimuli from the trauma all now connected inaccurately to danger and threat, as well as concepts of the various emotional and physiological symptoms of PTSD. The construct also includes inaccurate meanings about being incompetent due to their behaviour when the trauma occurred and their symptoms since. Treatment thus involves dismantling this fear construct through exposure and reprocessing, to reduce the overgeneralised sense of the world being dangerous and the patient being incompetent. Due to the nature of the therapy, there is no commonly used formulation diagram attached.

The treatment has a set course for the first three sessions. Session one focusses on psychoeducation regarding the rationale for treatment, gathering information about the trauma, the reactions of the patient to the trauma, and any prior relevant experiences before the trauma, and teaching the patient breathing retraining. This last aspect is then set as homework, so the patient can learn to breathe in a way that helps to control and reduce anxiety in their everyday life.

Session two helps the patient to make sense of common trauma symptoms via further psychoeducation so as to normalise their responses. It then goes on to cover the concept of in-vivo exposure to benign but feared real-world stimuli, with the therapist and patient creating a hierarchy of such stimuli, rating each against a SUDS scale (created as in Foa's treatment of OCD – see Chapter 16 for more detail). Exposure starts from this point, with an initial exercise set as homework along with further breathing retraining and reading more about common reactions to trauma.

Session three then focusses for the first time on the process of imaginal exposure, which will be a key feature in most subsequent sessions. In this, the patient is directed to imagine and describe the traumatic event as if it is occurring in the present moment, attempting to expose themselves to the trauma memory, ideally over the course of 45–60 minutes. Following this, the therapist and patient discuss the patient's associated thoughts and feelings, to support any changes in meaning. The description of the memory is recorded as the patient narrates it, so that they can re-expose themselves to it repeatedly over the week. Further homework from this session involves trying another in-vivo exposure to an item on their hierarchy.

Following these three sessions, therapy repeats the process of imaginal exposure to the trauma memory, focussing on making the reliving experience more vivid and detailed, and narrowing in on the hot spots – that is, the part of the memory most associated with fear and distress. Therapy homework continues to involve re-exposure to the recordings, and in-vivo exposure to higher items of the hierarchy (with some such exposure occurring in session if required). Therapy then ends with a final review of the trauma memory, exploring how the memory has changed, as well as how the process of reliving it feels different, along with a review of overall progress and a plan for relapse prevention.

An example of this work would be the case of Fred, a 45-year-old widower with two daughters, age 7 and 9. While being driven by a colleague to a work event, he was involved in a traumatic car accident, which caused his side of the car to become trapped under a lorry. The driver was knocked out, but then fairly quickly was removed from the car by emergency personnel. Fred stayed trapped for over an hour while they cut him out. He experienced loss of feeling in his legs, and thought he was paralysed. Actually, while there was some nerve damage, he eventually regained full functioning. Since the trauma, Fred has been highly avoidant of being in cars, the smell of petrol and sound of motorways and any tension or pain in his legs. He has regular nightmares and flashbacks, and feels embarrassed about how he is reacting.

Treatment started as described above, and Fred focussed on using his breathing retraining to manage the general stress he felt day to day, as well the heightened anxiety that came whenever he felt pain in his legs and when trying to fall asleep. In the second session his SUDS anchors were first determined, with 0 being watching his favourite movie in bed, 25 being a work meeting with a difficult customer, 50 realising a trade he's made has lost capital, 75 being the memory of his daughter falling off a swing and 100 being how he felt at the moment of going under the lorry. With these in place, Frederick and the therapist then created his in-vivo hierarchy, focussed on roads and exercise, which started with walking alone down a road with cars on, and built up to being a passenger in a car again, on a motorway like where the accident occurred (see Table 19.2). Homework started on this hierarchy immediately, with him trying out both the first and the second items, by walking his children to school each day rather than letting a friend take them as he had been.

Table 19.2 Fred's in-vivo exposure hierarchy

Item	SUDS
Walking down the road with cars going past alone	25
Walking down the road with cars going past with my daughters	35
Going for a gentle jog	40
Doing leg exercises at the gym	50
Going to the petrol station	50
Driving a car on a quiet street	60
Driving on a busy road	70
Driving on a motorway	80
Being a passenger on a motorway	95

Prolonged imaginal exposure started with going through the entire trauma in moderate detail, though the therapist noted that the level of details became slightly more limited when describing going under the lorry, became more detailed when describing the process of the friend being cut out of the car and the emergency personnel saying they'll both be okay and then became less detailed again from when he's told they can't cut him out as easily until they arrive at the hospital. Following the first exposure, the reprocessing discussion revolved around the difference in how much support the emergency personnel had given, compared to his previous feelings of being alone and abandoned. While the reliving had been distressing, noticing this difference helped Fred to value the process, and he was pleased that he had coped with thinking about it.

From this point, further reliving sessions focussed on each of the hotspots the therapist and patient had noted: of hitting the lorry, of being told they can't get him out, of the fireman's face looking worried, of the moment of being cut out and fearing what his legs would look like and of the journey to hospital where the paramedic didn't say anything when he asked if he was going to lose his legs. Each time, the process was initially distressing, but resulted in a reduction in fear of the memory, and new meanings of what was happening and how he'd responded, until by the final exposure in the twelfth session, he could remember and describe all parts with some sadness, but little fear. Having already reached the top of his in-vivo hierarchy as well, he focussed relapse planning on maintaining his gains, driving and being driven regularly, and joining an over-40s football team.

Resick, Monson and Chard

This model focusses on the cognitive dilemma that occurs during a trauma, when the individual is exposed to experiences that cannot be made sense of in terms of their prior beliefs. In everyday life, this results in accommodation, where our beliefs are helpfully modified to more accurately make sense of the world, helping us to learn and grow. When this occurs during trauma, two alternative shifts can also occur; either the information from the real world is distorted or changed to fit with the prior beliefs (assimilation) or the prior beliefs are excessively modified to fit with the new information (over-accommodation). Such assimilation and over-accommodation can result in difficult and unhelpful emotions, as well as behavioural changes in line with the new world- and self-views. Treatment thus focusses on talking, not about the trauma itself, but about each of these 'stuck points' – that is the beliefs caused by the assimilation and over-accommodation – to help the client to explore these in light of everything they know and come to more helpful accommodated options.

Treatment begins with psychoeducation regarding the nature of PTSD and the concept of stuck points, and then by briefly exploring what the key trauma was and formulating the problem. This formulation is not diagrammatic, but via a written impact statement created as the first session's homework – a description of why the patient believes the trauma happened, the causes and their resultant beliefs about safety, trust, power and control, esteem and intimacy.

Once the impact statement has been created, the therapist and patient will work together to determine a list of stuck points, and then will explore each of these one by one using cognitive restructuring, with specific additional questions used to target key issues in PTSD cognitions, such as whether the thought is focussed on unrelated parts of the story, or if the concepts are coming from an unreliable source. Stuck points are generally worked on in a set order, starting with the specific trauma cognitions involving assimilation, and then moving through the over-accommodated beliefs about each of the five areas in turn. When working on the main themes, there are various useful tools to complement general restructuring, such as behavioural experiments, the trust star and a complements exercise, all of which help bring flexibility and change into the rigid negative thinking that trauma can cause. Final sessions focus as ever on relapse prevention, and on reformulating the experience with a new impact statement, which helps to summarise the new accommodated beliefs.

An example of a suitable client for this work is Rachel, a third-year student who was raped while she was drunk at a house party in her first year. The memory is quite blurred, but she does remember that after it happened, she eventually left the bedroom it occurred in, and heard the rapist telling his friends that he'd 'hit that' and them seemingly congratulating him (he had lied about the event, and told them she'd begged him for it – being drunk themselves they had not realised it was rape). Since the event, she has experienced significant guilt, shame and rumination, especially in this year, as she heard that another student is claiming he raped her. Ever since the trauma, she has avoided relationships and any situations where she feels vulnerable, such as drinking or being alone with a man.

Rachel's initial impact statement was as follows:

> For a long time, I questioned if this was rape at all; I guess I still do. I feel to blame for it all – if I hadn't been drinking it wouldn't have happened. I keep thinking back over how I was acting that night; I was too flirty, too slutty. It was my fault. I feel even worse since hearing about the other girl – if I'd done more, maybe she wouldn't have gone through this. I told my parents, and now they seem so upset; I've hurt them, I shouldn't have made this into such a big deal. I feel dirty, and then I feel stupid for feeling that way.
>
> At the same time, I'm so angry at him, at them, at all men. Men seem all powerful, and I can't trust them. They just want to hurt us. No one cares – the people in charge won't believe me, they always blame the victim. The only solution is to keep myself safe – I can't risk being close to any man again, I have to ensure no one ever has the chance to hurt me.

From this, the following stuck point list was devised:

- It wasn't really rape (assimilated)
- It was all my fault that this happened (assimilated)
- I'm slutty and dirty (assimilated)
- I'm selfish and I have hurt others (assimilated)
- I'm weak and stupid for being so upset (over-accommodated)
- Men are more powerful than me (over-accommodated)
- Men all want to hurt me (over-accommodated)
- Others will blame me, not help me (over-accommodated)
- I have to constantly protect myself (over-accommodated)
- If I get close to others, they will hurt me (over-accommodated)

The therapist and Rachel started by looking at the process of thought challenging, then worked through her assimilated beliefs, helping her to come to new conclusions about why the trauma happened and its meaning about her by going through each of the recommended challenging questions for each of the beliefs. They then worked through each of the five themes in turn, both using cognitive discussion techniques to restructure as before, and adding in additional techniques as needed. For example, in response to the belief 'if I trust a man, they will hurt me' they used trust stars to draw out the variable meanings of trust along different dimensions for a given man (her friend's boyfriend). In doing this, they helped to break away from the concept of trust as a binary issue, and the concept that any lack of trustworthiness (such as being late occasionally) means that the person will hurt them in a damaging way. Meanwhile for the beliefs around herself and others being of low esteem, she was encouraged to actively look to give others compliments, and to note if others complimented her. In doing so, she noticed how much more caring and supportive those around her were, compared to what she had been believing previously.

Having worked through each theme, Rachel was encouraged to summarise her learning by re-writing her impact statement, with what she now believed about the causes of the trauma and each of the key areas. Her new statement read:

> I was raped at a party with my friends; I'd been having fun in what I'd thought was a safe environment. The guy took advantage of me and lied about what happened – it was his fault this occurred, and no one else's. I wish I'd spoken out about it sooner, but I can see why I didn't; I can see why I'd have thought it was my fault, even though this wasn't true. It's not my responsibility to keep everyone else safe, and it's not my fault if knowing what happened makes others sad – that's just because they love me.
>
> I'm still angry at him, but it doesn't help me to focus on this. I'll never know why he did this, but he's clearly broken in some major way. However, he is not all men – most men can be trusted in most ways, and some truly love me and want what's best for me. I should take reasonable steps to keeping myself safe, but it's okay to take some risks, and be intimate with those who've shown they can generally be trusted. I don't have to be in control all the time.

This new statement was one she could truly believe, and she felt that it was reasonable rather than overly positive, which is important in all restructuring. Importantly, it fitted with living her life in a way that brought her happiness and opportunities, rather than avoidance, guilt and shame.

Ehlers and Clark

As mentioned above, this model of PTSD (Figure 19.1) proposes that how a traumatic event is processed (or perhaps more accurately incompletely processed) and excessively negative appraisals of the event and its consequences create a sense of current threat for the individual despite the fact that the trauma is over. At the time of trauma, a variety of factors – including the often emotionally heightened state of the individual in combination with learned and automatic reactions, prior beliefs and actions taken or not taken – can lead to partial and distorted processing of the events, resulting in a fragmented memory without sufficient time-coding or meaning making for it to be 'stored' like other non-traumatic memories. The memory can be easily triggered by stimuli that are a close match for sensory elements present at the time of the trauma and so intrusive distressing memories are frequently experienced in the presence of such triggers and when they are it feels like the events are happening again. Whilst trauma is, by definition, always negative, the individual has excessively negative appraisals at the time of the trauma (for example, that they are going to die) or since the trauma (for example, that they are responsible for the trauma or other negative consequences of the trauma). These negative appraisals heighten the sense of current threat and underpin further negative emotional reactions. Furthermore, the model proposes that the strategies adopted to reduce this sense of threat, much like 'safety-seeking behaviours' in models of many other anxiety disorders, paradoxically keep this sense of

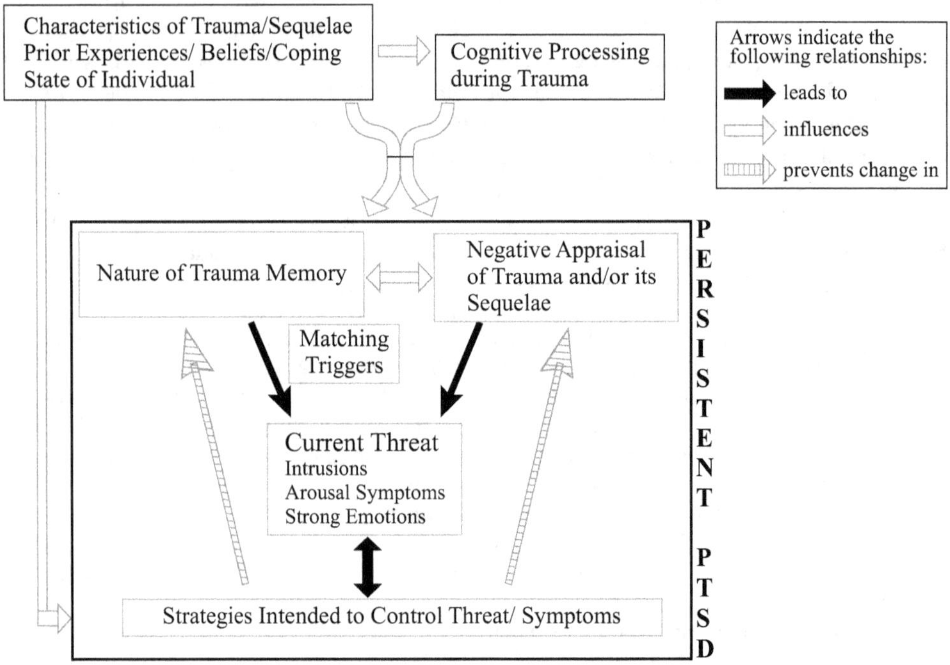

Figure 19.1 Cognitive model of PTSD.

threat alive. Typically, the individual with PTSD who experiences this sense of current threat will avoid thinking about the trauma and reminders of the trauma and in doing so eliminate opportunities to fully process the traumatic events and correct their excessively negative appraisals, further maintaining their strong sense of threat.

The treatment based on this model therefore targets these key maintaining factors; processing the trauma memory, discriminating trauma triggers, reappraising excessively negative cognitions and reversing the unhelpful strategies adopted to try and make the individual feel safer. Treatment often follows a typical sequencing of interventions or 'protocol', but importantly is underpinned by the individual presentation and formulation so that the therapist may adopt interventions flexibly in line with this.

Typically the treatment starts with a 'reclaiming your life' intervention in which the individual is encouraged to return to valued activities that have ceased since the trauma. The intervention serves a number of functions, including contextualising the trauma in the broader context of their life, exposing them to avoided stimuli and trauma reminders and testing out excessively negative appraisals, for example, about how the trauma has necessarily had a lasting negative impact on previously enjoyed relationships or activities. Reclaiming activities continue to be developed throughout the course of therapy.

Treatment then targets the processing of the trauma memory through a process known as 'reliving'. During reliving, the individual is encouraged to recall and recount the trauma, usually with their eyes closed and in the present tense to aid recall and facilitate emotional exposure, focussing on the events in order, sensory details and the thoughts and emotions experienced at that time. In doing so, the individual not only elaborates and contextualises the details of the memory but also identifies excessively negative cognitions experienced at the time of the trauma. The worst moments or 'hot spots' associated with these negative cognitions are then explored further and, through Socratic dialogue, data gathering and experimentation, they are updated to reflect more accurately the less threatening information that the individual has now. This information is usually then inserted back into the memory through further reliving to enhance the memory processing and meaning change.

Alongside these interventions, individuals are encouraged to reverse avoidance behaviours including avoidance of trauma memories, trauma triggers and activities and places related to the trauma. In the latter stages of therapy this may become a more significant focus of the treatment alongside reversing behaviours intended to control threat. For example, the individual may return with the therapist to the site of the trauma, discriminate triggers of the trauma memories from stimuli actually present at the time of the trauma and drop safety behaviours such as constantly checking for threat or danger and carrying out behavioural experiments to help them reassess the level of threat in the environment.

If not already completed the final stages of therapy often include a visit to the site of the trauma (where possible) and, as with all good CBT interventions, a review of learning and relapse prevention with a particular focus on triggers that may not yet have been encountered or typically challenging scenarios such as anniversaries of the traumatic event.

An example of an individual for whom this approach was successful is Clem. Clem presented for treatment about a year after he experienced a racially motivated assault when he, a black man, was out for an evening with his girlfriend, a white woman. Clem was terrified for his life during the attack when he was held down, kicked and punched. He felt breathless and thought that he would be killed by the blows. He was also fearful about what was happening to his girlfriend whilst he was being restrained and feared that she might also have been beaten up or sexually assaulted. He felt guilty that he was unable to protect her. Following the attack he was haunted by the fears and guilt he had during the event and felt guilty that they had been in that situation in the first place as he had suggested that they had walked that particular route home together, blaming himself for putting them in harm's way. He had frequent intrusive images of the attack and nightmares of being overpowered and killed. Since the event he avoided going out at all at night, rarely went out with his girlfriend, scanned his environment constantly for danger, in particular groups of white men, and withdrew from physical activities that he enjoyed prior to the trauma such as playing football and physical intimacy with his girlfriend. He no longer felt like the man he used to be.

Clem's initial reclaiming activities focussed on returning to physical exercise and team sport. Initially he was concerned about being around other people in the gym and at football so he took smaller steps towards these goals, exercising at home and attending the gym when it was quiet at first and gradually experimenting with busier sessions and training with one or two friends from his football team. Feeling breathless during exercise reminded him of some panicky feeling he had had during the trauma, so some psychoeducation about panic attacks was completed to help him understand that the physiological arousal he was experiencing was not dangerous. He also began to go out for short trips with his girlfriend to areas he considered safe during the day.

Early in the sessions Clem's therapist introduced the concept of reliving the trauma and although Clem was anxious about recalling the events he talked through the assault in great detail. Through completing the reliving Clem was able to bring to mind some information that he had previously not recalled, that his girlfriend had managed to run away almost as soon as the men had attacked him to try and raise the alarm and find help. In fact, he had told her to go. He remembered that when she returned she was unharmed but upset to see him so badly hurt. He was able to explore these memories and his guilt with her between sessions and she was shocked to hear that he had been feeling this way, reassuring him that he had done everything he could to ensure her safety and that in fact she had felt guilty for leaving him alone during the attack.

Clem was able to identify a number of hotspots during the assault, first when he was first being attacked and knocked down, he thought he needed to protect his girlfriend and that she must be being assaulted or raped and he felt weak, guilty and fearful. Second, being held down, he thought he was going to either die from suffocation or from the blows he was receiving to his body. He thought he would never see his girlfriend and his family again and felt terror and sadness. Third, as he lay on the ground alone afterwards he felt debased and ashamed, and had the thought 'I'm no longer a human being' due to the treatment he had received and the comments made by the attackers.

The first hotspot was readily updated with the information that he had recalled that his girlfriend had run away, and that she had done so because he had told her to, to protect her. In fact, he remembered putting his body in between the assailants and his girlfriend to shield her from them as they approached. It also became clear from the narrative and from the comments made by the assailants that he, not his girlfriend, was their target.

The second hotspot was updated with the information that he did not die during the attack and the fact that although severe, his injuries had not been life-threatening. Careful exploration of the attack and the behaviour of the assailants suggested additionally that there had been some attempts to limit the risk to life, despite the apparent frenzy of their behaviour. The fact that the assailants had left despite the fact he was still clearly alive and comments they made when they left also suggested that it had not been their intention to kill him. He was able to update the memory further with the information that he still saw his girlfriend on a daily basis and that he had seen his family many times since and they had supported him through his recovery.

The third hotspot was updated through exploring what it meant to him to be human and whether the behaviour and the comments of his assailants said more about his humanity or their inhumanity. This hotspot also linked to earlier experiences of racial abuse and microaggressions and Clem spent time exploring the meaning and impact of these events with his therapist and other individuals he respected from the racial background with which he identified.

All three hotspots were revisited in reliving and the new information was brought to mind. Clem's fear and guilt reduced in line with his new beliefs that he had not been weak and in fact had been brave and remarkably composed in the face of the attack and had done everything he could to protect his girlfriend and that he had not died but in fact survived and recovered well physically from the attack. Clem no-longer felt ashamed or debased by the attack in line with his new belief that the attack reflected badly only on the assailants, not on him, however, his shame was very naturally replaced with strong feelings of anger. Clem was encouraged to express his angry thoughts, which he did both verbally and in an unsent letter to his assailants, and his anger was validated by the therapist as an appropriate response to what was an abhorrent racist attack. As he now wished to, Clem was supported to report the attack, which he had not done at the time due to his feelings of shame and guilt.

Following this memory work, Clem and his therapist revisited the site of the trauma, re-tracing the route that he and his girlfriend had taken that night. At the site visit it became apparent that the route Clem had chosen was well lit and open, in contrast to the alternative route they could have taken, and he recalled that he had made that decision in order to keep them safe, even though he had not anticipated any significant risk that night. Clem undertook some research about crime statistics in the area and discovered that this was in fact a relatively safe area. This new information modified Clem's appraisal that it was his fault that they were subject to the attack in the first place along with reattribution of the responsibility of the attack to the assailants who were also not local to the area.

Clem continued to expand his 'reclaiming life' activities and experimented with going out more frequently and at night with his friends and his girlfriend. Whilst doing this he deliberately dropped his hypervigilance to threat, no longer scanning the environment for would-be assailants, sitting with his back to the wall in restaurants or looking for the nearest exits in enclosed spaces. Clem discovered that he did not need to be constantly on alert for danger and that this, in fact, was keeping his fear alive. He had understandably become more aware of racially motivated crime and found it helpful to modify his extreme appraisals of danger through talking to others amongst his family and friends whom he respected about their appraisal of and approach to such risks.

At the end of therapy, Clem was no longer experiencing intrusive memories of the attack or related nightmares, he had re-engaged in his previously enjoyed activities and was enjoying a more intimate relationship with his girlfriend. Whilst he still felt understandably angry about the attack this did not consume him or interfere with his life. The therapy blueprint included consideration of what he might do should future reports of racial violence or aggression remind him of the attack and the degree to which he personally wished to become involved in campaigning for racial equality and educating others about the impact of such events.

Concluding Remarks

PTSD is a difficulty centred on misprocessed memories which are connected with over-accommodating or assimilated beliefs, leading in turn to mood changes and being maintained by avoidance and unnecessary safety behaviours. Treatment focusses on changing these symptoms via emotional processing of the memory, cognitive restructuring techniques, and exposure to avoided stimuli. Specific protocols focus respectively on habituation to the memory and triggers, cognitive reappraisal across a number of important themes, or a combination of the two. In all cases, successful treatment does not mean forgetting that the trauma occurred, but means experiencing the memory as if it happened in the past, and with new accommodated beliefs.

Further Reading

Ehlers A, Clark DM. A cognitive model of posttraumatic stress disorder. *Behav Res Ther.* 2000;**38** (4):319–345.

Foa E, Hembree E, Rothbaum BO. *Prolonged Exposure Therapy for PTSD: Emotional Processing of Traumatic Experiences Therapist Guide.* Oxford: Oxford University Press; 2007.

Resick PA, Monson CM, Chard KM. *Cognitive Processing Therapy for PTSD: A Comprehensive Manual.* New York: Guilford Publications; 2017.

References

1. Rado S. Pathodynamics and treatment of traumatic war neurosis (traumatophobia). Psychosom Med. 1942;**4**(4):362–368.
2. Page HW. *Injuries of the Spine and Spinal Cord without Apparent Mechanical Lesion, and Nervous Shock*. London: J. & A. Churchill; 1883.
3. American Psychiatric Association Staff. *Diagnostic and Statistical Manual of Mental Disorders* (DSM-III). Washington, DC: American Psychiatric Publishing; 1980.
4. American Psychiatric Association. *Diagnostic and Statistical Manual of Mental Disorders* (DSM-5). Washington, DC: American Psychiatric Association; 2013.
5. World Health Organization. *International Classification of Diseases*, Eleventh Revision (ICD-11). World Health Organization; 2019.
6. Brady KT, Killeen TK, Brewerton T, Lucerini S. Comorbidity of psychiatric disorders and posttraumatic stress disorder. J Clin Psychiatry. 2000;**61**:22–32.
7. Kessler RC, Sonnega A, Bromet E, Hughes M, Nelson CB. Posttraumatic stress disorder in the national comorbidity survey. Arch Gen Psychiatry. 1995;**52**(12):1048–1060.
8. Breslau N. Epidemiology of trauma and posttraumatic stress disorder. In: R Yehuda (Ed.), *Psychological Trauma* (pp. 1–29). Washington, DC: American Psychiatric Press; 1998.
9. Breslau N, Davis GC, Andreski P, Peterson E. Traumatic events and posttraumatic stress disorder in an urban population of young adults. Arch Gen Psychiatry. 1991;**48**(3):216–222.
10. Goldstein RB, Smith SM, Chou SP, Saha TD, Jung J, Zhang H, et al. The epidemiology of DSM-5 posttraumatic stress disorder in the United States: Results from the National Epidemiologic Survey on Alcohol and Related Conditions-III. Soc Psychiatry Psychiatr Epidemiol. 2016;**51**:1137–1148.
11. McManus S, Bebbington PE, Jenkins R, Brugha T. Mental health and wellbeing in England: the adult psychiatric morbidity survey 2014. NHS digital; 2016.
12. Brewin CR, Miller JK, Soffia M, Peart A, Burchell B. Posttraumatic stress disorder and complex posttraumatic stress disorder in UK police officers. Psychol Med. 2022;**52**(7):1287–1295.
13. Weathers FW, Litz BT, Keane TM, Palmieri PA, Marx BP, Schnurr PP. National Center for PTSD. The PTSD checklist for DSM-5 (PCL-5). 2013. Scale available from the National Center for PTSD at www.ptsd.va.gov.
14. Blevins CA, Weathers FW, Davis MT, Witte TK, Domino JL. The posttraumatic stress disorder checklist for DSM-5 (PCL-5): Development and initial psychometric evaluation. J Trauma Stress. 2015;**28**(6):489–498.
15. Marx BP, Lee DJ, Norman SB, Bovin MJ, Sloan DM, Weathers FW, et al. Reliable and clinically significant change in the clinician-administered PTSD Scale for DSM-5 and PTSD Checklist for DSM-5 among male veterans. Psychol Assess. 2022;**34**(2):197–203.
16. The National Collaborating Centre for Mental Health. The Improving Access to Psychological Therapies Manual. Mental Health Policy Team, Operations and Information Directorate; 2018.
17. Cloitre M, Shevlin M, Brewin CR, Bisson JI, Roberts NP, Maercker A, et al. The International Trauma Questionnaire: Development of a self-report measure of ICD-11 PTSD and complex PTSD. Acta Psychiatr Scand. 2018;**138**(6):536–546.
18. Foa EB, Ehlers A, Clark DM, Tolin DF, Orsillo SM. The Posttraumatic Cognitions Inventory (PTCI): Development and validation. Psychol Assess. 1999;**11**(3):303–314.
19. OxCADAT Resources [Internet]. 2024 [accessed 11 January 2025]. OxCADAT Resources for cognitive therapy for PTSD, social anxiety disorder and panic disorder. Therapy Process Measures.

https://oxcadatresources.com/therapy-process-measures/.

20. Foa EB, Jameson JS, Turner RM, Payne LL. Massed vs. spaced exposure sessions in the treatment of agoraphobia. Behav Res Ther. 1980;**18**(4):333–338.

21. Foa, EB, Kozak MJ. Treatment of anxiety disorders: Implications for psychopathology. In: A Hussain Turna and Jack D Maser (eds), *Anxiety and the Anxiety Disorders* (pp. 421–452). New York: Routledge; 1985.

22. Foa EB, Kozak MJ. Emotional processing of fear: Exposure to corrective information. Psychol Bull. 1986;**99**(1):20–35.

23. Foa EB, Steketee G, Rothbaum BO. Behavioral/cognitive conceptualizations of post-traumatic stress disorder. Behav Ther. 1989;**20**(2):155–176.

24. Foa EB, Rothbaum BO. *Treating the Trauma of Rape: Cognitive-Behavioral Therapy for PTSD*. New York: Guilford Publications; 1998.

25. Resick PA, Schnicke MK. Treating symptoms in adult victims of sexual assault. J Interpers Violence. 1990;**5**(4):488–506.

26. Janoff-Bulman R. *Shattered Assumptions: Towards a New Psychology of Trauma*. New York: Free Press; 1992.

27. Hollon SD, Garber J. Cognitive therapy. In: Lyn Y Abramson (ed.), *Social Cognition and Clinical Psychology: A Synthesis* (pp. 204–253). New York: Guilford Press; 1988.

28. Resick PA, Schnicke MK. Cognitive processing therapy for sexual assault victims. J Consult Clin Psychol. 1992;**60**(5):748–756.

29. Resick PA, Schnicke M. *Cognitive Processing Therapy for Rape Victims: A Treatment Manual*. London: SAGE Publications; 1993.

30. Resick PA, Monson CM, Chard KM. *Cognitive Processing Therapy for PTSD: A Comprehensive Manual*. New York: Guilford Publications; 2017.

31. Resick PA, Galovski TE, Uhlmansiek MO, Scher CD, Clum GA, Young-Xu Y. A randomized clinical trial to dismantle components of cognitive processing therapy for posttraumatic stress disorder in female victims of interpersonal violence. J Consult Clin Psychol. 2008;**76**(2):243–258.

32. Ehlers A, Clark DM. A cognitive model of posttraumatic stress disorder. Behav Res Ther. 2000;**38**(4):319–345.

33. Öst LG, Enebrink P, Finnes A, Ghaderi A, Havnen A, Kvale G, et al. Cognitive behavior therapy for adult post-traumatic stress disorder in routine clinical care: A systematic review and meta-analysis. Behav Res Ther. 2023;**166**:104323.

34. Cusack K, Jonas DE, Forneris CA, Wines C, Sonis J, Middleton JC, et al. Psychological treatments for adults with posttraumatic stress disorder: A systematic review and meta-analysis. Clin Psychol Rev. 2016;**43**:128–141.

35. National Institute for Health and Care Excellence. Post-traumatic stress disorder [Internet]. 2018, p. 54. Report No.: NG116. www.nice.org.uk/guidance/ng116/resources/posttraumatic-stress-disorder-pdf-66141601777861.

36. Foa EB, Rothbaum BO, Furr JM. Augmenting exposure therapy with other CBT procedures. Psychiatr Ann. 2003;**33**(1):47–53.

37. Foa E, Hembree E, Rothbaum BO. *Prolonged Exposure Therapy for PTSD: Emotional Processing of Traumatic Experiences Therapist Guide*. New York: Oxford University Press; 2007.

Chapter 20

Depression

In this chapter we will help you to be able to:

- Explain what major depressive disorder is, and how it can present.
- Choose and use appropriate formulation models for CBT for depression.
- Describe the importance of monitoring and scheduling activities in any treatment plan.
- Develop a treatment plan for CBT for depression, using appropriate measures.

Introduction

Depression has been considered a pathological condition since ancient Greece, where it was described under the term melancholia [1]. Various aspects of how this is classified have changed over the subsequent two and a half millennia, in terms of required duration or exemptions from diagnosis [2]. However, in terms of presentation, much remains unchanged since Hippocrates, such as the primary symptom being 'depression that is prolonged' [3] and there being a link between 'aversion to food ... sleeplessness ... restlessness ...' and 'the mind being affected by melancholy' [4]. Treatment for depression likewise has a long history, and it was the first disorder conceptualised in what would now be considered CBT, with ongoing research into the disorder ever since. This chapter will explore this history and the developments made, before reviewing the key modern protocols of cognitive therapy for depression and behavioural activation, and how these can be applied with specific individuals.

What Is Depression?

As noted, above, depression has a long diagnostic history. In modern texts, the key criteria are for patients to have either a depressed mood most or all of the day, or significantly diminished interest or pleasure in most or all activities, nearly every day for at least two weeks [5]. Furthermore, they must have a total of at least five symptoms, including the mood and/or loss of interest, and:

- Tiredness or loss of energy
- Disturbed sleep
- Significant increase or decrease in appetite, or significant change in weight unaccounted for by dieting
- Feelings of excessive worthless or guilt

- Difficulty concentrating
- Psychomotor agitation or retardation
- Suicidal ideation

Global meta-analyses of depression put lifetime prevalence at approximately 11% [6], though it appears that this may be increasing over time [7]. Age of onset is typically between 19–44 years old, with a median of 32 [8], which is similar to generalised anxiety disorder, but later than all other anxiety disorders or substance misuse disorders. Earlier onset has been associated with greater lifelong impact of the disorder, including quality of life, marital and occupational impacts and comorbidity, both of other mental health difficulties and in terms of physical health [9], and so should not be trivialised by mental health professionals. Across the world, it is found to affect more women than men [10], though this appears to reverse after menopause [11]. Unlike many of the anxiety disorders described previously depression has a median duration of only three months, though around 20% of individuals will go on to remain depressed for over two years [12]. However, following recovery, the majority of those experiencing one episode of depression will go on to experience another [13], highlighting the importance of comprehensive relapse prevention work in this group.

Comorbidity is the rule, not the exception, in depression, with the most common comorbidities being generalised anxiety disorder, panic disorder and social anxiety disorder [14]. In these cases, consideration of which disorder is primary is useful, as well as considering whether any treatment approaches may help with shared underlying mechanisms – for example, treating rumination/worry as an unhelpful behaviour. While NICE guidelines recommend treating the depression first when there are simply comorbid symptoms, often it is recommended to treat the anxiety disorder first as this may improve the depressive symptoms [15].

There are many different measures used in research and clinical practice to assess for depression. One of the most user-friendly weekly measures is the Patient Health Questionnaire – 9 (PHQ-9), a 9-item measure that looks at the frequency of each of the key diagnostic symptoms over the past two weeks [16]. Alternatively, the Beck Depression Inventory II (BDI-II) is a significantly longer measure, but covers a wider range of common symptoms that may be therapeutically valuable to assess, such as feelings of being punished, crying and loss of sex-drive [17].

Treatment of Depression

Prior to the 1950s, psychological treatment for depression was commonly based on psychoanalysis. However, increasingly some clinicians became dissatisfied with this approach, both due to how long treatment took to be effective, and due to the difficulty in proving the underlying theories of how psychoanalysis explained depression [18,19]. In response to this, a range of behavioural approaches were developed, based on the concepts of classical and operant conditioning, resulting in learnt helplessness problems with self-control [20,21,22]. Contemporaneously, a range of cognitive approaches were trialled, based on the concepts of Beck and Ellis [23,24,25].

On the behavioural side, depression was conceptualised as maintained by a lack of positive reinforcement of rewarding activities, and an increase in negative reinforcement of withdrawal, resulting in a reduction of meaningful and rewarding behaviours and so a loss of opportunities for happiness, and an increase in practical problems. On the cognitive side, depression was conceptualised as maintained by depressogenic thinking, which is driven by negative core beliefs about the self, the world and the future, leading to a biased way of interpreting events on a day-to-day basis. These thoughts then result in lower mood, unhelpful behaviours and reduced motivation, which in turn reinforce the negative bias and core beliefs.

During the 1970s, a number of overall treatment packages were developed, which contained features of both cognitive and behavioural change (such as Control Your Depression [26]), including the seminal text *Cognitive Therapy of Depression* by Aaron T. Beck [27].

Cognitive therapy for depression was found to be highly effective and well proven, resulting in it becoming commonly used across North America and much of Europe [28,29]. While the approach contained both behavioural and cognitive tools, the assumption was that it was the cognitive approaches that were fundamental to its efficacy, as its central premise is that depression is caused by cognitive distortions and underlying schema, and that behavioural changes are important ultimately because they otherwise maintain the negative beliefs [27]. This assumption was then evaluated by the use of a component analysis, where patients were given treatment focussing either on just the behavioural tools, the tools for behavioural change and modifying automatic thoughts, or the full treatment including tools focussed on changing core beliefs [30]. Contrary to expectations, all treatments were found to be equally effective, and all caused changes to negative thinking and attributional style, regardless of whether cognitive work was actively used.

From this, the premise that treatment requires overt cognitive work was called into question, and new pure behavioural activation (BA) protocols were created, drawing from the full breadth of theories and treatment approaches from the 1970s and earlier [31]. When this was tested against Beckian cognitive therapy (CT), it resulted in higher recovery rates, due to increased efficacy with the more severely depressed patients [32]. While subsequent meta-analyses have failed to replicate this difference in efficacy [33], cost and outcome studies have shown that BA may be a more cost-effective approach, due to reductions in training requirements to effectively provide the therapy compared to CT [34]. As such, for fully trained cognitive behavioural therapists, there is an ongoing choice to make regarding treatment for depression – CT or BA – with both approaches commonly taught on many modern training programs.

Efficacy Data for CBT for Depression

As CBT first reported research into treatment outcome in 1977 [35] there have been a substantial number of RCTs, systematic reviews and meta-analysis published examining outcome (efficacy) for CBT for depression. As such it is beyond the scope of this book to exhaustively review that evidence here. A review published in 2023 [36] provides a comprehensive and contemporary account of the evidence of CBT for depression and as it reports on more than 400 individual studies, it is one of the largest reviews of its type. All studies entered into this review compared CBT with a control condition although how active these conditions were varied. The majority of participants in the studies entered into the review met diagnostic criteria for major depressive disorder, with a majority of participants female (69%). This review had the majority of studies included dated from 2011 onwards so the data is likely to meet more recent standards for RCTs. Most studies examined individual delivered CBT. The evidence base for CBT for depression is undoubtedly efficacious. When compared to other psychotherapies CBT reported a slight advantage in terms of treatment outcome. When comparing CBT with pharmacotherapy there was no difference in outcome at end of treatment but at 6–12 months follow-up there was again some evidence suggesting CBT was more efficacious. When combined CBT and pharmacotherapy was compared to CBT alone there was no difference in outcome. One needs to be very conservative when looking at these results as there is a lot of what is termed heterogeneity reported for the effect sizes which suggests there is a lot of variation of outcome.

Picking a Protocol

As described above, there are a range of ways of conceptualising depression, and so a range of possible ways to structure therapy. Currently, the most commonly used manualised approaches for treatment of depression in the UK are:

- Beck, Rush, Shaw and Emery's (1979) guide *Cognitive Therapy of Depression* [27]

And

- Martell, Addis and Jacobson's (2001) guide *Depression in Context; strategies for Guided Action* [31].

Each of these specific protocols has its strengths, and both have a good evidence base for their efficacy. As Beckian therapy has a much longer history, it likewise has a far broader evidence base, but as noted above, studies have shown variable results on which approach has greater efficacy. A summary of how these two approaches compare is given in Table 20.1.

As opposed to many of the protocols described in the previous three chapters, these two approaches are quite significantly different, with BA shifting away from the concept of evaluating the content of cognitions, and focussing instead on the function of behaviours, including mental behaviours such as ruminating. However, it is important to remember that both protocols do cause changes in thinking at all levels of cognitions; the key difference is where the overt focus best lies for the patient, not on whether they have dysfunctional beliefs at all.

Cognitive Therapy of Depression

As discussed above, this protocol focusses on the concept that depression is caused by negative core beliefs about the self, the world and the future, leading to dysfunctional assumptions and negative automatic thoughts, as well as unhelping coping strategies and depressogenic patterns of behaviour.

Treatment aims throughout to increase flexibility in thinking, and gently explore and modify core beliefs, so that the client is more able to view themselves, the world and the future in a balanced way. However, as core beliefs are generally difficult to work on directly, therapy usually follows the general therapy course as described in Chapter 7, from activities and negative automatic thoughts (NATs), through intermediate beliefs, and then core beliefs. Before all of this, the therapist will socialise the patient to the model, by exploring how thoughts drive our reactions – behavioural, emotional and physiological – so that they can see the value of the work. This can be done by going though simple explorations of everyday situations which have made the patient feel low, noting how the thoughts they had in this situation made them feel, and what they did as a result.

Within activity scheduling, there are several steps. Firstly, the patient will be asked to monitor their activity hourly, and rate for each hour their sense of pleasure and mastery/achievement. Following this, the therapist and patient will explore their completed diary,

Table 20.1 Comparison of main individual CBT approaches for depression. *Number of sessions taken from NICE guidelines for more severe depression [29]

Protocol	Beck: Cognitive Therapy of Depression [27]	Martell: Depression in Context [31]
Most Recent Therapist Guide	Cognitive Therapy: Basics and Beyond [37]	Behavioural Activation for Depression: A Clinician's Guide [38]
Theory of depression	Depression is maintained by negative beliefs about the self, the world and the future, resulting in changes to motivation, behaviour, physiology, cognitive processes and emotion.	Depression is maintained by changes in interactions with the world, resulting in loss of opportunities for positive outcomes, and so changes in mood, energy and thinking.
Aim of treatment	Increase flexibility in thinking, and explore and modify core beliefs, so that the client is more able to view themselves, the world and the future in a balanced way.	Determine what activities (in which specific circumstances) will be most rewarding for the patient, and how to schedule these to best promote them occurring. Break avoidance cycles, problem solve issues and manage rumination.
Recommended structure of therapy*	16 sessions, each 60-minute duration, starting weekly or twice weekly, tapering to monthly.	12–16 sessions, each 60-minute duration, starting weekly or twice weekly, tapering to monthly.
Interventions used	• Activity scheduling • Cognitive restructuring • Challenging Intermediate beliefs • Core belief work	• Functional analysis • TRAP/TRAC analysis • Problem solving • Managing rumination
Helpful when	The patient has overt, ego-dystonic cognitions at various levels, such as 'I am unlovable'.	The patient struggles with verbalising or endorsing negative ego-dystonic cognitions, and where behaviour is overtly limiting opportunities for positive outcomes.

exploring whether there is a good balance of pleasure and achievement, and noticing any specific behaviours which seem to bring neither pleasure nor mastery (often things such as lying in bed, watching TV or reviewing social media), as well as any missing behaviours which used to bring pleasure or achievement. The therapist will explore what thoughts are attached to doing these unhelpful behaviours, and withdrawing from the previously valued behaviours, to help make sense of the changes. From this, the therapist and patient can devise experiments to tests these thoughts and see what actually happens when alternative activities are tried out. The following week, the therapist and patient can review how these experiments went, gathering more information about what can improve the patient's mood, as well as beginning to modify the patient's view of themselves and world.

Cognitive restructuring of NATs follows the process described in Chapter 6. Initially, the process is usually focussed on thoughts connected to unhelpful or avoided activities, or on difficult situations that may have occurred in the week, and is led by the therapist. Over time, as the patient begins to see the value of challenging NATs, they can be asked to record thoughts outside of sessions, and eventually trained to be able to identify key cognitions, evaluate them and devise balanced thoughts independently of the therapist. Especially with more depressed clients, it can be helpful to take this process one step at a time, ensuring the patient is aware of which thoughts to work on before asking them to try and restructure thoughts on their own.

Working on intermediate beliefs generally starts by creating a fuller cognitive conceptualisation (Figure 20.1), which expands on the situational explorations from earlier in therapy, and finds the shared meaning of the NATs the patient commonly experiences – their core beliefs. Exploration then typically flows both upwards, to the likely early experiences that helped form these beliefs, and down to the associated conditional assumptions and rules that the patient has developed to manage their core beliefs, as well as their coping strategies use to help meet these assumptions. By doing this prior to working on intermediate beliefs, the therapist and patient can be confident that they are focussing their work on key assumptions central to the overall problem.

Modifying intermediate beliefs can involve all of the same tools as the cognitive restructuring above. In addition to this, it can be helpful to explore pros and cons of the assumption, and to use more general guided discovery (as described in Chapter 6). Therapists may also want to use continua, to challenge all or nothing thinking, and rational-emotional role plays, to help the patient believe the rational side of the evidence at a gut level. Exploring how assumptions do or don't fit with other people can help to challenge their validity, and considering whether the patient would want loved ones to follow the same assumptions can help them to see what might be unhelpful in a different light; this is described as using others as a reference point. Once some change in belief has begun, getting the patient to act as if a more balanced assumption is true, or to set up behavioural experiments to test what happens if the new belief is followed, can help solidify the change.

Core beliefs work focusses not just of evaluating old, negative core beliefs, but on actively working towards new, more helpful and balanced core beliefs, and so these will often be devised at the outset of this stage of work, to focus the work. Modification of old core beliefs and support of new core beliefs can involve all the preceding techniques from NAT and intermediate belief work. In addition to these, it can be helpful to use tools such as a Core Belief Worksheet [39], which lists evidence that supports the new belief, and also the evidence that had been considered to support the old belief, but with a reframe on each piece of evidence to explain how else it can be understood. These worksheets can be used on current situations and experiences, and also used to summarise and explore historical evidence for each belief, which may have been part of maintaining the old core belief. It can also be helpful to explore some of these past events in more detail, including restructuring early memories and helping the patient to talk to their younger selves, to help meaningfully change how the patient understands these events, and what they mean about themselves.

Throughout treatment, the therapist and patient will be building an understanding of what helps the patient to think more helpfully and so feel better. Towards the end of therapy, they will want to ensure this information has been summarised, and troubleshoot any expected future roadblocks, to support the patient in maintaining their new more balanced view of themselves, the world and the future.

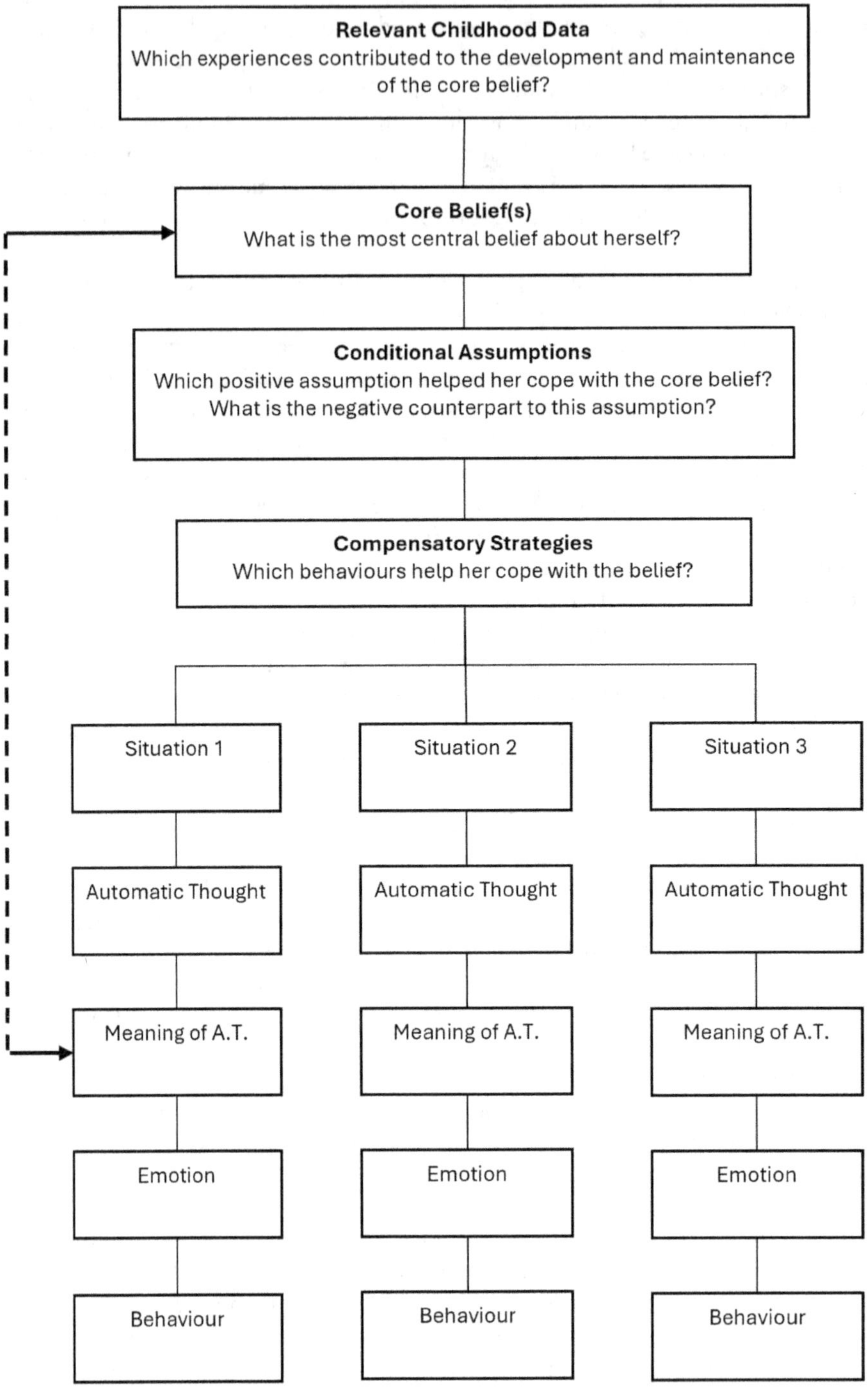

Figure 20.1 Generic Beckian cognitive conceptualisation, reproduced with permission from J. Beck (1995).

An appropriate client for this approach would be Jenny, who we met back in Chapter 8. After socialising Jenny to the concepts of how thoughts, behaviours and feelings interact, they started with activity scheduling, looking at re-engaging with social activities that Jenny used to go to, and any new opportunities that presented themselves. Activity scheduling also involved reducing time on some activities – namely working or looking at social media – so that Jenny could make time to engage in self-care, such as taking bubble-baths and going for walks. Throughout, the underlying therapeutic focus was on exploring how these changes did or didn't fit with her predictions, such as 'they won't want to spend time with me', 'I'm too tired to do that' and 'I don't deserve to take a break'.

Then therapy moved on to NAT work, teaching Jenny to challenge NATs such as 'I'm a burden' and 'I'm ruining the party for everyone'. The therapist and Jenny challenged these on logical, empirical and pragmatic grounds, first off with significant support in session, and then increasingly independently outside of sessions. Jenny became good at this, to the extent that she was more able to disengage from such thoughts when they were occurring. The therapist was also aware of Jenny's common thinking errors of 'should' and 'must' and so explored this as a concept and the impact these types of thoughts had on feelings of guilt and resentment. They agreed that as this happened, Jenny would instead think about how to reframe these into pairs of 'would likes'. For example, when Jenny was invited out by a friend, and had the automatic thought of 'I should be going to the gym', she quickly reframed this into 'I would like to keep in shape, but I also would like to go to the movies with my friend'. This allowed her to then consider which one of the two desires was more important to her overall, without the sense of guilt and resentment that the original thought engendered.

The therapist then collaboratively developed a fuller formulation with Jenny, as shown in Figure 20.2, to help make sense of why and how her problem had developed, and to confirm what core belief (I'm unlovable) and conditional assumptions were driving this, as well as the lifelong compensatory strategies she had been using to avoid feeling unlovable.

Having pinned these down, they then explored each conditional assumption, and what more flexible and helpful rules might be possible to follow, coming to ideas like 'People care about more than what I do for them – I'm allowed to say no'. These ideas were tested out by experiments where she said no to difficult-to-manage requests, first with newer friends, then with colleagues at work, and lastly with her mother. Whilst she did get some negative reactions to this from her mother, she could see how most people were accepting of her even when she said no, and that her mother did still love her.

Finally, the therapist and Jenny directed explored the core belief 'I'm unlovable', and a more helpful new belief of 'I am lovable'. They explored past events that appeared to reinforce the old belief, and reframed each, such as how her father leaving was because he had stopped loving her mother and fallen in love with another woman, and not because of anything about her as a person. They also explored past events that reinforced the idea that she was lovable, such as previous close friendships, and her relationships with her grandparents. They likewise explored current evidence on both sides, again reframing the evidence in support of being unlovable, and considered how she could best live her life as if she was lovable, and as if she loved herself as she was.

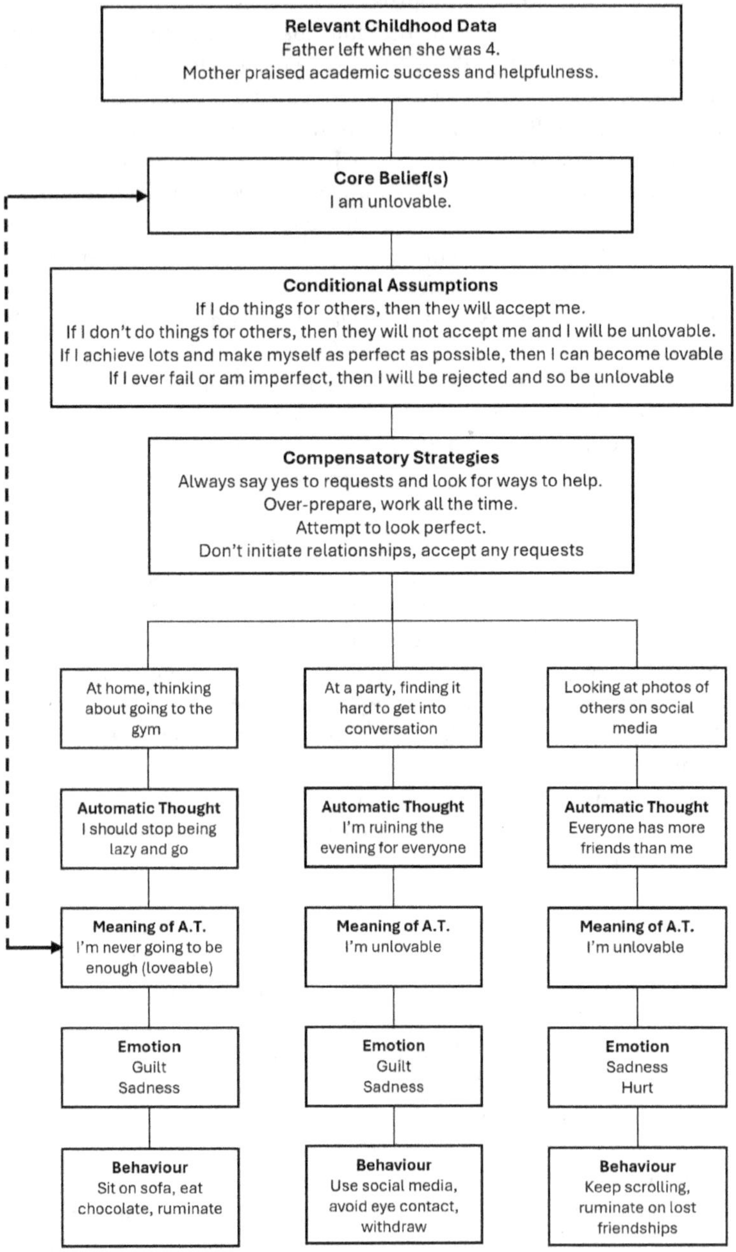

Figure 20.2 Beckian cognitive conceptualisation for Jenny, adapted with permission from J. Beck (1995).

Behavioural Therapy: Depression in Context

Behavioural therapy generally begins by conceptualising depression from a behavioural perspective, where life events are seen as initially causing change in mood, by increasing stressors and reducing reward in life. Following this, depression becomes maintained due to

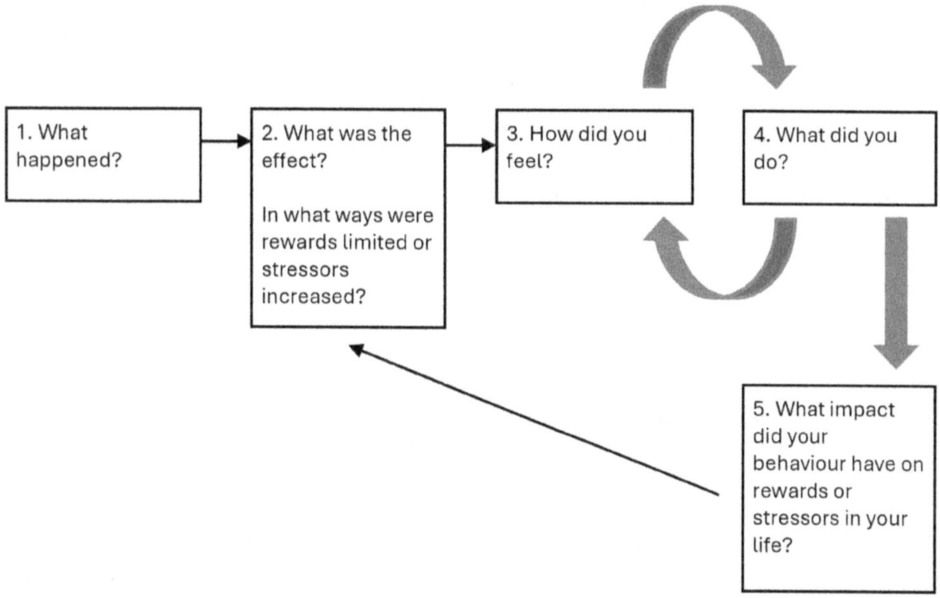

Figure 20.3 Generic BA conceptualisation, from Martell, Dimidjian and Herman-Dunn (2010), reproduced with permission from Guilford Press.

behavioural changes, which both further worsen mood, and also further reduce reward and increase stress. This can be drawn out for clients using the model shown in Figure 20.3.

From this point, the problem is first monitored using activity diaries and mood ratings, and then broken down and changed using a range of tools as needed. Often early therapy will include a focus on functional analysis, in order to determine what activities (in which specific circumstances) will be most rewarding for the patient, and then working out how to schedule these into the coming week to best promote them occurring. Each following week, previous attempts are reviewed, using the information to further refine the activities and timings to maximise reward.

Problem solving strategies will be used throughout behavioural therapy, to overcome barriers to engaging in coping and rewarding activities. Problem solving tools (as described in Chapter 6) are applied flexibly, using the aspect and stages that the client is lacking at any given point. To manage stressors long term, behavioural therapy will explore recurring problems using the concepts of triggers, responses and either avoidance patterns or alternative coping – known as TRAP and TRAC. Helping a client to move from unhelpful avoidance of stressors, to coping strategies that actually change the likelihood of the trigger recurring, can help break the cycle of ever-increasing stress and anxiety, common in depression.

Thinking processes are also worked on as needed in behavioural therapy, but are conceptualised as the behaviour rumination. Rather than engaging with and challenging the content of rumination, clients are taught to notice it, and determine if the process is being helpful – is it solving a problem, or increasing their understanding of the issue, or making them feel better? If not, it is likely unhelpful rumination, at which point clients can be encouraged to try alternative behaviours when they notice themselves ruminating. Such alternatives may to actively problem solve the situation, or to refocus externally on what they are doing and their senses, as well as to add in additional distractions on which to focus such as music or mental exercises.

Therapy finishes with creating a plan to maintain the gains from therapy, and to manage any future problems or lapses. This will include considering all the idiosyncratic aspects of what has helped this patient to feel less depressed, including which behaviours to keep increasing and which to decrease/keep minimised. They'll also consider the contexts that tend to lead to feeling more depressed, and the situations in which it is easier to do rewarding activities, so as to work towards creating the more helpful situations more often.

An example of this approach would be the case of Maida, a married stay at home mother of three. A year ago, she moved from her hometown to a new city with her family, in response to her husband getting a new role. Her kids all settled in well at the new school, and her husband's work was challenging but rewarding, resulting in him committing to long hours to achieve the goals set. Maida, however, struggled in the new city. She felt no longer able to do the old activities she used to enjoy, as they all either involved her husband, her family or her old friends. Feeling let down by her husband, and finding it too much work to build a new social network, she increasingly stayed at home doing housework and watching TV, or scrolling through social media seeing what everyone else was up to. In addition to feeling lower and less energetic, she realised that the change in activity has meant that she'd gained quite a lot of weight. Embarrassed about the changes, she increasingly avoided her family and old friends, and her husband's new work colleagues, for fear of what they would think of her.

The therapist started work by helping Maida make sense of what had happened and how her depression was now being maintained. They conceptualised how the move, and all the connected changes, had made life less rewarding for Maida, resulting in a natural shift in mood, and then an understandable change in activities. This in turn resulted in ever lower mood, and other changes such as the weight gain which made life less rewarding again, and added more stressors and blocks to the activity which might most help. They agreed that while the primary problem had been the mood, there were now secondary problems which might be more amenable to change, and agreed to start monitoring activity and mood each day to see what opportunities there could be.

Explorations of these initial mood diaries found that watching TV was, surprisingly to Maida, only minimally rewarding, and that time on social media was even less rewarding, despite her prior assumption that social media would be helping her to feel connected to her old friends and family. Following this, early changes involved getting up and changed each day, working out at home for 20 minutes mid-morning, and cooking herself and her family some of her favourite balanced meals. These activities helped her to start feeling better about herself and her body, and also less embarrassed about how she was spending her day. Following these 'quick wins' they then explored adding more high-effort new activities, such as joining a local women's swimming group. To maximise the chance of this being effective, they explored Maida's typical avoidance patterns when around new people, which were being driven by fears that the new people would reject her. They then explored and tried out new ways of coping, first with Maida's husband's work colleagues and partners, and then at the swimming group. While these coping behaviours had mixed results, no scenarios resulted in outright rejection or humiliation, and she did end up making friends with two women from the swimming group, who were also new to the area, leading to regular coffee dates after swimming. Towards the end of the therapy, once

Maida was feeling less ashamed of her new life, she worked on organising trips back to her hometown to see her old friends, and re-engaged with social media in a more active way and positive way, messaging friends and family and video-calling people regularly. She practised before these events dealing with any difficult conversations that might come up, balancing being honest with not being overwhelmed by the conversation or feeling dragged into rumination.

Conclusion

Depression is a broadly defined disorder, focussed on generalised and persistent low mood and a loss of pleasure or interest in activities, as well as a number of co-occurring cognitive and somatic symptoms. CBT understands depression as being maintained by negative thinking and unhelpful behavioural changes, including withdrawal, avoidance, and rumination. There are two fairly different treatment approaches that have been shown to be effective in depression, focussing either on the cognitions or the behaviours as the primary focus. Both approaches can be helpful at causing meaningful and lasting change, and due to the interconnection of thoughts and behaviours, either treatment will impact both areas for the patient.

Further Reading

Beck AT. *Cognitive Therapy of Depression.* New York: Guilford Press; 1979.

Beck JS. *Cognitive Behavior Therapy, Second Edition: Basics and Beyond.* 2nd ed. New York: Guilford Press; 2011.

Martell CR, Addis ME, Jacobson NS. *Depression in Context: Strategies for Guided Action.* New York: WW Norton & Co; 2001.

Martell CR, Dimidjian S, Herman-Dunn R. *Behavioral Activation for Depression: A Clinician's Guide.* New York: Guilford Press; 2013.

References

1. Jackson SW. *Melancholia and Depression: From Hippocratic Times to Modern Times.* JSTOR; 1986.
2. Horwitz A, Wakefield J, Lorenzo-Luaces L. History of depression. In DR Strunk, RJ DeRubeis (eds.), *The Oxford Handbook of Mood Disorders.* p. 11–23. Oxford: Oxford University Press; 2017.
3. Hippocrates, Heracleitus. *Hippocrates, Volume IV: Nature of Man.* Reprint edition. Cambridge, MA: Harvard University Press; 1931.
4. Hippocrates. *Hippocrates, Volume I: Ancient Medicine.* Cambridge, MA: Harvard University Press; 1923.
5. American Psychiatric Association. *Diagnostic and Statistical Manual of Mental Disorders: DSM-5.* American Psychiatric Association; 2013.
6. Lim GY, Tam WW, Lu Y, Ho CS, Zhang MW, Ho RC. Prevalence of depression in the community from 30 countries between 1994 and 2014. Sci Rep. 2018;**8**(1):2861.
7. Moreno-Agostino D, Wu YT, Daskalopoulou C, Hasan MT, Huisman M, Prina M. Global trends in the prevalence and incidence of depression:a systematic review and meta-analysis. J Affect Disord. 2021;**281**:235–43.

8. Kessler RC, Berglund P, Demler O, Jin R, Merikangas KR, Walters EE. Lifetime prevalence and age-of-onset distributions of DSM-IV disorders in the national comorbidity survey replication. Arch Gen Psychiatry. 2005;**62**(6):593–602.

9. Zisook S, Lesser I, Stewart JW, Wisniewski SR, Balasubramani GK, Fava M, et al. Effect of age at onset on the course of major depressive disorder. Am J Psychiatry. 2007;**164**(10):1539–1546.

10. Üstün TB, Ayuso-Mateos JL, Chatterji S, Mathers C, Murray CJL. Global burden of depressive disorders in the year 2000. Br J Psychiatry. 2004;**184**(5):386–392.

11. Bebbington PE, Dunn G, Jenkins R, Lewis G, Brugha T, Farrell M, et al. The influence of age and sex on the prevalence of depressive conditions: report from the National Survey of Psychiatric Morbidity. Psychol Med. 1998;**28**(1):9–19.

12. Spijker J, Graaf RD, Bijl RV, Beekman ATF, Ormel J, Nolen WA. Duration of major depressive episodes in the general population: Results from the Netherlands Mental Health Survey and Incidence Study (NEMESIS). Br J Psychiatry. 2002;**181**(3):208–213.

13. Mueller TI, Leon AC, Keller MB, Solomon DA, Endicott J, Coryell W, et al. Recurrence after recovery from major depressive disorder during 15 years of observational follow-up. Am J Psychiatry. 1999;**156**(7):1000–1006.

14. Brown TA, Campbell LA, Lehman CL, Grisham JR, Mancill RB. Current and lifetime comorbidity of the DSM-IV anxiety and mood disorders in a large clinical sample. J Abnorm Psychol. 2001;**110**(4):585–599.

15. Recommendations | Depression in adults: treatment and management | Guidance | NICE [Internet]. NICE; 2022 [accessed 3 June 2023]. www.nice.org.uk/guidance/ng222/chapter/Recommendations#behavioural-couples-therapy-for-depression.

16. Kroenke K, Spitzer RL, Williams JBW. The PHQ-9: Validity of a brief depression severity measure. J Gen Intern Med. 2001;**16**(9):606–613.

17. Beck AT, Steer RA, Brown GK. BDI-II, *Beck Depression Inventory: Manual*. San Antonio: Psychological Corporation, Harcourt Brace; 1996.

18. Beck JS, Fleming S. A brief history of Aaron T. Beck, MD, and cognitive behavior therapy. Clin Psychol Eur. 2021;**3**(2):e6701.

19. Beck AT. *Depression: Clinical, Experimental and Theoretical Aspects*. New York: Harper and Row; 1967.

20. Miller WR, Seligman ME. Depression and learned helplessness in man. J Abnorm Psychol. 1975;**84**(3):228–238.

21. Klein DC, Fencil-Morse E, Seligman ME. Learned helplessness, depression, and the attribution of failure. J Pers Soc Psychol. 1976;**33**(5):508–516.

22. Rehm LP. A self-control model of depression. Behav Ther. 1977;**8**(5):787–804.

23. Beck AT. Thinking and depression: I. Idiosyncratic content and cognitive distortions. Arch Gen Psychiatry. 1963;**9**(4):324–333.

24. Beck AT. Thinking and depression: II. Theory and therapy. Arch Gen Psychiatry. 1964;**10**(6):561–571.

25. Ellis A. Rational psychotherapy. J Gen Psychol. 1958;**59**(1):35–49.

26. Lewinsohn PM. *Control Your Depression*. Hoboken, NJ: Prentice-Hall; 1978.

27. Beck AT, Rush J, Shaw BF, Emery G. *Cognitive Therapy of Depression*. New York: Guilford Press; 1979.

28. Guideline Development Panel for the Treatment of Depressive Disorders. APA Clinical Practice Guideline for the Treatment of Depression Across Three Age Cohorts: (505892019-001) [Internet]. American Psychological Association; 2019 [accessed 3 February 2023]. http://doi.apa.org/get-pe-doi.cfm?doi=10.1037/e505892019-001.

29. National Institute for Health and Care Excellence. Depression in adults: treatment and management [Internet]. NICE; 2022

Jun. Report No.: NG222. www.nice.org.uk/guidance/ng222.

30. Jacobson NS, Dobson KS, Truax PA, Addis ME, Koerner K, Gollan JK, et al. A component analysis of cognitive-behavioral treatment for depression. J Consult Clin Psychol. 1996;**64**(2):295–304.

31. Martell CR, Addis ME, Jacobson NS. *Depression in Context: Strategies for Guided Action*. New York: WW Norton & Co; 2001.

32. Dimidjian S, Hollon SD, Dobson KS, Schmaling KB, Kohlenberg RJ, Addis ME, et al. Randomized trial of behavioral activation, cognitive therapy, and antidepressant medication in the acute treatment of adults with major depression. J Consult Clin Psychol. 2006;**74**(4):658–670.

33. Cuijpers P, Van Straten A, Andersson G, Van Oppen P. Psychotherapy for depression in adults: A meta-analysis of comparative outcome studies. J Consult Clin Psychol. 2008;**76**(6):909–922.

34. Richards DA, Ekers D, McMillan D, Taylor RS, Byford S, Warren FC, et al. Cost and outcome of behavioural activation versus cognitive behavioural therapy for depression (COBRA): A randomised, controlled, non-inferiority trial. The Lancet. 2016;**388**(10047):871–880.

35. Rush AJ, Beck AT, Kovacs M, Hollon S. Comparative efficacy of cognitive therapy and pharmacotherapy in the treatment of depressed outpatients. Cogn Ther Res. 1977;**1**:17–37.

36. Cuijpers P, Miguel C, Harrer M, Plessen CY, Ciharova M, Ebert D, et al. Cognitive behavior therapy vs. control conditions, other psychotherapies, pharmacotherapies and combined treatment for depression: A comprehensive meta-analysis including 409 trials with 52,702 patients. World Psychiatry. 2023;**22**(1):105–115.

37. Beck JS. *Cognitive Behavior Therapy: Basics and Beyond*. 2nd ed. New York: Guilford Press; 2011.

38. Martell CR, Dimidjian S, Herman-Dunn R. *Behavioral Activation for Depression: A Clinician's Guide*. New York: Guilford Press; 2013.

39. Beck JS. *Cognitive Behavior Therapy: Basics and Beyond*. 1st ed. New York: Guilford Press; 1995.

Chapter 21

CBT for Psychosis and Complex Mental Health (PCMH)

A Synthesis of Practice and Therapist Guide

Sean Harper and David Carmichael

Introduction

This chapter outlines a model of service structure and adapted cognitive therapy approaches for people who present to secondary care services with difficulties associated with psychosis and complex mental health (PCMH). We include in this context diagnoses associated with schizophrenia spectrum disorders, bi-polar disorders and personality disorders and the complexity of co-morbidities that will present to secondary care services from acute in-patient admissions, crisis teams and community mental health teams. Our view is that this is a coherent PCMH service delivery pathway allowing continuity of applied psychological approaches, interventions and therapies directly for the patient groups, but also more widely across multi-disciplinary teams and systems that provide care and support. Our clinical experience indicates that when specialist adapted CBT is applied across the pathway in this way the benefits to users of our services can be maximised, providing a coherence of psychological care which improves not only direct therapy outcomes, but also multi-disciplinary knowledge and understanding of the psychology of severe and complex mental health. There are also additional important systemic benefits observed such as improved flow and efficiency of discharge from acute in-patient hospital to community services. There is also little doubt that the maintenance of improvement and wellness in PCMH conditions lies beyond the realms and scope of health service provision and that the links with third sector agencies provides crucial value thereafter.

The task then is to design a service structure that has a clear psycho-bio-social pathway throughout with an evidence-based, balanced focus on psychological, symptomatic, social and vocational recovery. The pathway needs also to be designed flexibly to ensure that PCMH services are easily and rapidly accessible for those clients that might require periodic or episodic service support. The concept of early intervention is never more relevant than in this context given the evidence of the negative impact that repeated relapses, associated hospital admissions and coercive treatments can have. The PCMH service structure then underpins the conceptual framework for provision of CBT for PCMH and is presented to the reader as a frame of reference for which to consider their clinical activity and thus improvements and challenges that might be encountered. We will therefore describe in this chapter an introduction in how to apply CBT across the PCMH pathway from acute and crisis teams to Community Mental Health Teams with disorder specific approaches outlined in context.

The orientation here is to offer some generic principles and concepts which underpin adapted CBT applied across the PCMH pathway and disorder specific considerations for the cognitive therapist to begin the journey towards expertise in this area. We do not attempt to describe specific treatment protocols, as this is done so in much more detail elsewhere and to which the reader is duly referred.

Cognitive Therapy for Psychosis and Complex Mental Health Problems: Key Underlying Principles

The key to all cognitive therapy success is obviously effective engagement and alliance building, but there are some particular adaptations required in the therapist approach to PCMH worthy of initial consideration. Psychosis spectrum disorders may present with problems, symptomatically described as delusions or hallucinations, which may be difficult for the therapist to fully understand and thus formulate. The alliance may be at risk if the therapist does not demonstrate an ability to grasp the client's internal reality which may at times appear at odds with objective reality. There is therefore a fundamental approach to engagement that requires extra attention with this client group where the therapist must withhold judgement and enter into the client's internal world in order to fully make the effort to understand where the client's beliefs and experiences most likely arose, how they were developed, maintained and elaborated. It is our contention that through a genuine and demonstrable therapist interest and curiosity that is not contaminated by therapist's own beliefs on reality or otherwise, that the therapist can fully engage effectively and work therapeutically with psychotic presentations. Access to expert supervision is a key component to provide a forum where therapists can explore their own beliefs and how they may be interfering with the therapeutic process. These principles will be returned to throughout this chapter.

Part of the issue of engagement with psychosis also relates to therapist's beliefs about aetiology. Again, any firmly held beliefs are likely to risk contaminating the therapeutic alliance and so should be held in the context of the evidence-base which remains equivocal. The research evidence regarding psychosis in general indicates that there are known to be a wide range of psychological, social and biological factors which may combine in differential ways for different people that lead to a triggering of psychotic experience. Equally, recovery from psychosis takes many different forms and trajectories such that some people will experience a single episode, others multiple episodes and others may have more persistent psychotic experience associated with much greater disability. It is therefore incumbent upon the cognitive therapist to retain an optimistic stance regarding all conceptualisations of recovery at any point in the clients' journey through PCMH services. Holding aetiological ambivalence and recovery optimism are therefore central to the engagement and effectiveness of CBT for PCMH at the outset and require particular attention and careful idiosyncratic formulation. Again the need for access to expert supervision is crucial to explore and manage these issues.

Whilst we have focussed on psychosis thus far, we would contend that much the same principles for effective engagement are required for bi-polar disorder (which may present with psychotic features). Engagement with personality disorders (PD) may present a different and distinct challenge. Personality disorder diagnoses are partly defined by major difficulties in forming and maintaining relationships, so inevitably the potential for challenge to engagement may quite quickly become manifest in the building of the therapeutic alliance. The client may for example appear disengaged, or critical of the therapist in the initial sessions and therefore challenge the alliance formation. The cognitive therapist must hold in mind at all times that such presentations are very likely the manifestation of the problems associated with PD enacted in the context of the therapeutic alliance and are therefore a key part of the formulation. Thereafter, interpersonal and relational aspects of therapy are central to therapy agendas and process and thus the material and focus of therapy. These issues will be discussed in more detail on the relevant section below.

Key Psychological Theories to Consider in Context

Core psychological theory may usefully be applied in the PCMH context to make sense of relational challenges in alliance formation, in particular attachment theory. CBT formulation can very helpfully articulate attachment styles (e.g. [1]) in ways which allow the alliance to be maintained but also to provide the medium with which manifest relational challenges can be worked upon within therapy often before the client is able to test out new ways of interacting in their external real world relationships outside of therapy. The therapeutic alliance becomes then a useful microcosm of the client's problems where formulation driven strategies can be tested in relative safety before embarking on the work outside of the therapy room.

The application of multi-level theories of emotional processing for example interacting cognitive systems (ICS) theory articulated by Teasdale [2] are also centrally important in formulating severe and complex mental health presentations. The importance of applying the implications of ICS here allows a validating discussion with clients around implicational meaning or 'felt sense' emotional experiences which can often help with the exploration of some of the key challenges of cognitive therapy approaches where clients may gain cognitive insight over the course of therapy but remain at an emotional level limited in progress. When this scenario arises the therapist is able to discuss more directly how implicational meaning or 'felt sense' experience may follow cognitive insight, but that improvement is likely to take longer to impact at that level, with a genuine rationale for repetition of CBT targeting the most highly emotively charged relational experiences. Within the core conceptualisation frameworks of adapted CBT that follow in this chapter there is much that can be done by understanding the application of these two key psychological theories and principles in the context of CBT and the reader is recommended to reflect in supervision how these concepts can be incorporated into CBT effectively (e.g. [3]).

Diagnosis

The cognitive therapist working in PCMH often may face the dilemma of how to discuss diagnosis with clients who may want to know the therapist opinion on these issues. There are of course a wide range of client perspectives on diagnosis; those who embrace the diagnostic conceptualisation of their difficulties to those who refute diagnoses entirely. There is therefore no standard way to deal with these issues and each client requires a careful and considered assessment of their beliefs associated with diagnosis and how this impacts on their psychological well-being. Clearly the alliance can easily be fractured if the therapist holds a particular perspective strongly, and thus it is a key moment in the process to be reminded of the importance of the core therapeutic skill of withholding judgement and engaging with the clients perspective on reality however challenging that might be. For example, in psychosis there may be external system level pressures to 'encourage' a client to accept diagnosis and associated treatment through the therapeutic process. Whilst this may appear superficially beneficial to the client from a symptom management perspective, the cognitive therapist must ascertain the psychological impact of accepting such a diagnosis as there can be significant and potentially risk related attributions for some clients which need careful consideration. Equally some clients find personality disorder diagnoses helpful to explain long-term relational difficulties and emotion dysregulation whereas others may find the diagnosis extremely distressing and pejorative in nature. Again the task of the cognitive therapist is to remain neutral, and where necessary assess impact of diagnosis and the utility of such for each individual client. When assessed and formulated well the diagnosis can form a useful part of the therapeutic agenda and process which can contribute to the clients well-being but also wider multi-disciplinary team (MDT) engagement and benefit. However that should not be a goal of the therapeutic process but rather a potential outcome of a successful therapy if formulation dictates that it should be so.

Supervision in PCMH

As mentioned above, it is really important to highlight that expertise in PCMH is a necessary pre-requisite for any supervisor of a cognitive therapist developing skills in this area. The notion of the expert supervisor [4,5] is hugely important such that the some of the key issues and challenges articulated in the above sections can be discussed, explored and considered thoroughly in alliance building, formulation and therapeutic planning. Peer supervision is therefore not recommended.

Sessional Planning

The nature of working with PCMH clients involves significant therapist effort in engagement, as many of our clients may be ambivalent about therapy and/or somewhat hopeless about the possibility of change for many and varied reasons. We would therefore push firmly against contemporary concepts of 'readiness for therapy' that can be prevalent in service operational policies focussed on waiting list management. In contrast, we would see it as the first task of therapy in PCMH to engage the client and this may very legitimately require four to six sessions before more targeted CBT can commence. This might involve initially meeting outside of the therapy room to encourage a client to engage. Indeed active therapy outside of the therapy room may well be extremely helpful for engagement and treatment phases. We know that PCMH clients have very often found it difficult to access therapy services for a variety of reasons [6,7] and it may be important for the cognitive therapist to identify clients who may benefit where services are under-developed in accordance with [8,9] guidelines for psychological therapies for PCMH.

Overall the evidence base for CBT adapted for PCMH clients indicates a duration of treatment between 20 and 30 sessions [8,9], thus a service model of delivery should be constructed with those parameters in mind, allowing some reasonable flexibility incorporated to allow clinician discretion and judgement. That said, we would not advocate for therapy to extend significantly beyond these limits as there is risk of appointments becoming more supportive than therapeutic in orientation which is not clearly in the remit of the cognitive therapist nor clearly, from an evidence-based point of view, likely to be helpful in the long term. There may be requirements for longer-term support for people with PCMH difficulties post-therapy and the links between the constituent parts of the PCMH pathway accounted for in this chapter and third sector organisations should be clear and coherent at the outset. Clients entering into the PCMH pathway should have clear information that CBT is part of an overall package of support with clear rationale as to when, and for how long, each component can be accessed throughout a PCMH pathway. A detailed and well-articulated service pathway is hugely important if therapeutic benefit is to be maximised.

Summary

Having described some fundamental principles for the practice of CBT in PCMH we will now outline an overview of adapted CBT approaches for acute in-patients, psychosis, bi-polar disorder and personality disorder. These descriptions should be considered as starting points to assist the developing cognitive therapist navigate into this specialist field holding the above guidance and principles in mind at all times. Further reading is strongly encouraged via the reference list at the end of this chapter where disorder specific and acute in-patient approaches are described in much greater detail. Further professional learning and development as well as access to specific training in each of the PCMH areas described in the following is also encouraged for those wishing to develop expertise in this area of work.

Finally many presenting problems and approaches to cognitive therapy are hugely overlapping in PCMH work and this chapter is therefore recommended to be read as a whole in order to derive most benefit. Whilst of course mental health clinical pathways are non-linear the reader might usefully consider the first section on acute in-patient CBT as a starting point on the client's journey to access therapy with the following sections providing additional learning depending on the nature of the presenting problem and thus focus of the ongoing therapeutic work.

CBT in Acute Inpatient Wards and Crisis Teams Understanding the Role of Psychological Intervention in Inpatient and Crisis Settings

People may require inpatient mental health treatment when there is a risk associated with their difficulties that can no longer be safely managed within the community. These may include: risk of suicide or self-harm; risk of violence and aggression towards others; risk of violence and aggression or retribution from others; risk of neglect or to dignity. Admissions can occur on an informal (voluntary) or formal basis under the Mental Health Act [10,11]. Typical diagnosis or presenting problems in inpatient settings often include psychosis, mania, borderline personality disorder, complex PTSD, severe depression, severe presentations of more common mental health problems (such as OCD), self-harm and suicidality.

Crisis services have a similar role and remit to inpatient admission, however in crisis services the aim is to provide intensive home treatment or 'hospital at home' as an alternative to inpatient admission [12]. Crisis services also offer early supported discharge from inpatient settings. Whether inpatient admission or intensive home treatment with a crisis service is indicated is often dependent on the intensity of clinician input felt to be required to keep an individual safe. This may vary from multiple visits per week, daily visits, multiple visits per day up to the requirement for 24-hour continuous staff input associated with inpatient mental health wards.

People with experience of mental health crisis treatment report that, while they recognise the role of psychiatric/medical treatment, what they most value is the opportunity to talk to someone, to be listened to, for people to help them feel safe and for someone to help them to make sense of and to help them understand their experiences [13]. Despite this, adult inpatient mental health services have previously been heavily criticised for their lack of therapeutic activity and input [14], where it has been suggested this may account for the high rates of re-admission often experienced by these services [15,16].

In response to these concerns, clinicians and regulatory bodies have suggested that access to dedicated, intensive psychological interventions during acute inpatient admissions and crisis may improve outcomes [17,18,19,20]. Despite this, while the majority of people with psychosis and complex mental health problems report psychological therapy to be of significant benefit or view this option as potentially beneficial both patients and multidisciplinary colleagues report significant difficulty in accessing psychological therapy and clinical psychology [21,22,23].

On the basis of the above, it would appear that there is a clear role for therapists in inpatient mental health services and crisis teams, where psychological therapy is recommended in the treatment of the mental health difficulties typically encountered in inpatient and settings, such as psychosis, bipolar disorder, personality disorders, c/PTSD and severe depression [8,9,24,25,26,27,28]. Concerns have been raised however regarding the feasibility of psychological therapies on an inpatient basis. Professional guidelines typically recommend at least six months of therapy as an outpatient for PCMH (20–30 sessions, see [29]), where the average length of acute psychiatric admissions is thought to range from 39 to 49 days [30]. While 30–40 days may appear to be a reasonable time frame for meaningful psychological intervention, in practice there is considerable variation, where some admissions may be as short as 72 hours.

Working within a brief and time limited structure can present challenges for cognitive therapy application in conceptualising the scope, focus and remit of interventions in inpatient settings. One way to address this challenge is to consider the role of inpatient or crisis cognitive therapy within the context of phased-based models of intervention.

Readers will likely be familiar with the phased-based model of intervention for complex PTSD, where the phases of intervention include Phase 1: Safety & Stabilisation, Phase 2: Reprocessing and Phase 3: Reintegration/Reconnecting [24]. More recently, however, this model has been adapted to provide a framework for conceptualising and organising the phases of care and treatment for borderline personality disorder. This adapted phased-based model [31] suggests that Phase 1 Safety and Stabilisation should be broken down into three sub-phases which include:

1) **Safety:** Interventions to ensure the safety of the patient and others.
2) **Containment:** Interventions based primarily on general treatment strategies such as validation and stabilising the environment in order to contain behavioural and affective instability. Medication may be appropriate. This stage may also include social interventions aimed at achieving safety, stability and containment including housing or financial needs.
3) **Regulation and control:** Behavioural, cognitive and occasionally pharmacological interventions to reduce symptoms and improve self-regulation of affects and impulses.

This adapted phased-based model of intervention is outlined in Figure 21.1. This model may be a particularly useful framework for cognitive therapists in conceptualising their role in inpatient settings. Rather than attempting to provide a complete course of psychological therapy, the aim is to provide a psychological formulation of the mental health crisis and

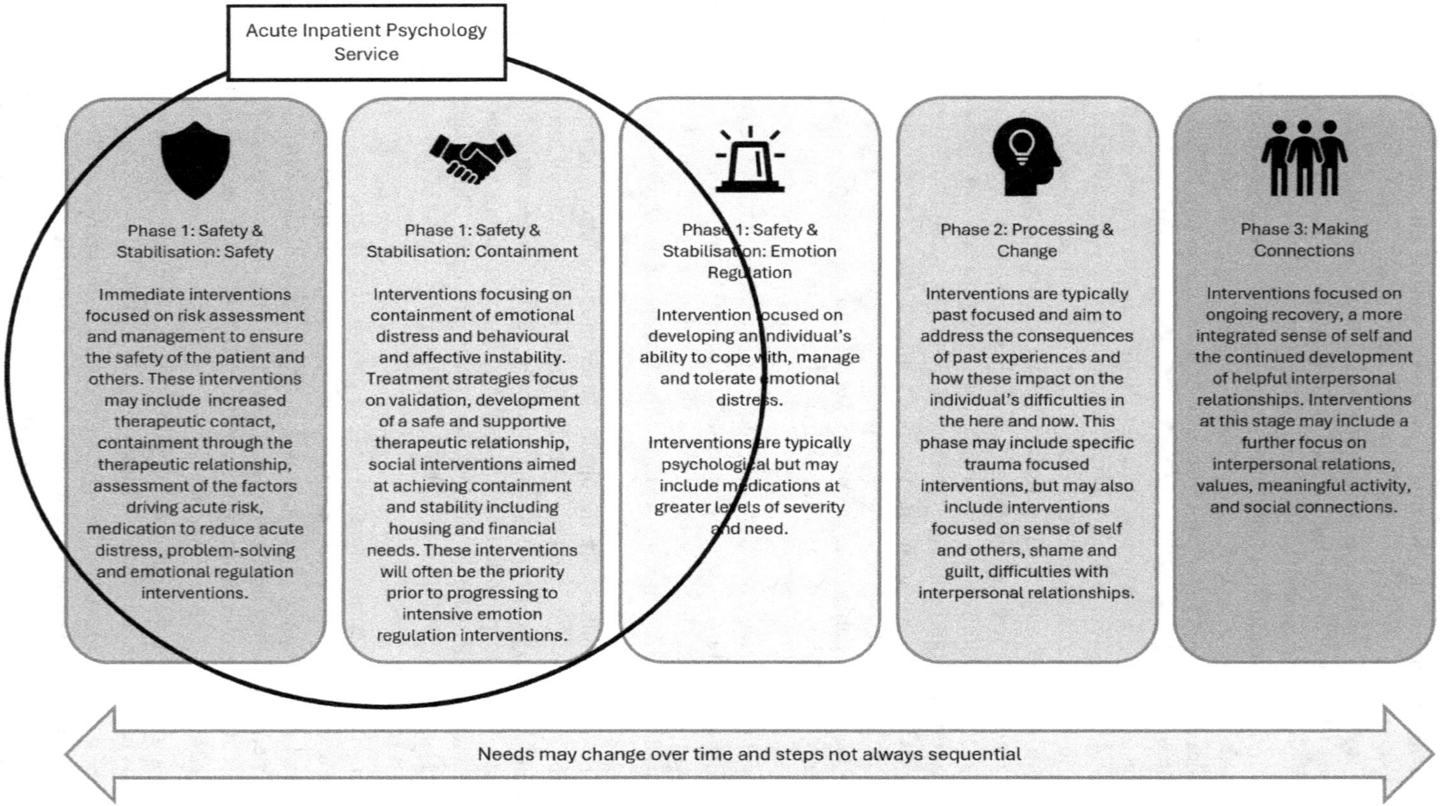

Figure 21.1 Adapted phased-based model of intervention applied to acute inpatient and crisis services ([32]; adapted from [31]).

associated risk. In the same way that our colleagues aim to resolve the crisis through medication and intensive nursing support, inpatient/crisis cognitive therapy aims to provide care and treatment in the form of a validating and containing therapeutic relationship, and psychological interventions targeting acute emotional distress.

Formulating and Conceptualising Risk

The cognitive therapist's goal is to work with patients to resolve the mental health crisis by reducing the distress driving risk. While many cognitive therapists will be skilled at risk assessment and immediate safety planning, *risk formulation* can often feel more unfamiliar. The section below will outline key theoretical models and psychological processes that may be of benefit to consider when conceptualising and developing collaborative formulations of risk.

The Integrated Motivational-Volitional (IMV) Model of Suicide [33] highlights the role of defeat, entrapment and hopelessness in the development of suicidal ideation and intent. That is, where people view themselves as defeated by their emotional distress, experience this distress as intolerable and overwhelming, feel trapped in their current circumstances and cannot see this changing in the future, this may give rise to suicidal ideation or intent. The role of the inpatient/crisis cognitive therapist thus requires a formulation of an individual's difficulties with a particular focus on maintaining factors. The identification of maintaining factors allows the proposal of interventions to break the vicious cycles maintaining an individual's difficulties, where the aim is to reduce risk by targeting the individual's sense of defeat, entrapment and hopelessness.

Understanding the functions of self-harm can also be key when working in inpatient/crisis settings. In a review of the literature, Klonsky [34] identified seven functions of self-harm or non-suicidal self-injury including:

1) **Affect-regulation:** To alleviate high levels of acute emotional distress or arousal.
2) **Anti-dissociation:** To manage or end the experience of depersonalisation or dissociation.
3) **Anti-suicide:** To replace, compromise with or avoid thoughts of impulses to complete suicide.
4) **Interpersonal Boundaries:** To assert one's autonomy or a distinction between self and others.
5) **Interpersonal Influence:** To communicate or seek help or care from others.
6) **Self-punishment:** To express or cope with anger towards the self.
7) **Sensation Seeking:** To generate positive sensation (exhilaration or excitement) to replace acute emotional distress or negative affect.

Patients who self-harm can often describe significant shame and guilt in relation to these coping strategies. The development of a collaborative formulation recognises and validates the function of these coping strategies, but identifies formulation driven psychological interventions that serve a parallel function to self-harm but avert the longer-term negative consequences. A useful axiom for therapists to promote engagement in this context is captured in the following: 'If you were deprived of the opportunity to learn and internalise helpful emotion regulation and self-soothing strategies … it is no wonder and it makes sense that you were forced to find alternatives.'

Acute psychosis and mania may also be key considerations for formulating risk in inpatient settings. For example, people experiencing persecutory beliefs that others intend to cause them harm may present with significant violence and aggression due to a deeply help belief that they may need to protect themselves from harm. Conversely, people who experience grandiose delusions may be at risk of harm if they strongly believe they have special powers or abilities and engage in behaviours to test these beliefs (e.g. patients may have the belief that they are able to fly or invulnerable to harm). Acute mania can often be associated with risk to others. If, for example, the individual experiences a reduced tolerance for delays and frustrations and responds to these through violence and aggression, or the patient presents as sexually disinhibited, this may place them at risk of harm from others. Finally, acute mental health crisis can often result in individuals being unable to recognise or act upon basic needs for food, water, self-care and shelter.

Core Components and Key Features of Inpatient and Crisis Psychological Services

The role of cognitive therapy for inpatient or crisis services has to go beyond that of a 'visiting therapist'. Rather, the therapist should be a fully integrated member of the inpatient or crisis MDT in order to provide a psychological perspective into all aspects of inpatient or crisis care.

The key features of an effective inpatient/crisis inpatient CBT/psychology service is therefore required to be:

1. Accessible and integrated
2. Responsive
3. Flexible
4. Time limited and risk/crisis focussed
5. Formulation-driven

The British Psychological Society (BPS) and Association of Clinical Psychologists UK (ACP-UK) have developed commissioning guidelines that further develop and outline the core components of psychology services across the acute care pathway [35]. They propose that inpatient and crisis psychology services should offer the following:

1. *Direct Psychological Interventions:* Direct psychological interventions include individual assessment, formulation and therapy or group psychological interventions
2. *Indirect Psychological Interventions:* Indirect psychological interventions refer to interventions focussed on the system around the patient and often are in collaboration with colleagues, such as case consultations or team formulation meetings.
3. *Trauma-Informed Care:* Therapist working in acute and crisis settings should work with MDT colleagues to integrate reflective, compassionate and trauma-informed care into the multidisciplinary team culture.
4. *Reflective Practice and Staff Support:* Therapists working in inpatient and crisis settings should offer psychologically led reflective practice, supervision and post-incident support to MDT colleagues in order to promote wellbeing, resilience and retention of staff and ameliorate the emotional impact of working in challenging environments.

5. *Teaching, Training and Supervision:* Inpatient and crisis cognitive therapists should have the capacity to contribute to teaching and training for MDT colleagues and to provide clinical supervision of low intensity psychological therapies.

Individual Assessment, Formulation and Intervention

The challenges of delivering psychological therapy in acute inpatient and crisis settings are outlined above. Isobel Clarke's [36] Comprehend, Cope, Connect (CCC) model of psychological therapy has been specifically developed for brief, intensive, time-limited psychological therapy in crisis.

The CCC model proposes that an overwhelming, powerful and intolerable 'horrible feeling' is at the heart of acute mental health crises and that it is this horrible feeling that can result in the risk associated with mental health crisis. For example, if an individual feels worthless or alone, experienced as intolerable and overwhelming (entrapment) and does not believe this will ever change, they may view ending their life as the only remaining escape. In the same manner, should an individual experience a sudden and intense implicational meaning 'felt-sense' related to rejection, abandonment or loneliness, and experience this emotion as overwhelming and unbearable, they may resort to short-term coping strategies such as self-harm to alleviate distress.

Conceptualising risk and mental health crisis within the context of an acute and overwhelming 'horrible' feeling can also be applied to psychotic experiences within the CCC model, where significant emotional distress might result in increased vulnerability to anomalous perceptual experiences. The individual may interpret these experiences as indicating they are at risk of harm and may attempt to cope with this distress through violence and aggression to protect themselves and reduce feelings of vulnerability or threat.

The CCC model is a third-wave CBT intervention that integrates elements of ACT, mindfulness, CBT, DBT, CFT and CAT. The model has an explicit focus on formulating vicious cycles that maintain the horrible feeling. Interventions aim to provide 'exits' from these vicious cycles, thereby reducing the intensity of the overwhelming emotion. In acute mental health crisis, the model suggests that the 'implicational' or 'felt sense' driven meaning making system is dominant. According to this rationale, emotion-focussed intervention techniques such as mindfulness, distress tolerance and emotion regulation interventions are more appropriate at this stage of intervention than more traditionally cognitive focussed techniques such as cognitive restructuring.

The CCC formulation model is outlined in Figure 21.2.

A detailed therapeutic manual and session guide is outlined in Clarke and Nicholls [36] and we shall not attempt to replicate these here. Rather, we offer some insights and reflections below that may be of benefit to cognitive therapists new to formulating using this model in inpatient settings.

Contracting

Many individuals receiving inpatient mental health treatment may be detained under the mental health act against their will. In addition, challenges with interpersonal relationships may be a significant aspect of the individuals' difficulties. In this context, explicit and clear therapy contracting is critical. The therapist should ensure the

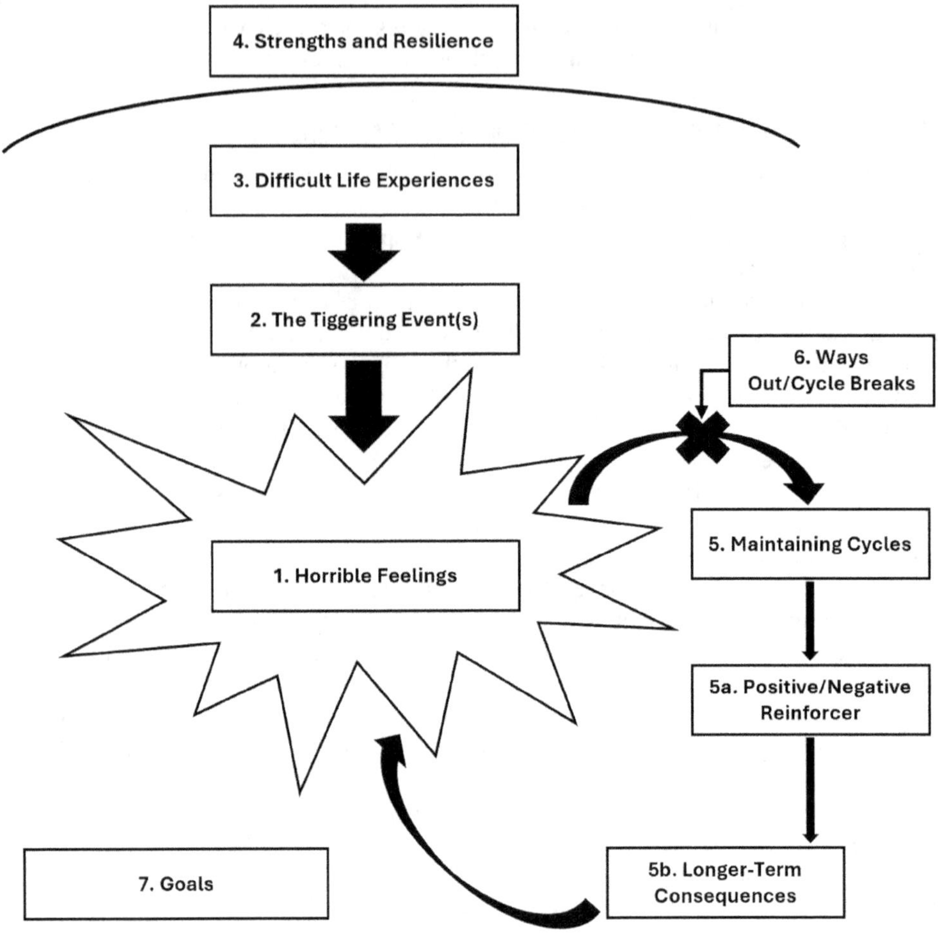

Figure 21.2 Comprehend, Cope, Connect (CCC) formulation model [37]. Reproduced with permission from Harris, Clarke and Riches.

patient is aware that engagement in psychological therapy is a choice; there will be no negative consequences should they choose not to engage with therapy; there is a planned frequency and duration of sessions, there are clear limits and parameters of confidentiality and information sharing with the wider MDT to inform treatment.

Pacing

The pacing and timing of assessment and formulation can be a particular challenge when working in time-limited inpatient settings, particularly when attempting to develop a 'good enough' formulation prior to discharge. Figure 21.2 outlines a process for developing a CCC formulation through the assessment process. In line with this approach, we would propose that an initial session should focus on precipitants for an individual's difficulties and beginning to develop a detailed 'here and now' formulation of the individual's difficulties.

Rather than looking for triggers over one specific period, there may be three layers of precipitants that are of interest. Examining precipitants in this increased level of detail may aid in developing a formulation of concepts such as defeat, entrapment, hopelessness, threat or vulnerability developed over time. These three layers of precipitant might include:

- What was happening in the person's life when their difficulties began?
- When did things get worse and were there any additional stressors at this point in time?
- What happened on the day of admission and why was the person admitted to hospital?

When people are experiencing acute and overwhelming emotional distress, it is unsurprising that they may struggle to give a chronological account of their difficulties. The DBT chain analysis [38] technique can often be of benefit during the assessment and formulation process as a result. In addition to identifying precipitants and the evolution of risk over time, examining the individual's reasons for dying or the emotions driving self-harm can assist in the identification of the 'horrible feeling' driving the persons distress and associated risks.

Once an understanding of precipitants for the individual's distress and the 'horrible feeling' has been progressed, the focus of assessment can turn to developing a detailed 'Here and Now' five systems level formulation of the thoughts, feelings, physical symptoms and behaviours associated with an individual's difficulties [39]. A more detailed focus on coping behaviours, examining both short-term benefits of these behaviours and longer-term consequences is of particular benefit when attempting to develop formulations of the vicious cycles maintaining the horrible feeling at the heart of an individual's distress and associated risks as outlined in stage 5a and 5b of the CCC formulation model.

Identification of precipitating factors, 'the horrible feeling' and beginning five areas of assessment of the individuals' difficulties to identify maintenance cycles should ideally begin in Session 1. Continuing this approach and assessment of predisposing factors should be the focus of Session 2 and 3. In inpatient settings, the aspiration would be to be in the position to collaboratively develop a CCC formulation diagram with patients by Session 4.

Adaptations to Therapy in Inpatient Settings

Individuals experiencing acute mental health crisis may struggle to tolerate the traditional therapy hour. Poor sleep or sedation as a result of medication may also impact upon the time of day patients prefer to be seen for appointments. Furthermore, the therapist should be aware of the other demands on the patient on the same day as a planned appointment (e.g. ward round, MDT meetings or trialling passes for the first time) and consider whether a therapy session in addition to these demands is within the patient's window of tolerance. Given the above challenges, a collaborative approach to the day, timing and during of sessions is key in facilitating access to inpatient psychological therapies and developing a therapeutic relationship.

Managing Disagreement with Diagnosis or Detention

Many individuals receiving inpatient mental health treatment under the mental health act will disagree with their diagnosis or detention status. This can present a particular challenge when attempting to develop a collaborative formulation of the individuals' difficulties. Further guidance on the development of collaborative formulations with people experiencing psychosis is available in the CBT for psychosis section and the introductory section. The cognitive therapist should attempt to adopt a curious therapeutic stance and focus upon developing an understanding of the individual's attitudes, thoughts, feelings and perspective on their diagnosis and the need for inpatient care. Patients may often have been told very little about their working diagnosis and it can be helpful for the therapist to provide psychoeducation regarding diagnostic criteria and seek further feedback on the individuals' thoughts regarding diagnosis following the provision of more detailed information.

Personal History Assessments and Predisposing Factors

Adverse childhood experiences (ACEs) and interpersonal trauma have been found to be highly prevalent in inpatient psychiatric settings (e.g. [40]). In addition, experiences of interpersonal trauma and adversity are thought to play a key role in the development of psychosis and complex mental health difficulties [41,42,43,44,45,46,47,48,49,50,51, 52,53].

The CCC model advocates for taking a limited approach to personal history assessment, formulation of predisposing factors and exploration of trauma [36]. This is perhaps understandable due to concerns that detailed assessment may not be within an individual's window of tolerance during an acute mental health crisis or due to concerns regarding the appropriateness of this discussion within the context of a time-limited, brief psychological intervention.

However, with due respect to the above concerns, many individuals recognise that past events likely impact their current difficulties and value the opportunity for these experiences to be given their place in the formulation process. The trauma informed practice principles of choice, collaboration and empowerment [54] are important considerations at this stage of the formulation process, where the cognitive therapist should discuss the rationale for personal history assessment and collaboratively agree with the patient to what degree this should be explored during the formulation process.

Therapists need to be flexible in their approach to assessment. It may be more appropriate in this context to avoid the more structured approach to personal history assessment typically outlined in therapy manuals and simply to ask the patient whether they believe there are any past experiences that may be important for the therapist to know.

A comprehensive approach to personal history and trauma assessment, including recommendations for managing barriers or anxieties in relation to this process is outlined in Read et al. [55], where the authors recommend adopting the funnel-based approach outlined in Figure 21.3.

Early life emotional neglect or invalidation has been identified as a significant predisposing factor, particularly in the case of borderline personality disorder [56,57,58]. Assessment of these experiences however can often feel challenging. We would advocate for asking patients what would happen when they were upset, angry or anxious as a child (did other people notice? What did they do?) as a particular assessment question for emotional abuse and invalidation. In addition, we would recommend that experiences at school and possible bullying experiences are explored given the potential impact of these experiences in the development of core beliefs regarding self and others and associated relational threat-based beliefs (see for example [59]).

In the section above, the role of an inpatient psychological therapist is considered within the context of phased-based models of intervention. We would recommend therapists hold this model in mind when completing personal history assessments. For example, therapists

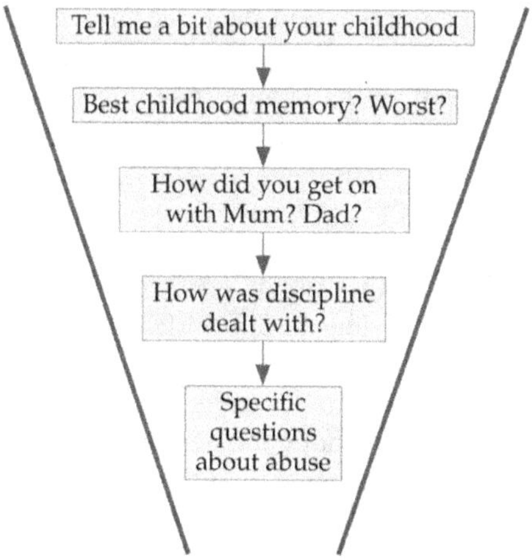

Figure 21.3 Read et al. [55] 'Funnel approach' to trauma assessment. Reproduced with permission from Cambridge University Press.

may collaboratively agree with patients that phase 1 safety and stabilisation interventions (such as grounding and relaxation) are important to introduce and practice prior to personal history assessment.

Finally, in some cases, particularly where shame and guilt are key features of the individuals' difficulties or where validating the impact of early life experiences and their relationship to difficulties in the here and now is felt to be particularly important, it may be helpful to include assessment of past experiences and relationship with recent triggers to develop compassionate and validating shared formulations. When this is indicated, the therapist might wish to outline three key impacts:

1. Beliefs: Core beliefs about the self, world and others.
2. Emotion Regulation: How did this person learn to manage their emotions?
3. Relationships: How did these experiences impact of how the person views others, what they might expect from relationships and what they might do to prevent themselves being hurt in future relationships.

For example, when working with a patient who presents with comorbid substance use difficulties with associated shame and guilt, it can be helpful in the formulation to consider how substance use might serve as a function for an individual in managing the impact of past experiences.

Formulating Maintenance Cycles

A detailed above, here and now 'five areas' formulation of the individuals' difficulties should allow the therapist working within the CCC model to explore vicious maintenance cycles with patients. For example, a maintenance cycle may start with eliciting thoughts, feelings and physical symptoms associated with the patient's difficulties. Then focus on the coping strategies/behaviours, recognising the short-term benefits/function, and highlighting the longer-term negative consequences that exacerbate, reinforce and maintain the horrible feeling at the heart of the individual's acute crisis.

This approach can be adapted to be suitable for psychotic experiences by including 'unusual experience', and 'how I made sense of it', prior to eliciting feelings, physical symptoms and coping behaviours, short-term benefits/function and longer-term negative consequences. Within this approach, increased vulnerability to anomalous perceptual experiences would be formulated within the context of overwhelming emotion or 'the horrible feeling'. It can also be of benefit to consider formulating relational difficulties, including those with staff teams.

Identification of Exits and Psychological Interventions

A key emphasis of the CCC formulation model is the identification of 'exits' (or interventions) that can break vicious cycles maintaining the individuals' difficulties. These are introduced in the form of arrows that break the relationship between thoughts, feelings, physical symptoms and coping behaviours. Often they will aim to deliver the same or similar short-term functions to previous coping strategies, but without longer-term negative consequences. Therapists should identify the range of psychological interventions that may be of benefit to the patient; even where it will not be feasible to explore each of these during the inpatient admission. Therapist and patient should prioritise interventions based upon those that are likely to have the greatest immediate benefit on reducing emotional distress. In line with the CCC approach, these will often be 'felt sense' or 'implicational system' focussed interventions such as grounding, distress tolerance or emotion regulation interventions.

As a member of an inpatient MDT, the inpatient psychological therapist should share this formulation with colleagues to inform to overall care and treatment plan and include interventions offered by other professions as exists in CCC formulations. This might include for example: medication as a possible exit from overwhelming emotion and/or physical symptoms; psychologically informed interventions offered by nursing colleagues; inpatient group therapies; meaningful occupation/behavioural activation delivered by occupational therapy colleagues.

Inpatient and Crisis Psychological Therapy Groups

Limited resource and the gap between demand and capacity will be familiar challenges to therapists working in inpatient settings. It will rarely be possible to offer all patients on the ward at any one period of time individual intervention. Access to inpatient psychology intervention can therefore be expanded by offering interventions on a group basis. Transdiagnostic psychological therapy groups, such as emotional coping skills (ECS; [60]) have been found to significantly reduce distress, improve recovery self-efficacy, reduce rates of re-admission and result in improved patient satisfaction and ward atmosphere [18,20,61].

Adaptations are often required to ensure feasible psychological therapy groups in inpatient settings, where running groups on a rolling 'open basis' may be more acceptable to patients. Selection of co-facilitators can also be a key consideration, where co-facilitators from other professions can promote the dissemination of psychological approaches and interventions across the wider MDT.

Case Consultation and 'Indirect Psychological Interventions'

The role of a therapist working in an inpatient setting is broader than the delivery of psychological therapies alone [35]. Rather, the role of the inpatient therapist is to provide formulation-driven psychological advice regarding all aspects of inpatient care and treatment.

In order to do so, the inpatient therapist should seek to integrate themselves into the inpatient team by their presence and contribution towards clinical case discussions during ward rapid rundowns/'safety briefs', weekly ward rounds and MDT meetings, making themselves available to colleagues for consultation, advice/clinical supervision to staff offering psychologically informed interventions. These forms of clinical activity may be referred to as 'indirect' psychological interventions of which team formulation and reflective practice are examples.

In line with this approach and conceptualising the role of an inpatient therapist within phased-based models of intervention, the inpatient therapist should actively be involved in the process of contributing towards discharge planning. The therapist should use their formulation of the individuals' difficulties to inform what is required from community services in order for the patient to feel contained, for any ongoing risks to be effectively managed and to identify interventions targeting the factors felt to be maintaining the individual's difficulties, including further cognitive therapy.

In addition, the wider MDT can serve as a particularly useful sense check when attempting to formulate an individual's difficulties in inpatient settings. MDT colleagues may have information regarding an individual's presenting difficulties of which the inpatient therapist may not immediately be aware. Furthermore, discussing working formulations with MDT colleagues and gathering their perspectives and feedback can be an important method of testing formulation hypotheses.

Team Formulation

Team formulation is the process of facilitating a group or team of professionals to construct a shared understanding of an individual's difficulties [62]. The benefits of team formulation over individual psychological formulation are thought to include [63]:

- The formulation is based upon the knowledge and experience of a variety of different professions and roles within the team and is likely to be a more comprehensive understanding of a person's difficulties.
- It allows the team the time and space to gather our knowledge and understanding together in one place.
- Helps the team develop a shared understanding of a person's difficulties and achieve a consistent team approach towards treatment.
- Helps the team to identify and deal with core issues rather than just managing crises.
- Helps the team to identify, predict and manage risk.
- Helps to challenge unfounded myths or beliefs about a particular patient.
- Helps to plan and consider multi-disciplinary approaches towards treatment.
- Helps to explain why some people may be experienced as particularly complex or challenging to work with and how the team can support one another.
- Aims to increase team morale and hope for positive change.

Studies evaluating the impact of team formulation meetings in adult inpatient mental health wards have reported that when patients difficulties have been discussed in team formulation meetings; staff experience lower rates of burnout and patients report significantly stronger therapeutic relationships with staff, and rate the ward atmosphere as significantly more positive than patients who were not discussed in team formulations [64]. More recently, a five-year evaluation of trauma-informed team formulations and staff training in low-intensity emotion regulation interventions found significant reductions in self-harm (reduced by 55.91%), seclusion (reduced 28.66%) and restraint (reduced 19.82%) [65].

A number of professional practice guidelines have been developed to support staff offering team formulation meetings [63,66]. As a result, this chapter will focus on recommendations for establishing and facilitating team formulation meetings on adult acute psychiatric and intensive psychiatric care units.

We would recommend the 5 Ps approach for team formulation meetings [67]. We recommend this model as it is likely that this approach to formulation may be familiar to MDT colleagues and also that a generic, rather than modality-specific, formulation approach can allow for the integration of different models of psychological therapy that may be accessible (e.g. CBT/Systemic/CAT). We would advocate however that in addition to the 5 Ps, inpatient therapists should consider adding 'relationships' and 'risk of re-traumatisation/strategies to reduce the risk of re-traumatisation' as additional variables in their formulation templates. There is emerging evidence of the use and value of relational formulation approaches for inpatient ward staff, for example, Duffy et al. [68].

Team formulations should focus on the MDT developing a shared understanding and formulation of the problem together. The formulation should be informed by the expertise of all members of the MDT and should be inclusive of psychological factors, biological/medication and social intervention strategies. For team formulation meetings to be effective and to inform diagnosis and inpatient care and treatment, the key 'decision-makers' in the individuals care and treatment need to be involved, namely senior nursing colleagues, the patient's consultant psychiatrist and/or the responsible medical officer/approved clinician. This often requires consultation with colleagues to identify feasible timing for team formulation meetings within the wider functioning of the ward. In addition, consideration should be given to community colleagues who may know the patient well which assists smooth discharge back to the community and agreement on the care and treatment plan on discharge.

We have found that 1.5 hours is typically required to develop a formulation (1 hour) and to discuss the associated intervention plan (30 minutes). The inpatient therapist should prepare by completing rapid case note review prior to team formulation meetings, where the focus is upon gathering information regarding predisposing factors and recent triggers. Team formulation meetings present the opportunity to offer a psychological perspective of an individual's difficulties and to develop balanced psycho-bio-social treatment plans.

The following structure for team formulation meetings is recommended in inpatient settings.

1. **Background to admission:** Focus on identifying possible precipitants.
2. **Presenting problem:** Prompts might include mood (elated versus depressed?), psychotic experiences including hallucinations, delusions, negative symptoms, suicidality and/or self, sleep, appetite, concentration, ability to engage in activities of daily living (self-care, eating, drinking), how the individual spends time on the ward and engagement with staff.
3. **Relationships:** Discussion amongst staff on what it is like to work with the patient, discuss progress to developing therapeutic relationship, barriers to this process and any interpersonal challenges.
4. **Predisposing:** Discussion of pre-disposing factors.

5. **Formulating:** Discussion of the impact of past experiences, how this might impact on an individual's sense of self and other (core beliefs), ability to manage emotions and relationships in the here and now. Discuss how these past experiences may be related to difficulties in the here and now and how recent triggers may have resulted in the current difficulties.
6. **Perpetuating:** Discussion of the factors thought to be maintaining the individuals' difficulties.
7. **Intervention**: Discussion of intervention plan including the risk of re-traumatisation and potential strategies to reduce the risk of re-traumatisation.

There is often uncertainty as to how best to conceptualise an individual's difficulties in inpatient settings. A team formulation has the potential to clarify the most appropriate diagnosis (should that be indicated as helpful) through the process of formulation-driven hypothesis testing. Typical differential diagnoses in inpatient settings might include: drug-induced psychosis versus psychotic spectrum condition; mania versus impulsivity and anger associated with BPD; BPD versus complex PTSD or co-morbidity. Formulation-hypothesis testing can be of benefit in seeking evidence from the MDT to consider what might be observed in support of each diagnosis. Tools such as the Adult Coventry Grid [69] or recent articles on the conceptual overlap between complex PTSD and BPD [70] can be of particular benefit in supporting the inpatient therapist with this process of formulation hypothesis testing.

Finally, one of the most important considerations in team formulation is patient involvement in the team formulation process. Professional guidelines recommend that patients are involved in the team formulation process as far as possible. Whilst patient inclusion should be the priority, it may not be feasible or appropriate initially to include patients experiencing acute psychosis or mania or presenting with extreme distress and associated risk. Any team-based clinical decision not to include a patient directly in the creation of their formulation should be recorded and justified from a 'risk outweighing benefit' perspective and that a regular review process should be included as acuity reduces and the patient improves.

Summary

This section has provided an overview of the direct and indirect application of Cognitive Therapy to the acute in-patient and crisis PCMH context. The range of direct and indirect, team and consultation based applied psychological work described is pertinent to the whole PCMH pathway of care and the following sections should be viewed as additional learning which should be integrated with that presented thus far.

CBT for Psychosis

Taking full account of the key engagement issues highlighted above provides the necessary pre-conditions for the development of a collaborative CBT formulation of psychosis. In the process of developing a formulation the therapist is recommended to familiarise themselves with background literature highlighting some of the particular psycho-social stressors and developmental experiences associated with psychosis, in particular trauma and neglect (e.g. [71,72,73]). Whilst such adversity does not feature in all psychotic presentations, there is a high prevalence in the populations who access the PCMH service pathway as described, and thus should be considered as having potential assessment utility and explanatory power in psychological formulation. Enquiry regarding adversity is comprehensively recommended.

The task, then, is to formulate the impact of trauma in the manifestation of cognitive, behavioural and psychotic experiences. There are no hard and fast rules but as broad proxies to consider, voice hearing can often be associated with more specific abusive experiences, whereas emotional neglect may more often associate with paranoia and persecutory delusions. Voice hearing and persecutory beliefs may co-exist and the formulation should aim to articulate the complexity of presentations where possible.

A carefully collaboratively constructed developmentally based formulation can be extremely helpful for clients and therapists to share a hypothesis of the origins of psychotic experience, which can in itself be significantly therapeutic. Of course a clear developmental history in relation to psychosis is not always possible nor necessarily appropriate depending on the presentation and client preferences. Some clients may not wish nor require to explore their background so the therapist must be adaptive to differential approaches to formulation and potentially take a more present-focussed, five-system approach as appropriate. Either way, client-identified distress is the focus of formulation and problems that can be translated into goals for therapy via formulated maintenance cycles will most likely become the therapeutic targets thereafter.

The key in the formulation process is to identify the source of the distress, that which is most troubling or distressing for the client. It may be tempting for the therapist to focus on psychotic experience per se as the source of distress, where it may be more important to assess and formulate the clients' interpretation or attributions of unusual experiences. Thus the therapist needs to be alert in formulating individual sense-making of psychotic experiences to fully understand the client perspective and to identify targets for therapeutic intervention. These targets are usually constructed in one form of maintenance cycle or another where the client's existing approach to dealing with their experience might provide access to potential hypothesis testing based interventions which may have either a cognitive or behavioural focus. A final point to bear in mind, as with all CBT of course, is that the client must be fully on board with any identified goal linked to identified maintenance cycles and formulation which can then provide the forum for therapeutic collaborative empiricism consistent with the CBT approach.

The following formulation model [74] provides an excellent framework and is presented here as a key starting point for the reader to work with CBT for psychosis. For further contemporary approaches to working with paranoia and persecutory delusions the reader is referred to the evidence-base developed to support the CBT approach summarised in The Feeling Safe Programme [75] which has hugely advanced the field and evidence-base in CBT for persecutory delusions.

Morrison's model allows flexibility in formulation as discussed above but essentially takes a normalising approach to anomalous experience that may fit with, but is not dependant on, a developmental context or explanation. Thus the psychotic phenomena per se is considered a normal response to stress of one sort or another and that the formulation seeks to understand through functional analyses of key cognitive attributions and behavioural responses predicted to be maintaining associated distress. See Figure 21.4.

Once a collaborative formulation is agreed upon with client and therapist a list of goals and therapeutic targets can be agreed. This is a further area where considerable therapist skill is required to identify achievable goals. So, for example, a client may wish to identify a goal of stopping some other person or organisation persecuting them or to remove the experience of hearing voices. Whilst undeniably desirable, such outcomes are unlikely to be

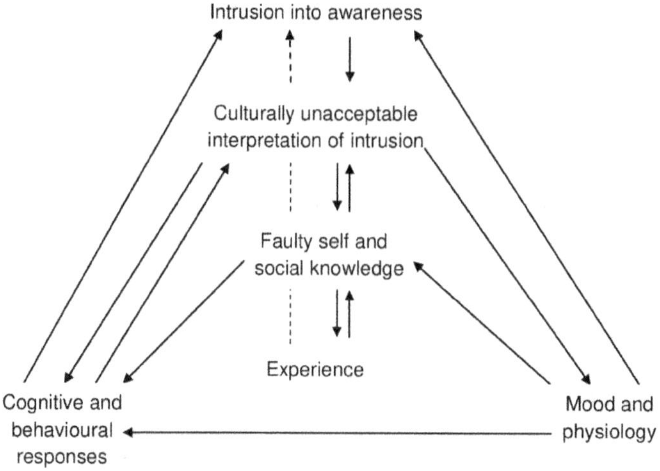

Figure 21.4 Morrison, 2001 model. Reproduced with permission.

achievable through CBT. Thus the therapist must try to orientate the client towards a normalisation of psychotic experience (e.g. [76]) and identify goals focussed on reduction of distress and improved functioning. Once established, therapist and client can work through each goal in turn, identifying potential cognitive and behavioural maintenance factors associated with each problem and measure impact session to session via formal psychometrics, and often more usefully, through simple session by session measures such as Likert scales. Client and therapist may then assess progress and review goals and approaches accordingly. Of course it is well worth establishing at the outset what progress would look like from a measurable perspective in terms of distress reduction and/or improved functioning. It is helpful to agree and contract six sessions at a time to assess progress and review goals of therapy to ensure there is a mutually agreed focus of therapy moving forward and that a change-based direction is maintained.

CBT Psychosis

Sessions 1–6

As described above there may be considerable attention required to create a therapeutic alliance initially and this may take four to six sessions and indeed may require consistent attention throughout the course of therapy. During the alliance building process the therapist should aim to build a formulation that identifies key sources of distress for the client which should relate directly to identified client goals. Sources of distress may relate directly to psychotic experience: voices, paranoia and unusual beliefs. However distress may also relate to experiences in relation to others' reactions; disbelief or disdain for example. Attributions in relation to mental illness, diagnoses, hospital admission and treatment orders or indeed the psycho-social context of peoples' lives may actually be more troubling than psychosis and it is the task of the cognitive therapist to identify key idiosyncratic cognitive and behavioural maintenance cycles linked to agreed therapy goals in order that therapy has an identified direction and measurable process.

Sessions 6–24

The heart of the therapy process will involve systematically working through each client goal with targeted interventions focussed on the key maintenance cycles identified. Voice hearing may be formulated through close attention to patient reactions to voices which may provide the opportunity for testing out new ways of reacting hypothesised to reduce distress. Paranoid and persecutory beliefs are not usually easily addressed directly though standard evidence gathering approaches and thus formulating fear at the core of persecutory beliefs may allow reasonable focus on systematic exposure and re-attribution of fear related stimuli which may often be best progressed in-vivo, outside of the therapy room. Therapists are thus encouraged to accompany patients on exposure-based activities with well-constructed behavioural experiments eliciting key meaning and counter evidence as part of the process. There is considerable therapeutic gain and credibility to be gained through engaging fully with clients in such activity. Measurement is key to ensure progress is observable and simple Likert scales aligned to testable beliefs and goals are usually most useful for clients and therapists alike.

Sessions 24–30

This phase of cognitive therapy for psychosis should have a key focus on staying well. The therapist should summarise the work of therapy and review the context and trigger for the acute psychosis clearly, such that a preventative relapse prevention approach can be shared. Each patient will have a unique cognitive and behavioural and emotional pattern of possible early signs of deterioration and these should be explicitly detailed and link directly to the work covered in therapy. Thus the aim is to demonstrate to the patient that the more they can continue to practise successful interventions covered in therapy the more likely they are to remain well. Of course there are no guarantees and patients should be very clear on the support available to them should that be necessary in the future. A written therapy summary/staying well plan with all necessary contact information should be detailed for each client at the end of therapy. Consistent with all endings in therapy the meaning and impact for each client should be elicited and worked upon directly to manage this process as helpfully as possible.

CBT for Personality Disorder

The conceptualisation of core beliefs and cognitive schemas are arguably at their most important when it comes to CBT formulation and provision of therapy for personality disorders (PD). Whilst definitions of these concepts may differ somewhat in the literature, for the purposes of this section we will consider core beliefs to be fundamentally cognitive in nature and schemas to be of wider scope to include cognitive, behavioural, emotional and physiological features. These differential conceptual descriptions are really important to consider when working with PD clients and have become the main focus of adapted CBT for PD, in particular schema therapy [77,78]. The schema therapy approach identifies potential schema modes [77] which may become manifest within the therapy session and indeed in the context of difficulties described relationally in clients' lives which often are the key sources of distress and emotion dysregulation. Self-harming behaviours may be part of presenting problems which may serve a wide variety of functions and require careful assessment, formulation and functional analyses.

In addition, the problem constellations that are typically associated with different types of personality disorder diagnoses (e.g. [79]) are also helpful for therapists to familiarise themselves as it may give further information with which to understand presentations alongside hypotheses regarding schema modes. Using diagnostic and schema mode information may help therapists develop formulations as well as treatment approaches. Detailed consideration of the relational aspects of therapy are crucial for reflection and learning in clinical supervision and to assist in the challenge of providing effective therapy for this client group.

The focus of therapy is then to initially build the therapeutic alliance in such a way that the client is engaged in the process of change whilst recognising clearly the boundaries of therapy which may be particularly challenging for the therapist to maintain. The PD clients' relational problems may very easily become manifest in the client therapist relationship and the need to conceptualise this dynamic in CBT terms may therefore be required early on the process. Once the relational interaction between client and therapist is well understood this can be formulated in session and therapy can begin to progress within the relative safety of the clinic. Thus, the task of transferring learning into real world relationships can be somewhat less daunting for clients who will likely have experience of lifelong relational challenges and associated emotional dysregulation.

Formulation then seeks to understand the relationship between key developmental experiences and manifest relational problems. Childhood trauma and neglect may be common features in the developmental histories for this client group, but not always, and thus the therapist may be required to unravel much more subtle patterns of relational development to arrive at a coherent formulation of the manifest difficulties a client may experience. Again attachment theory applied to CBT may be useful

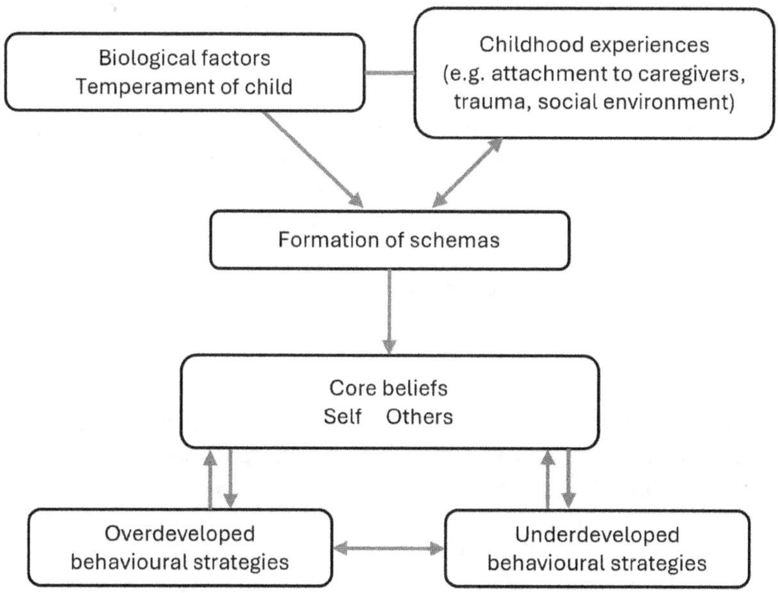

Figure 21.5 Davidson 2008 model. Reproduced with permission from Elsevier.

underlying theory for the therapist to be familiar in application to CBT formulations (e.g. [1]). The best evidence for CBT for PD has been developed through the seminal work of Davidson [80] and readers are referred to her excellent manual for further detailed protocol (Figure 21.5). In addition, the developments in CBT described by Padesky [81,82] in her work on transforming personality provide an excellent frameworks for developing competence in this clinical field. Developing competence in schema therapy [77,78] may be a useful professional development opportunity for the more experienced cognitive therapist.

CBT for PD

Sessions 1–6

The first four to six sessions are much in line with all PCMH work in that the engagement process may be complicated for clients who may have accessed the mental health system on multiple occasions with little derived benefit. The initial engagement process then aims to instil hope and optimism whilst maintaining therapeutic boundaries and gradually socialising the client to the CBT model. During this early therapy phase the formulation is developing as described above with a key focus on understanding the links between developmental experiences and the formation of core beliefs/schemas. Typically the problems clients describe relate directly to schema activation in the relational world which are associated with high levels of emotional distress and typically difficulties in emotion regulation and resultant relationship challenges. Formulation usually indicates that clients with PD who enter PCMH pathways experience an immersed negative sense of self, which can be very hard to work with in standard CBT approaches identifying vicious cycles and potential exit strategies. It is often really helpful to use a strengths-based CBT framework and approach [82] to focus therapy on a more positive model of self. Essentially the therapists' task is to identify even the smallest of positive experiences of self and extrapolate a positive self-formulation which can be used as a template for focussed CBT aiming to expand positive self-experience. The negative self-formulation is considered equitably and requires validation in therapy. The negative self can be conceptualised as the part of self that has been damaged through no fault of the client and thus therapeutic interventions focus on detached awareness, mindful and nurturing responses, in an effort to 'heal' the damaged part of the self. The negative self is usually not available for cognitive challenge when activated in PD clients, such is the extent of associated emotional overwhelm. Thus the overall approach is towards building the positive self and management of the negative self with an aim to find a better balance in experience of self in the relational world. Positive self-experimentation utilises positive self-log and behavioural experiments at the core of the work which aim to create a more expanded experience of the positive self.

Sessions 6–24

During the formulation development, the client should be encouraged to recognise, monitor and record experiences of schema activation. Through this process clients will become more familiar with the nature of negative schema activation and how this impacts on their day-to-day life. In so doing, a degree of objectivity can be developed and the client can be encouraged to consider alternative cognitive and behavioural responses to activating situations usually best conceptualised in the form of behavioural experiment where the client can test out new ways of being and interacting relationally. This, of course, is a major challenge and may be experienced by the client as a significant interpersonal threat given that their established relational interactions have been developed to protect the self and thus, underlying assumptions and associated behaviours have a clear function and exist, as Padesky has described, for 'good reasons'. Thus at the heart of the therapeutic process is a requirement to understand and recognise schema operation and associated underlying assumptions. Focussing positive self-behavioural experiments to test out new ways of being in the relational world provides the context of the therapeutic endeavour. As alluded to earlier the therapeutic relationship may be the initial forum where behavioural experiments may be tested out before translation into the real-world context. Therapeutic progress should be measured, initially by identifying client goals in relation to positive self-experience. So, if a client were to be able to experience more of life in the positive self what might that allow the client to be doing with themselves in practical behavioural terms? Such goals provide ideal anchors with which to measure therapeutic progress. It may also be helpful to take a simple measure of current experience of positive versus negative self-experience at the start of therapy in order to track change. Taking a percentage of life experienced in positive versus negative self with a realistic goal for change can be very powerful for clients, and indeed therapists, to see the change more clearly and be mindful of the negative self threatening to interfere with progress.

This approach takes the view that both the negative and positive selves are legitimate and valid parts of the self, and that due to no fault of their own, clients have experienced large parts of their lives through the lens of the negative self, with cognitive and behavioural patterns subconsciously developed to protect the self, but which inadvertently lead to distress, anxiety and depression. Through the therapeutic process the idea is to help clients understand that whilst protective on one level, these deeply established schema driven patterns are at the same time likely to be reinforcing negative self schema and associated distress. It therefore takes considerable courage for clients to test out new ways of being and it requires a particularly robust therapeutic alliance to create the conditions for such change to occur.

Sessions 24–30

This phase of therapy requires a particular focus on ending therapy and should be a key item on the agenda for at least six sessions. Whilst the relatively short-term nature of CBT should always be clear to clients at the outset and sessions agreed in chunks of six sessions to ensure therapeutic clarity and direction of travel, the ending phase of therapy can be particularly challenging for those with PD. Understandably, inter-personal relationships are usually at the heart of the problem manifestation in PD and thus the therapist-client relationship is particularly important and sensitive to change. The therapist should ensure that there is explicit discussion regarding how ending might feel and be experienced by the client. It may be helpful for the therapist to be explicit in acknowledging their own concerns regarding the end of therapy. This can be usefully formulated again and considered in context of the work covered in therapy to assist the client retain and experience a positive ending in therapy, which may well be a novel experience and thus of high therapeutic value. Additional techniques for ending therapy is to encourage the client to take control of the agenda and the therapist should aim to be increasingly Socratic in approach to maximise the learning and empowerment for the client to be taken from therapy. The use of therapy letters can also be extremely powerful. The client can be invited to write to the therapist to summarise the important aspects of therapy and vice versa. The therapist can take the opportunity to write a summary of key therapy points and some personal narrative, which in combination, can provide the client with a useful summary to continue the work post therapy and hopefully a sense of the importance and value of the relational process. Two or three sessions before the final appointment the client and therapist can exchange therapy letters and discuss each other's perspective and iron out any outstanding issues that may arise. This can provide excellent material for final therapeutic discussions. Finally, it may be helpful to offer the final sessions less frequently such that the client can gradually take further control of continuing the work progressed in therapy (e.g. [3]). The final session may or may not be attended and whilst clearly conjecture, it may be that non-attendance is a sign that the client may feel more ready to move on in their lives post-therapy and should not be considered a negative therapeutic outcome.

CBT for Bi-Polar Disorder

Bi-polar disorder is characterised by periods of elation, over activity and mania, contrasted with periods of severe low mood and depression. There may be psychotic features present in which case the reader is referred to the above section on CBT for psychosis as a framework to be used for focussed work should such presentations be part of the clinical picture and formulation. Equally, models describing CBT for severe depression should be utilised when working with clients where depression is the most prevalent problem identified through assessment and formulation. The following CBT approach described here aims to provide the reader with additional considerations when working with bi-polar disorder, with therapy essentially focussed on well-being and staying well.

The engagement and assessment phase aims as always in PCMH where possible to develop a longitudinal developmental formulation, paying particular attention to the context and precursors to episodes of bi-polar disorder and clients' cognitive attributions in relation to controllability of disorder and emotion. Key to the CBT formulation then is to identify in detail the nature of cognitive, behavioural and emotional processes that provide hypotheses about the interactions that might be implicated in acceleration of mood elation or indeed mood decline. The idea then is to assist clients in maintaining an equilibrium of well-being and a preventative approach to episodes of mania or depression. Typically therapy aims to assist clients to learn to self-monitor their reactions to experience of emotion, both positive and negative, that may be hypothesised to link to depression and mania. In so doing, a staying well metaphor is often useful to conceptualise CBT in this context. Clients who may have experienced multiple episodes of bi-polar disorder may have very limited belief in controllability and such beliefs are important to elicit and work upon as an additional layer of cognition that might be best conceptualised at the meta-cognitive level. Client beliefs in the function of holding meta-cognitive beliefs is additionally important to assess. Further, those clients with longer-term experience of bi-polar disorder may have very understandable worry attached to relapse and so worry-based cognition and associated safety behaviours are another important consideration. Of further particular note, people who have experienced mania may have found the experience initially positive, associated with unusual amounts of energy and thus the cognitive attributions attached to possible early signs of mania are important to elicit. In contrast, behaviours during manic spells may be considered out of character in retrospect, and link with cognition in relation to shame and humiliation, all of which need careful elicitation with potential implications for post mania depression. The overall clinical picture in bi-polar disorder may reflect a disconnect generally between a client and their personal experience and management of emotion, that may link to key developmental experiences which may have led to dysfunctional patterns of emotional self-relating. Formulation that considers staying well and emotion at the centre of the problem is often a very useful framework [83,84]. Formulation templates are not prevalent in the literature but a useful approach is described by Mansell [85] and reproduced in Figure 21.6.

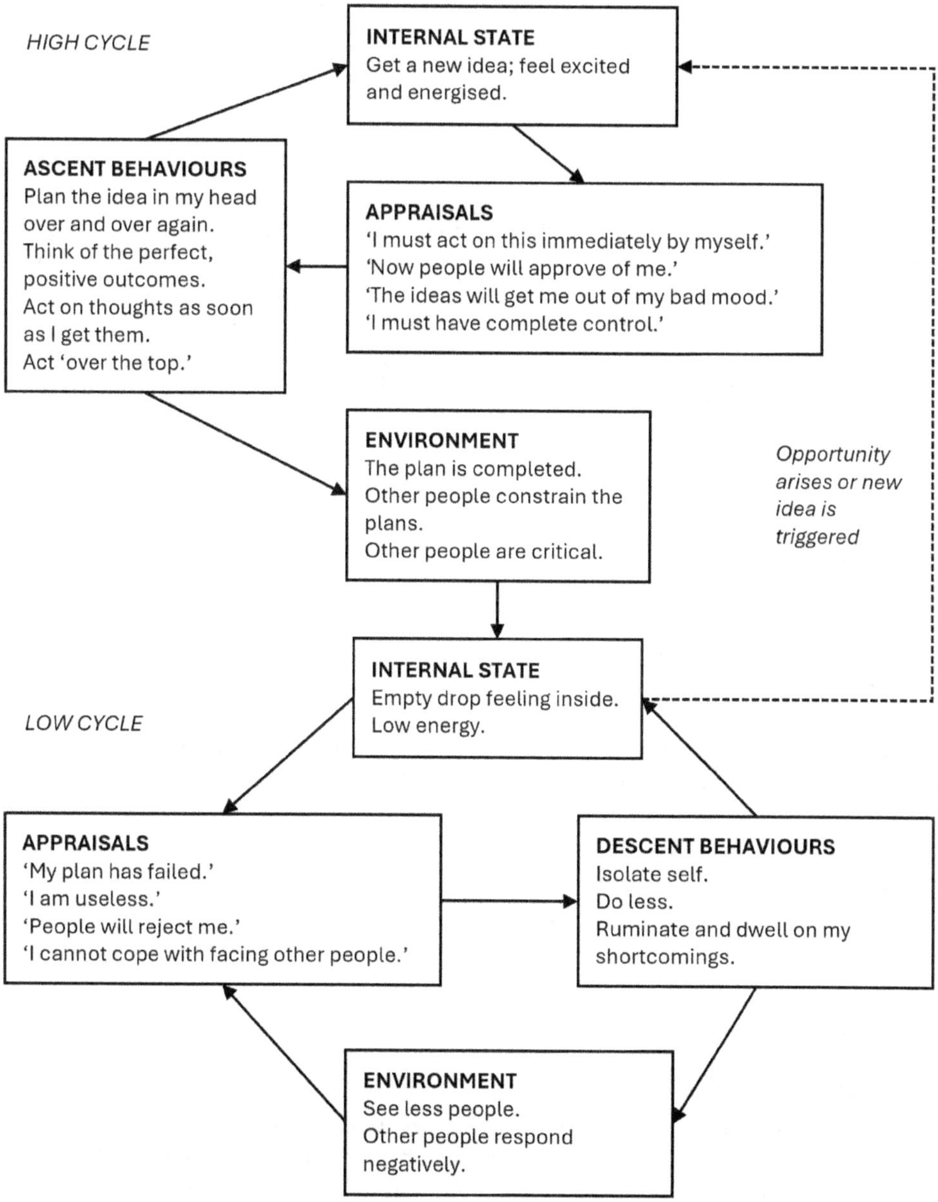

Figure 21.6 Mansell 2007 formulation template adapted from Mansell [85]. Reproduced with permission from John Wiley & Sons.

Sessions 1–6

In parallel with the previous sections the engagement and formulation process involves instillation of hope with a particular focus on the potential controllability of bi-polar disorder as clients may have limited belief that they can influence relapse through psychological approaches. Therapy goals will of course vary from client to client, but will tend to focus on a staying well rationale broadly to fit with the evidence base. As ever in CBT we advise taking a hypothesis-driven approach to beliefs around control and test formulation-driven hypotheses to develop evidence to support control and emotional management.

The formulation then seeks to identify possible cognitive, behavioural and emotional patterns implicated in relapse and further potential maintenance beliefs and behaviours that may likely relate to control of disorder and safety in the experience of emotions.

Sessions 6–24

Therapy then focusses on close monitoring of perceived changes in cognition, behaviour and emotion, that allow active experimentation directly challenging that which is hypothesised to be implicated in relapse or maintenance of a problematic perspective on emotion, the self or the disorder. Progress should be measured closely to ascertain improvements gained and linked to identified therapeutic goals. As a further reminder, evidence-based approaches to CBT psychosis and CBT for depression are recommended, as appropriate to the clinical presentation/formulation and can be woven into therapy for bi-polar disorder as described in this section.

Sessions 24–30

Similar to the other sections described in this chapter a staying well plan-based approach is recommended for the final phase of therapy. The work covered during therapy can be usefully summarised into a staying well plan shared with the client towards the end of therapy either as a standalone document or as part of an ending therapy letter (as described in the CBT for PD section). The overall aim is to encourage the client to continue the work post therapy such that improved ways of managing bi-polar disorder and/or experience of emotions may be incorporated into client's lives, ultimately experienced as a natural way of being, consistent with the aims and orientation of an effective Socratic method in practise.

Digital Applications

Finally the reader is referred to the very promising emerging evidence-base for digital CBT applications which in due course, we predict will provide extremely helpful adjuncts to CBT especially for psychosis. There is very promising emerging evidence for the efficacy of Avatar Therapy for hearing voices [86], Slo-Mo for paranoia and persecutory delusions [87] and Careloop to help prevent relapse in psychosis [88].

Concluding Remarks

PCMH clients typically find it challenging to access CBT and they may often find it very difficult to engage in therapy. It is therefore the primary task of the cognitive therapist to engage and provide effective services for this client group. It is our contention that engagement is the job of the therapist in PCMH and difficulties in so doing should not be attributed to the client. The question that should always be considered pertains to why our approach/

service is not working to engage the client rather than vice versa. Complexity is by definition the PCMH client group and we recommend that all clients on the pathway have access to the full range of mental health disciplines where a genuine and equitably balanced application of psycho-bio-social approaches underpin the service model and pathway. Ideally all MDT members will have access to training in psychological models, formulations and interventions at all levels of intensity such that a therapeutic milieu is the lens through which formulations and care plans are conceptualised and implemented across the PCMH pathway. This is probably best observed currently in early intervention in psychosis services but we can see no reason theoretically why equivalent models cannot be achieved across in-patient, crisis team and CMHT settings as described in our PCMH pathway. Whilst progress within secondary care systems where PCMH services tend to be commissioned, can be extremely challenging, the value of this work in our view is unequivocal for those cognitive therapists motivated to apply psychological skills and knowledge for PCMH clients who are often most in need and access disadvantaged. Adapted CBT as described in this chapter, plays a central part at both the individual, team and system level alongside all evidence-based treatments for PCMH. We hope this chapter inspires the reader to embark on the journey of developing CBT expertise for PCMH and assist with the still necessary endeavour to create psychologically informed pathways and CBT services for some of our most disadvantaged clients. The challenges and rewards, in our experience, are equal and unparalleled.

Further Reading

Morrison AP (Ed.). *A Casebook of Cognitive Therapy for Psychosis*. Hove: Brunner-Routledge; 2002.

Lam DH, Jones SH, Hayward P. *Cognitive Therapy for Bipolar Disorder: A Therapist's Guide to Concepts, Methods and Practice*. Chichester: John Wiley & Sons; 2010.

Davidson KM. Cognitive–behavioural therapy for personality disorders. *Psychiatry*, 2008;**7**(3):117–120.

Clarke I, Nicholls H. *Third Wave CBT Integration for Individuals and Teams: Comprehend, Cope, and Connect*. New York: Routledge; 2018.

British Psychological Society (BPS) & Association of Clinical Psychologists UK (ACP UK). *Psychological Services within the Acute Adult Mental Health Care Pathway: Guidelines for Service Providers, Policy Makers and Decision Makers*. Leicester: BPS; 2021.

References

1. Newman-Taylor K, Harper S, Maguire T, Sivyer K, Sapachlari C, Carnelley KB. Attachment-based CBT models for psychosis: A PPI-informed approach for acute care settings. *The Cognitive Behaviour Therapist*, 2022:**15**;e55.
2. Teasdale JD. Emotion and two kinds of meaning: Cognitive therapy and applied cognitive science. *Behaviour Research and Therapy*, 1993;**31**(4):339–354.
3. Harper SF. Integrating theories and concepts: Formulation driven CBT for a client with a diagnosis of schizo-affective disorder. *Clinical Psychology & Psychotherapy*, 2013;**20**(1):77–86.
4. Milne DL. *Evidence-Based Clinical Supervision: Principles and*

Practice. Chichester: John Wiley & Sons; 2009.

5. Murr S, Nicklas L, Harper S. How does supervision aid cognitive behaviour therapy skill development? Perspectives of CBT trainees: A thematic analysis. *The Cognitive Behaviour Therapist*, 2020:**13**; e45. https://doi.org/10.1017/S1754470X20000422.
6. Braehler C, Harper SF. Identifying psychological needs in psychosis: Perceptions and priorities of CMHT workers. *Clinical Psychology Forum* 2008;**182**:13–17.
7. Switzer F, Harper SF. A narrative review of the barriers to the implementation of cognitive behavioural therapy for psychosis. *Psychosis*, 2019;**11**(2):151–161. https://doi.org/10.1080/17522439.2019.1578400.
8. National Institute for Health and Care Excellence (NICE) Psychosis and schizophrenia in adults: Prevention and management. 2014. www.sign.ac.uk/assets/sign131.pdf.
9. Scottish Intercollegiate Guidelines Network (SIGN) Management of schizophrenia: A national clinical guideline. 2013. www.sign.ac.uk/assets/sign131.pdf.
10. Mental Health (Scotland) Act. 2015. www.legislation.gov.uk/asp/2015/9/contents/enacted.
11. Mental Health Act. 1983. www.legislation.gov.uk/ukpga/1983/20/contents.
12. Royal College of Psychiatry. *Practice Guidelines for Crisis Line Response and Crisis Resolution and Home Treatment Teams*. London: Royal College of Psychiatry; 2022.
13. Mind. *Listening to Experience: An Independent Inquiry into Acute and Crisis Mental Healthcare*. London: Mind; 2011.
14. Schizophrenia Commission. *The Abandoned Illness: A Report from the Schizophrenia Commission*. London: Rethink Mental Illness; 2012.
15. Information Services Division Scotland. Mental health inpatient activity: A national statistics publication for Scotland. 2019. www.isdscotland.org/Health-Topics/Mental-Health/Publications/2019-09-10/mental-health-inpatient-activity/data-explorer/.
16. Paterson C, Karatzias T, Harper S, Dougall N, Dickson A, Hutton P. A feasibility study of a cross-diagnostic, CBT-based psychological intervention for acute mental health inpatients: Results, challenges, and methodological implications. *British Journal of Clinical Psychology*, 2019;**58**(2):211–230.
17. British Psychological Society. *Commissioning and Delivering Clinical Psychology in Acute Adult Mental Health Care*. 2012.
18. Janner M. From the inside out: Star Wards – Lessons from within acute in-patient wards. *Journal of Psychiatric Intensive Care*,2007;**3**(2):75–78.
19. Mind. *Mental Health Crisis Care: Commissioning Excellence*. London: Mind; 2012.
20. Veltro F, Falloon I, Vendittelli N, Oricchio I, Scinto A, Gigantesco A, Morosini P. Effectiveness of cognitive-behavioural group therapy for inpatients. *Clinical Practice and Epidemiology in Mental Health*, 2006;**2**:16.
21. Mental Health Foundation. *A Review of Mental Health Services in Scotland: Perspectives and Experiences of Service Users, Carers and Professionals*. Glasgow: The Mental Health Foundation; 2016.
22. Mental Welfare Commission for Scotland *Adult Acute Themed Visit Report*. Edinburgh: Mental Welfare Commission for Scotland; 2017.
23. Mental Welfare Commission for Scotland. *Living with Borderline Personality Disorder*. Edinburgh: Mental Welfare Commission for Scotland; 2018.
24. NHS Education for Scotland. *The Matrix: A Guide to Delivering Evidence-Based Psychological Therapies in Scotland*. Edinburgh: NHS Education for Scotland; 2015.

25. National Institute for Health and Care Excellence. *Bipolar Disorder: Assessment and Management*. London: National Institute for Health and Care Excellence; 2018a.
26. National Institute for Health and Care Excellence. *Depression in Adults: Recognition and Management (CG90)*. London: National Institute for Health and Care Excellence2018b.
27. National Institute for Health and Care Excellence. *Post-traumatic Stress Disorder (NG116)*. London: National Institute for Health and Care Excellence; 2018c.
28. Scottish Intercollegiate Guidelines Network. *Non-pharmaceutical Management of Depression in Adults*. Edinburgh: Scottish Intercollegiate Guidelines Network; 2010.
29. Paterson C, Karatzias T, Dickson A, Harper S, Dougall N, Hutton P. Psychological therapy for inpatients receiving acute mental health care: A systematic review and meta-analysis of controlled trials. *British Journal of Clinical Psychology*, 2018;**57**(4):453–472.
30. Scottish Government. *Mental Health Inpatient Census 2023*. Edinburgh: Scottish Government; 2024.
31. Livesley WJ. *Practical Management of Personality Disorder*. London: Guilford Press; 2003.
32. Carmichael DA, Dalziel E, Al Sayegh A. *Unpublished Adaptation of Livesley, W. J. (2003). Practical Management of Personality Disorder*. London: Guilford Press; 2025.
33. O'Connor RC, Kirtley OJ. The integrated motivational–volitional model of suicidal behaviour. *Philosophical Transactions of the Royal Society B: Biological Sciences*, 2018;**373**(1754):20170268.
34. Klonsky ED. The functions of deliberate self-injury: A review of the evidence. *Clinical Psychology Review*, 2007;**27**(2):226–239.
35. British Psychological Society (BPS) & Association of Clinical Psychologists UK (ACP UK). *Psychological Services within the Acute Adult Mental Health Care Pathway: Guidelines for Service Providers, Policy Makers and Decision Makers*. Leicester: BPS; 2021.
36. Clarke I, Nicholls H. *Third Wave CBT Integration for Individuals and Teams: Comprehend, Cope, and Connect*. New York: Routledge; 2018.
37. Harris J, Clarke I, Riches S. Developing 'comprehend, cope and connect' training for acute and crisis mental health services: Staff, patient and carer perspectives. *Journal of Psychiatric Intensive Care*, 2023;**19**(1):33–50.
38. Rizvi SL, Ritschel LA. Mastering the art of chain analysis in dialectical behavior therapy. *Cognitive and Behavioral Practice*, 2014;**21**(3):335–349.
39. Williams C, Garland A. A cognitive–behavioural therapy assessment model for use in everyday clinical practice. *Advances in Psychiatric Treatment*, 2002;**8** (3):172–179.
40. Read J, van Os J, Morrison AP, Ross CA. Childhood trauma, psychosis and schizophrenia: A literature review with theoretical and clinical implications. *Acta Psychiatrica Scandinavica*, 2005;**112** (5):330–350.
41. Aas M, Henry C, Andreassen OA, Bellivier F, Melle I, Etain B. The role of childhood trauma in bipolar disorders. *International Journal of Bipolar Disorders*, 2016;**4**(1):2.
42. Agnew-Blais J, Danese A. Childhood maltreatment and unfavourable clinical outcomes in bipolar disorder: A systematic review and meta-analysis. *The Lancet Psychiatry*, 2016;**3**(4):342–349.
43. Beck AT, Rush AJ, Shaw BF, Emery G. *Cognitive Therapy of Depression*. New York: The Guilford Press; 1979.
44. Cattane N, Rossi R, Lanfredi M, Cattaneo A. Borderline personality disorder and childhood trauma: Exploring the affected biological systems and mechanisms. *BMC Psychiatry*, 2017;**17**(1):221.
45. Courtois CA. Complex trauma, complex reactions: assessment and treatment.

Psychological Trauma: Theory, Research, Practice, and Policy, 2008;**1**:86–100

46. Garety PA, Kuipers E, Fowler D, Freeman D, Bebbington PE. A cognitive model of the positive symptoms of psychosis. *Psychological Medicine*, 2001;**31**(2):189–195

47. Green JG, McLaughlin KA, Berglund PA, Gruber MJ, Sampson NA, Zaslavsky AM, Kessler RC. Childhood adversities and adult psychiatric disorders in the national comorbidity survey replication I: Associations with first onset of DSM-IV disorders. *Archives of General Psychiatry*, 2010;**67**(2):113–123.

48. Herman JL, Perry C, Van der Kolk BA. Childhood trauma in borderline personality disorder. *The American Journal of Psychiatry*, 1989;**146**(4):490–495.

49. Kessler RC. Childhood adversities and adult psychiatric disorders in the national comorbidity survey replication I: Associations with first onset of DSM-IV disorders. *Archives of General Psychiatry*, 2010;**67**(2):113–123.

50. Mansell W. An integrative formulation-based cognitive treatment of bipolar disorders: Application and illustration. *Journal of Clinical Psychology*, 2007;**63**(5):447–461.

51. McLaughlin P, Giacco D, Priebe S. Use of coercive measures during involuntary psychiatric admission and treatment outcomes: Data from a prospective study across 10 European countries. *PloS one*, 2016;**11**(12):e0168720.

52. Read J, Perry BD, Moskowitz A, Connolly J. The contribution of early traumatic events to schizophrenia in some patients: A traumagenic neurodevelopmental model. *Psychiatry: Interpersonal and Biological Processes*,2001; **64**(4):319–345.

53. Varese F, Smeets F, Drukker M, Lieverse R, Lataster T, Viechtbauer W et al. Childhood adversities increase the risk of psychosis: A meta-analysis of patient-control, prospective-and cross-sectional cohort studies. *Schizophrenia Bulletin*, 2012;**38** (4):661–671.

54. NHS Education for Scotland *Transforming Psychological Trauma: A Knowledge and Skills Framework for the Scottish Workforce*. Edinburgh: NHS Education for Scotland; 2017.

55. Read J, Hammersley P, Rudegeair T. Why, when and how to ask about childhood abuse. *Advances in Psychiatric Treatment*, 2007;**13**(2):101–110.

56. Bateman A, Fonagy P. Mentalization based treatment for borderline personality disorder. *World Psychiatry*, 2010;**9** (1):11–15.

57. Linehan MM. *Cognitive-Behavioural Treatment of Borderline Personality Disorder*. London: The Guilford Press; 1993.

58. Porter C, Palmier-Claus J, Branitsky A, Mansell W, Warwick H, Varese F. Childhood adversity and borderline personality disorder: A meta-analysis. *Acta Psychiatrica Scandinavica*, 2020;**141** (1):6–20.

59. Cunningham T, Hoy K, Shannon, C. Does childhood bullying lead to the development of psychotic symptoms? A meta-analysis and review of prospective studies. *Psychosis*, 2016;**8**(1):48–59.

60. Clarke I, Wilson H. (Eds.). *Cognitive Behaviour Therapy for Acute Inpatient Mental Health Units: Working with Clients, Staff and the Milieu*. London: Routledge; 2009.

61. Araci D, Clarke I. Investigating the efficacy of a whole team, psychologically informed, acute mental health service approach. *Journal of Mental Health*, 2016;**8237**:1–5.

62. Johnstone L, Dallos R. *Formulation in Psychology and Psychotherapy*. Hove: Routledge; 2014.

63. British Psychological Society Division of Clinical Psychology. *Good Practice Guidelines on the Use of Psychological Formulation*. Leicester: BPS; 2011.

64. Berry K, Haddock G, Kellett S, Roberts C, Drake R, Barrowclough C. Feasibility of a ward-based psychological intervention to improve staff and patient relationships in

psychiatric rehabilitation settings. *British Journal of Clinical Psychology*, 2016;**55** (3):236–252.

65. Nikopaschos F, Burrell G, Clark J, Salgueiro A. Trauma-informed care on mental health wards: The impact of power threat meaning framework team formulation and psychological stabilisation on self-harm and restrictive interventions. *Frontiers in Psychology*,2023;**14**:1145100.

66. Association of Clinical Psychologists UK. *Team Formulation: Key Considerations in Mental Health Services*. ACP-UK; 2022.

67. Kuyken W, Padesky CA, Dudley R. *Collaborative Case Conceptualization: Working Effectively with Clients in Cognitive-Behavioral Therapy*. New York: Guilford Press; 2011.

68. Duffy A, Goodall K, Carmichael D, Harper SF, Sivyer K, Carnelley K et al. Strengthening relationships within intensive psychiatric care: Staff perceptions of an attachment training intervention. *Journal of Psychiatric and Mental Health Nursing*, 2024;**32**(2):321–331. https://doi.org/10.1111/jpm.13109.

69. Cox C, Bulluss E, Chapman F, Cookson A, Flood A, Sharp A. The Coventry Grid for adults: A tool to guide clinicians in differentiating complex trauma and autism. *Good Autism Practice*, 2019;**20** (1):76–87.

70. Ford JD, Courtois CA. Complex PTSD and borderline personality disorder. *Borderline Personality Disorder and Emotion Dysregulation*, 2021;**8**(1):1–21.

71. Bentall RP, de Sousa P, Varese F, Wickham S, Sitko K, Haarmans M, Read J. From adversity to psychosis: Pathways and mechanisms from specific adversities to specific symptoms. *Social Psychiatry and Psychiatric Epidemiology*, 2014;**49**: 1011–1022.

72. Morrison AP, Frame L, Larkin W. Relationships between trauma and psychosis: A review and integration. *British Journal of Clinical Psychology*, 2003;**42** (4);331–353.

73. Larkin W, Read J. Childhood trauma and psychosis: Evidence, pathways, and implications. *Journal of Postgraduate Medicine*, 2008;**54**(4):287–293.

74. Morrison AP (Ed.). *A Casebook of Cognitive Therapy for Psychosis*. Hove: Brunner-Routledge; 2002.

75. Freeman D. Developing psychological treatments for psychosis. *The British Journal of Psychiatry*. 2024;**224**(5):147–149. http://doi.org/10.1192/bjp.2024.5.

76. Harper DJ. Realising the potential of general population research to reconceptualise the study of 'delusions': From normalising 'psychosis' to defamiliarising 'normality'. *Theory & Psychology*, 2021;**31**(6):887–911. https://doi.org/10.1177/09593543211000429.

77. Young JE, Klosko JS, Weishaar ME. *Schema Therapy: A Practitioner's Guide*. New York: Guilford Press; 2003.

78. Arntz A, Van Genderen H. *Schema Therapy for Borderline Personality Disorder*. Chichester: John Wiley & Sons; 2020.

79. Sperry L, Freeman A. *Cognitive Behavior Therapy of DSM-IV-TR Personality Disorders: Highly Effective Interventions for the Most Common Personality Disorders*. New York: Routledge; 2006.

80. Davidson KM. Cognitive–behavioural therapy for personality disorders. *Psychiatry*, 2008;**7**(3):117–120.

81. Padesky CA. Schema change processes in cognitive therapy. *Clinical Psychology & Psychotherapy*, 1994;**1**(5):267–278.

82. Padesky CA, Mooney KA. (2012). Strengths-based cognitive–behavioural therapy: A four-step model to build resilience. *Clinical Psychology*, 2012;**19**(4):283–290.

83. Power M. *Emotion-Focused Cognitive Therapy*. Chichester: John Wiley & Sons; 2010.

84. Lam DH, Jones SH, Hayward P. *Cognitive Therapy for Bipolar Disorder: A Therapist's Guide to Concepts, Methods and Practice*. Chichester: John Wiley & Sons; 2010.

85. Mansell W, Morrison AP, Reid G, Lowens I, Tai S. The interpretation of, and responses to, changes in internal states: An

integrative cognitive model of mood swings and bipolar disorders. *Behavioural and Cognitive Psychotherapy*, 2007;**35** (5):515–539.

86. Garety P, Edwards C, Jafari H, Emsley R, Huckvale M, Rus-Calafell M et al. Digital AVATAR therapy for distressing voices in psychosis: the phase 2/3 AVATAR2 trial. *Nature Medicine*, 2024;**30**:3658–3668.

87. Hardy A, Taylor KM, Grant A, Christie L, Walsh L, Gant T et al. Co-designing technology to improve psychological therapy for psychosis: SloMo, a blended digital therapy for fear of harm from others. *Schizophrenia Research*, 2024;**274**:526–534.

88. Gumley AI, Bradstreet S, Ainsworth J, Allan S, Alvarez-Jimenez M, Aucott L, et al. The EMPOWER blended digital intervention for relapse prevention in schizophrenia: A feasibility cluster randomised controlled trial in Scotland and Australia. *The Lancet Psychiatry*, 2022;**9**(6):477–486.

Chapter 22

Adaptations for Specific Populations

In this chapter we will help you to be able to:

- Approach how adaptations can be applied with specific populations, for example, older people, carers, CYP and so on, to enhance treatment outcomes explaining principles of this approach.
- Consider rationales suggesting need for adaptations and advantages in terms of applicability and/or augmentation of outcome.
- Consider adaptations that enhance access and address unmet need in specific populations.

In what way and under what circumstances should clinicians consider adaptations when applying CBT with specific populations, especially as the issue is rather complex and there may be a number of considerations to take heed of within the modality of CBT, with the applicability of techniques and in the culture of the population being served? Therapists may have to pause and consider whether evidence-based treatment protocols essentially designed for adult mental health populations are suitable without adaptation. Often the answer is that they are not, or not fully. Sometimes the answer is a nuanced one; sometimes cultural adaptations are necessary to ensure greater access with specific populations and sometimes adaptations require technical changes as to how CBT is practised with specific populations. Arundell [1] provides a helpful typology to use when considering adaptations and this paper provides us with a very thoughtful frame of reference from which to approach the question of adaptations. With older people, one could specify that adaptations are *unnecessary* as non-adapted CBT with older people has been shown to be equally efficacious with older people and adults of working age [2]. However, when one considers that older people are often a marginalised and under-valued section of society and there are often stereotypical biases that can prevent older people accessing evidence-based treatments the picture is much less clear cut and adaptations may be much needed. Additionally, there may be different theoretical contexts to consider when working with older people such as typical ageing, and similarly when working with children the developmental context is inescapable and adaptations become more compelling. Developmental adaptations when working with children as opposed to adults often take account of theoretical considerations such as Piagetian stages of cognitive development, Vygotsky's developmental theories and attachment theories. In this domain adaptations are theoretically driven and these considerations are given fuller consideration in the following chapters. If the question about adaptations is how one can improve on treatment outcomes the answer may be more focussed on what technological adaptations may be recommended and the question of how to evidence this becomes more complex [1]. Augmentation of outcome may also be an important necessary condition when working with specific populations who may present clinicians with challenges, as there may not be existing evidence-based protocols at hand such as when working with older people or those with dementia who have an anxiety disorder or a depression. Additionally, how to apply the principles of CBT for common mental health conditions may present some challenges due to the characteristics of specific populations such as dementia caregivers. Adaptations may take account of additional factors such as understanding typical ageing and attitudes to growing older. In dementia caregiving additional specific population knowledge necessary for clinicians is about types of dementias, prognosis and trajectory of living with a dementia. There are evidently general considerations to bear in mind in adaptations.

Additionally, we may wish to consider how cultural adaptations ought to be considered and implemented in a way that is respectful and celebratory of different viewpoints. Hinton and Patel [3] provide a very thoughtful and helpful consideration of how to work towards a contextually sensitive approach to adapting CBT.

Further Reading

The following source provides more in-depth coverage of the topics raised in this chapter.

Rathod S, Phiri P, Naeem F. An evidence-based framework to culturally adapt cognitive behaviour therapy. *The Cognitive Behaviour Therapist*. 2019;**12:e10**.doi:10.1017/S1754470X18000247.

References

1. Arundell LL, Barnett P., Buckman JEJ, Saunders R, Pilling S. The effectiveness of adapted psychological interventions for people from ethnic minority groups: A systematic review and conceptual typology. *Clinical Psychology Review*. 2021;**88**:102063.
2. Cuijpers P, Karyotaki E, Eckshtain D, Ng MY, Cortesellinia KA, Noma H, et al. Psychotherapy for depression across different age groups: A systematic review and meta-analysis. *JAMA Psychiatry*. 2020;**77**(7):694–702.
3. Hinton DE, Patel A. Cultural adaptations of cognitive behavioral therapy. *Psychiatric Clinics of North America*. 2017;**40**(4):701–714,

Chapter 23

Evidence-Based Age-Appropriate Cognitive Behavioural Therapy with Older People

This chapter will help you to be able to:

- Access essential information to add to your existing clinical knowledge and skills so as to more effectively work with older people using CBT.
- Work collaboratively with older people using CBT, planning treatment interventions unencumbered by stereotypical beliefs about ageing and older people and expect symptom reduction consistent with standard treatment protocols.
- Apply ideas from theories of the science of ageing (gerontology), such as wisdom and emotional development, in order to help your client make use of lifeskills when helping themselves overcome common mental health problems.
- Use and apply new techniques associated with a developmentally appropriate frame of reference when working with older people.

In this chapter, research and clinical evidence is synthesised to ensure you will feel confident in applying CBT with older people in a way that enhances your practice and more likely results in a positive treatment outcome. This chapter combines complimentary sources of evidence from CBT theory and gerontology to provide a more process-oriented account of the application of CBT with older people.

Gerontology is a multi-professional science of ageing. Its value to therapists with limited expertise in working with older people is as a source of facts about ageing and resource for challenging stereotypical beliefs and negative biases about ageing. Gerontological research evidence is drawn from community dwelling older people, often taking part in longitudinal follow-up studies, thus providing therapists with key insights into experiences and attitudes to ageing. Thus when CBT therapists want to help their older clients challenging unhelpful negative biases and stereotypes about ageing, gerontology provides the science to support alternative prosocial cognitions empowering and enhancing optimal functioning in later life.

Introduction

Older people are an engaging and positive group to work with – much to the surprise of many therapists who expect old age to be all about loss and decrepitude. While change and loss can be a feature of ageing, change is also very much possible when working with older people. Thus, the focus of CBT is empowering older people to make positive changes enhancing the quality of life regardless of chronological age. A focus entirely on geriatrics (the illnesses of old age) can often make working with older people a more intimidating prospect to therapists which can demotivate and demoralise. Recent research examining outcome of older people seeking help from National NHS Talking Therapies services suggest older people report as good, and often better outcomes than working age adults on key parameters such as treatment completion and recovery rate [1,2].

Gerontological theories may be useful to CBT therapists in a number of respects, but primarily because knowledge of normal aspects of ageing can act as a counterbalance to overcome negative ageist attitudes and beliefs. Unless knowledgeable about normative aspects of ageing, therapists who work with older people with emotional distress may become convinced that depression, anxiety and dementia are common consequences of ageing, with detrimental consequence for the expectation of change within treatment.

Ageing is a process rather than a state, and the experience of ageing is nuanced, complex and individual with there being as many experiences of ageing as there are older people. Indeed often people feel younger 'inside' than their chronological years [3], with people who have lower subjective perceptions often experiencing better wellbeing [4,5]. Consequently, we should approach working with this client group with a sense of curiosity and discovery. This chapter will aid your exploration of this process.

Late Life Mental Health

As a consequence of profound demographic change, people are living longer than previous generations. For example, by 2050, across the globe there will be twice as many people aged 65 and above compared to those aged 5 and under [6]. Life expectancy of men aged 65 years old is estimated to be 18.5 years and 21 years for women. A recent report in the Lancet predicted increases in life expectancy to continue to increase steadily within the UK up to 2030 and for the male-female longevity gap (i.e. age difference in life expectancy between men and women) to decrease [7]. However, inequalities in health are important in determining life expectancy, with the Marmot report [8] noting that areas with the greatest level of deprivation report the lowest levels of life expectancy, with deprivation having a much deeper impact on healthy life expectancy. This nuanced and changing picture suggests therapists are more likely to work with many more older clients than ever before, and with clients who are much older than previously, as the fastest growing demographic group in populations are the oldest old [9]. In primary care settings older people's psychological problems can often be seen as secondary to physical health conditions, with a result being mental health problems are poorly treated or overlooked [10], and unfortunately older people are often not offered approaches such as CBT.

Research data and treatment guidelines have very often failed to keep pace with the population demographic shift [11] but thankfully there is a relatively recent positive practice guide (2024) for psychological therapists working with older people (https://babcp.com/Therapists/Older-Adults-Positive-Practice-Guide) which contains a lot of contemporary detail and helpful guidance on how to use CBT with older people. Interested readers should also consult the APA (2024) guidelines for psychological practice with older adults [39]. Nevertheless, there remains a need for more texts on how to provide a developmentally appropriate CBT, that values the experiences older clients bring into therapy, takes account of challenges that may be associated with working with older people (cohort beliefs, multimorbidity, ageism etc.) and is respectful and empowering. While working with older people may sometimes require knowledge and understanding about long-term conditions and many may think dementia will be an inevitable problem to address (it isn't always), working with older people should be as much about enhancing positive affect as it is about reducing negative symptoms associated with depression and the anxiety disorders [11].

Late Life Emotional and Psychological Development

Contrary to expectations and challenging many stereotypes about ageing, most older people do not experience depression [12,13] as there are positive psychological and emotional gains associated with ageing [14,15]. Enhanced emotional competence and increased ability to down-regulate negative affect are in part due to experience in dealing with the consequences of previous challenges in regulating emotion and a prosocial appreciation for emotionally positive contexts through learning to use strategies that 'take the heat out of situations' [16].

As people age, they become more open and less set in their ways and more attuned to emotional and psychological nuances as they exist in human relationships [14]. As people age, they get better at emotion regulation [16,17] with longitudinal research demonstrating older people experience enhanced levels of emotional stability compared with younger age groups [14], perhaps as a consequence of preferential encoding of positive rather than negative information (termed the positivity effect). When working with older clients we may not see this positivity effect immediately if they are depressed, but an improvement in mood should see a return to previous (positively biased) affective state.

If research evidence suggests older people are better than working age adults at regulating emotion [18], proactively using strategies to prevent negative arousal [19], older people may be more attuned to the values and goals of cognitive restructuring in CBT, and more open to the suggestions of homework exercises for overcoming difficulties, and as such may make better candidates for CBT.

How Is CBT Different with Older People?

In a useful clinical reflection on working with older people [20] five Cs are used to explain how working with this group may be different. These can be useful for therapists to consider when treatment planning and in formulation (see Box for more details). One very real difference evident in working with older people is that of the age difference between therapist and client, which may be very large. For some therapists the age difference may be intimidating, as some may worry about taking a comprehensive history and becoming stuck with too much detail, or being enmeshed with past traumas. Another issue concerns multimorbidity and combined chronicity and comorbidity of physical and psychological conditions. Equally for therapists trained to work within evidence-based treatment protocols there may be a concern that these clients are not an optimal fit for services. Thankfully, as recent routine data from NHS Talking Therapies services demonstrates, older people report good, if not better, treatment outcome than that achieved by working age adults [1,2].

Sadavoy's 5 Cs of working with older people:

Complexity: interplay of psychological, social and physiological factors.

Chronicity: factors present in a client's presentation and history that may be enumerated in terms of decades.

Comorbidity: At least one physical comorbid condition is to be expected but often clients present with multi-morbidity. This can be complicated by the fact that practitioners (and clients) may often give primacy to physical conditions when understanding client presentation. Not all comorbid conditions have negative impact on clients.

Continuity: Referred to as the cumulative lifespan developmental impact. Choices made earlier in life may have ramifications/consequences later in life.

Context: The client and their problems can be considered in wider context and for older people this may be that we live in an ageist society that may result in barriers for help-seeking and receiving help for mental health conditions.

Another concern is that late onset mental health conditions will be more complicated to treat and reflect an underlying organic condition such as an early stage of dementia. For example, pseudodementia is a classic psychiatric disorder where people appear to present with a dementia but in fact are depressed. While in some instances the relationship between depression and dementias can be complex, therapists should always refer clients for a neuropsychological assessment where there is doubt.

Recent work from Saunders et al. [2] examined outcomes for older people receiving CBT via Improving Access to Psychological Therapy (IAPT) services across London and calculated better outcomes for older people in comparison to working age adults despite older people receiving fewer sessions. If long-term conditions (LTC) conditions are taken into account working age adult outcomes are more impacted compared to older people. With better outcomes and low attrition for treatment there is no longer any logical reason to deny older people access to CBT.

The vascular depression hypothesis, first proposed by Alexopoulos in 1997, is associated with a late onset depression (i.e. depression only occurring much later in life) but the data for this is complex as are the proposed neuropathological pathways [21] so it may be more important for therapists who suspect a late onset to take a very careful history, as many people who people who experience depression may not necessarily seek help from mental health services (e.g. [40]) and as such many late onset cases are people who have not come to the attention of services until now. Of note on this issue is that while more people are accessing help for common mental health conditions (over one third or 39.4%), according to an adult psychiatric morbidity survey in England and Wales [26], almost one half of people (46.8%) with an unmet treatment need request had received no mental health treatment.

Age-Appropriate CBT with Older People

An age-appropriate approach to CBT enhances the therapeutic relationship, overcomes any fear that may exist because of age differences between therapist and client, and augments treatment outcome to maximise therapeutic gains in treatment. Age-appropriate interventions with older people can consist of use of life skills and timelines (collectively known as wisdom enhancement in CBT), and problem-oriented elective loss-based strategies using selective optimisation with compensation (SOC). In this new approach to CBT with older people termed 'wisdom-enhancement' the aim is to encourage individuals to use their own life data to identify their resilience and the psychological growth that develops after dealing with adversity and overcoming challenges in life. By identifying these attributes and competences (resilience, compassion and self-acceptance) as attributes they possess, individuals are better placed to manage current difficulties and to feel empowered to meet any future challenges that ageing may bring their way.

Age-appropriate CBT based upon the traditional Beck model of CBT and underpinned by gerontological theory recognises older people can be empowered by CBT to bring about change in their circumstances *at any age, or at any life stage.*

Wisdom and CBT with Older People

Wisdom as a concept is valid and meaningful and from a lay perspective, positively associated with ageing. Research suggests that wisdom is associated with wellbeing [22] and is highly valued as a capability associated with elders in our society. However, wisdom is not something that is age-acquired [23]. Indeed wisdom may be more likely to develop in individuals who have had significant life experiences if they have reflected upon experiences and actions rather than something that is acquired passively as one ages. A recent study [23] addressed the erroneous belief that life experience is, by itself, sufficient for the development of wisdom. 'Most agree that wisdom is forged from life experience, yet life experience does not guarantee wisdom ... Wiser individuals process life challenges in an exploratory manner that emphasizes meaning and growth, even if that process may sometimes be unpleasant' [23, p. 811]. Wisdom, however, may be a resource and capability that could be taught and increased [24] and active engagement in reflection, review and change may result in acquisition of wisdom. Most importantly wisdom enhancement in CBT with older people is consistent with an approach that seeks to enhance positive affect as well as targeting and reducing negative affect. Individuals who acquire wisdom develop cognitive behavioural affective strategies, recruiting real life examples of a lifetime of dealing with and overcoming adversity, and these can be applied positively to bring about the most optimal solution to real life problems in the here and now.

Wisdom Enhancement: Life Skills

While a large age discrepancy between therapists and clients can seem daunting to younger therapists, the fact that clients have lived longer than their therapists may be used to advantage in the session and may even enhance therapeutic alliance. With increased age older people can be considered to possess *life skills.* These are emotional and psychological resources clients develop as they overcome adversity over the course of a lifetime. These life skills may not be initially recognised by clients, but a therapist can help a cultivate an appreciation of overcoming adversity and of having psychologically changed (grown) as a result of dealing with challenging situations. A collaborative, enquiring, compassionate stance adopted by the therapist may help the client to see they may have gained life skills from experiences that can be put to good use in the here and now when attempting to overcoming current mental health challenges. A client who has lived longer than the therapist will likely have faced and overcome many adversities over their lifetime (e.g. loss of spouse, changes to physical health and independence, role change, etc.), that the therapist may not yet have faced [11,25,27]. Therapists may reflect on how their client has navigated these significant life events and ponder as to how they would cope were similar circumstances to occur in their own experience. Life skills suggest that a person has overcome adversity and will have gained lessons about themselves and their coping capacity that may be helpful to the client when attempting to overcome their current difficulties [26,28]. In reviewing how a client has met life challenges and developed 'life skills' in the process, therapists may reflect upon the overgeneralised negative autobiographical standpoints our clients habitually adopt as they review their life circumstances. It is unfortunate that when viewed through a lens of anxiety or depression, a person will view their lives over-generally and negatively. When a client says, 'I should be strong enough not to need help at [age] 73', and 'I have such a struggle with my life and other people happen to be getting on fine', they are really communicating a sense of a failure in the fundamental pragmatics of life. Yet when working with clients who view themselves as weak, an observer of these narratives often adopts a different perspective when listening to how people overcome life's challenges, and instead see a resilient, surviving and coping individual. As a consequence, clients quickly lose sight of their own resources and strengths in having coped with 'objectively' difficult circumstances over a lifetime, and life skills can be reviewed and appreciated in a Socratic-type dialogue with the therapist. Thus, life skills can form part of the formulation and treatment approach within CBT.

The use of a timeline technique within CBT with older people [11,25,27,29], has been developed to make use of life skills that older people possess, the purpose of which is to actively help clients explore and challenge negative, overgeneralised appraisals about past experiences empowering the client to enhance functioning in the here and now by instead having a client recognise their prior skills, agency and competences developed from dealing with adversity over the course of their lifetime.

Wisdom Enhancement: Timelines

In CBT we *do not* tell people what to think or even how to think. We simply remind our clients that in CBT we believe there is seldom only one way to think about a situation. There are many different ways to think about a situation and examining a timeline may bring about new revelations and new thoughts about old experiences. Timelines draw upon research into autobiographical memory (e.g. [29,30,31]), and encourage people to reach a different perspective on events in their lives. This is consistent with research demonstrating that teaching people to be concrete thinkers enhances depression recovery and reduces self-criticism (see [32,33]). When events are appraised through a depression-lens symptom-contamination with biased cognitive appraisal is the norm and narratives of failure will be intense within an individual's recall. In older people this negative 'evidence' from the past may be used by the client to denigrate themselves both in terms of their 'character' but also in terms of their decision-making over past events with devastating and prolonged effects on one's confidence and sense of personal agency. It suggests that people will not necessarily reflect on past events and, as a consequence, valuable life-lessons may go unnoticed, or in extreme cases unlearned and as the common saying goes, those who do not learn from the past are doomed to repeat it.

A common example might be where a client says, 'When I look back over my life, all I see is a catalogue of failings.' In a more traditional approach within CBT, one would examine this statement for evidence and also look for evidence against. One might also wish to enquire, 'in what way have you failed?' This approach can be very effective, but it does not address the more general core underlying belief and it also ignores a context of negative age stereotypes. Timelines on the other hand provide the opportunity to assess the 'episodes' of failure and affords an opportunity to take a longer view of how a client has overcome a number of difficult episodes over their lifetime. Therapists are likely to observe that they do not agree with the client's negative appraisals and instead of seeing failures, they may be in awe of how resilient their client is. Asking clients to reflect on difficult life experiences within a structured format in CBT can help them to develop a more nuanced and elaborated account of their recall of overcoming past adversity with the aim of enhancing compassion towards oneself within a greater appreciation of oneself as a survivor.

Timelines Are . . .

Timelines fit within the historical and traditional philosophical approach to Beck CBT.
Timelines provide therapists with a pragmatic way of taking account of many years of life experience at assessment.
Timelines capture an individual's idiosyncratic appraisal of their life and identify nadir and peak points in life referenced as important life events.
Timelines are used as a way of enhancing positive affect (emotions) and positive actions such as self-acceptance and self-forgiveness.
Timelines help people to use evidence if how they have overcome adversity in the past that can be used to suggest they have psychological and emotional resources to deal with current problems and challenges.

As research suggests compassion towards oneself is associated with better psychological well-being [34,35]. Enhancing compassion may be important in augmenting treatment outcomes for depression and anxiety. Timelines use a client's own hard-won experience to engender a greater sense of compassion to oneself over a lifetime of dealing with challenges with timelines simultaneously reducing negative affect and increasing positive affect.

This new technique and approach has been developed over a number of years based on clinical experience, and especially clinical experience with older people with past experience of depression and who unfortunately self-identify as weak or having failed at life in some respect. However a review of overcoming adversity from the timeline may help a person create a more constructive narrative. Angela, a 79-year-old retired pharmacist, after reviewing her timeline, was able to remind herself, 'It won't always be like this. I've been through difficult things before when I felt life was hardly worth it. I can come through difficult things . . . I don't deserve this awfulness.' For more details about the development of this technique and read about a case example, see [37].

The technique of a timeline is straightforward enough in that it is simply a summary of a person's lifespan development history from an idiosyncratic here-and-now perspective of someone who is depressed or has an anxiety disorder. How a person views what is important rather than the veracity of these accounts is key. Timelines capture an individual's appraisal of their life and identify what points in their life they reference as important or significant.

Timelines can be incorporated in CBT as a homework task to be completed by the client and then brought into therapy. A timeline worksheet has been created in Table 23.1 that you can use when creating a timeline. There are a few steps to follow in the use of this new technique:

Steps to completing a timeline

- Step One: Develop a timeline (homework) – acknowledge strengths and resilience.
- Step Two: Consider specific experiences from the past that evoke some emotion – examine them as factually as possible.
- Step Three: When examining past experiences agree certain rules apply:

Table 23.1 A table listing suggested Socratic questions contextualised within a task-oriented frame of reference [11]. Timeline worksheet. Reproduced with permission from the American Psychological Association (APA).

Task	Timeline Socratic question
Factual reappraisal of event	Looking back on that event now, what does it tell you about yourself when you think about how you managed?
Enhancing sense of internal resources	If you could somehow go back in time as you are now and talk to your younger self, what would you say to your younger self about how you coped?
Learning from the past	Have you been in a similar position in the past? If so, how did that turn out? How might this help you manage your current problems?
Challenging negative narrative of self	Pick an event from the timeline. If someone would have told you that was about to happen, how would you have predicted how you would cope? . . . Looking at that event now, what did you actually do?
Self-acceptance	In the past in times of crisis, how, and in what way, has being self-critical in the midst of a crisis been helpful to you?
Reappraisal of self as a survivor	Looking back at this timeline, what do you learn from dealing with setbacks? What does that tell you?

  - Reflection rather than blame – shame is not helpful or constructive.
  - No hindsight bias – assess on what was known at the time.

- Step Four: Ask the client whether there was a time in their life when they did something wise . . . or when they coped with adversity?
- Step Five: Can these skills/competences in handling ambiguous situations help the client deal with their current problems?

To enable a more systematic approach to the use of timeline data within CBT a series of Socratic questions to be used [11] are written below when exploring a timeline with a client and to agree a coherent narrative that can subsequently emerge. Table 23.1 lists suggested Socratic questions and contextualises these within a task-oriented frame of reference.

There is no commentary or attitude required about events and experiences, as individuals are asked to list events they consider important. The viewpoint adopted by clients is encouraged by use of the following phrase. 'Everything you have lived through has helped to make you the person you are today.'

A worksheet for the timeline is introduced in Figure 23.1.

Timelines and Wisdom Enhancement in CBT

Example of Using Timelines in CBT with Older People

Geraldine, a 90-year-old widow living on her own, overcoming a fall from a broken pelvis, provides a good example of how to use timelines within CBT. Geraldine was originally referred by her family doctor for help with agoraphobia. Initially, Geraldine made good progress in treatment and was rapidly overcoming her anxiety symptoms. Unfortunately,

Name: ______________________ Date of Next Appointment:__/__/___

Life is full of ups and downs, and experiences may sometimes challenge our beliefs about ourselves or may 'teach' us something. Everything we live through helps make us the person we are today. This worksheet may help you review your own ups and downs in your own lifetime. When completing this sheet try not to evaluate whether the experience is good or bad or even whether you are good or bad. It may be that as you look back on your life (your timeline) you can identify a few key moments in life. These may be events you are proud, but equally they be events that evoke feelings of shame or embarrassment. Alternatively there may be some bittersweet moments. When you complete this task, think of your whole lifetime and add all that you think is important. If you need to, please use the back of this sheet to add additional events. Please complete the 'timeline' here by first put your date of birth at the top of the timeline and under the bottom horizontal line write todays date. Use this space tin-between to note events across your life you consider important. Use both sides of the line to make the most of the space. Your therapist will want to review your timeline with you at your next appointment.

DoB

Figure 23.1 Timeline worksheet. Reproduced with permission from the American Psychological Association (APA).

Geraldine fell and broke her pelvis and was admitted to hospital. She was treated in hospital for a few weeks and then discharged. Initially when she was discharged she said to her therapist 'Is it (life) going to be worth it now I can't walk?'

This was challenging for both therapist and client. The therapist having visited Geraldine in hospital prior to her discharge home had taken the opportunity to consult with medical and nursing staff about the prognosis and likelihood of Geraldine being able to walk. The nurse matron confirmed that Geraldine would walk again but may require a stick and it would take many months before she recovered her confidence. The timeline was useful for the therapist here in two main respects: first it reminded the therapist that the client had overcome adversity in the past and had resources they could encourage their client to dip into. In this respect this may just be enough to prevent therapists from becoming passive and to maintain an expectation for change over treatment. Second, the timeline reminds clients they have been in difficult circumstances before that they have overcome and this elicits hope for possible change. In the timeline created by Geraldine there are a number of experiences that can be recruited to be used to promote a sense of hope. From the timeline it is evident that losing her husband was a big event in her life and one that she dreaded. Geraldine was one such woman. She and her husband were married in the early 1950s and were unable to have children at a time when friends and relatives were having large families. At the age of 77 after 51 years of marriage she was left widowed and alone. Yet, Geraldine coped with this significant event and while she was affected by this she was not consumed by her sadness and loss: 'I don't know how I coped, I just did . . . we used to go everywhere together.' She did not present for help at this time and she managed by herself by engaging with her friends and creating a support network for herself, commenting that she 'made [her]self content'.

These events may be observed by the therapist with an appreciation for what the individual has overcome, all the while retaining a sense of wonder as to how one might cope with these events oneself. It may be that the therapist is left wondering how and to what extent they may cope as effectively as the client sitting in front of them. This is an essential starting point when working with older people. We need to recognise and respect the resilience and resources of the clients we work with.

It is interesting that one can recruit many experiences from Geraldine's timeline and this is generally true of all our older clients. A few months later Geraldine noted that some days she feels much improved overall, saying 'Ooh, I'm a lot better now.' In Geraldine's timeline (see Figure 23.2) there is evidence of her having overcome many difficult situations and evidence of personal strength and courage. In reviewing the event of her not being able to have children she had made a decision early on after consulting her doctor that protracted tests (in the 1950s) would not result in any positive outcome and she was concerned for the effect on her close relationship with her husband if it turned out that he was unable to father children. So she decided to say that *she* couldn't have children. When she was asked, if you could go back in time as you are now, and talk to your younger self at that time what would you say, she replied, 'I think I made the right decision, if asked I know I made the right decision.' It struck me how courageous and strong Geraldine was when talking about this.

She had not always been confident in herself and recalled that when she was very young she passed her 11+ and was given a scholarship to attend a grammar school where she felt inferior as the other girls were from more affluent families, and in 1930s Britain the distinction between working class and middle class could be quite sharp. Going back to her younger self she would say now, 'Forget it and get on with it.' This may at first glance seem quite harsh but it was said in an affirmative manner, in that she was acknowledging

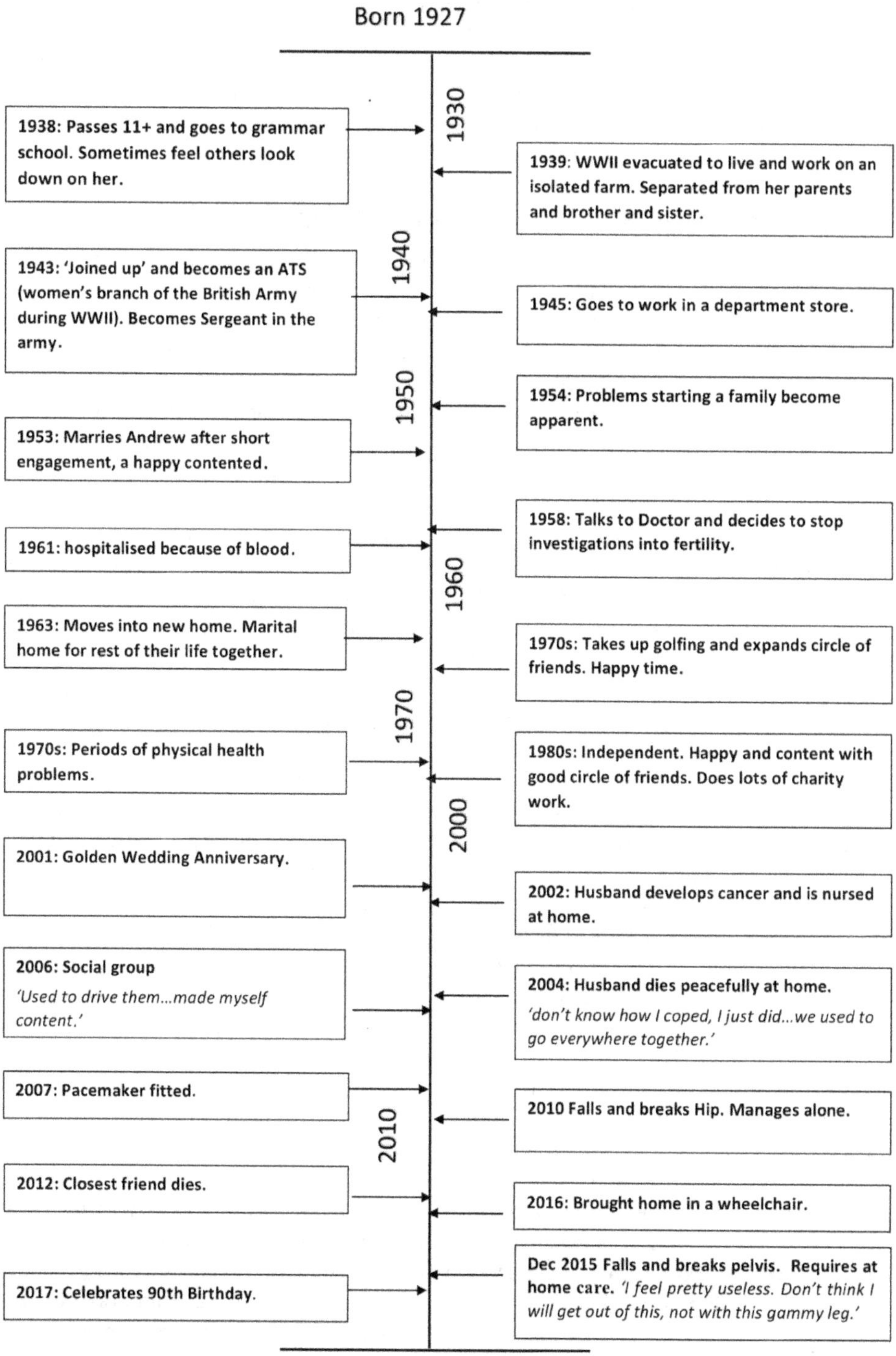

Figure 23.2 Example of Geraldine's completed timeline.

that she couldn't change the attitudes of others but that shouldn't hold her younger self back. Her schooling was interrupted by the war.

By the time Geraldine was ready for discharge she was able to say she was '[I am]More in control of myself now than when you first came to see me . . . Didn't seem to be able to make my mind up to do anything [then], was as low as it was possible to get . . . Doing so much more now. Convinced I am better in my self.'

Selection, Optimisation with Compensation

Selection, optimisation with compensation (SOC) is a meta-theory of ageing first proposed by Baltes and colleagues [36] where older people faced with age-related challenges proactively employ three loss-based self-regulatory processes (i.e. Selection, Optimisation, Compensation) in order to manage the effects of age-related losses (Loss-based SOC) and to optimise functioning in valued roles and goals (Elective SOC). When individuals are confronted by a potential loss in a valued activity, they proactively allocate resources to mitigate the impact on them. In this instance, selection (**S**) focuses upon potential types and a range of strategies that may permit continued engagement in valued roles and goals. Additionally, if one intentionally engages more time and effort in a focussed selection of actions this allows an individual to optimise functioning (**O**). Finally as it not always possible to continue in valued roles and goals as one had done earlier in life, compensation (**C**) means an individual may attempt to change how they do things in order to continue to function optimally in valued roles and goals. Baltes [36] cites the example of Arthur Rubinstein who intuitively applied all three elements of SOC in order to continue to function as a world-renowned pianist and to continue playing to audiences to great acclaim throughout his life. As noted by Baltes [36], Rubinstein was aware of age challenging his virtuosity. In response and in order to continue to function in a valued area of his life, when touring, he selected (S) his large musical repertoire into a more manageable size, and so as to maintain optimal performance he was able to practice his selected repertoire more frequently, thus optimising (O) his performance. To compensate (C) for potential losses of dexterity he would imperceptibly (to audiences at least) slow his playing prior to changes in tempo during performances so that people perceived him to perform as he had as a younger man. A clinical example of SOC in CBT comes from 82-year-old Alasdair. He has been living with degenerative spinal disease and chronic pain for many years. He is a retired astronomer and is writing a book for interested non-experts. His pain intrudes upon his ability to concentrate and to sit and write his book. At times he has forced himself to sit at his computer for hours so as to complete his book, but this has caused pain and recently progress has been very slow, so he is now very demoralised about the prospect of ever finishing his book and this impacts on his low mood. When his therapist talked to Alasdair about using SOC as a means of progressing his book, the therapist explained SOC by using the example of Rubinstein and this was an intriguing idea to him. This was an intriguing idea to him. Alasdair and his therapist came up with a plan based on SOC. Alasdair would **select** the most optimal time of the day to work (this took some time to find the best time), he would **optimize** his progress by working on his book every day of a working week. To compensate for his pain and lowered concentration levels, Alasdair agreed with his therapist to reduce his time spent sitting at his computer working on his manuscript. The plan was for him to work between 10-20 minutes in the first instance and to gradually increase this but within limits. This compensatory strategy aims to ensure that work completed is better quality and progress on a regular basis may become more motivating. This type of work often requires modification and adjustment. Initial good progress was reported but changes to circumstances proved additional challenges. This work is ongoing. SOC is a problem-oriented strategy that can be used with CBT to deal with the reality of challenging life circumstances and by employing a purposeful approach resulting in how we approach valued roles and goals we can maintain engagement in these resulting in minimised loss, and enhanced well-being.

Concluding Remarks

The idea of wisdom enhancement in CBT with older people is a new idea that makes use of a simple timeline technique. The timeline is a positive psychological intervention to enable an individual to recognise their strengths and resilience. It enables an individual to reframe their sense of self and to take ownership of the past. It can help the therapist build a strong therapeutic relationship with their clients as it engenders respect for the competences that have been gained over a lifetime (life skills). It is based on a very simple technique that requires little in the way of technology as a timeline can be completed by anyone who can write simply.

Timelines remind therapists and clients that they can use past experiences to cope better in the present and the future. Timelines help people learn lessons and develop wisdom in the process by encouraging reflection on dealing with adversity and encouraging attentional deployment towards growth and resilience.

Timelines help therapists and clients recognise that our clients have developed 'life skills' after dealing with adverse circumstances. Life skills develop after adversity through overcoming challenging life circumstances, once people have been able to reflect on what they have learned from these experiences. As such people may be wiser than they think and may also be stronger than they give themselves credit. Consequently, reflecting on events from the past as life lessons affords a chance to develop psychological growth and a better appreciation of how to tackle difficult life events as they arise.

Learning Log: Reflection and Review

- Consider completing a timeline using your own life to see how it feels and to see what wisdom you may already possess? Remember wisdom is not an outcome of age. Use the timeline worksheet and start to trace out significant events from your own life. List them chronologically but do not necessarily start at the top and work down. Add in events as you remember them.
- Be honest with yourself in completing this task. Add in the events you are most proud of. It can be your first job, or a significant event like a marriage or birth of a child. It may not be a big event to other people but it will be significant to you. These are called 'peak events'. Now add in events that you are less proud of. It may be the failure of an important task or role, or it may involve not having been able to help a client or a friend or a loved one. It may involve having lost someone, it may involve regret because of what you did, or even perhaps what you didn't do. You may look back and see this as a time when you did not live up to your ideals for self or your values. These are called 'nadir events'.
- Be forgiving of yourself. If this was someone else what would you say to help them in this circumstance? Self-forgiveness will improve your psychological health. The goal is to become more self-accepting. It means accepting ourselves for our flaws as well as our weaknesses. See yourself as a work in progress and accept as being the same. It is good to be forgiving of others, but is important to be forgiving of ourselves. Remember that 'being human means being flawed and imperfect and learning from one's mistakes' [38, p. 26].

- Use the techniques outlined and reflect on how your view of yourself may have changed. If you plan to use this technique with others when applying CBT then it is really helpful for you to explore how it feels to engage in this task.

Further Reading

You may wish to take your reading further. Here are some recommendations.

The following sources provide more in-depth coverage of topics raised in this chapter.

Laidlaw K. *Cognitive Behaviour Therapy for Older People: An Introduction*. London: SAGE Publications; 2015.

Reynolds 3rd CF, Jeste, DV, Sachdev PS, Blazer DG. Mental health care for older adults: recent advances and new directions in clinical practice and research. *World Psychiatry*. 2022;***21*** (3):336–363.

Steffen A, Thompson LW, Gallagher-Thompson D. *Treating Later-Life Depression: A Cognitive-Behavioral Therapy Approach*. 2nd ed. New York: Oxford University Press;2021.

AGE UK/NHSE (2024). *Positive Practice with Older People Guideline*. https://babcp.com/Therapists/Older-Adults-Positive-Practice-Guide.

Marmot M, Allen J, Boyce T, Goldblatt P, Morrison J. *Health Equity in England: The Marmot Review Ten Years On*. London: Institute of Health Equity; 2020.

References

1. Chaplin R, Farquharson L, Clapp M, Crawford M. Comparison of access, outcomes and experiences of older adults and working age adults in psychological therapy. *International Journal of Geriatric Psychiatry*, 2015;**30**:178–184.
2. Saunders R, Buckman JEJ, Stott J, Leibowitz J, Aguirre E, John A, et al. Older adults respond better to psychological therapy than working age adults: Evidence from a large sample of mental health service attendees. *Journal of Affective Disorders*, 2021;**294**:85–93.
3. Rubin D, Berntsen D. People over forty feel 20% younger than their age: Subjective age across the lifespan. *Psychonomic Bulletin & Review*, 2006;**13**(5):776–780.
4. Kornadt AE, Albert I, Hoffmann M, Murdock E, Nell J. Ageism and older people's health and well-being during the COVID-19-pandemic: The moderating role of subjective aging. *European Journal of Ageing*, 2021;**18**(2):173–184.
5. Kotter-Grühn D, Kornadt A, Stephan Y. Looking beyond chronological age: Current knowledge and future directions in the study of subjective age. *Gerontology*, 2016;**62**:86–93.
6. United Nations, Department of Economic and Social Affairs, Population Division. World Population Prospects 2022, Data Sources. UN DESA/POP/2022/DC/NO. 9.
7. Bennett JE, Guianquan L, Foreman K, Best N, Kontis V, Pearson C, et al. The future of life expectancy and life expectancy inequalities in England and Wales: Bayesian spatiotemporal forecasting. *Lancet*, 2015;**386** (9989):P163–170.
8. Marmot M, Allen J, Boyce T, Goldblatt P, Morrison J. *Health Equity in England: The Marmot Review Ten Years On*. London: Institute of Health Equity; 2020.
9. Robine JM. Ageing populations: We are living longer lives, but are we healthier? United Nations, Department of Economics and Social Affairs, Population Division, 2021; UN DESA/POP/2021/TP/NO. 2.

10. Frost R, Beattie A, Bhanu C, Walters K, Ben-Shlomo B. Management of depression and referral of older people to psychological therapies. A systematic review of qualitative studies. *British Journal of General Practice*, 2019;e171.

11. Laidlaw K. CBT with Older People. In A Wenzel (Ed.), *The American Psychological Association's Handbook of Cognitive Behavioral Therapy, Vol. 2 Applications*. Washington DC: APA; 2021.

12. Rodda J, Walker Z, Carter J. Depression in older adults. *BMJ-British Medical Journal*, 2011;**343**(8):d5219.

13. Haigh EAP, Bogucki OE, Sigmon ST, Blazer DG. Depression among older adults: A 20-year update on five common myths and misconceptions. *American Journal of Geriatric Psychiatry*, 2018;**26**(1):107–122.

14. Carstensen LL. Socioemotional selectivity theory: The role of perceived endings in human motivation. *The Gerontologist*, 2021;**61**(8):1188–1196.

15. Sims T, Hogan CL, Carstensen LL. Selectivity as an emotion regulation strategy: Lessons from older adults. *Current Opinion in Psychology*, 2015;**3**:80–84.

16. Stretton J, Schweizer S, Dalgleish T. Age-related enhancements in positive emotionality across the lifespan: Structural equation modelling of brain and behaviour. *Journal of Neuroscience*, 2022;**42**(16):3461–3472.

17. Urry HL, Gross JJ. Emotion regulation and older age. *Current Directions in Psychological Science*, 2010;**19**:352–357.

18. Sims T, Carstensen LL. The elusiveness of a life-span model of emotional regulation. *ISSBD Bull.* 2014;**38**(3):30–32.

19. Scheibe S, Sheppes G, Staudinger UM. Distract or reappraise? Age-related differences in emotion-regulation choice. *Emotion*, 2015;**15**:677–681.

20. Sadavoy J. An integrated model for defining the scope of psychogeriatrics: the five Cs. *International Psychogeriatrics*, 2009;**21**:805–812.

21. Salo KI, Scharfen J, Wilden I, Schubotz R, Holling H. Confining the concept of vascular depression to late-onset depression: A meta-analysis of MRI-defined hyperintensity burden in major depressive disorder and bipolar disorder. *Frontiers in Psychology*, 2019;**10**.

22. Jeste DV, Lee EE. The emerging empirical science of wisdom: Definition, measurement, neurobiology, longevity, and interventions. *Harvard Review of Psychiatry*, 2019; **27**(3):127–140.

23. Weststrate NM, Glück J . Hard-earned wisdom: Exploratory processing of difficult life experience is positively associated with wisdom. *Developmental Psychology*, 2017;**53**(4):800–814.

24. Glück J, Weststrate NM. The wisdom researchers and the elephant: An integrative model of wise behavior. *Personality and Social Psychology Review*, 2022;**26**(4):342–374.

25. Laidlaw K. *Cognitive Behaviour Therapy for Older People: An Introduction*. London: SAGE Publications; 2015.

26. Lubian K, Weich S, Stansfeld S, Bebbington P, Brugha T, Spiers N, McManus, S, Cooper C. Chapter 3: Mental health treatment and services. In: McManus S, Bebbington P, Jenkins R, Brugha T (eds.), *Mental Health and Wellbeing in England: Adult Psychiatric Morbidity Survey 2014*. Leeds: NHS Digital; 2016.

27. Laidlaw K, Kishita N. Age appropriate augmented CBT for enhancing treatment outcome with older people. *Geropsych: The Journals of Gerontopsychology and Geriatric Psychiatry*. 2015;**28**:57–66.

28. Bilbrey AC, Laidlaw K, Cassidy-Eagle E, Thompson LW, Gallagher-Thompson D. Cognitive behavioral therapy for late life depression: Evidence, issues, and recommendations. *Cognitive & Behavioral Practice*, 2022;**29**(1):128–145. https://doi.org/10.1016/j.cbpra.2020.02.003.

29. Kadri A, Leddy A, Gracey F, Laidlaw K. (2022). Wisdom enhancement and lifeskills to augment CBT outcomes for depression in later life: A series of N-of-1 trials.

Behavioural & Cognitive Psychotherapy, 2022;**50**:508–527.

30. Williams JMG, Barnhopfer T, Crane C, Hedrmans D, Raes F, Watkins E, Dalgleish T. Autobiographical memory specificity and emotional disorder. *Psychological Bulletin*, 2007;**133**:122–144, https://doi.org/10.1037/0033-2909.133.1.122.
31. Wisco BE, Nolen-Hoeksema S. (2010). Valence of autobiographical memories: the role of mood, cognitive reappraisal, and suppression. *Behaviour Research and Therapy*, **48**(4):335–340. doi.10.1016/j.brat.2009.11.009.
32. Edward R. Watkins ER. Depressive rumination: Investigating mechanisms to improve cognitive behavioural treatments. *Cognitive Behaviour Therapy*, 2009;**38**: S1:8–14.
33. Watkins E. *Rumination-Focused Cognitive-Behavioral Therapy for Depression*. New York: Guilford; 2016.
34. Barnard LK, Curry JF. Self-compassion: Conceptualizations, correlates, and interventions. *Review of General Psychology*, 2011;**15**(4): 289–303.
35. Phillips WJ, Ferguson SJ (2012). Self-compassion: A resource for positive aging. *The Journals of Gerontology Series B: Psychological Sciences and Social Sciences*, 2012. doi.10.1093/geronb/gbs091.
36. Baltes PB, Baltes MM. Psychological perspectives on successful aging: The model of selective optimization with compensation. In Baltes PB, Baltes MM (eds.), *Successful Aging: Perspectives from the Behavioral Sciences*. pp. 1–34. New York: Cambridge University Press; 1990.
37. Laidlaw K. Self-acceptance and aging: Using self-acceptance as a mediator of change in CBT with depressed and anxious older people. In Bernard ME (ed.), *The Strength of Self-Acceptance*. Melbourne: Springer Publications; 2013.
38. Neff KD, Vonk R. Self-compassion versus global self-esteem: Two different ways of relating to oneself. *Journal of Personality*, 2009;**77**(1):23–50.
39. American Psychological Association (2024). Guidelines for Psychological Practice with Older Adults. Retrieved from https://www.apa.org/practice/guidelines/older-adults.pdf.
40. Boerema, A.M., Kleiboer, A., Beekman, A. T., van Zoonen, K., Dijkshoorn, H., Cuijpers P. (2016). Determinants of help-seeking behavior in depression: a cross-sectional study. BMC Psychiatry. 23, 16:78. doi: 10.1186/s12888-016-0790-0.

Chapter 24

Using Cognitive Behavioural Therapy with Family Caregivers of Persons Living with Dementia

Dolores Gallagher-Thompson, Jennifer Ramsey, Ann Choryan Bilbrey and Julian Montoro-Rodriguez

This chapter will help you to be able to:

- Describe an overview of the approach to using CBT with dementia caregivers.
- Critically appraise the evidence-base for CBT for caregivers.
- Exercise choice of use of CBT with a range of issues affecting dementia caregivers based on the evidence-base for CBT.
- Function more confidently as an evidence-based practitioner of CBT working with a range of dementia caregivers.

Introduction

According to the World Health Organization, dementia is a global problem affecting an estimated 50 million people worldwide, with the prevalence of Alzheimer's disease and related dementias (ADRD) expected to double in the next 30 years [72]. Dementia itself is an umbrella term used to encompass several neurological disorders, of which Alzheimer's disease is most common, followed by vascular dementia and dementia with Lewy bodies [2]. Although the various subtypes have unique characteristics which distinguish them, all persons living with dementia (PLWD) experience progressive cognitive deficits (e.g. memory loss and issues with planning and organisation) plus a variety of behavioural problems (e.g. repetitive questioning, wandering) and neuropsychiatric symptoms (e.g. delusional thinking, suspiciousness) that result in progressive inability to care for oneself and consequent reliance on family, friends, and other sources of support. Most PLWD reside at home so that the community and family members play a vital role in maintaining their quality of life [2,3].

As of 2021, there were an estimated 260 million informal caregivers in the 18 member countries of the International Alliance of Carer Organizations (IACO) [31]. Care recipients may suffer from a variety of physical, mental and/or neurological disorders requiring various kinds of ongoing assistance, including emotional and organisational help, financial support and, in some instances, personal care. Extent and type of specific care needs depends on the nature of the care recipients' chronic illness and where they are in the progression of their disease. In this chapter we will use the term *caregiver* and will focus on the mental health of family members caring for an older adult with ADRD. There are several reasons for this including the fact that most research describing the impact of caregiving on caregivers' mental health focuses on those caring for an ADRD relative or friend, as does most published intervention research [60,61].

While it is difficult to describe the typical caregiver of a PLWD, sources from the US and internationally [2,3] suggest that a few generalisations are appropriate. First, most caregivers are women. This may reflect the fact that in most cultures, women fulfil caregiving roles throughout their lives. Women report more negative impacts from caregiving on their mental health compared to male caregivers. Second, because of this, women request more support and seek mental health services more often. Third, caregivers can be of any age, socioeconomic strata and socio-cultural background; extant research shows that distress is common in virtually all groups studied [72]. Prior to the pandemic, most caregivers were either spouses, or middle-aged daughters or daughters-in-law taking care of aging parents. Since the pandemic began, more younger individuals, age 18–34, became caregivers and often need specific help navigating services including finding peer connections [66]. Fourth, about two-thirds of middle-aged caregivers, age 35–54, are caught between caring for parents and young children. Often employed as well, they have challenging schedules and demands to meet. Known as the *sandwich generation* this group is generally highly stressed [61] and often seek mental health services for their distress. Finally, the next largest group of caregivers is comprised of spouses, whose caregiving experience is very different from that of adult children. Faced with the increasing loss of life as they knew it with their husband or wife, these caregivers often experience feelings of depression and loss. Many of the older generation of spouses (those 75+) have significant medical issues themselves, adding to the burden of care. Recent studies have found that about 20% of older caregivers are uncomfortable with technology – though this percentage is higher in many minoritised groups around the world, due in part to what has been termed the *digital divide* [50]. This discomfort with technology interfered with help-seeking during the pandemic when most, if not all, supportive services were no longer offered face-to-face but only virtually through telehealth platforms.

In summary, caregiving for a PLWD is an international concern since the bulk of long-term care is provided by overworked and often ill-prepared families and community supports. Recent enactment of the National Strategy to Support Family Caregivers by the US Congress (2022) provides both leadership and funding to better address the many unmet needs of this highly diverse group. Other international initiatives are in progress, such as the iSupport on-line program for caregivers worldwide, under the auspices of the WHO (www.who.int/teams/mental-health-and-substance-use/treatment-care/isupport).

Impact of Caregiving on the Caregiver

Caring for a PLWD has both positive and negative effects. On the positive side, many report feeling grateful to be able to 'give back' to a person who loved and cared for them; others report that caregiving gives meaning to their life and strengthens their relationship with the care recipient [67]. At the same time, a number of negative impacts on both mental and physical health have been reported in the literature. These are summarized in the book by Schulz and Eden [61] and in research reports such as Larson and Stroud [35].

A number of factors influence how caregiving is experienced, including the caregiver's cultural background and the value that culture places on the caregiving role [51]; whether the caregiver feels trapped in their role [54]; number of resources available to both caregiver and care recipient [71]; and quantity and quality of the available support network [45]. It is important to note that not all caregivers are depressed, highly anxious or experiencing other negative emotions.

An initial intake (or assessment interview) is helpful to understand these factors and how they interact in the individual caregiver/client you are meeting with. Questions should be included about the following factors: cultural background and identity; relationship to the PLWD; living arrangements; severity of care recipient's cognitive and behavioural problems; amount and intensity of care required; level of subjective burden reported by the caregiver; available resources; and evaluation of caregivers' levels of depression and anxiety, as these are often problematic. Specific recommendations for what information to obtain in the initial interview can be found in *Family Caregiver Distress* by Gallagher-Thompson et al. [20].

Chronic Stress

Chronic stress is an ongoing issue for most caregivers. A recent survey of caregivers for PLWD found that 59% reported high or very high emotional stress from the activities associated with day-to-day caregiving [2]. For many, the caregiving journey is a long one that can take a decade or more. Many of the dementias are progressive and will require more personal hands-on care and increased supervision over time. Everyday care needs of the PLWD and therefore the caregivers' tasks and responsibilities, change over time in what is referred to as the *caregiving trajectory* resulting in significant stress for many, especially caregivers with low resilience and overwhelmed coping skills [25].

Depression and Anxiety

Significant levels of depressive symptoms were first reported about 30 years ago in a study where structured clinical interviews were conducted with dementia family caregivers. The prevalence of clinically significant depression was found to be about 50% [23]. Subsequent work by many researchers found rates between 30–50% depending on the measure used [30]. Certain factors increase the risk of depression: being female, caring for a male care recipient, and being the care recipient's spouse [59].

Anxiety is also common among caregivers. Brodaty and Donkin [73] reviewed several studies that found prevalence of significant anxiety symptoms to be between 16–45% depending on the assessment measures used. In a 2021 review on anxiety, del-Pino-Casada and colleagues found an association between subjective caregiver burden and anxiety symptoms across all informal caregiver groups [18]. It is noteworthy that these researchers could not determine if the caregiver's anxiety elevated their perception of burden or vice-versa.

Strain and Burden

In a 2020 concept analysis of burden, Liu and colleagues define caregiving burden or strain as 'the level of multifaceted strain perceived by the caregiver from caring for a family member and/or loved one over time' [38, p. 442]. Perception of burden differs not only between types of caregivers [55] but also according to stressors such as care demands, caregiver motivation, coping style, and external support ([54]; see Figure 24.1). High burden is associated with lower reported wellbeing, higher rates of depression and anxiety and lower resilience [60]. However, burden is not equally endorsed by all caregivers. Many find it discordant with their cultural values and beliefs to think about, much less talk about, caregiving in this way. For example, cultural groups that strongly endorse the value of filial piety, such as many Asian groups, do not typically report high burden, although they often endorse depressive symptoms [69].

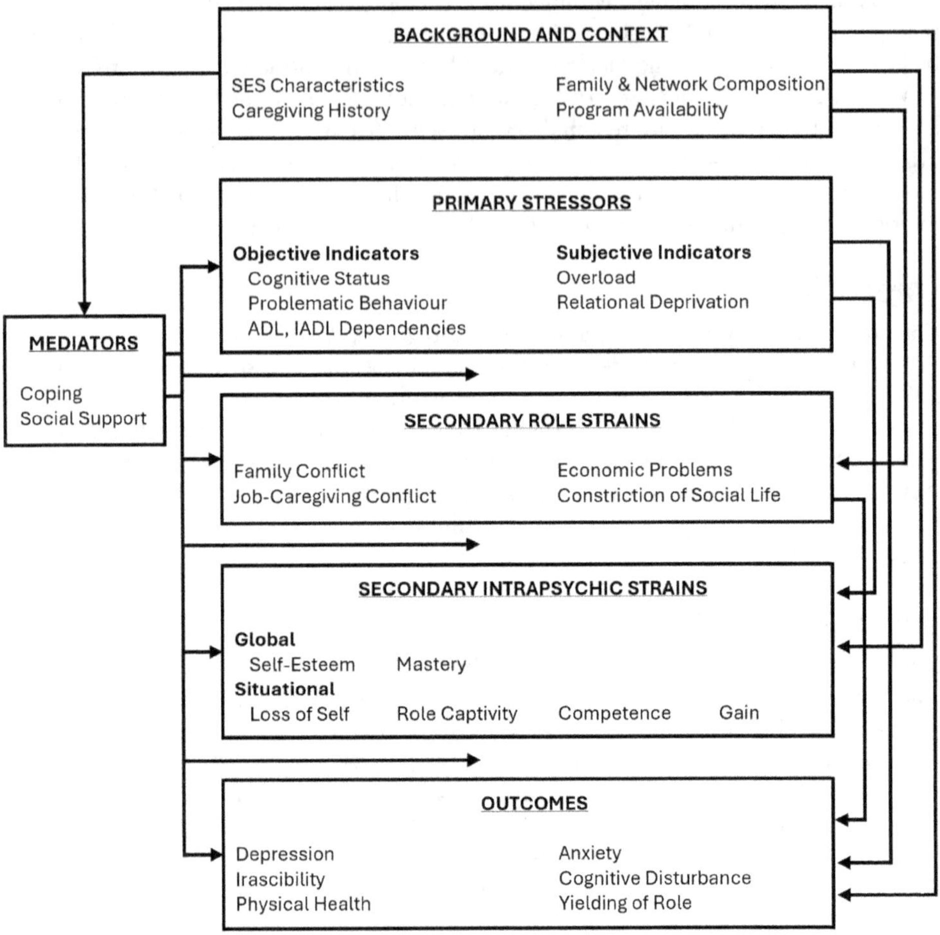

Figure 24.1 Stress process model of caregiving (adapted from [54]). Reproduced with permission from Oxford University Press.

Theoretical Models

Folkman and Lazarus [36] first described the basic 'stress and coping' model that launched caregiving research. They posited that one's response to a stressor depends both on one's perception of the threat and one's perceived coping resources to handle it. If the latter become overwhelmed, significant distress results. In 1990, Pearlin and associates developed the stress-process model to include the fact that 'stress' for caregivers is often multifactorial. As well, response to stressors varies with several factors in addition to one's coping abilities, such as available social and instrumental supports ([54]; see Figure 24.1). Around the same time Bandura published his theory of self-efficacy, which refers to an individual's belief in their capacity to execute behaviours necessary to produce specific results [7,8]. Individuals lacking that confidence are more likely to experience distress in challenging situations. Several caregiver intervention researchers studied the relationship of perceived self-efficacy to improvement in distress indices (e.g. depressive symptoms) and found that it played

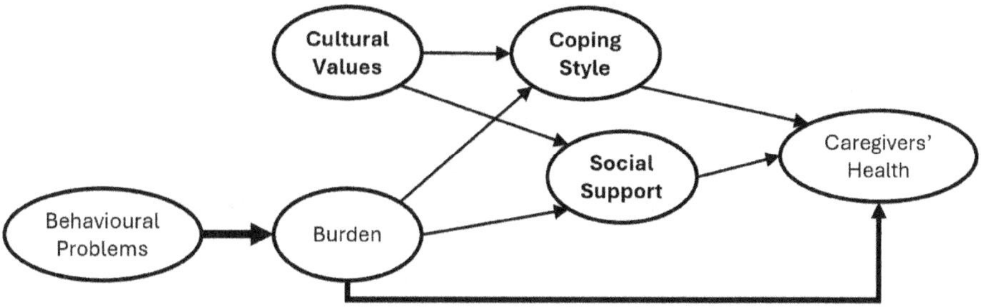

Figure 24.2 The Revised Sociocultural Stress and Coping Model for Caregivers. Reproduced with permission from Oxford University Press.
Note. The revised sociocultural stress and coping model presented here includes only key variables, with the three variables believed to vary across cultural groups presented in bold. Adapted from [34].

a mediating role. Caregivers with low self-efficacy before and after intervention had poorer outcomes compared to those whose self-efficacy increased. Self-efficacy improves when intervention programs teach specific coping skills relevant to caregiving, such as stress management techniques and improving communication [6,70,43]. In general, higher self-efficacy is associated with a stronger, more positive response to a variety of intervention methods including psychotherapy and psychoeducational programs [16].

It is noteworthy that these models did not take account of how diverse cultural values and beliefs could affect caregivers' distress. Aranda and Knight [74] developed a sociocultural model of caregiver stress which emphasised the importance of knowing about elements of diversity in the caregiver's background – such as their ethnic and/or racial identity – and understanding how that affects role expectations, willingness to seek help, and access to services (see Figure 24.2). Subsequent research by Pinquart and Sorenson [56] found many differences along these lines based on race, ethnicity and/or cultural identity. For example, racial/ethnic minority caregivers of PLWD often report higher levels of depression as well as less outside help, more caregiving hours, and more complex tasks due to comorbidity of other health problems along with dementia, as well as lower levels of formal service use [19].

Taken together, these theoretical advances led to development of several effective interventions to reduce distress. However, the majority did not employ methods of psychotherapy; rather, psychoeducational programs became prominent and are still widely used today both in the US and internationally [2,16,73]. Their efficacy has been reviewed in recent publications [15,16,17,64,65].

There are several reasons for the popularity of psychoeducational programs, including the fact that many are considered evidence-based or evidence-informed by professional organisations evaluating such programs, such as the Benjamin Rose Institute on Aging's Best Practice Caregiving website which is specific to intervention programs for dementia caregivers: https://benrose.org/best-practice-caregiving. As well, they are less costly to provide since master's level clinicians can be effectively trained, in contrast to providers with more advanced training (such as MDs or PhDs) whose time is compensated at a higher level. In addition, many are delivered by staff in agencies that provide other services to dementia caregivers, such as respite care or support groups, rather than by providers in private practice. Having a trusted provider recommend participation in such programs likely increases caregivers' acceptance.

Table 24.1 Psychological intervention categories

Counselling and Psychotherapy	For individuals, family, and CGs by trained providers Targets: significant mental health problems including CG specific distress/burden, depression, anxiety, and stress
Psychoeducation	For small groups of 6–12 CGs by trained facilitator Provides education and instruction in adaptive skills within a structured format Possible Components: education, skills training in a variety of topics benefiting CG or the CR, or goal setting
Multicomponent Interventions	For CGs and Family by trained providers Several established intervention strategies blended into one program Possible Components: education, skills training, counselling, problem-solving, support group, or home modifications
Mindfulness-based Interventions	For individuals CGs or groups of CGs May be part of individual therapy or psychoeducational program Possible Components: breathing techniques, relaxation exercises, or meditation
Support Groups	For Groups of CGs lead by providers, facilitators or peers Goal is to provide support to CGs Possible Components: non-judgemental listening, info on community services, or education

Note: Adapted from [15] and [16].

Finally, many caregivers are reluctant to seek help for themselves, putting their care recipient's needs ahead of their own, so are unlikely to go to a mental health clinic or provider [52]. Psychoeducational programs were designed partly to address this barrier. They are promoted as educational in nature rather than as a form of therapy and so are accepted by many caregivers. Table 24.1 depicts the various forms of psychological intervention that have been used to improve dementia caregivers' mental health. Explanations of these categories are found in Cheng et al. [16].

Effective Forms of Psychotherapy for Dementia Family Caregivers

Both cognitive-behavioural therapy (CBT) and acceptance and commitment therapy (ACT) are efficacious to reduce depression in dementia caregivers. There is some evidence that ACT also significantly reduces anxiety. In this chapter we focus exclusively on CBT, although it is well to keep in mind that ACT is considered a 'third wave' of CBT. In contrast to original CBT, ACT helps the caregiver to notice and accept difficult thoughts and feelings – rather than questioning or changing or modifying them. ACT helps clients identify what they value in life (e.g. a positive relationship with their care recipient) and act in ways that are consistent with those values (e.g. keep a gratitude journal focussed on what the caregiver is grateful for, in their relationship with the PLWD). This approach is very relevant to dementia caregivers who often must accept many things that they cannot change about their care recipient, their lives, and their future. The interested reader is referred to Losada [42,43] for more in-depth discussion of how ACT can be used effectively with dementia caregivers.

CBT for Caregiver Depression: Individual and Group Psychotherapy

CBT is theoretically rooted in the work of Aaron T. Beck and colleagues [9] which was developed to treat clinical depression in adult outpatients. It posits that depressed persons have unrealistically negative views of themselves, their future, and the world around them. Cognitive therapy teaches skills to evaluate one's thoughts and develop more realistic views. It focuses on the here and now rather than on the past and is goal-oriented and time-limited, which makes it appealing to people who are dealing with real-life challenges such as long-term caregiving. Lewinsohn and colleagues [37] added a behavioural component, having observed that depression is sustained when there is limited positive reinforcement from the environment and from oneself. His view is that engaging in positive activities on a regular basis will improve mood by providing the person with this much-needed positive reinforcement.

Our work with depressed caregivers always includes behavioural activation as a key component, based largely on Lewinsohn's model. See Bilbrey et al. [11] for a detailed description of this approach. In brief, behavioural activation with depressed caregivers consists of helping them to identify key positive activities that they used to enjoy but are no longer doing or doing less frequently because of their caregiving responsibilities. These include activities that are meaningful, pleasurable and/or rewarding. The focus is first on small things that can be incorporated into everyday life, such as listening to music or going for a walk. Caregivers rate whether or not these activities actually lift their mood. Once they see the relationship between activities and mood, their personal list can be expanded to include more complex things such as going to lunch with a friend, which requires planning, particularly in later stages of dementia when the PLWD cannot be left unsupervised. Besides identifying and scheduling these activities, caregivers learn to anticipate barriers and to problem solve so that the activity can actually occur. Usually, this approach requires four to six sessions. It can be done over a secure telehealth platform or in person. For some caregivers, this is sufficient to improve their depression so CBT is terminated at that time.

However, in our experience, most caregivers who are significantly depressed require a full CBT approach where their thoughts, as well as their behaviours, are addressed. Several therapeutic issues that arise in this situation are discussed in two recent books on CBT with middle aged and older adults [62,63] and in a new volume *Family Caregiver Distress* for clinicians [20].

There is a growing body of research that illustrates the efficacy of using CBT with distressed caregivers. Both individual and group CBT can be efficacious. Akkerman and Ostwald [1] found that anxious caregivers randomised to a nine-week group CBT program reported improvement in anxiety on self-report and clinician-administered measures, both at post-test and at nine-month follow up. In a group CBT intervention targeting dysfunctional thinking, several studies found that caregivers reported fewer dysfunctional thoughts about caregiving and less depressive symptomatology [43,44,57]. CBT group interventions can also be culturally tailored as illustrated by the study done by Gonyea and colleagues [27] which successfully targeted neuropsychiatric symptom management for Latinos.

Efficacy of CBT with Individual Caregivers

An early randomized controlled trial by Gallagher-Thompson and Steffen [24] enrolled caregivers with a diagnosis of major depressive disorder and compared short term psychodynamic therapy with CBT of comparable length to evaluate comparative efficacy. Results indicated that length of time as a caregiver was a key mediating variable: those who had been in the caregiving role for four years or more responded more effectively to CBT in terms of reduced symptoms of depression and fewer caregivers meeting criteria for major depression at post-evaluation. In contrast, those who were caregivers for a shorter time benefitted more from the psychodynamic approach. Authors hypothesised that in the early stages of caregiving, the theme of loss is often dominant and psychodynamic therapy can focus on that type of distress, whereas longer-term caregivers may need the active coping skills approach of CBT to help maintain hope that there are still things they can do to improve quality of life for themselves and their loved one.

A landmark study conducted by Losada and colleagues [42] compared CBT and ACT for depressed caregivers of PLWD. Results indicated that both were efficacious in reducing caregivers' depression at post evaluation. In addition, ACT had a significant effect on caregivers' anxiety, suggesting that different mechanisms may be operative in the two approaches.

More recently, Meichsner and colleagues [46] conducted a CBT-based therapist-guided intervention via the internet that was tailored to caregivers' individual needs. They found significant effects for coping with the anticipated death of the care recipient and for greater utilisation of psychosocial resources at conclusion of therapy. However, no treatment effect was found for depression or burden.

Taken together, the fact that there are so few studies of CBT with depressed and/or anxious caregivers underscores the fact that these individuals find it difficult to prioritize their own mental health needs. As well, practical issues such as accessibility (being able to attend appointments in person as long as there is someone to stay with the PLWD for the time needed) and cost most likely limit their participation. Yet the work that has been done clearly supports the efficacy of CBT to treat significant depression in dementia caregivers (see Table 24.2).

CBT for Caregiver Depression: Psychoeducational Programs

These programs incorporate key elements of CBT (such as behavioural activation, re-appraisal of negative thoughts about caregiving and use of goal setting to facilitate home practice) but are not considered psychotherapy. They are termed 'psychoeducation' because they provide information and teach relevant skills. They also provide caregivers with opportunities to interact with and learn from one another in a small group which fosters supportive relationships. They are de-stigmatizing in that caregivers do not have to declare themselves to need psychological help in order to participate, and many are offered by agencies that provide other caregiver services such as respite. This co-location factor likely increases accessibility.

There are several evidence-based psychoeducational programs that reduce distress in dementia caregivers, including reducing symptoms of depression, anxiety, stress or burden. Several such programs that are in fairly widespread use in the US include 'Coping with Caregiving' [10,21,22] and its on-line derivative 'Caregiver TLC: Thrive, Learn, Connect' [49], as well as 'Savvy Caregivers' [28,53], and 'Building Better Caregivers' [41]. All have in common that they are closed groups (e.g. 8–12 caregivers typically) and time-limited (e.g.

Table 24.2 Effectiveness of CBT by delivery format, delivery modality and intensity

Studies Providing Cognitive-Behaviour Therapy				
Delivery format	**Delivery modality**	**Intensity**	**Outcomes**	**References**
group	face-to-face	medium-high & high/intensive	anxiety; burden; depressive symptoms; dysfunctional thoughts; mental health	Akkerman & Otswald [1]; Arango-Lasprilla et al. [5]; Losada et al. [43]; Márquez-González et al. [44]; Rodriguez-Sanchez et al. [57]
group	face-to-face & telephone	medium-high	depressive symptoms	Gonyea et al. [27]
individual	Internet delivery	high/intensive	acceptability; depression; coping with pre-death; utilization of resources; burden; emotional wellbeing	Meichsner et al. [46]
individual	face-to-face	medium-high & high/intensive	anxiety; depressive symptoms; dysfunctional thoughts; experiential avoidance	Gallagher-Thompson and Steffen [24]

Notes: Intensity classifications are based on Brodaty and colleagues [12]: as minimal (1–2 sessions); moderate (3–5 sessions), medium-high (6–10 sessions), or high/intensive (>10 sessions).

4–8 sessions); meet weekly for a set period of time; are led by trained facilitators; and use a combination of education, caregiver interaction and home practice to teach a specific set of skills known to affect caregiver resilience. Skills vary by program but in general, all include strategies for stress management and caregiver self-care as well as methods for handling difficult care recipient behaviours, and ways to improve communication with the care recipient, other family members and/or care providers.

Several have been culturally adapted for different racial/ethnic groups and when appropriate, translated into other languages including Spanish and Chinese. Comparable outcomes are reported among these diverse groups as with non-Hispanic whites for whom they were originally developed [47]. A similar psychoeducational program developed and implemented in the UK found analogous results. The START (STrAtegies for RelaTives) has shown long-term effectiveness in reducing depressive and anxiety symptoms and is utilised in many parts of UK [39,40]. Other effective psychoeducational programs include one that uses problem-solving to decrease depressive and anxiety symptoms and negative problem-orientation [26], and a benefit finding intervention that uses positive psychology principles and thought-modification [14,15] to achieve beneficial effects with dementia caregivers in Hong Kong. In addition to using CBT-based psychoeducational programs with dementia family caregivers, others have successfully employed them with grandparents caring for grandchildren who are without parent(s) due to death, incarceration, abandonment, or work schedules that leave the child alone for long periods of time [48].

Psychoeducational Programs for Grandparents as Caregivers

An unprecedented number of grandparents across developed countries have assumed the primary caregiving role of raising their grandchildren during the past decades. They report positive rewards such as an increased sense of meaning in their lives and feelings of reassurance that their grandchildren receive adequate care; however, they also experience multiple physical, emotional and financial strains, leading to high levels of psychological distress. Researchers have developed programs to support the mental health and quality of life of grandparent caregivers, and a few evidence-based interventions reporting moderate levels of efficacy have emerged. Despite methodological limitations, the best available evidence suggests that grandparent caregiver's interventions within the cognitive-behavioural spectrum have the most empirical support. For example, recent work by Montoro-Rodriguez et al. [48], evaluated the efficacy of a goal-setting psychoeducational skill-training program. Caregivers attended six weekly small group sessions to learn how to identify healthy ways to reduce stress, improve communication skills, learn positive parenting practices, manage their grandchildren's behavioural problems and seek help from others. Grandparents who received this program reduced their level of depression, improved their parental efficacy and increased their ability to choose effective goals. Success was related to the dual emphasis on goal setting and solution-based thinking in each session.

Case Example: CBT with a Moderately Depressed Caregiver (PHQ9 = 20)

The following case example illustrates that therapists need to be flexible and employ a variety of CBT skills to ensure a successful outcome.

At the start of therapy, Helen is a 55-year-old primary school teacher in a medium size city whose 80-year-old widowed mother lives with her and her husband John. Helen's two adult children do not live nearby. She has one brother who is a lawyer with a busy practice who spends little time assisting with caregiving for their mother Joan who is the middle stages of dementia due to Alzheimer's disease. Joan is unable to manage her medications, can no longer drive and has little ability to plan ahead. Her judgement is poor: she often wanders away from home and cannot find her way back and she upsets her daughter and son-in-law by calling out for people who aren't there when she's agitated in the evening.

At the start of CBT, Helen had been her mother's caregiver for five years. Initially Joan lived independently but as the dementia progressed that became a safety issue, so two years ago Joan was moved into a room in Helen's home. Helen was initially able to manage her job, caregiving and her marriage. But over time, Joan's increasing dependence and behavioural issues made Helen frustrated and worried about the future. She attended a monthly support group but became increasingly depressed as she saw her life 'narrowing'. Her marriage became more tense as she spent less time with her husband, and her job was harder after a new principal arrived who was not empathic about Helen's need to leave early or take a full day off for caregiving. The last straw was Helen's being reprimanded due to excessive absences; this sent her to her primary doctor for help. She was prescribed anti-depressant medication, but it interacted with other medicines she had to take so it was discontinued, with the recommendation that she seek counselling. One of her friends told her about CBT and suggested a provider in the area.

Helen was seen for 18 sessions of individual CBT spread out over 12 months – mainly because of scheduling challenges. Behavioural activation was done initially so that at least some of her (limited) free time could be spent doing things that were meaningful, enjoyable or rewarding. However, success was limited because of her mother's unpredictable behaviour which made it hard for Helen to maintain her own schedule. Resentment towards her mother was increasing, as Helen realised that the future would see a worsening of the dementia. She shared several of her unhelpful thoughts such as: 'No matter what I do things will only get worse' and 'it's hopeless – John will find someone else who he can play golf with and do other things we used to enjoy together that I can't do anymore'. Methods such as examining the evidence and learning to see things in less 'all or none' terms were used to help Helen get a different perspective on her situation. Through regular completion of thought diaries Helen learned what triggered her negative thoughts and feelings which in turn increased her confidence as a caregiver. For example, 'things will only get worse' was modified into: 'I am a resilient person. I can learn to manage what's ahead just like I'm learning to manage things better now.' And 'I'm focusing only on the negatives with my mother – we've had a good relationship all these years. I will find some positives in all of this and try to build on them.' As far as her relationship with John, she realised she needed to carve out time to do activities with him that they both enjoyed. To do that she would have to make arrangements for someone to be with Joan, who could not be left alone for any length of time.

Teaching Helen techniques for problem-solving was important as well, including how to find reputable in-home supportive care and how to ask for help from her brother. Finally, Helen was encouraged to explore essential community-based resources so she could balance competing demands. Her therapist guided her to find these resources; they also discussed pros and cons of memory care placement in the future as dementia progressed.

Helen's PHQ-9 at termination was 8. She said she was better able to manage her thoughts, feelings and behaviours. About a year later, Helen contacted the therapist for four additional sessions because of a new behavioural issue that had arisen – her mother's incontinence following an episode of bladder cancer. Helen felt she could not manage that at home along with keeping her job and marriage intact. With the help of a social worker in the community, Helen arranged placement for Joan in an excellent memory care facility for which she and her brother split the ongoing costs. She said this was a 'good outcome' and although she felt some guilt, her CBT skills enabled her to make an appropriate decision.

There are several key take-away points from this case example: first, the therapist had to be familiar with appropriate community resources so she could guide this client to find the supplemental help she needed. Second, she had to be flexible about rescheduling appointments that needed to be changed due to caregiving demands. Third, both cognitive and behavioural strategies were helpful to counteract frequent negative thinking and low engagement in positive activities. Fourth, Helen complied well with most home practice assignments which gave her opportunity to learn by doing, thus increasing her sense of self-efficacy over time. Setting up do-able home practice is a key element of success in CBT with caregivers, as it is with other clients. Fifth, this client returned for more CBT when her caregiving situation changed. That occurs often as new challenges may feel overwhelming at first. A CBT 'tune-up' really helps!

Concluding Remarks

This chapter describes the many ways in which CBT itself, as well as non-traditional CBT-based interventions, can improve the mental health of dementia family caregivers. Basic CBT skills seem applicable to a wide variety of caregivers, including those from minoritised communities. Availability of smart phones and increasingly sophisticated apps for them present unique opportunities (and challenges) as the field moves forward. Exciting developments in technology hold promise for making CBT and its derivatives available to larger numbers of caregivers, many of whom lack resources to engage in traditional CBT psychotherapy. Although there will always be some caregivers who need psychotherapy because of the nature and/or severity of their mental health issues, there are many who can benefit from these alternative forms of intervention that employ CBT principles and practices, but do so in innovative ways, with less reliance on highly trained providers and more reliance on caregivers themselves to improve their quality of life.

Further Reading

The following sources provide more in-depth coverage of topics raised in this chapter.

Bilbrey AC, Cassidy-Eagle E, Gallagher-Thompson D. Working with depressed caregivers: Behavioral activation. In LB Dunn, E Cassidy-Eagle (Eds.). *Practical Strategies in Geriatric Mental Health: Cases and Approaches* (pp. 31–41). Washington, DC: American Psychiatric Association Press; 2020.

Bilbrey AC, Laidlaw K, Cassidy-Eagle E, Thompson LW, Gallagher-Thompson D. Cognitive behavioral therapy for late-life depression: Evidence, issues, and recommendations. *Cognitive and Behavioral Practice*, 2022;**29**(1):128–145.

Gallagher-Thompson D, Bilbrey AC, Qualls SH, Ghatak R, Trivedi RB, Waelde LC. *Distressed Family Caregivers*. Newburyport: Hogrefe; 2023.

Laidlaw K, Wilkinson P. Cognitive behavioural therapy. *Oxford Textbook of Old Age Psychiatry* (p. 253). Oxford: Oxford University Press; 2020.

Steffen AM, Dick-Siskin LP, Bilbrey AC, Thompson LW, Gallagher-Thompson D. *Treating Later-Life Depression: A Cognitive-Behavioral Therapy Approach, Workbook*. Oxford: Oxford University Pres; 2021.

Steffen AM, Thompson LW, Gallagher-Thompson D. *Treating Later-Life Depression: A Cognitive-Behavioral Therapy Approach, Clinician Guide*. Oxford: Oxford University Press; 2021.

References

1. Akkerman RL, Ostwald SK. Reducing anxiety in Alzheimer's disease family caregivers: The effectiveness of a nine-week cognitive-behavioral intervention. *American Journal of Alzheimer's Disease & Other Dementias*, 2004;**19**(2):117–123.
2. Alzheimer's Association. 2022 Alzheimer's disease facts and figures. *Alzheimer's & Dementia*, 2022;**18**(4):700–789. https://doi.org/10.1002/alz.12638.
3. Alzheimer's Disease International. *World Alzheimer Report 2022: Life after diagnosis: Navigating treatment, care and support*, 2022. www.alzint.org/resource/world-alzheimer-report-2022/.

4. Aranda MP, Kremer IN, Hinton L, Zissimopoulos J, Whitmer RA, Hummel CH et al. Impact of dementia: Health disparities, population trends, care interventions, and economic costs. *Journal of the American Geriatrics Society*, 2021;**69** (7):1774–1783. https://doi.org/10.1111/jgs.17345.

5. Arango-Lasprilla JC, Panyavin I, Merchán EJ, Perrin PB, Arroyo-Anlló EM, Snipes DJ, Arabia J. Evaluation of a group cognitive-behavioral dementia caregiver intervention in Latin America. *American Journal of Alzheimer's Disease and Other Dementias*, 2014;**29**(6):548–555. https://doi.org/10.1177/1533317514523668.

6. Au A, Lai MK, Lau KM, Pan PC, Lam L, Thompson L, Gallagher-Thompson D. Social support and well-being in dementia family caregivers: The mediating role of self-efficacy. *Aging & Mental Health*, 2009;**13**(5):761–768. https://doi.org/10.1080/13607860902918223.

7. Bandura A. *Social Foundations of Thought and Action: A Social Cognitive Theory*. Englewood Cliffs: Prentice Hall; 1986a.

8. Bandura A. The explanatory and predictive scope of self-efficacy theory. *Journal of Social and Clinical Psychology*, 1986b;**4** (3):359–373. https://doi.org/10.1521/jscp.1986.4.3.359.

9. Beck AT (Ed.). *Cognitive Therapy of Depression*. New York: Guilford Press; 1979.

10. Belle SH. Enhancing the quality of life of dementia caregivers from different ethnic or racial groups: A randomized controlled trial. *Annals of Internal Medicine*, 2006; **145** (10):727. https://doi.org/10.7326/0003-4819-145-10-200611210-00005

11. Bilbrey AC, Cassidy-Eagle E, Gallagher-Thompson D. Working with depressed caregivers: Behavioral activation. In LB Dunn, E Cassidy-Eagle (Eds.), *Practical Strategies in Geriatric Mental Health: Cases and Approaches* (pp. 31–41). Washington, DC: American Psychiatric Association Press; 2020.

12. Brodaty H, Green A, Koschera A. Meta-analysis of psychosocial interventions for caregivers of people with dementia. *Journal of the American Geriatrics Society*, 2003;**51**:657–664. https://doi.org/10.1034/j.1600-0579.2003.00210.x

13. Brodaty H, Donkin M. Family caregivers of people with dementia. *Dialogues in Clinical Neuroscience*, 2022;**11**(2):217–228. https://doi.org/10.31887/DCNS.2009.11.2/hbrodaty.

14. Cheng ST, Chow PK, Song YQ, Edwin CS, Chan AC, Lee TM, Lam JH. Mental and physical activities delay cognitive decline in older persons with dementia. *The American Journal of Geriatric Psychiatry*, 2014;**22**(1):63–74. https://doi.org/10.1016/j.jagp.2013.01.060.

15. Cheng ST, Au A, Losada A, Thompson LW, Gallagher-Thompson D. Psychological interventions for dementia caregivers: What we have achieved, what we have learned. *Current Psychiatry Reports*, 2019;**21**:1–12.

16. Cheng S-T, Li K-K, Losada A, Zhang F, Au A, Thompson LW, Gallagher-Thompson D. The effectiveness of nonpharmacological interventions for informal dementia caregivers: An updated systematic review and meta-analysis. *Psychology and Aging*, 2020;**35**(1):55–77. https://doi.org/10.1037/pag0000401.

17. Cheng ST, Zhang F. A comprehensive meta-review of systematic reviews and meta-analyses on nonpharmacological interventions for informal dementia caregivers. *BMC Geriatrics*, 2020;**20** (1):1–24.

18. del-Pino-Casado R, Priego-Cubero E, López-Martínez C, Orgeta V. Subjective caregiver burden and anxiety in informal caregivers: A systematic review and meta-analysis. *PLoS One*, 2021;**16**(3), https://doi.org/10.1371/journal.pone.0247143.

19. Dilworth-Anderson P, Moon H, Aranda MP. Dementia caregiving research: Expanding and reframing the lens of diversity, inclusivity, and intersectionality. *The Gerontologist*, 2020;**60**(5):797–805. https://doi.org/10.1093/geront/gnaa050.

20. Gallagher-Thompson D, Bilbrey AC, Qualls SH, Ghatak R, Trivedi RB,

Waelde LC. *Distressed Family Caregivers.* Newburyport: Hogrefe, 2023.

21. Gallagher-Thompson D, Coon DW, Solano N, Ambler C, Rabinowitz Y, Thompso L. W. Change in indices of distress among Latino and Anglo female caregivers of elderly relatives with dementia: Site-specific results from the REACH National Collaborative Study. *The Gerontologist*, 2003;**43**(4):580–591. https://doi.org/10.1093/geront/43.4.580.
22. Gallagher-Thompson D, Gray HL, Dupart T, Jimenez D, Thompson LW. Effectiveness of cognitive/behavioral small group intervention for reduction of depression and stress in Non-Hispanic White and Hispanic/Latino women dementia family caregivers: Outcomes and mediators of change. *Journal of Rational-Emotive & Cognitive-Behavior Therapy*, 2008;**26**(4), 286–303. https://doi.org/10.1007/s10942-008-0087-4.
23. Gallagher D, Rose J, Rivera P, Lovett S, Thompson LW. Prevalence of depression in family caregivers. *The Gerontologist*, 1989;**29**(4):449–456. https://doi.org/10.1093/geront/29.4.449.
24. Gallagher-Thompson D, Steffen AM. Comparative effects of cognitive-behavioral and brief psychodynamic psychotherapies for depressed family caregivers. *Journal of Consulting and Clinical Psychology*, 1994;**62**(3):543–549. https://doi.org/10.1037/0022-006X.62.3.543.
25. Gallagher-Thompson D, Bilbrey AC, Apesoa-Varano EC, Ghatak R, Kim KK, Cothran F. Conceptual framework to guide intervention research across the trajectory of dementia caregiving. *The Gerontologist*, 2020;**60**(Supplement_1):S29–S40. https://doi.org/10.1093/geront/gnz157.
26. Garand L, Rinaldo DE, Alberth MM, Delany J, Beasock SL, Lopez OL et al. Effects of problem solving therapy on mental health outcomes in family caregivers of persons with a new diagnosis of mild cognitive impairment or early dementia: A randomized controlled trial. *The American Journal of Geriatric Psychiatry*, 2014;**22**(8):771–781. https://doi.org/10.1016/j.jagp.2013.07.007.
27. Gonyea JG, López LM, Velásquez EH. The effectiveness of a culturally sensitive cognitive behavioral group intervention for Latino Alzheimer's caregivers. *Gerontologist*, 2016;**56**(2):292–302. https://doi.org/10.1093/geront/gnu045.
28. Hepburn K, Lewis M, Tornatore J, Sherman CW, Bremer KL. The Savvy Caregiver program: The demonstrated effectiveness of a transportable dementia caregiver psychoeducation program. *Journal of Gerontological Nursing*, 2007;**33**(3):30–36. https://doi.org/10.3928/00989134-20070301-06.
29. Hopkinson MD, Reavell J, Lane DA, Mallikarjun P. Cognitive behavioral therapy for depression, anxiety, and stress in caregivers of dementia patients: A systematic review and meta-analysis. *The Gerontologist*, 2019;**59**(4):e343–e362. https://doi.org/10.1093/geront/gnx217.
30. Huang SS. Depression among caregivers of patients with dementia: Associative factors and management approaches. *World Journal of Psychiatry*, 2022;**12**(1):59–76. https://doi.org/10.5498/wjp.v12.i1.59.
31. International Alliance of Carer Organizations. *Global State of Caring. International Alliance of Carer Organizations*. 2021. https://internationalcarers.org/wp-content/uploads/2021/07/IACO-Global-State-of-Caring-July-13.pdf.
32. Kajiyama B, Fernandez G, Carter EA, Humber MB, Thompson LW. Helping Hispanic dementia caregivers cope with stress using technology-based resources. *Clinical Gerontologist*, 2018;**41**(3):209–216. https://doi.org/10.1080/07317115.2017.1377797.
33. Kajiyama B, Thompson LW, Eto-Iwase T, Yamashita M, Mario J di, Tzuang YM, Gallagher-Thompson D. Exploring the effectiveness of an internet-based program for reducing caregiver distress using the iCare Stress Management e-Training Program. *Aging and Mental Health*, 2013;**17**(5):544–554. https://doi.org/10.1080/13607863.2013.775641.

34. Knight BG, Sayegh P. Cultural values and caregiving: The updated sociocultural stress and coping model. *The Journals of Gerontology Series B: Psychological Sciences and Social Sciences*, 2010;**65B**(1):5–13. https://doi.org/10.1093/geronb/gbp096.

35. Larson EB, Stroud C. Meeting the challenge of caring for persons living with dementia and their care partners and caregivers: A report from the National Academies of Sciences, Engineering, and Medicine. *JAMA*, 2021;**325**(18):1831–1832. https://doi.org/10.1001/jama.2021.4928.

36. Lazarus RS, Folkman S. *Stress, Appraisal, and Coping*. New York: Springer; 1984.

37. Lewinsohn PM, Clarke GN, Hoberman HM. The Coping With Depression Course: Review and future directions. *Canadian Journal of Behavioural Science/Revue canadienne des sciences du comportement*, 1989;**21**(4):470–493. https://doi.org/10.1037/h0079846.

38. Liu Z, Heffernan C, Tan J. Caregiver burden: A concept analysis. *International Journal of Nursing Sciences*, 2020;**7**(4), 438–445. https://doi.org/10.1016/j.ijnss.2020.07.012.

39. Livingston G, Barber J, Rapaport P, Knapp M, Griffin M, King D et al. Clinical effectiveness of a manual based coping strategy programme (START, STrAtegies for RelaTives) in promoting the mental health of carers of family members with dementia: pragmatic randomised controlled trial. *BMJ*, 2013;**347**. https://doi.org/10.1136/bmj.f6276.

40. Livingston PM, Osborne RH, Botti M, Mihalopoulos C, McGuigan S, Heckel L et al. Efficacy and cost-effectiveness of an outcall program to reduce carer burden and depression among carers of cancer patients [PROTECT]: Rationale and design of a randomized controlled trial. *BMC Health Services Research*, 2014;**14**(1):1–8.

41. Lorig KR, Ritter PL, Laurent DD, Yank V. Building better caregivers: A pragmatic 12-month trial of a community-based workshop for caregivers of cognitively impaired adults. *Journal of Applied Gerontology*, 2019;**38**(9):1228–1252. https://doi.org/10.1177/0733464817741682.

42. Losada A, Márquez-González M, Romero-Moreno R, Mausbach BT, López J, Fernández-Fernández V et al. Cognitive–behavioral therapy (CBT) versus acceptance and commitment therapy (ACT) for dementia family caregivers with significant depressive symptoms: Results of a randomized clinical trial. *Journal of Consulting and Clinical Psychology*, 2015;**83**(4):760–772. https://doi.org/10.1037/ccp0000028.

43. Losada A, Márquez-González M, Romero-Moreno R. Mechanisms of action of a psychological intervention for dementia caregivers: Effects of behavioral activation and modification of dysfunctional thoughts. *International Journal of Geriatric Psychiatry*, 2011;**26**:1119–1127. https://doi.org/10.1002/gps.2648.

44. Márquez-González M, Losada A, Izal M, Pérez-Rojo G, Montorio I. Modification of dysfunctional thoughts about caregiving in dementia family caregivers: Description and outcomes of an intervention programme. *Aging & Mental Health*, 2007;**11**:616–625. http://dx.doi.org/10.1080/13607860701368455.

45. Mehta R. Who do you care for and who cares for you? Atlas of Caregiving. 2018. https://atlasofcaregiving.com/caremap/.

46. Meichsner F, Töpfer NF, Reder M, Soellner R, Wilz G. Telephone-based cognitive behavioral intervention improves dementia caregivers' quality of life. *American Journal of Alzheimer's Disease & Other Dementias*, 2019;**34**(4):236–246. https://dio.org/10.1177/1533317518822100.

47. Montoro-Rodriguez J, Gallagher-Thompson D. Stress and coping: Conceptual models for understanding dementia among Latinos. In Adames HY, Tazean YN (eds.), *Caring for Latinxs with Dementia in a Globalized World: Behavioral and Psychosocial Treatments* (pp. 231–246). New York: Springer; 2020.

48. Montoro-Rodriguez J, Hayslip Jr B, Ramsey J, Jooste JL. The utility of solution-oriented strategies to support

grandparents raising grandchildren. *Journal of Aging and Health*, 2021;**33** (9):647–666. https://doi.org/10.1177/08982643211004817.

49. Montoro-Rodriguez J, Ramsey J, Bilbrey AC, Kajiyama B, Thompson LW, Gallagher-Thompson D. Caregiver Thrive, Learn, & Connect: Testing the Efficacy of an Online Psychoeducational Program for Family Caregivers. Clin Gerontol. 2024;47 (1):39–49.

50. Muller C, Aguiar JC. *What is the digital divide?* 2022, March 3. www.internetsociety.org/blog/2022/03/what-is-the-digital-divide.

51. Ng R, Indran N. Societal perceptions of caregivers linked to culture across 20 countries: Evidence from a 10-billion-word database. *PLoS One*, 2021;**16**(7), https://doi.org/10.1371/journal.pone.0251161.

52. Oliveira MC, Lima EM, de Paiva MLN, Valente KDR. Factors associated with caregiver burden of adults with epilepsy in a middle-income country. *Seizure*, 2022;**98**:1–7. https://doi.org/10.1016/j.seizure.2022.03.015.

53. Ostwald SK, Hepburn KW, Burns T. Training family caregivers of patients with dementia: A structured workshop approach. *Journal of Gerontological Nursing*, 2003;**29**(1):37–44. https://doi.org/10.3928/0098-9134-20030101-11.

54. Pearlin LI, Mullan JT, Semple SJ, Skaff MM. Caregiving and the stress process: An overview of concepts and their measures. *The Gerontologist*, 1990;**30** (5):583–594. https://doi.org/10.1093/geront/30.5.583.

55. Pinquart M, Sörensen S. Spouses, adult children, and children-in-law as caregivers of older adults: A meta-analytic comparison. *Psychology and Aging*, 2011;**26** (1):1–14. https://doi.org/10.1037/a0021863.

56. Pinquart M, Sörensen S. Ethnic differences in stressors, resources, and psychological outcomes of family caregiving: A meta-analysis. *The Gerontologist*, 2005;**45** (1):90–106. https://doi.org/10.1093/geront/45.1.90.

57. Rodriguez-Sanchez E, Patino-Alonso MC, Mora-Simón S, Gómez-Marcos MA, Pérez-Peñaranda A, Losada-Baltar A, García-Ortiz L. Effects of a psychological intervention in a primary health care center for caregivers of dependent relatives: a randomized trial. *The Gerontologist*, 2013;**53**(3):397–406. https://doi.org/10.1093/geront/gns086.

58. Romero-Moreno R, Márquez-González M, Mausbach BT, Losada A. Variables modulating depression in dementia caregivers: A longitudinal study. *International Psychogeriatrics*, 2012;**24** (8):1316–1324. https://doi.org/10.1017/S1041610211002237.

59. Sallim AB, Sayampanathan AA, Cuttilan A, Ho RCM. Prevalence of mental health disorders among caregivers of patients with Alzheimer disease. *Journal of the American Medical Directors Association*, 2015;**16**(12):1034–1041. https://doi.org/10.1016/j.jamda.2015.09.007.

60. Schulz R, Beach SR, Czaja SJ, Martire LM, Monin JK. Family caregiving for older adults. *Annual Review of Psychology*, 2020;**71**:635–659. https://doi.org/10.1146/annurev-psych-010419-050754.

61. Schulz R, Eden J., National Academies of Sciences, Engineering, and Medicine. Family caregiving roles and impacts. In *Families Caring for an Aging America.* Washington, DC: National Academies Press (US); 2016.

62. Steffen AM, Gallagher-Thompson D, Thompson LW. Theoretical support and practical strategies for CBT with depressed older adults. In NA Pachana, V Molinari, LW Thompson, D Gallagher-Thompson (Eds.), *Psychological Assessment and Treatment of Older Adults* (pp. 43–68). Newburyport: Hogrefe; 2021.

63. Steffen AM, Thompson LW, Gallagher-Thompson D. *Treating Later-Life Depression: A Cognitive-Behavioral Therapy Approach, Clinician Guide.* Oxford: Oxford University Press; 2021.

64. Sun Y, Ji M, Leng M, Li X, Zhang X, Wang Z. Comparative efficacy of 11 non-pharmacological interventions on

depression, anxiety, quality of life, and caregiver burden for informal caregivers of people with dementia: A systematic review and network meta-analysis. *International Journal of Nursing Studies*, 2022;104204. https://doi.org/10.1016/j.ijnurstu.2022.104204.

65. Verreault P, Turcotte V, Ouellet MC, Robichaud LA, Hudon C. Efficacy of cognitive-behavioural therapy interventions on reducing burden for caregivers of older adults with a neurocognitive disorder: A systematic review and meta-analysis. *Cognitive Behaviour Therapy*, 2021;**50**(1):19–46. https://doi.org/10.1080/16506073.2020.1819867.

66. Wang H, Li T, Barbarino P, Gauthier S, Brodaty H, Molinuevo JL, Yu, X. Dementia care during COVID-19. *The Lancet*, 2020;**395**(10231):1190–1191. https://doi.org/10.1016/S0140-6736(20)30755-8.

67. Wang J, Li X, Liu W, Yang B, Zhao Q, Lü Y, Xiao M. The positive aspects of caregiving in dementia: A scoping review and bibliometric analysis. *Frontiers in Public Health*, 2022;**10**. https://doi.org/10.3389/fpubh.2022.985391.

68. World Health Organization. *Dementia*. (2022, September 20). www.who.int/news-room/fact-sheets/detail/dementia.

69. Yeo G, Gerdner LA, Gallagher-Thompson D. (Eds.) *Ethnicity and the Dementias*. New York: Routledge; 2019.

70. Zhang H, Xiong RH, Hujiken S, Zhang JJ, Zhang XQ. Psychological distress, family functioning, and social support in family caregivers for patients with dementia in the mainland of China. *Chinese Medical Journal*, 2013;**126**(18):3417–3421.

71. Zimmerman S, Sloane PD, Ward K, Beeber A, Reed D, Lathren C et al. Helping dementia caregivers manage medical problems: Benefits of an educational resource. *American Journal of Alzheimer's Disease & Other Dementias*, 2018;**33**(3):176–183. https://doi.org/10.1177/1533317517749466.

72. Global status report on the public health response to dementia. Geneva: World Health Organization; 2021. Licence: CC BY-NC-SA 3.0 IGO.

73. Brodaty H, Donkin M. (2009). Family caregivers of people with dementia. *Dialogues in Clinical Neuroscience*, 2009:**11**(2);217–228. https://doi.org/10.31887/DCNS.2009.11.2/hbrodaty.

74. Aranda MP, Knight BG. The influence of ethnicity and culture on the caregiver stress and coping process: A sociocultural review and analysis. *Gerontologist*, 1997;**37**:342–354.

Chapter 25

Cognitive Behavioural Therapy for Children and Young People

Mike Turnbull and Markku Wood

In this chapter we will help you to be able to:

- Describe the developmental context of working with children and young people (CYP).
- Assess and formulate using developmentally sensitive CBT theory.
- Explain the evidence underpinning intervention with CYP and their families.
- Adapt CBT for working with CYP and families at different ages (including considerations around neurodiversity).

Introduction

Cognitive behavioural therapy for CYP is proving to be one of the most effective treatments for mental health (MH) difficulties across multiple disorders and presentations [1]. Effective adaptations to CBT practice have been developed across low mood, anxiety, trauma, obsessive compulsive and related disorders (OCRD), bereavement, physical health, eating disorders and many more presentations, proving CBT to be one of the most diverse modalities of treatment for CYP. With advances now in third wave CBT therapies and transdiagnostic approaches CBT continues to advance. Historically, the evidence-base for CBT for CYP has emerged from adaptations to CBT for adults [2], however, there is now a growing pool of research specifically for CYP [1]. To this end there is commitment by NHS-England to increase the psychological workforce to meet the growing need for MH support in the CYP population. The long-term plan [3], CYP-IAPT initiative and the recent green paper [4], for instance, in England have led to the training of thousands more high and low intensity CBT therapists and practitioners over the last decade. These national projects, facilitated by the emergence and now fast expanding speciality of ;ow intensity CBT for CYP (discussed in more detail below), focus heavily on increasing access to evidence-based therapies in schools and community settings. This chapter will summarise the evidence-base for CBT for CYP and discuss how to make adaptations in assessment, formulation and treatments.

Considering Childhood Development in Working with CYP Using CBT

Much of this book focuses on interventions with adults and there is much we can learn from working with adults, as long as the therapist takes careful consideration of developmental factors impacting the CYP.

Like adult models of CBT, CBT for CYP is based on the conceptual and scientific integration of cognitive and behavioural theory and practice. It is important to note the heterogeneity and diversity of CYP when assessing, formulating and planning interventions. Key indicators of success in therapy include therapeutic alliance, effective communication (taking into account that therapeutic language can be abstract and hypothetical in nature) and the use of the most appropriate emotional, cognitive and behavioural skills (based on formulation). Neurodiversity, intellectual disability and executive/cognitive functioning difficulties are important considerations when agreeing collaborative treatment plans, however, it is good practice not to make assumptions with any CYP, regardless of age or assumed cognitive and development ability. The CYP's emotional literacy (including access to appropriate descriptions of their own emotions) is also important to ascertain. Consider too the impact of traumatic events on a child's development. It is now clear that traumatic events can impact on a CYP's normative development and can cause delays in emotional and cognitive/brain development [5,6,7,8,9,10]. One helpful way of beginning to understand the impact of difficult past events is to use the adverse childhood experiences (ACEs) structure/model [11]. The ACEs model includes key factors for the therapist to consider (such as neglect or abuse from adults or peers in the CYP's life).

When planning treatment, consider the CYP's developmental stage on a case-by-case basis. Consider the emotional, cognitive and social skills that the CYP has already mastered and those which need support to be developed. Vygotsky [12] proposed the zone of proximal development (ZPD), which helps us as therapists conceptualise how close a CYP might be to mastering a skill (e.g. the ability to understand their own thoughts and then challenges negative thinking bias). The therapist can then present new information, scaffolding the process to improve the uptake of new learning, supporting the child to move into the ZPD. Supporting a CYP to a ZPD requires a good therapeutic relationship/alliance (discussed in more detail below) so that they can feel safe to learn and develop.

Piagetian theory can also help to adapt your CBT practice and interventions. Piaget's stages of cognitive development [13] and its application suggest that CYP progress through interactions with the environment, passing through developmental stages; it is further proposed that affect develops alongside this progress. By creating a suitable platform, by which a CYP can learn and progress, they will develop their own schemata (a blueprint for understanding the world). This will shape how they interact with the world around them. Through better understanding of how children's schemata have developed negatively we can create an environment by which CBT can help the CYP develop skills in challenging and changing negative cognitive biases.

Attachment theory can also help us understand better how the CYP has come to a state of discord and distress. Bowlby [14], proposes that it is through interactions with the primary care giver that a CYP form a view of their self, world and others. Negative experiences of parenting and subsequently peer relationships have been shown to have a significant impact on distress, readiness to change and treatment outcomes [15]. Assessment that includes gathering information around a CYP's experiences of being parented and how well they make and retain friendships can support you to better understand how they perceive the world and how they might engage in a therapeutic alliance or not, based on their attachment experiences.

By considering cognitive and behavioural theory and the evidence-base for CBT with CYP we can take into account important factors such as cognitive readiness, and access to thoughts, feelings and behaviours.

Engagement, Assessment and Formulation with CYP

In general, the aims, underpinning principles, structure and processes of assessment are similar to those discussed for adults within Chapter 8. In terms of the structure and process, the CYP's CBT therapist needs to move from the collection of background information in assessment (as described in Chapter 8), through to the development of a theoretically and developmentally informed idiosyncratic CBT formulation of the CYP's difficulties, tightly defined therapeutic goals and an evidence-based plan for treatment. Formulation for children and young people should still answer the six key questions posed in Chapter 8 (highlighted below) but do it with greater developmental and systemic consideration.

- 'What are the problems?'
- 'What is causing the problems?'
- 'How is this causing the problems?'
- 'What made the problems happen at that point?'
- 'What made the problems happen to them?' and
- 'What might get in the way of fixing the problems?'

As with adults, the thorough assessment of risk and safety planning is an integral part of this process, although the therapist should be mindful that risks might present differently from adult populations, for example, increased risk from others. Moreover, the assessment process should also be seen as a continuous process that doesn't end at the start of treatment but is ongoing until the point of discharge; as we should be learning about difficulties and adapting our formulations from beginning to end [16].

When assessing CYP, it is even more essential, than with adults, to consider the interaction between the system and CYP. CYP rely heavily upon the systems they are in, such as families and schools, and as a result the impact from the system can be higher. CYP's difficulties can also have a profound impact upon those systems in terms of parental stress and practical considerations in managing mental health difficulties. It is especially important that the CBT therapist considers the neurodevelopmental stage of the young person and whether there might be any underpinning co-morbidities such as ASD, ADHD and/or intellectual difficulties/disabilities. In some instances, it might be that the young person requires diagnostic or neuropsychological assessment to inform the best approach. We should also be mindful of these difficulties within the parent or carer themselves, as they will potentially be a crucial part of CYP assessment, formulation and intervention, as we will see.

The use of routine outcomes measures in assessment, whilst always deemed important, has become more embedded in standard practice in CYP services since the advent of CYP-IAPT in 2011. Whilst there are multiple measures for CYP, CYP-IAPT has led to the more consistent use of the recommended measures, highlighted in Table 25.1, by making it a core part of the training and implementation model. These measures are also accompanied by an array of 'symptom trackers' that allow the therapist to track symptomatology for a broad spectrum of specific conditions, for example, social anxiety, OCD and depression. All measures are available and easily accessible on the Child Outcomes Research Consortium (CORC) website (www.corc.uk.net). The use of parent/carer and teacher report measures is an important consideration and often an extremely helpful addition. Diagnostic interviews, such as the Kiddie-Schedule for Affective Disorders and Schizophrenia (K-SADS [17]), are also at the disposal of the therapists although in routine clinical practice rarely used.

Table 25.1 Primary outcome measures recommended for use in CYP-IAPT downloadable from the CORC website (www.corc.uk.net)

Measure	Description
Revised Child Anxiety and Depression Scale: Child and Parent versions (RCADS- Child, RCADS- Parent/Carer; [18]	A 47-item self-report measure used to assess anxiety and low mood in CYP between ages 8–18 years. Subscales: major depressive disorder (MDD), generalised anxiety disorder (GAD), obsessive compulsive disorder (OCD), panic disorder (PD), separation anxiety disorder (SAD), social phobia (SP).
Goal-Based Outcomes [19]	GBO are used to evaluate CYPs idiosyncratic goals progress using a 10-point Likert scale (0 presents no goal progress, 10 represent goal completion).
Session Rating Scale (SRS [20])	The SRS is a brief measure of the therapeutic alliance. CYP are asked to indicate function by marking on a 10cm analogue scale.
Outcome Rating Scale (ORS) & Child Outcomes Rating Scale (CORS) [21]	ORS and CORS are used to assess CYPs function across 4four scales: Individual, Interpersonal, Social and Overall function. ORS and CORS use a similar analogue scale to the SRS.

Assessment and formulation also give us the first, and arguably the most important, opportunity to build the therapeutic alliance and socialise CYP to therapy and the CBT model. To this end, we need to consider the adaptions and accommodations discussed below and the expectations of CYP who are often referred by others with little discussion and/or consideration of their understanding of therapy or CBT. CYP are used to being in situations and environments where adults direct their activities, such as in education. As a result, they can often arrive at therapy expecting to be a passive recipient of therapy. Hence, time should be devoted to socialising them to a more collaborative way of working both by overt discussion and gradual socialisation as part of the therapy process. We also need to consider CYP's willingness to take part in CBT, their readiness to change [22] and how cultural and demographic factors might influence expectations and engagement.

Whilst the aim of formulation should always be to develop parsimonious understanding of the patient's difficulties, this is even more important with CYP due to the fact that they are developing their cognitive and emotional abilities as discussed above. Indeed, assessment and formulation with CYP present us with a golden opportunity to understand these abilities and consider how well CYP can access thoughts, feelings and behaviours and make links between these areas. Hence, having a simple understandable formulation is key to the success of therapy. Moreover, we need to make sure that the formulation makes sense to those systemically involved in the therapeutic process, for example, a parent supporting therapy. Practically, this often means that formulations are simplified to account for CYP's learning needs and zone of development. Figure 25.1 gives an example of a simplified generic CBT formulation including consideration of thoughts, feelings and behaviours [23]. Moreover, Fuggle, Dunmuir and Curry [16] suggest that formulations for CYP should pay careful attention to systemic factors such as parent/carer's beliefs and expectations. In some instances, parents and carers' thoughts/expectations, feelings and behaviours might well be part of the shared formulation as they might be key

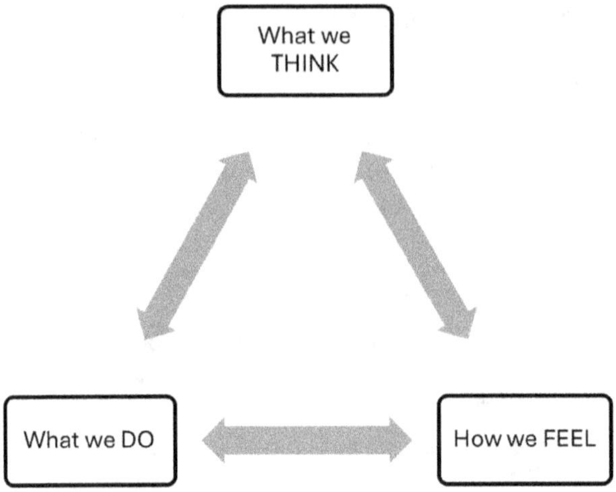

Figure 25.1 An example of CYP-friendly generic formulation adapted from Stallard [23]. Reproduced with permission from John Wiley & Sons.

parts of the maintenance cycle. Once a shared and understood formulation and treatment goals have been arrived at, it is then time to develop the intervention plan.

Intervention with CYP

Following on from formulation and as highlighted above, whilst there is evidence for the effectiveness of CBT interventions with CYP, generally speaking the research is more limited, and the effect sizes smaller than for adult interventions. This is at least in part due the complexities of conducting research with CYP, meaning that models and interventions in some cases are adapted from the adult literature [24]. The implementation of intervention can also be diluted by a range of factors including systemic and developmental considerations as discussed above. Table 25.2 and Table 25.3 provide a brief summary of helpful models, books and protocols that might be useful in informing practice, some of which will require adaptation from adult models.

Low Mood

One area where we have seen recent advancements is within the treatment of adolescent depression with the development of brief behavioural activation (BA) for adolescents [25,26], an approach developed specifically for adolescents. In a recent systematic review and meta-analysis, Tindall and colleagues [27] concluded that BA may be an effective treatment for young people with depression although caution should be exercised due methodological limitations within the literature. More recently, Oud et al. [28], in a systematic review and meta-regression analysis, looked at CBT for CYP depression more generally, concluding CBT to be an effective treatment for young people with depression. They [28] went on to suggest that effectiveness might be improved when interventions contain elements of BA and thought challenging where carers are involved. These findings highlight the need to work behaviourally with CYP and to involve families within CBT. This becomes more important the younger the child is, with higher levels of scaffolding being required for younger CYP. In terms of specific CBT protocols for children experiencing low mood, there are good texts out there, for example Verdyn, Rogers and Wood [29], but more updated attention would be welcome.

Table 25.2 Summary of key CBT models, literature and protocols

Low Mood	Panic	GAD	Social Phobia	Separation Anxiety
Behavioural Activation (Pass et al. [25]; Pass and Reynolds [26])	Clark [86]	Robichaud [87]	Clark and Wells [88]	Stallard [45]; Stallard [23]
Cognitive Behaviour Therapy (Beck and Beck [89]; Verduyn et al. [29])	Waite and Clark [38]	Parent Led CBT Individually (Halldorsson et al. [49]), groups (Halldorsson et al. [50]), self-help book (Creswell and Willetts [48])	Leigh and Clark [36]	Parent Led CBT individually (Halldorsson et al. [49]), groups (Halldorsson et al. [50]), self-help book (Creswell and Willetts [48])
		Coping Cat (Kendall [44])	Parent Led CBT individually (Halldorsson et al. [49]), groups (Halldorsson et al. [50]), self-help book (Creswell and Willetts [48]),	Coping Cat (Kendall [44])
			Coping Cat (Kendall [44])	

Table 25.3 Summary of key CBT models, literature and protocols (cont'd)

Specific Phobia	Body Dysmorphic Disorder	OCD	Trauma/ PTSD	Health Anxiety
Parent Led CBT individually (Halldorsson et al. [49]), groups (Halldorsson et al. [50]), self-help book (Creswell and Willetts [48])	Wilhelm et al. [91]	Turner et al. [63]	Ehlers and Clark [90]	Warwick and Salkovskis [92]
A cognitive model of specific phobia (Kirk and Rouf [93])	Maudsley Hospital National and Specialist OCD, BDD and Related Disorders Service	OCD and ASD Jassi [84]	Smith et al. [70]	Salkovskis et al. [94]
One Session Treatment (Davis et al. [41]; Davis et al. [42]; Ollendick et al. [39])		March and Mulle [95]	Cohen et al. [71]	Haig-Ferguson et al. [96]; Wells [97]

An Example of an Adapted Intervention for Low Mood: Brief Behavioural Activation for Adolescents [26]

To give an example of an intervention that has been adapted for adolescents, it might be helpful to provide more in-depth consideration to brief BA for adolescents [26]. BA for adolescents follows an eight-session protocol (not including assessment or post treatment review) that is underpinned by behavioural theories of depression as discussed in Chapter 20. Parents and carers are explicitly asked to attend various sessions, including psychoeducational sessions and reviews, although CYP, therapists and families can often agree for parents to attend more than these three sessions.

The protocol starts with psychoeducation and providing a rationale for BA facilitated by using the child-friendly BA model in Figure 25.2. As homework from this first session, the CYP is asked to keep an activity diary which is reviewed at the second session in order to try and identify activities that are likely to be positively reinforcing and therefore anti-depressant. In session two, the therapist reviews the log paying particular attention to activities linked to increased sense of achievement, closeness to others and enjoyment. As homework from session two, the young person is encouraged to build on activities linked to positive reinforcement, whilst monitoring this through continued use of the activity diary. At the next session, this diary is again reviewed, and the therapist attempts to diversify avenues of positive reinforcement by completing a values assessment with the young person. The values identified are then translated into potentially valued and reinforcing activities that the young person can try to engage with during the course of therapy. As a homework task from session three, the young person is asked to identify one task from the values exercise to try between sessions, for example going to football training or joining a book club. Activities are normally graded, starting with easier activities that are likely to provide quick wins. This is recorded on achievement, closeness to others and enjoyment logs (ACE Logs) ready for review at the next session.

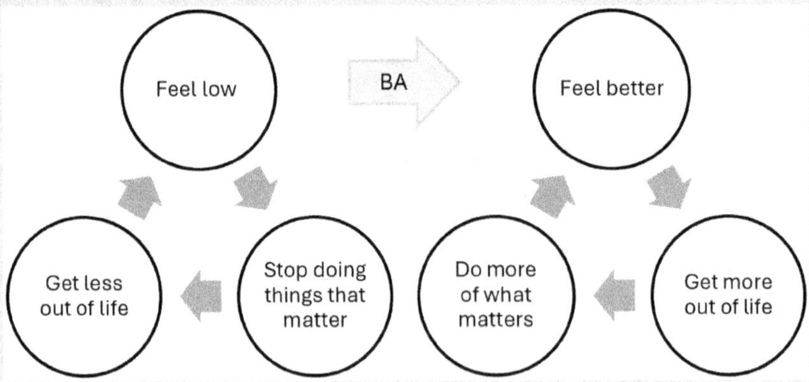

Figure 25.2 Brief BA for Adolescents' model [26]. Reproduced with permission from Jessica Kingsley Publishers.

From session three onwards, the process becomes one of reviewing the completed ACE logs and setting new valued activities to do and/or repeat. The protocol sets a progress review with parents in session six, alongside additional work on problem solving. From there, the process of setting and reviewing valued activities continues until relapse prevention, with parents or carers, in session eight. Whilst the protocol is eight sessions in total, the dose of BA delivered can be, and often is, increased by delivering further sessions focussed on reviewing and scheduling valued activities as described above.

Anxiety Disorders

As with depression, CBT for CYP with anxiety is found to be effective [1,24] and is widely held as the treatment of choice [30]. However, most evidence in support of CBT for CYP explores populations with a broad variety of anxiety disorders rather than focussing on specific disorders such social anxiety, panic disorder, generalised anxiety disorder and specific phobia [1]. As a result, it is harder to draw a firm conclusion around the effectiveness of specific CBT interventions for specific conditions and more research is needed in this area [1]. That said, some evidence does exist for the effective treatment of specific anxiety disorders, for example panic disorder [31,32] and separation anxiety disorder [33,34]. More recent efforts have focussed on developing more condition specific treatments for CYP including, for example, treatments for social anxiety [35,36] and panic disorder [37,38]. In terms of specific phobia, multi-session CBT has long been held as gold standard treatment for children and young people [39,40], and recent studies have shown the potential for one session treatments (OST) [39,41,42,43].

An Example of Guided Parent Delivered CBT for Younger Children Experiencing Anxiety: Parent Led CBT (PL-CBT)

As well as disorder specific approaches, there is an emerging evidence-base and literature focussed on the development of more transdiagnostic approaches such as Coping Cat [44] and there have been a number of helpful practical texts produced [23,45]. Whilst these generic interventions have been popular within Child and Adolescent Mental Health Services (CAMHS), particularly for younger children, in recent years we have seen welcome and exciting advancements in relation to Parent-Delivered/Parent-Led CBT (PL-CBT) that focuses on up-skilling parents and carers to support primary school aged children [46]. The PL-CBT approach can be delivered in individual, group and online formats [47] and is supported by an excellent and accessible guide for parents and carers [48].

Primarily, aimed at CYP between the ages of 5–12 experiencing anxiety disorders (specific phobia, generalised anxiety disorder, social anxiety disorder and separation anxiety disorder), PL-CBT supports parents and carers to develop their own skills in CBT in order to support their young person. Based on the inhibitory learning model and the principles that parents and carers are experts in their children and that they are the ones spending most of their time with their CYP, PL-CBT supports parents and carers to, in effect, become the CYP's therapists. PL-CBT promotes exposure through four core components of psychoeducation, identification and examination of negative automatic thoughts, developing graded hierarchies and reward systems and problem solving. The programme, delivered on an individual basis, requires the parent or carer to attend seven sessions, which are delivered either face to face or over the telephone/video consultation. On top of this, many parents and carers are asked to attend an information session that allows them to hear about the programme and consider if it is a good match for them and their CYP. Home tasks, for parents and carers to complete with CYP, are set at the end of each appointment and reviewed at the next.

The first face to face session of the programme focuses on psychoeducation, attuning the parent or carer to the principles of CBT applied to the treatment of anxiety disorders in CYP. In many ways, this first session is akin to a formulation session helping the parent or carer understand their CYP difficulties whilst developing idiosyncratic treatment goals collaboratively with their CYP outside of the session. In session two, the therapist and parent focus on understanding the young person's thoughts and understanding what they need to learn to get better. The aim of this is to promote 'have a go' behaviour supported by rewards. In session three, the parent focuses on the development of exposure hierarchies or 'step-by-step' plans which are then developed by parents and carers outside of the session in collaboration with CYP.

Session four is delivered remotely, either by telephone or by video consolation, and focuses on reviewing progress and supporting the development and progress of 'step-by-step' plans. Session five, which is conducted face to face, introduces problem solving techniques whilst reviewing previously set home tasks and setting new home tasks. Session six is a review similar to session four but also prepares the family for discharge. Session seven, sees the end of the programme with coverage of relapse prevention and next steps. Thought is also given as to whether any further input might be required from wider services or whether the CYP is to be discharged.

As it stands at the time of writing, parent PL-CBT can be deliver individually [49], in groups [50] and online via the online support and intervention for child anxiety (OSI) platform. Work continues on adapting this approach for children and young people experiencing ASD and OCD [51] and offers us the potential of further advancement.

OCD

Cognitive behavioural therapy for CYP has also made advances around obsessive-compulsive and related disorders, with NICE [52] recommending CBT as the treatment of choice for CYP experiencing OCD and body dysmorphic disorder (BDD). Whilst evidence for CBT for BDD in CYP is limited [53,54] more evidence does exist for CBT for OCD [55,56,57,58]. Evidence and guidance also highlight the importance of including exposure response prevention (ERP) as an active ingredient of intervention for CYP with OCD [52,57]. Practically speaking, this is another instance where more behavioural approaches like ERP tend to work better with younger age groups than more cognitively based approaches. There have been several protocols written specifically for CYP over the years [59,60,61] with evidence to support [56,61,62]. More recently, we have seen the contemporary and helpful development of child specific resources to support therapy such as the CBT workbook 'OCD tools to help you fight back' [63].

PTSD

Trauma focussed CBT (TF-CBT) is cited as the primary treatment for CYP with trauma [64] and has a robust evidence-base [55,65]. Two recent meta-analyses conducted by Mavranezouli and De Haun colleagues, respectively [66,67], suggested that TF-CBT was the most effective treatment for managing symptoms of PTSD in young people, above Eye Movement Desensitisation and Reprocessing (EMDR) and supportive counselling. In addition, TF-CBT has been shown to be one of the most cost-effective treatments for children and young people with trauma related mental health difficulties compared with supportive counselling and a family therapy approach [66,68,69]. As with other disorder specific interventions, CYP models and interventions are largely based on adult models although adaptation and CYP specific models [70,71] are now well established. Interventions are also emerging in CCBT-based treatments amongst other areas of innovation, widening the access and treatment options for CYP.

Treatment protocols are adapted to CYP, taking into account intellectual and developmental stage of the individual or group. Comprehensive assessment of PTSD should include interviewing CYP/carers/others with increased awareness of how to conduct this in an engaging and sensitive way for young people with trauma. In PTSD, rapport building with CYP and family and establishing a strong trusting relationship is particularly important in preparation for interventions which will, necessarily, cause moderate to high levels of distress. Psychoeducation is a key foundational stage of treatment and can include videos and use of metaphors to increase validation, therapeutic alliance, helping to develop a shared rationale for the intervention.

Developing a collaborative timeline and setting up and delivering the reliving of each memory, using imaginal approaches, written narratives and drawings are useful tools in assessment, development of the formulation and initial treatment stages. Cognitive skills then involve reliving to identify the CYP's hotspots, updating the negative appraisals and associated meanings using various CBT skills including Socratic questions, surveys, behaviour experiments, pie charts with considerations of rumination, anger, shame and guilt. As with adult treatments reprocessing through reliving and updating, supports the CYP to find new meanings and appraisals which is key to helping the CYP move beyond the trauma. Skills in imagery rehearsal and re-scripting, in-vivo exposure are important here allowing the YP to identify the difference between now and the traumatic events helping them move forward with new more functional beliefs and behaviours.

Finally, as with all conditions, constructing appropriate homework tasks to support the CYP with all of the work described (e.g. activity diaries; intrusion diaries; listening to reliving; writing narratives, etc.) is key in supporting the CYP to embed the learning and skills learning in sessions.

Innovations and CYP Specific Recommendations in CBT with CYP

In addition to the interventions mentioned, there is a growing evidence-base for new ways of working with CYP. There are also clear and helpful adaptations that can be utilised in CYP to improve outcomes.

Beyond the common mental health problems described above, the application of CBT has in recent times diversified to several other areas ranging from supporting CYP with neurodevelopmental comorbidities, such as ASD [1] to supporting CYP with long-term health problems such as diabetes, epilepsy, persistent physical symptoms and/or chronic pain [72]. With reference to the later, CBT has become one of the primary interventions within pain management services with research evidence and guidance supporting its use and effectiveness in reducing levels of experienced pain [73]. Within clinical practice, much attention has also been given to third wave CBT approaches such as acceptance and commitment therapy (ACT) with evidence slowly building to support this.

Including Parents in Your Intervention

Although it is historically unclear whether parental involvement in therapy improves outcomes for CYP [74], as discussed above in terms of brief BA for adolescents and PL-CBT, there is emerging evidence that when parental involvement is developed in a meaningful and structured way, outcomes can be significantly improved. Take for instance OCD, where the safety-seeking behaviours and neutralising behaviours can be maintained (albeit with benign intent) by the parent. Parents can for instance incorporate neutralising behaviours into the daily routine for the whole family, thereby maintaining the perceived threat of not engaging in the safety-seeking behaviours. Consider bringing the parent into sessions on a regular basis to talk about the collaborative formulation and if needed model skills of interaction with their child. In OCD, parents can play a key role in making sure that ERP plans are followed. As discussed above the successes of the PL-CBT approach strongly suggest that parental involvement can be key to outcomes for the CYP.

Low Intensity CBT

Innovations in the development of low intensity CBT interventions for CYP have formed an important part of getting effective treatments to CYP early and has also shaped the largest part of workforce expansion for psychological professions in recent years. Roles include the community specialist children's wellbeing practitioner (CWP; based in the community), the education mental health practitioner (EMHP; based in schools) the youth intensive psychological practitioner, and now the senior wellbeing practitioner (SWP) where CWPs and EMHPs can learn to expand their breadth of practice to a wider variety of MH conditions. CBT is adapted to brief and parsimonious interventions, that still rely on a collaborative approach. The emerging evidence-base primarily exists in low mood and anxiety, but is expanding to a greater breadth [75].

Computerised CBT (CCBT)

As discussed in previous adult focussed chapters, computerised or digital CBT is a fast-developing area for CYP. The use of online tools, learning, interactive content and even video/online games is developing at an extraordinary pace, particularly since the pandemic. CCBT can allow a CYP to access treatment from their home or another safe location, extending the reach and increasing access to evidence-based treatments for CYP [76]. That said, some have argued that CCBT can lead to a range of cultural and social-economic inequalities [77].

In response to the considerable advantages of CCBT, NICE [78], in their early value assessment of 'Guided self-help digital cognitive behavioural therapy for children and young people with mild to moderate symptoms of anxiety or low mood' recommended four packages for use whilst further evidence is collected. These packages include:

- Lumi Nova (BfB labs)
- Online social anxiety cognitive therapy for adolescents (OSCA)
- Online support and intervention for child anxiety (OSI)
- (SilverCloud) space from anxiety for teens, space from low mood for teens, space from low mood and anxiety for teens

Whilst the process of collecting evidence remains in its infancy for CCBT with CYP the pace of development and research is encouraging.

Making CBT Developmentally Sensitive

As discussed earlier in this chapter, when working with CYP of different ages or those who are impacted by developmental difficulties, it is important to consider a thorough assessment of where the CYP is in their emotional, social and cognitive development to best ensure collaborative and appropriate treatment. Key to effective CBT is genuine collaboration and therapeutic alliance, therefore adaptations should be considered based on good information gathering, assessment and formulation. Assessment needs to include getting a good understanding of the YP's preferred means of communication, that is, visually, verbally or through play, for instance. This will improve engagement and create the therapeutic setting, which has the best chance of making a meaningful impact on goals and distress levels.

Assessing Developmental Needs

When assessing the developmental needs of a CYP, consider including neuropsychological assessments such as the Weschler Intelligence Scale for Children (V WISC-V) [79]. These measures can support better understanding of a CYP, using data about their cognitive and learning profiles and intellectual abilities. For instance, better understanding their capacity to learn, retain and reflect on the content of sessions. However, (if completed in isolation) these assessments can have limitations in the scope of understanding all of the emotional components needed for effective engagement in therapy. There is little substitute for dialogue, focussed on getting a measure of whether the CYP has access to and can explain their thoughts, feelings, and behaviours. Techniques such as Socratic questioning can be effectively adapted for CYP to see if they have the ability to generate their own learning and new meanings [80]. If the CYP does not appear to be developmentally able to access this information, consider going back a step in therapy and teaching them these skills. Taking the time to support the CYP to develop skills such as expanding their emotional literacy, teaching them to recognise and manage difficult emotions and better understand the potentially difficult language used in therapy can improve therapeutic alliance and therefore outcomes [81].

Attachment

As discussed earlier in this chapter, the life events that the CYP has experienced can significantly impact their ability to engage in therapy and the therapeutic relationship with the therapist. Consider that the only other experiences the CYP may have had with adults could have been inconsistent, aggressive/abusive or neglectful; this can, understandably, impact how they relate with the therapist. Holding these factors in mind and taking the time, where needed, to build trust in the therapeutic relationship can create the safe environment needed for meaningful change and new learning to take place and allow the platform for the CYP to test their concept of self, world and others. Consider discussing explicitly the expectations for therapy and how the relationship with the therapist differs from that of the parent, caregiver and teacher. Remind them that the therapy space is a safe environment, one that is compassionate, confidential, and collaborative. Positive therapeutic attachment and relationship can significantly improve outcomes for the CYP [82].

Language

Bear in mind that CBT is largely a language-based therapeutic intervention, which can be abstract, hypothetical, jargon and metaphor heavy and technically challenging. CYP friendly metaphors and analogies can help the CYP engage with abstract concepts, for instance, how our thoughts and feelings can impact one another, or how something difficult that happens earlier in our lives can impact how we see the world later in life. As long as interventions are evidence-based and formulation driven, it is appropriate to use the CYP's own interests to maintain engagement and improved understanding. Discussing for instance how a CYP's favourite superhero might manage a challenging situation, negative thought or their negative sense of self can support CYP to gain new understanding for CYP and make abstract ideas more accessible.

Therapeutic Environment, Breaks and Session Length

As well as adaptations to language, key to creating a safe and nurturing space for CYP is considering if adaptations are needed in the environment. CYP may appreciate more child sensitive spaces with activities to engage them such as arts, crafts, toys and so on. It may be necessary to consider shorter sessions or regular breaks if the CYP has a shorter attention span, particularly if they have working memory or executive functioning difficulties and/or neurodevelopmental difficulties. At the beginning of the session, consider including in your agenda: agreeing with the CYP and family how long they can manage and whether they would like breaks in the session and to stick to these agreed parameters.

Play and Creativity

Play is critical to child development in learning how to manage relationships, develop cognitive representations for understanding the world and process their experiences. These mechanisms can be particularly powerful in helping with engagement and facilitating change [83]. Activities around play can allow the CYP to better conceptualise abstract constructs that are necessary for new learning in effective CBT. Play can also be used as a reward for hard work in therapy sessions and can take the form of games, board games, imaginative play; feel free to be creative. As long as the play is led by the formulation, it is appropriate to create a fun and engaging environment which will ultimately benefit the CYP. There are many helpful resources and ideas for supporting communication of and learning around potentially complex CBT ideas in the literature (for example Stallard 'Thinking Good – Feeling Better' [23] which will give advice and illustrations to help you to better socialise and help CYP engage with the content of sessions). It is appropriate to allow the CYP to suggest the nature of the play, this can support the development and maintenance of the therapeutic alliance and will add to the richness of ongoing assessment and formulation.

Neurodiversity: Adaptations in CBT

ASD, ADHD and other neuro-developmental difficulties can have a significant impact on how a CYP processes the world around them and how they, think, feel and behave. ASD affects social interaction and communication, and causes repetitive and restrictive behaviours impacting flexibility and rigidity in thinking styles: important for CBT to be effective. There is a growing body of research that suggests that, when adapted, evidence-based psychological interventions can be effective in the treatment of a range of common mental health problems experienced by autistic people. Much of the clinical research is related to interventions within a cognitive behavioural framework with a focus on anxiety problems (e.g. [85]).

When considering appropriate adaptations, all of the recommendations above (for CYP overall) are applicable in working with CYP with neurodevelopmental difficulties. Although not always necessary, consider that you might need a greater number of sessions when working with neurodiversity. Take the time to make sure language, particularly abstract/hypothetical language is sufficiently understood by the CYP and their family. Your collaborative formulation and assessment will be key here. Understanding for instance the difference between a functional sensory coping behaviour (reducing distress in a perceived chaotic world) and a safety-seeking behaviour (maintaining distress by avoiding perceived threat), could shape the collaborative treatment plan in, for example, OCD. In this case, resources, such as those in 'Challenge your OCD' [84], can be helpful.

Taking into account of all the above considerations to create a therapeutically idiosyncratic treatment plan, relevant and developmentally appropriate resources can improve engagement and collaboration in sessions. A recent paper [85] surveyed therapists and identified several key recommendations for adapting CBT to work with autistic people. These include having a concrete approach, not deviating too much from the agenda and not being overly abstract. If the CYP is having difficulties accessing and understanding their thoughts, it can be helpful to focus more of behavioural strategies so that the CYP can act as an agent in their change. Language should be 'plain', saying what you mean and again not being too abstract. Using the hobbies or the CYP's special/circumscribed interest can increase engagement in the session, but also including family members wherever possible.

Conclusion

In this chapter, we have considered the developmental context of working with CYP and the implication those considerations have upon how we deliver CBT. In particular, we have discussed the importance of including the CYP's parents, carers, schools and other systems such as wider health and social care provision during the assessment, formulation, intervention, relapse prevention and evaluation phases of CBT. Whilst the historical evidence-base for CBT with CYP is largely extrapolated and adapted from the adult literature, we have seen that in recent years more child specific interventions are being developed and researched. These interventions are designed to be developmentally sensitive in terms of developmental stage, language, emotional literacy and the inclusion of others within treatment protocols. Moreover, there has also been a growth in the application of third wave CBT, for example ACT, for CYP with range of conditions. The advent of CYP-IAPT in 2011 led to an explosion in the training of CBT therapist trained specifically to work with CYP. Perhaps evermore exciting has been the development of low intensity CBT since the expansion of CYP-IAPT to train low intensity practitioners such has CWPs and EMHPs. Utilising new health technologies such as CCBT, this new workforce, perhaps, heralds a new and promising advancement in early intervention using CBT.

Further Reading

Creswell C, Willetts L. *Helping Your Child with Fears and Worries: A Self-Help Guide for Parents.* 2nd ed. London: Robinson; 2019.

James AC, Reardon T, Soler A, James G, Creswell C. Cognitive behavioural therapy for anxiety disorders in children and adolescents. Cochrane Database of Systematic Reviews, 2020;**11**, CD013162. https://pubmed.ncbi.nlm.nih.gov/33196111/.

Fuggle P, Dunmuir S, Curry V. *CBT with Children and Young People and Families.* London: Sage; 2013.

Rapee RM, Creswell C, Kendall PC, Pine DS, Waters AM. Anxiety disorders in children and adolescents: A summary and overview of the literature. Behaviour Research and Therapy, 2023;**168**:104376, https://doi.org/10.1016/j.brat.2023.104376.

Stallard P. *Anxiety: Cognitive Behaviour Therapy with Children and Young People (CBT with Children, Adolescents and Families)*. Hove: Routledge; 2009.

Stallard P. *Thinking Good, Feeling Better: A Cognitive Behavioural Therapy Workbook for Adolescents and Young Adults*. John Wiley & Sons; 2018.

References

1. James AC, Reardon T, Soler A, James G, Creswell C. Cognitive behavioural therapy for anxiety disorders in children and adolescents. Cochrane Database Syst Rev [Internet]. 2020 [accessed 26 January 2024]; (11). www.cochranelibrary.com/cdsr/doi/10.1002/14651858.CD013162.pub2/abstract.
2. Stallard P. Think good, feel good: *A Cognitive Behavioural Therapy Workbook for Children and Young People*. Chichester: John Wiley & Sons; 2002.
3. NHS. The NHS long term plan [Internet]. 2019. www.longtermplan.nhs.uk/.
4. Department of Health, Department for Education. Transforming_children_and_young_people_s_mental_health_provision.pdf [Internet]. Department of Health, Department for Education; [accessed 26 January 2024]. Report No.: CM 9525. https://assets.publishing.service.gov.uk/media/5a823518e5274a2e87dc1b56/Transforming_children_and_young_people_s_mental_health_provision.pdf.
5. Atkinson J. Trauma-informed services and trauma-specific care for Indigenous Australian children. Aust Inst Health Welf [Internet]. 2013 [accessed 26 January 2024]; https://apo.org.au/sites/default/files/resource-files/2013-07/apo-nid35109.pdf.
6. Cook A, Blaustein M, Spinazzola J, van der Kolk B. Complex trauma in children and adolescents: White paper from the national child traumatic stress network complex trauma task force. Los Angel Natl Cent Child Trauma Stress. 2003;**35**(5):390–398.
7. Cook A, Spinazzola J, Ford J, Lanktree C, Blaustein M, Cloitre M, et al. Complex Trauma in Children and Adolescents. Psychiatr Ann [Internet]. 2005 [accessed 26 February 2024]; https://psycnet.apa.org/record/2005-05449-004.
8. Perry BD. Applying principles of neurodevelopment to clinical work with maltreated and traumatized children: The neurosequential model of therapeutics. In: NB Webb (Ed.), *Working with Traumatized Youth in Child Welfare*, 1st ed. (pp. 27–52). New York: Guilford Press; 2005.
9. Perry BD. Examining child maltreatment through a neurodevelopmental lens: Clinical applications of the neurosequential model of therapeutics. J Loss Trauma. 2009;**14**(4):240–255.
10. van der Kolk BA, Pynoos RS, Cicchetti D, Cloitre M, D'Andrea W, Ford JD, et al. Proposal to include a developmental trauma disorder diagnosis for children and adolescents in DSM-V. Unpubl Manuscr Verfügbar Unter Httpwww Cathymalchiodi Comdtdnctsn Pdf Zugriff 205 2011 [Internet]. 2009 [accessed 22 February 2024]; https://complextrauma.org/wp-content/uploads/2019/03/Complex-Trauma-Resource-3-Joseph-Spinazzola.pdf.
11. Bellis MA, Lowey H, Leckenby N, Hughes K, Harrison D. Adverse Childhood Experiences: Retrospective Study to Determine Their Impact on Adult Health Behaviours and Health Outcomes in a UK Population. 2013 [accessed 26 January 2024]; https://api.taylorfrancis.com/content/chapters/edit/download?identifierName=doi&identifierValue=10.1201/b18768-16&type=chapterpdf.
12. Vygotsky LS. Mind in Society: The Development of Higher Psychological Processes [Internet]. Harvard University Press; 1978 [accessed 26 February 2024]. https://books.google.co.uk/books?hl=en&lr=&id=Irq913lEZ1QC&oi=fnd&pg=PR13&ots=HcAsy0Ehrb&sig=ZQVoUNGb7qTXTnyhN99qD0WP4bk.

13. Piaget J, Inhelder B. *Psychology of the Child.* New York: Basic Books; 1969.
14. Bowlby J. Developmental psychiatry comes of age. Am J Psychiatry. 1988;**145**(1):1–10.
15. Denton R, Frogley C, Jackson S, John M, Querstret D. The assessment of developmental trauma in children and adolescents: A systematic review. Clin Child Psychol Psychiatry. 2017;**22**(2):260–287.
16. Fuggle P, Dunsmuir S, Curry V. *CBT with Children, Young People and Families.* London: Sage; 2013.
17. Kaufman J, Birmaher B, Axelson D, Perepletchikova F, Brent D, Ryan N. The Kiddie Schedule for Affective Disorders and Schizophrenia Present and Lifetime Version (KSADS-PL DSM5) [Internet]. Advanced Center for Intervention and Services Research (ACISR) for Early Onset Mood and Anxiety Disorders Western Psychiatric Institute and Clinic; https://pre.pediatricbipolar.pitt.edu/sites/default/files/assets/AH/AK/KSADS_DSM_5_SCREEN_Final.pdf.
18. Chorpita BF, Yim L, Moffitt C, Umemoto LA, Francis SE. Assessment of symptoms of DSM-IV anxiety and depression in children: A revised child anxiety and depression scale. Behav Res Ther. 2000;**8**(38):835–855.
19. Law D, Jacob J. *Goals and Goal Based Outcomes (GBOs).* London: CAMHS Press; 2013.
20. Duncan B, Miller S, Sparks J, Claud D, Reynolds L. The session rating scale: Preliminary psychometric properties of a 'working' alliance measure. J Brief Ther. 2003;**3**:3–12.
21. Miller SD, Duncan BL. *The Outcome Rating Scale.* Chicago; Authors: 2000.
22. Prochaska JO, DiClemente CC. Transtheoretical therapy: Toward a more integrative model of change. Psychother Theory Res Pract. 1982;**19**(3):276–288.
23. Stallard P. *Thinking Good, Feeling Better: A Cognitive Behavioural Therapy Workbook for Adolescents and Young Adults.* Chichester: John Wiley & Sons; 2018.
24. Rapee R, Creswell C, Kendall PC, Pine DS, Waters AM. Anxiety disorders in children and adolescents: a summary and overview of the literature. Behav Res Ther [Internet]. 2023 [accessed 26 January 2024]; **168**. https://ora.ox.ac.uk/objects/uuid:5218be78-b857-4c15-b3e8-53e275fa39b7.
25. Pass L, Lejuez CW, Reynolds S. Brief behavioural activation (Brief BA) for adolescent depression: A pilot study. Behav Cogn Psychother. 2018;**46**(2):182–194.
26. Reynolds S, Pass L. Brief Behavioural Activation for Adolescent Depression: A Clinician's Manual and Session-by-session Guide [Internet]. Jessica Kingsley Publishers; 2020 [accessed 22 February 2024]. https://books.google.co.uk/books?hl=en&lr=&id=0qPsDwAAQBAJ&oi=fnd&pg=PP1&dq=Brief+Behavioural+Activation+for+Adolescent+Depression:+A+Clinician%27s+Manual+and+Session-by-Session+Guide&ots=DZtKtXXa5d&sig=yn401uojuW4m5IlWOWhtMyWsIfQ.
27. Tindall L, Mikocka-Walus A, McMillan D, Wright B, Hewitt C, Gascoyne S. Is behavioural activation effective in the treatment of depression in young people? A systematic review and meta-analysis. Psychol Psychother Theory Res Pract. 2017;**90**(4):770–796.
28. Oud M, De Winter L, Vermeulen-Smit E, Bodden D, Nauta M, Stone L, et al. Effectiveness of CBT for children and adolescents with depression: A systematic review and meta-regression analysis. Eur Psychiatry. 2019;**57**:33–45.
29. Verduyn C, Rogers J, Wood A. *Depression.* 1st ed. London: Routledge; 2009.
30. NHS. nhs.uk. 2023 [accessed 22 February 2024]. Anxiety disorders in children. www.nhs.uk/mental-health/children-and-young-adults/advice-for-parents/anxiety-disorders-in-children/.
31. Chase RM, Whitton SW, Pincus DB. Treatment of adolescent panic disorder: A nonrandomized comparison of intensive versus weekly CBT. Child Fam Behav Ther. 2012;**34**(4):305–323.

32. Pincus DB, May JE, Whitton SW, Mattis SG, Barlow DH. Cognitive-behavioral treatment of panic disorder in adolescence. J Clin Child Adolesc Psychol. 2010;**39**(5):638–649.

33. Schneider S, Blatter-Meunier J, Herren C, In-Albon T, Adornetto C, Meyer A, et al. The efficacy of a family-based cognitive-behavioral treatment for separation anxiety disorder in children aged 8–13: A randomized comparison with a general anxiety program. J Consult Clin Psychol. 2013;**81**(5):932–940.

34. Giani L, Caputi M, Forresi B, Michelini G, Scaini S. Evaluation of cognitive-behavioral therapy efficacy in the treatment of separation anxiety disorder in childhood and adolescence: A systematic review of randomized controlled trials. Int J Cogn Ther. 2021;**15**(1):57–80.

35. Leigh E, Clark DM. Cognitive therapy for social anxiety disorder in adolescents: A development case series. Behav Cogn Psychother. 2016;**44**(1):1–17.

36. Leigh E, Clark DM. Cognitive Therapy for Social Anxiety Disorder in Adolescents [Internet]. 2018. https://oxcadatresources.com/wp-content/uploads/2018/11/CT-SAD-A-MANUAL.pdf.

37. Waite P. Protocol for a randomised controlled feasibility study examining the efficacy of brief cognitive therapy for the treatment of panic disorder in adolescents (PANDA). Pilot Feasibility Stud. 2022;**8**(1):49.

38. Waite P, Clark DM. Cognitive Therapy for Panic Disorder in Adolescents, (Version 1). [Internet]. Oxcadatresources; 2023. https://oxcadatresources.com/wp-content/uploads/2023/09/Brief-Cognitive-Therapy-for-Panic-Disorder-in-Adolescents-Clinician-Manual-and-Session-by-Session-Guide-Version-1.0_15-08-23.pdf.

39. Ollendick TH, Cowart M, Milliner E. Specific phobias. In: RA Vasa, AK Roy (Eds.), *Pediatric Anxiety Disorders: A Clinical Guide.* (pp. 113–128). New York: Springer Science & Business Media; 2013.

40. NHS. nhs.uk. 2023 [accessed 22 February 2024]. Treatment – Phobias. www.nhs.uk/mental-health/conditions/phobias/treatment/.

41. Davis TE, Ollendick TH, Öst LG. Intensive treatment of specific phobias in children and adolescents. Cogn Behav Pract. 2009;**3**(16):294–303.

42. Davis TE, Ollendick TH, Öst LG. *Intensive One-Session Treatment of Specific Phobias.* New York: Springer; 2012.

43. Wang HI, Wright B, Tindall L, Cooper C, Biggs K, Lee E, et al. Cost and effectiveness of one session treatment (OST) for children and young people with specific phobias compared to multi-session cognitive behavioural therapy (CBT): Results from a randomised controlled trial. BMC Psychiatry [Internet]. 2022 [accessed 22 February 2024];**22**(1). https://eprints.keele.ac.uk/id/eprint/11263/.

44. Kendall PC. *Coping Cat Workbook.* 2nd ed. Ardmore, PA: Workbook Pub Inc; 2006.

45. Stallard P. *Anxiety: Cognitive Behaviour Therapy with Children and Young People* [Internet]. Routledge; 2009. https://books.google.co.uk/books?id=LwnbAAAAMAAJ.

46. Thirlwall K, Cooper PJ, Karalus J, Voysey M, Willetts L, Creswell C. Treatment of child anxiety disorders via guided parent-delivered cognitive–behavioural therapy: Randomised controlled trial. Br J Psychiatry. 2013;**203**(6):436–444.

47. Hill C, Chessell C, Percy R, Creswell C. Online support and intervention (OSI) for child anxiety: A case series within routine clinical practice. Behav Cogn Psychother. 2022;**50**(4):429–445.

48. Creswell C, Willetts L. *Helping Your Child with Fears and Worries: A Self-Help Guide for Parents.* 2nd ed. London: Robinson; 2019.

49. Halldorsson B, Elliott L, Chessell C, Willetts L, Creswell C. Helping your child with fears and worries: a self-help guide for parents treatment manual for therapists [Internet]. the authors; 2019 [accessed 22 February 2024]. https://centaur.reading.ac.uk/id/eprint/87041.

50. Halldorsson B, Elliott L, Chessell C, Willetts L, Creswell C. Helping your child with fears and worries: Guided self-help manual for Therapists working with groups [Internet]. The authors; 2021 [accessed 29 February 2024]. https://centaur.reading.ac.uk/65533/.

51. Chessell C, Harvey K, Halldorsson B, Farrington A, Creswell C. Parents' experiences of parenting a preadolescent child with OCD: A qualitative study. Emot Behav Difficulties. 2023;**28**(1):68–85.

52. National Institute for Health and Care Excellence. Obsessive-compulsive disorder and body dysmorphic disorder: treatment. Clinical Guidance [Internet]. NICE; 2005 Nov. Report No.: CG31. www.nice.org.uk/guidance/cg31.

53. Harrison A, de la Cruz LF, Enander J, Radua J, Mataix-Cols D. Cognitive-behavioral therapy for body dysmorphic disorder: A systematic review and meta-analysis of randomized controlled trials. Clin Psychol Rev. 2016;**48**:43–51.

54. Mataix-Cols D, de la Cruz LF, Isomura K, Anson M, Turner C, Monzani B, et al. A pilot randomized controlled trial of cognitive-behavioral therapy for adolescents with body dysmorphic disorder. J Am Acad Child Adolesc Psychiatry. 2015;**54**(11):895–904.

55. James AC, James G, Cowdrey FA, Soler A, Choke A. Cognitive behavioural therapy for anxiety disorders in children and adolescents. Cochrane Database Syst Rev. 2015;**2015**(2):CD004690.

56. Öst LG, Riise EN, Wergeland GJ, Hansen B, Kvale G. Cognitive behavioral and pharmacological treatments of OCD in children: A systematic review and meta-analysis. J Anxiety Disord. 2016;**43**:58–69.

57. Reid J, Laws K, Drummond LM, Vismara M, Grancini B, Mpavaenda D, et al. Cognitive behavioural therapy with exposure and response prevention in the treatment of obsessive-compulsive disorder: A systematic review and meta-analysis of randomised controlled trials. Compr Psychiatry [Internet]. 2021 [accessed 22 February 2024]; http://uhra.herts.ac.uk/handle/2299/23969.

58. Uhre CF, Uhre VF, Lønfeldt NN, Pretzmann L, Vangkilde S, Plessen KJ, et al. Systematic review and meta-analysis: Cognitive-behavioral therapy for obsessive-compulsive disorder in children and adolescents. J Am Acad Child Adolesc Psychiatry. 2020;**59**(1):64–77.

59. March JS, Mulle K. OCD in children and adolescents: A cognitive-behavioral treatment manual. [Internet]. New York: Guilford Press; 1998 [accessed 22 February 2024]. https://psycnet.apa.org/record/1998-07740-000.

60. Barrett PM, Healy-Farrell L, Piacentini J, March J. Obsessive-compulsive disorder in childhood and adolescence: Description and treatment. In: P Barrett, T Ollendick (Eds.), *Handbook of Interventions That Work with Children and Adolescents: Prevention and Treatment.* (pp. 187–216). Chichester: Wiley Online Library; 2004.

61. Barrett P, Farrell L, Dadds M, Boulter N. Cognitive-behavioral family treatment of childhood obsessive-compulsive disorder: Long-term follow-up and predictors of outcome. J Am Acad Child Adolesc Psychiatry. 2005;**10**(44):1005–1014.

62. Williams TI, Salkovskis PM, Forrester L, Turner S, White H, Allsopp MA. A randomised controlled trial of cognitive behavioural treatment for obsessive compulsive disorder in children and adolescents. Eur Child Adolesc Psychiatry. 2010;**19**(5):449–456.

63. Turner C, Volz C, Krebs G. OCD-Tools to Help You Fight Back!: A CBT Workbook for Young People [Internet]. Jessica Kingsley Publishers; 2019 [accessed 22 February 2024]. https://books.google.co.uk/books?hl=en&lr=&id=zg5UDwAAQBAJ&oi=fnd&pg=PP2&dq=OCD+-+Tools+to+Help+You+Fight+Back!:+A+CBT+Workbook+for+Young+People&ots=UxpDVCqS86&sig=YxGVgVqUqduIAOGpRrOQueL7WyQ.

64. National Institute for Health and Care Excellence. Post-traumatic stress disorder [Internet]. 2018, p. 54. Report No.: NG116.

www.nice.org.uk/guidance/ng116/resources/posttraumatic-stress-disorder-pdf-66141601777861.

65. Xian-Yu CY, Deng NJ, Zhang J, Li HY, Gao TY, Zhang C, et al. Cognitive behavioral therapy for children and adolescents with post-traumatic stress disorder: Systematic review and meta-analysis. J Affect Disord. 2022;308:502–511.

66. Mavranezouli I, Megnin-Viggars O, Daly C, Dias S, Stockton S, Meiser-Stedman R, et al. Psychological and psychosocial treatments for children and young people with post-traumatic stress disorder: A network meta-analysis. J Child Psychol Psychiatry. 2020;**61**(1):18–29.

67. Haan A de, Meiser-Stedman R, Landolt MA, Kuhn I, Black MJ, Klaus K, et al. Efficacy and moderators of efficacy of cognitive behavioural therapies with a trauma focus in children and adolescents: An individual participant data meta-analysis of randomised trials. Lancet Child Adolesc Health. 2024;**8**(1):28–39.

68. Meiser-Stedman R, Smith P, McKinnon A, Dixon C, Trickey D, Ehlers A, et al. Cognitive therapy as an early treatment for post-traumatic stress disorder in children and adolescents: A randomized controlled trial addressing preliminary efficacy and mechanisms of action. J Child Psychol Psychiatry. 2017;**58**(5):623–633.

69. Shearer J, Papanikolaou N, Meiser-Stedman R, McKinnon A, Dalgleish T, Smith P, et al. Cost-effectiveness of cognitive therapy as an early intervention for post-traumatic stress disorder in children and adolescents: A trial based evaluation and model. J Child Psychol Psychiatry. 2018;**59**(7):773–780.

70. Smith P, Perrin S, Yule W, Clark DM. *Post Traumatic Stress Disorder: Cognitive Therapy with Children and Young People.* 1st ed. London: Routledge; 2009.

71. Cohen JA, Mannarino AP, Deblinger E. *Treating Trauma and Traumatic Grief in Children and Adolescents* [Internet]. New York: Guilford Publications; 2017 [accessed 29 February 2024]. https://books.google.co.uk/books?hl=en&lr=&id=hf6PDAAAQBAJ&oi=fnd&pg=PP1&ots=aUbjE2UCyM&sig=LJgfQ8b5gm4qqeTA-wka1rzvR6Y.

72. Bennett S, Shafran R, Coughtrey A, Walker S, Heyman I. Psychological interventions for mental health disorders in children with chronic physical illness: A systematic review. Arch Dis Child. 2015;**100**(4):308–316.

73. Lonergan A. The effectiveness of cognitive behavioural therapy for pain in childhood and adolescence: A meta-analytic review. Ir J Psychol Med. 2016;**33**(4):251–264.

74. Thulin U, Svirsky L, Serlachius E, Andersson G, Öst LG. The effect of parent involvement in the treatment of anxiety disorders in children: A meta-analysis. Cogn Behav Ther. 2014;**43**(3):185–200.

75. Turnbull M, Kirk H, Lincoln M, Peacock S, Howey L. A pilot evaluation of the role of a children's wellbeing practitioner (CWP) in a child and adolescent mental health service (CAMHS). Clin Child Psychol Psychiatry. 2023;**28**(3):1150–1159.

76. Bevan Jones R, Hussain F, Agha SS, Weavers B, Lucassen M, Merry S, et al. Digital technologies to support adolescents with depression and anxiety. BJPsych Adv [Internet]. 2022 [accessed 26 January 2024]; https://eprints.gla.ac.uk/263327/.

77. Aisbitt GM, Nolte T, Fonagy P. Editorial perspective: The digital divide–inequalities in remote therapy for children and adolescents. Child Adolesc Ment Health. 2023;**28**(1):105–107.

78. National Institute for Health and Care Excellence. Guided self-help digital cognitive behavioural therapy for children and young people with mild to moderate symptoms of anxiety or low mood: early value assessment [Internet]. NICE; 2023 [accessed 22 February 2024]. Report No.: HTE3. www.nice.org.uk/guidance/hte3.

79. Wechsler D. *Wechsler Intelligence Scale for Children.* 5th ed. Bloomington, MN: Pearson; 2014.

80. McLachlan NH, Eastwood L, Friedberg RD. Socratic questions with

children: Recommendations and cautionary tales. J Cogn Psychother. 2016;**30**(2):105–119.

81. Lieberman AF, Horn PV. *Psychotherapy with Infants and Young Children: Repairing the Effects of Stress and Trauma on Early Attachment.* 1st ed. New York: Guilford Press; 2011.

82. Ryan R, Berry K, Hartley S. Review: Therapist factors and their impact on therapeutic alliance and outcomes in child and adolescent mental health – a systematic review. Child Adolesc Ment Health. 2023;**28**(2):195–211.

83. Knell SM, Dasari M. Cognitive-behavioral play therapy for anxiety and depression. In: *Empirically Based Play Interventions for Children*, 2nd ed. (pp. 77–94). Washington, DC: American Psychological Association; 2016.

84. Jassi A. *Challenge Your OCD! A CBT Workbook for Young People with ASD.* Illustrated ed. London: Jessica Kingsley Publishers; 2020.

85. Cooper K, Loades ME, Russell AJ. Adapting psychological therapies for autism-therapist experience, skills and confidence. Res Autism Spectr Disord. 2018;**45**:43–50.

86. Clark DM. A cognitive model of panic attacks. In: S Rachman, JD Maser (eds.), *Panic: Psychological Perspectives* (pp. 71–89). Hillsdale, NJ : Lawrence Erlbaum Associates, Inc.; 1988.

87. Robichaud M. *Cognitive Behavioral Treatment for Generalized Anxiety Disorder: From Science to Practice.* New York: Routledge; 2019.

88. Clark DM, Wells A. A cognitive model of social phobia. In: RG Heimberg, MR Liebowitz, DA Hope, FR Schneier (eds.), *Social Phobia: Diagnosis, Assessment, and Treatment* (pp. 69–93). New York: Guilford Publications; 1995.

89. Beck JS, Beck AT. *Cognitive Behavior Therapy: Basics and Beyond.* 3rd ed. New York: Guilford Press; 2020.

90. Ehlers A, Clark DM. A cognitive model of posttraumatic stress disorder. *Behav Res Ther.* 2000;**38**(4):319–45.

91. Wilhelm S, Phillips KA, Steketee G. *Cognitive-Behavioral Therapy for Body Dysmorphic Disorder: A Treatment Manual.* New York: Guilford Press; 2013.

92. Warwick HM, Salkovskis PM. Hypochondriasis. *Behav Res Ther.* 1990;**28**(2):105–117.

93. Kirk J, Rouf K. Specific phobias. In: J Bennett-Levy, G Butler, M Fennell, A Hackmann, M Mueller, D Westbrook (eds.), *Oxford Guide to Behavioural Experiments in Cognitive Therapy* (pp. 161–182). Oxford: Oxford University Press; 2004.

94. Salkovskis PM, Warwick H, Deale AC. Cognitive-behavioral treatment for severe and persistent health anxiety (hypochondriasis). *Brief Treatment and Crisis Intervention.* 2003;**3**(3):353–367.

95. March JS, Mulle K. *OCD in Children and Adolescents: A Cognitive-Behavioral Treatment Manual.* New York: Guilford Press; 1998.

96. Haig-Ferguson A, Cooper K, Cartwright E, Loades ME, Daniels J. Practitioner review: Health anxiety in children and young people in the context of the COVID-19 pandemic. *Behav Cogn Psychother,* 2021;**49**(2):129–143.

97. Wells A. Hypochondriasis: Health anxiety. In: *Cognitive Therapy of Anxiety Disorders: A Practice Manual and Conceptual Guide* (pp. 79–96). 1st ed. Somerset: Wiley; 2013.

Chapter 26

Adaptations for Specific Events: Immediately after a Traumatic Event

Rachel Handley

In this chapter we will help you to be able to:

- Describe NICE recommendations for responding immediately after trauma.
- Utilise guidelines in your clinical practice and developing service policy.
- Offer pragmatic and compassionate responses to individuals presenting with very recent trauma exposure.

Introduction

Post-traumatic stress disorder (PTSD) has been described and recognised as psychiatric diagnosis for a relatively brief period of time compared to other psychological disorders. More recently, however, the disorder has become much more spoken about and recognised, not only in psychological services but also in the public domain. It is frequently portrayed in books and films and TV programmes, often in the context of war stories but also across a variety of traumatic events such as childhood and adult sexual assault and road traffic accidents. It is often referenced in the news media reporting on traumatic events such as terrorist incidents and other large-scale disasters.

This growing recognition of PTSD is welcome as it reflects a growing awareness of the fact that PTSD is not only a disorder of war – that it can impact anyone exposed to any type of trauma – and has also highlighted the availability of good evidence-based treatments that can radically alter the course of the disorder for individuals, particularly if accessed early.

However, as PTSD is spoken about more frequently, both in common parlance and in mental health services, 'trauma' has sometimes become synonymous with 'PTSD'. Two unhelpful assumptions can be made when these concepts are used interchangeably; first, that 'trauma' is a psychological disorder rather than an event that can, but does not inevitably, lead to psychological symptoms, and second, that PTSD is the inevitable consequence of trauma. These insidious ideas can equally unhelpfully lead to well-meaning but unhelpful responses immediately after trauma.

'Trauma' is a description of an event type with a specific definition within diagnostic descriptions of PTSD. DSM-5 describes the experience of trauma as 'Exposure to actual or threatened death, serious injury, or sexual violence' that can be experienced directly, witness or learned about, if occurring to a 'close family member or close friend' and also 'violent or accidental' [1]. PTSD, on the other hand, is one of the potential negative psychological consequences of the experience of trauma which is neither inevitable nor the only disorder associated with these negative life events. The symptoms and diagnostic criteria for PTSD, in both the DSM-5 and ICD-11, have been described in Chapter 19 [1,2].

The Most Common Response to Trauma Is Resilience

Exposure to traumatic events meeting the DSM-5 criteria is very common, being reported by up to 90% of individuals [3], and symptoms of PTSD in the immediate aftermath of trauma are common, but only a minority of trauma survivors go on to develop persistent PTSD. The proportion of trauma survivors who do develop PTSD has been shown to vary with the type of traumatic event; for example, traumas involving interpersonal violence are associated with higher rates of PTSD than those involved in natural disasters [4]. By far the most common outcome for individuals experiencing trauma is psychological recovery or resilience in terms of PTSD. This does not mean that interventions in the immediate aftermath of trauma are unnecessary or unhelpful, but it does mean that it is useful to think carefully about what interventions will be helpful and for whom.

Disasters versus Individual Traumas

Much of the literature around immediate responses to trauma has focussed on large-scale disasters or group traumas and/or in populations at high risk of trauma exposure such as the emergency services. Disasters and group trauma provoke a natural desire to help as we see and hear them reported. They present a challenge for authorities and emergency responders to know what response is appropriate. The significant occupational risk of trauma exposure, employer's duty of care and potential for negative occupational outcomes are compelling reasons for programmes to be developed to support emergency and military personnel. Programmes to intervene in the immediate aftermath of trauma have been variously effective.

Prevention versus Early Intervention

Broadly speaking early responses to trauma can be conceptualised as either attempts to prevent the development and persistence of PTSD symptoms or early interventions to treat these symptoms, although these categories are overlapping.

Prevention

Critical Incident Stress Debriefing (CISD) was developed in the 1980s to support emergency personnel following exposure to disasters and was subsequently applied more broadly to other populations post-trauma. The approach which was designed to be implemented very soon after the traumatic event (24–72 hours) includes assessment of the individuals' experience of and early reactions to and coping with the event, providing space to talk about thoughts, emotions and experiences and providing validation of their unique experience. The approach has face-validity given that trauma-focussed cognitive interventions all involve the reversal of avoidance of talking and thinking about the trauma experienced and reappraising unhelpful, often self-judging, cognitions about the event. However, studies of the impact of single-session debriefing interventions on PTSD outcomes have been equivocal with most suggesting no benefit and some a potentially a harmful impact, with the result that debriefing is not recommended by the National Institute for Health and Care Excellence guidelines [5].

Psychological First Aid

Young describes psychological first aid (PFA) as 'the use of pragmatic oriented interventions delivered during the immediate-impact phase (first 4 weeks) to individuals who are experiencing acute stress reactions or who appear at risk for being unable to regain sufficient functional equilibrium by themselves, with the intent of aiding adaptive coping and problem solving' [6]. Psychological first aid is embedded in systems and organisations that might normally come into contact with disaster survivors in the normal course of events which, depending on context, might for example include emergency services, medical services, charitable organisations or social services. Disaster mental health workers seek out survivors in these settings and informally assess risk through talking about their immediate concerns. The goals of PFA are to first help trauma survivors establish basic physical safety (e.g. signposting away from change and towards basic needs such as food and warmth). Second, PFA targets extreme acute stress reactions where they are perceived to be occurring, for example talking and listening in an empathic manner to those who have experienced sudden bereavement, protecting survivors from exposure to frightening or disgust-triggering stimuli and education about coping with memory triggers, helping them move their attention away from re-experienced aspects of the event and reframing negative appraisals of the event or subsequent coping. Reduction of stress-related reactions may also include interventions such as relaxation training and psychoeducation about normal stress reactions and stress management and could include psychopharmacology. Third, PFA signposts survivors to further psychosocial resources and services that can support them with basic needs relating to the trauma and, if needed, mental health supports.

Again, this approach has face-validity and although it has not been empirically evaluated it has been endorsed by experts in the field [6]. Many of the interventions proposed are recommended with caveats, for example, relaxation may exacerbate symptoms and psychoeducation about symptoms alone may be unhelpful. It is likely, therefore, that a thorough understanding of the risk and maintenance factors for PTSD (such as avoidance and suppression of intrusive memories) would be important in delivering them successfully.

Organisational Support

For those at high risk of trauma exposure, for example, those working in emergency services or the military there may be an opportunity to enhance detection of and early intervention with PTSD and other adverse mental health outcomes through programmes training managers. Programmes that help managers to understand risk factors and to recognise the signs and symptoms of PTSD may help them put measures in place to mitigate the impact of trauma and in the early period post-trauma, reduce stigma and enhance social support and help-seeking [7]. One such programme is the Trauma Risk Management (TRiM) programme, which originated in the UK military and has been applied in emergency services and other organisations where employees are at high risk of exposure to traumatic events. This programme trains peer supporters to provide psychological first aid in the aftermath of traumatic incidents including being able to assess for potential risk factors for developing psychological problems and to put in place effective support from managers and colleagues. The programme does not aim to prevent PTSD, but may help change perceptions of mental health problems and support help-seeking when needed [8].

Early Intervention

Given the existence of effective and psychological interventions for PTSD, a credible alternative approach to the prevention or maintenance of PTSD in the early days and weeks following a trauma might be to offer individuals with mild, or 'subclinical', PTSD symptoms early access to interventions such as trauma-focussed Cognitive Therapy. However, given that intrusive memories and other PTSD-related symptoms are a common experience after traumatic events, that these may be considered normal and perhaps even adaptive, and given that not all individuals with go on to develop PTSD this would be potentially an unnecessary, burdensome, intrusive and aversive experience for the individuals offered the treatment, and represent unnecessary and costly healthcare expenditure. Indeed, NICE guidance recommends 'active monitoring' for individuals who have symptoms PTSD that would be considered subthreshold when less than a month since the trauma has elapsed [5].

One such example of active monitoring was implemented on a large scale following the terrorist attacks on the London transport system on 7 July 2005. A novel Screen and Treat programme was set up by a Psychosocial Steering Group including leading experts in PTSD research and treatment [9]. The aim was to identify all trauma-exposed persons to enable follow-up and screening for psychological problems and to offer those who needed it evidence-based treatment. This 'screen and treat' approach emphasised outreach due to low treatment-seeking rates for PTSD. The authors of the study noted that few referrals came to the service through 'normal' referral channels (i.e. general practitioners) and many more were identified through the outreach programme. Analysis of outcomes indicated treatment outcomes similar to those reported in randomised controlled trails of PTSD treatment.

On an individual level, the implementation of 'active monitoring' – also sometimes referred to as 'watchful waiting' – is likely to fall to the GP. Given the fact that individuals may not present for support following traumatic experiences for a wide variety of reasons (e.g. being unaware that support may be accessible or a sense of shame associated with the trauma itself) public health approaches may be helpful to educate others they may come into contact with (managers, co-workers, family members, community groups) about the signs and symptoms of PTSD and the availability of effective evidence-based therapies.

An individual trauma-focussed CBT intervention is, however, recommended by NICE guidelines for those who have more significant symptoms of PTSD within the first month, that is, meeting criteria for Acute Stress Disorder (ASD) or 'clinically important' symptoms of PTSD. The DSM-5 criteria for ASD are very similar to those for PTSD, with the most notable, and relevant to this text, difference being the timing of the onset and duration of the problem [1]. ASD can be diagnosed if the individual's symptoms had their onset between three days and one month after the traumatic event and persist for at least three days. If the symptoms persist beyond one month after the trauma exposure, then PTSD would be assessed, and they would no longer have a diagnosis of ASD. The term 'clinically important symptoms' is adopted by NICE to refer to cases where individuals may have been assessed to meet threshold criteria for PTSD on based on validated self-report measures rather than through a diagnostic clinical interview [5].

The basis of these recommendations are studies that have shown positive outcomes for this early intervention, with reduced incidence of PTSD post-treatment and at follow-up. One such study to treat ASD, for example, was carried out by Bryant and colleagues [10]. Participants were randomly allocated to either five sessions of CBT or five sessions of supportive counselling less than two weeks after exposure to a traumatic event (either road traffic or industrial accidents). The CBT sessions included common elements of trauma-focussed cognitive therapy, that is, psychoeducation about trauma reactions, imaginal exposure to trauma memories, cognitive restructuring of fear appraisals and exposure to avoided situations as well as progressive muscle relaxation training. Of participants in the CBT condition only 8% met criteria for PTSD at the end of treatment and 17% at six months post-trauma. Fewer participants in the CBT group than the supportive counselling group met criteria for PTSD at each time point. The authors compared the results to a previous study they carried out indicating that 78% of participants experiencing ASD after road traffic accidents continued to suffer from PTSD at six months post-trauma. A four-year follow-up study by the same showed similar positive results and sustained benefits of the treatment (although there was no wait list control) [11].

Current and Future Areas of Research

A wealth of research into the consolidation and re-consolidation of memories and interventions that can disrupt and enhance these processes is emerging. A thorough review is beyond the scope of this chapter, but for an overview see Monfils and Holmes [12]. Interesting experimental applications have included disrupting or blocking memory consolidation and re-consolidation using pharmacological and novel behavioural approaches such as the use of propanol during memory exposure or playing Tetris to inhibit intrusive memories during re-consolidation of memories [13].

Given the importance of social support as a risk factor for PTSD further research into what constitutes effective social support and how interventions could be designed to enhance social support in the aftermath of trauma would potentially be very useful [14].

Conclusion: Pulling It Together – What to Do in the Early Aftermath of Trauma?

In conclusion, it is still the case that in the very early days after trauma, there is little we know definitively with respect to the best interventions to prevent trauma and how to identify those that might most benefit from them. What is clear from the literature and clinical guidelines currently is that debriefing is not likely to be helpful, and may be harmful, while psychological first aid may be helpful but should be applied with caution and by individuals with expertise in trauma reactions. Watchful waiting or active monitoring for those exposed to trauma but not displaying clinically important symptoms of PTSD is advised and may be enhanced by 'public health' interventions that improved general understanding of the risk factors for and signs and symptoms of PTSD. Where individuals do indeed develop clinically important symptoms of PTSD or ASD in the immediate aftermath of trauma, trauma-focussed CBT interventions are recommended, although it is still difficult to predict who might otherwise go on to develop 'full-blown' PTSD.

Further Reading

National Institute for Health and Care Excellence. Post-traumatic stress disorder: Recommendations [NICE Guideline No. 116]. 2018. www.nice.org.uk/guidance/ng116/chapter/recommendations.

References

1. American Psychiatric Association. *Diagnostic and Statistical Manual of Mental Disorders: DSM-5.* Washington, DC: American Psychiatric Association; 2013.
2. World Health Organization. *International Classification of Diseases*, 11th Revision (ICD-11). World Health Organization; 2019.
3. Kilpatrick DG, Resnick HS, Milanak ME, Miller MW, Keyes KM, Friedman MJ. National estimates of exposure to traumatic events and PTSD prevalence using DSM-IV and DSM-5 criteria. J Trauma Stress. 2013;**26**(5):537–547.
4. Kessler RC, Sonnega A, Bromet E, Hughes M, Nelson CB. Posttraumatic stress disorder in the national comorbidity survey. Arch Gen Psychiatry. 1995;**52**(12):1048–1060.
5. National Institute for Health and Care Excellence. Post-traumatic stress disorder [Internet]. 2018 Dec p. 54. Report No.: NG116. www.nice.org.uk/guidance/ng116/resources/posttraumatic-stress-disorder-pdf-66141601777861.
6. Young BH. The immediate response to disaster: Guidelines for adult psychological first aid. In: EC Ritchie, PJ Watson, MJ Friedman (Eds.), *Interventions Following Mass Violence and Disasters: Strategies for Mental Health Practice* (pp. 134–154) [Internet]. New York: Guilford Publications; 2006.
7. Brooks SK, Rubin GJ, Greenberg N. Traumatic stress within disaster-exposed occupations: Overview of the literature and suggestions for the management of traumatic stress in the workplace. Br Med Bull. 2019;**129**(1):25–34.
8. Greenberg N, Langston V, Everitt B, Iversen A, Fear NT, Jones N, et al. A cluster randomized controlled trial to determine the efficacy of Trauma Risk Management (TRiM) in a military population. J Trauma Stress. 2010;**23**(4):430–436.
9. Brewin CR, Scragg P, Robertson M, Thompson M, d'Ardenne P, Ehlers A. Promoting mental health following the London bombings: A screen and treat approach. J Trauma Stress. 2008;**21**(1):3–8.
10. Bryant RA, Harvey AG, Dang ST, Sackville T, Basten C. Treatment of acute stress disorder: A comparison of cognitive-behavioral therapy and supportive counseling. J Consult Clin Psychol. 1998;**66**:862–866.
11. Bryant RA, Moulds ML, Nixon RV. Cognitive behaviour therapy of acute stress disorder: A four-year follow-up. Behav Res Ther. 2003;**41**(4):489–494.
12. Monfils MH, Holmes EA. Memory boundaries: Opening a window inspired by reconsolidation to treat anxiety, trauma-related, and addiction disorders. Lancet Psychiatry. 2018;**5**(12):1032–1042.
13. Iyadurai L, Blackwell SE, Meiser-Stedman R, Watson PC, Bonsall MB, Geddes JR, et al. Preventing intrusive memories after trauma via a brief intervention involving Tetris computer game play in the emergency department: A proof-of-concept randomized controlled trial. Mol Psychiatry. 2018;**23**(3):674–682.
14. Guay S, Billette V, Marchand A. Exploring the links between posttraumatic stress disorder and social support: Processes and potential research avenues. J Trauma Stress Off Publ Int Soc Trauma Stress Stud. 2006;**19**(3):327–338.

Chapter 27

Cognitive Behavioural Therapy in Primary Care

In this chapter we will help you to be able to:

- Explain the rationale for the development of a national primary care mental health service.
- Describe the concept of stepped care.
- Reflect on the progress and future for programmes such as NHSTT both in England and worldwide.

Introduction

CBT is an effective treatment approach for common mental health problems but is not routinely available at the levels required to support everyone. England's National Health Service Talking Therapies for Anxiety and Depression (NHSTT – previously IAPT) programme is an attempt at rectifying this issue, arguing that the economic benefits of providing widescale therapy outweighs the cost. A key part of this concept is the stepped care model, where patients are offered the least burdensome (and cheapest) effective treatments first, to maximise how many people can be helped by each therapist. This chapter will review the rationale for NHSTT and its progress to date, as well as exploring the future of programmes such as NHSTT, both in its country of origin and worldwide.

The Rationale for a National Primary Care Mental Health Service

Mental health issues such as depression and anxiety disorders are highly prevalent in modern society, imposing a significant impact on quality of life and overall wellbeing. They are also financially costly to society, in terms of lost productivity, sick pay and unemployment benefits, which between them can cover up to 4% of a country's gross domestic product [1]. Guidelines on how to effectively treat such disorders [2,3] all indicate that psychological treatments are an effective treatment that should be offered as an option, and evidence suggests that when offered the choice, three quarters of patients would prefer this to medication [4].

The UK consists of four devolved nations: England, Scotland, Wales and Northern Ireland, each with its own government responsible for healthcare services, including psychological therapies, and all following the ethos that healthcare should be free to users at point of access. Whilst the NHS is the overarching healthcare system, each nation manages its own NHS, leading to variations in policy, funding and service provision. Each nation offers similar services but emphasises different models. Despite differences, all nations of the UK aim to improve access to mental health care and reduce waiting times. In England, where there were previously major gaps in psychological therapy provision, it was argued that it would be cost-effective to offer therapy for individuals experiencing common mental health problems, as the cost of training therapists and providing evidence-based therapies would be cheaper than allowing those mental health difficulties to remain untreated [5]. Indeed, it was determined that if only 4% of the individuals receiving such therapies improved their employment status because of the treatment, that would offset the cost of the treatment for all. It would also of course enhance population wellbeing and quality of life and allow for equity between physical and mental health.

To test this theory, two pilot sites were created. Following NICE guidance, each site offered both traditional CBT and low-intensities therapies such as guided self-help, as well as group psychoeducation and computerised CBT (see Chapters 28 and 31 for further information on these treatment approaches). Therapy was carried out within primary care and community settings, to minimise any barriers to access, and patients were also allowed to self-refer into therapy. All patients were asked to complete questionnaires measuring depression (PHQ-9; [6]) and anxiety symptoms (GAD-7; [7]) at every appointment, so that recovery rates could be accurately assessed for the project.

The sites were both highly successful [8]. Large numbers of patients were seen, especially via the therapists offering the low intensity therapy approaches. Recovery rates (patients going from above cut-off on at least one measure, to below cut-off on both measures) were measured at 55% in one and 56% at the other, which were both above the hoped-for target of 50%. The self-referral option resulted in a more diverse patient profile, in line with the communities as a whole. Last, 5% of those treated changed employment status, ensuring that the programme was self-funding.

Based on this success, the government agreed to invest in a nationwide expansion of therapy services, called the Improving Access to Psychological Therapies programme – IAPT.

The Stepped Care Approach

In line with NICE guidance, and the success of lower-intensity therapies at the pilot sites, current NHSTT services run on a Stepped Care system. The fundamental principle of this is that all patients should first be offered the least intrusive intervention (step) that is likely to be effective for them. In general, most NICE guidelines for common mental health problems have four steps, as follows:

Step 1: Assessment and Diagnosis, Monitoring and Psychoeducation

The initial step for all patients is of course assessment and diagnosis, to determine what type of problem they are experiencing and so being able to know which treatment approach may work best. For some disorders, such as depression [2] and generalised anxiety disorder (GAD) [3], this step also involves providing basic education about the nature of their disorder, and a period of active monitoring, to review whether the problem improves by this alone. For other disorders, active monitoring is not part of the process, and so recommendations may be to move the patient to step 2 immediately (e.g. Panic Disorder [3]); or even straight to step 3 (e.g. Social Anxiety Disorder [9]; PTSD [10]).

Step 2: Low Intensity Psychological Interventions and Medication

Step 2 generally involves a range of low intensity therapy options, such as non-facilitated or guided self-help, psychoeducational groups or computerised CBT, generally involving less than eight hours of therapist time. In England, these therapies are provided by practitioners specifically trained in these approaches, called psychological wellbeing practitioners (PWP). Step 2 approaches can also involve pharmacological approaches prescribed by the patient's general practitioner, which may be supplemented by medication management support from the PWP.

While most of the psychological approaches offered at step 2 are based on the principles of CBT, they are at the same time qualitatively different from traditional CBT. Due to the various formats used, they focus on teaching standardised versions of CBT interventions that have been found to be effective for the disorder in question but are not specifically tailored to the patient's idiosyncratic formulation. Therapist time is focussed on this skills training, rather than on applying the interventions with the patient in-session. Such approaches have been found to be highly effective and allow many patients to recover without a more intrusive treatment approach. However, it can be useful to keep the distinction clear, so that patients who have not benefitted from one approach may still be willing to consider the other.

Step 3: High Intensity Psychological Interventions and Medication

Step 3 is where traditional CBT is found, along with various other evidence-based high intensity therapeutic approaches, such as interpersonal therapy, counselling and couple's therapy. Step 3 often also involves pharmacological approaches, either separately or in conjunction with psychological support. As with step 2, the exact options offered at step 3 will depend on the disorder the patient is experiencing; for example, counselling is noted as an effective treatment approach for depression, but not for GAD.

A referral to step 3 should be made for those for whom step 2 was ineffective, or for those were step 2 approaches are not recommended. In NHSTT, step 3 therapies are often offered in the same service as step 2, so that rapid and seamless movement between steps can occur.

Step 4: Combined Treatment, Multidisciplinary Care and Inpatient Services

While the services offered within NHSTT at steps 2 and 3 are effective for most individuals with common mental health problems, there are some who require yet more intensive approaches. Step 4 is thus provided by specialist mental health services, who can offer multidisciplinary care and treatment in a range of settings, such as home treatment and inpatient services. Treatment at step 4 can include pharmacological approaches from a psychiatrist, as well as further psychological approaches, or even treatments such as electro-convulsive therapy (ECT).

The benefit of a stepped care system for the provider is obviously reduced costs, and when applied correctly, greater cost efficiency. However, the approach is also of benefit to the patient, requiring less intrusion and disruption of their lives, and involving reduced waiting times for treatment. Conversely, the risk of a stepped care approach is in providing a subtherapeutic initial dose of treatment, which can result in a longer waiting time for the patient before receiving the appropriate treatment. In the worst case, this can result in patients dropping out of treatment altogether prior to being referred to the right step for them. A key focus should thus be on using the stepped care approach as written; that is, referring patients directly to the step that their condition and severity warrants, rather than trying to treat all patients at step 2 first.

NHSTT: Current Picture and Future Hopes

England's NHSTT programme provides an unparalleled level of data collection and performance monitoring, allowing it to prove its successes, but also highlighting any and all issues [11]. At the time of writing, the most annual recent data is for 2023/2024 [12]. Within this year, NHSTT was accessed by 1.26 patients, with 90.5% starting their treatment within 6 weeks, and 50.1% reaching recovery by the end. These numbers are all above the targets initially planned for what was IAPT, but the goal is now higher still. By 2028/29, the aim is for NHSTT to see almost 400,000 additional patients a year, with 53% reaching not just recovery, but reliable recovery [13]. As with the pilot sites, NHSTT services continue to predominantly offer CBT based approaches, but almost all now also offer at least one other modality in line with NICE guidelines, including counselling for depression, couples therapy, interpersonal therapy and brief psychodynamic therapy.

While the current national picture is reasonably promising, the local view highlights significant inequality, with recovery rates ranging from one area to another from as low as 35% to as high as 63% [14]. From this information, key recovery factors can be determined [15], such as how experienced therapists are, how many sessions patients get, how quickly patients start treatment after contacting the service, how well the step-up process is used, how carefully modalities are chosen (e.g. not giving counselling to patients with GAD) and how fully individuals are diagnosed. Many of these factors in turn correlate to funding levels – areas of England with better general health can afford to put more of their budget into NHSTT, in turn allowing for NHSTT to follow NICE and NHSTT manual guidelines, and so provide a more effective service. Social deprivation as a whole has also been shown to be a factor in recovery rates, though whether this is in addition to variabilities in funding, or due to this, has not been determined.

The NHSTT manual [13] states that NHSTT services should expect to offer therapy to patients experiencing mental health conditions such phobias (including agoraphobia), depression, OCD and BDD, GAD, IAD, panic disorder, PTSD, social anxiety disorder and mixed depression and anxiety (aka sub-syndromic depression and anxiety). In addition to this, NHSTT therapists should also be trained to offer psychological therapy to patients experiencing chronic fatigue syndrome, irritable bowel syndrome and other medically unexplained symptoms, as well as supporting patients with depression/anxiety and other comorbid long term physical health conditions (LTCs). Such therapy has a double benefit to the country's economy and wellbeing; not only may it help individuals in terms of employment status, but it can also improve their ability to effectively self-manage their conditions, and so reduce the need to use physical health services. As with the core NHSTT conditions, the data regarding treatment of those with co-morbid LTCs is promising, both in terms of recovery rates and in patient and staff experience [16].

Further development is also occurring in terms of child and adolescent mental health, via the children and young people's IAPT (CYP-IAPT) programme, which previously followed the low and high intensity model from adult NHSTT, but now also includes educational mental health practitioners (EMHP) based directly in schools [17]. Due to the comparative infancy of these programmes, and the evidence base on which they are based, it is unsurprising that there remain challenges in proving the efficacy of such services [18]. CBT training is also being increasingly focussed on treatment for severe and enduring mental health conditions (SEMHC), such as eating disorders, bipolar, personality disorders and psychosis. Due to the multidisciplinary needs of many such clients, it is likely that these practitioners will remain part of secondary care rather than joining core NHSTT service.

Despite its shortcomings, NHSTT has been a revolution in terms of centralised therapy provision, resulting in similar programmes being developed in other countries. Australia's 'NewAccess' programme has successfully filled the gap between the step 1 and step 3 systems that existed previously, with even higher recovery rates than NHSTT despite the difficulties presented by Australian geography [19]. Likewise Norway has created prompt mental health care (Rask Psykisk Helsehjelp), which is also showing great promise in its various pilot sites [20].

Concluding Remarks

Mental health problems are one of the leading causes of reduced quality of life, as well as being costly to society in terms of gross domestic product. Psychological therapies, and in particular CBT, are often the most effective treatment of choice. As such, national therapy services, such as England's NHSTT programme, can be an effective way to enhance quality of life and a country's economic status at the same time. While NHSTT initially focussed purely on common mental health issues for working age adults, it is now expanding into supporting those with LTCs, working with all ages, and training therapists to treat SEMHCs. NHSTT's success has resulted in similar programmes in other countries, such as Norway and Australia.

Further Reading

Layard R, Clark DM. *Thrive: The Power of Evidence-Based Psychological Therapies.* London: Penguin UK; 2014.

Bennett-Levy J, Richards D, Farrand P, Christensen H, Griffiths K, Kavanagh D, et al., *Oxford Guide to Low Intensity CBT Interventions.* Oxford: Oxford University Press; 2010.

References

1. Hewlett E, Moran V. Making Mental Health Count [Internet]. Paris: OECD Publishing; (OECD Health Policy Studies). www.oecd-ilibrary.org/content/publication/9789264208445-en.
2. National Institute for Health and Care Excellence. Depression in adults: recognition and management [Internet]. NICE; 2009 Oct. Report No.: CG90. www.nice.org.uk/guidance/cg90.
3. National Institute for Health and Care Excellence. Generalised anxiety disorder and panic disorder in adults: management [Internet]. 2020, p. 47. Report No.: CG113. www.nice.org.uk/guidance/cg113/resources/generalised-anxiety-disorder-and-panic-disorder-in-adults-management-pdf-35109387756997.
4. McHugh RK, Whitton SW, Peckham AD, Welge JA, Otto MW. Patient preference for psychological vs pharmacologic treatment of psychiatric disorders: A meta-analytic review. J Clin Psychiatry. 2013;**74**(6):13979.
5. Layard R. *Mental Health: Britain's Biggest Social Problem?* London: Centre for Economic Performance; 2005.

6. Kroenke K, Spitzer RL, Williams JBW. The PHQ-9: Validity of a brief depression severity measure. J Gen Intern Med. 2001;**16**(9):606–613.
7. Spitzer RL, Kroenke K, Williams JB, Löwe B. A brief measure for assessing generalized anxiety disorder: The GAD-7. Arch Intern Med. 2006;**166**(10):1092–1097.
8. Clark DM, Layard R, Smithies R, Richards DA, Suckling R, Wright B. Improving access to psychological therapy: Initial evaluation of two UK demonstration sites. Behav Res Ther. 2009;**47**(11):910–920.
9. National Institute for Health and Care Excellence. Social anxiety disorder: Recognition, assessment and treatment [Internet]. 2013, p. 39. Report No.: CG159. www.nice.org.uk/guidance/cg159/resources/social-anxiety-disorder-recognition-assessment-and-treatment-pdf-35109639699397.
10. National Institute for Health and Care Excellence. Post-traumatic stress disorder [Internet]. 2018, p. 54. Report No.: NG116. www.nice.org.uk/guidance/ng116/resources/posttraumatic-stress-disorder-pdf-66141601777861.
11. Clark DM. Realizing the mass public benefit of evidence-based psychological therapies: The IAPT program. Annu Rev Clin Psychol. 2018;**14**(1):159–183.
12. NHS England Digital [Internet]. [accessed 11 January 2025]. NHS Talking Therapies, for anxiety and depression, Annual reports, 2023–24. https://digital.nhs.uk/data-and-information/publications/statistical/nhs-talking-therapies-for-anxiety-and-depression-annual-reports/2023-24.
13. National Collaborating Centre for Mental Health. The NHS Talking Therapies for anxiety and depression manual. Mental Health Policy Team, Operations and Information Directorate; 2024. 151 p.
14. NHS Digital IAPT Team. Psychological Therapies, Annual report on the use of IAPT services 2019–20 [Internet]. 2020 Jul. https://digital.nhs.uk/data-and-information/publications/statistical/psychological-therapies-annual-reports-on-the-use-of-iapt-services/annual-report-2019-20.
15. Clark DM, Canvin L, Green J, Layard R, Pilling S, Janecka M. Transparency about the outcomes of mental health services (IAPT approach): An analysis of public data. The Lancet. 2018;**391**(10121):679–686.
16. Clarke K, Furmaniak K, Pilling S. IAPT-LTC Early Implementers Programme: Report on the implementation and process evaluation of Wave 1 early implementer sites [Internet]. University College London; 2018. www.ucl.ac.uk/pals/sites/pals/files/iapt-ltc-early-implementers-programme-report.pdf.
17. Ludlow C, Hurn R, Lansdell S. A current review of the children and young people's improving access to psychological therapies (CYP IAPT) program: Perspectives on developing an accessible workforce. Adolesc Health Med Ther. 2020;**11**:21–28.
18. Wolpert M, Jacob J, Napoleone E, Whale A, Calderon A, Edbrooke-Childs J. Child- and Parent-reported Outcomes and Experience from Child and Young People's Mental Health Services 2011–2015 [Internet]. London: CAMHS Press; 2016. www.corc.uk.net/media/1544/0505207_corc-report_for-web.pdf.
19. Baigent M, Smith D, Battersby M, Lawn S, Redpath P, McCoy A. The Australian version of IAPT: Clinical outcomes of the multi-site cohort study of NewAccess. J Ment Health. 2020;**32**(1):341–350.
20. Knapstad M, Lervik LV, Sæther SMM, Aarø LE, Smith ORF. Effectiveness of prompt mental health care, the Norwegian version of improving access to psychological therapies: A randomized controlled trial. Psychother Psychosom. 2020;**89**(2):90–105.

Chapter

28

Group Cognitive Behavioural Therapy

In this chapter we will help you to be able to:

- Describe the development of group CBT.
- Explain the costs and benefits of group CBT to both the provider and client.
- Apply best practice when running CBT groups.

Introduction

As discussed in Chapter 27, there is an ever-increasing push to improve access to CBT. One of the oldest methods of achieving this is group CBT, which has been proposed as a format of delivery from the beginning. This chapter will explore the history and theory of group CBT, and the evidence base to date for its use in various disorder. It will then discuss the overarching benefits and costs of group formats for CBT, before exploring the practical considerations to be made when setting up such a group.

Development of Group CBT

Group therapy has existed in some format since the early 1930s [1], and has been used in countless settings with a range of modalities. There are many possible therapeutic benefits to the group setting. Yalom lists these as the 'installation of hope, [the sense of] universality, imparting information, [experiencing] altruism, the corrective recapitulation of the primary family group, development of socialising techniques, imitative behaviour, interpersonal learning, group cohesiveness, catharsis, [and] existential factors' [2, p. 1].

Applying CBT in a group setting has likewise been a part of the therapeutic approach since its inception, with a chapter of Beck et al.'s seminal work *Cognitive Therapy of Depression* [3] being devoted to applying cognitive therapy in a group setting. The most obvious reason for doing this, as given in the original chapter, is that it allows for therapists to support more patients at the same time.

The initial focus in CBT groups was on teaching CBT material – helping patients to learn the CBT techniques relevant to the disorder they were experiencing. As such, the assumption was that the success of the group would rely predominantly on the content of the taught material, and the therapeutic benefits of the group itself was less of a focus. Groups are set up to follow the same concepts as individual CBT – they have agendas and homework tasks, involve working collaboratively, use formulations and goal setting and focus on cognitive and behavioural techniques.

More recently, the additional impact of various group factors has begun to be considered [4]. Such factors include the patient, the leader, the structure of the group and the processes occurring in the group. Each of these factors can interact with each other, as well as the protocol being followed, and then in turn affect how successful the group therapy will be.

Modern group CBT has diversified significantly from the original concept described by Hollon and Shaw [3]. Current groups range from mostly didactic large-group psychoeducation (such as stress control groups [5]), to highly interactive small-group CBT with only a few patients each. The trade-off of supporting ever more patients, against the therapeutic limitations imposed by such large group settings, is hotly debated [6].

Efficacy Data for Group CBT

Group CBT has been shown to be effective (and cost effective) in a number of settings. As this evidence has built up, group CBT has increasingly been accepted as an effective treatment for a number of disorders, as determined by bodies such as NICE. However, in other disorders, group CBT has either not been proven effective, or has actively been proven to be an ineffective choice. For a summary of the current guidelines, see Table 28.1.

Given the wide range of group structures being used, and the large number of confounding factors, it is unsurprising that the efficacy data for groups is mixed. Many CBT protocols have not been tested for group efficacy at all, and when they have, it will often be with one particular format in terms of numbers of group members and facilitators, with one set of group rules and one level of didacticism/interactivity. The formats chosen are often decided

Table 28.1 Summary of the current NICE guidelines for group CBT

Disorder	NICE guidelines including group treatment	Details
Depression	Yes [7]	NICE guidelines state: 'Should be based on a structured model such as "Coping with Depression"' (see [24] for details of this) Should involve groups of 8–10 patients with 2 facilitators, with 10–12 sessions. Not recommended for severe depression.
OCD and BDD	Yes [8]	As with individual CBT, should be a protocol that includes ERP. Only recommended as a low intensity option for those with mild functional impairment.
GAD	Yes [9]	Only recommended as a low intensity option in GAD, run as psychoeducational groups with a ratio of one practitioner to 12 patients. Group would run for six two-hour sessions.
Panic Disorder	No [9]	Not currently recommended due to apparent greater efficacy of individual treatment.
Social Anxiety	No [10]	Not currently recommended due to apparent greater efficacy of individual treatment.
PTSD	No [11]	Not currently recommended due to apparent greater efficacy of individual treatment.

by the constraints of the trial centre, and how the facilitators have previously run group therapy, rather than being based on theoretical consideration of an optimum set up given the clinical presentations. When the format chosen then performs less well than individual therapy, all this has actually proven is that this exact group set up is not optimal, not that group therapy itself cannot work for the disorder in question.

On the other hand, most studies that are presented as showing equivalence of group therapy to individual are actually just failing to prove difference. Due to the low participant numbers involved in these studies, a lack of statistically significant difference may itself not be statistically significant. Given the direction of the non-significant differences in many such studies, it could still be reasonable to assume that individual therapy has the higher effectiveness, simply not by a large enough magnitude to show in a small sample [12].

Benefits of Group CBT

Just as with any group psychotherapy, CBT can have several benefits from being run in a group setting, which can support recovery above and beyond that provided by the same protocol given to individuals. How much each of these benefits will apply to any given group will depend on how the group is set up – its size, the specificity of its focus and how carefully group members are selected. However, each of these factors will impact each benefit differently; every type of group will involve a trade-off.

First, being part of a group of individuals who are all experiencing a similar problem can be highly normalising, and the value of this on group members has been shown extensively [6,13,14,15]. This benefit can increase with larger groups, especially if socialising between members is facilitated. However, if the size of group is being achieved by having a very diverse set of clinical presentations, said normalising may be impaired.

Likewise, many group therapy set-ups can reduce the stigma of accessing therapy. Coming to large group psycho-educational workshops, such as stress control [5], often doesn't require extensive referral and assessment processes and can even be offered in workplaces and in physical health settings. This should reduce barriers for entry, meaning that treatment can be accessed by those who might otherwise never do so. In practice this bears out, as such outreach groups are found to be attended by individuals with diagnosable mental health disorders who hadn't disclosed such issues to their GP [16]. Beyond the issue of barriers, some patients simply find group therapy less intrusive and find group therapy more anonymous, as they do not have to personally expose each aspect of their difficulties with the therapist [17]. Here, both larger and less selective groups will most effectively provide this benefit.

Group CBT also offers enhancements to the techniques of CBT itself. When planning out behavioural experiments, having a ready-made group may allow for better testing options [18]. Indeed, for problems such as social anxiety disorder, the group itself can be a useful source of exposure [18], though this is not always found to be the case [19]. Groups also allow for vicarious learning of the tools from observing others making positive behavioural and cognitive changes [13], while active involvement in supporting others to make change can provide an early sense of mastery with CBT tools [3]. Such benefits will each be dependent on the exact set up of the group, and how skilfully the group leaders support patient interaction.

Group therapy also offers benefits to the provider. As proposed from the start, group therapy has been shown to take on average 50% less therapist time [6], thus allowing services to provide therapy to more people with any given number of therapist hours. For those disorders where group CBT is sufficiently effective, this efficiency translates into cost effectiveness, with each unit change for clients costing less [12]. While efficiency is largely driven purely by group size, cost effectiveness may not scale so linearly, as some large groups do not reach the same per-patient effect sizes.

Costs and Contraindications for Group CBT

Group CBT also has its costs, which can limit its effectiveness in some circumstances, and mean that it is positively contraindicated in others. For example, in almost all cases, group CBT will not be as tightly formulation driven as individual CBT. While this can be less exposing for patients, it also means that it may miss the important idiosyncrasies of each patient's presentation, as therapy will inevitably focus more on the cognitions and behaviours common to the group as a whole, with only limited time, if any, spent on individual examples.

Likewise, the idiosyncratic difficulties each patient may experience, such as difficulties completing homework, or acknowledging highly problematic cognitions, will be given less time than in individual therapy, especially if the individual feels uncomfortable exposing these with the group [6,14,15]. As such features are often key to recovery, group CBT can end up leaving some patients behind. These two issues are particularly true in larger and more diverse groups, counter-acting some of the benefits above.

Despite apparent lower costs for group CBT, the lower efficacy in various scenarios limits the overall cost effectiveness. While group therapy is likely to be cost effective in depression as mentioned above, some would argue that its effectiveness for anxiety disorders is debatable [12]. One reason for this debate is due to the hidden costs to group CBT which are often missed when being compared to individual therapy. Such costs include the additional therapist time that groups can take more therapist time due to set up and preparation. There may also be increased costs to clients – such as those imposed by the increased overall contact time and lack of flexibility in group CBT appointment times – both of which may impose a cost on the group members. As such, overall cost-efficiency is hard to define, with upfront group therapy costs hiding larger losses elsewhere.

A further cost to groups is the additional training that may be needed to ensure competence. As discussed below, there are many facets to running a successful group that go beyond the skills required for individual therapy. Most therapists will be first taught how to do CBT for individuals, and so there is either a cost in providing further training, or the cost of running groups with untrained staff. Even with training, competence may be difficult to ensure, as the inconclusive evidence base makes it harder to be certain what skills are needed, and so groups may still be run ineffectively.

Patient factors also influence whether groups are effective, and not all patients will be suited to groups. Whitfield [17] summarised a number of key factors for patient suitability to group CBT. These included:

- Communication difficulties
- Interaction difficulties, such as either dissociating, aggression, or high levels of competitiveness
- Risk issues (both suicidal ideation and active self-harm)
- Comorbidity
- Anxiety surrounding groups
- Patient preference

Assessing for these features will inevitably add to the time taken to set up groups. Excluding all such individuals may result in insufficient patient numbers to run a cost-effective group at any given time, especially in rural areas. Even beyond these exclusion factors, there also needs to be a general fit of the clients in relation to each other; if one client is much more severe or demographically different from the others, this may impact group cohesion, and impair any sense of normalising.

Providing Group CBT

As discussed above, there are numerous different group CBT protocols, each with their own recommendations on the structure and process of the group. As such, the first step in creating any new group is to explore the specific literature related to the population and setting in question. However, there are also a number of more general considerations, from deciding whether a group should be created at all, contracting with the group, managing the group members and working through the different stages of a group.

When deciding whether to create a group, it is important to weigh up both the possible benefits and likely costs, both according to the literature, and in relation to the local population who might be attending. Given the impact of waiting for longer than 4–6 weeks on treatment efficacy [25], one key question is how many suitable patients for any given group will access the service providing it in any given month. If it will take longer than the average waiting time for individual therapy to fill a group, then the group is unlikely to be cost-effective in that setting.

In parallel with this decision, it will be important to determine what the group criteria will be, and how to screen potential patients. As discussed above, the more similar a group is, the more normalising and targeted it can be, but this limits the relevant population, takes additional time and may add barriers to entry that put off possible members. If screening is done, it may be helpful to consider the patient suitability factors described above, as well as the patient's clinical presentation.

At the start of any group, a contract will need to be agreed with the group members, covering topics such as lateness and attendance, behaviour during sessions (including use of drugs and alcohol), and managing risk issues and any extreme emotional reactions. Prior to the start of the group, the therapist(s) may want to consider what will be didactically imposed, versus what will be agreed as a group. They may also want to have a co-therapist involved, to focus on these processes while they focus on the group content.

Once the group has started, it will be important to manage any problematic behaviours from group members as they arise. While group members often share common symptoms of a mental health disorder, they are likely to vary in most other ways. As such, how the group leaders manage the group, and manage each member, will need to account for this, as it will affect how participants engage and progress, which in turn will affect the group as a whole.

The typical ways in which patients present within a group have been described and classified in several ways [2,20,21], focussing on the recurring behaviours of each. Many texts recommend standardised responses to each member type, to try and limit the problematic interaction patterns, or lessen their impact on the group [21]. However, such responses do not consider the underlying cause of each behaviour, and so risk producing alternative, equally problematic behaviours. From a cognitive perspective, the key to adaptively changing behaviour is formulating its function in relation to the patient's underlying beliefs, to consider if there is a way to meet their needs without reinforcing the disruptive behaviour. Often, tactful individual discussion of these may be most effective, as it will allow the leader to either determine new ways to interact with the member or provide a collaborative agreement to interact differently.

Following the original description by Benne and Sheats (20), Box 28.1 provides a such a list of problematic member roles, as well as the key considerations for the leader, and some possible initial Socratic questions to ask.

Box 28.1 Defining and Formulating Problematic Member Roles

Aggressor – attacks or demeans the group work or ideas. *Are these things making them angry or anxious? What rule is being broken for them?* 'How do you feel about the group discussions today?' 'If these ideas were implemented, what would be the worst thing about that?'

Blocker – disagreeing or going against the group ideas without any clear reason. *This implies they don't want the concepts to be true – why? What might it mean about them if it was?* 'What's stuck out to you most in today's discussions?' 'What do you think about that?' 'If that were true, what would that mean to you?'

Recognition seeker – works to get positive attention. *Is there an 'if . . . then' rule here? What does it mean about them if they don't get positive attention, either in this situation or in general?* 'How are you feeling in these sessions?' 'I notice you focus a lot on what's going well/where you agree with others. I wonder if there are ever any negative things for you that you don't feel as comfortable mentioning?'

Self-confessor – uses group as an opportunity to express feelings and beliefs unrelated to the group agenda. *What does the client value about this opportunity to express themselves? What are their beliefs about doing this in other situations? What are their beliefs about self-expression?* 'I noticed you told us all quite a lot today. How are you feeling about that?' 'Are these topics you feel able to discuss in other situations?'

Playboy – actively shows disengagement from the group focus, by joking, playing around or being cynical. *What would it mean if they took the group seriously? What are the risks to them of fully committing?* 'How are you feeling about being part of a therapy group?'

Dominator – trying to take control of the group members or discussion and behaving as if superior to the others. *What does it mean to them to not be in control? What does it mean to not be superior?* 'How do you feel about how the group is running?' 'How do you feel about your place in the group?'

Help-Seeker – rather than meaning to seek help in a pragmatic sense, this is where the member appears to be aiming for sympathy from the rest of the group. *What do they believe would happen if others did not pity them?* 'How do you see yourself in the group?' 'How do you feel about the other group members?'

Special Interest Pleader – where the member repeatedly verbalises minority opinions, but not from their own perspective. *Are these their own opinions? If so, what prevents them from verbalising them as their own? What are the underlying concerns about these opinions having not been verbalised already?* 'I noticed you raised some interesting points of view today. What are your views on [topic]?'

Silent member* – group member who does not volunteer information and replies to direct questions in a minimal way. *How do they view sharing information with the group? How do they feel about their relative quietness compared to others?* 'How helpful are you finding the group?' 'Are there any points where you'd want any further help, or where you want to add anything?'

*While not part of the original list of problematic members, silent members are commonly a concern for group therapy leaders (e.g. [21]). While this can be a sign of a problem, it can also be a valid learning style (see [26] for a discussion of quiet learners) and so should be explored with curiosity rather than assumed to be an issue from the start.

Groups of all kinds tend to change over time, following a fairly universal set of stages. Initially described by Tuckman [22] as forming, storming, norming and performing, the fifth stage adjourning was subsequently added [23]. These stages can be considered as follows:

Forming: The initial stage where being part of the group is new, and where rules and boundaries are typically being defined and understood.

Storming: Once the newness has worn off, issues with the rules and boundaries as well as interpersonal conflicts come to light. The group tasks and necessary interpersonal intimacy may be resisted at this point, often through behavioural reactions as described in the Problematic Member Roles (Box 28.1).

Norming: As the interpersonal conflicts are resolved, and rules and structures are modified or accepted, the group can become more interpersonally effective and open.

Performing: With the group members having become interpersonally sensitive and willing to be open and engage, the group can now focus on the group tasks and aims.

Adjourning: With the group tasks hopefully finished, the group members begin to focus on and react to the upcoming ending, which can result in negative emotions and the range of ending styles seen in therapy in general.

In a more task-oriented therapy group such as CBT, the preferred stage is typically that of performing, where active therapy work is occurring, and change can be made in regards to the problems brought. However, it is important for group therapists to be aware of the other stages that need to be worked through to get here. Clarity in rule setting, and time to explore issues with boundaries in early sessions, can help to smooth the path, as can a measured but purposeful development towards increasing openness. Clear time dedicated to the process of ending, and early acknowledgement of the possible issues this brings, can likewise help the group through the adjourning phase, so that it does not result in dismantling of the earlier work done.

Concluding Remarks

Group therapy has a long history, and there are many proposed benefits to the group experience, from greater learning and normalisation, to greater cost-efficacy and improved access. Following this, CBT has been trialled in various group formats for various clinical presentations, but there are still many limitations to the evidence-base. As such, therapists should consider not only whether group CBT has proven efficacy for the disorder they will be treating, but also the overarching benefits and costs of group CBT and how these will relate to the various group formats that they could potentially set up. If group CBT is provided, then considerations should be made regarding how to understand problematic group behaviours, and how to best guide the participants through the typical group stages.

Further Reading

Bieling P, McCabe R, Antony M. *Cognitive Behavioural Therapy in Groups*. New York: Guildford Press; 2006.

Yalom I. *The Theory and Practice of Group Psychotherapy*. 4th ed. New York: Basic Books; 1995.

References

1. Slavson SR. *An Introduction to Group Therapy*. New York: International Universities Press; 1943.
2. Yalom ID. *The Theory and Practice of Group Psychotherapy*. 4th ed. [Internet]. New York: Basic Books; 1995. https://books.google.co.uk/books?id=KXhHAAAAMAAJ.
3. Shaw BF, Hollon SD. Group cognitive therapy for depressed patients. In: AT Beck, J Rush, G Emery (Eds.), *Cognitive Therapy of Depression* (pp. 328–353). New York: Guilford Press; 1979.
4. Burlingame GM, Strauss B, Joyce A. Change mechanisms and effectiveness of small group treatments. Bergin Garfield's Handb Psychother Behav Change. 2013;6:640–689.
5. White J. Stress control manual. South East Glasgow NHS Trust; 2005.
6. Morrison N. Group cognitive therapy: Treatment of choice or sub-optimal option? Behav Cogn Psychother. 2001;29(3):311–332.
7. National Institute for Health and Care Excellence. Depression in adults: recognition and management [Internet]. NICE; 2009. Report No.: CG90. www.nice.org.uk/guidance/cg90.
8. National Institute for Health and Care Excellence. Obsessive-compulsive disorder and body dysmorphic disorder: treatment. Clinical Guidance [Internet]. NICE; 2005. Report No.: CG31. www.nice.org.uk/guidance/cg31.
9. National Institute for Health and Care Excellence. Generalised anxiety disorder and panic disorder in adults: management [Internet]. 2020, p. 47. Report No.: CG113. www.nice.org.uk/guidance/cg113/resources/generalised-anxiety-disorder-and-panic-disorder-in-adults-management-pdf-35109387756997.
10. National Institute for Health and Care Excellence. Social anxiety disorder: recognition, assessment and treatment [Internet]. 2013, p. 39. Report No.: CG159. www.nice.org.uk/guidance/cg159/resources/social-anxiety-disorder-recognition-assessment-and-treatment-pdf-35109639699397.
11. National Institute for Health and Care Excellence. Post-traumatic stress disorder [Internet]. 2018, p. 54. Report No.: NG116. www.nice.org.uk/guidance/ng116/resources/posttraumatic-stress-disorder-pdf-66141601777861.
12. Tucker M, Oei TPS. Is group more cost effective than individual cognitive behaviour therapy? The evidence is not solid yet. Behav Cogn Psychother. 2007;35(1):77–91.
13. Lewinsohn PM, Clarke GN. Psychosocial treatments for adolescent depression. Clin Psychol Rev. 1999;19:329–342.
14. Toseland RW, Siporin M. When to recommend group treatment: A review of the clinical and the research literature. Int J Group Psychother. 1986;36(2):171–201.
15. Vinogradov S, Yalom ID. Group Therapy. In RE Hales, SC Yudofsky, JA Talbott (Eds.), *American Psychiatric Press Textbook of Psychiatry* [Internet] (pp. 1143–1175). American Psychiatric Press; 1994. https://books.google.co.uk/books?id=WZaLzQEACAAJ.
16. Brown JSL, Boardman J, Elliott SA, Howay E, Morrison J. Are self-referrers just the worried well? Soc Psychiatry Psychiatr. 2005;40(5):396–401.
17. Whitfield G. Group cognitive-behavioural therapy for anxiety and depression. Adv Psychiatr Treat. 2010;16(3):219–227.
18. Heimberg RG, Salzman DG, Holt CS, Blendell KA. Cognitive-behavioral group treatment for social phobia: Effectiveness at five-year follow up. Cogn Ther Res. 1993;17(4):325–339.
19. Stangier U, Heidenreich T, Peitz M, Lauterbach W, Clark D. Cognitive therapy for social phobia: Individual versus group treatment. Behav Res Ther. 2003;41(9):991–1007.
20. Benne KD, Sheats P. Functional roles of group members. J Soc Issues. 1948;4:41–49.

21. Bieling PJ, McCabe RE, Antony MM. Cognitive-Behavioral Therapy in Groups [Internet]. New York: Guilford Publications; 2006. https://books.google.co.uk/books?id=pCdtAAAAMAAJ.

22. Tuckman BW. Developmental sequence in small groups. Psychol Bull. 1965;63:384–399.

23. Tuckman BW, Jensen MAC. Stages of small-group development revisited. Group Organ Stud. 1977;2(4):419–427.

24. Lewinsohn PM, Clarke GN, Hoberman HM. The coping with depression course: Review and future directions. *CAN J BEHAV SCI/Revue canadienne des sciences du comportement*. 1989;21(4):470–493.

25. Clark DM. Realizing the mass public benefit of evidence-based psychological therapies: The IAPT Program. *Annu Rev Clin Psychol.* 2018;14(1):159–183.

26. Cain S. *Quiet: The Power of Introverts in a World That Can't Stop Talking*. London: Penguin; 2012.

Chapter

29

Conjoint Format: Couple's Therapy

In this chapter we will help you to be able to:

- Describe the development of cognitive, behavioural and integrative approaches to couple's therapy.
- Apply a range of dyadic formulation processes to couples.
- Apply the key interventions in couple's therapy, including empathic joining, unified detachment and dyadic behavioural change processes.

Introduction

CBT is generally concerned with the thoughts, feelings and behaviours of an individual. However, when the problem is caused by, or is causing, significant relationship distress, it can be more effective to focus on the relationship than either partner on their own.

This chapter will explore the development of couples therapy, and the various ways in which couple dynamics can be formulated. It will then explore the key interventions used with couples, both to help develop understanding of behaviours and their underlying causes, and to build up the frequency of positive experiences.

Development of Cognitive and Behavioural Couple's Therapy

In general, being married has been shown to result in higher average levels of happiness than not being married [1]. However, this happiness disappears when the marriage is unsatisfying, and marital dissatisfaction is strongly associated with higher levels of depression [2]. In such cases, traditional cognitive therapy is found to be less effective than usual [3]; it doesn't appear to be helpful to try and change one person's outlook when the perceived issue is the relationship.

Couple's therapy – initially called marital therapy [4] but now applied to any significant couple relationship – is an alternative cognitive behavioural approach that aims to meet this need. There are multiple formats of this type of therapy, but all work on the essential feature that the problem is not located in the thoughts or behaviours of one individual or the other, but in the dyadic relationship between them. As such, therapy will work on making sense of the dyadic problem, and then finding ways to change the problem from both sides.

Traditional behavioural couple's therapy (TBCT [4]) focusses predominantly on behavioural change. The key issue is seen as the comparative lack of positive interactions in the relationship, compared to the quantity of negative interactions. This is managed through communication training (to create more positive interactions in communicating), problem solving (to prevent negative interactions caused by ongoing problems) and behaviour exchange procedures (to actively increase the number and type of positive behaviours each experience from the other). In addition, the aversiveness of some negative behaviours can be reduced through paradoxical directives.

Developing on from this, cognitive behavioural couple's therapy (CBCT [5]) employs many of the same general techniques, but also specifically focuses on key areas of problematic cognition and emotion typical in distressed relationships. One of the most features of this model, for all cognitive therapists, is the classifying of cognitions into five main types:

- Perceptions (including the result of selective attention) – that is, thoughts about what has occurred
- Attributions – opinions about why things have occurred
- Expectancies – predictions about what will occur in the future
- Assumptions – beliefs about what the world is like
- Standards – beliefs about what the world should be like

Cognitive behavioural couple's therapy also puts a focus on the different emotions experienced as a result of these thoughts, particularly depression, anxiety, anger and jealousy.

Current approaches now focus on more of an integrative approach than pure CBT, as this has been shown to be more effective at creating the desired change [6]. The two main models most commonly used are integrative behavioural couple therapy (IBCT; [7]) and couple's therapy for depression (CTfD; [8]). CTfD is itself based on the earlier version of IBCT [9], while also incorporating key competencies from other efficacious (non-CBT) models, and was created by expert consensus after reviewing across all the available studies.

In both ICBT and CTfD, the focus of therapy is on understanding what is causing the distress in the relationship and helping both individuals to see the situation from a more detached perspective, as well as understanding how each other feel in situations and responding to this empathically. These two processes are called unified detachment and empathic joining. In doing this, the therapy helps partners to go from seeing problems as a result of their partner being fundamentally flawed, to something more concrete and understandable. Following on from this, both models focus more on acceptance and understanding of problematic patterns than active change, as any such change tends to occur best as a result of seeing things differently, rather than by external rules.

The key defining principles of all the models above have been summarised as [6]:

1. See the couple's problem as dyadic
2. Aim to change behaviours which are dangerous, disruptive or emotionally driven
3. Explore and work with behaviours resulting from hidden emotions
4. Aim to improve communication
5. Encourage positive behaviours, building on current strengths

By following these key concepts, each of the models allows for couples to improve their relationship satisfaction without putting blame or responsibility on either individual.

Efficacy Data for Couple's Therapy CBT

England's IAPT programme regularly collects treatment and outcome data for every patient seen, and this can then be analysed to explore which treatment results in the greatest rates of recovery. Given that the data collected in IAPT looks at symptom reduction, rather than relationship satisfaction, it would be reasonable to assume that couple's therapy would perform poorly. However, the reverse has actually been found; couple's therapy had the highest recovery rates, of 61.8% for anxiety disorders, and 58.8% for depression, against overall IAPT recovery rates of 48.8% and 46.7% [10]. Being real-world data, it is important to note that treatments were not randomly assigned, and couple's therapy patients were specifically selected for the treatment. They will also likely have had more sessions in total, and by the nature of the therapy, must have had a partner at least slightly motivated to support change. Nonetheless, the data is compelling evidence that, in these circumstances, couple's therapy is an effective choice, whether the patient is experiencing depression or an anxiety disorder.

In the US, more rigorous studies have explored the comparative benefit of the traditional couple's therapy (TBCT) against the newer integrative approach (IBCT). While these studies have found that both approaches have similar acute affects, IBCT results in better maintenance over the following two years [11,12,13].

Typical Course of Therapy

Couple's therapy does not have a set duration, though NICE guidelines recommend that a course of treatment should typically be between 15 and 20 sessions, spaced over 5–6 months [14]. During this time, the treatment will typically go through four stages – assessment, feedback, intervention and ending. Assessment is typically carried out over three sessions, one with the couple together, and then one with each half of the couple separately. Feedback is then generally the focus of the next one to two sessions, where the therapist will present their proposed dyadic formulation to the couple and then edit this as needed to create a shared understanding of the difficulties, and allow the couple to make a decision about whether they would like to work on the issues being raised. From here, the active intervention stage begins, helping couples to increase their levels of acceptance and tolerance, and finding ways to change behaviour as needed. Finally, treatment enters the termination phase, where the couple are helped to see the changes they have made, and explore how they will manage future challenges independently.

Dyadic Formulation Processes

As with most types of CBT, couples therapies begin with formulation, helping to make sense of how the problem developed and is maintained. There is a number of different ways of formulating the key difficulties in a couple relationship, but each will focus on the dyadic nature of the problem – how the two individuals interact and impact each other.

The **nine areas model** is one of the simplest forms of dyadic formulation, and is based on the cognitive model for individual CBT [15], which shows the interaction of the environment, thoughts, mood, behaviour and physical sensations. Applying this to couples [16] involves the same cycle, but with the thoughts, behaviours, mood and sensations of each partner being considered in turn, and then exploring the interaction between the behaviour of each and the thoughts of the other. A visual summary of this is shown in Figure 29.1.

This model is purely a maintenance cycle, and so doesn't explain where problems have started from, but it can be very helpful in explaining how, once the problem has started, each person's behaviour can influence the other's thinking, and so result in further behaviours that reinforce the initial thinking.

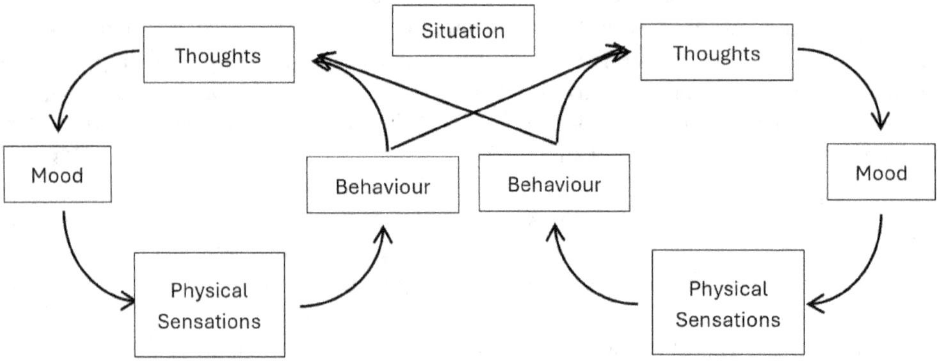

Figure 29.1 The nine-areas formulation [16] reproduced with permission Grimmer [16]. The nine-part model: A tool for sharing dyadic formulations. Retrieved from www.bristolcbt.co.uk/publications/the-nine-part-modeldyadic-formulation.

Formulation statements focussing on polarisation are the primary conceptualisation used in CTfD [8]. These statements tend to cover a number of key areas, such as the issues that divide the couple, their varying childhood experiences, the reasons why these issues divide the couple, the strengths of the relationship and how therapy can help the couple. Throughout the statement, there will be a focus on a central theme regarding how the couple's natural differences have become a source of conflict. Such differences are not seen as problems in themselves, but they become problematic when each partner starts to see the difference as meaning something negative, and become increasingly divided over it. Once each partner begins to view their own standpoint as the right one, and the other as wrong or bad, the difference tends to widen and become an increasingly major issue for the couple. This process is known in CTfD as polarisation, and it is one of the therapist's first goals to determine and name this polarisation.

An example of this would be a couple where one partner (Bill) generally prefers to save money for a rainy day, while his partner (Freida) tends to spend money on shared pleasures. Freida may initially see Bill as responsible and like how safe he makes her feel, while Bill may see Freida as happy go lucky and enjoy how the events she sets up bring colour to his life. This may be a positive facet of their relationship for many years, until such a time as they hit financial stress. At this point, Bill may become more focussed on saving than usual, and Freida may take from this that spending money on nice things for the couple will no longer be appreciated by Bill, or that it only causes arguments. As Freida doesn't see the need to save as much as Bill does, she may start to spend in secret, either hiding the purchases altogether, or lying about the costs. Bill eventually finds out and takes from this situation that he can't trust her with money at all, and needs to be fully in control of the finances. This then reinforces to Freida that he is excessively preoccupied by money, and so she feel compelled to continue lying about expenditure. Such a couple's polarisation on the spectrum of responsible to happy-go-lucky started with a valued difference, but stress caused it to polarise.

DEEP analysis – In IBCT, a similar formulation statement is used, with the key areas of the levels of distress being experienced by each part of the couple, the level of commitment of the couple, core issues and theme (often a point of polarisation), a 'DEEP analysis' of the core issues, and finally the couple's strengths. Central to this formulation is the DEEP analysis; that is, an exploration of the couple's differences, emotional sensitivities, external stressor and circumstances and patterns of communication or interaction [7].

The differences focussed upon in this analysis could be due to any number of things, such as personality, libido, connection to family of origin, stress management style or each partner's interests. While couples often have things in common, they also will inevitably have differences between them; some valued, some unnoticed, some tolerated. Differences are not a problem in and of themselves, and so not every difference will be part of the analysis.

However, differences can result in problems due to the emotional sensitivities of each partner. These are things such as abandonment issues, being sensitive to criticism, having a fragile sense of one's own value, feeling an enhanced need for recognition, being concerned about attractiveness, being sensitive to a sense of being controlled or being preoccupied by one's own competency. Most individuals will have some emotional sensitivities without this causing any issues, but they are more likely to cause difficulties if they align poorly with the natural differences in the couple. For example, if a couple differs on libido, this will be more likely to result in issues if there is also emotional sensitivity regarding attractiveness on the side of the partner whose libido is higher. Cultural, socio-economic and gender norms can also heighten such sensitivities, for example if a female partner feels that it is culturally wrong for her to initiate sex, she may be especially sensitive to a partner lower libido.

External stressors and circumstances can then exacerbate the impact of differences over time, or heighten an emotional sensitivity. Such stressors and circumstances could be almost anything, from moving house or getting a promotion, to the birth of a child or health issues. The key is how such circumstances interact with the emotionally charged difference. For example, the birth of a child could simultaneously impact libido due to increased stress, and worsen concerns about attractiveness.

Finally there is the key feature of patterns of communication and interaction within the couple as they attempt to resolve the issue. Normally open discussion will be attempted at some point by the couple, and in many situations will work. For the difference in question however, with the connected emotional sensitivities and external factors, open discussion becomes seemingly impossible or fails to solve the issue. At this point, partners will move onto other types of interaction, such as criticism, appeasing the other, invading privacy or avoidance. Each of these processes can end up solving the issue at hand, either short-term or long-term, but become problematic in that they bring about further cyclical patterns of interaction that cause distress. These patterns can be symmetrical, where both partners attack each other or avoid, or can be asymmetrical (such as attack-avoid, or pursue-avoid). When such interactions cause distress, there will then need to be some kind of recovery process to heal the rupture, and this too can be a source of problematic difference. For example, couples may disagree over whether, in a 'good relationship' the issue should be discussed, if acts of repair are needed, or if things should be quickly forgotten.

Through a DEEP analysis, the couple can start to see how the difference in question interacts with their emotional sensitivities and external stressors, all of which will be targets of acceptance and tolerance building. Through this, the couple can then begin to work on changing the distressing or dysfunctional patterns of interaction.

Key Interventions for Couple's Therapy

Having shared a formulation and come to an agreement on the key issues, therapy will then move into the intervention stage. Couple's therapy protocols rarely encourage set interventions in a set order, but there are a range of key interventions to be applied as needed. In general, these interventions can be split into tools that focus on promoting acceptance – such as empathic joining, unified detachment, building tolerance, coping methods and exploring sexual problems – and those that promote behavioural change, such as problem solving, behavioural activation and communication training. The intervention stage will typically start with the acceptance and tolerance building tools first, to reduce the sense of polarisation and distress and so allow the couple to become more receptive to change.

Empathic joining is a process in which one partner makes an emotional disclosure, which is then heard and responded to empathically by the other in a way that is noted by the initial speaker. Such a process can be difficult, but is key in helping couples to understand each other and allows for partners to behave supportively, forgive and/or show acceptance in response to what might previously have been rupturing experience.

Empathic joining work starts from the assessment, being modelled implicitly by the therapist when they reflect and so make visible the emotional reactions that each partner describes having to situations. This then continues in the weekly treatment sessions, with the therapist focussing in through questioning and reflection on the known internal experience that each partner describes feeling, rather than their beliefs about the other's experience or motivations. At times this can include actively suggesting what might be being felt by the speaker, as often one of the issues in the relationship is that the individual finds it difficult to articulate how they feel or perceive things. It can also involve helping to lead the client to disclose a wider range of emotions – helping an angry partner to disclose the hurt they are also feeling, or helping the seemingly calm client verbalise the anger they typically repress (which may help their partner to realise they at least do care!).

In general, therapists will start by encouraging disclosure from the person experiencing stronger emotions, as this avoids them feeling supressed. Alternatively, a therapist may start with the person more able to express emotions, to allow for a quick win, and to model such expression being a safe process. Last, some situations benefit from starting with the person who is more likely to shut down in response to the reactions and opinions of the other. In all cases, the aim is to discover the reactions occurring in one or both of the couple, and then break the usual cycle from here by adding empathy for the emotions being experienced. In an ideal scenario, this empathy will come from the partner in response to the therapist asking them to summarise what thoughts and emotions they've heard from their other half. At other times, especially earlier on in the process, the empathy can be modelled by the therapist, without forcing the partner to take the same step.

Unified detachment is a different way of having a couple explore a situation, where the therapist aims to get the couple to both see the situation with a bit of distance and without the usual value judgments that can occur. To achieve this unified detachment, the therapist will explore and draw out a sequence of events leading up to a rupture, with a focus on the earlier and more understandable actions. The therapist then may help the couple to compare the intent and impact of actions, or explore differences between various recurrences of a typical cycle to see what the comparative costs and benefits are of these. Throughout, the therapist will be attempting to explore action and reaction without value judgements, and may use analogies (such as dancing) to help the couple to see the patterns from a more detached viewpoint. Again, while such unified detachment can result in spontaneous behavioural change, the key goal is to enhance each partner's ability to understand why the cycles actually happen, so that they are less distressing.

Building tolerance. While helping partners to understand and empathise with each other is useful, it is unlikely to completely neutralise the effects of all unpleasant or unwanted behaviours. In these circumstances, the next step can be to actively help clients to become more tolerant of the others' negative behaviour, even if it were not what they would prefer. This can be similar to building tolerance of uncertainty in anxiety disorder, or habituating to feared items in a phobia; the individual may never grow to love it, but they may reach a point where it doesn't actively cause distress.

One strategy to help build tolerance to unwanted behaviours can be to re-enact them in isolation, when they are not being done in response to an emotionally charged situation. By doing this, both partners can see the behaviour more objectively, and see it from different angles. This should make it possible for the partner experiencing this behaviour to more easily tolerate it, as it is just a simple behaviour, rather than part of a chain of events with assumed meanings. As a side effect, this can also result in the behaviour occurring less, as the individual whose behaviour it is can more easily see the result of the behaviour while not in an emotional state themselves. However, reducing the behaviour is not the active aim of the process, as this will likely only cause resentment when the behaviour recurs due to habit.

Such a process can either occur in the therapy session, or can be planned as a homework task, where each of the partners will do one problematic behaviour unprompted on a random occasion, and then actively observe how the other reacts, and then show empathy for their experience of it. By having this as a task that both partners carry out, the focus is kept on the idea of dyadic change, and both parts of the couple have to both show empathy and tolerate an unwanted behaviour. Importantly, this process should be used for behaviours that are problematic predominantly due to what they mean (such as eye rolling, sighing, or asking for reassurance) rather than those which are innately problematic of themselves, such as physical violence.

Coping methods. In tandem with helping to reduce the emotional power of unwanted behaviours, it can also help to build up coping methods in each of the partners independently of each other. While support, understanding and empathy from within the couple dynamic is important, it is likely in all relationships that there will be points where the partner cannot automatically meet the other's needs either due to being the cause of the stress, or being equally stressed by an external trigger themselves. As such, having planned coping methods can ensure that there is a back-up route available.

Typical options include leaving problematic situations and self-soothing, getting support elsewhere or assertively stating ones needs to the partner, rather than expecting them to know. None of these options are perfect, and so it is important that the coping methods already being used and possible alternatives are explored fully, to consider what is most likely to be useful in most situations, and when an alternative will be better.

It can also be helpful to consider how the couple can manage stress together. To do this, the therapist will start from what has worked for either or both members of the couple in the past, both in terms of what each other has done for them, and what helps them on their own. Next the therapist will explore a specific situation where one partner felt stressed, helping them to identify and verbalise the impact that being stressed has on them emotionally. The therapist will ask the non-stressed partner to respond to this and attempt to support the stressed partner, and then ask the stressed partner for feedback. Using this feedback, the therapist can help the non-stressed partner to modify how they respond, to maximise the effective of the support from the stressed partner's perspective. Options for support could include positive reframing of the situation, promoting a sense of solidarity, telling the partner how appreciated they are for carrying the burden, pointing out positives in the partner, giving the partner options to relax, or making problem solving suggestions. Each of these options will be helpful to different people in different situations, and there is no right or wrong choice; it is about ensuring both clients learn how their partner most feels supported and knowing they have the ability to provide this.

Sexual problems. Sexual dysfunction, or the absence of a wanted sexual relationship, can reduce couple satisfaction in a relationship by up to 75% [17]. This is unsurprising, as sex is often one of the unique features of a romantic relationship, which sets it apart from all other relationships in life, and so the loss of it can bring into question whether the relationship is viable. The topic is also a particularly taboo one, often tied up in shame and fixed ideas about gender roles and how relationships should work. As such, it is key that couple's therapists actively broach and explore the topic, whether or not it is brought up by the couple. The fundamental aim is to help couples have 'Good Enough Sex' [18] in the sense that they have varying levels of satisfaction when having sex, and are accepting of the less satisfying while working towards having and celebrating the most satisfying.

To achieve this, the therapist will first explore how each partner sees their sex life, often during the shared and then each individual assessment session. In this, it is important to explore how both individuals feel about their sex life and how they interpret the other's behaviour. The therapist will want to note if one or both clients has an overly narrow view of what counts as acceptable sex, and help both to come to a broader definition – ideally to the point of counting any intimate contact that they both find pleasurable. While broadening the definition of sex, the therapist will also aim to broaden the rules around sex – who can initiate, what it can mean if one partner does not want sex, and what positions and actions are appropriate for each partner. Therapy can also offer a safe place to discuss what each partner finds enjoyable, so that the other has a better chance of being able to make contact pleasurable.

The therapist stance when discussing sexual problems should generally be that where any mutually pleasurable activity between consenting adults is a positive thing. While the therapist is not expected to be an expert on all aspects of sexuality, it can be helpful for them to offer basic psycho-sexual education where needed for reassurance's sake, regarding common yet taboo fantasies or the normalcy of masturbation. Therapy typically will work on acceptance and understanding of sexual problems more than on explicit behaviour change, though sometime therapists will make suggestions – with the agreement of both partners – trying out low level sexual behaviours to see if this can help rebuild a cycle of intimacy.

Working on sexual problems can be uncomfortable for some couple's therapists, who are not used to broaching such topics. However, studies into the effects of therapy on sexual and relationship satisfaction have shown that it is generally a topic that would benefit from greater focus [19], and so it can be worthwhile for the therapist to become practiced and at ease with this.

Problem solving. Once the couple have made significant steps towards acceptance and tolerance, and they are at least somewhat less divided on the central issues, the therapist can start moving towards active change. Couple problem solving is one commonly used tool to support this. Couple problem solving cannot be applied to all problems, but instead should be focussed specifically on situations where both parties see the issue as one worth solving, and where they have some control. The problem must also be one where both sides can 'win' at least in part, and so issues where there are limited possible options, such as whether to have a child for example, do not typically fit.

As in individual CBT, problem solving involves first defining the problem, and then attempting to solving it. In defining the problem, it is helpful to start by stating a relevant positive, such as 'I like spending time with you, so miss you when you're away', rather than directly critiquing, such as 'you're always leaving me alone'. This keeps the tone balanced, and reminds the partner what is valued about them as well as what is being brought up as an issue. It is also important for the problem describer to stick to behavioural specifics, and express their own emotional reactions to these. Ideally, the describer should be encouraged to avoid going further than this, such as by describing their perceptions on why the behaviour occurs, or on related issues.

Once the problem has been defined, the next step will be for each partner to acknowledge their role in the problem, as by definition any issue is only one because of how the other perceives it. The couple should then stick to this issue, and neutrally try to make sense of the problem, focussing on possible solutions each of them could try. The couple can then explore the pros and cons of each solution, with the aim of finding a compromise solution where both partners agree to make some changes, that together should improve the situation.

Behavioural activation. For many couples, more general behavioural changes occur naturally in response to empathic joining, unified detachment and building tolerance. Such changes will generally be prompted for by the therapist every session, and explored when they occur, to help reinforce and consolidate changes. However, other couples may need a more structured approach to behavioural change, to increase the frequency and perceived value of caring behaviours.

Such approaches will often start with asking the clients to make a list of undemanding gestures that they each feel they could make and that their partner may appreciate. The requirements for these gestures are that they are things that can be done daily, independent of reciprocation and are overt enough that they can be recognised by the other. Possible examples include making someone a cup of coffee, asking how their day has gone or smiling and making eye contact when their partner is talking to them. To ensure the activities meet these requirements, each client will discuss their list with the therapist, who will then help to make gestures concrete and ensure that the list hasn't missed anything important that has already been mentioned in therapy. While the partner is present for this discussion, they are asked to make no input, either verbally or non-verbally. The therapist will then set the couple the homework of trying out one or more items from the list, and making an active note of whether it was noticed by their partner and how it was received, as well as how it felt for them to do it. The following week, the outcomes are discussed, at which point the receivers of each activity can express how they felt about the chosen behaviours, and offer any other ideas to add to the lists.

In following this process, each client gets to experience both having things done for them without requesting it, and providing an unprompted positive experience to their partner. They learn how to evaluate their partner reactions to any chosen behaviour, and so weigh up the comparative value of different behaviours to find options that are genuinely rewarding. Hopefully, such exchanges can result in an increase of positive experiences without having to formally set this as homework long term.

Communication training was a core skill within TBCT, and focussed on for several sessions, yet was rarely used outside of the therapy office, or after treatment had ended. Despite this, communication training is still considered to be an important part of the couple therapy process. This is because it gives couples an experience of being able to communicate with each other, and of relating intimately, which they can then take forwards without the formal processes.

Communication training involves both speaking skills and listening skills. Speaking skills involve using clear 'I' statements, making concrete and specific requests for change, speaking concisely, editing out negative statements and speaking calmly. Meanwhile, listening skills include summarising what has been said, reflecting on what this means and is being felt, validating whatever can be empathically understood and asking questions to support understanding further. Each of these concepts will need to be explained to the couple, and then practised while speaking about a comparatively low emotion topic, with the therapist actively interjecting to offer suggested improvements where needed. Over time, patients can often move on to more emotive and central concerns.

To take this a step further, some couples will benefit from the use of the Dialogue Guide [20]. This is a set of statement starters to be used in turn, beginning with 'I notice' and 'I assume' and moving through a range of prompts finishing with 'I realize' and 'I hope'. The various prompts encourage the expression of a range of different reactions and aspects to a problem, starting with identifying a problematic behaviour, then moving onto reflecting on the emotional and cognitive reaction to it and then finishing with defining and reflecting on a possible solution. This can help bring a sense of specificity and completeness to exploring a problem, which can be missed when speaking more naturally.

Conclusion

Couple distress can be a key issue for those in relationships, resulting in depression or anxiety disorders. Relationship issues are also a common result of mental health difficulties experienced by one or both partners. In such circumstances, a CBT therapist may opt to work on the relationship itself rather than the individual's problem. Couple therapy is founded on the premise that the problem is dyadic – that is, that the problem lies within the interaction between the partners, not in either individual themselves. As such, helping a couple to better understand their problematic interactions, and empathically make sense of why they each react as they do, can be a major part of relieving the distress and reducing unhelpful spirals. More structured change approaches, such as problem solving, behavioural activation and communication training, can then support couples to adjust how they interact in line with their new understanding of each other.

Further Reading

Christensen A, Doss BD, Jacobson NS. *Integrative Behavioral Couple Therapy: A Therapist's Guide to Creating Acceptance and Change*. New York: WW Norton & Company; 2020.

Hewison D, Clulow C, Drake H. *Couple Therapy for Depression: A Clinician's Guide to Integrative Practice*. Oxford: Oxford University Press; 2014.

References

1. Stack S, Eshleman JR. Marital status and happiness: A 17-nation study. J Marriage Fam. 1998;**60**(2):527–536.
2. Whisman, MA. The Association Between Depression and Marital Dissatisfaction. In SRH Beach (Ed.), *Marital and Family Processes in Depression: A Scientific*

Foundation for Clinical Practice. Washington, DS: American Psychological Association; 2001.

3. Addis ME, Jacobson NS. Reasons for depression and the process and outcome of cognitive–behavioral psychotherapies. J Consult Clin Psychol. 1996;**64**(6):1417–1424.
4. Jacobson NS, Margolin G. *Marital Therapy: Strategies Based on Social Learning and Behavior Exchange Principles* [Internet]. New York: Brunner/Mazel; 1979. https://books.google.co.uk/books?id=DrlkEazTHQYC.
5. Baucom DH, Epstein N. *Cognitive-Behavioral Marital Therapy*. Levittown: Brunner/Mazel; 1990.
6. Jacobson NS, Christensen A, Prince SE, Cordova J, Eldridge K. Integrative behavioral couple therapy: An acceptance-based, promising new treatment for couple discord. J Consult Clin Psychol. 2000;**68**:351–355.
7. Christensen A, Doss B, Jacobson NS. *Integrative Behavioral Couple Therapy – A Therapist's Guide to Creating Acceptance and Change*, 2nd ed. New York: W. W. Norton & Company; 2020.
8. Hewison D, Clulow C, Drake H. *Couple Therapy for Depression: A Clinician's Guide To Integrative Practice*. 1st ed. Oxford: Oxford University Press; 2014.
9. Jacobson NS, Christensen A. *Integrative Couples Therapy – Promoting Acceptance & Change: Promoting Acceptance and Change*. New York: W. W. Norton & Company; 1996.
10. Baucom DH, Fischer MS, Worrell M, Corrie S, Belus JM, Molyva E, et al. Couple-based intervention for depression: An effectiveness study in the National Health Service in England. Fam Process. 2018;**57**(2):275–292.
11. Christensen A, Atkins DC, Berns S, Wheeler J, Baucom DH, Simpson LE. Traditional versus integrative behavioral couple therapy for significantly and chronically distressed married couples. J Consult Clin Psychol. 2004;**72**:176–191.
12. Christensen A, Atkins DC, Yi J, Baucom DH, George WH. Couple and individual adjustment for 2 years following a randomized clinical trial comparing traditional versus integrative behavioral couple therapy. J Consult Clin Psychol. 2006;**74**:1180–1191.
13. Christensen A, Atkins DC, Baucom B, Yi J. Marital status and satisfaction five years following a randomized clinical trial comparing traditional versus integrative behavioral couple therapy. J Consult Clin Psychol. 2010;**78**:225–235.
14. Recommendations | Depression in adults: treatment and management | Guidance | NICE [Internet]. NICE; 2022 [accessed 3 June 2023]. www.nice.org.uk/guidance/ng222/chapter/Recommendations#behavioural-couples-therapy-for-depression.
15. Padesky C, Mooney KA. Presenting the cognitive model to clients. Cogn Ther Newsl Int. 1990;**6**:13–14.
16. Grimmer A. The nine-part model: A tool for sharing dyadic formulations. www.bristolcbt.co.uk/publications/the-nine-part-model-dyadic-formulation/.
17. McCarthy BW, Thestrup M. Couple therapy and the treatment of sexual dysfunction. In: AS Gurman, JL Lebow, DK Snyder (Eds.), *Clinical Handbook of Couple Therapy* (pp. 591–617). 4th edition. New York: Guilford Press; 2008.
18. McCarthy B. *Sex Made Simple: Clinical Strategies for Sexual Issues in Therapy*. Eau Claire: PESI Publishing & Media; 2015.
19. Rothman K, Cicila LN, McGinn M, Hatch SG, Christensen A, Doss BD. Trajectories of sexual satisfaction and frequency during and after couple therapy for relationship distress. J Sex Marital Ther. 2021;**47**(3):209–223.
20. Gordon LH, Satir VM, Frandsen J. *Passage to Intimacy: A Practical Guide to Repairing and Rekindling Your Most Important Relationship* [Internet]. New York: Simon & Schuster; 1993. https://books.google.co.uk/books?id=7X9okk0LENEC.

Chapter

30

Internet and Telephone Delivery

In this chapter we will help you to be able to:

- Describe the development of remote delivery CBT, both by phone, video-conferencing and text-based systems.
- Explain the costs and benefits of the various remote formats to both the provider and client.
- Help your clients choose the most appropriate format for their therapy.

Introduction

Initially all CBT, whether for individuals or groups, was carried out face to face. However, this was costly, and limited the availability of therapy to those who were able to physically attend such sessions, or who could afford to have therapists come to them. In particular, this poses challenges for those in more remote settings, and became a global issue during the COVID-19 pandemic [1]. As such, alternative methods of delivery have been trialled, to see if more accessible formats could be equally effective. Initially this focussed on phone work, but then developed from this into both video-conferencing therapy and text-based therapy. This chapter will explore the different remote-delivery formats available, exploring the benefits each provide, as well as the costs and limitations imposed.

Telephone Therapy

Telephone therapy, at its simplest, is individual therapy provided via telephone call. Sessions can be set up to mirror face to face therapy in many ways, including having an agenda, engaging in homework review and homework setting and applying active change methods. There are several main benefits of telephone therapy over the more traditional face to face format. First, telephone appointments improve accessibility; there is no requirement for either the patient or the therapist to spend time travelling, and so sessions can fit into the shortest possible time no matter how remote the client. Linked to this are the low hardware and digital literacy requirements of a phone call, which makes this format more accessible for patients than other remote formats. This is important, as the remote locations or mobility issues which often make remote therapy desirable may also impair the feasibility of using a more technological approach. Within this accessible format there is also the option to remain comparatively anonymous; the patient could feasibly engage with therapy having provided little or no information at all, and is not required to enter a potentially stigmatising location such as a medical centre or therapy building.

Of course, this anonymity can also be a detractor from telephone therapy, as the therapist is likewise anonymous to some extent, which for some clients can raise concerns about whether the therapist is truly qualified or can be trusted [2]. More widely, the lack of visual information can be considered to be doing therapy with one's eyes closed. That is, the lack of visual interaction can make it harder to keep emotional arousal in the optimal zone, to notice subtle cues regarding safety behaviours or to share visual information such as formulations or written summaries. Due to these factors, telephone work is more generally used in low intensity CBT with the addition of pre-written guided self-help resources.

Video-Conferencing CBT

Video-conferencing therapy involves carrying out CBT via a video-conferencing platform. These may be those used more generally in business, such as Zoom, Webex or Microsoft Teams, or be tools specifically designed for healthcare providers, such as Attend Anywhere, Zoom for Healthcare or Theraplatform. Video-conferencing differs from telephone therapy as the therapist regains full use of the visual medium for interaction, making the process more analogous to face to face therapy [3]. While this form of therapy can still feel very new, trials involving video-conferencing therapy have actually been occurring for more than 20 years [4], and meta-analyses of these showed that the clinical outcomes were equivalent to traditional CBT [5]. However, until recently this form of therapy was not widely adopted, due to shortcomings in easily accessed videoconferencing tools, and by barriers imposed by digital literacy levels and resultant attitudes towards videoconferencing from both patients and therapists [5].

In the last few years, as video-conferencing quite suddenly became an everyday part of many people's lives, and as the software improved, video-therapy has become far more mainstream. This has been vital for the continuation of services during periods where face-to-face therapy was impossible, as it retained many of the benefits of face-to-face therapy, while removing travel requirements. Even after face-to-face therapy became once-again available, many chose to stay online, as the ability to have therapy in one's own home, without travel or the risk of stigma, is highly attractive. Likewise for therapists, the ability to remotely enter the patient's home offers a unique opportunity to carry out virtual home visits while working in services where this might be prevented due to costs or safety considerations. As issues are generally more likely to be happening in the patient's home than in the therapy office (especially for disorders such as OCD and hoarding), online therapy can get to the heart of the situation, and provides opportunities for experimenting and exposure that are harder to simulate in person.

However, the move of services to predominantly online therapy has also created digital divide, where those unable to access this – due to digital literacy issues, lack of private space or poor IT set ups – cannot benefit. As such, the need for face-to-face therapy as an alternative to online work continues.

Text-Based Therapy

Text-based therapy is also relatively new, but rapidly proliferating. This mode of therapy involves communicating one-on-one with a therapist via text chat, either via simple text messaging, a messaging app or a dedicated computer program with its own chat rooms. A number of organisations are now offering this, either as a primary system (e.g. IESO) or as a major component of their overall support packages (e.g. Better Help). Many of the costs and benefits of this form of therapy are the same as those of telephone and video-conferencing therapy. Text-based therapy in particular may be attractive to some as it allows for anonymity beyond even telephone therapy – while the systems still generally require basic information about clients for payment and safety reasons, it can be possible to do all of therapy without ever being seen or heard by the therapist. Conversely, this also means that the therapy cannot benefit from either visual and tonal communication; often used to support meaning and empathy in traditional therapy. Despite this, the evidence-base shows that it can be an effective modality, both in terms of group therapy [6] and in individual therapy [7].

Providing Remote-Delivery CBT

As explored above, there are a range of costs and benefits to offering remote-delivery CBT, whether this be via telephone, video call or text. Each of these should be carefully considered, in terms of whether remote access should be used at all, and which format could be most appropriate. When such a format has been chosen, it is important to consider how to provide it most effectively.

Some of the requirements for remote delivery are very similar to that of face-to-face work. Therapy should be done with full focus on the client and the work, in a way that ensures that the therapist is fully present in the session and the patient can feel safe [8]. These requirements can become neglected in remote delivery work, especially in those where the therapist is not seen by the patient, but this can significantly reduce the efficacy of the work. Ideally, therapy should be carried out in a private space, with all communication routes turned off, other than that being used to contact the client (that is, no email accounts open, no web chat clients, and phones out of the way and on mute). Such a set up can be challenging, but it is worth attempting to gain this for both therapist and client, as a sense of being present has been shown to correlate with session outcomes [9].

Likewise, as in face-to-face therapy, it is important to have a mechanism by which outcome measures and any paperwork associated with the homework tasks can be shared with the therapist. While in face-to-face therapy, this can be done by simply handing the paperwork to the therapist, in remote therapy alternatives will need to be agreed. There are a number of apps and computer programs that allow for this type of data to be shared in a secure way. On the other end of the technology spectrum, a simple photograph attached to an email can also do the job.

A specific requirement of remote CBT is that the therapist be familiar with the software and hardware. Overall, technical difficulties and a lack of familiarity with the technology is associated with the software has been shown to correlate with a loss of efficacy, so practice is essential [10,11]. This may be explained by the impact of delays caused by such issues; these can impact patient views of the therapist, attributing the issues to not being fully present or engaged in the process [12].

A consideration that may be needed for therapy happening in people's homes or offices is that of transition; how they will mentally close off the time in therapy before returning to their life. In traditional therapy, this is generally a given in terms of the journey home, whereas in remote therapy the client may be immediately thrust back into other activities unless a plan is put in place. As such, it can be helpful to explore options for transition for the client, such as staying at their computer/phone for a few minutes to reflect, or to go for a walk.

To make the most of the unique benefits of video-therapy, it is important to optimise the visual information being shared; how much you and the client can see of each other.

In terms of the client seeing the therapist, this allows for the use of body language showing empathy and mirroring. In terms of the therapist seeing the patient, this enhances the ability to pick up on non-verbal cues and safety behaviours. In practice, this first involves paying attention to lighting, distance from camera and the screens being used on each side [8]. To also allow for a sense of eye-contact, it is helpful to have both the camera and screen approximately at eye level, and then check with the client if unsure [8].

Concluding Remarks

Therapy was initially provided face-to-face but now can be accessed via a range of delivery formats. Each has benefits, such as greater accessibility, anonymity and reduced costs, but can also reduce the richness of communication, and risks leaving behind those without access to the necessary resources or technical ability. As such, patients are best provided for when there is a range of formats available, with information about the costs and benefits of each clearly provided. If therapy is to be carried out remotely, care should be given to ensuring the optimum set up for both therapist and client, so that it can provide the benefits of remote working without losing efficacy.

Essential Reading

Geller S. Cultivating online therapeutic presence: Strengthening therapeutic relationships in teletherapy sessions. Counselling Psychology Quarterly, 2021;***34***(3–4):687–703.

References

1. Cromarty P, Gallagher D, Watson J. Remote delivery of CBT training, clinical supervision and services: In times of crisis or business as usual. Cogn Behav Ther. 2020;**13**:e33.
2. Bee PE, Lovell K, Lidbetter N, Easton K, Gask L. You can't get anything perfect: 'User perspectives on the delivery of cognitive behavioural therapy by telephone'. Soc Sci Med. 2010;**71**(7):1308–1315.
3. Himle JA, Fischer DJ, Muroff JR, Van Etten ML, Lokers LM, Abelson JL, et al. Videoconferencing-based cognitive-behavioral therapy for obsessive-compulsive disorder. Behav Res Ther. 2006;**44**(12):1821–1829.
4. Manchanda M, McLaren P. Cognitive behaviour therapy via interactive video. J Telemed Telecare. 1998;**4**(1_suppl):53–55.
5. Chakrabarti S. Usefulness of telepsychiatry: A critical evaluation of videoconferencing-based approaches. World J Psychiatry. 2015;**5**(3):286–304.
6. Zerwas SC, Watson HJ, Hofmeier SM, Levine MD, Hamer RM, Crosby RD, et al. CBT4BN: A randomized controlled trial of online chat and face-to-face group therapy for bulimia nervosa. Psychother Psychosom. 2016;**86**(1):47–53.
7. Catarino A, Bateup S, Tablan V, Innes K, Freer S, Richards A, et al. Demographic and clinical predictors of response to internet-enabled cognitive–behavioural therapy for depression and anxiety. BJPsych Open. 2018;**4**(5):411–418.
8. Geller S. Cultivating online therapeutic presence: Strengthening therapeutic relationships in teletherapy sessions. Couns Psychol Q. 2021;**34**(3–4):687–703.
9. Geller SM, Greenberg LS, Watson JC. Therapist and client perceptions of therapeutic presence: The development of a measure. Psychother Res. 2010;**20**(5):599–610.

10. Cipolletta S, Frassoni E, Faccio E. Construing a therapeutic relationship online: An analysis of videoconference sessions. Clin Psychol. 2018;**22**(2):220–229.

11. Etzelmueller A, Radkovsky A, Hannig W, Berking M, Ebert DD. Patient's experience with blended video-and internet based cognitive behavioural therapy service in routine care. Internet Interv. 2018;**12**:165–175.

12. Schoenenberg K, Raake A, Koeppe J. Why are you so slow? Misattribution of transmission delay to attributes of the conversation partner at the far-end. Int J Hum-Comput Stud. 2014;**72**(5):477–487.

Chapter 31

Computerised CBT Self-Help Approaches

with Bruno Kajiyama

In this chapter we will help you to be able to:

- Describe computerised CBT and its evidence-base to date.
- Weigh up the benefits and costs of computerised CBT to both the provider and client.

Introduction

As with both group and remote delivery approaches, computerised CBT (cCBT) developed out of need to disseminate CBT more widely and reduce costs. Many studies have been carried out exploring how effective cCBT is, both in controlled trial environments and in practice settings. Through this, a range of additional benefits of the approach have been discovered that can make it more helpful for some than traditional CBT, though there are also potential costs and limitations.

What Is Computerised CBT?

CBT has always involved helping patients to understand how their difficulties are being maintained, and then applying tools to change the cycle. As such, much of therapy is learning pre-defined concepts and skills. Self-help resources have thus been added to therapy as an adjunct since its inception, such as the use of the booklet 'Coping with Depression' in the original CBT protocol for depression [1]. Over time, the pressure has mounted to complete more therapy faster, and so further self-help materials have been added. These self-help guides mean that sessions themselves can be focussed on the application of skills and reflection rather than on psychoeducation, and so reduce the overall therapist time required. Self-help guides have the added advantage that, being pre-written in accordance with the chosen protocol, they clearly lay out what should be covered and in what order, and so help keep therapy focussed on proven techniques and known priorities.

cCBT was an expansion of this, allowing for even more of the standard therapy processes to be done outside of the therapy session, as the majority of the learning and skills acquisition aspects of therapy are achieved by working through a computer program. Such programs include filling in and getting feedback on outcome measures, psychoeducation and interactive tools such as thought diaries and activity schedules, which the patient will be taken through step by step. They often also include fillable formulations with case examples and related videos. Typically, cCBT involves completing a set amount of the program each week, often in a single chunk like a therapy session, with or without additional therapist support after each section has been completed. As with any other form of CBT, there will be homework tasks to complete between each section of the program, so as to apply the skills being learnt to everyday life.

Efficacy Data for Computerised CBT

The efficacy of cCBT has undergone a number of phases. Initial studies looking at efficacy were done in conjunction with program developers, and these studies showed results from cCBT as superior to treatment as usual, as reviewed in meta-analysis of such studies [2]. Latter pragmatic trials exploring efficacy in routine practice, however, have shown limited efficacy compared to GP support alone – that is none, if GP support is being compared to pure cCBT [3], and small to moderate effects if the cCBT is telephone assisted [4]. When compared to the evidence-base regarding non-computerised low intensity psychological interventions [5] the overall effect size of cCBT effect size is comparable, but not superior.

A number of factors appear to impact the efficacy of cCBT [6], with one of the key drivers being how much the patients engage with the program. This in turn is affected by the attractiveness of the user interface, and how intuitive it is to use. It is also impacted by the patient's beliefs about whether cCBT (and the exact program in question) will be helpful, and so practitioner training in developing patient confidence is vital, as is patient choice.

Benefits of Computerised CBT

There are several possible advantages to the use of cCBT over other self-help and CBT approaches. First, cCBT can involve less therapist time than many forms of CBT or guided self-help [7], and so more individuals can be supported by the same number of therapists. When considering pure cCBT with no therapist involvement, there is theoretically no limit on the number of patients that can be supported, allowing for an infinitely scalable process which can help with large-scale difficulties such as common mental health problems. In addition to this, the reduced (or removed) need for direct synchronous time between a patient and therapist allows for cCBT to more easily fit into an individual's busy life – it can be worked on at 8pm as easily as between 9am and 5pm [8].

cCBT can also be less exposing. For some individuals, it is far easier to tell their deepest fears to a mindless computer, rather than to a person. This is especially relevant in more isolated communities, where it can be difficult to achieve anonymity with traditional services [9]. It can also be highly normalising to have that same mindless computer then provide relevant information about the problem in question – going some way to proving that the problems are understandable and shared by others. These two concepts can be particularly powerful in disorders such as social anxiety disorder, where the therapist themselves can otherwise be a phobic object, and where reassurance from people is often hard to believe. Last, the mindless computer, by definition, can't modify therapy based on instinct, and so will usually have a higher fidelity to the protocol than other therapies, which may be a strength.

Costs and Contraindications for Computerised CBT

cCBT also has some disadvantages in comparison with other CBT approaches. While cCBT (and other guided self-help approaches) can be very effective at providing information and skills, it cannot react dynamically to how the patient receives the information; it cannot troubleshoot difficulties or empathise. It also cannot fully assess if information has been understood and applied correctly. As such, while it can be a useful adjunct to live therapist contacts, it is difficult to use optimally as a fully standalone treatment. Its flexibility can also be a drawback; as the session can be done at any time, it can easily be postponed, and so treatment can become more spread out than designed, reducing effectiveness.

cCBT in particular also has the barrier that it requires IT skills and resources. As such, it is unsuitable for anyone without these two things, and so it is problematic when services rely on it as a primary treatment approach.

These drawbacks play out in recent large-scale trials comparing cCBT to GP check-ups, where the addition of the cCBT to the check-ups, when done without therapist input, did not improve outcomes [3]. In a follow-up study, efficacy was improved by the addition of telephone therapist support [4] but it was still only comparable to other forms of guided self-help. Given the higher cost of cCBT programs compared to paper self-help guides, this would suggest that cCBT is not more cost effective than traditional guided self-help done via a booklet. This backs up earlier work, which had also shown a strong correlation between therapist input and outcome [10]. Of course, there may be some individuals who will benefit more from one version over the other, and more research may help to better define when each approach is warranted.

AI and cCBT

As discussed, a key issue with cCBT is that it can't react responsively to what patient is doing. If the patient is misunderstanding what they're being taught, the program cannot spot this, and nor can a program idiosyncratically troubleshoot issues when a patient is stuck. A developing answer to this is cCBT programs which incorporate artificial intelligence (AI).

Until recently, therapy was considered one of the least automatable professions [11] but will this continue? Already, some services are trialling use of AI chat bots to enhance cCBT programs, such as Woebot, with promising results [12]. On the other hand, experiments simulating the experience of chatbot-provided therapy have been met with negative reactions from clients in comparison to therapist-driven text-based therapy [13], despite the 'chatbot' in question actually being driven by a therapist. Of course, it is hard to know if this shows that AI can't replace therapists, or if therapists can't effectively replicate AI.

The key risk of fully automated therapy is that it may miss things that therapists would catch, such as implicit communication and the more nebulous links between concepts, which don't follow a programmable pattern. However, AI also won't allow for personal biases and prejudices to influence therapy, and so it may be able to have a higher fidelity to the theoretical model. It also won't make erroneous links based on the therapist's personal experiences, which may make for a more genuine Socratic dialogue.

For patients who avoid discussing problem with others, and dislike personal interaction, will all of this be better than working with a human? Given that current routes into therapy do involve personal interaction, there may be a hidden market here, so long as the technology can catch up.

Technologically Supported CBT Approaches with Caregivers

Technology-based CBT (TB-CBT), which includes cCBT and other related options, can be used as a tool or key component of self-help programs for populations that may find it difficult to attend face-to-face sessions. An example of this is TB-CBT for caregivers (CGs).

Some benefits of TB-CBT over traditional CBT include enhanced access to psychotherapy for those CGs who may not be willing, do not have time or do not have services in their local area to receive face-to-face CBT. These factors may ultimately improve caregivers' engagement and enhance compliance with the intervention. A current example is the iCare program (www.icarefamily.com) which incorporates multiple sources of information (e.g. videos, articles, podcasts, etc.) that demonstrate poor versus more effective ways to manage care recipient behaviours, a notebook of home practice exercises and a series of structured learning opportunities focussing on increasing caregivers' use of adaptive cognitive and behavioural coping strategies. Results indicated reduced stress and better self-reported coping skills among caregivers who completed the program [14].

As an accessible non-consumable resource that can be shared widely, video training offers many benefits to complement and expand the reach of CBT programs, such as distributing information, explaining concepts and engaging clients with role-playing examples that are likely to increase generalisation and motivation. Key elements of behavioural activation are also integral, to encourage CGs to identify, plan and do activities to bring energy back and maintain positive mental strength.

Mobile Apps Specifically for Caregivers

As personal devices which caregivers typically carry with them, smartphones provide a powerful mechanism to deliver personalised programs, enable supportive interactions and facilitate client engagement before, during, and after CBT therapy sessions, or as stand-alone programs. A mobile app that is dedicated to CGs of people living with a Dementia, is the Dementia Caring Response App (DCRA) developed by Photozig, Inc. (available at www.photozig.com/app). DCRA contains a self-paced program to help caregivers of individuals with Alzheimer's disease to understand and deal with difficult behaviours of their care recipients. CBT strategies in the DCRA training help caregivers to learn how to respond to these behaviours, such as agitation, aggression, anxiety, confusion and irritability. Specific CBT content includes identification of unhelpful thoughts and cognitive restructuring, which are facilitated by interactive features of the mobile app that enable caregivers to learn more about a challenging behaviour, select possible responses and choose alternative thought patterns that are more helpful (see Figure 31.1 for example screenshots).

There are several factors to consider when deciding whether to incorporate technology into CBT work with caregivers. Some important limitations are noted to include the assumption that caregivers know how to use devices, such as internet browsers and smartphones, to access relevant content [15]. This limitation is becoming less problematic as caregivers are more comfortable with digital approaches. Caregivers also need reliable internet service for online programs and mobile apps, but this is not always affordable. In addition, nuances of communication may be lost or reduced when technology alone is used to convey CBT principles and techniques. Lack of therapist-client interaction can be problematic for those who need a more hands-on approach to their problems. When compared to a live therapy session, technology may never replace the human interaction, compassionate response, expert counselling and active care that a therapist can provide. The choice of whether or not to incorporate technology into CBT depends on clinical judgement; in many cases, technology can complement the intervention program and enhance positive outcomes.

Figure 31.1 Examples of the CBT strategies in the Dementia Caring Response App (DCRA).

Concluding Remarks

cCBT has developed out of the long tradition in CBT of providing psychoeducation and skills information via additional written resources. The use of cCBT programs, versus attending traditional CBT, can make therapy more accessible and scalable, but at the same time, it loses its idiosyncrasy, and so can end up less effective unless supplemented with therapist support.

In addition to generic cCBT, specific tools have been designed to either replace or complement therapy with specific populations, such as caregivers. These tools can be specialised to the information and interventions more commonly needed for these groups, providing a level of specialist information that may not be easily accessible in the local area, but the suitability of a digital approach needs to be considered both for the group as a whole, and on a case-by-case basis.

Further Reading

Klein B, Proudfoot J. Guided CBT Interventions using the Internet. In Bennett Levy J, Richards D, Farrand P, Christensen H, Griffiths K, Kavanagh D, et al. *Oxford Guide to Low Intensity Interventions*. Oxford: OUP; 2010.

References

1. Beck AT, Rush J, Shaw BF, Emery G. *Cognitive Therapy of Depression*. New York: Guilford Press; 1979.
2. Kaltenthaler E, Brazier J, De Nigris E, Tumur I, Ferriter M, Beverley C, et al. Computerised cognitive behaviour therapy for depression and anxiety update: A systematic review and economic evaluation. Health Technol Assess Winch Engl. 2006;**10**(33):iii–xi.
3. Gilbody S, Littlewood E, Hewitt C, Brierley G, Tharmanathan P, Araya R, et al. Computerised cognitive behaviour therapy (cCBT) as treatment for depression in primary care (REEACT trial): Large scale pragmatic randomised controlled trial. *BMJ*. 2015;**351**:h5627.
4. Brabyn S, Araya R, Barkham M, Bower P, Cooper C, Duarte A, et al. The second randomised evaluation of the effectiveness, cost-effectiveness and acceptability of computerised therapy (REEACT-2) trial: Does the provision of telephone support enhance the effectiveness of computer-delivered cognitive behaviour therapy? A randomised controlled trial. Health Technol Assess. 2016;**20**(89):1–64.
5. Cuijpers P, van Straten A, van Schaik A, Andersson G. Psychological treatment of depression in primary care: A meta-analysis. Br J Gen Pract. 2009;**59**(559):e51–60.
6. Klein B, Proudfoot J. Guided CBT Interventions using the internet. In: J Bennett-Levy, D Richards, P Farrand, H Christensen, K Griffiths, D Kavanagh, et al. (Eds.), *Oxford Guide to Low Intensity CBT Interventions* (pp. 225–264). Oxford: OUP; 2010.
7. Andrews G, Davies M, Titov N. Effectiveness randomized controlled trial of face to face versus Internet cognitive behaviour therapy for social phobia. Aust N Z J Psychiatry. 2011;**45**(4):337–340.
8. McClay CA, Waters L, McHale C, Schmidt U, Williams C. Online cognitive behavioral therapy for bulimic type disorders, delivered in the community by a nonclinician: qualitative study. J Med Internet Res. 2013;**15**(3):e2083.
9. Aisbett D, Boyd CP, Francis KJ, Newnham K. Understanding barriers to mental health service utilization for adolescents in rural Australia. Rural Remote Health. 2007;**7**(1):1–10.
10. Palmqvist B, Carlbring P, Andersson G. Internet-delivered treatments with or without therapist input: Does the therapist factor have implications for efficacy and cost? Expert Rev Pharmacoecon Outcomes Res. 2007;**7**(3):291–297.

11. Frey CB, Osborne MA. The future of employment: How susceptible are jobs to computerisation? Technol Forecast Soc Change. 2017;**114**:254–280.

12. Fitzpatrick KK, Darcy A, Vierhile M. Delivering cognitive behavior therapy to young adults with symptoms of depression and anxiety using a fully automated conversational agent (Woebot): A randomized controlled trial. JMIR Ment Health. 2017;**4**(2): e7785.

13. Bell S, Wood C, Sarkar A. Perceptions of chatbots in therapy. CHI'19 Extended Abstracts, May 4–9, 2019, Glasgow, Scotland UK. https://advait.org/files/bell_2019_chatbots_therapy.pdf.

14. Kajiyama B, Thompson LW, Eto-Iwase T, Yamashita M, Di Mario J, Marian Tzuang Y, et al. Exploring the effectiveness of an internet-based program for reducing caregiver distress using the iCare Stress Management e-Training Program. Aging Ment Health. 2013;**17**(5):544–554.

15. Hopkinson MD, Reavell J, Lane DA, Mallikarjun P. Cognitive behavioral therapy for depression, anxiety, and stress in caregivers of dementia patients: A systematic review and meta-analysis. The Gerontologist. 2019;**59**(4):e343–62.

Chapter 32

Developing and Progressing as a Cognitive Behavioural Therapy Therapist

In this chapter we will help you to be able to:

- Explain the meaning of therapist competence and meta-competence.
- Differentiate the experiences required to enhance competence based on the DPR model of skills development.
- Define the value of CPD, patient feedback, supervision and self-practice/self-reflection (SP/SR) in furthering therapist competence.
- Maximise your own learning opportunities in relation to identified gaps.

Introduction:

Thus far, this book has been predominantly focussed on providing the key declarative knowledge required to effectively carry out CBT, as well as examples and pointers to illustrate the practical application of this knowledge. However, development as a CBT therapist is a broader endeavour than learning theory and protocols, and is likely to continue long past the end of a book, or even of a standard CBT training course.

This chapter will focus on the meaning of competence within CBT, considering this in terms of not just knowledge, but also skills and reflective processes. It will then summarise the key methods for acquiring and maintaining this therapeutic knowledge, skills and reflectivity across a lifetime, and what can help to make each of these methods most effective.

What Is Therapist Competence and Meta-Competence?

Competent therapists, like competent vehicle drivers, are those who can use the tools they have available to get someone to their aimed-for destination, both safely and as quickly as safety and comfort allows. While competence as a therapist is no guarantee of patient recovery, there is some evidence that competent therapists do have better therapeutic outcomes, such as in reduced symptoms and disability in panic disorder [1] and improved outcomes and ability to manage comorbidity in depression [2]. To be competent, therapists will need to have theoretical knowledge, procedural skills and the ability to use these effectively and dynamically with the patient in front of them [3]. As they progress, they also will need to develop meta-competence – the ability to use evidence and skills to go beyond the basics, to adapt to the specific clients in front of them when they don't fit the clear categories or rule [4]. Generally, this involves being formulation and underlying principle driven so as to achieve meta-competent adherence – that is, following the underlying principle of a treatment approach based on the formulation of the client, even when the exact mechanics of the approach are adapted or altered [5].

Developing Competence

Becoming an ever-more competent and meta-competent practitioner is hopefully the aim of all those working in the caring professions, to ensure that our patients get the most from our work with them and the best chance of recovery. However, while the evidence-base for what makes good therapy is well-established, there was until recently less known and proven regarding what will best develop a practitioner [6].

One comparatively recent model of therapist development is the declarative-procedural-reflective (DPR) model [7]. The DPR model states there are three interconnected systems that all need developing to become a skilled practitioner – declarative knowledge, procedural skills and reflective practice. Declarative knowledge – 'knowing that' – is the facts and theory that is learnt in lectures, watching videos and reading texts like the book in front of you. Having this knowledge is important in knowing what therapy should involve, and updating this knowledge is key to ensuring that the therapy given is the most effective version available.

Procedural knowledge is the set of related rules about 'how to' and 'when to'. This is the knowledge about using skills directly and is essential in applying declarative knowledge in practice. Unlike declarative knowledge, this can often be learnt without explicit conscious awareness of what the rules in question are, as many CBT lecturers discover when they are first asked to verbalise these how's and when's while teaching! Such procedural knowledge can be learnt in several ways, often initially via observing the skill being modelled and then the learner attempting role play with a partner, ideally with feedback provided [7,8]. To embed these skills, supervised practice in real world clinical settings is then helpful.

To develop this procedural knowledge further however, one then needs the third system – reflective practice. In a nutshell, this is the practice of comparing a concrete experience to current knowledge (declarative and procedural) to determine what discrepancies exist, and then pulling new conceptual learning from this to make sense of the situation [9]. The concept of this type of thinking on the refinement and modification of habit is something that has been described for more than 100 years [10], and has long been considered by some as key to effective learning [11,12]. It is now increasingly accepted as vital to ongoing development in counselling and psychotherapy, making the difference between those who continue to develop into experts, and those who remain average despite many years of practice [13]. Reflection is a skill that occurs both in-action (that is, during experiences) and on-action (after experiences), and conscious practice of reflection on-action can assist with more effective and rapid reflection in-action [9]. Reflection can be undertaken individually, and on any clinical experience, but is often greatly enhanced by the use of reflective supervision and dyadic or group self-practice self-reflection (SPSR) [8].

All parts of the learning process can also be enhanced by the collection and examination of patient feedback – both of how they are experiencing the therapy, and how their symptoms and goal achievement are changing over time. This can then be taken to supervision or reflected upon in and after the situation, to further refine competence with this case and in the future.

Continuing Professional Development (CPD)

On graduation from an appropriately detailed and comprehensive training programme, such as a Level 2 BABCP accredited CBT programme in the UK, or a similarly accredited course in many other countries, a therapist will hopefully have proven themselves to have a decent starting level of declarative knowledge and procedural skills, sufficient to write academically about their treatment of clients, and to pass assessments of their skills in vivo [14]. However, to become a truly competent therapist, it will be important to supplement this starting knowledge via continuing professional development. This will help in a range of ways:

1. The total amount of knowledge and skills taught on a comprehensive training course is enormous, and trainees typically will not have the opportunity to apply or be assessed on every component [14]. As such, CPD can be focussed on areas where initial training failed to become embedded, broadening the therapist's knowledge to all areas that they will benefit from understanding.
2. Best practice will change over time, as new protocols are developed and proven to have greater efficacy than what came before – without ongoing updates to knowledge, the therapy offered will be less and less effective compared to the newer possibilities.
3. Old declarative knowledge can become inaccurate in our memories over time, and so reviewing known models and knowledge will help to guard against this and keep knowledge accurate.

The range of activities that could be counted as CPD are almost endless; the BABCP for example list 42 different suggested options that could be considered CPD from attending workshops and reading journals and textbooks, to acting as an examiner or helping to publicise CBT in the media [15]. Generally, for CPD to be maximally effective, it will need to include at least some skills practice, and be reflected upon, and as such evidence of these may be required for reaccreditation as a therapist depending on your national body [16].

Patient Feedback

As noted above, competence may be linked (at least loosely) to patient outcomes, especially at the extremes of competence [17]. Outcomes are also affected by whether patients remain in therapy to completion, or drop out, which in turn correlates to their satisfaction in the treatment process [18]. As such, patient feedback, both on how their symptoms are changing, and how they feel about the process of therapy, is invaluable.

More formal methods of patient feedback include general and disorder specific self-report measures, goal-based outcome monitoring [19] and patient/session satisfaction ratings [20]. These rating-based self-report measures are subjective, and can take time to complete, but they offer valuable insight into how therapy is helping clients towards symptom reduction and valued goals, and whether there are issues with how the therapy is proceeding that may benefit from discussion. Depending on the patient and therapeutic context, different measures may be used either within the session (at beginning or the end) to allow for instruction on how to use the measure, or between sessions, to avoid using up therapy time. They can be used every session, at regular intervals, or just at the beginning and end of treatment. They can also be given to other involved individuals, such as parents, teachers or carers, to get a broader view of the changes occurring.

In addition to these formal measures, informal feedback elicitation can be used, both at regular intervals and in response to perceived shifts in symptoms or satisfaction. Simple questions such as 'what changes have you noticed in your difficulties?' or 'what was most/least useful about today's session for you?' and 'how are you finding the therapy so far?' can help patients to feel more comfortable giving feedback, though of course the feedback given must then be positively reinforced by the therapist.

All feedback, both positive and negative, should then be reflected upon, to consider what learning can be taken from it. If a patient is recovering faster than expected, what can that tell us about the method of delivery we have applied, or what patient factors might have made the therapy a better fit? Likewise, if recovery is slower than expected, or deterioration is occurring, how can that be made sense of in the light of the patient's context and difficulties, and the way in which therapy is being delivered? If a patient is enjoying therapy, what is making this the case, and is this correlated to therapeutic gains (or possibly collusion)? Meanwhile, if a patient is struggling with the process, can this be modified without risking efficacy? While many of these questions may be answerable on private reflection, they can also prompt us to take the case to supervision, another key feature of ongoing and increasing therapist competence.

Supervision

Supervision is a common feature in many healthcare roles, especially those involving therapy and counselling. Due to the broad use of it across varying setting and professions, its definition is likewise broad, from

> an intervention provided by a more senior member of a profession to a more junior member or members of that same profession. This relationship is evaluative, extends over time, and has the simultaneous purposes of enhancing the professional functioning of the more junior person(s), monitoring the quality of professional services offered to the clients, she, he, or they see, and serving as a gatekeeper for those who are to enter the particular profession. [21]

to

> a distinct professional activity in which education and training aimed at developing science-informed practice are facilitated through a collaborative interpersonal process. It involves observation, evaluation, feedback, facilitation of supervisee self-assessment, and acquisition of knowledge and skills by instruction, modelling, and mutual problem-solving. Building on the recognition of the strengths and talents of the supervisee, supervision encourages self-efficacy. [22]

One well-accepted way of considering supervision is by its three main aims, which are:

- formative – the development and refinement of knowledge and skills,
- normative – the monitoring performance and fidelity,
- restorative – provision of emotional support, including normalisation and validation [23].

In comparison to the evidence base regarding CBT itself, there is a lack of evidence about what constitutes effective CBT supervision [24]. Derek Milne in particular has been working to address this, and has devised and disseminated evidence-based guidelines that could support new supervisors in being more effective [24,25,26]. These include how to train supervisors effectively, how to support a supervisory alliance, goal setting in supervision, how to facilitate learning in supervision, giving feedback and providing evaluation in supervision and support and guidance in supervision [26]. Within each there are then concrete recommendations – for example, within the alliance guidelines are recommendations to 'clarify the learning agreement ... agree on tasks and create structure ... build a collaborative bond ... provide a role model ... facilitate reflection ... provide formative feedback ... [and] set the supervision relationship in context' [26].

Another place to look to for what is likely to constitute good supervision is randomised control trials – here, where those leading the trial are highly invested in ensuring that the therapy is done as effectively as possible, the four following features are generally expected:

- skills development including role play
- live observation or watching recordings
- fidelity monitoring, and
- outcome monitoring [27]

In particular, the value of live observation or watching recordings cannot be undersold. Various studies have shown the difficulty for therapists to accurately assess their own competence, and that therapists may either over assess it [28] or under assess it [29]. In either case, a supervisor who can see the therapist's actual performance can offer insight into what the therapist is missing – either the gaps in their skills and knowledge, or the strengths they may be unconscious of, and in either case, this then allows for reflection and the refinement of the rules being used to drive future practice.

We can also consider what guidance is in place in large-scale CBT providers. For example, England's NHS Talking Therapies for Anxiety and Depression has a manual for best practice across services, and this includes a sizable number of recommendations regarding supervision, including that it is weekly, with every case reviewed at least every four weeks, that it makes use of outcome measures, and that it should consider cultural competence [30].

SP/SR

SP/SR is increasingly being recognised as one of the most powerful ways for therapists to deepen their understanding and appreciation of CBT, as well as enhancing their skills in using this model in a sensitive and empathetic way [31]. SP/SR is a two-part process, involving first applying CBT techniques to oneself (SP) and then reflecting back on the process (SR) [32]. Pragmatically, this involves several steps. First, participants to choose a personal or professional problem that they would like to work on, one which they feel emotionally able to explore without a formal therapy process in place (though it can be useful to have a plan of who to talk to if the process does unearth something more challenging, such as one's GP). They then need to create a regular space to work on this problem where they are in the right emotional space to do so. Either alone or with the partner, they will use various CBT techniques to explore, conceptualise, evaluate and finally test out their beliefs and behaviours connected to this problem, working towards a 'new way of being'. Throughout the process, the participants should take time to reflect as deeply as they can about what they have noticed and experienced in using the tools of CBT on themselves, either with their SP/SR partner or on their own. These reflections can focus on their learning about themselves but should also explore what they have learnt about the process of CBT, about what it is like to explore one's own beliefs and use various tools, and what makes things work better and worse. Sharing these process-based reflections in a wider group can help consolidate the learning, as well as normalising the difficulties experienced.

Through using this process, participants have noted six major benefits:

- Improved procedural CBT ability
- Improved ability to explain the conceptual framework
- Enhanced therapeutic flexibility
- Better understanding and focus on the therapeutic relationship
- Being more attuned to the patient's emotional state
- Enhanced self-reflection [31]

Given the comparative difficulty of acquiring these benefits through lectures and role plays, it is unsurprising that SP/SR is being increasingly encouraged in trainee and qualified therapists, and beginning to be required as part of accredited courses.

Concluding Remarks

Becoming a competent therapist is a lifelong endeavour, requiring the ongoing maintenance and refinement of current knowledge and skills, along with constant updating of both to keep up with the evidence base. While literature such as this book can be a useful starting point especially for declarative knowledge, the development of procedural and reflective skills will be aided by more hands on and interactive methods. Therapists who wish to continue developing should prioritise attending CPD events, gathering and reviewing patient feedback and engaging in meaningful supervision and SP/SR. All therapists will have their own specific fluctuating strengths and weaknesses, and so should ask themselves regularly what their greatest specific learning needs are at present, and which of the concepts above could best support them with it.

Further Reading

Bennett-Levy J, McManus F, Westling BE, Fennell M. Acquiring and refining CBT skills and competencies: Which training methods are perceived to be most effective? Behav Cogn Psychother. 2009;**37**(5):571–583.

Milne DL, Reiser RP. *A Manual for Evidence-Based CBT Supervision.* Chichester: John Wiley & Sons; 2017.

Bennett-Levy J. *Experiencing CBT from the Inside Out: A Self-Practice/Self-Reflection Workbook for Therapists.* New York: The Guilford Press; 2014.

References

1. Grey N, Salkovskis P, Quigley A, Clark DM, Ehlers A. Dissemination of cognitive therapy for panic disorder in primary care. Behav Cogn Psychother. 2008;**36**(5):509–520.
2. Kuyken W, Tsivrikos D. Therapist competence, comorbidity and cognitive-behavioral therapy for depression. Psychother Psychosom. 2008;**78**(1):42–48.
3. Muse K, Kennerley H, McManus F. The why, what, when, who and how of assessing CBT competence to support lifelong learning. Cogn Behav Ther. 2022;**15**:e57.
4. Roth A, Pilling S. The CBT competencies framework for depression and anxiety

disorders. Lond UK Cent Outcome Res Eval. 2007. www.ucl.ac.uk/pals/research/clinical-educational-and-health-psychology/research-groups/competence-frameworks-0.

5. Whittington A, Grey N. *How to Become a More Effective CBT Therapist: Mastering Metacompetence in Clinical Practice.* Chichester: John Wiley & Sons; 2014.
6. O'donovan A, Dyck M. Effective training in clinical and counselling psychology: Not as simple as it sounds. Aust Psychol. 2001;**36**(2):92–98.
7. Bennett-Levy J. Therapist skills: A cognitive model of their acquisition and refinement. Behav Cogn Psychother. 2006;**34**(1):57–78.
8. Bennett-Levy J, McManus F, Westling BE, Fennell M. Acquiring and refining CBT skills and competencies: Which training methods are perceived to be most effective? Behav Cogn Psychother. 2009;**37**(5):571–583.
9. Schon DA. *The Reflective Practitioner: How Professionals Think in Action.* New York: Basic Books; 1983.
10. James W. *The Principles of Psychology.* H. Holt; 1890.
11. Dewey J. *Democracy and Education: An Introduction to the Philosophy of Education* [Internet]. New York: MacMillan; 1916. (Text-book series). https://books.google.co.uk/books?id=MUz7CnO-4iMC.
12. Dewey J. *Experience and Education* [Internet]. New York: Macmillan; 1938. https://books.google.co.uk/books?id=GS8EAQAAIAAJ.
13. Skovholt TM, Rønnestad MH, Jennings L. Searching for expertise in counseling, psychotherapy, and professional psychology. Educ Psychol Rev. 1997;**9**(4):361–369.
14. Kalpakoglou T. Standards for Training and Accreditation of Cognitive and/or Behaviour Therapists. EABCT. https://eabct.eu/wp-content/uploads/2019/01/Thomas-Kalpakoglou-Training-and-Accreditation-2002-2013.pdf.
15. Acceptable CPD Activities and Evidence [Internet]. [accessed 14 September 2023]. www.babcp.com/Accreditation/CBT-Practice-Supervision-CPD/CPD-Guidance/Acceptable-CPD-Activities-and-Evidence.
16. Reaccreditation Guidelines [Internet]. [accessed 14 September 2023]. www.babcp.com/Accreditation/Reaccreditation/Reaccreditation-Guidelines.
17. Branson A, Shafran R, Myles P. Investigating the relationship between competence and patient outcome with CBT. Behav Res Ther. 2015;**68**:19–26.
18. Zieve GG, Persons JB, Yu LAD. The relationship between dropout and outcome in naturalistic cognitive behavior therapy. Behav Ther. 2019;**50**(1):189–199.
19. Law D, Jacob J. *Goals and Goal Based Outcomes (GBOs).* London: CAMHS Press; 2013.
20. Duncan B, Miller S, Sparks J, Claud D, Reynolds L. The session rating scale: Preliminary psychometric properties of a 'working' alliance measure. J Brief Ther. 2003;**3**:3–12.
21. Bernard JM, Goodyear RK. *Fundamentals of Clinical Supervision.* Boston: Allyn & Bacon; 1998.
22. Falender CA, Shafranske EP. *Clinical Supervision: A Competency-Based Approach.* Washington, DC: American Psychological Association; 2004.
23. Inskipp F, Proctor B. *Making the Most of Supervision.* Twickenham: Cascade Publications; 1993.
24. Milne D. *Evidence-Based Clinical Supervision: Principles and Practice.* Chichester: BPS Blackwell; 2009.
25. Milne D, Dunkerley C. Towards evidence-based clinical supervision: The development and evaluation of four CBT guidelines. Cogn Behav Ther. 2010;**3**(2):43–57.
26. Milne DL, Reiser RP. *A Manual for Evidence-Based CBT Supervision.* Chichester: John Wiley & Sons; 2017.
27. Dorsey S, Pullmann MD, Deblinger E, Berliner L, Kerns SE, Thompson K, et al. Improving practice in community-based settings: A randomized trial of supervision–study protocol. Implement Sci. 2013;**8**(1):1–11.
28. Brosan L, Reynolds S, Moore RG. Self-evaluation of cognitive therapy

performance: Do therapists know how competent they are? Behav Cogn Psychother. 2008;**36**(5):581–587.

29. McManus F, Rakovshik S, Kennerley H, Fennell M, Westbrook D. An investigation of the accuracy of therapists' self-assessment of cognitive-behaviour therapy skills. Br J Clin Psychol. 2012;**51**(3):292–306.
30. National Collaborating Centre for Mental Health. *The Improving Access to Psychological Therapies Manual.* UK NCCMH. 2018.
31. Bennett-Levy J, Lee N, Travers K, Pohlman S, Hamernik E. Cognitive therapy from the inside: Enhancing therapist skills through practising what we preach. Behav Cogn Psychother. 2003;**31**(2):143–158.
32. Bennett-Levy J. *Experiencing CBT from the Inside Out: A Self-Practice/Self-Reflection Workbook for Therapists.* New York: The Guilford Press; 2014.

Index

www.ingramcontent.com/pod-product-compliance
Lightning Source LLC
LaVergne TN
LVHW052221200926
848481LV00001B/178
* 9 7 8 1 0 0 9 0 8 8 3 5 0 *